for my Mother
Ida Mack
1946-1995

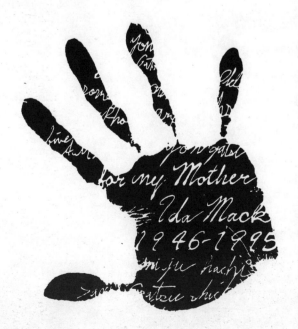

KABUKI

CIRCLE OF BLOOD

writer and artist
DAVID MACK

editor
CONNIE JIANG

Letterers
STEVE STEGELIN
JOE MARTIN
DAVID MACK

image

Publisher:
JIM VALENTINO
Art Director:
DOUG GRIFFITH
Director of Production:
BRENT BRAUN
Graphic Design:
KENNY FELIX
Controller:
TRACI HALE
Accounting Asst:
CYNDIE ESPINOZA
Director of Marketing:
ANTHONY BOZZI

film output
TONY KELLY and KELL-O-GRAPHICS

KABUKI Circle of Blood is published by Image Comics,
1071 North Batavia Street, Suite A, Orange, CA 92867

3rd Printing

ISBN 1-88-7279-80-6

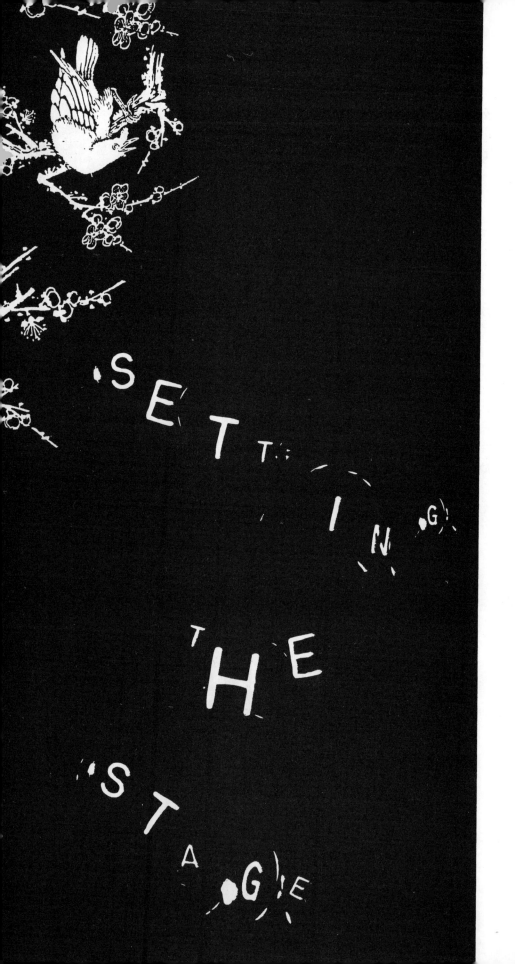

SETTING THE STAGE

Introduction by Steranko

What could David Mack be thinking of ?

Reading any issue of **Kabuki** immediately evokes a myriad of questions, beginning with a query asking *what* the work is really about.

Because it often articulates the abstract, answers will vary, but a consensus would undoubtedly confirm that the series is an exploration of the senses. While the new wave of New-Wave comic-book artists strives to make heard their scream of primal rage, the ultimate effect is too often nothing more than the crybaby yowl of teen angst. In today's four-color universe, where "normal" is usually over the top and defined by pinhead musclemen with terminally constipated expressions, **Kabuki's** approach is absolutely against the grain.

What could David Mack be thinking of ?

Personal expression comes to mind, an aspect which often defines the ultimate status and staying power of an artist's work. A careful look at the **Kabuki** saga reveals the effort to which its creator has gone to achieve that expression.

Consider his choices. Schooled in the visual arts (he graduated with a BFA in graphic design and a minor in English also studying Japanese language, theater, and working summers as packaging designer for a toy company in Hong Kong), Mack opted to shun the commercial-agency route to become a storyteller--using the comic page as his forum. And rather than following his peers into grunge-heroland, he decided, with his initial creator-owned project, to generate an offbeat, cross-cultural epic--exotic but remote to the American audience. Then, rather than adapting to the current storytelling style--in which storytelling is almost nonexistent--he created a foundation upon which storytelling is crucial.

Risky business for a neophyte in a depressed market.

His exploration of Japanese tradition (Mack transcends the stereotypes with his authority on the subject matter), is a calculated combination of fantasy, violence, and psychodrama, overlaid with sexual leitmotifs which hook readers with a touch of the conventional, while taking them far from what they expect.

From blood-splattered action scenes to evocative, emotional nuances, **Kabuki** inevitably finds a way to surprise, often shock, even those who have become jaded with comics' predictability. Using an approach which ranges from the cinematic to the surreal, Mack has forged a new visual syntax in an art form starved for protean development.

What could David Mack be thinking of ?

How many contemporary artists, for example, actually modify or change rendering styles to compliment their characters or storylines ? Out of arrogance, carelessness, or inability, most simply develop a *single* artistic style and flog it mercilessly to smithereens on every assignment, from superheroes to the supernatural, from romance to horror--never realizing that style and subject matter could be powerfully linked into a unified vision.

Mack takes the concept a step further, deliberately changing styles to underscore specific scenes, sometimes depicting a tight, controlled line when the story warrants or taking a more casual, even chaotic, direction when his characters undergo dramatic trauma.

To change the mood of a sequence or even a panel, he will employ a different rendering medium. The process suggests a much richer integrity than most comics ever offer, let alone deliver.

This is not to suggest that all his experiments are successful. Even those which fail, however, should be treated as honorable attempts to enrich the reading experience. Rather than the same reprocessed panels that clutter most books littering comic-shop shelves, **Kabuki** is a tapestry of visual paradoxes, metaphors, transitions, and icons. Although it employs action sequences as a kind of commercial epoxy, page for page, **Kabuki** has more authentic storytelling ideas than an armful of top-40 comics.

What could David Mack be thinking of ?

To reiterate a point, **Kabuki** is an exploration of the senses, an excursion beyond the purely visual, a voyage that attempts to touch *all* of his readers' perceptions. One of Mack's techniques is to bring us so close to his characters that we can almost *hear* their breath, *smell* their sweat, *feel* their heartbeat. Unlike many other hot-button draftsmen--whose styles range from in-your-face to down-your-throat--Mack approaches his subjects slowly patiently, allowing readers to fully ingest the nuances with which he overlays their lives. (One of the pleasures of the **Kabuki** saga is observing its creator develop from book to book, each of which represents an artistic plateau of both rendering technique and storytelling mastery).

Today's comics have blurred the line between form and function, often delivering little more substance than a cheeze doodle and about as poetic as lint--not exactly soul nourishing material. From a certain viewpoint, one cannot fail to conclude that Mack's work is either a statement of great courage or great folly. Most artists never achieve either.

Calling upon a complex fabric of influences from fine art to pop music, Mack structures **Kabuki**'s narrative passages like an architect, interlocking layer upon layer of intriguing images, labyrinthine subplots, historic details, and symbolic references, constantly refining information until it achieves artistic weight.

Additionally, the series is uncommonly well-written. Mack has substituted the bombast of incessant and arrogant wisecracking with insightful introspection. He has carefully unified his themes, content, and esthetics into an elaborate and expressive spectacle sustained throughout by a breath of vision and intellectual energy. The result is an intensely personal work of somber tonality and penetrating elegance.

What could David Mack be thinking of ?

STERANKO

February 1996

As a filmmaker, Steranko has collaborated with such director's as Steven Spielberg and Francis Ford Coppola, working on **Raiders of the Lost Ark, Brahm Stoker's Dracula** and George Lucas' **Star Wars and Empire Strikes Back.** His strong sense of color, motion and composition made a lasting friend of Italian director Federico Fellini (who wrote the introduction to Steranko's comic-book history series).
Steranko has won numerous awards for his work in every field of endeavor, from magic to comic art to commercial design, both in America and in Europe. His work has been displayed internationally at more than 160 exhibitions worldwide including the Louvre in Paris. In the 60's, Steranko drew a secret agent strip called Nick Fury, Agent of S.H.I.E.L.D. and turned it into a tour de force of graphic surprises that changed the direction of the comics medium. In his journalistic efforts as publisher, editor, designer, and award winning typographer of **PREVUE** magazine, Steranko has interviewed a galaxy of filmmakers from Arnold Schwarzenegger to Sharon Stone to Harrison Ford.

PROLOGUE

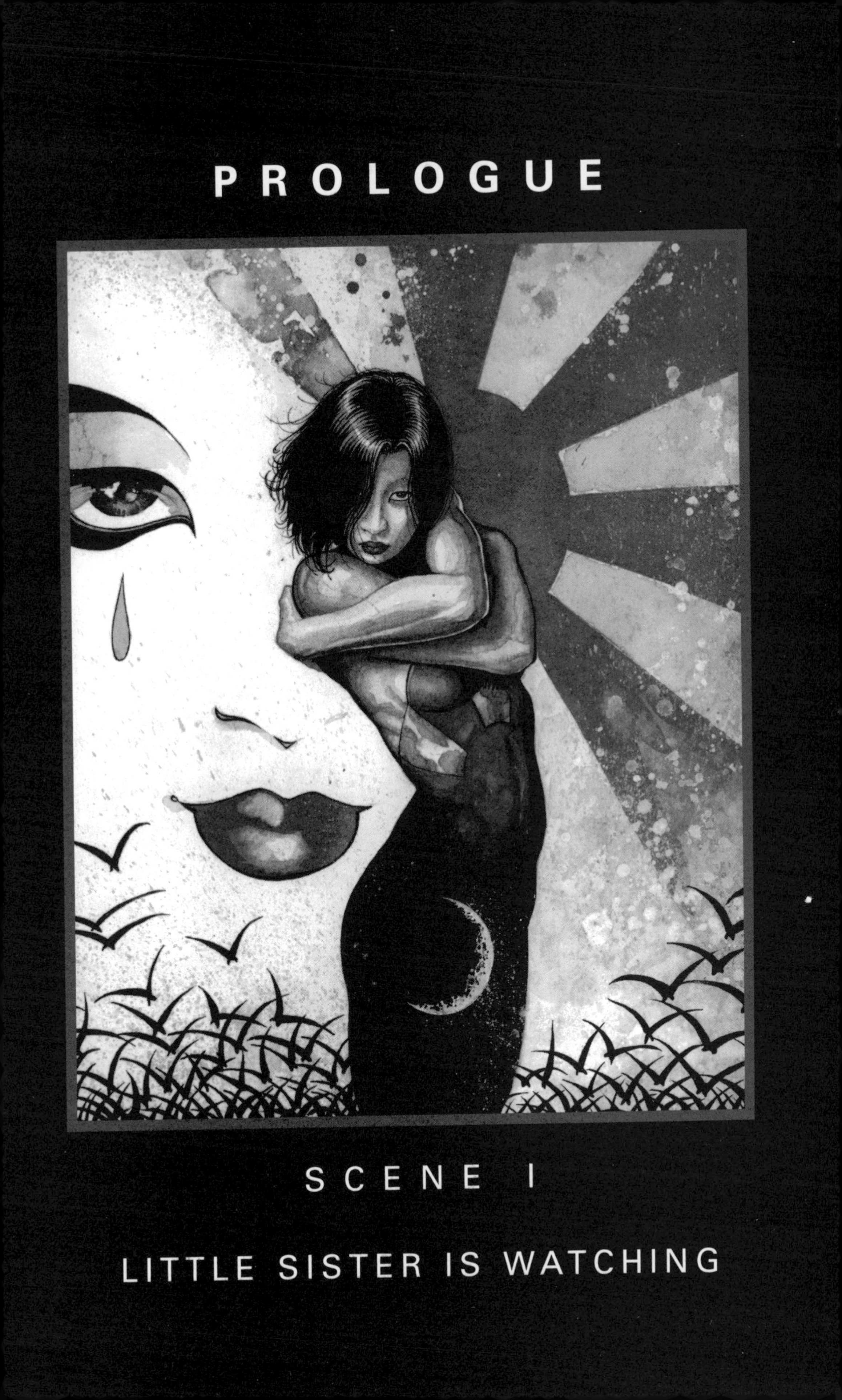

SCENE I

LITTLE SISTER IS WATCHING

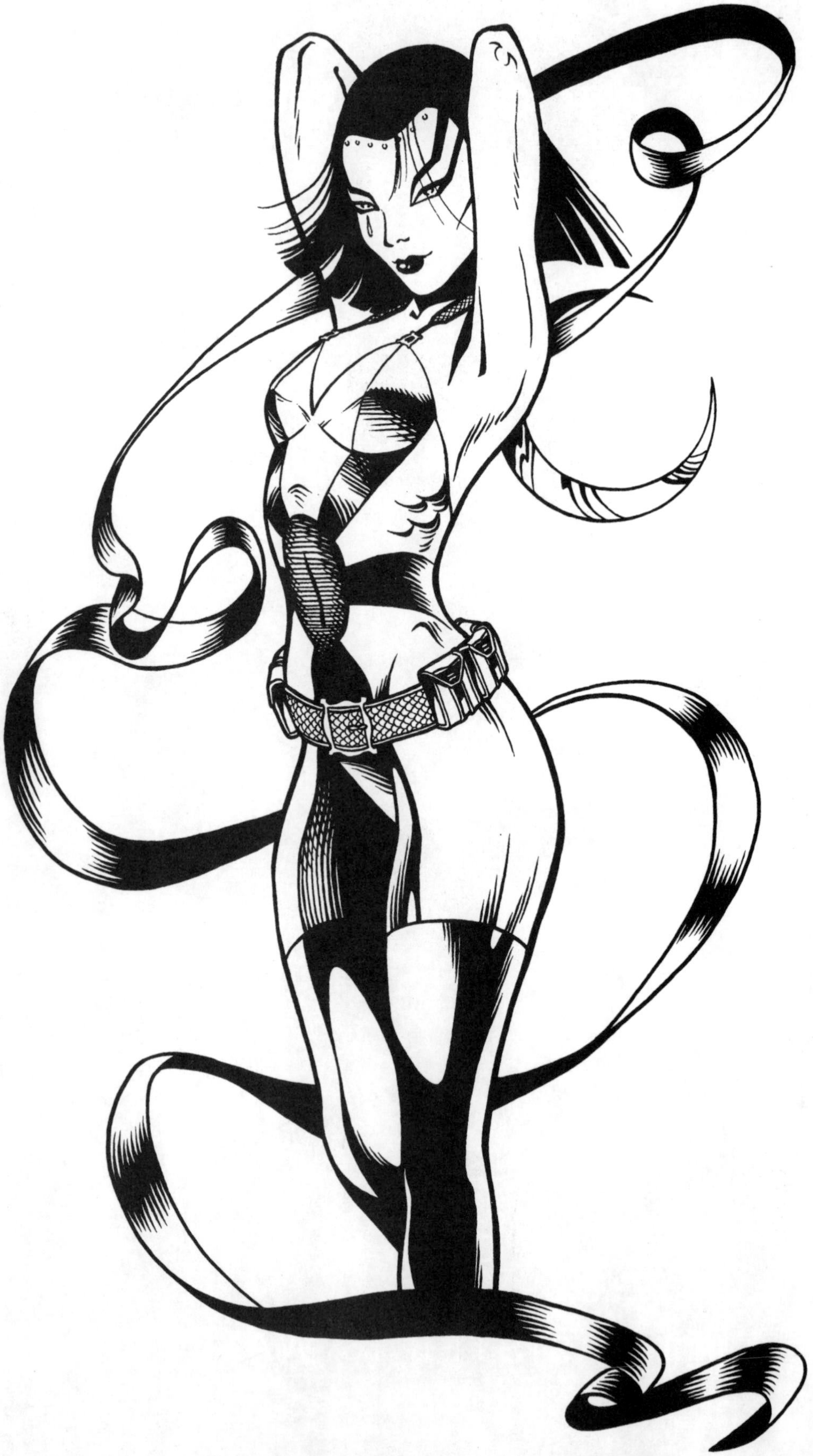

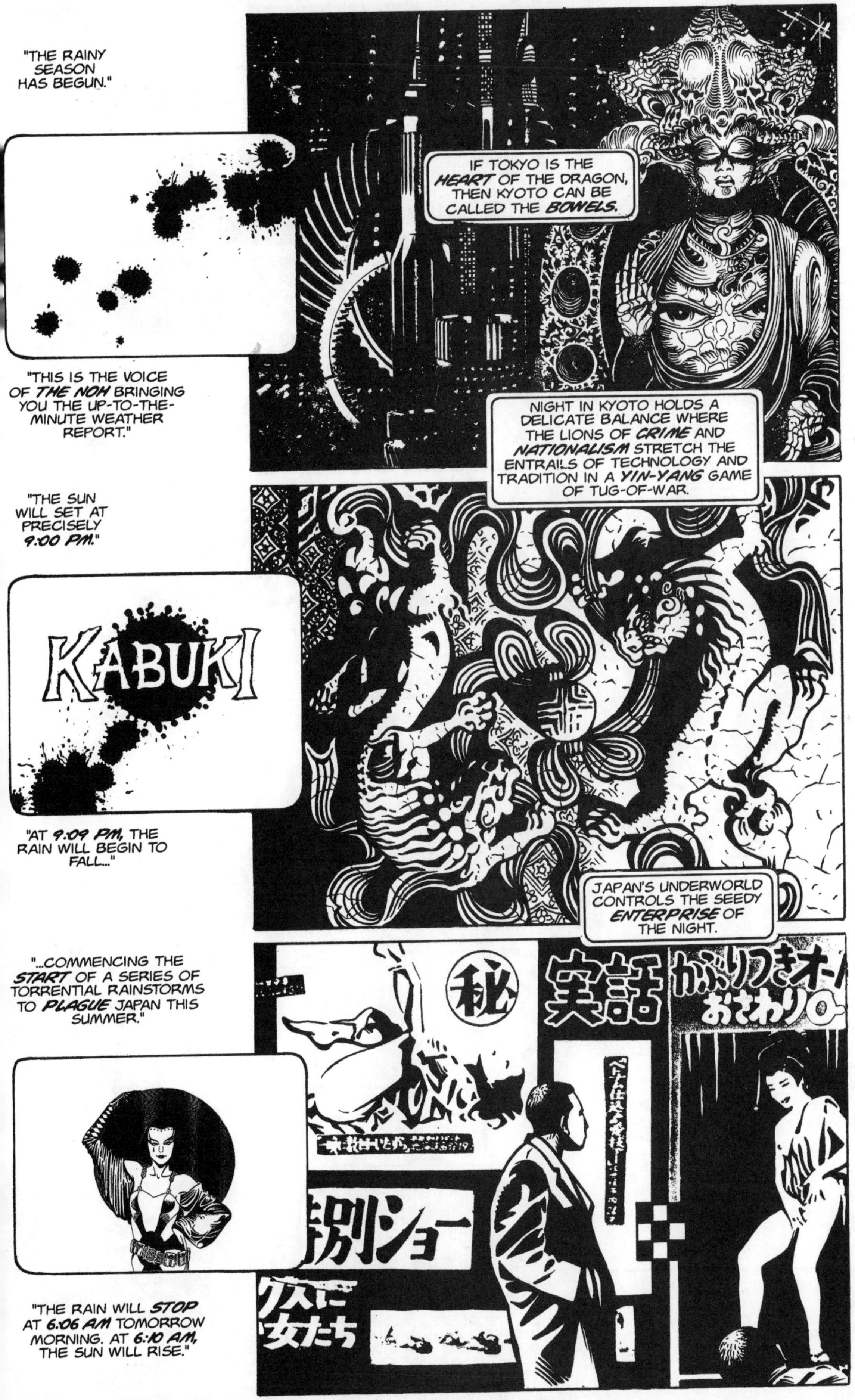
"THE RAINY SEASON HAS BEGUN."
IF TOKYO IS THE HEART OF THE DRAGON, THEN KYOTO CAN BE CALLED THE BOWELS.
"THIS IS THE VOICE OF THE NOH BRINGING YOU THE UP-TO-THE-MINUTE WEATHER REPORT."
NIGHT IN KYOTO HOLDS A DELICATE BALANCE WHERE THE LIONS OF CRIME AND NATIONALISM STRETCH THE ENTRAILS OF TECHNOLOGY AND TRADITION IN A YIN-YANG GAME OF TUG-OF-WAR.
"THE SUN WILL SET AT PRECISELY 9:00 PM."
KABUKI
"AT 9:09 PM, THE RAIN WILL BEGIN TO FALL..."
JAPAN'S UNDERWORLD CONTROLS THE SEEDY ENTERPRISE OF THE NIGHT.
"...COMMENCING THE START OF A SERIES OF TORRENTIAL RAINSTORMS TO PLAGUE JAPAN THIS SUMMER."
秘
実話
かぶりつきオー
おさわり
別ショー
女たち
"THE RAIN WILL STOP AT 6:06 AM TOMORROW MORNING. AT 6:10 AM, THE SUN WILL RISE."

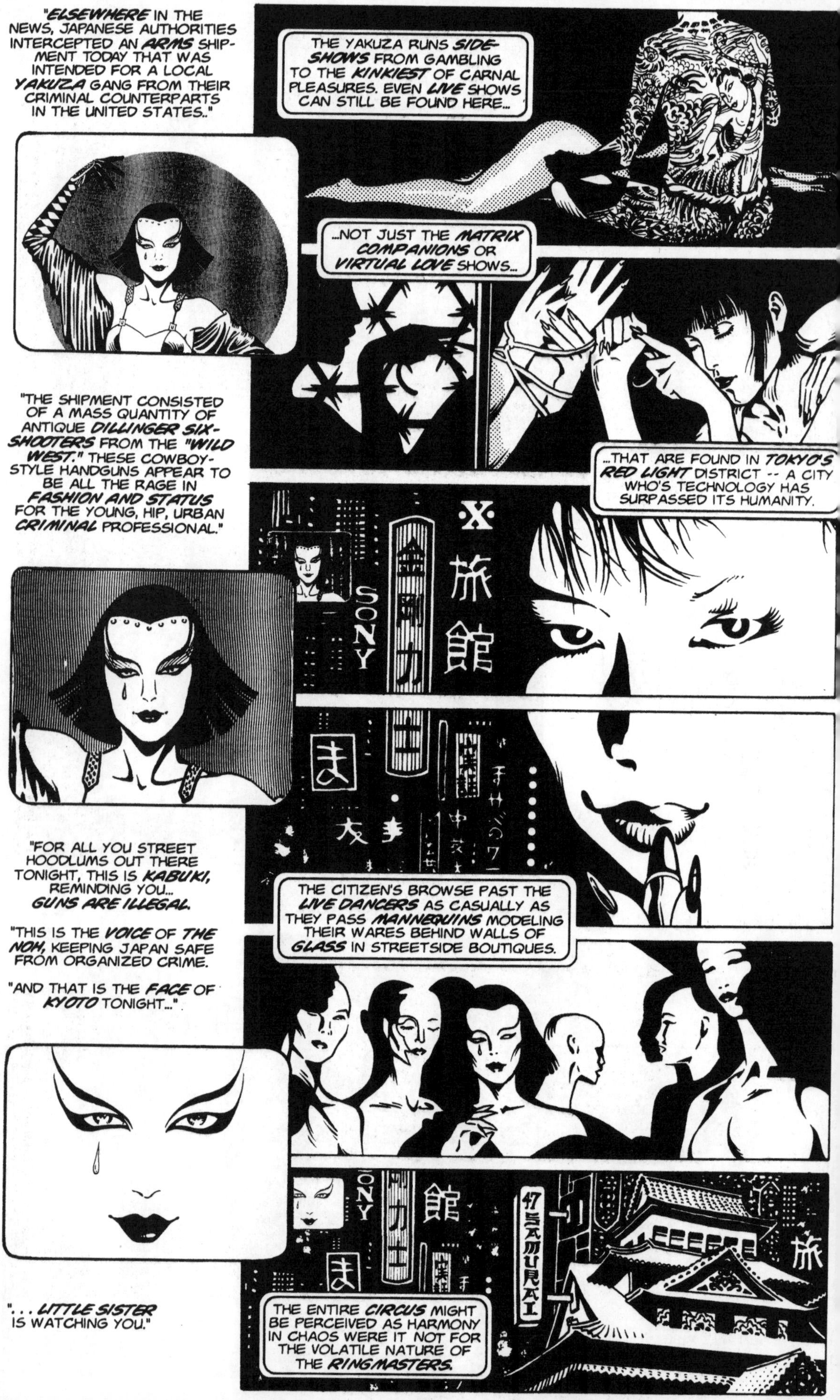
"ELSEWHERE IN THE NEWS, JAPANESE AUTHORITIES INTERCEPTED AN ARMS SHIPMENT TODAY THAT WAS INTENDED FOR A LOCAL YAKUZA GANG FROM THEIR CRIMINAL COUNTERPARTS IN THE UNITED STATES.."
THE YAKUZA RUNS SIDESHOWS FROM GAMBLING TO THE KINKIEST OF CARNAL PLEASURES. EVEN LIVE SHOWS CAN STILL BE FOUND HERE...
...NOT JUST THE MATRIX COMPANIONS OR VIRTUAL LOVE SHOWS...
...THAT ARE FOUND IN TOKYO'S RED LIGHT DISTRICT -- A CITY WHO'S TECHNOLOGY HAS SURPASSED ITS HUMANITY.
"THE SHIPMENT CONSISTED OF A MASS QUANTITY OF ANTIQUE DILLINGER SIX-SHOOTERS FROM THE "WILD WEST." THESE COWBOY-STYLE HANDGUNS APPEAR TO BE ALL THE RAGE IN FASHION AND STATUS FOR THE YOUNG, HIP, URBAN CRIMINAL PROFESSIONAL."
X
旅館
SONY
THE CITIZEN'S BROWSE PAST THE LIVE DANCERS AS CASUALLY AS THEY PASS MANNEQUINS MODELING THEIR WARES BEHIND WALLS OF GLASS IN STREETSIDE BOUTIQUES.
"FOR ALL YOU STREET HOODLUMS OUT THERE TONIGHT, THIS IS KABUKI, REMINDING YOU... GUNS ARE ILLEGAL.
"THIS IS THE VOICE OF THE NOH, KEEPING JAPAN SAFE FROM ORGANIZED CRIME.
"AND THAT IS THE FACE OF KYOTO TONIGHT..."
"... LITTLE SISTER IS WATCHING YOU."
47 SAMURAI
THE ENTIRE CIRCUS MIGHT BE PERCEIVED AS HARMONY IN CHAOS WERE IT NOT FOR THE VOLATILE NATURE OF THE RINGMASTERS.

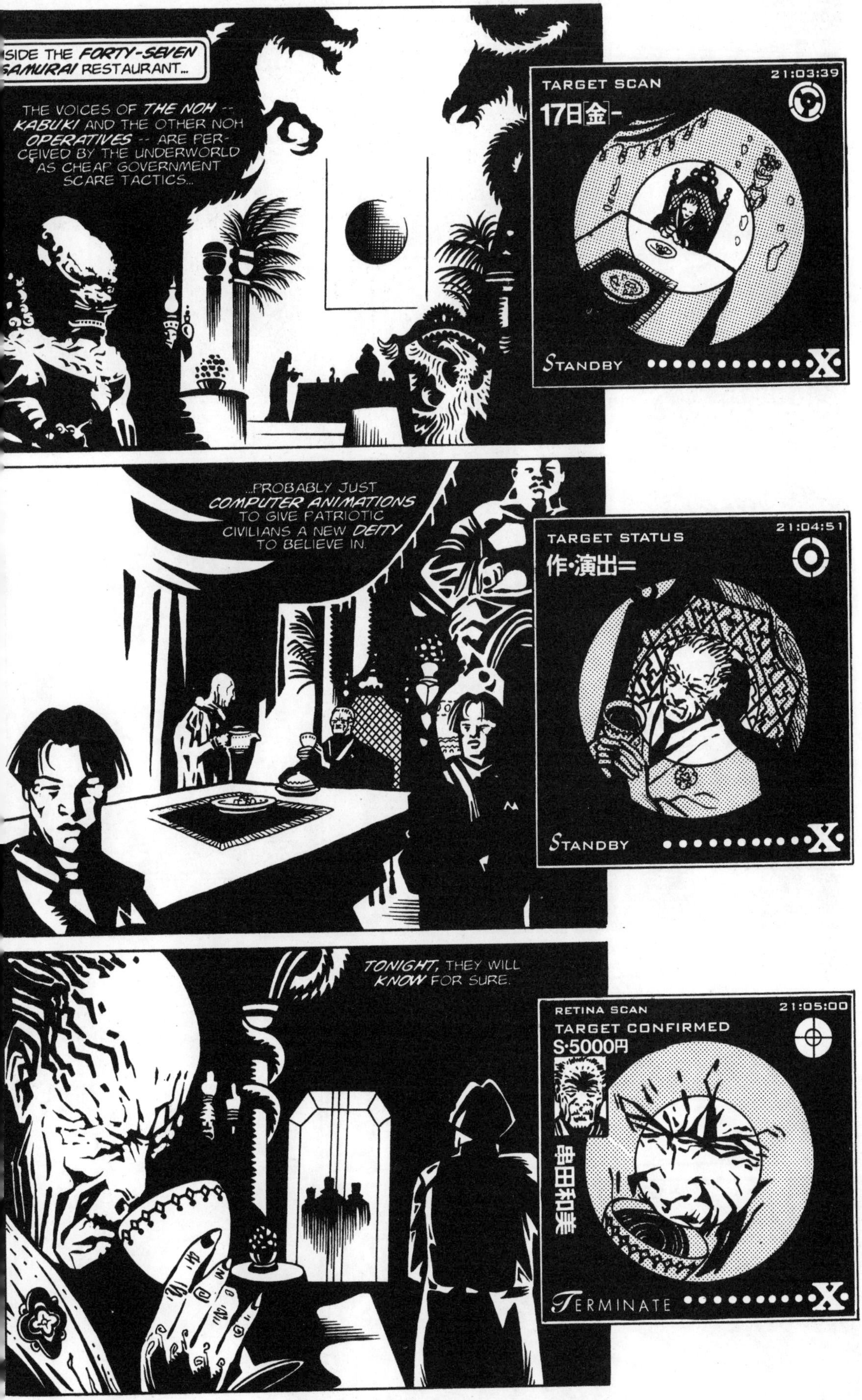
SIDE THE FORTY-SEVEN
SAMURAI RESTAURANT...
THE VOICES OF THE NOH -- KABUKI AND THE OTHER NOH OPERATIVES -- ARE PERCEIVED BY THE UNDERWORLD AS CHEAP GOVERNMENT SCARE TACTICS...
TARGET SCAN
21:03:39
17日[金]ー
STANDBY
X
...PROBABLY JUST COMPUTER ANIMATIONS TO GIVE PATRIOTIC CIVILIANS A NEW DEITY TO BELIEVE IN.
TARGET STATUS
21:04:51
作・演出＝
STANDBY
X
TONIGHT, THEY WILL KNOW FOR SURE.
RETINA SCAN
21:05:00
TARGET CONFIRMED
S・5000円
串田和美
TERMINATE
X

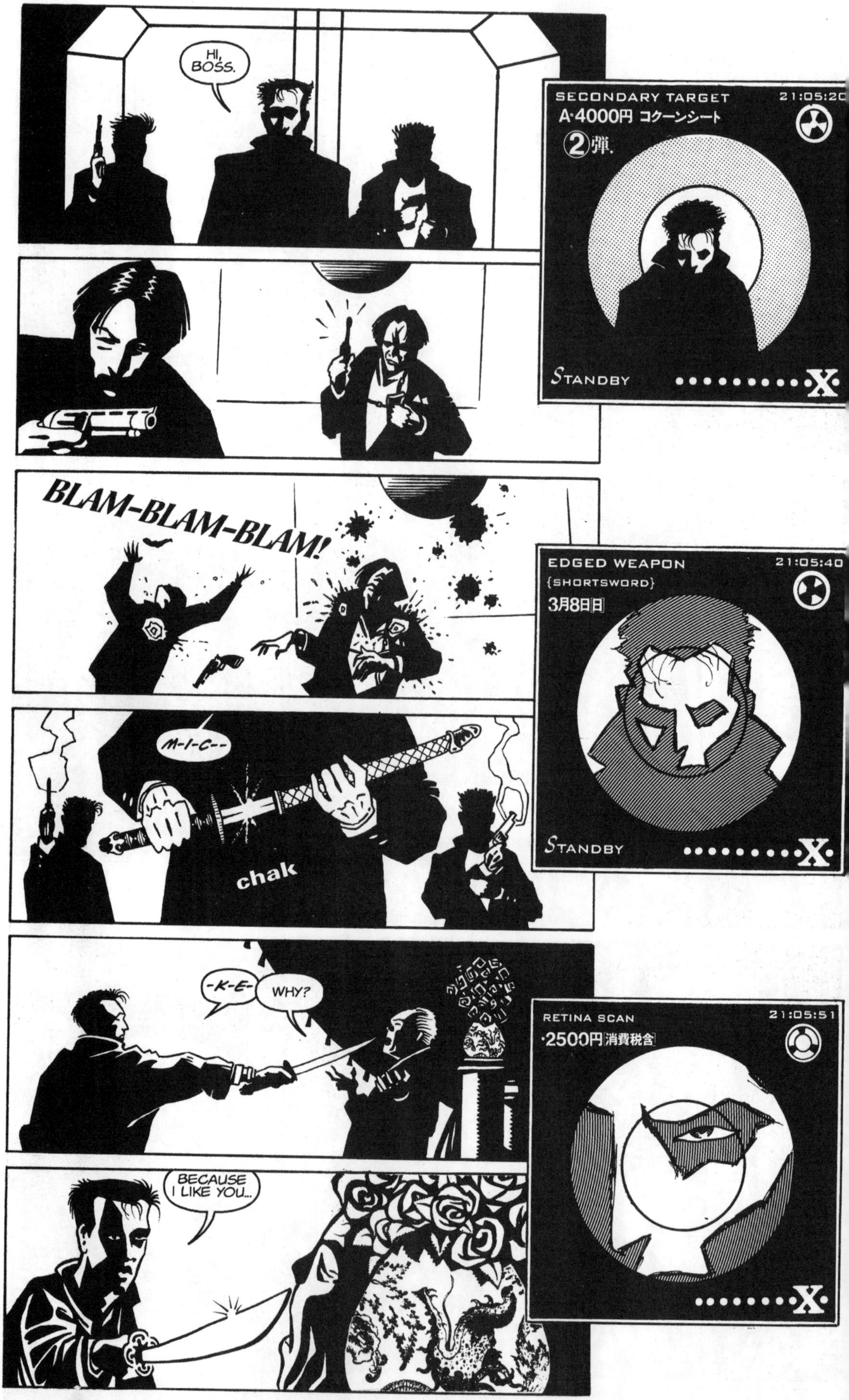
HI, BOSS.
SECONDARY TARGET
21:05:20
A·4000円 コクーンシート
②弾.
STANDBY
X
BLAM-BLAM-BLAM!
EDGED WEAPON
{SHORTSWORD}
21:05:40
3月8日(日)
STANDBY
X
M-I-C--
chak
-K-E-
WHY?
RETINA SCAN
21:05:51
·2500円[消費税含]
X
BECAUSE I LIKE YOU...

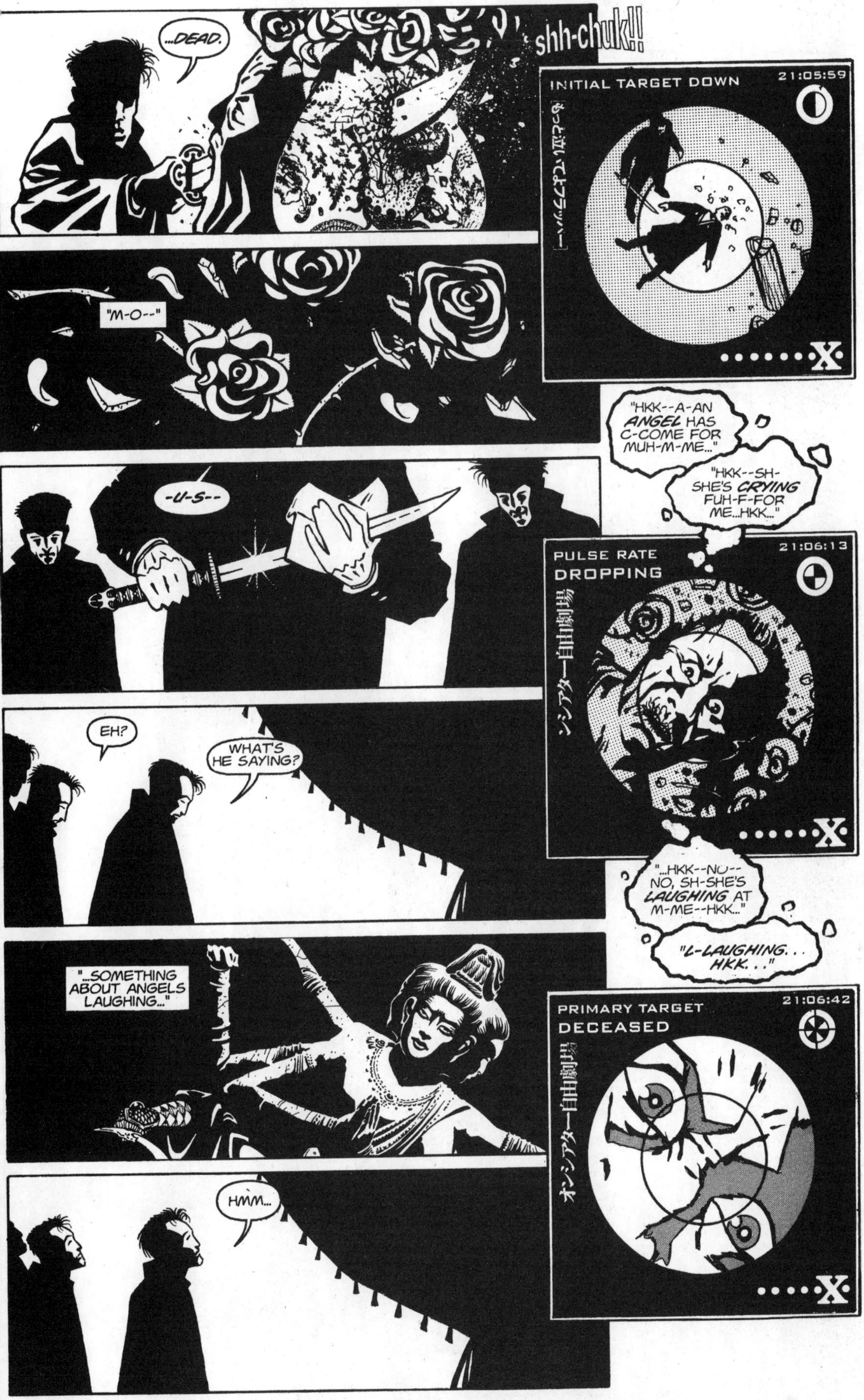
...DEAD.
shh-chuk!!
INITIAL TARGET DOWN
21:05:59
"M-O--"
"HKK--A-AN ANGEL HAS C-COME FOR MUH-M-ME..."
"HKK--SH-SHE'S CRYING FUH-F-FOR ME...HKK..."
-U-S--
PULSE RATE DROPPING
21:06:13
EH?
WHAT'S HE SAYING?
"...HKK--NO--NO, SH-SHE'S LAUGHING AT M-ME--HKK..."
"L-LAUGHING... HKK..."
"...SOMETHING ABOUT ANGELS LAUGHING..."
PRIMARY TARGET DECEASED
21:06:42
オンシアター自由劇場
HMM...

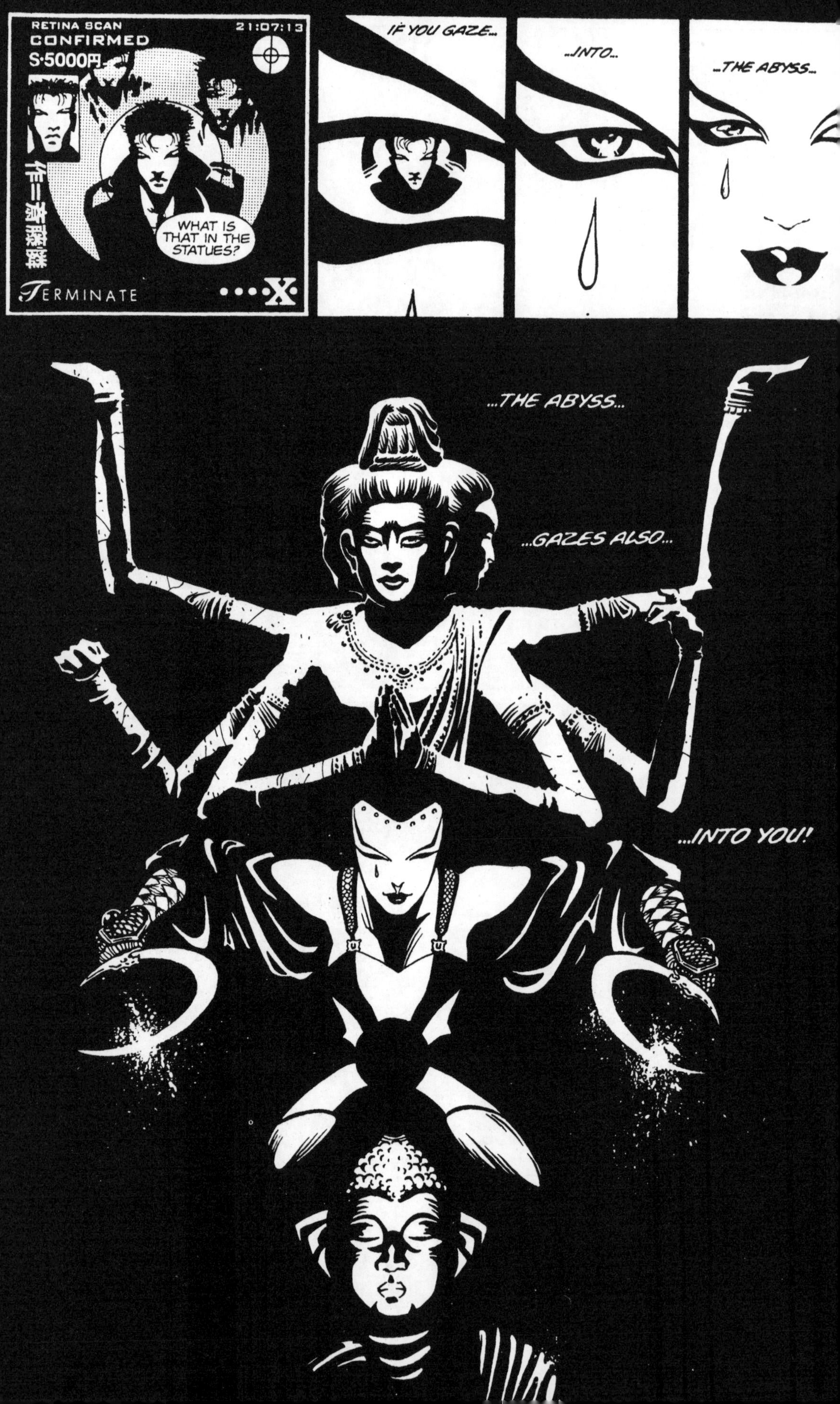
RETINA SCAN
21:07:13
CONFIRMED
S·5000円
作=斎藤鱗
WHAT IS THAT IN THE STATUES?
TERMINATE
IF YOU GAZE...
...INTO...
...THE ABYSS...
...THE ABYSS...
...GAZES ALSO...
...INTO YOU!

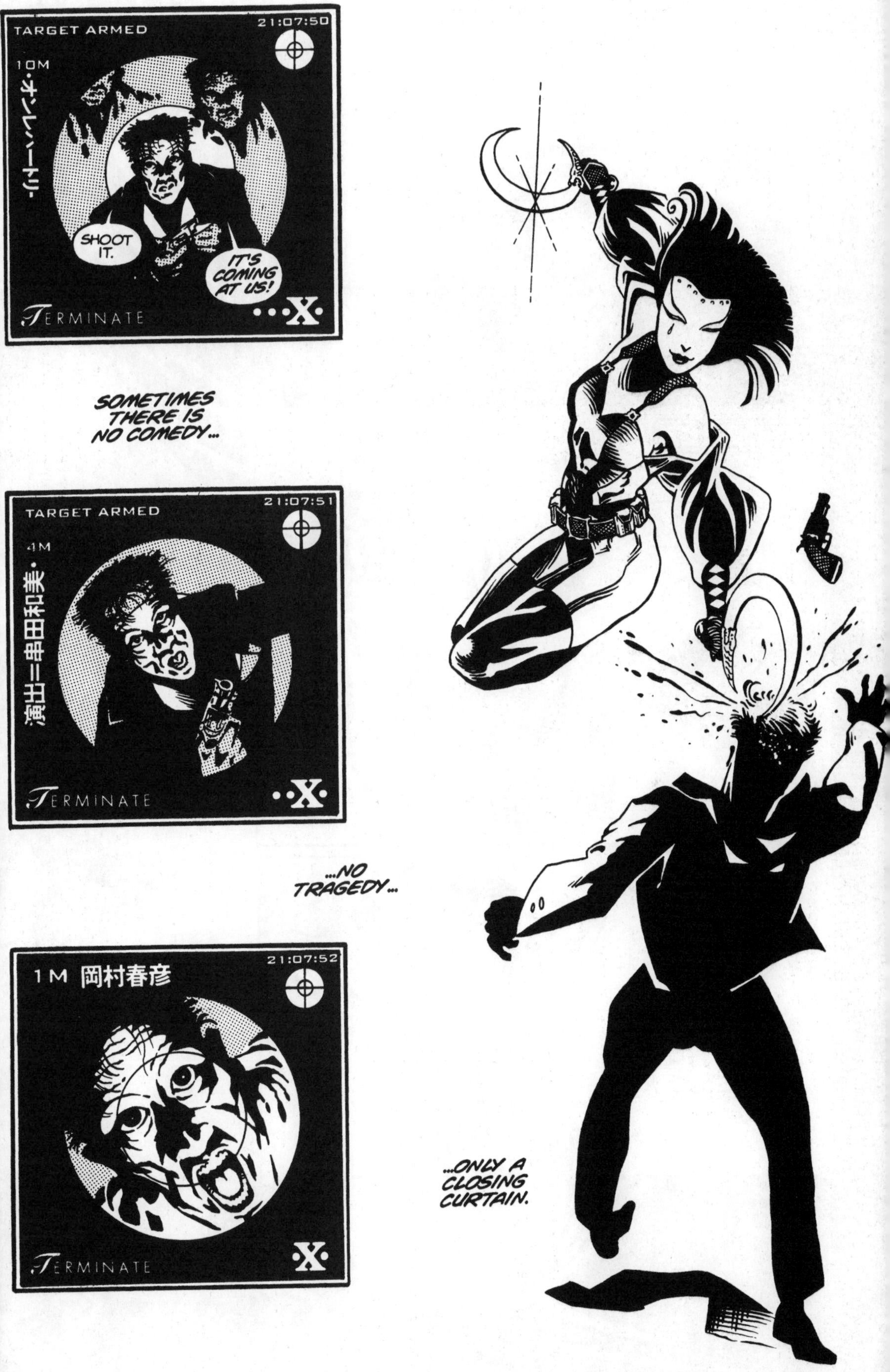

TARGET ARMED
21:07:50
10M
・オンレハートリ・
SHOOT IT.
IT'S COMING AT US!
TERMINATE
X
SOMETIMES THERE IS NO COMEDY...
TARGET ARMED
21:07:51
4M
演出＝串田和美・
TERMINATE
X
...NO TRAGEDY...
1M 岡村春彦
21:07:52
TERMINATE
X
...ONLY A CLOSING CURTAIN.

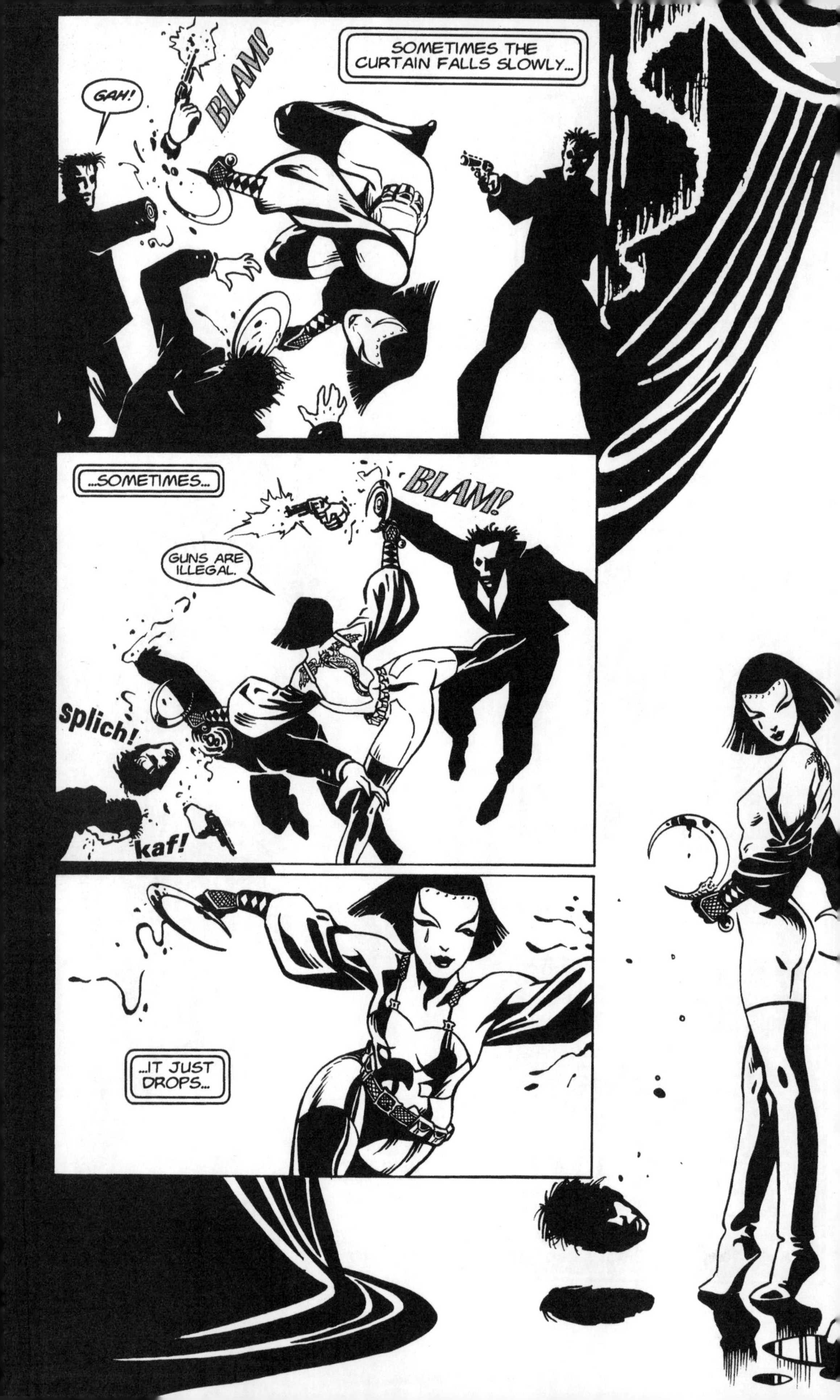
SOMETIMES THE CURTAIN FALLS SLOWLY...
GAH!
BLAM!
...SOMETIMES...
BLAM!
GUNS ARE ILLEGAL.
splich!
kaf!
...IT JUST DROPS...

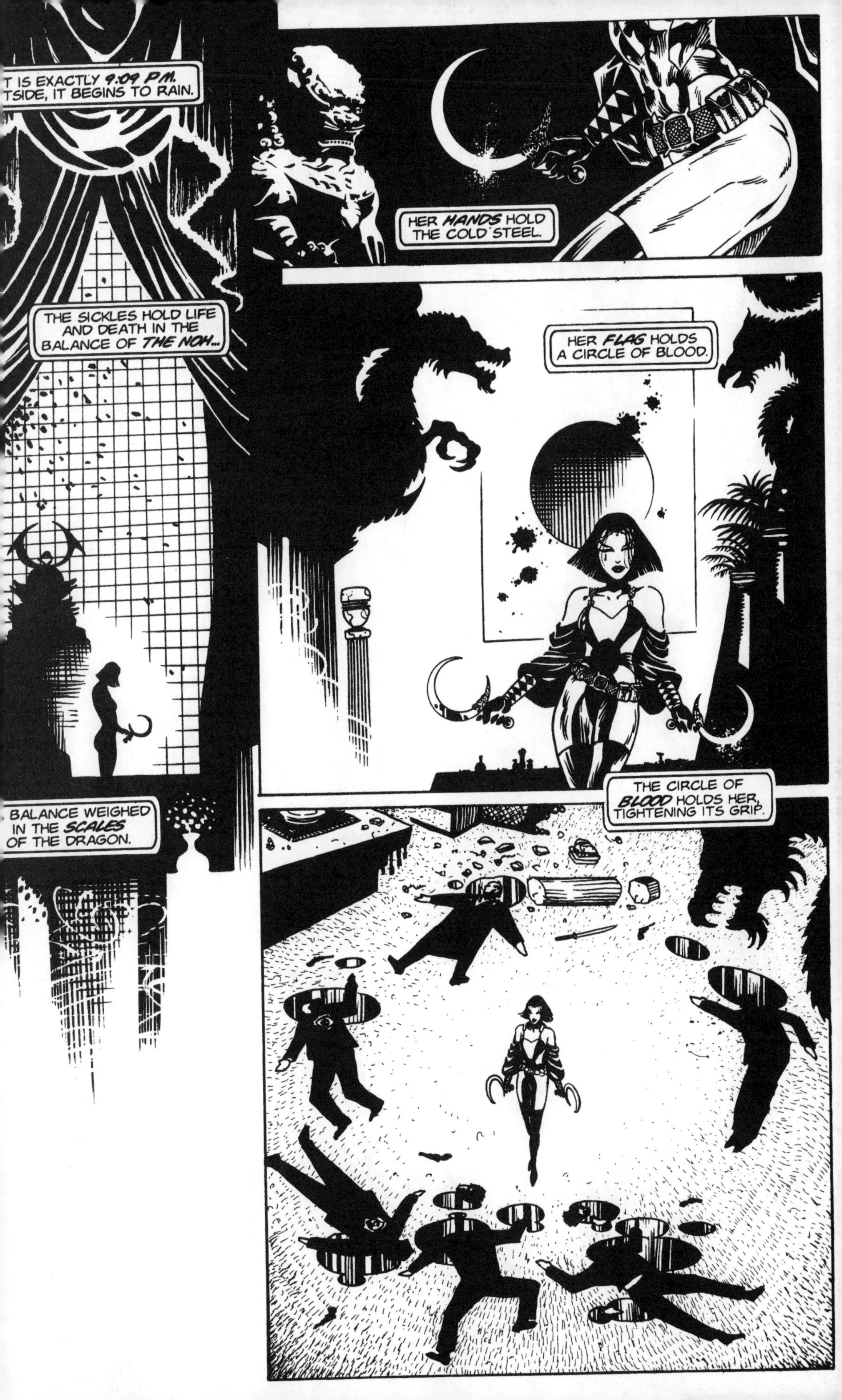
T IS EXACTLY 9:09 P.M. TSIDE, IT BEGINS TO RAIN.
HER HANDS HOLD THE COLD STEEL.
THE SICKLES HOLD LIFE AND DEATH IN THE BALANCE OF THE NOH...
HER FLAG HOLDS A CIRCLE OF BLOOD.
BALANCE WEIGHED IN THE SCALES OF THE DRAGON.
THE CIRCLE OF BLOOD HOLDS HER, TIGHTENING ITS GRIP.

SCENE II
DEALING WITH THE DEVIL

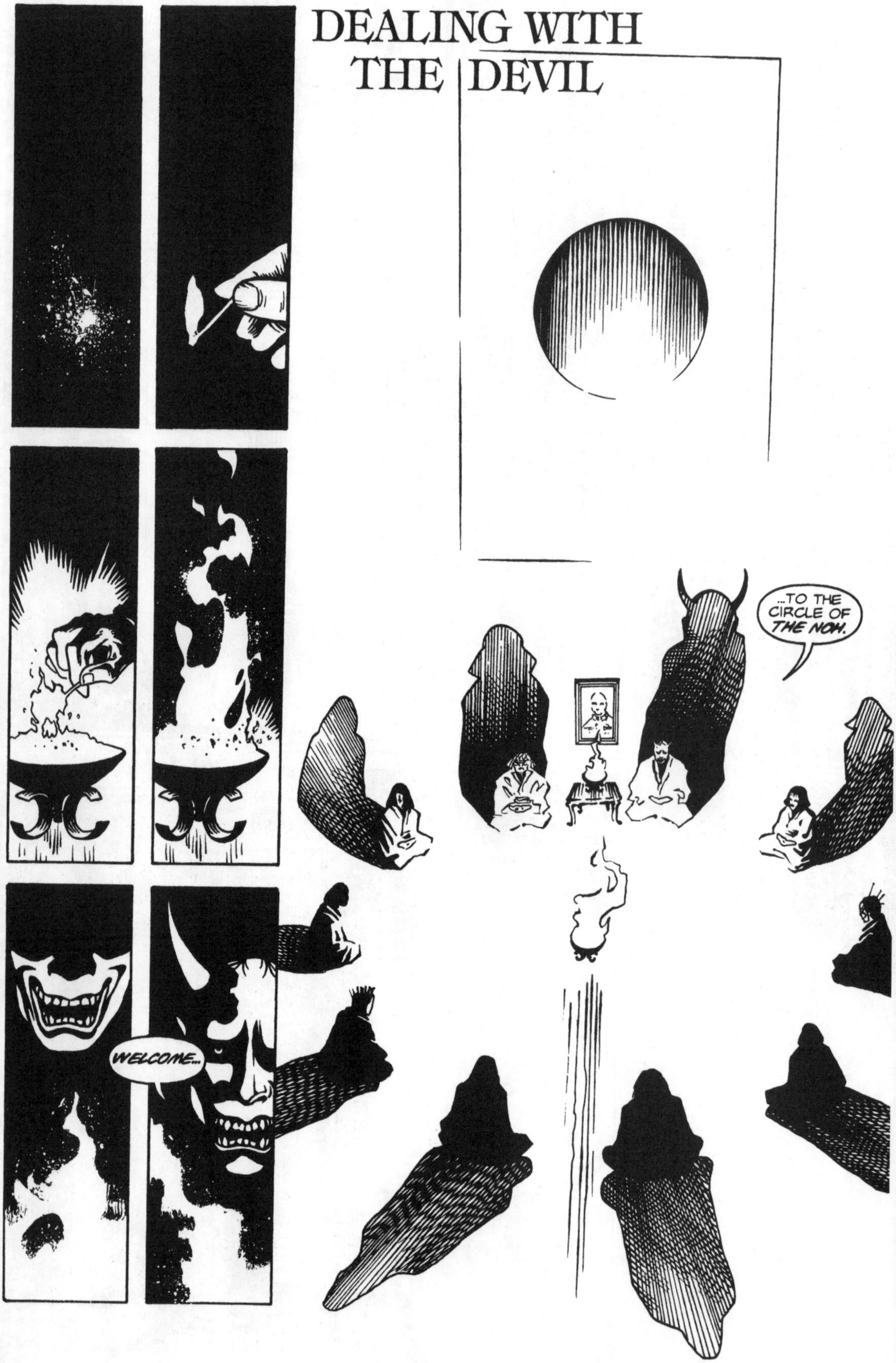
WELCOME...
...TO THE CIRCLE OF THE NOW.

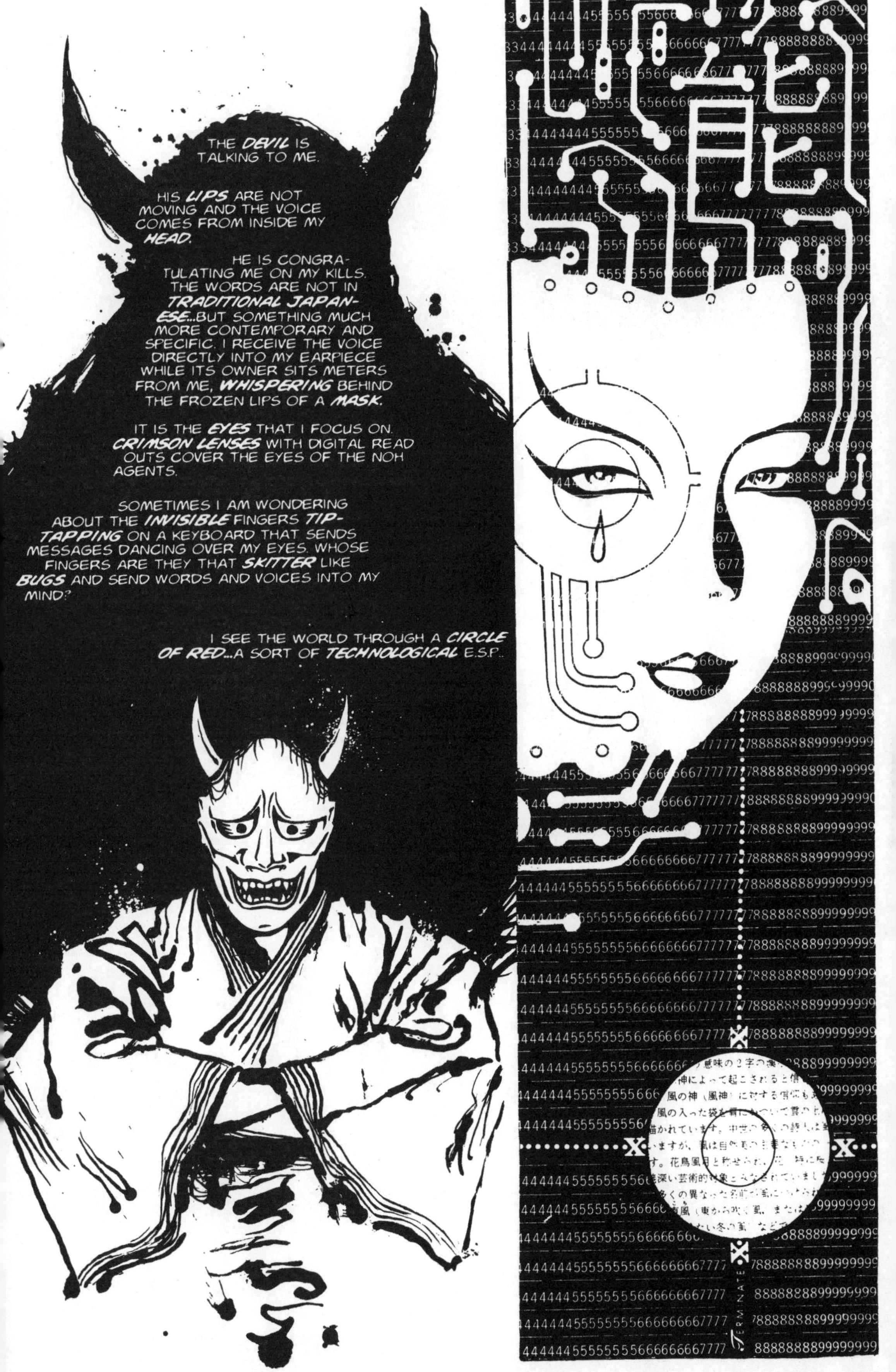
THE DEVIL IS TALKING TO ME.
HIS LIPS ARE NOT MOVING AND THE VOICE COMES FROM INSIDE MY HEAD.
HE IS CONGRATULATING ME ON MY KILLS. THE WORDS ARE NOT IN TRADITIONAL JAPANESE...BUT SOMETHING MUCH MORE CONTEMPORARY AND SPECIFIC. I RECEIVE THE VOICE DIRECTLY INTO MY EARPIECE WHILE ITS OWNER SITS METERS FROM ME, WHISPERING BEHIND THE FROZEN LIPS OF A MASK.
IT IS THE EYES THAT I FOCUS ON. CRIMSON LENSES WITH DIGITAL READ OUTS COVER THE EYES OF THE NOH AGENTS.
SOMETIMES I AM WONDERING ABOUT THE INVISIBLE FINGERS TIP-TAPPING ON A KEYBOARD THAT SENDS MESSAGES DANCING OVER MY EYES. WHOSE FINGERS ARE THEY THAT SKITTER LIKE BUGS AND SEND WORDS AND VOICES INTO MY MIND?
I SEE THE WORLD THROUGH A CIRCLE OF RED...A SORT OF TECHNOLOGICAL E.S.P...
能
TERMINATE

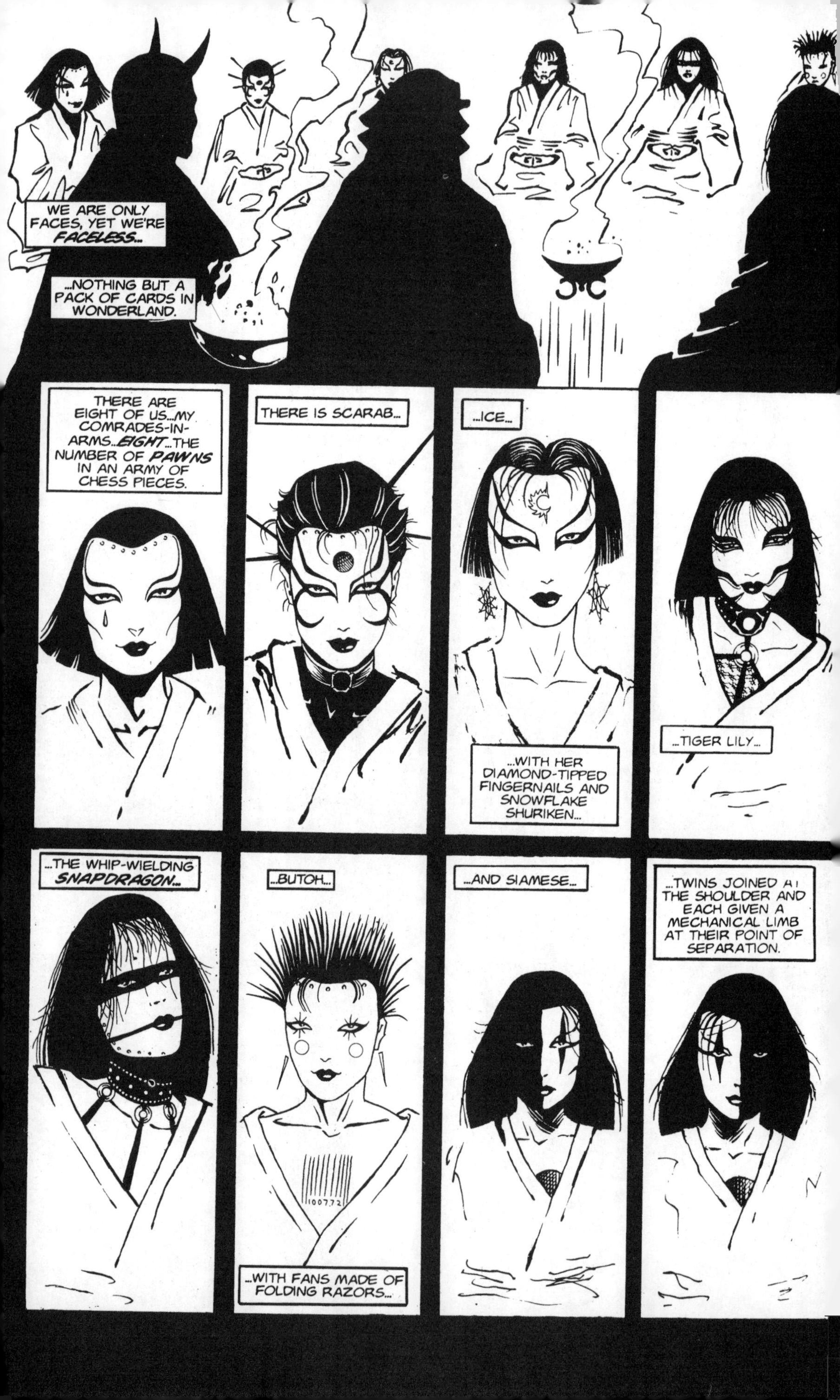
WE ARE ONLY FACES, YET WE'RE FACELESS...
...NOTHING BUT A PACK OF CARDS IN WONDERLAND.
THERE ARE EIGHT OF US...MY COMRADES-IN-ARMS...EIGHT...THE NUMBER OF PAWNS IN AN ARMY OF CHESS PIECES.
THERE IS SCARAB...
...ICE...
...WITH HER DIAMOND-TIPPED FINGERNAILS AND SNOWFLAKE SHURIKEN...
...TIGER LILY...
...THE WHIP-WIELDING SNAPDRAGON...
...BUTOH...
1007.72
...WITH FANS MADE OF FOLDING RAZORS...
...AND SIAMESE...
...TWINS JOINED AT THE SHOULDER AND EACH GIVEN A MECHANICAL LIMB AT THEIR POINT OF SEPARATION.

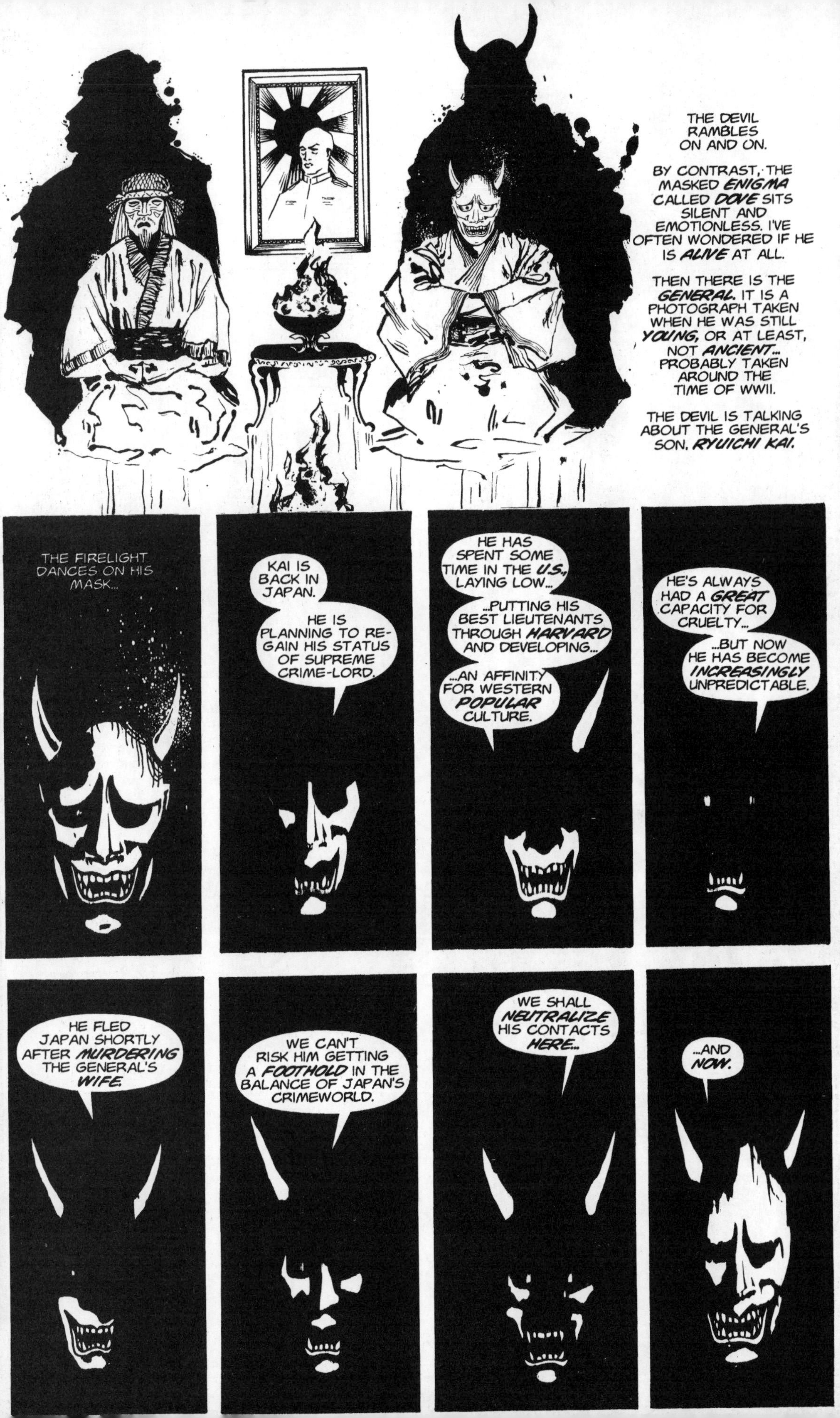
THE DEVIL RAMBLES ON AND ON.
BY CONTRAST, THE MASKED ENIGMA CALLED DOVE SITS SILENT AND EMOTIONLESS. I'VE OFTEN WONDERED IF HE IS ALIVE AT ALL.
THEN THERE IS THE GENERAL. IT IS A PHOTOGRAPH TAKEN WHEN HE WAS STILL YOUNG, OR AT LEAST, NOT ANCIENT... PROBABLY TAKEN AROUND THE TIME OF WWII.
THE DEVIL IS TALKING ABOUT THE GENERAL'S SON, RYUICHI KAI.
THE FIRELIGHT DANCES ON HIS MASK...
KAI IS BACK IN JAPAN.
HE IS PLANNING TO RE-GAIN HIS STATUS OF SUPREME CRIME-LORD.
HE HAS SPENT SOME TIME IN THE U.S., LAYING LOW...
...PUTTING HIS BEST LIEUTENANTS THROUGH HARVARD AND DEVELOPING...
...AN AFFINITY FOR WESTERN POPULAR CULTURE.
HE'S ALWAYS HAD A GREAT CAPACITY FOR CRUELTY...
...BUT NOW HE HAS BECOME INCREASINGLY UNPREDICTABLE.
HE FLED JAPAN SHORTLY AFTER MURDERING THE GENERAL'S WIFE.
WE CAN'T RISK HIM GETTING A FOOTHOLD IN THE BALANCE OF JAPAN'S CRIMEWORLD.
WE SHALL NEUTRALIZE HIS CONTACTS HERE...
...AND NOW.

"THIS IS A PHOTOGRAPH OF THE MAN CALLED *SNOW*. KAI HAD *LEGITIMIZED* HIS ORGANIZATION THROUGH SNOW'S TELEVISION STATION.

"SNOW BEGAN HIS CAREER AS A *DRUGLORD* FROM WHICH HE GAINED HIS BUSINESS *ALIAS*. THE TELEVISION STATION SERVED AS A FRONT FOR LAUNDERING MONEY.

"WITH THE ADVANCEMENTS OF *TECHNOLOGY*, SNOW WASHED HIS HANDS CLEAN OF THE DRUG BUSINESS ALTOGETHER AND CONCENTRATED ON HIS COMPANY'S PORNOGRAPHIC *'PAY PER PLAY'* VIRTUAL REALITY VIDEO PROGRAMS.

"THE INTERACTIVE PROGRAMS PROVED TO BE VERY *ADDICTIVE*, AND SNOW CORNERED THE MARKET ON HOME ENTERTAINMENT.

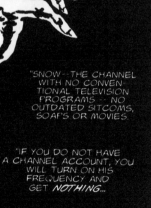

"SNOW--THE CHANNEL WITH NO CONVEN-TIONAL TELEVISION PROGRAMS -- NO OUTDATED SITCOMS, SOAPS OR MOVIES.

"IF YOU DO NOT HAVE A CHANNEL ACCOUNT, YOU WILL TURN ON HIS FREQUENCY AND GET *NOTHING*...

"...ONLY *SNOW*...

"...*CHANNEL* SNOW."

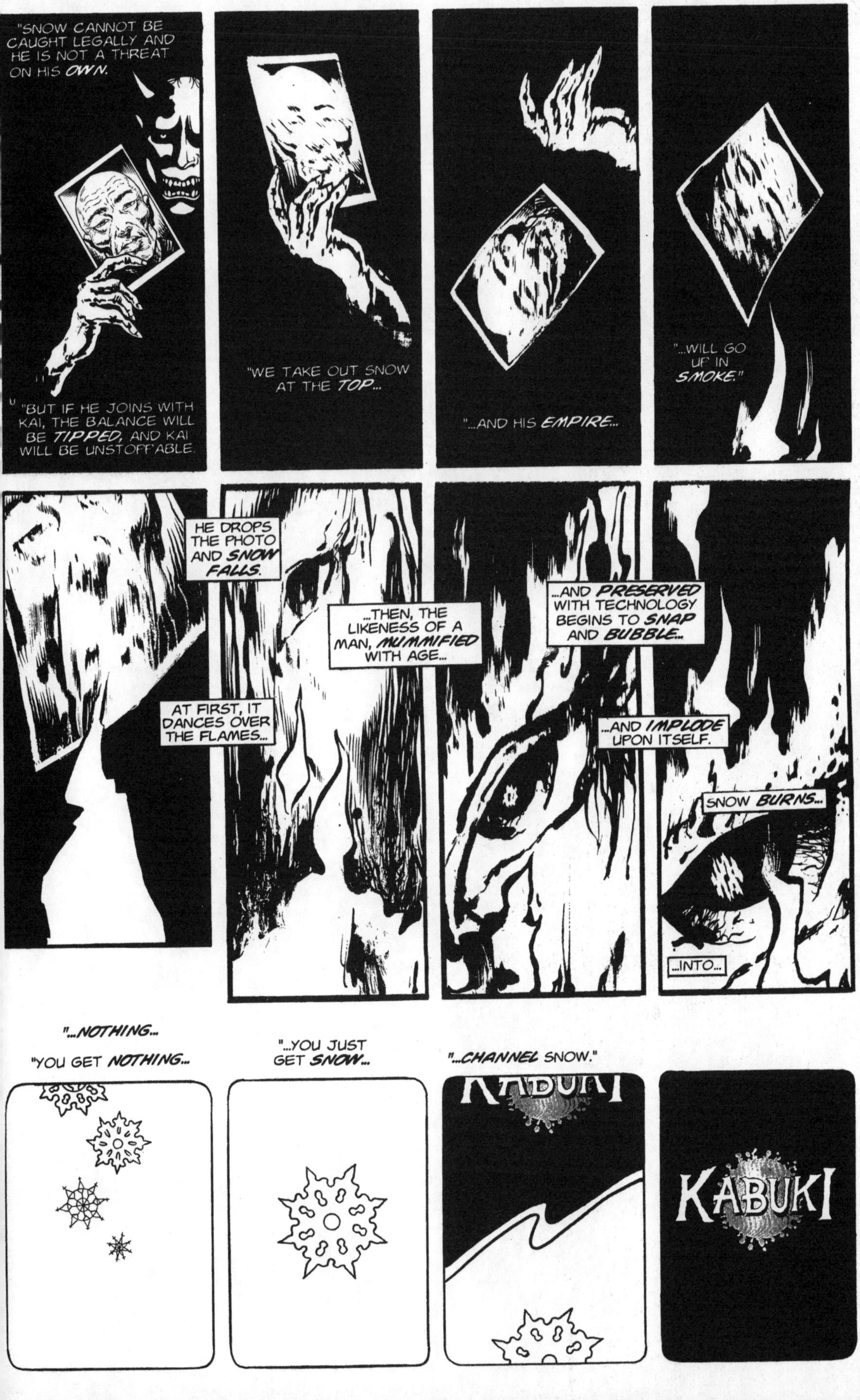
"SNOW CANNOT BE CAUGHT LEGALLY AND HE IS NOT A THREAT ON HIS OWN.
"BUT IF HE JOINS WITH KAI, THE BALANCE WILL BE TIPPED, AND KAI WILL BE UNSTOPPABLE.
"WE TAKE OUT SNOW AT THE TOP...
"...AND HIS EMPIRE...
"...WILL GO UP IN SMOKE."
HE DROPS THE PHOTO AND SNOW FALLS.
AT FIRST, IT DANCES OVER THE FLAMES...
...THEN, THE LIKENESS OF A MAN, MUMMIFIED WITH AGE...
...AND PRESERVED WITH TECHNOLOGY BEGINS TO SNAP AND BUBBLE...
...AND IMPLODE UPON ITSELF.
SNOW BURNS...
...INTO...
"...NOTHING...
"YOU GET NOTHING...
"...YOU JUST GET SNOW...
"...CHANNEL SNOW."
KABUKI

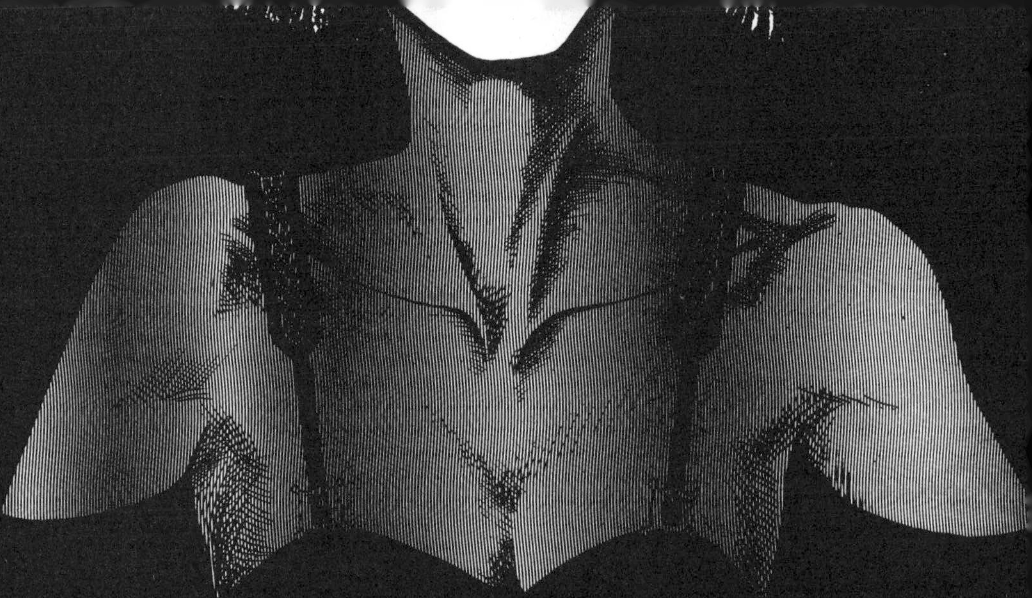

KABUKI

SCENE III
SNOWFALL

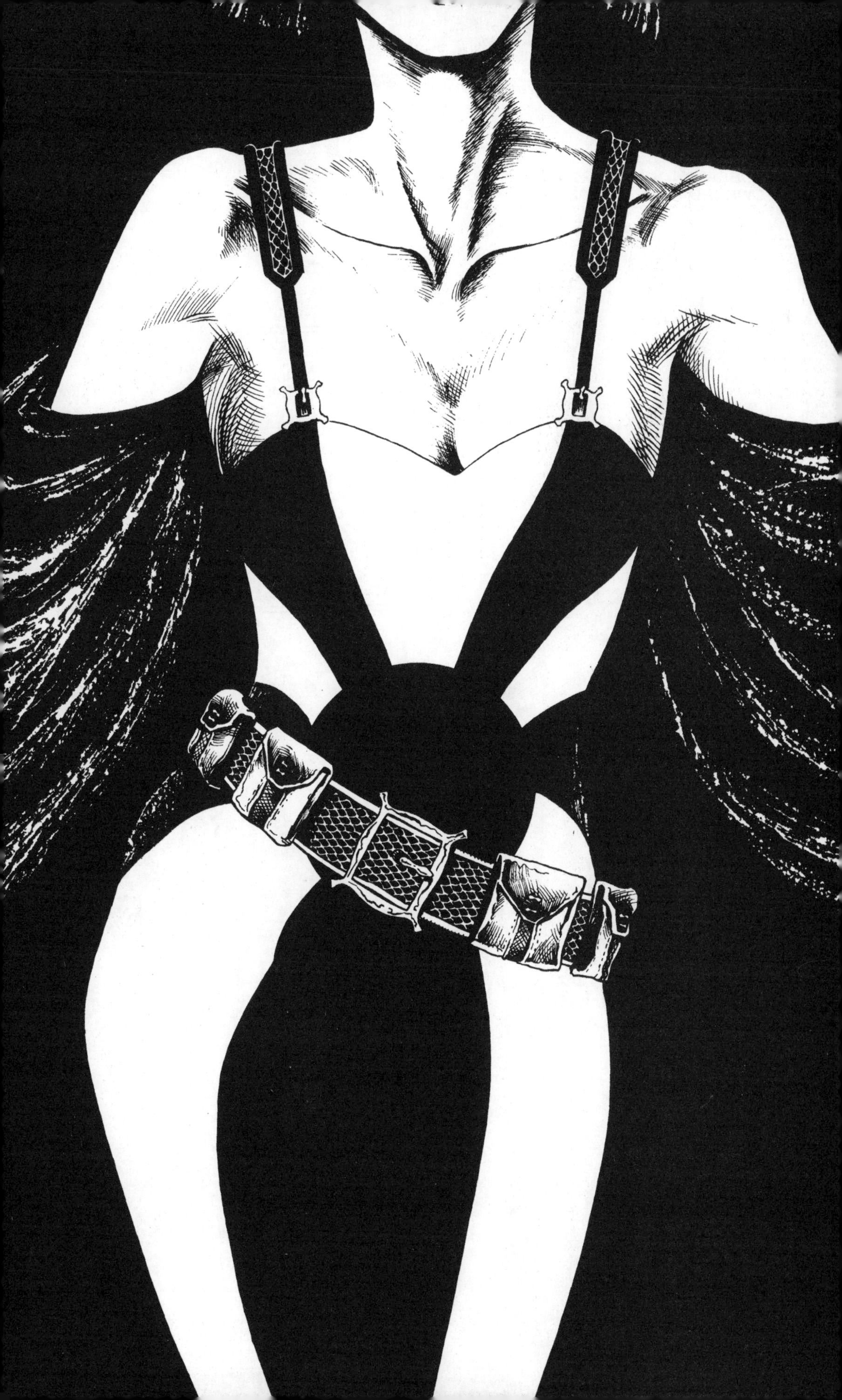

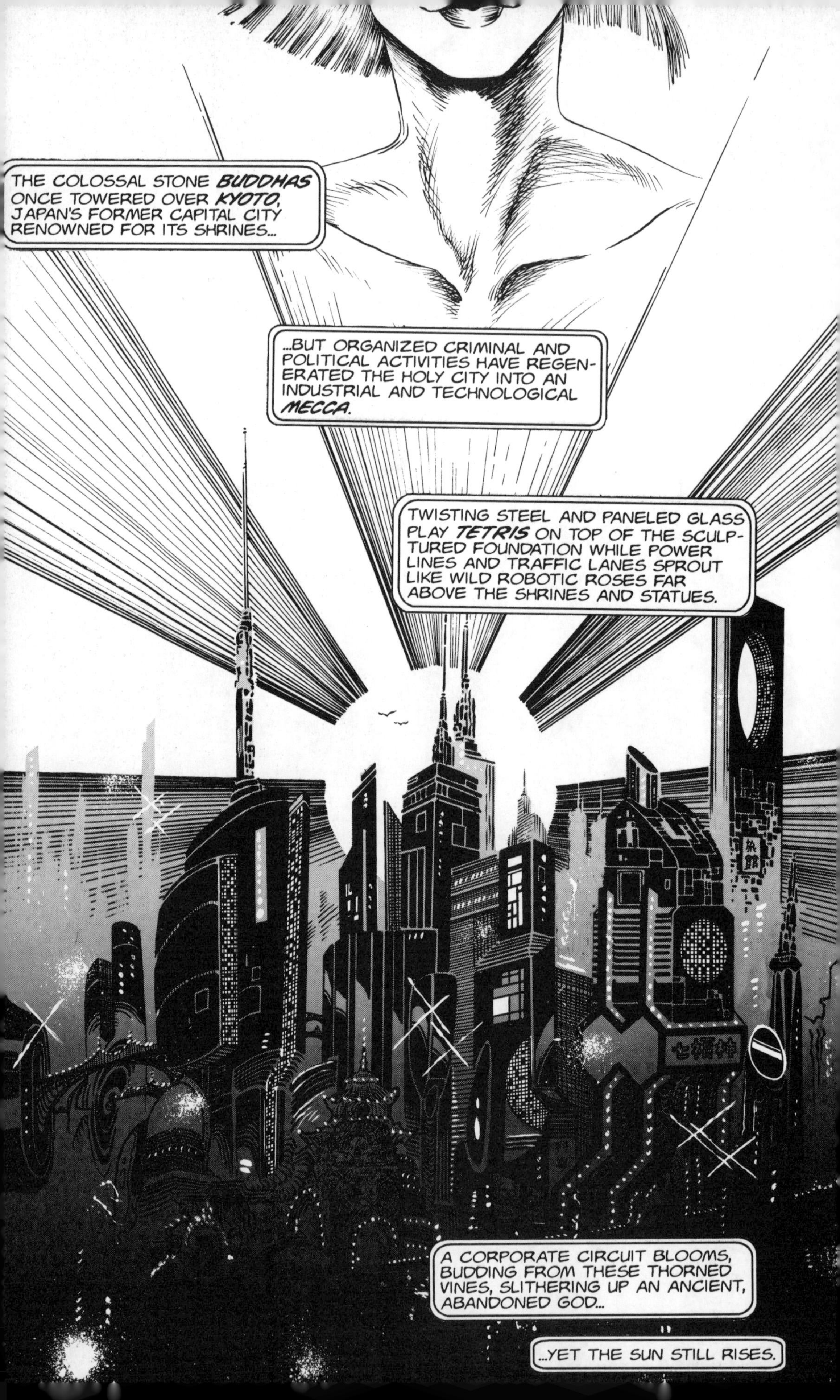

THE COLOSSAL STONE BUDDHAS ONCE TOWERED OVER KYOTO, JAPAN'S FORMER CAPITAL CITY RENOWNED FOR ITS SHRINES...
...BUT ORGANIZED CRIMINAL AND POLITICAL ACTIVITIES HAVE REGEN-ERATED THE HOLY CITY INTO AN INDUSTRIAL AND TECHNOLOGICAL MECCA.
TWISTING STEEL AND PANELED GLASS PLAY TETRIS ON TOP OF THE SCULP-TURED FOUNDATION WHILE POWER LINES AND TRAFFIC LANES SPROUT LIKE WILD ROBOTIC ROSES FAR ABOVE THE SHRINES AND STATUES.
A CORPORATE CIRCUIT BLOOMS, BUDDING FROM THESE THORNED VINES, SLITHERING UP AN ANCIENT, ABANDONED GOD...
...YET THE SUN STILL RISES.

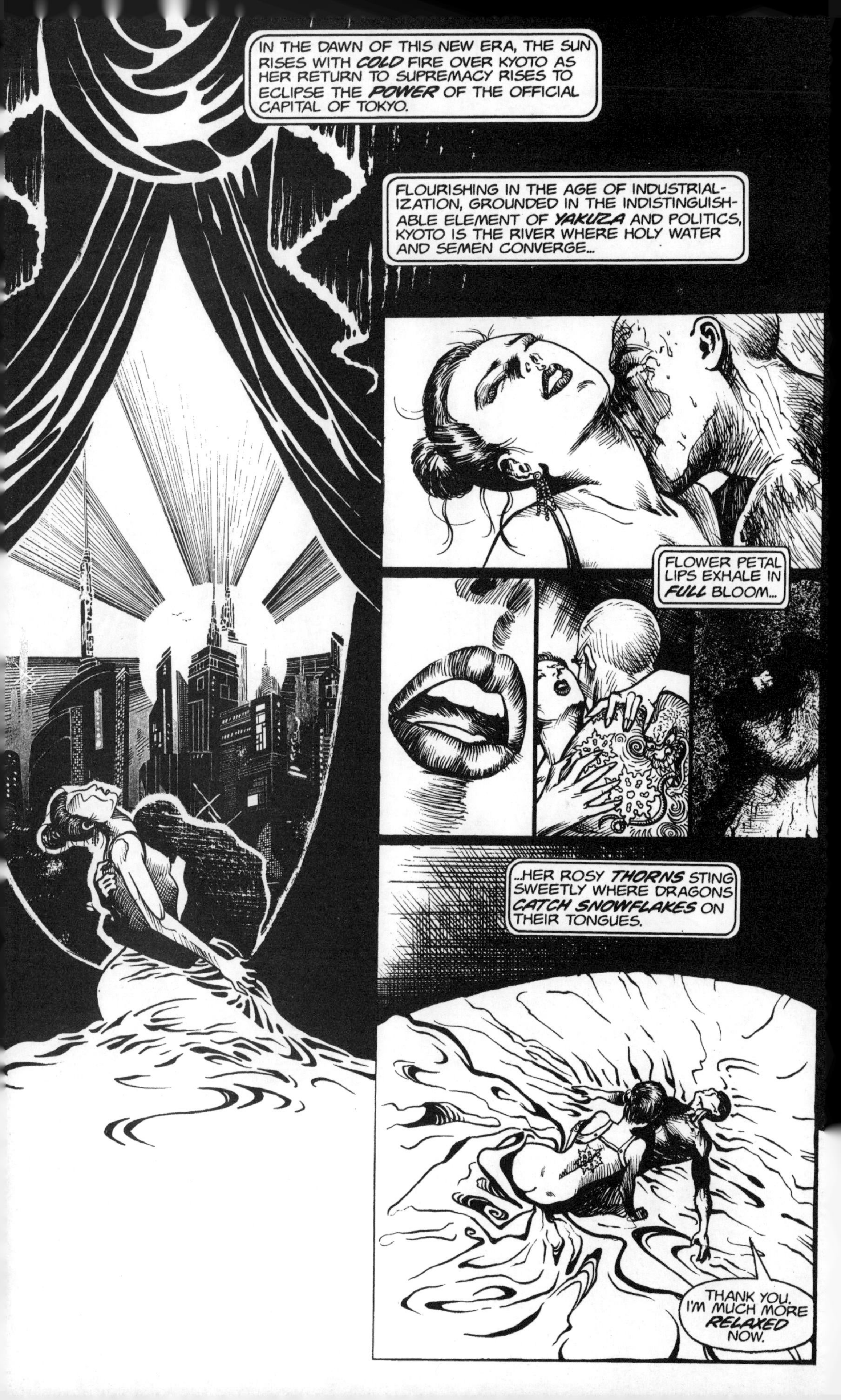
IN THE DAWN OF THIS NEW ERA, THE SUN RISES WITH COLD FIRE OVER KYOTO AS HER RETURN TO SUPREMACY RISES TO ECLIPSE THE POWER OF THE OFFICIAL CAPITAL OF TOKYO.
FLOURISHING IN THE AGE OF INDUSTRIALIZATION, GROUNDED IN THE INDISTINGUISHABLE ELEMENT OF YAKUZA AND POLITICS, KYOTO IS THE RIVER WHERE HOLY WATER AND SEMEN CONVERGE...
FLOWER PETAL LIPS EXHALE IN FULL BLOOM...
...HER ROSY THORNS STING SWEETLY WHERE DRAGONS CATCH SNOWFLAKES ON THEIR TONGUES.
THANK YOU. I'M MUCH MORE RELAXED NOW.

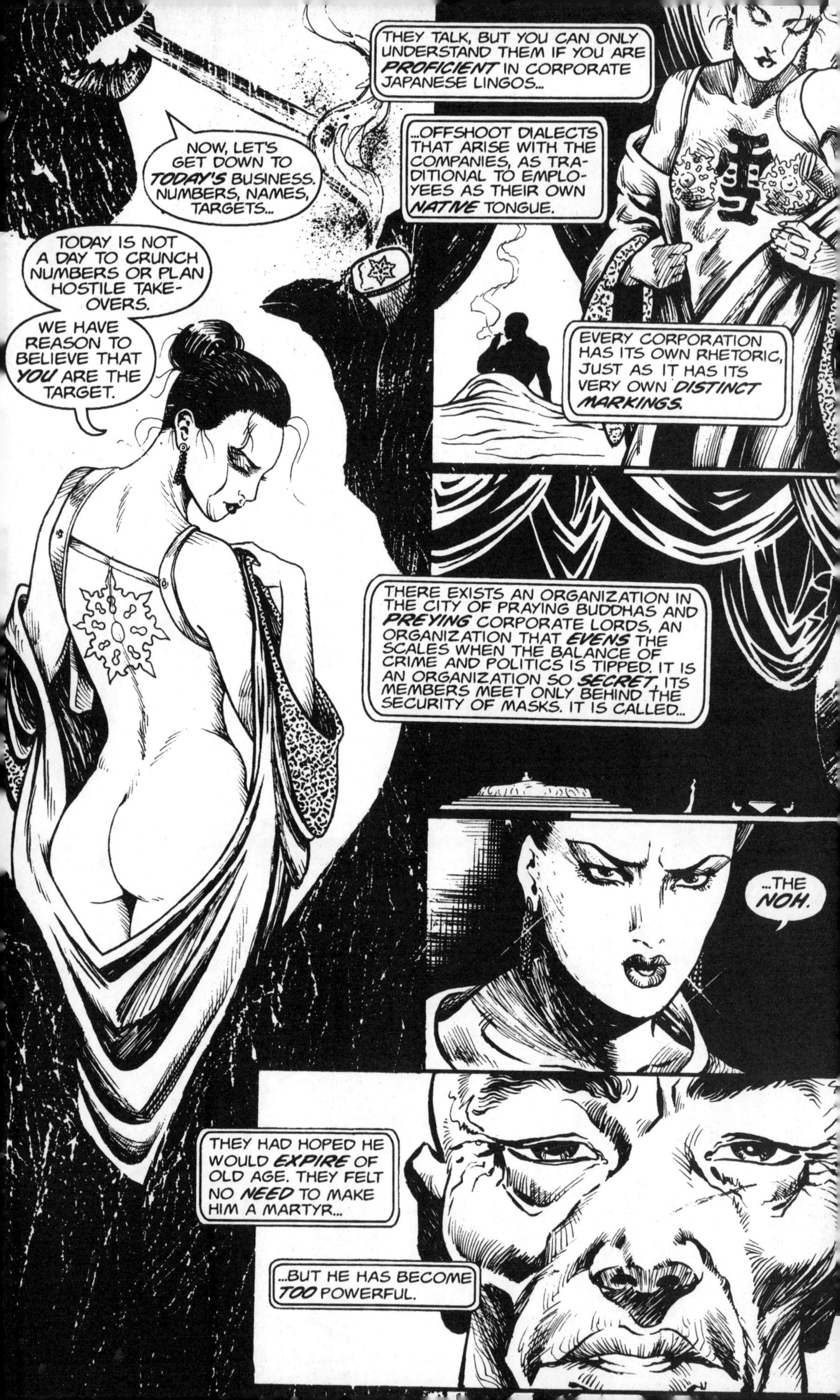

NOW, LET'S GET DOWN TO TODAY'S BUSINESS. NUMBERS, NAMES, TARGETS...
THEY TALK, BUT YOU CAN ONLY UNDERSTAND THEM IF YOU ARE PROFICIENT IN CORPORATE JAPANESE LINGOS...
...OFFSHOOT DIALECTS THAT ARISE WITH THE COMPANIES, AS TRADITIONAL TO EMPLOYEES AS THEIR OWN NATIVE TONGUE.
TODAY IS NOT A DAY TO CRUNCH NUMBERS OR PLAN HOSTILE TAKE-OVERS.
WE HAVE REASON TO BELIEVE THAT YOU ARE THE TARGET.
EVERY CORPORATION HAS ITS OWN RHETORIC, JUST AS IT HAS ITS VERY OWN DISTINCT MARKINGS.
THERE EXISTS AN ORGANIZATION IN THE CITY OF PRAYING BUDDHAS AND PREYING CORPORATE LORDS, AN ORGANIZATION THAT EVENS THE SCALES WHEN THE BALANCE OF CRIME AND POLITICS IS TIPPED. IT IS AN ORGANIZATION SO SECRET, ITS MEMBERS MEET ONLY BEHIND THE SECURITY OF MASKS. IT IS CALLED...
...THE NOH.
THEY HAD HOPED HE WOULD EXPIRE OF OLD AGE. THEY FELT NO NEED TO MAKE HIM A MARTYR...
...BUT HE HAS BECOME TOO POWERFUL.

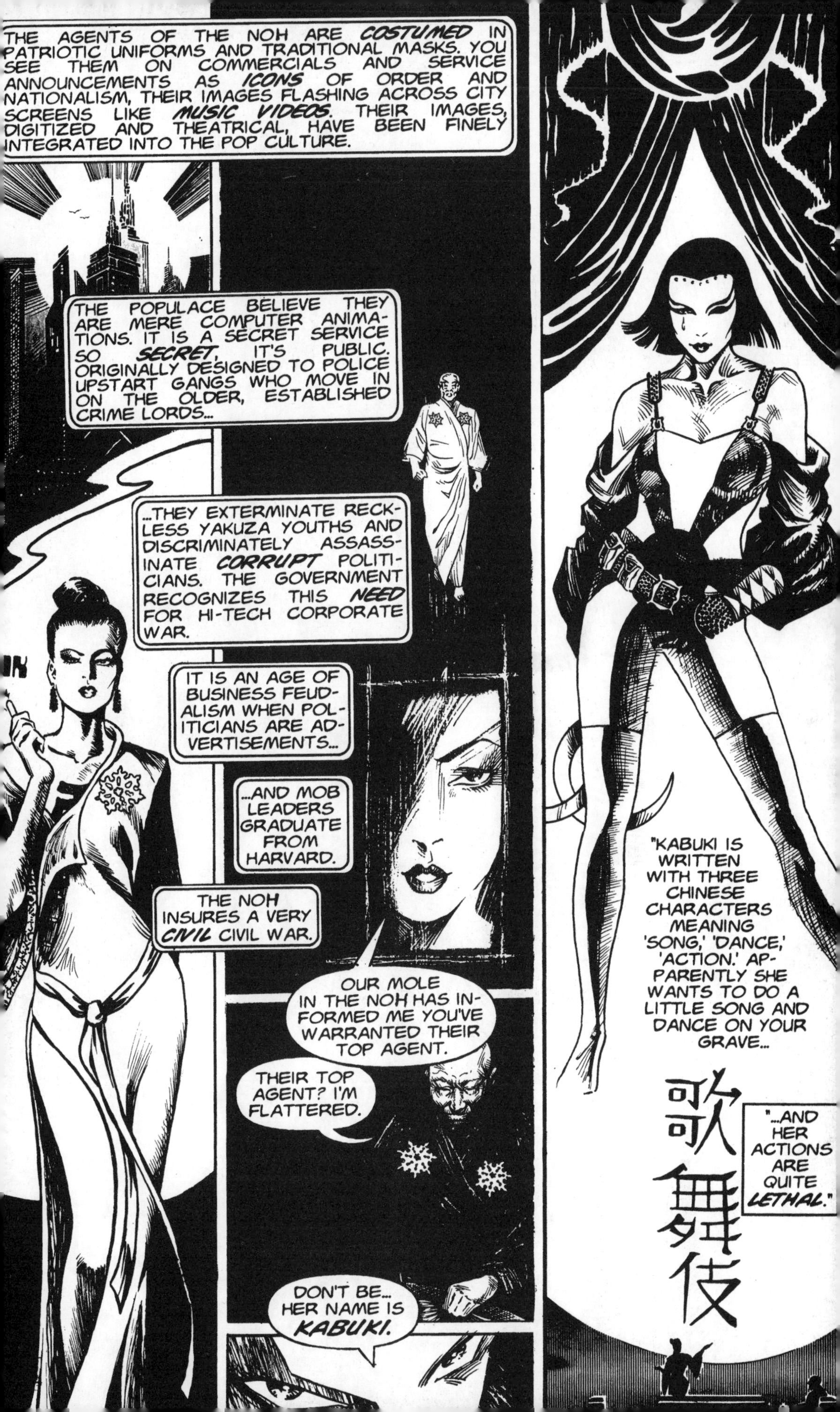
THE AGENTS OF THE NOH ARE COSTUMED IN PATRIOTIC UNIFORMS AND TRADITIONAL MASKS. YOU SEE THEM ON COMMERCIALS AND SERVICE ANNOUNCEMENTS AS ICONS OF ORDER AND NATIONALISM, THEIR IMAGES FLASHING ACROSS CITY SCREENS LIKE MUSIC VIDEOS. THEIR IMAGES, DIGITIZED AND THEATRICAL, HAVE BEEN FINELY INTEGRATED INTO THE POP CULTURE.
THE POPULACE BELIEVE THEY ARE MERE COMPUTER ANIMATIONS. IT IS A SECRET SERVICE SO SECRET, IT'S PUBLIC. ORIGINALLY DESIGNED TO POLICE UPSTART GANGS WHO MOVE IN ON THE OLDER, ESTABLISHED CRIME LORDS...
...THEY EXTERMINATE RECKLESS YAKUZA YOUTHS AND DISCRIMINATELY ASSASSINATE CORRUPT POLITICIANS. THE GOVERNMENT RECOGNIZES THIS NEED FOR HI-TECH CORPORATE WAR.
IT IS AN AGE OF BUSINESS FEUDALISM WHEN POLITICIANS ARE ADVERTISEMENTS...
...AND MOB LEADERS GRADUATE FROM HARVARD.
THE NOH INSURES A VERY CIVIL CIVIL WAR.
OUR MOLE IN THE NOH HAS INFORMED ME YOU'VE WARRANTED THEIR TOP AGENT.
THEIR TOP AGENT? I'M FLATTERED.
DON'T BE... HER NAME IS KABUKI.
"KABUKI IS WRITTEN WITH THREE CHINESE CHARACTERS MEANING 'SONG,' 'DANCE,' 'ACTION.' APPARENTLY SHE WANTS TO DO A LITTLE SONG AND DANCE ON YOUR GRAVE...
歌舞伎
"...AND HER ACTIONS ARE QUITE LETHAL."

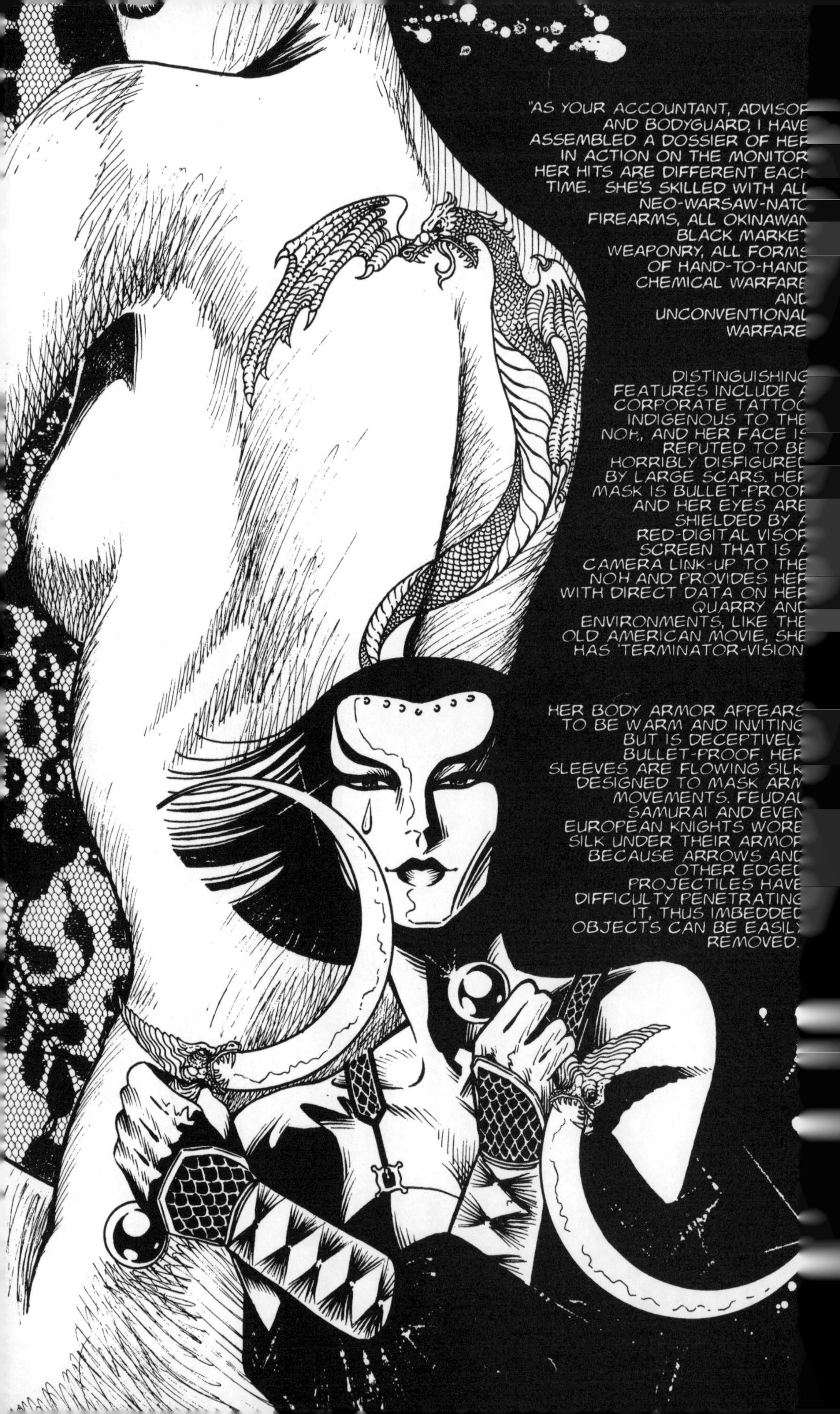

"AS YOUR ACCOUNTANT, ADVISOR AND BODYGUARD, I HAVE ASSEMBLED A DOSSIER OF HER IN ACTION ON THE MONITOR. HER HITS ARE DIFFERENT EACH TIME. SHE'S SKILLED WITH ALL NEO-WARSAW-NATO FIREARMS, ALL OKINAWAN BLACK MARKET WEAPONRY, ALL FORMS OF HAND-TO-HAND, CHEMICAL WARFARE AND UNCONVENTIONAL WARFARE.
DISTINGUISHING FEATURES INCLUDE A CORPORATE TATTOO INDIGENOUS TO THE NOH, AND HER FACE IS REPUTED TO BE HORRIBLY DISFIGURED BY LARGE SCARS. HER MASK IS BULLET-PROOF AND HER EYES ARE SHIELDED BY A RED-DIGITAL VISOR SCREEN THAT IS A CAMERA LINK-UP TO THE NOH AND PROVIDES HER WITH DIRECT DATA ON HER QUARRY AND ENVIRONMENTS. LIKE THE OLD AMERICAN MOVIE, SHE HAS 'TERMINATOR-VISION.'
HER BODY ARMOR APPEARS TO BE WARM AND INVITING BUT IS DECEPTIVELY BULLET-PROOF. HER SLEEVES ARE FLOWING SILK DESIGNED TO MASK ARM MOVEMENTS. FEUDAL SAMURAI AND EVEN EUROPEAN KNIGHTS WORE SILK UNDER THEIR ARMOR BECAUSE ARROWS AND OTHER EDGED PROJECTILES HAVE DIFFICULTY PENETRATING IT, THUS IMBEDDED OBJECTS CAN BE EASILY REMOVED.

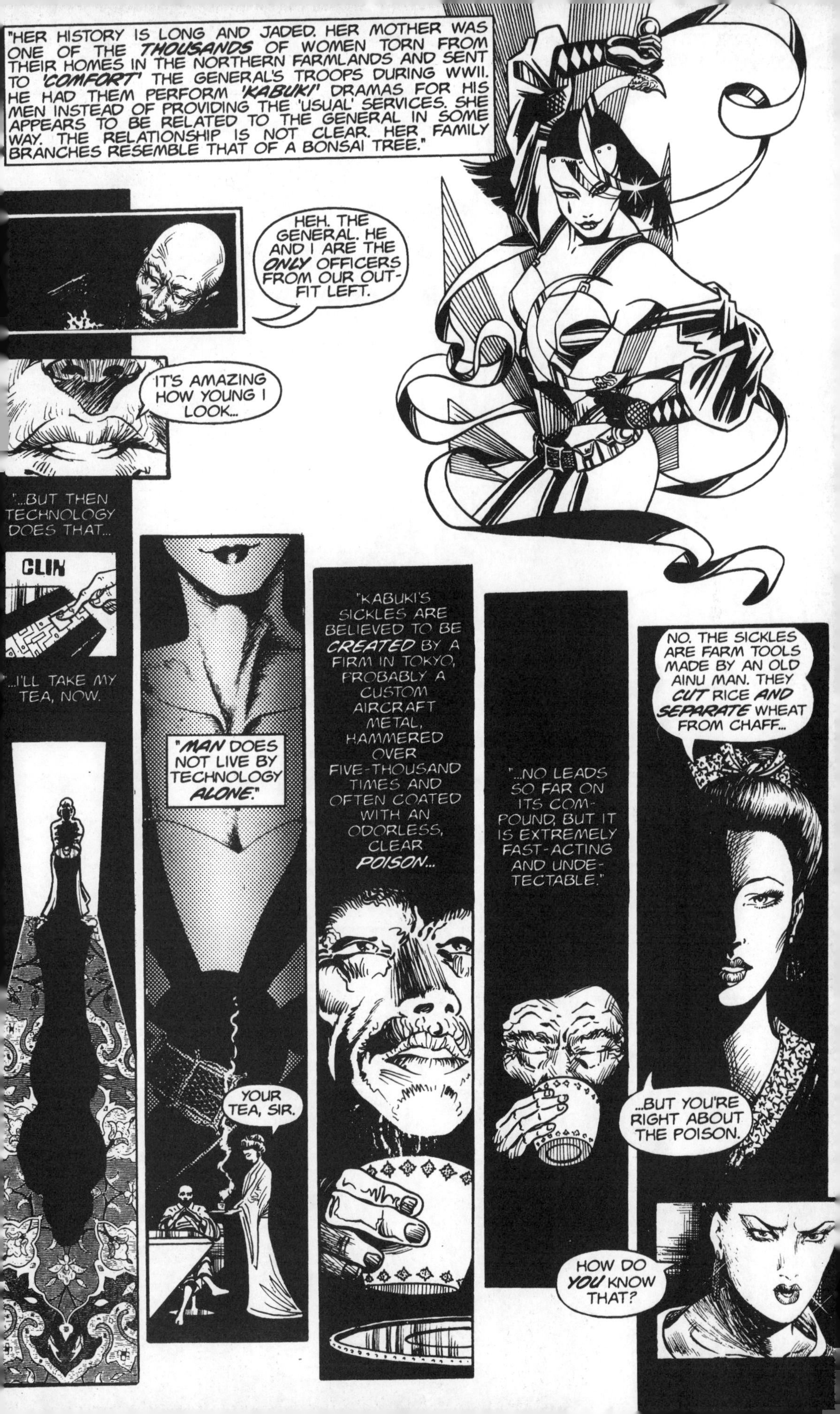
"HER HISTORY IS LONG AND JADED. HER MOTHER WAS ONE OF THE THOUSANDS OF WOMEN TORN FROM THEIR HOMES IN THE NORTHERN FARMLANDS AND SENT TO 'COMFORT' THE GENERAL'S TROOPS DURING WWII. HE HAD THEM PERFORM 'KABUKI' DRAMAS FOR HIS MEN INSTEAD OF PROVIDING THE 'USUAL' SERVICES. SHE APPEARS TO BE RELATED TO THE GENERAL IN SOME WAY. THE RELATIONSHIP IS NOT CLEAR. HER FAMILY BRANCHES RESEMBLE THAT OF A BONSAI TREE."
HEH. THE GENERAL. HE AND I ARE THE ONLY OFFICERS FROM OUR OUT-FIT LEFT.
IT'S AMAZING HOW YOUNG I LOOK...
"...BUT THEN TECHNOLOGY DOES THAT...
CLIK
...I'LL TAKE MY TEA, NOW.
"MAN DOES NOT LIVE BY TECHNOLOGY ALONE."
YOUR TEA, SIR.
"KABUKI'S SICKLES ARE BELIEVED TO BE CREATED BY A FIRM IN TOKYO, PROBABLY A CUSTOM AIRCRAFT METAL, HAMMERED OVER FIVE-THOUSAND TIMES AND OFTEN COATED WITH AN ODORLESS, CLEAR POISON...
"...NO LEADS SO FAR ON ITS COM-POUND, BUT IT IS EXTREMELY FAST-ACTING AND UNDE-TECTABLE."
NO. THE SICKLES ARE FARM TOOLS MADE BY AN OLD AINU MAN. THEY CUT RICE AND SEPARATE WHEAT FROM CHAFF...
...BUT YOU'RE RIGHT ABOUT THE POISON.
HOW DO YOU KNOW THAT?

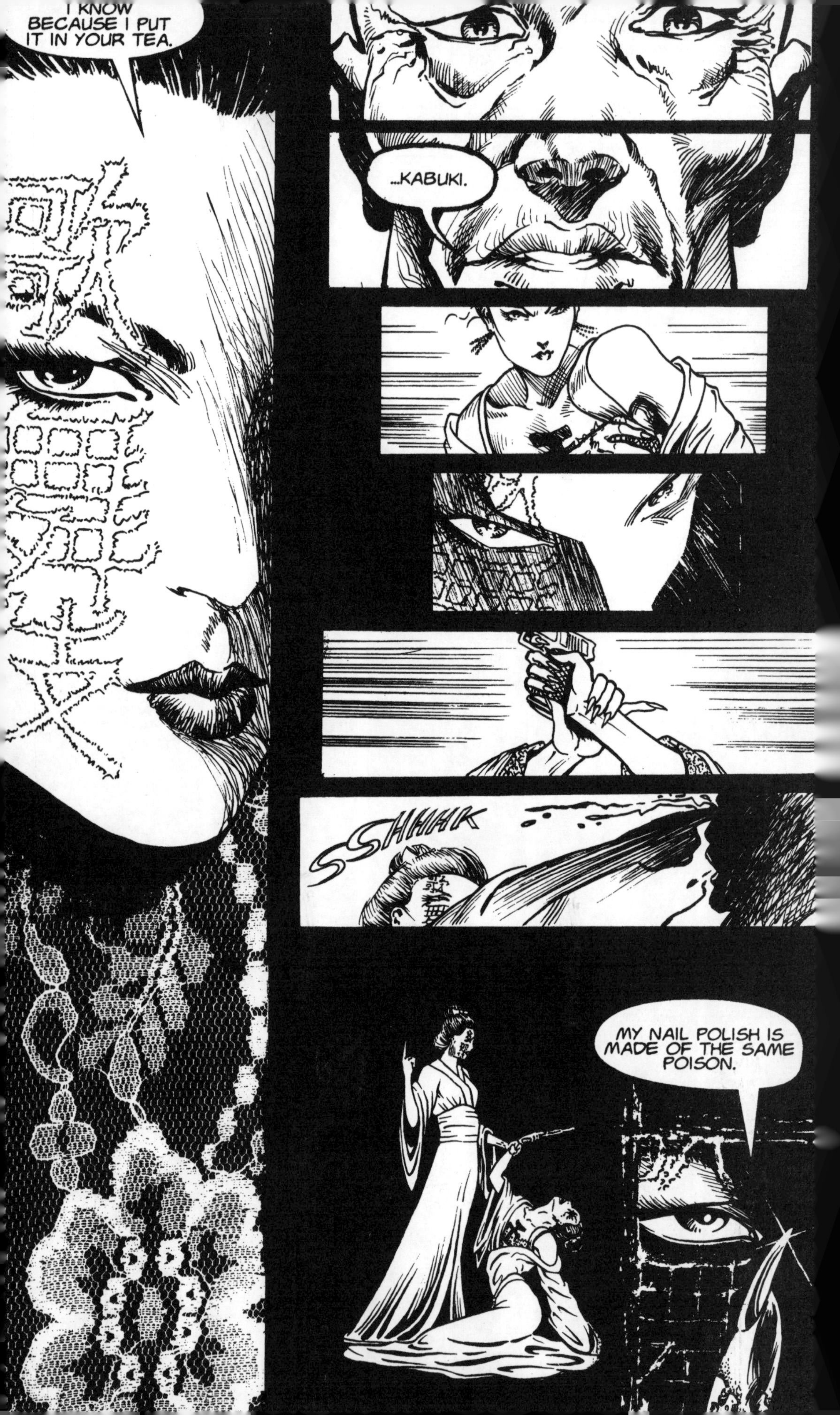
I KNOW BECAUSE I PUT IT IN YOUR TEA.
...KABUKI.
SSHHHK
MY NAIL POLISH IS MADE OF THE SAME POISON.

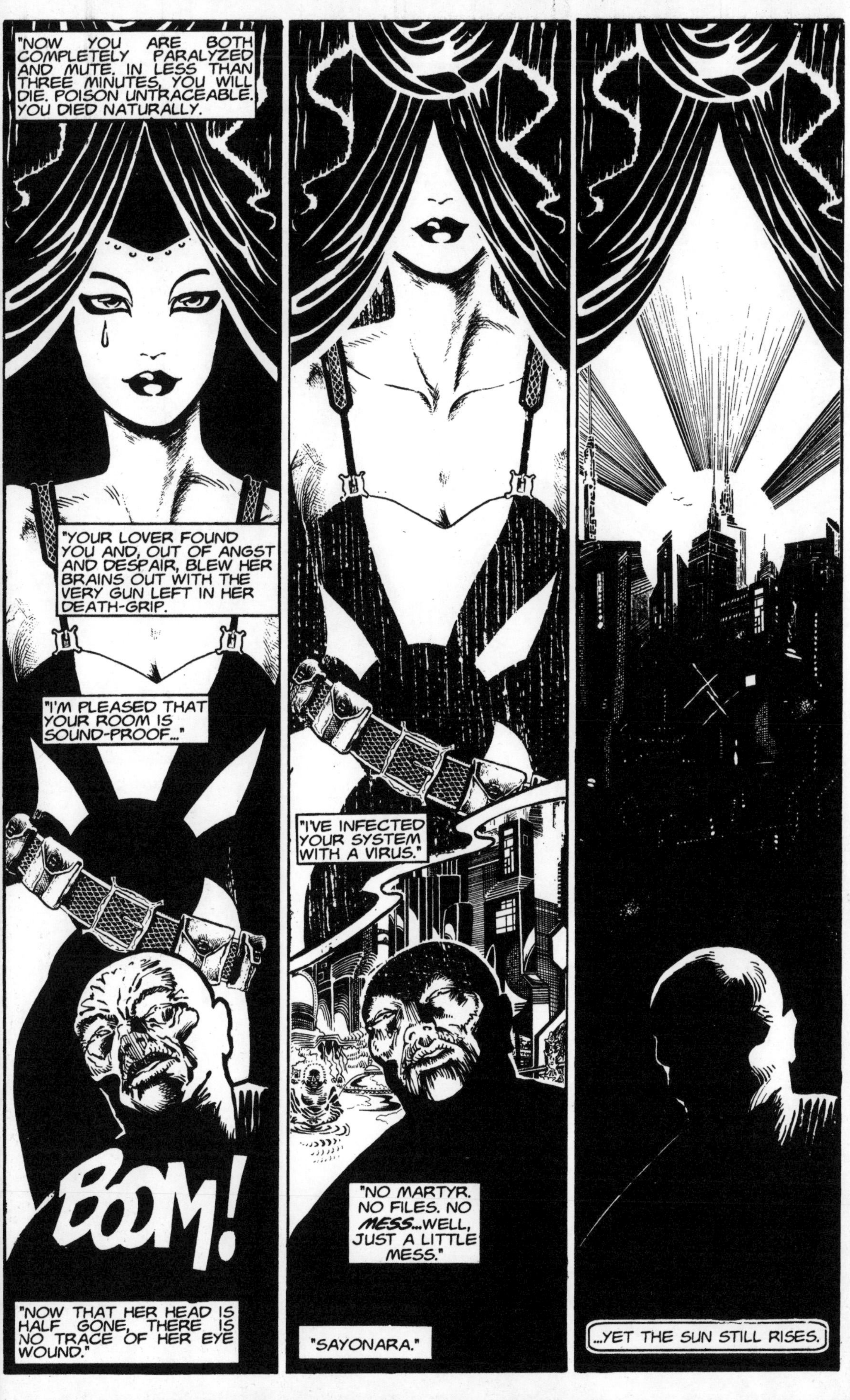
"NOW YOU ARE BOTH COMPLETELY PARALYZED AND MUTE. IN LESS THAN THREE MINUTES, YOU WILL DIE. POISON UNTRACEABLE. YOU DIED NATURALLY.
"YOUR LOVER FOUND YOU AND, OUT OF ANGST AND DESPAIR, BLEW HER BRAINS OUT WITH THE VERY GUN LEFT IN HER DEATH-GRIP.
"I'M PLEASED THAT YOUR ROOM IS SOUND-PROOF..."
BOOM!
"NOW THAT HER HEAD IS HALF GONE, THERE IS NO TRACE OF HER EYE WOUND."
"I'VE INFECTED YOUR SYSTEM WITH A VIRUS."
"NO MARTYR. NO FILES. NO MESS...WELL, JUST A LITTLE MESS."
"SAYONARA."
...YET THE SUN STILL RISES.

SCENE IV
THROUGH THE LOOKING GLASS

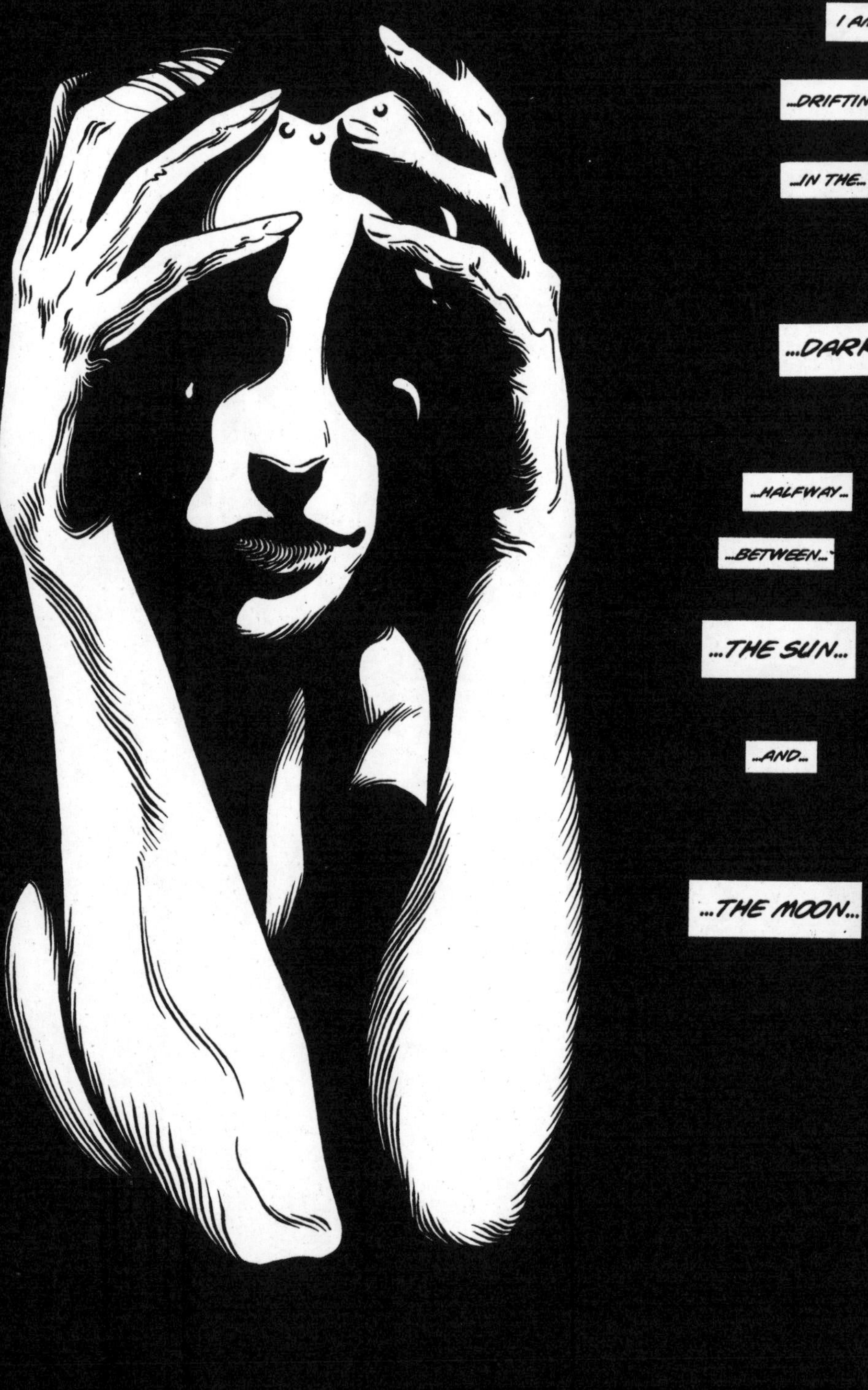
I AM...
...DRIFTING...
...IN THE...
...DARK...
...HALFWAY...
...BETWEEN...
...THE SUN...
...AND...
...THE MOON...

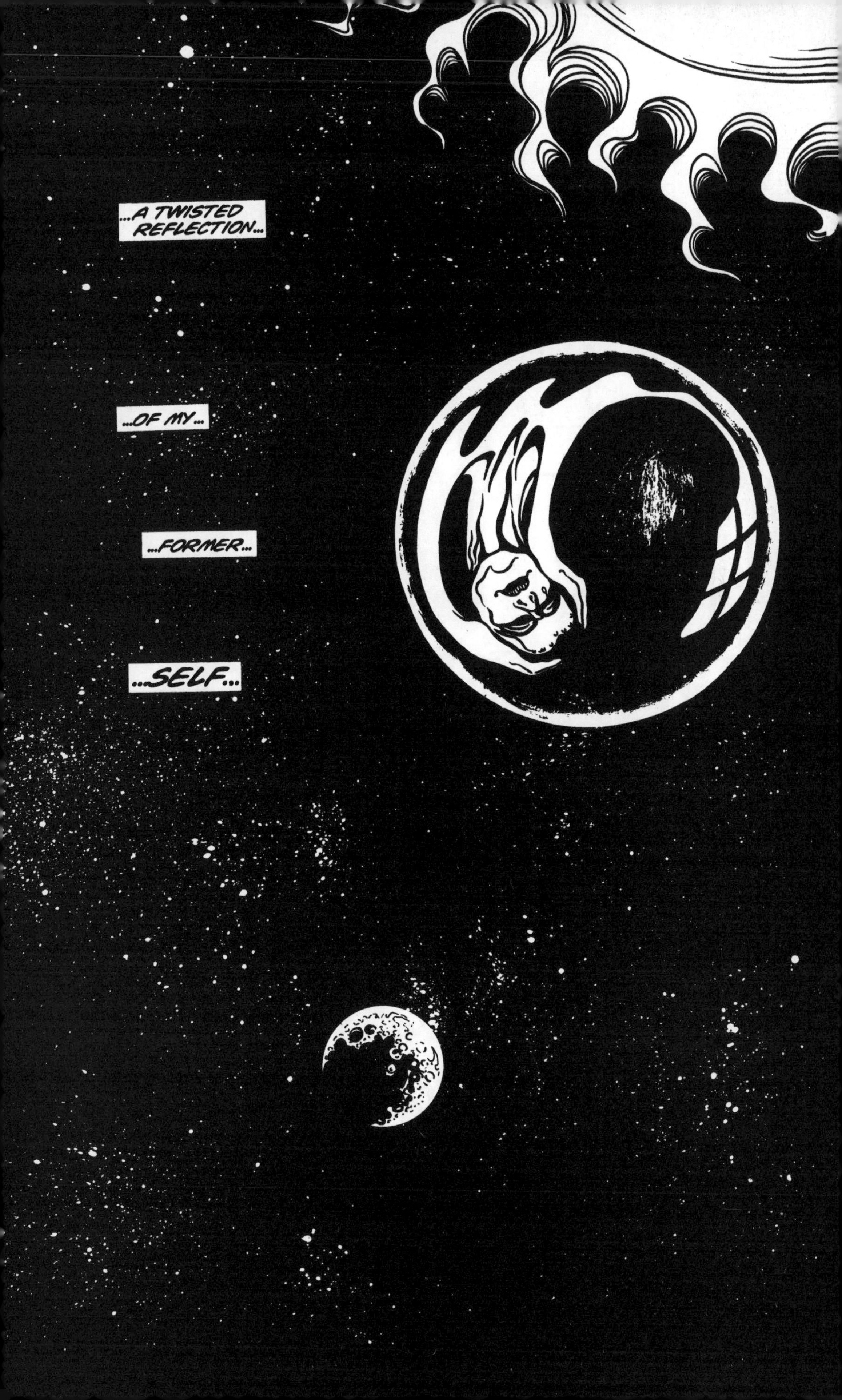

...A TWISTED REFLECTION...
...OF MY...
...FORMER...
...SELF...

...A *REFLECTION* THAT IS CAUGHT...
...IN THE SPHERICAL *URN*...
...AT MY MOTHER'S *GRAVE*.
月子

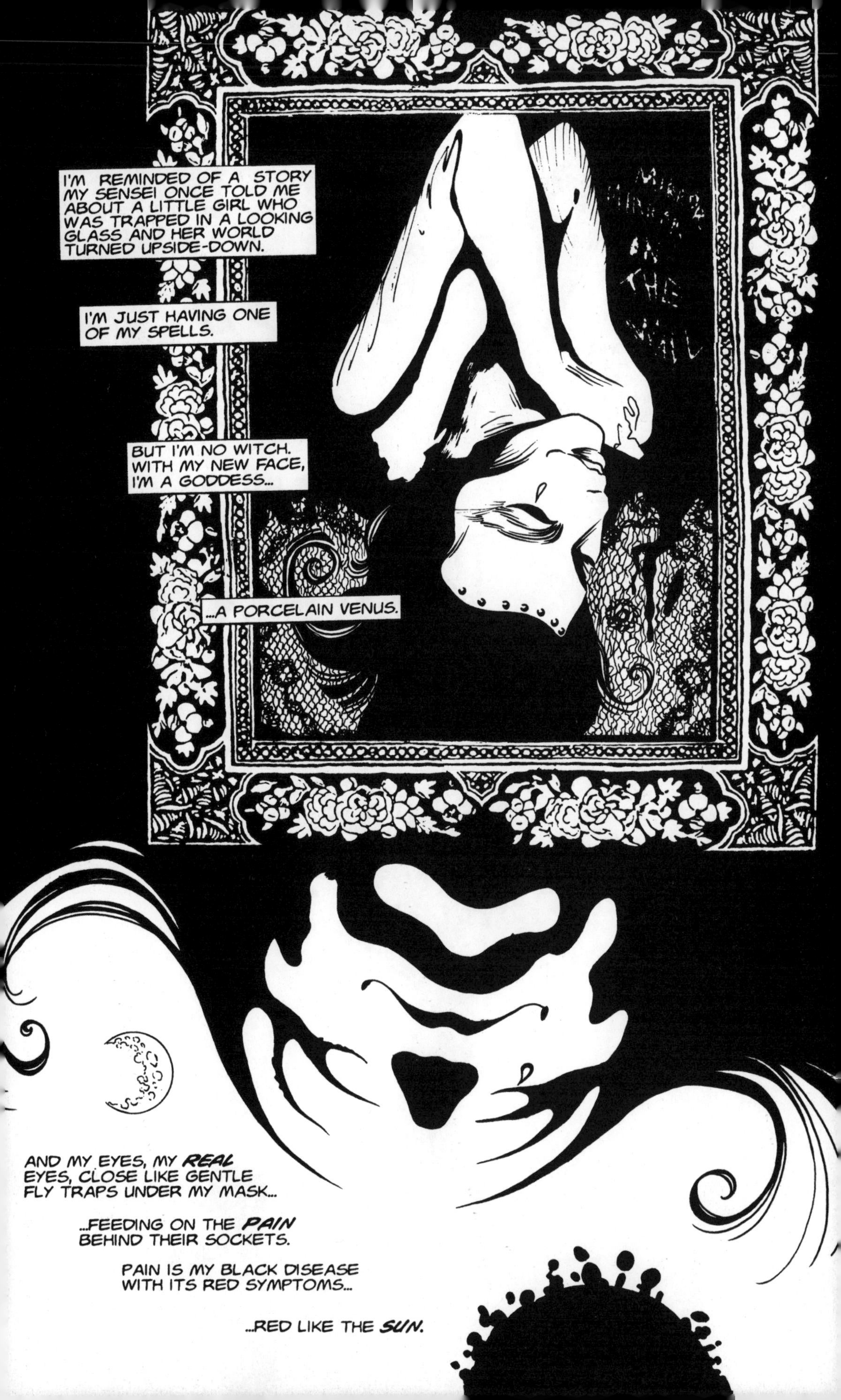
I'M REMINDED OF A STORY MY SENSEI ONCE TOLD ME ABOUT A LITTLE GIRL WHO WAS TRAPPED IN A LOOKING GLASS AND HER WORLD TURNED UPSIDE-DOWN.
I'M JUST HAVING ONE OF MY SPELLS.
BUT I'M NO WITCH. WITH MY NEW FACE, I'M A GODDESS...
...A PORCELAIN VENUS.
AND MY EYES, MY REAL EYES, CLOSE LIKE GENTLE FLY TRAPS UNDER MY MASK...
...FEEDING ON THE PAIN BEHIND THEIR SOCKETS.
PAIN IS MY BLACK DISEASE WITH ITS RED SYMPTOMS...
...RED LIKE THE SUN.

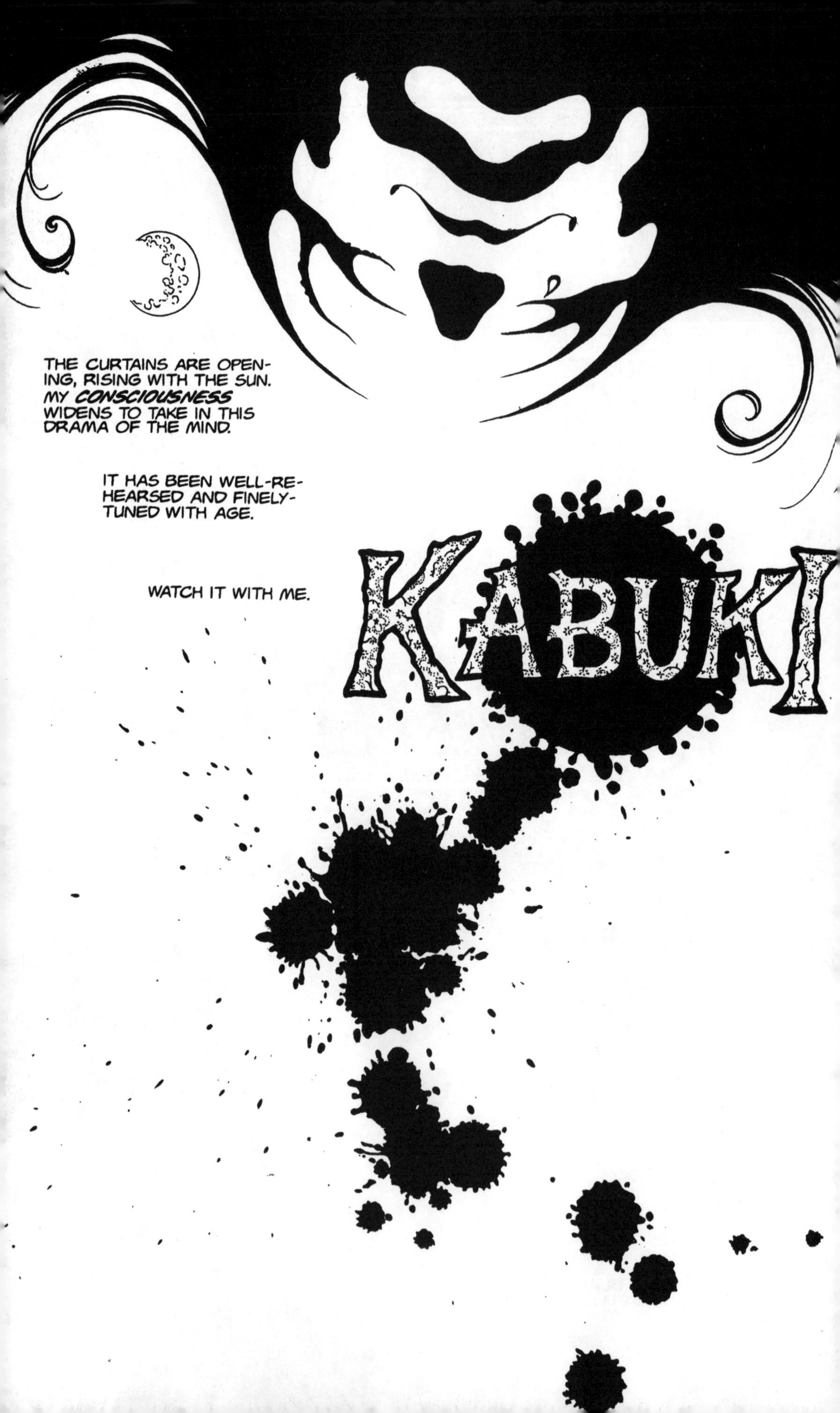

THE CURTAINS ARE OPENING, RISING WITH THE SUN. MY CONSCIOUSNESS WIDENS TO TAKE IN THIS DRAMA OF THE MIND.
IT HAS BEEN WELL-REHEARSED AND FINELY-TUNED WITH AGE.
KABUKI
WATCH IT WITH ME.

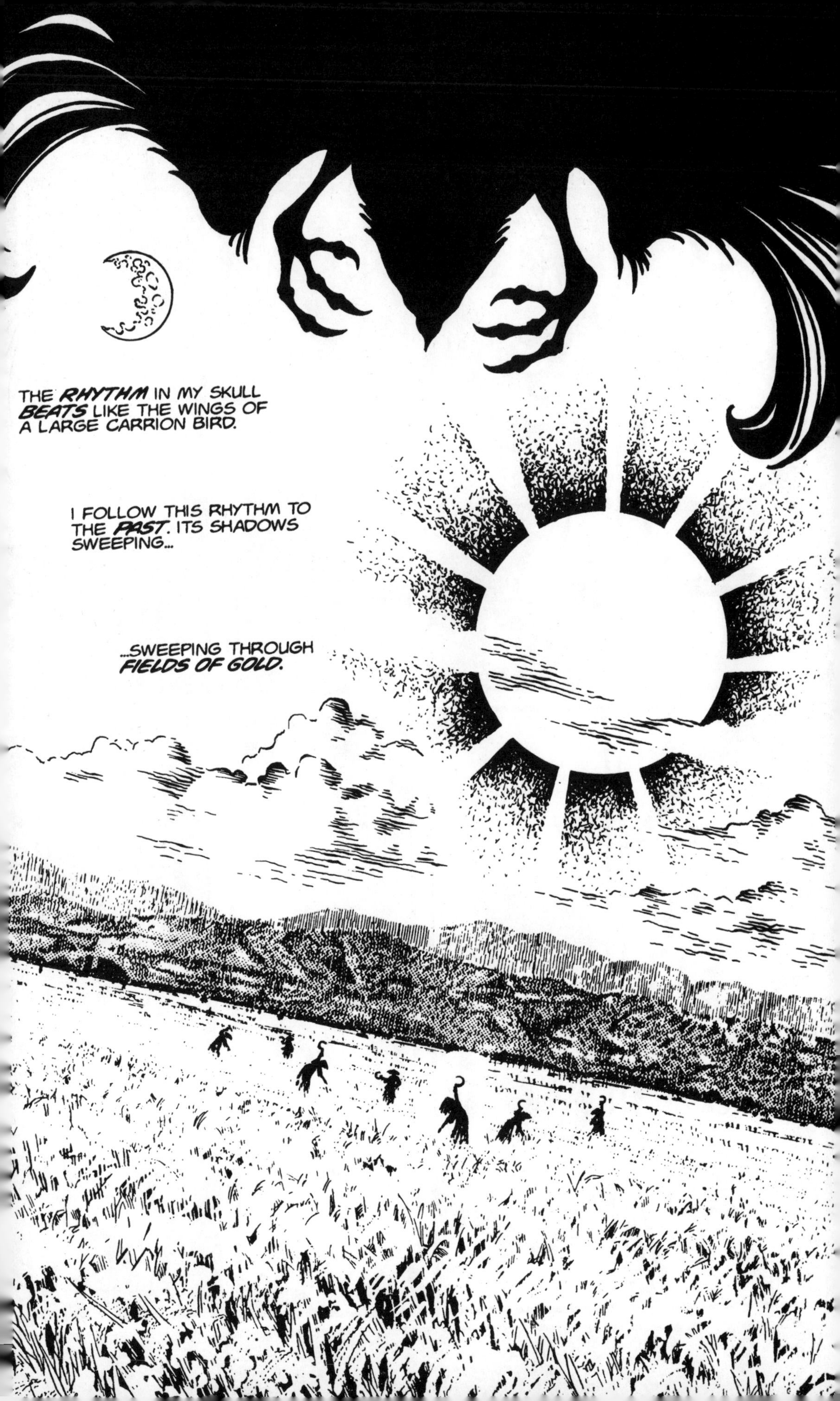
THE RHYTHM IN MY SKULL BEATS LIKE THE WINGS OF A LARGE CARRION BIRD.
I FOLLOW THIS RHYTHM TO THE PAST. ITS SHADOWS SWEEPING...
...SWEEPING THROUGH FIELDS OF GOLD.

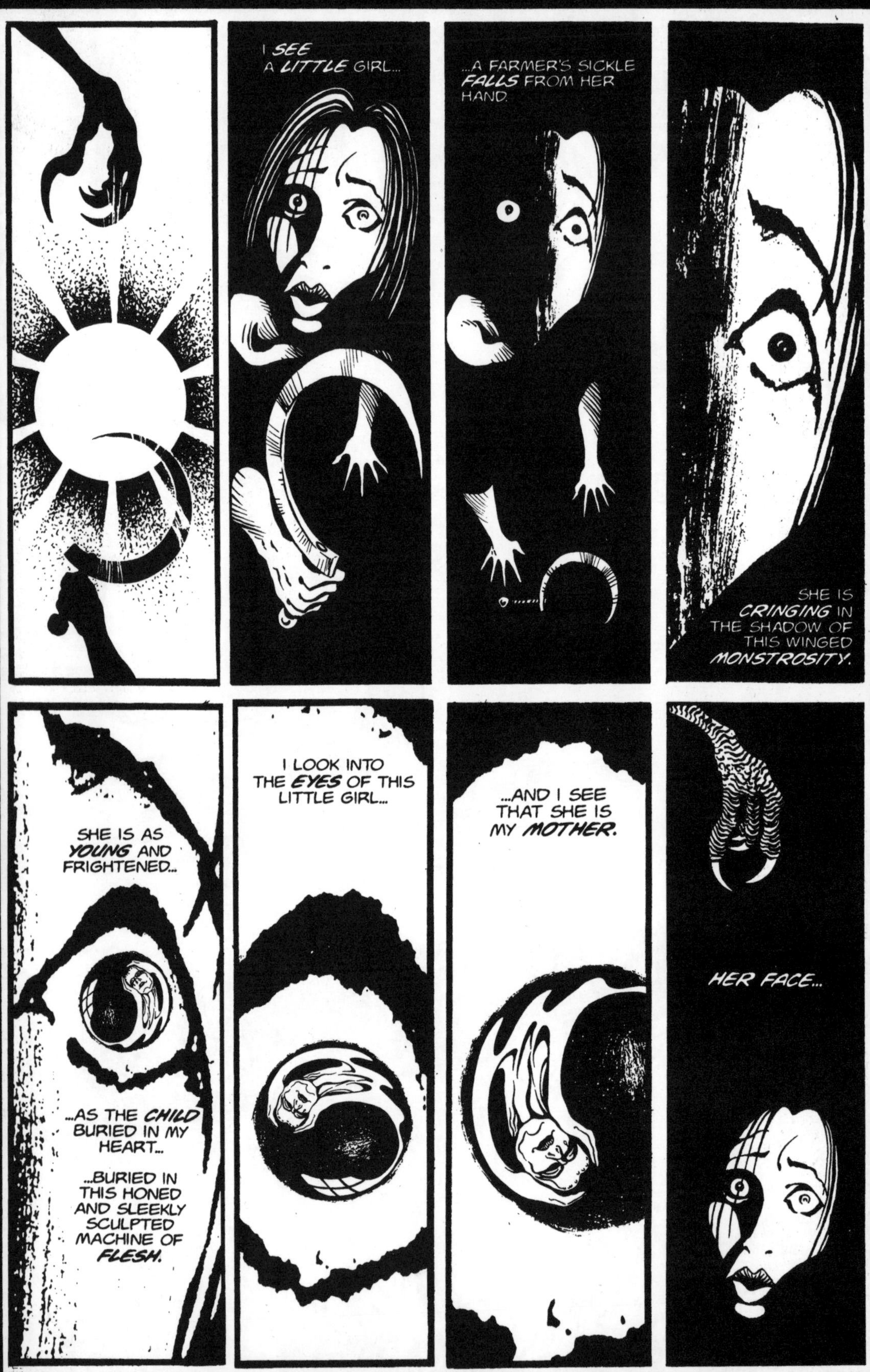
I SEE A LITTLE GIRL...
...A FARMER'S SICKLE FALLS FROM HER HAND.
SHE IS CRINGING IN THE SHADOW OF THIS WINGED MONSTROSITY.
SHE IS AS YOUNG AND FRIGHTENED...
...AS THE CHILD BURIED IN MY HEART...
...BURIED IN THIS HONED AND SLEEKLY SCULPTED MACHINE OF FLESH.
I LOOK INTO THE EYES OF THIS LITTLE GIRL...
...AND I SEE THAT SHE IS MY MOTHER.
HER FACE...

HER FACE IS ONE IN A FRIGHTENED *SEA* OF FACES.

IT IS WWII.

YOUNG FARM GIRLS WERE *UPROOTED* FROM THEIR PARENTS BY FORCE AND SHIPPED IN MASS QUANTITIES TO *JAPANESE* MILITARY OUTPOSTS.

THESE GIRLS WERE EXPECTED TO *PERFORM* THEIR DUTY TO KEEP THE *SOLDIERS* IN GOOD SPIRITS JUST AS THE SOLDIERS ACCEPT THEIR CALL TO *FIGHT* FOR THEIR COUNTRY.

THESE GIRLS, DUBBED *COMFORT* WOMEN...

...WERE, IN EFFECT...

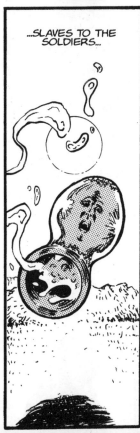

...SLAVES TO THE SOLDIERS...

...AND THEIR *WORLD CAME CRASHING DOWN.*

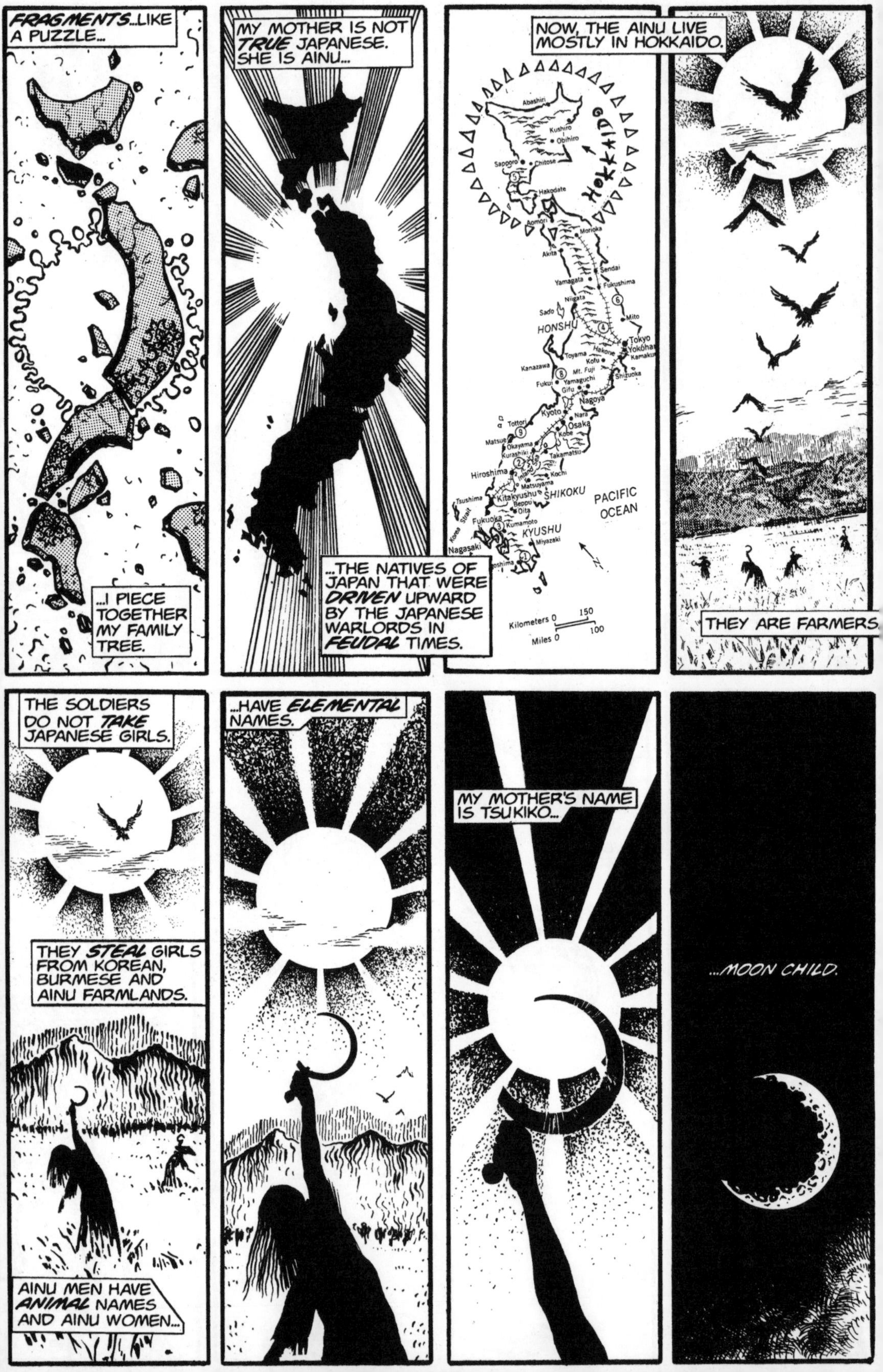
FRAGMENTS...LIKE A PUZZLE...
...I PIECE TOGETHER MY FAMILY TREE.
MY MOTHER IS NOT TRUE JAPANESE. SHE IS AINU...
...THE NATIVES OF JAPAN THAT WERE DRIVEN UPWARD BY THE JAPANESE WARLORDS IN FEUDAL TIMES.
NOW, THE AINU LIVE MOSTLY IN HOKKAIDO.
HOKKAIDO
Abashiri
Kushiro
Obihiro
Sapporo
Chitose
Hakodate
Aomori
Morioka
Akita
Sendai
Yamagata
Fukushima
Niigata
Sado
HONSHU
Mito
Tokyo
Toyama
Hakone
Kofu
Kanazawa
Mt. Fuji
Shizuoka
Fukui
Yamaguchi
Gifu
Nagoya
Tottori
Kyoto
Nara
Osaka
Matsue
Okayama
Kobe
Kurashiki
Takamatsu
Hiroshima
Inland
Kochi
Matsuyama
Tsushima
Kitakyushu
SHIKOKU
Beppu
Oita
Fukuoka
Korea Strait
Kumamoto
KYUSHU
Nagasaki
Miyazaki
PACIFIC OCEAN
Kilometers 0 150
Miles 0 100
THEY ARE FARMERS.
THE SOLDIERS DO NOT TAKE JAPANESE GIRLS.
THEY STEAL GIRLS FROM KOREAN, BURMESE AND AINU FARMLANDS.
AINU MEN HAVE ANIMAL NAMES AND AINU WOMEN...
...HAVE ELEMENTAL NAMES.
MY MOTHER'S NAME IS TSUKIKO...
...MOON CHILD.

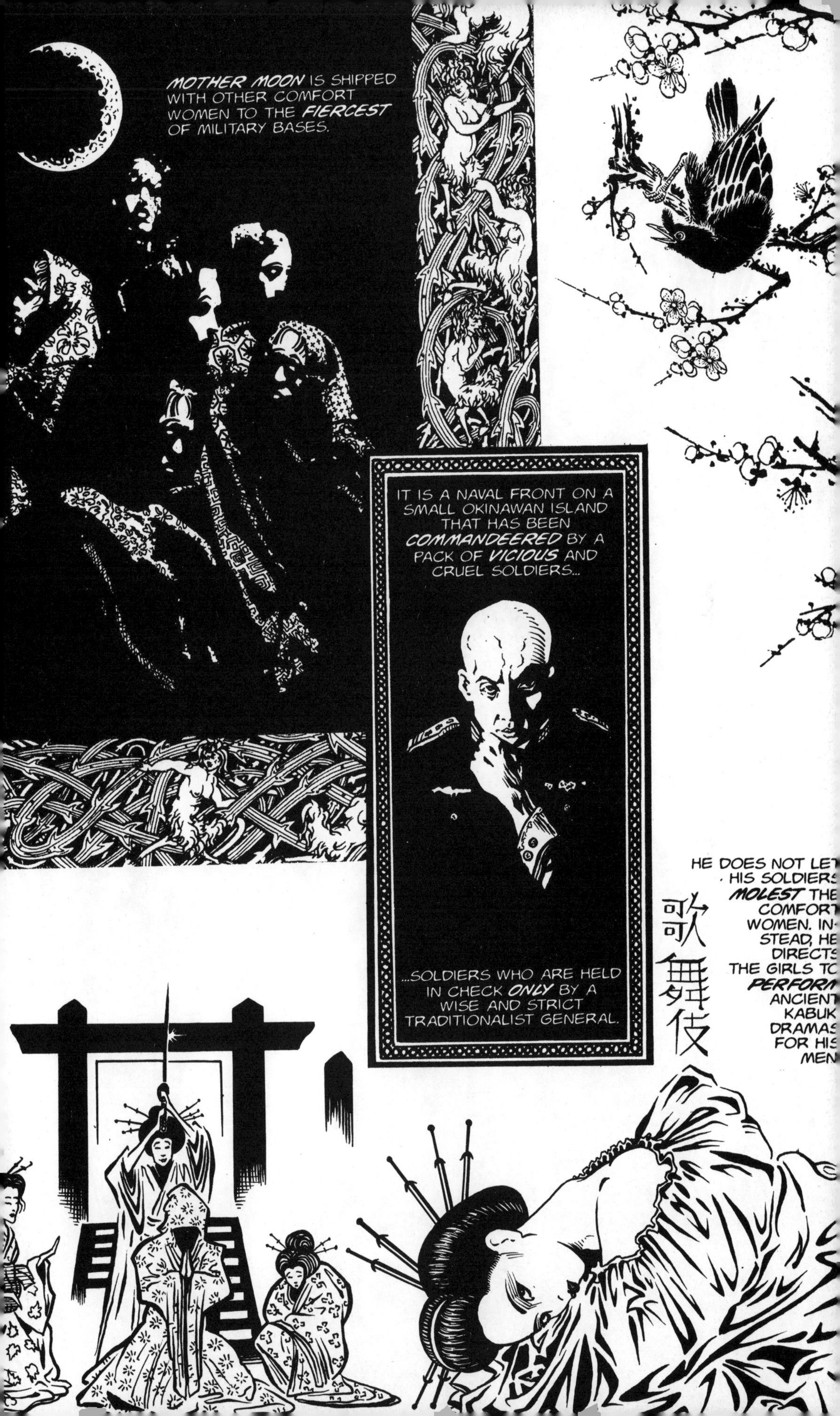
MOTHER MOON IS SHIPPED WITH OTHER COMFORT WOMEN TO THE FIERCEST OF MILITARY BASES.
IT IS A NAVAL FRONT ON A SMALL OKINAWAN ISLAND THAT HAS BEEN COMMANDEERED BY A PACK OF VICIOUS AND CRUEL SOLDIERS...
...SOLDIERS WHO ARE HELD IN CHECK ONLY BY A WISE AND STRICT TRADITIONALIST GENERAL.
HE DOES NOT LET HIS SOLDIERS MOLEST THE COMFORT WOMEN. IN-STEAD, HE DIRECTS THE GIRLS TO PERFORM ANCIENT KABUK DRAMAS FOR HIS MEN
歌舞伎

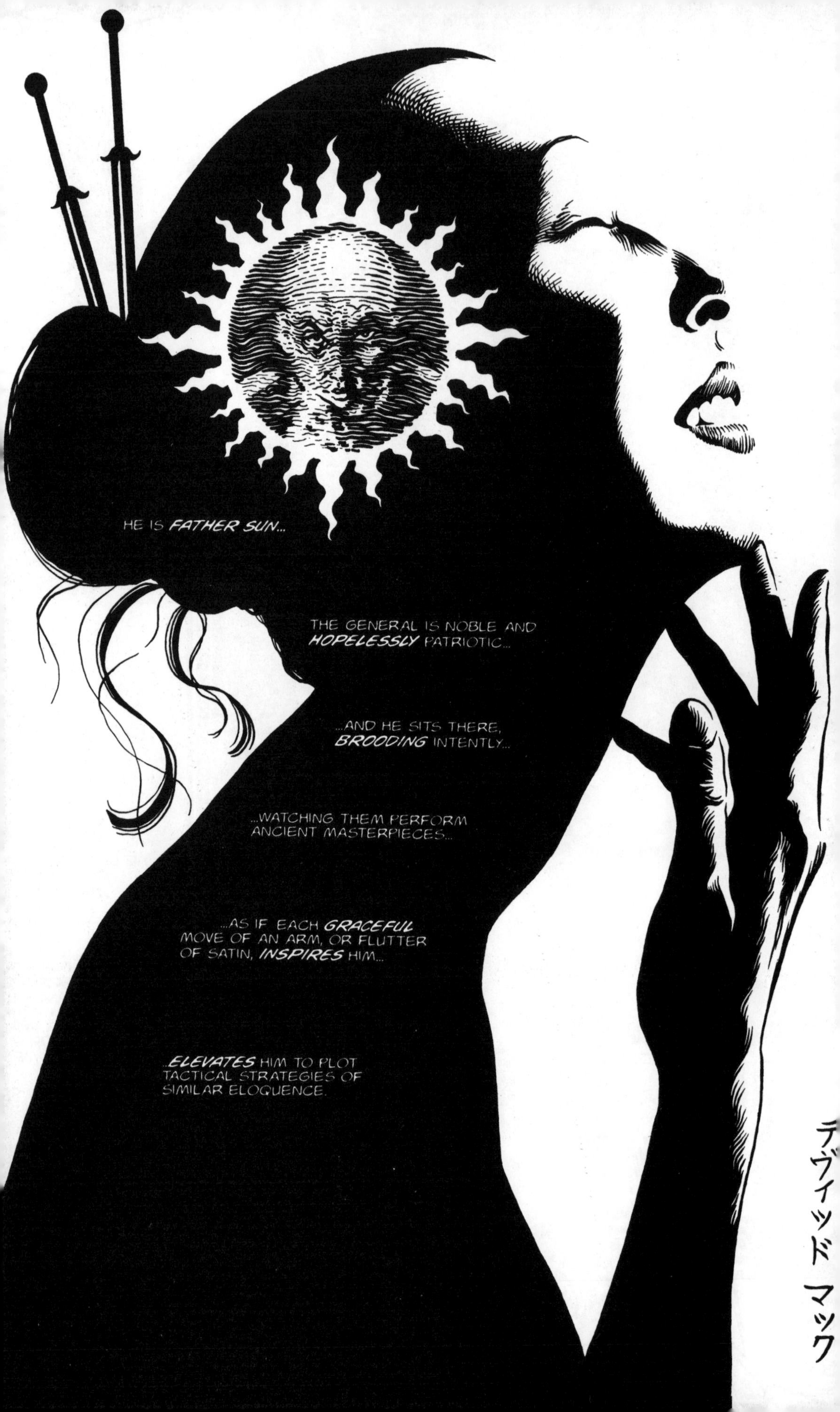
HE IS FATHER SUN...
THE GENERAL IS NOBLE AND HOPELESSLY PATRIOTIC...
...AND HE SITS THERE, BROODING INTENTLY...
...WATCHING THEM PERFORM ANCIENT MASTERPIECES...
...AS IF EACH GRACEFUL MOVE OF AN ARM, OR FLUTTER OF SATIN, INSPIRES HIM...
...ELEVATES HIM TO PLOT TACTICAL STRATEGIES OF SIMILAR ELOQUENCE.
デヴィッド マック

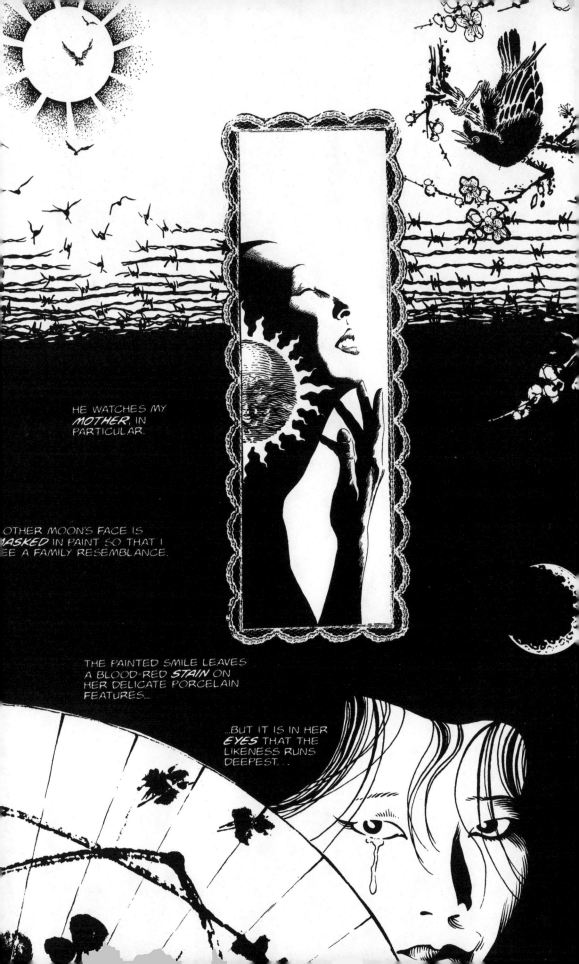

HE WATCHES MY *MOTHER*, IN PARTICULAR.

OTHER MOON'S FACE IS *MASKED* IN PAINT SO THAT I EE A FAMILY RESEMBLANCE.

THE PAINTED SMILE LEAVES A BLOOD-RED *STAIN* ON HER DELICATE PORCELAIN FEATURES...

...BUT IT IS IN HER *EYES* THAT THE LIKENESS RUNS DEEPEST...

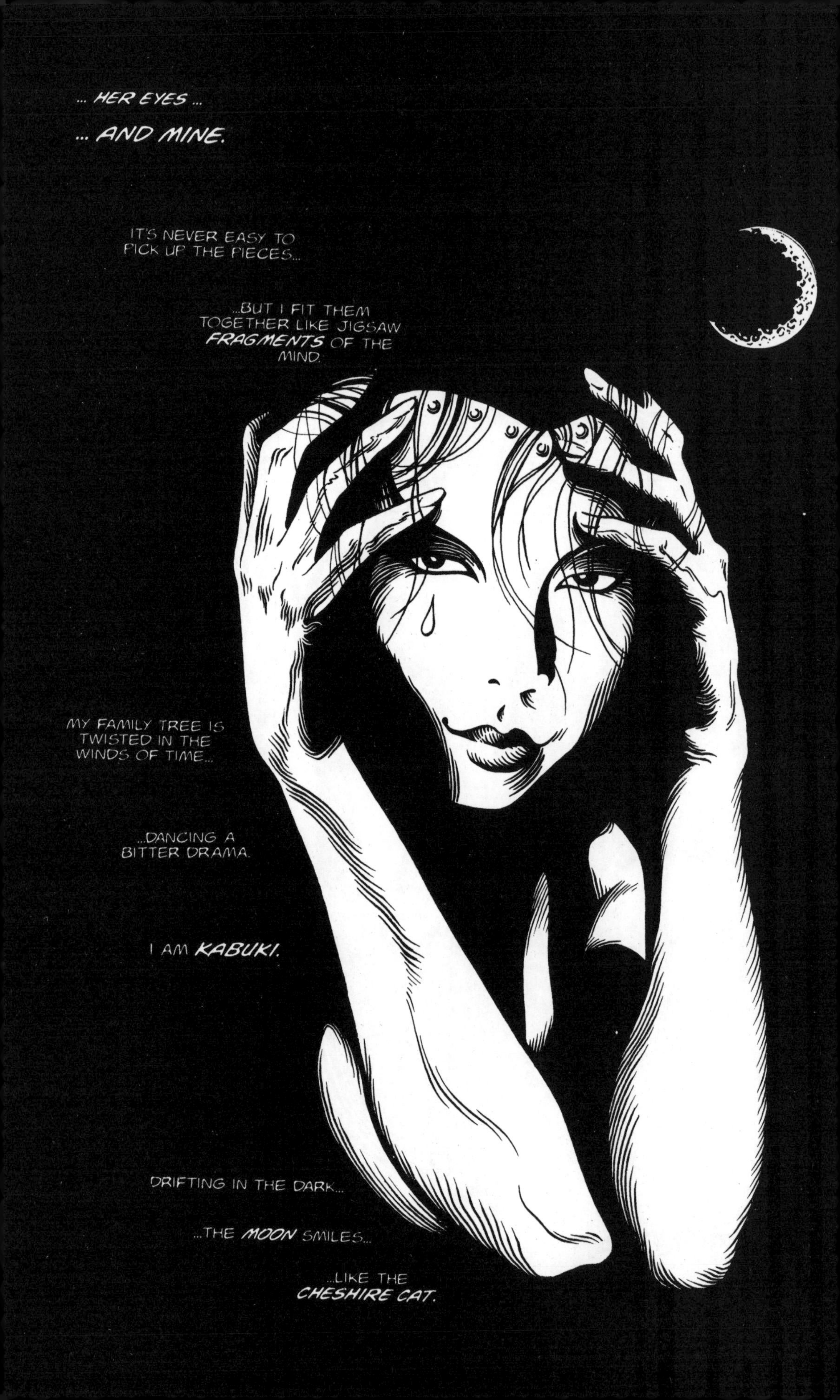
... HER EYES ...
... AND MINE.
IT'S NEVER EASY TO PICK UP THE PIECES...
...BUT I FIT THEM TOGETHER LIKE JIGSAW FRAGMENTS OF THE MIND.
MY FAMILY TREE IS TWISTED IN THE WINDS OF TIME...
...DANCING A BITTER DRAMA.
I AM KABUKI.
DRIFTING IN THE DARK...
...THE MOON SMILES...
...LIKE THE CHESHIRE CAT.

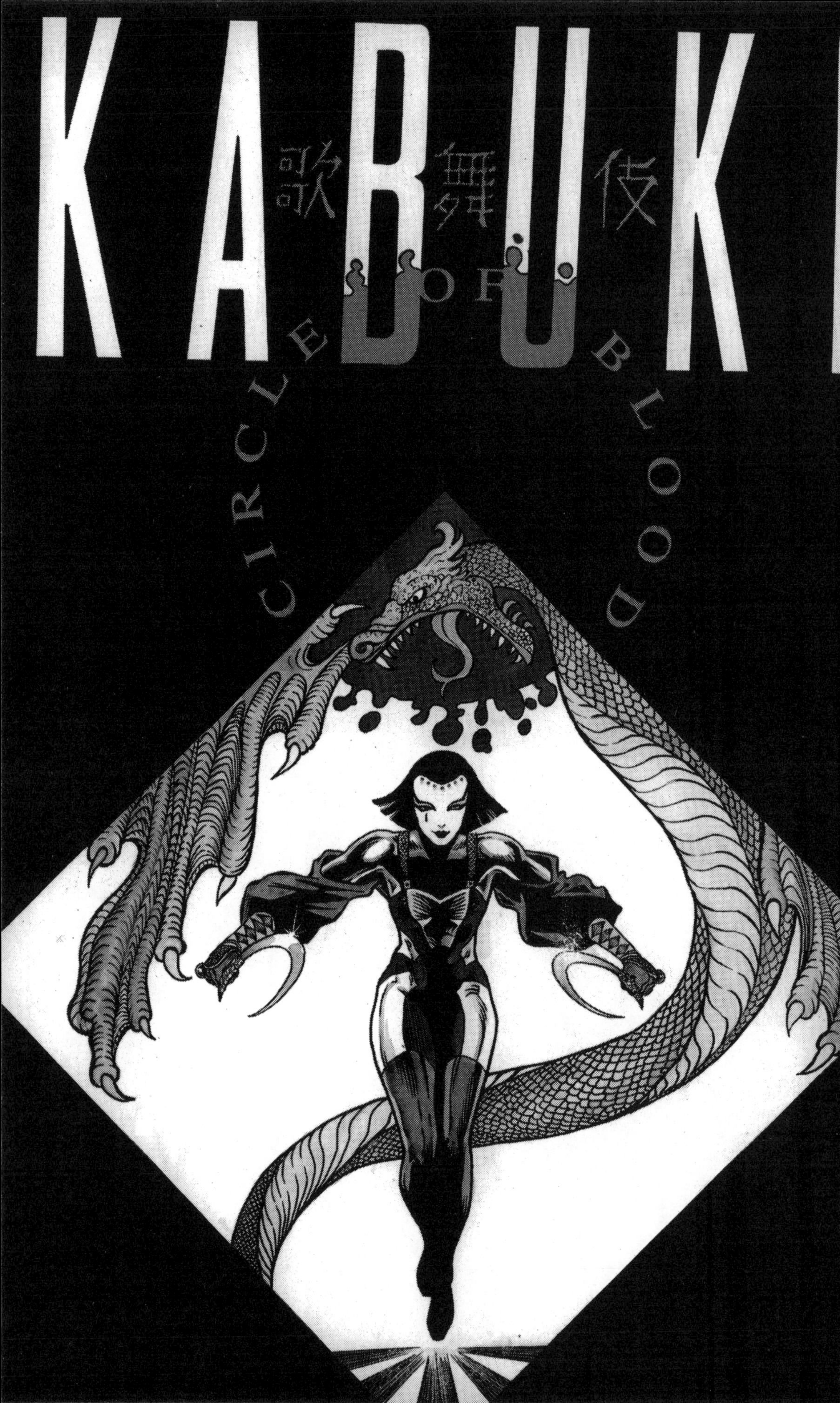
KABUKI
歌舞伎
CIRCLE OF BLOOD

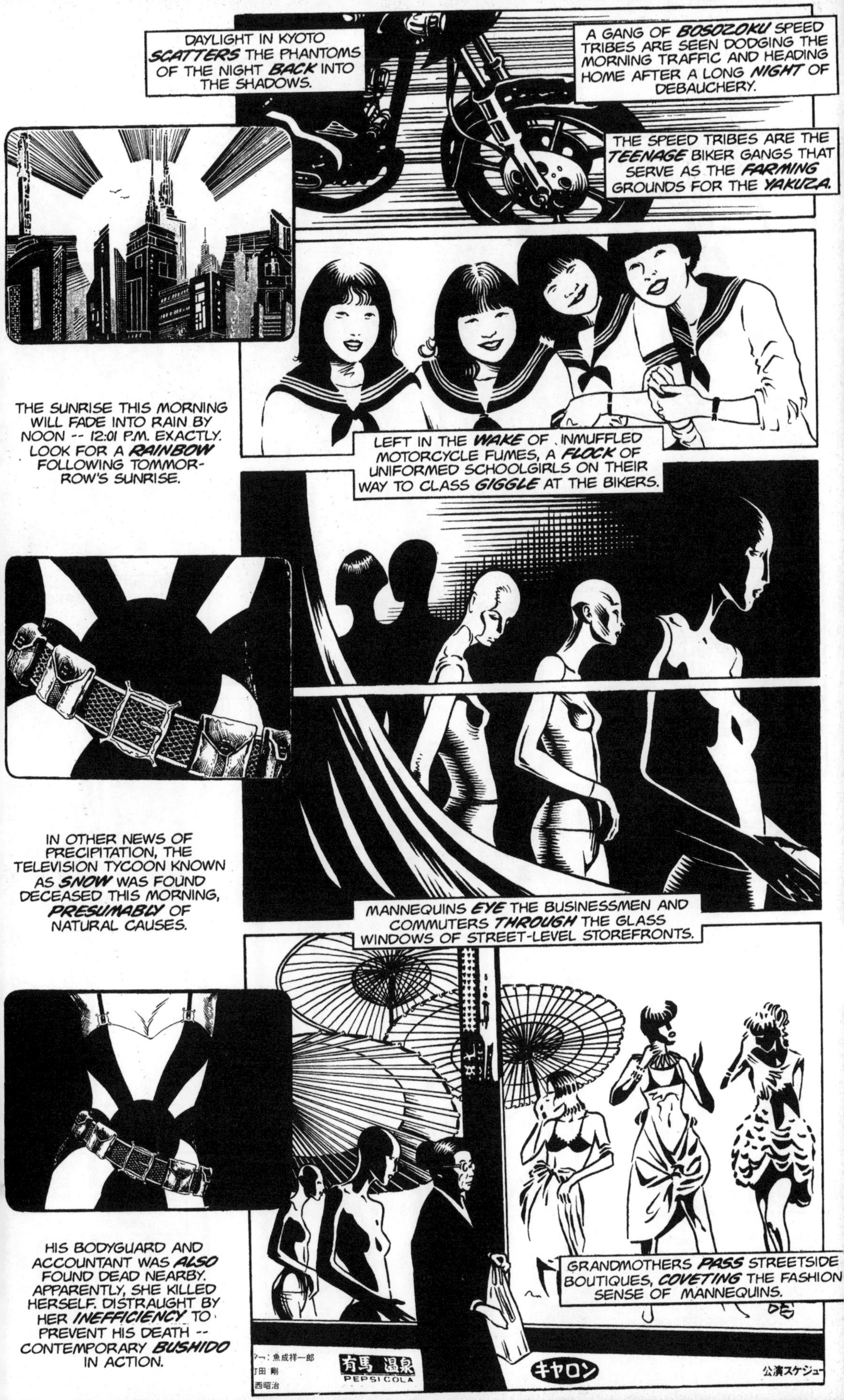

DAYLIGHT IN KYOTO SCATTERS THE PHANTOMS OF THE NIGHT BACK INTO THE SHADOWS.
A GANG OF BOSOZOKU SPEED TRIBES ARE SEEN DODGING THE MORNING TRAFFIC AND HEADING HOME AFTER A LONG NIGHT OF DEBAUCHERY.
THE SPEED TRIBES ARE THE TEENAGE BIKER GANGS THAT SERVE AS THE FARMING GROUNDS FOR THE YAKUZA.
THE SUNRISE THIS MORNING WILL FADE INTO RAIN BY NOON -- 12:01 P.M. EXACTLY. LOOK FOR A RAINBOW FOLLOWING TOMMOR-ROW'S SUNRISE.
LEFT IN THE WAKE OF UNMUFFLED MOTORCYCLE FUMES, A FLOCK OF UNIFORMED SCHOOLGIRLS ON THEIR WAY TO CLASS GIGGLE AT THE BIKERS.
IN OTHER NEWS OF PRECIPITATION, THE TELEVISION TYCOON KNOWN AS SNOW WAS FOUND DECEASED THIS MORNING, PRESUMABLY OF NATURAL CAUSES.
MANNEQUINS EYE THE BUSINESSMEN AND COMMUTERS THROUGH THE GLASS WINDOWS OF STREET-LEVEL STOREFRONTS.
HIS BODYGUARD AND ACCOUNTANT WAS ALSO FOUND DEAD NEARBY. APPARENTLY, SHE KILLED HERSELF. DISTRAUGHT BY HER INEFFICIENCY TO PREVENT HIS DEATH -- CONTEMPORARY BUSHIDO IN ACTION.
GRANDMOTHERS PASS STREETSIDE BOUTIQUES, COVETING THE FASHION SENSE OF MANNEQUINS.
魚成祥一郎
西昭治
有馬 温泉
PEPSI COLA
キャロン
公演スケジュ

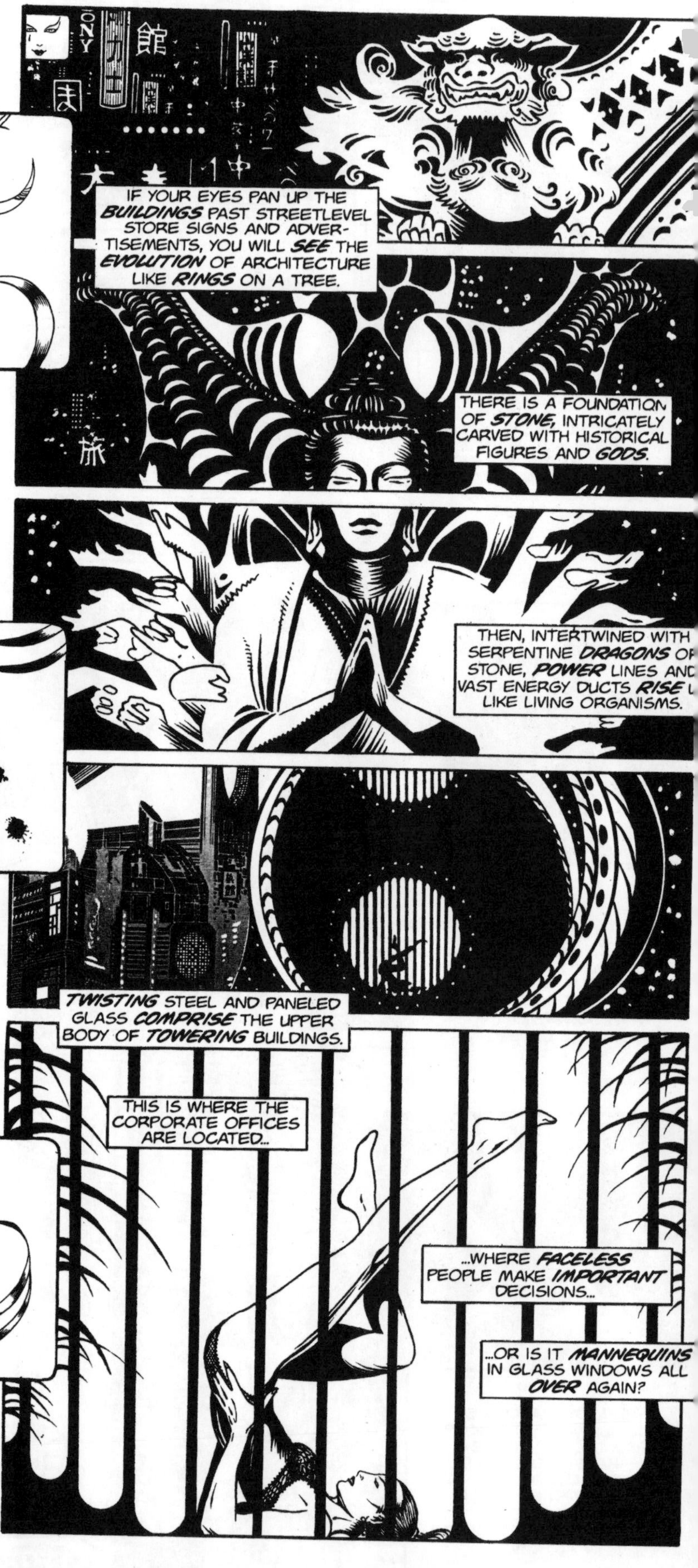
IF YOUR EYES PAN UP THE BUILDINGS PAST STREETLEVEL STORE SIGNS AND ADVERTISEMENTS, YOU WILL SEE THE EVOLUTION OF ARCHITECTURE LIKE RINGS ON A TREE.
THERE IS A FOUNDATION OF STONE, INTRICATELY CARVED WITH HISTORICAL FIGURES AND GODS.
THEN, INTERTWINED WITH SERPENTINE DRAGONS OF STONE, POWER LINES AND VAST ENERGY DUCTS RISE UP LIKE LIVING ORGANISMS.
TWISTING STEEL AND PANELED GLASS COMPRISE THE UPPER BODY OF TOWERING BUILDINGS.
THIS IS WHERE THE CORPORATE OFFICES ARE LOCATED...
...WHERE FACELESS PEOPLE MAKE IMPORTANT DECISIONS...
...OR IS IT MANNEQUINS IN GLASS WINDOWS ALL OVER AGAIN?

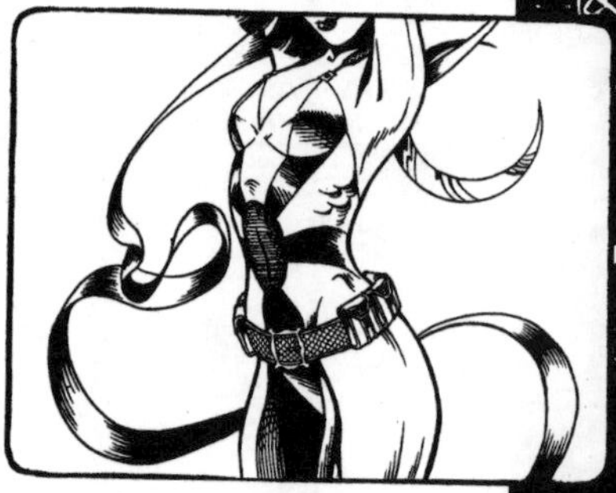

SNOW'S LIFE UP TO THE AGE OF ***NINETY-NINE*** YEARS OF AGE WAS ***REMARKABLE*** FOR A MAN OF HIS GENERATION.

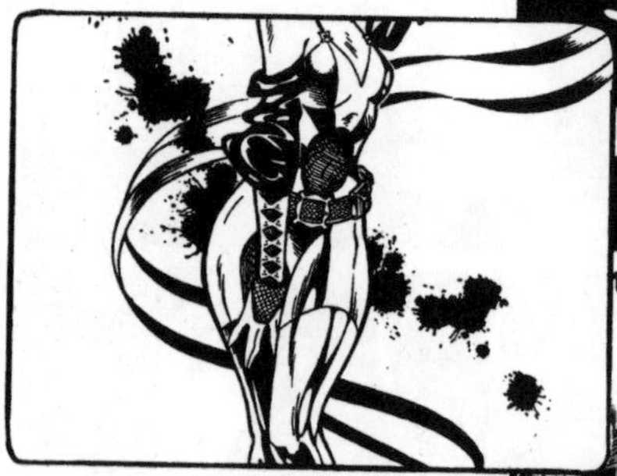

IT HAD BEEN MADE ***POSSIBLE*** BY THE REJUVENATING EFFECTS OF BREAKTHROUGH LONGEVITY ***DRUGS*** THAT HAVE BEEN AVAILABLE IN JAPAN'S LAST TWO DECADES.

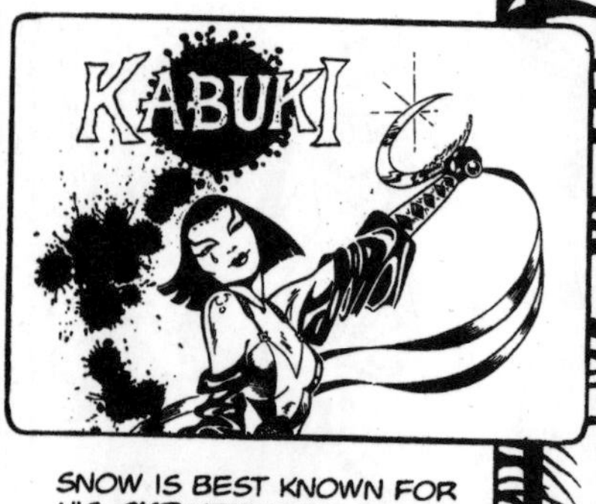
KABUKI

SNOW IS BEST KNOWN FOR HIS ***AVR*** NETWORK CALLED ***CHANNEL SNOW.*** AVR, A COMBINATION OF ADULT VIDEO AND VIRTUAL REALITY, RENOWNED HIM AS THE ***"HUGH HEFNER"*** OF HIS GENERATION.

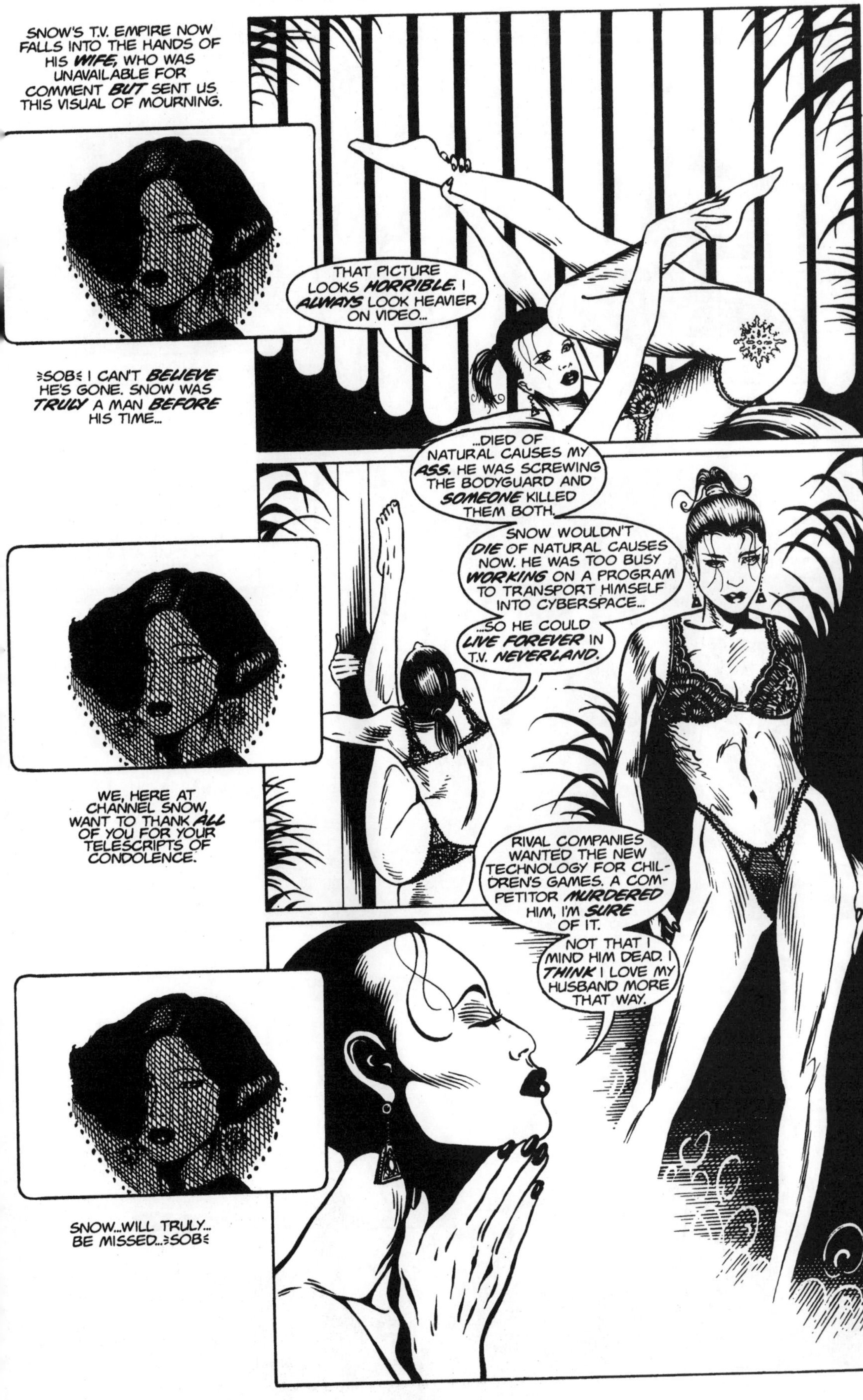

SNOW'S T.V. EMPIRE NOW FALLS INTO THE HANDS OF HIS WIFE, WHO WAS UNAVAILABLE FOR COMMENT BUT SENT US THIS VISUAL OF MOURNING.
THAT PICTURE LOOKS HORRIBLE. I ALWAYS LOOK HEAVIER ON VIDEO...
≥SOB≤ I CAN'T BELIEVE HE'S GONE. SNOW WAS TRULY A MAN BEFORE HIS TIME...
...DIED OF NATURAL CAUSES MY ASS. HE WAS SCREWING THE BODYGUARD AND SOMEONE KILLED THEM BOTH.
SNOW WOULDN'T DIE OF NATURAL CAUSES NOW. HE WAS TOO BUSY WORKING ON A PROGRAM TO TRANSPORT HIMSELF INTO CYBERSPACE...
...SO HE COULD LIVE FOREVER IN T.V. NEVERLAND.
WE, HERE AT CHANNEL SNOW, WANT TO THANK ALL OF YOU FOR YOUR TELESCRIPTS OF CONDOLENCE.
RIVAL COMPANIES WANTED THE NEW TECHNOLOGY FOR CHIL-DREN'S GAMES. A COM-PETITOR MURDERED HIM, I'M SURE OF IT.
NOT THAT I MIND HIM DEAD. I THINK I LOVE MY HUSBAND MORE THAT WAY.
SNOW...WILL TRULY... BE MISSED...≥SOB≤

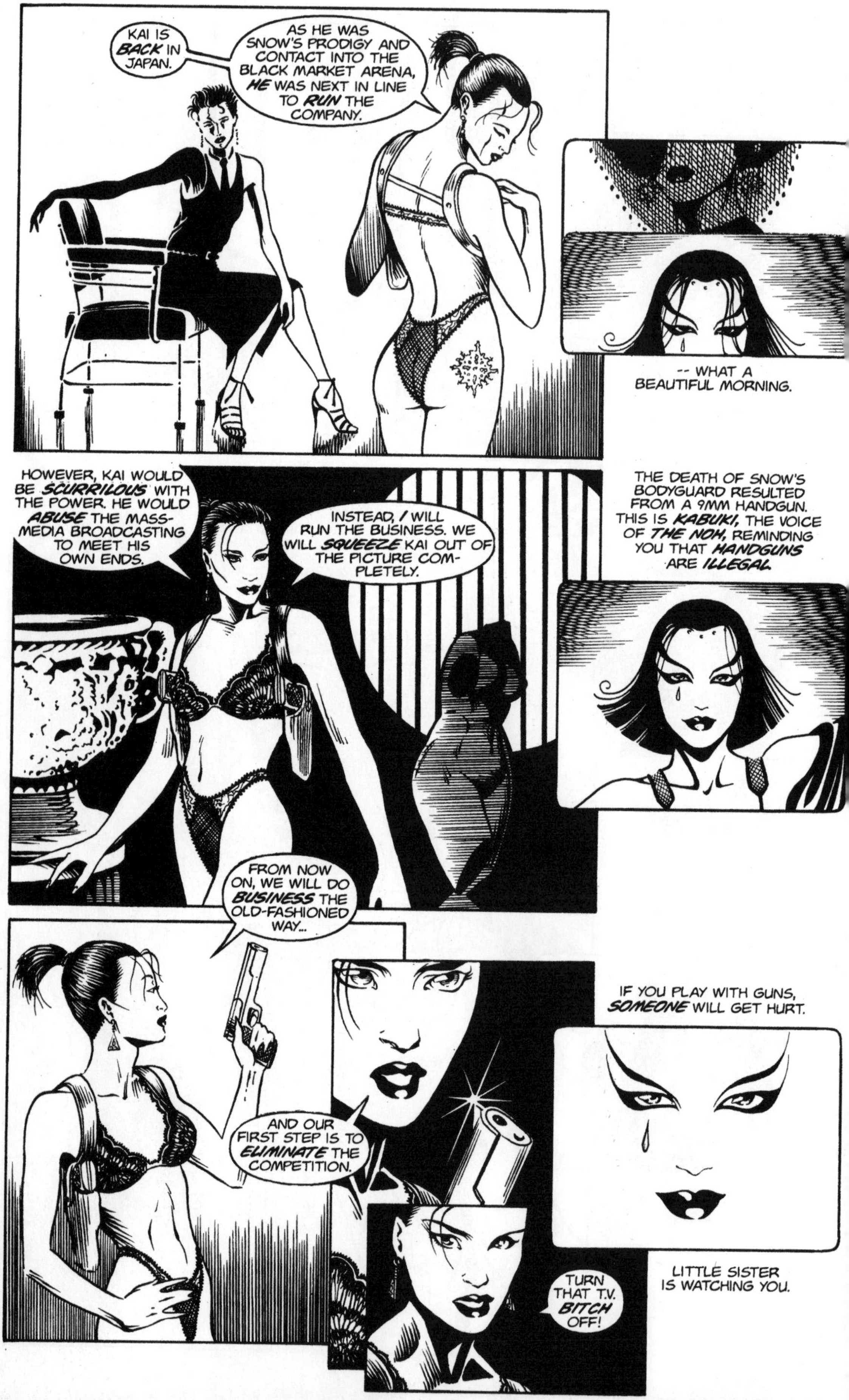
KAI IS BACK IN JAPAN.
AS HE WAS SNOW'S PRODIGY AND CONTACT INTO THE BLACK MARKET ARENA, HE WAS NEXT IN LINE TO RUN THE COMPANY.
-- WHAT A BEAUTIFUL MORNING.
HOWEVER, KAI WOULD BE SCURRILOUS WITH THE POWER. HE WOULD ABUSE THE MASS-MEDIA BROADCASTING TO MEET HIS OWN ENDS.
INSTEAD, I WILL RUN THE BUSINESS. WE WILL SQUEEZE KAI OUT OF THE PICTURE COMPLETELY.
THE DEATH OF SNOW'S BODYGUARD RESULTED FROM A 9MM HANDGUN. THIS IS KABUKI, THE VOICE OF THE NOH, REMINDING YOU THAT HANDGUNS ARE ILLEGAL.
FROM NOW ON, WE WILL DO BUSINESS THE OLD-FASHIONED WAY...
AND OUR FIRST STEP IS TO ELIMINATE THE COMPETITION.
IF YOU PLAY WITH GUNS, SOMEONE WILL GET HURT.
LITTLE SISTER IS WATCHING YOU.
TURN THAT T.V. BITCH OFF!

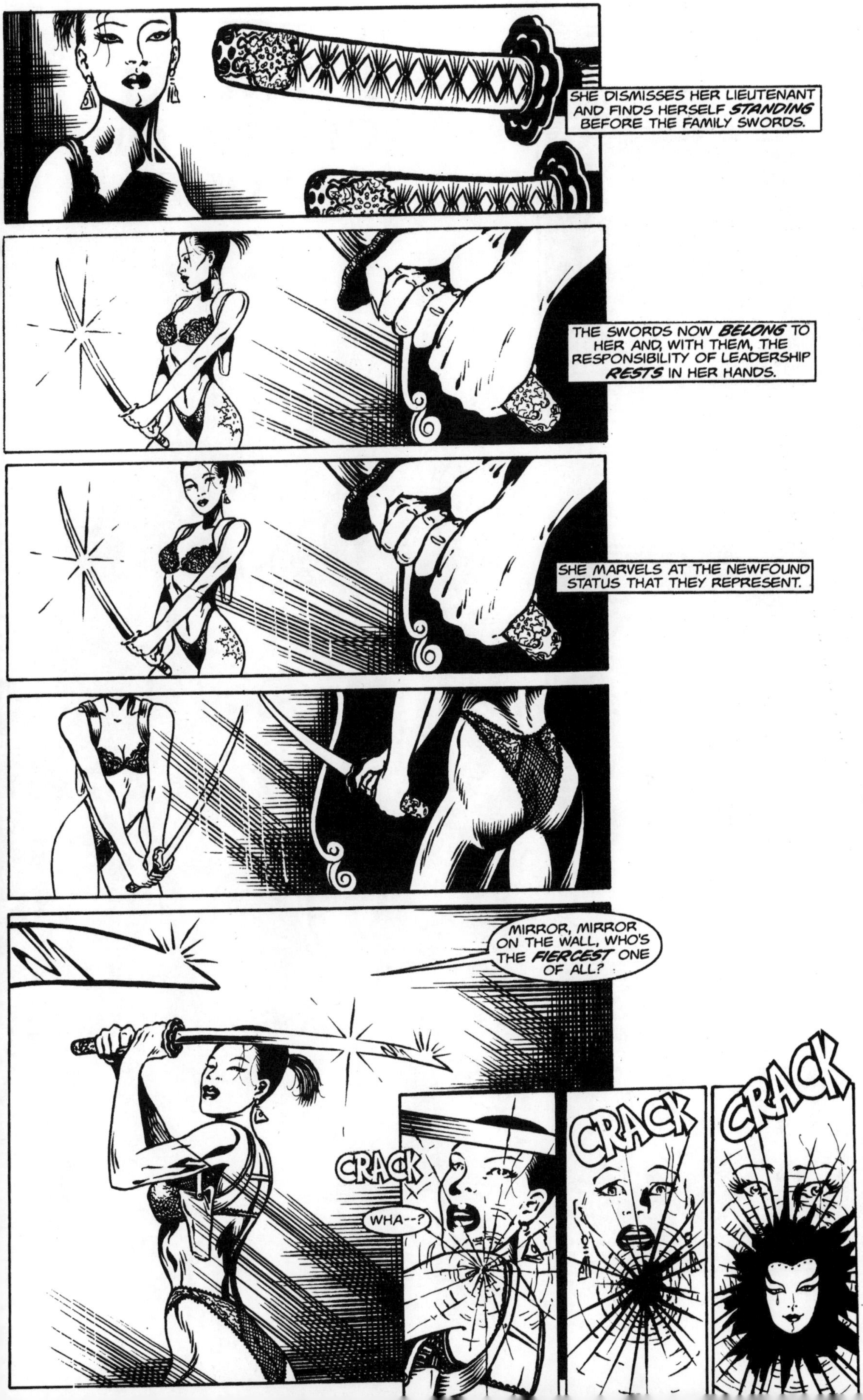
SHE DISMISSES HER LIEUTENANT AND FINDS HERSELF STANDING BEFORE THE FAMILY SWORDS.
THE SWORDS NOW BELONG TO HER AND, WITH THEM, THE RESPONSIBILITY OF LEADERSHIP RESTS IN HER HANDS.
SHE MARVELS AT THE NEWFOUND STATUS THAT THEY REPRESENT.
MIRROR, MIRROR ON THE WALL, WHO'S THE FIERCEST ONE OF ALL?
CRACK
WHA--?
CRACK
CRACK

KABUKI: CIRCLE OF BLOOD

ACT 1
GHOSTS IN THE LOOKING GLASS

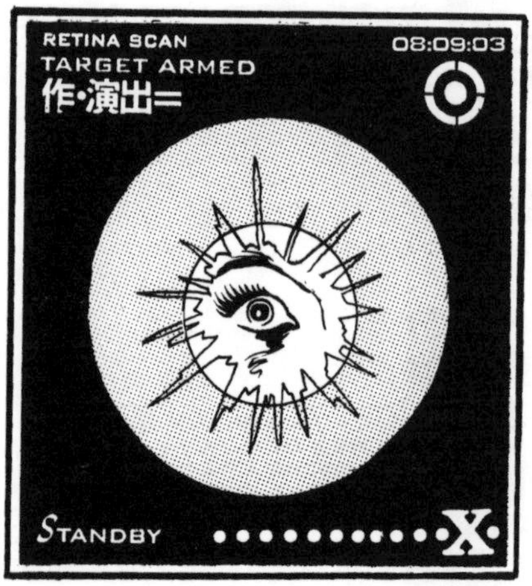
RETINA SCAN
08:09:03
TARGET ARMED
作・演出＝
STANDBY
X

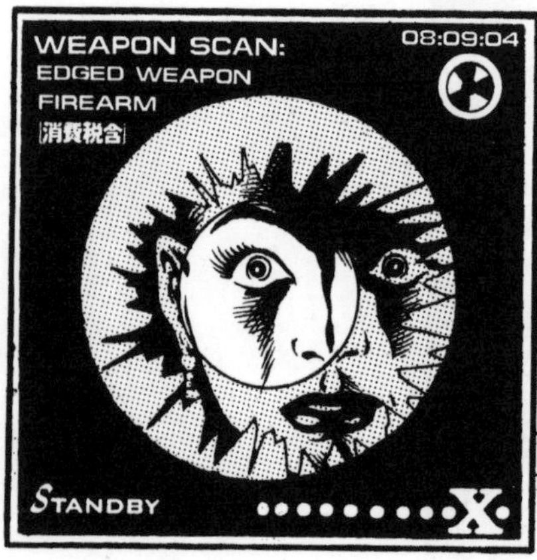
WEAPON SCAN:
08:09:04
EDGED WEAPON
FIREARM
[消費税含]
STANDBY
X

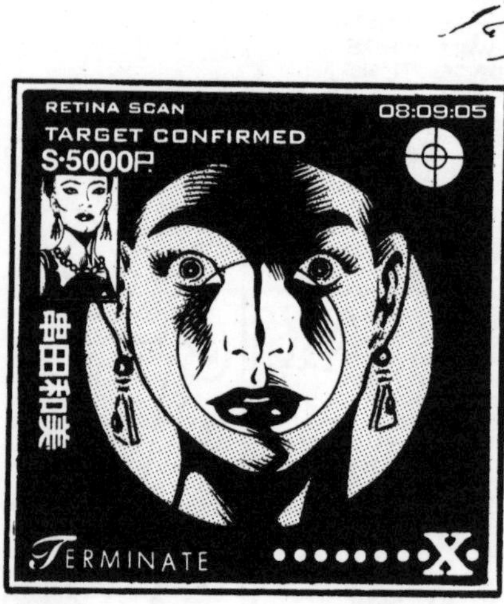
RETINA SCAN
08:09:05
TARGET CONFIRMED
S·5000円
串田和美
TERMINATE
X

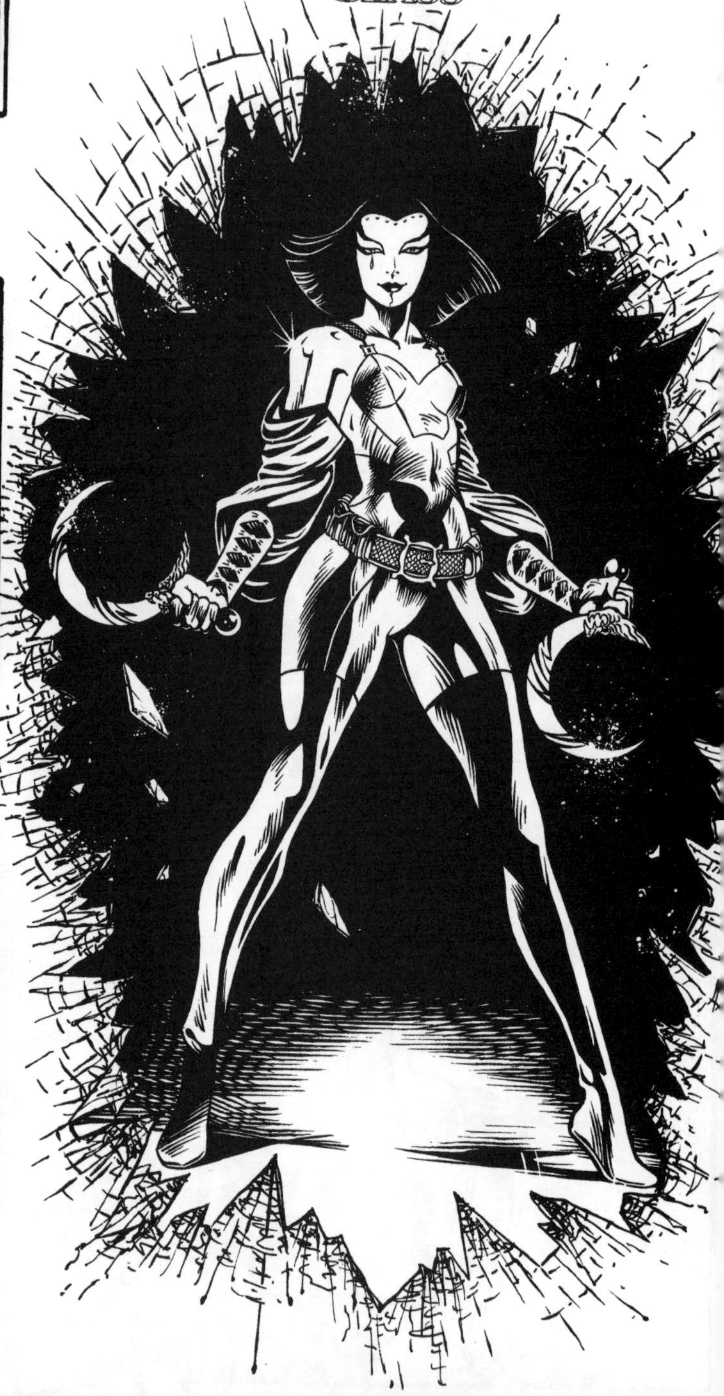

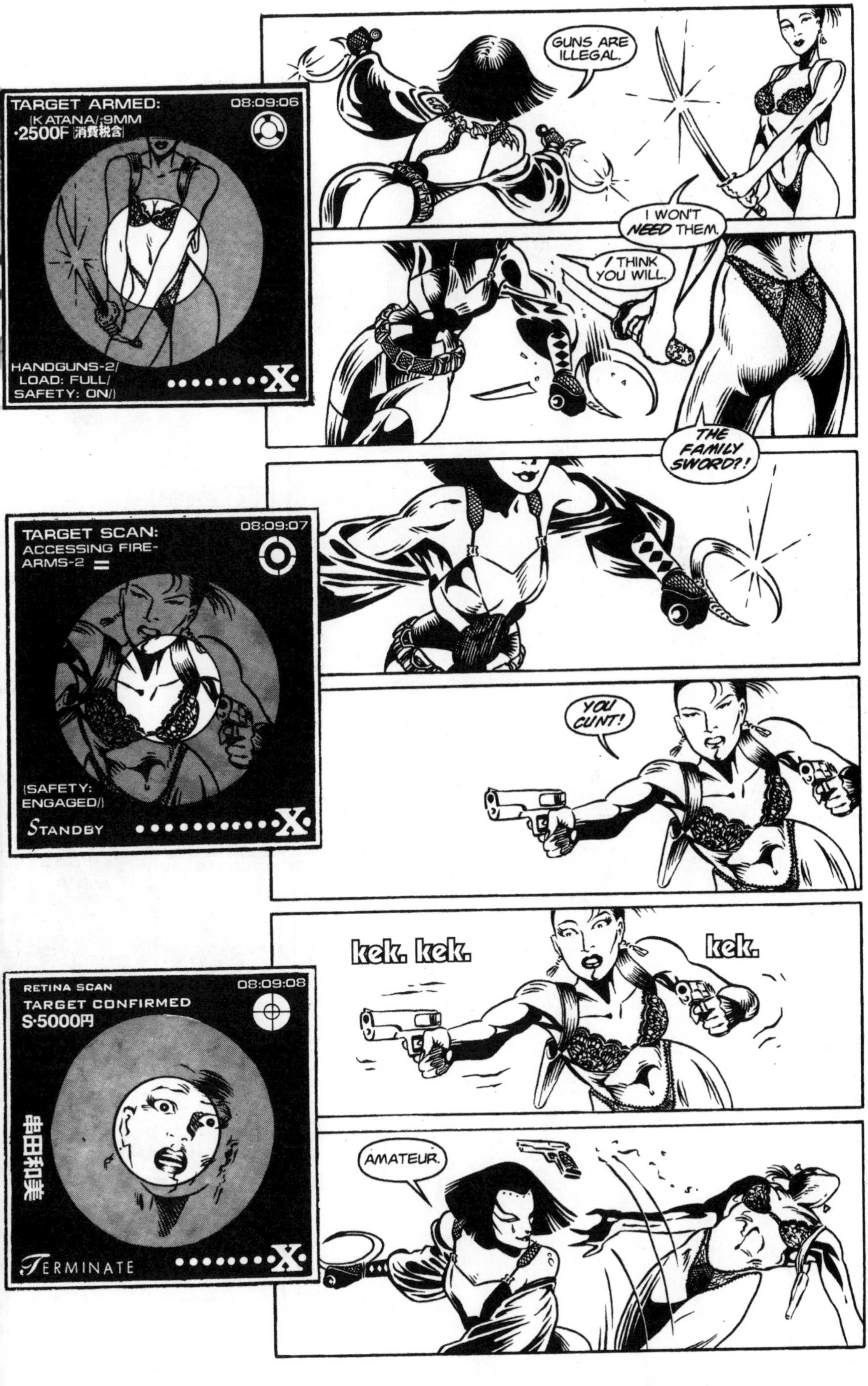

TARGET ARMED:
08:09:06
(KATANA/-9MM
•2500F [消費税含]
HANDGUNS-2/
LOAD: FULL/
SAFETY: ON/)
X
GUNS ARE ILLEGAL.
I WON'T NEED THEM.
I THINK YOU WILL.
THE FAMILY SWORD?!
TARGET SCAN:
08:09:07
ACCESSING FIRE-ARMS-2 =
(SAFETY: ENGAGED/)
STANDBY
X
YOU CUNT!
kek. kek.
kek.
RETINA SCAN
08:09:08
TARGET CONFIRMED
S·5000円
串田和美
TERMINATE
X
AMATEUR.

TARGET SCAN:
>NEUTRALIZED<
>NEUTRALIZED<

08:09:09

串田和美

TERMINATE

•••X

THE DATA READOUT DISPLAY ON HER CRIMSON LENSES *CONFIRMS* HER KILL. THE OPERATIVE KNOWN AS KABUKI VIEWS LIFE AND DEATH THROUGH A FIBEROPTIC *CIRCLE* OF RED...

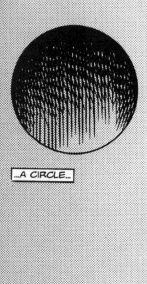

...A CIRCLE...

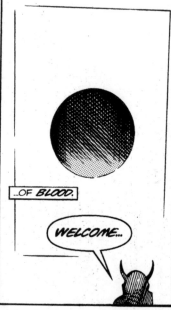

...OF *BLOOD.*

WELCOME...

...TO THE *CIRCLE* OF THE *NOH.*

IN 1997, WHEN THE *BAMBOO CURTAIN* OF *COMMUNIST* CHINA FELL OVER HONG KONG...

...THE TRIADS LEFT LIKE RATS IN A FIRE, *FLOODING* THE PACIFIC RIM -- HAWAII, CALIFORNIA, JAPAN... THEY HAVE *TIPPED* THE BALANCE OF POWER TO A *VOLATILE* STATE.

SINCE THE FLOW OF THE TRIADS INTO THE *JAPANESE* UNDERWORLD *BEGAN,* SHORTLY BEFORE CHINA *RECLAIMED* HONG KONG...

...THERE HAS BEEN *CONSTANT* TURF WARS *BETWEEN* THE CHINESE AND JAPANESE SYNDICATES.

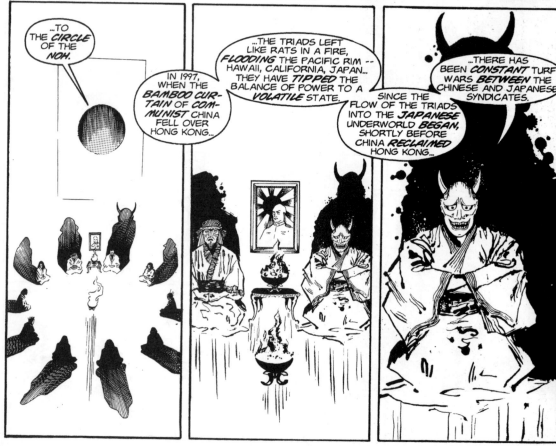

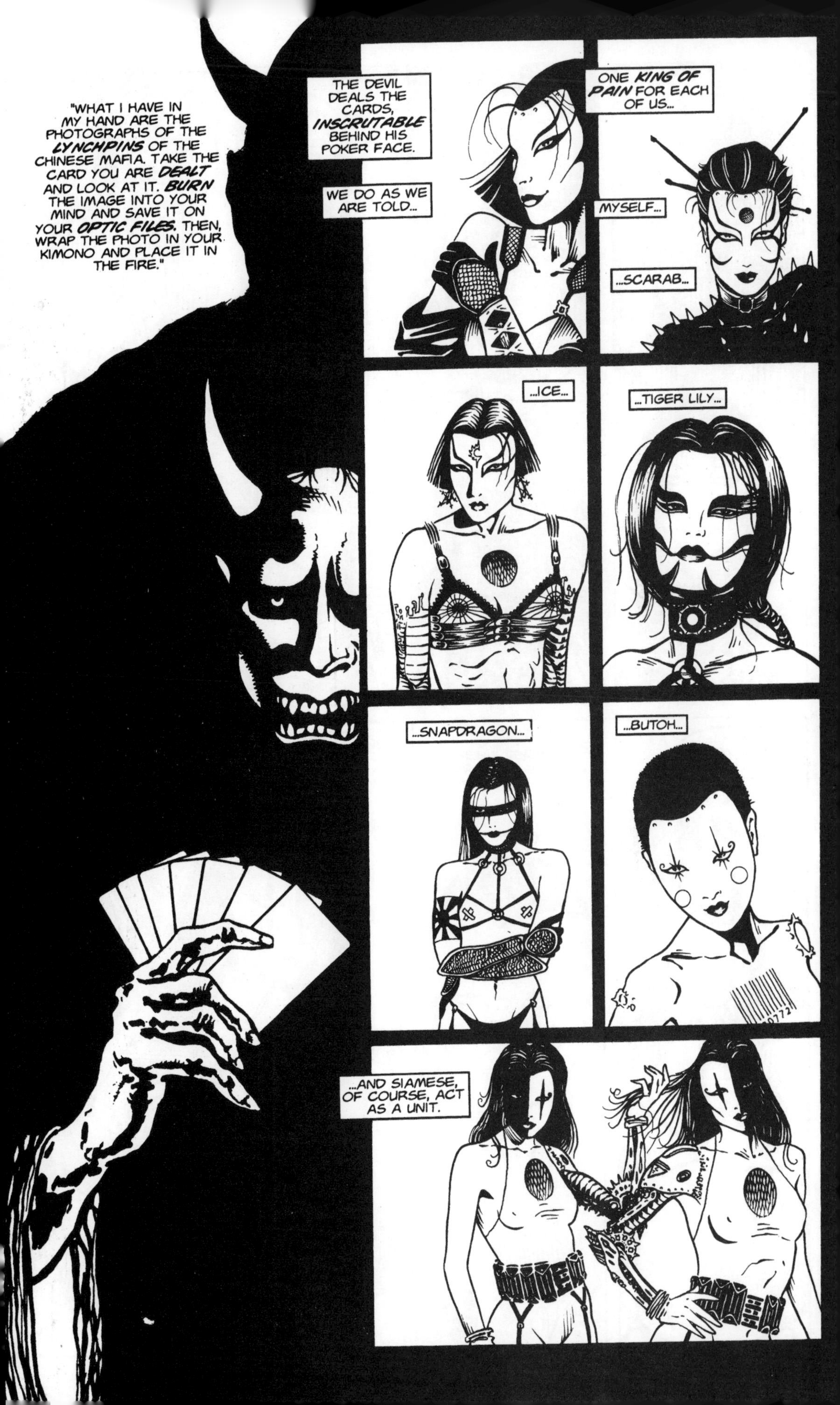
"WHAT I HAVE IN MY HAND ARE THE PHOTOGRAPHS OF THE LYNCHPINS OF THE CHINESE MAFIA. TAKE THE CARD YOU ARE DEALT AND LOOK AT IT. BURN THE IMAGE INTO YOUR MIND AND SAVE IT ON YOUR OPTIC FILES. THEN, WRAP THE PHOTO IN YOUR KIMONO AND PLACE IT IN THE FIRE."
THE DEVIL DEALS THE CARDS, INSCRUTABLE BEHIND HIS POKER FACE.
WE DO AS WE ARE TOLD...
ONE KING OF PAIN FOR EACH OF US...
MYSELF...
...SCARAB...
...ICE...
...TIGER LILY...
...SNAPDRAGON...
...BUTOH...
...AND SIAMESE, OF COURSE, ACT AS A UNIT.

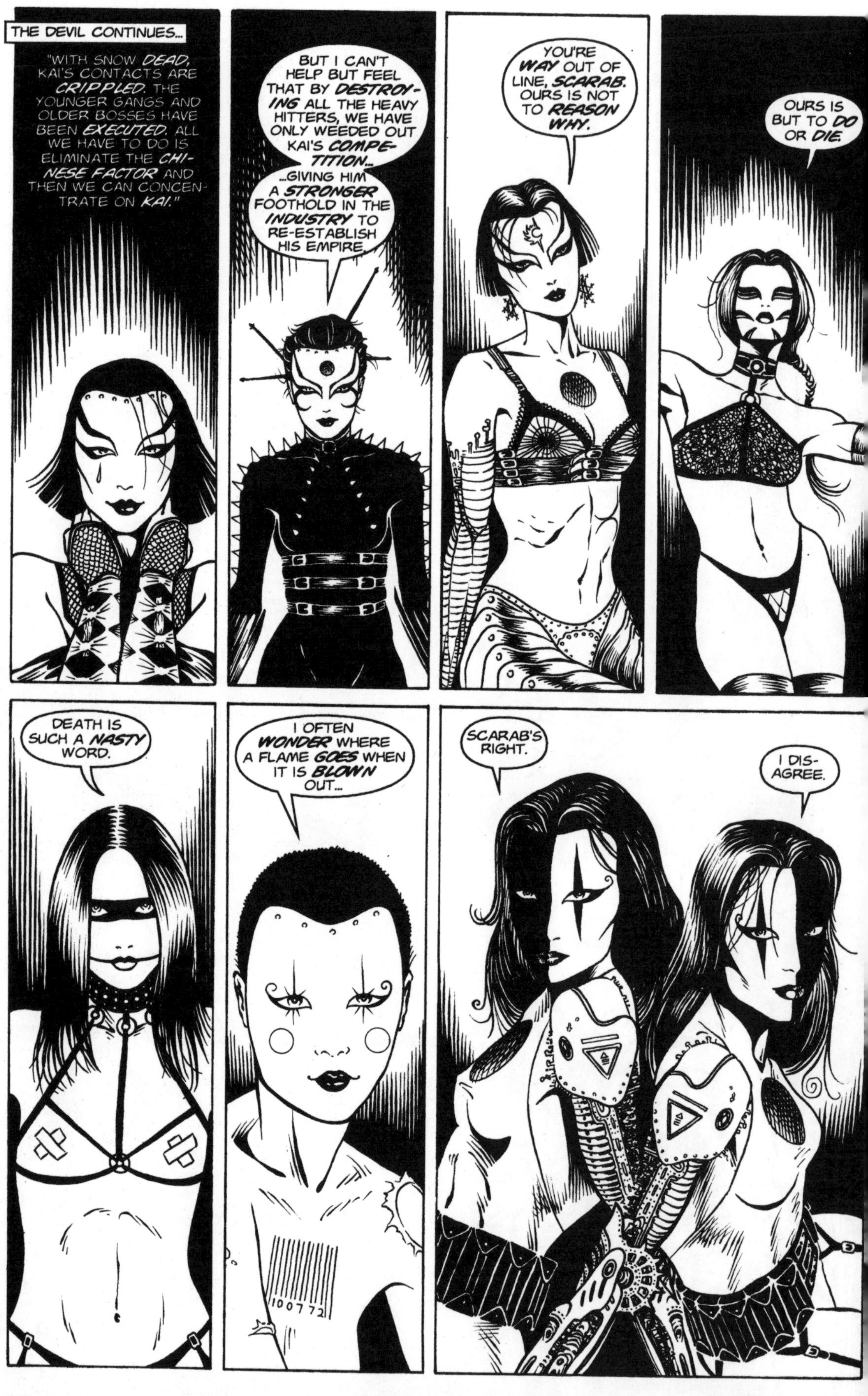

THE DEVIL CONTINUES...
"WITH SNOW DEAD, KAI'S CONTACTS ARE CRIPPLED. THE YOUNGER GANGS AND OLDER BOSSES HAVE BEEN EXECUTED. ALL WE HAVE TO DO IS ELIMINATE THE CHINESE FACTOR AND THEN WE CAN CONCENTRATE ON KAI."
BUT I CAN'T HELP BUT FEEL THAT BY DESTROYING ALL THE HEAVY HITTERS, WE HAVE ONLY WEEDED OUT KAI'S COMPETITION...
...GIVING HIM A STRONGER FOOTHOLD IN THE INDUSTRY TO RE-ESTABLISH HIS EMPIRE.
YOU'RE WAY OUT OF LINE, SCARAB. OURS IS NOT TO REASON WHY.
OURS IS BUT TO DO OR DIE.
DEATH IS SUCH A NASTY WORD.
I OFTEN WONDER WHERE A FLAME GOES WHEN IT IS BLOWN OUT...
SCARAB'S RIGHT.
I DISAGREE.

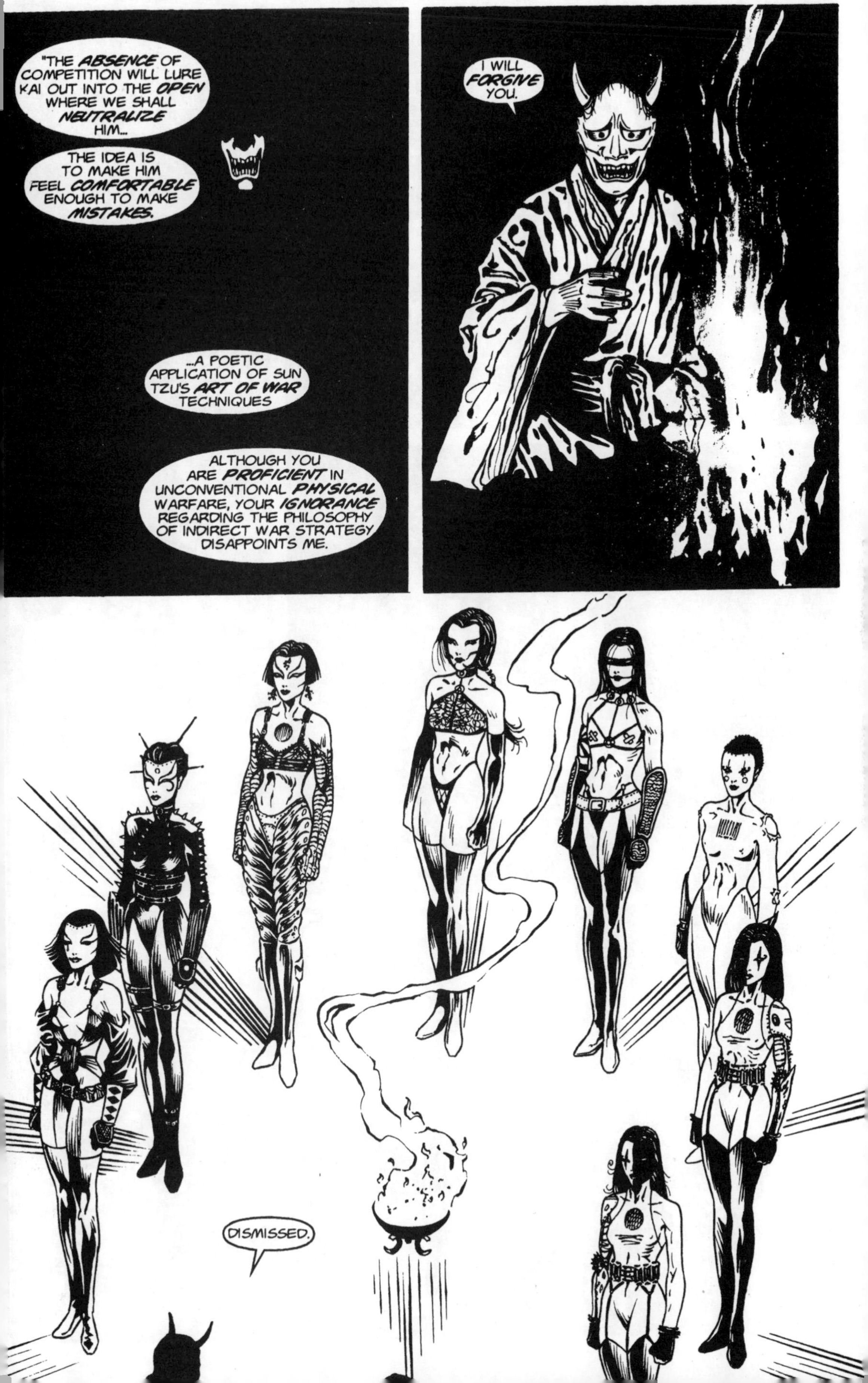
"THE ABSENCE OF COMPETITION WILL LURE KAI OUT INTO THE OPEN WHERE WE SHALL NEUTRALIZE HIM...
THE IDEA IS TO MAKE HIM FEEL COMFORTABLE ENOUGH TO MAKE MISTAKES.
...A POETIC APPLICATION OF SUN TZU'S ART OF WAR TECHNIQUES
ALTHOUGH YOU ARE PROFICIENT IN UNCONVENTIONAL PHYSICAL WARFARE, YOUR IGNORANCE REGARDING THE PHILOSOPHY OF INDIRECT WAR STRATEGY DISAPPOINTS ME.
I WILL FORGIVE YOU.
DISMISSED.

THE PIECES ARE MOVED WITH THE GRACEFUL *ELEGANCE* OF A HAND WELL EXPERIENCED IN THE STRATEGIC ARTS. THE *HAND*, WRINKLED AND HEAVY WITH THE WEIGHT OF *AGE*, BELONGS TO THE MAN BEHIND THE *MASKS*.

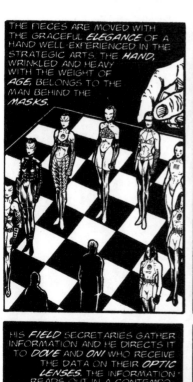

HE IS THE *FOUNDER* OF THE SECRET GOVERNMENT DIVISION CALLED *THE NOH*.

THE NOH IS THERE TO *EVEN* THE SCALES WHEN THE *BALANCE* OF CRIME AND POLITICS IS *TIPPED*.

OFFICIALLY, THE NOH EXISTS ONLY AS *TELEVISION ICONOGRAPHY*. IT IS AN ORGANIZATION SO *SECRET*, THE MEMBERS MEET ONLY BEHIND THE *ANONYMITY* OF *MASKS*. THIS MAN IS SO SECRET, HE IS MET BY *NO ONE*.

HIS *FIELD* SECRETARIES GATHER INFORMATION AND HE DIRECTS IT TO *DOVE* AND *ONI* WHO RECEIVE THE DATA ON THEIR *OPTIC LENSES*. THE INFORMATION READS OUT IN A CONTEMPORARY *SPLINTER DIALECT* CALLED *NOH-SPEAK*. DOVE AND ONI ARE THEN RESPONSIBLE FOR USING THIS TO *FORMULATE* FIELD DIRECTIVES TO THE MASKED AGENTS.

HE IS REFERRED TO AS "*THE GENERAL*," ALTHOUGH IT'S BEEN *GENERATIONS* SINCE HE'S LED MEN INTO BATTLE. BUT HE WEARS HIS *ANTIQUE MEDALS* AND *MILITARY INSIGNIA* AND SITS IN A DARK ROOM FULL OF ELABORATE MECHANISMS AND BLINKING ARTIFICIAL LIGHTS.

HE THINKS. HE *PLANS*. HE MOVES *PIECES* ON A *CHESSBOARD*.

SOMETIMES HE THINKS ABOUT HOW TO WEED OUT CORRUPT POLITICIANS IN THE DIET WHO ARE THE *PUPPETS* OF THE OLDER CRIME BOSSES. HE HAS PREVENTED MANY SCANDALS WITH HIS *INVISIBLE* CIVIL WAR. SOMETIMES HE THINKS OF HOW HE HAS HELPED JAPAN BECOME MORE INTERNATIONALLY INDEPENDENT.

BUT SOMETIMES HE LETS HIMSELF THINK ABOUT *MASKED WOMEN* DRESSED IN FLAGS PERFORMING *UNSPEAKABLE* ACTS. SOMETIMES HE THINKS ABOUT A LITTLE GIRL STARING INTO THE REFLECTIVE URN AT HER *MOTHER'S* GRAVESTONE.

HE *THINKS* OF THIS AND HE *SHIVERS*.

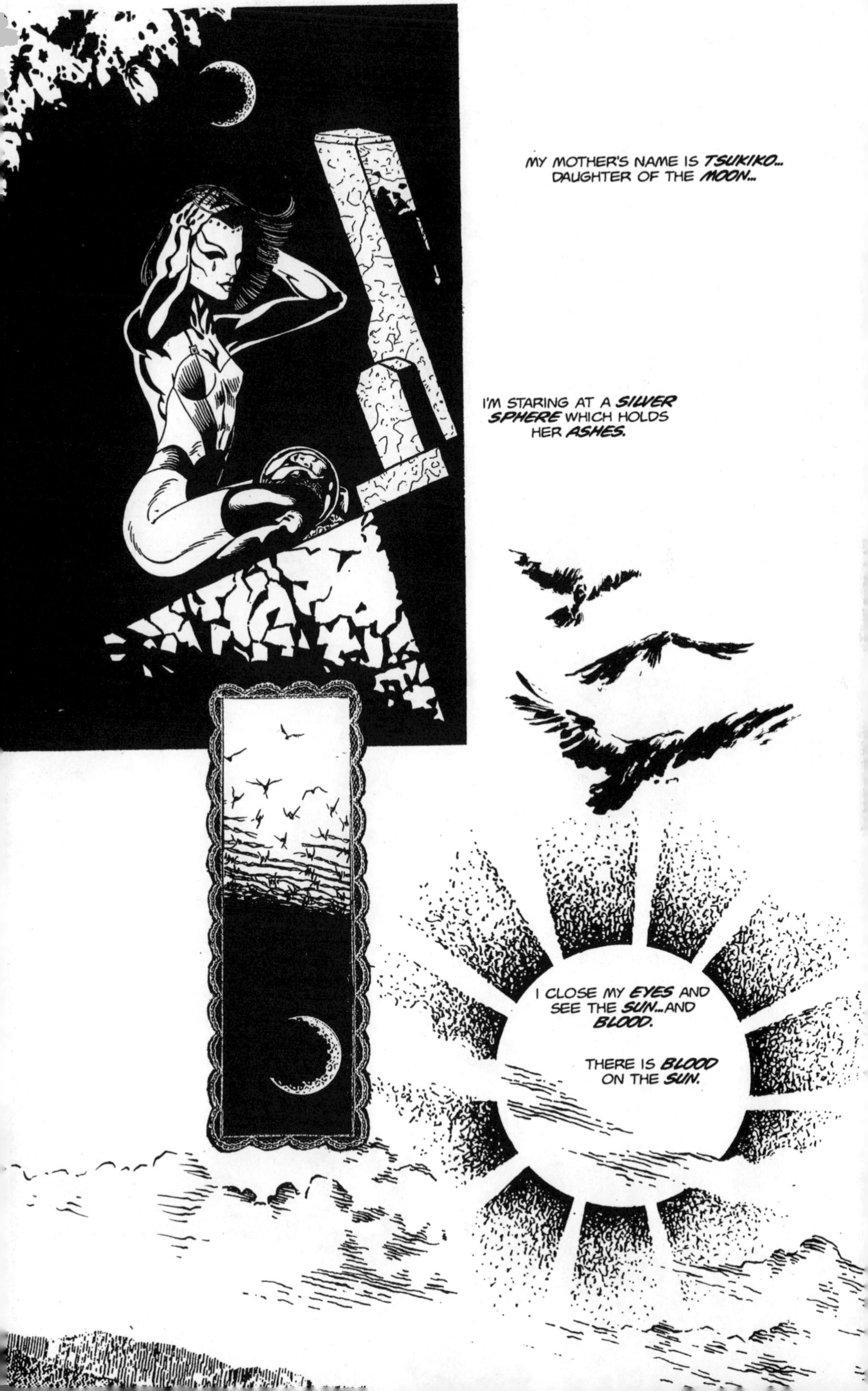
MY MOTHER'S NAME IS TSUKIKO... DAUGHTER OF THE MOON...
I'M STARING AT A SILVER SPHERE WHICH HOLDS HER ASHES.
I CLOSE MY EYES AND SEE THE SUN...AND BLOOD.
THERE IS BLOOD ON THE SUN.

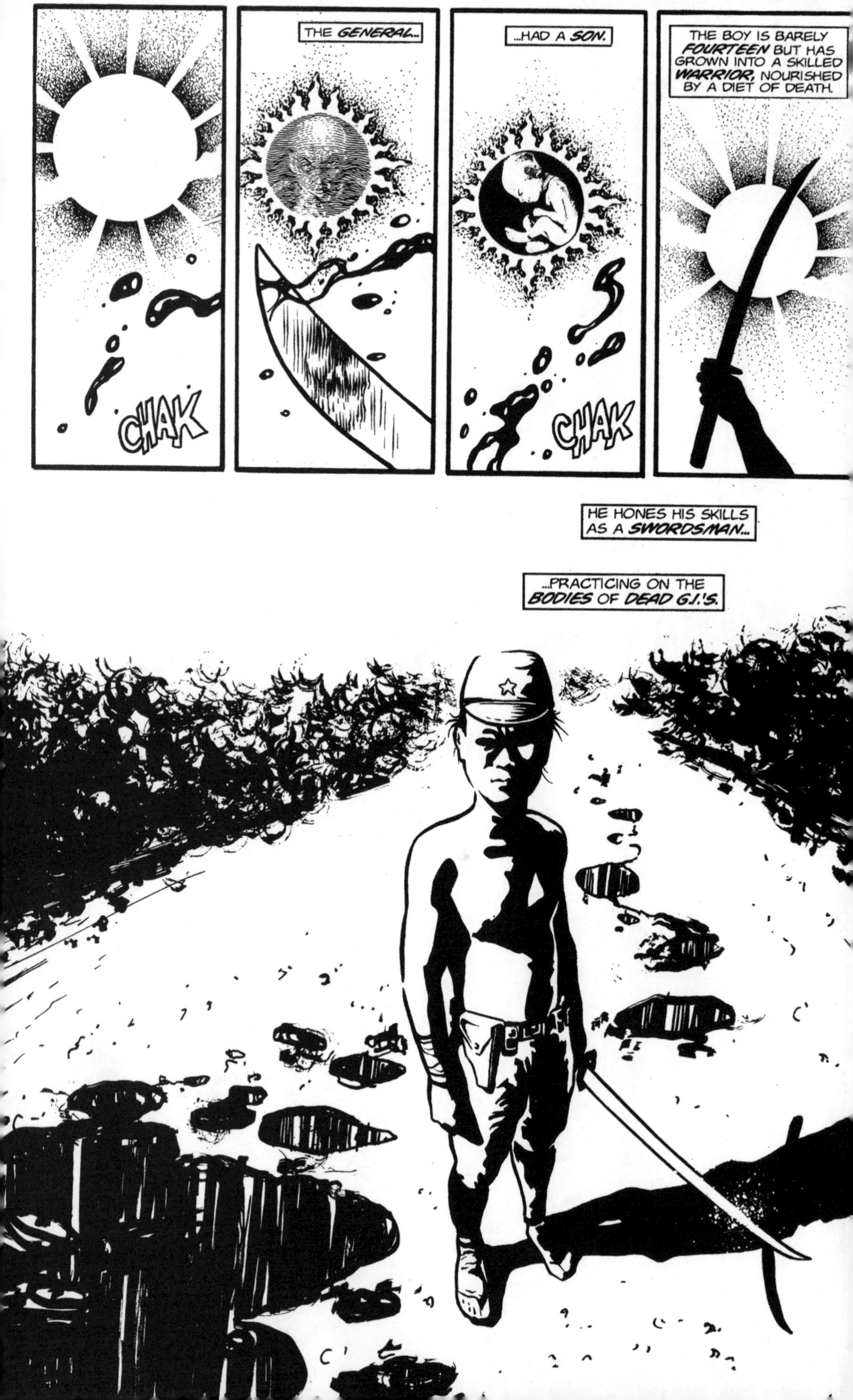
CHAK
THE GENERAL...
...HAD A SON.
CHAK
THE BOY IS BARELY FOURTEEN BUT HAS GROWN INTO A SKILLED WARRIOR, NOURISHED BY A DIET OF DEATH.
HE HONES HIS SKILLS AS A SWORDSMAN...
...PRACTICING ON THE BODIES OF DEAD G.I.'S.

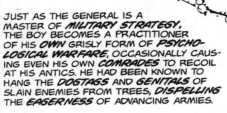

JUST AS THE GENERAL IS A MASTER OF *MILITARY STRATEGY,* THE BOY BECOMES A PRACTITIONER OF HIS *OWN* GRISLY FORM OF *PSYCHO-LOGICAL WARFARE,* OCCASIONALLY CAUSING EVEN HIS OWN *COMRADES* TO RECOIL AT HIS ANTICS. HE HAD BEEN KNOWN TO HANG THE *DOGTAGS* AND *GENITALS* OF SLAIN ENEMIES FROM TREES, *DISPELLING* THE *EAGERNESS* OF ADVANCING ARMIES.

THE BLOODY *HANDS* OF WAR MOLD HIM INTO THE *MESS-ENGER* OF DEATH.

HE IS YOUNG AND EAGER TO *BOAST* OF HIS *KILLS,* DIS-PLAYING HIS OWN RED *BADGES* OF *COURAGE.* HE BECOMES A *"TROPHY-TAKER."*

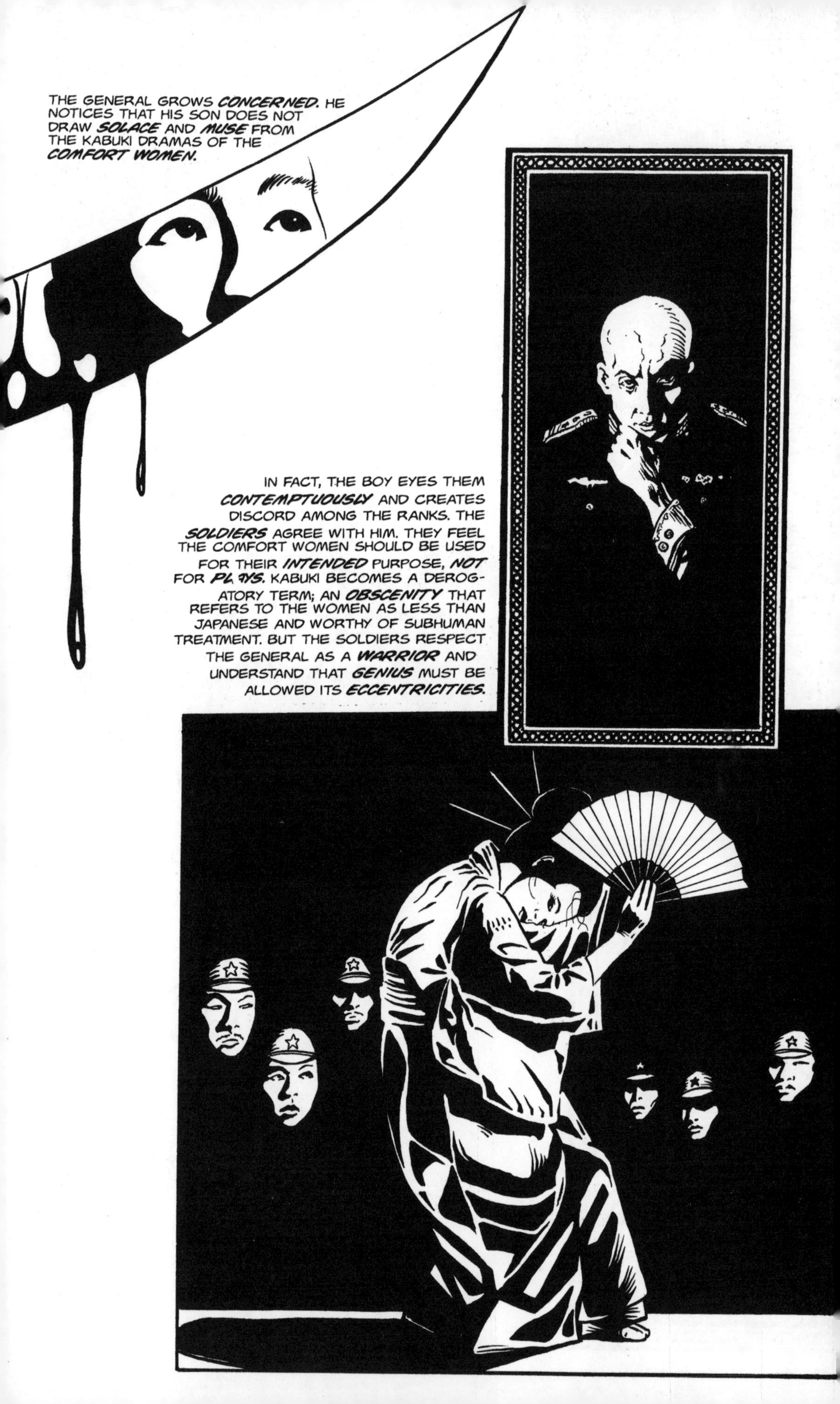
THE GENERAL GROWS *CONCERNED.* HE NOTICES THAT HIS SON DOES NOT DRAW *SOLACE* AND *MUSE* FROM THE KABUKI DRAMAS OF THE *COMFORT WOMEN.*
IN FACT, THE BOY EYES THEM *CONTEMPTUOUSLY* AND CREATES DISCORD AMONG THE RANKS. THE *SOLDIERS* AGREE WITH HIM. THEY FEEL THE COMFORT WOMEN SHOULD BE USED FOR THEIR *INTENDED* PURPOSE, *NOT* FOR *PLAYS.* KABUKI BECOMES A DEROGATORY TERM; AN *OBSCENITY* THAT REFERS TO THE WOMEN AS LESS THAN JAPANESE AND WORTHY OF SUBHUMAN TREATMENT. BUT THE SOLDIERS RESPECT THE GENERAL AS A *WARRIOR* AND UNDERSTAND THAT *GENIUS* MUST BE ALLOWED ITS *ECCENTRICITIES.*

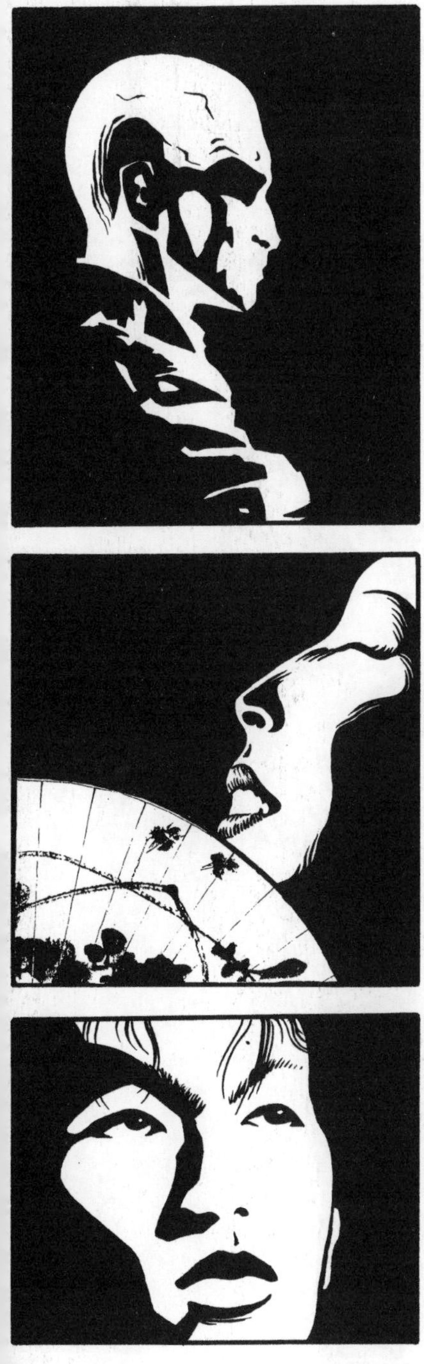

THE GENERAL IS *ENTRANCED* BY MY MOTHER'S *PERFORMANCE.* THE BOY IS SICKENED BY THE AFFECTION HE SENSES BETWEEN THEM, *DISTURBED* THAT HIS FATHER PAYS SO MUCH ATTENTION TO THIS WOMAN.

THEY ARE COMFORT WOMEN. THEY ARE NOT *JAPANESE.* THEY ARE NOT PART OF THE COLLECTIVE *"WA"* OF THE *REGIMENT.* THEY ARE *DOGS* AND SHE IS WORSE. SHE IS *AINU.*

THEY SHOULD BE TREATED AS *PETS* AND *NOTHING MORE.* THE SOLDIERS *AGREE,* SAYING THE WOMEN ARE *WASTED* ON THE *PERFORMANCES.*

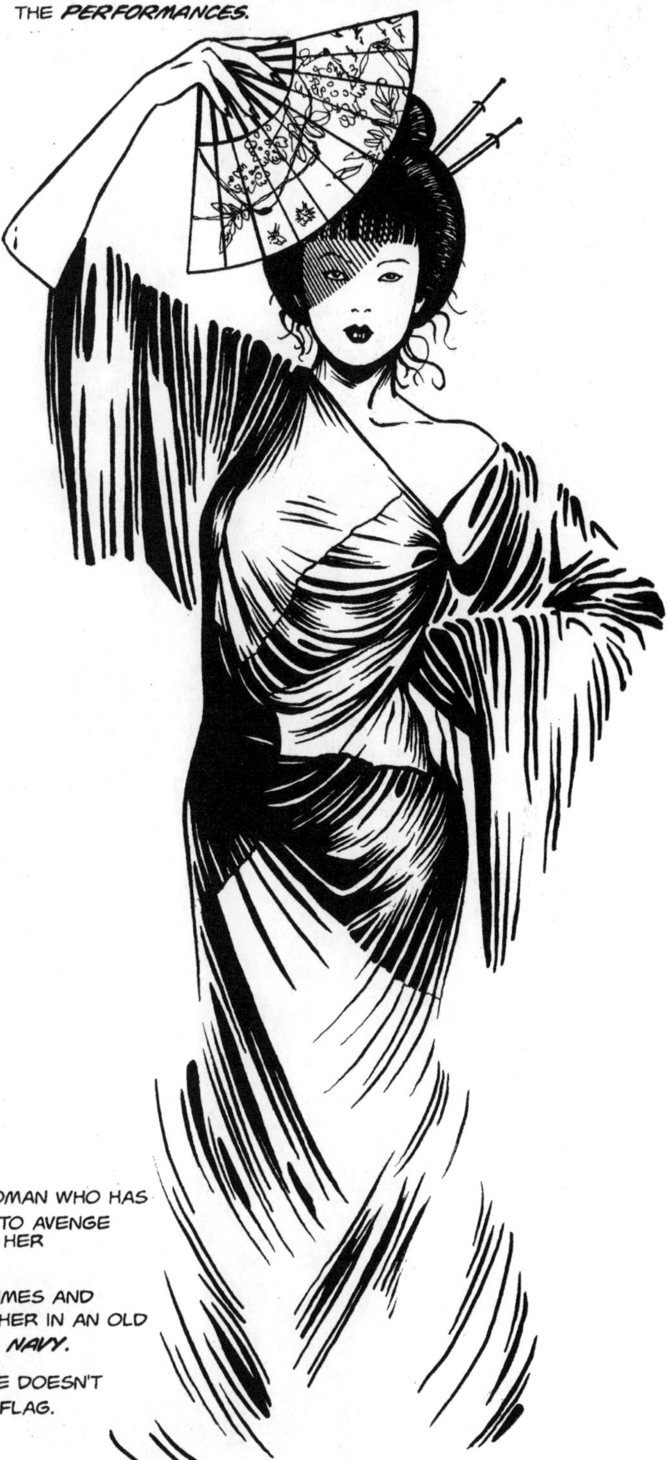

MY *MOTHER* PLAYS A WOMAN WHO HAS RETURNED AS A *GHOST* TO AVENGE HER FAMILY. THIS WILL BE HER *LAST PERFORMANCE.*

THEY RUN OUT OF COSTUMES AND IMPROVISE BY DRESSING HER IN AN OLD *FLAG* OF THE *IMPERIAL NAVY.*

HIS THOUGHTS *BURN.* SHE DOESN'T *DESERVE* TO WEAR THE FLAG.

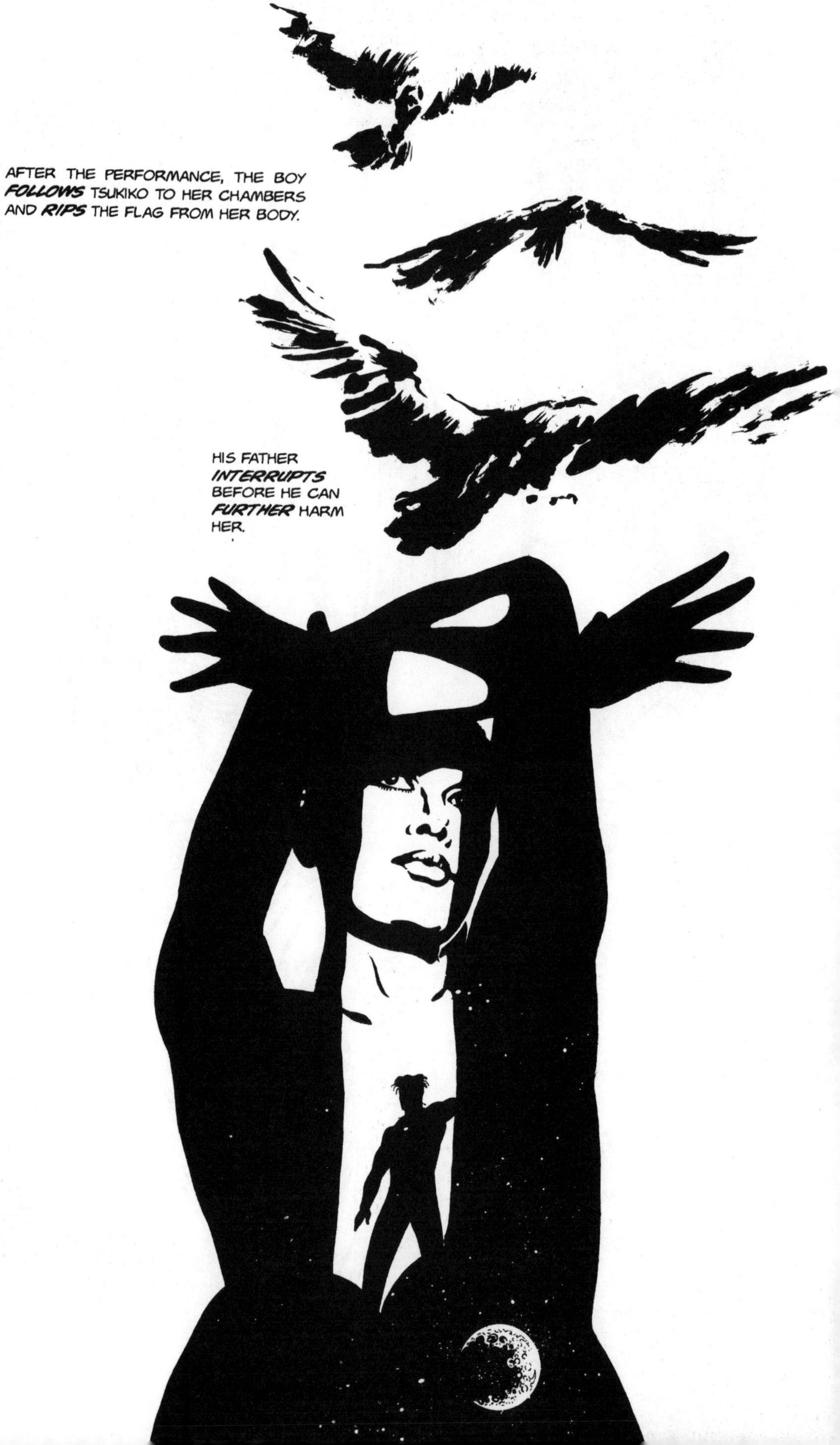
AFTER THE PERFORMANCE, THE BOY FOLLOWS TSUKIKO TO HER CHAMBERS AND RIPS THE FLAG FROM HER BODY.
HIS FATHER INTERRUPTS BEFORE HE CAN FURTHER HARM HER.

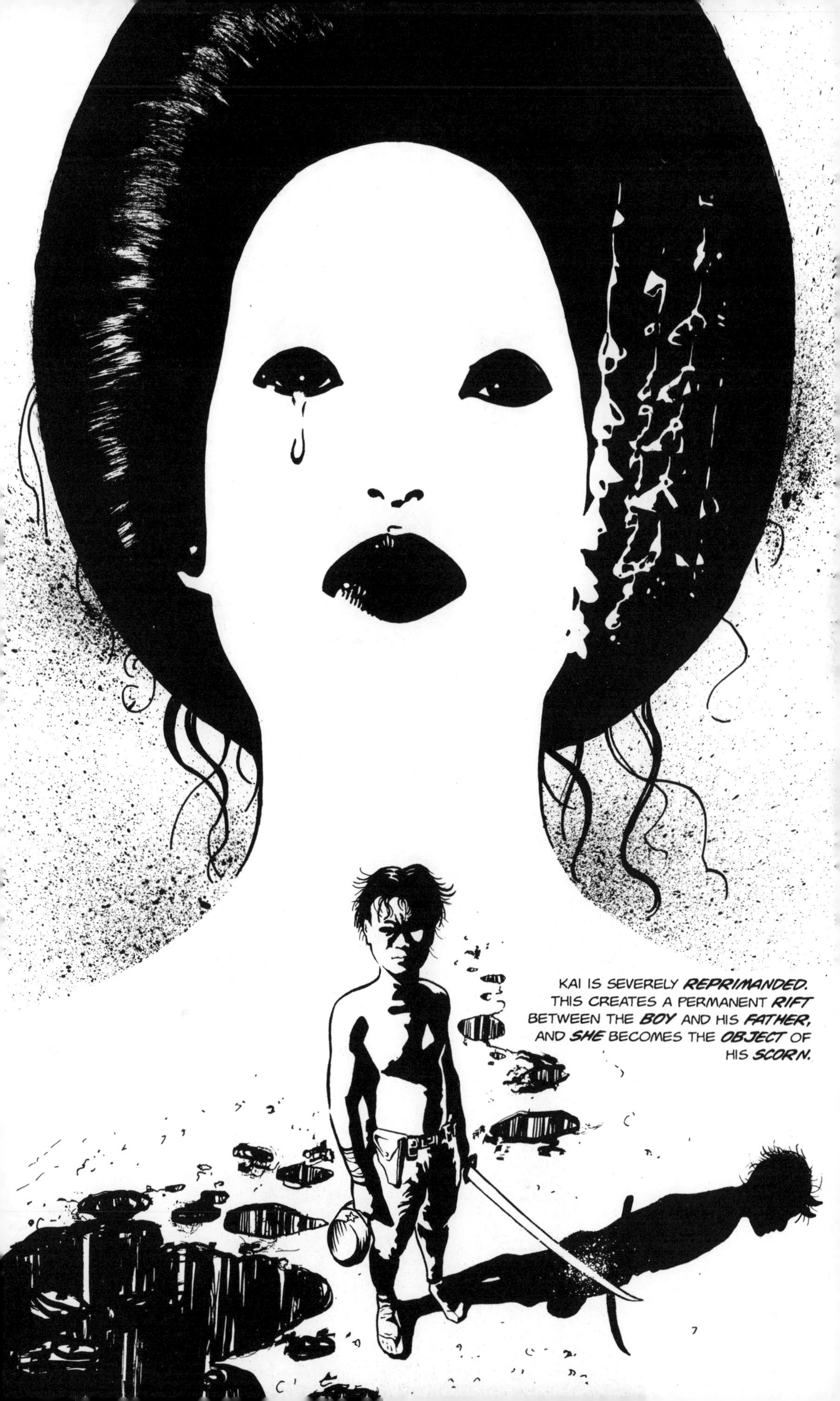
KAI IS SEVERELY REPRIMANDED.
THIS CREATES A PERMANENT RIFT
BETWEEN THE BOY AND HIS FATHER,
AND SHE BECOMES THE OBJECT OF
HIS SCORN.

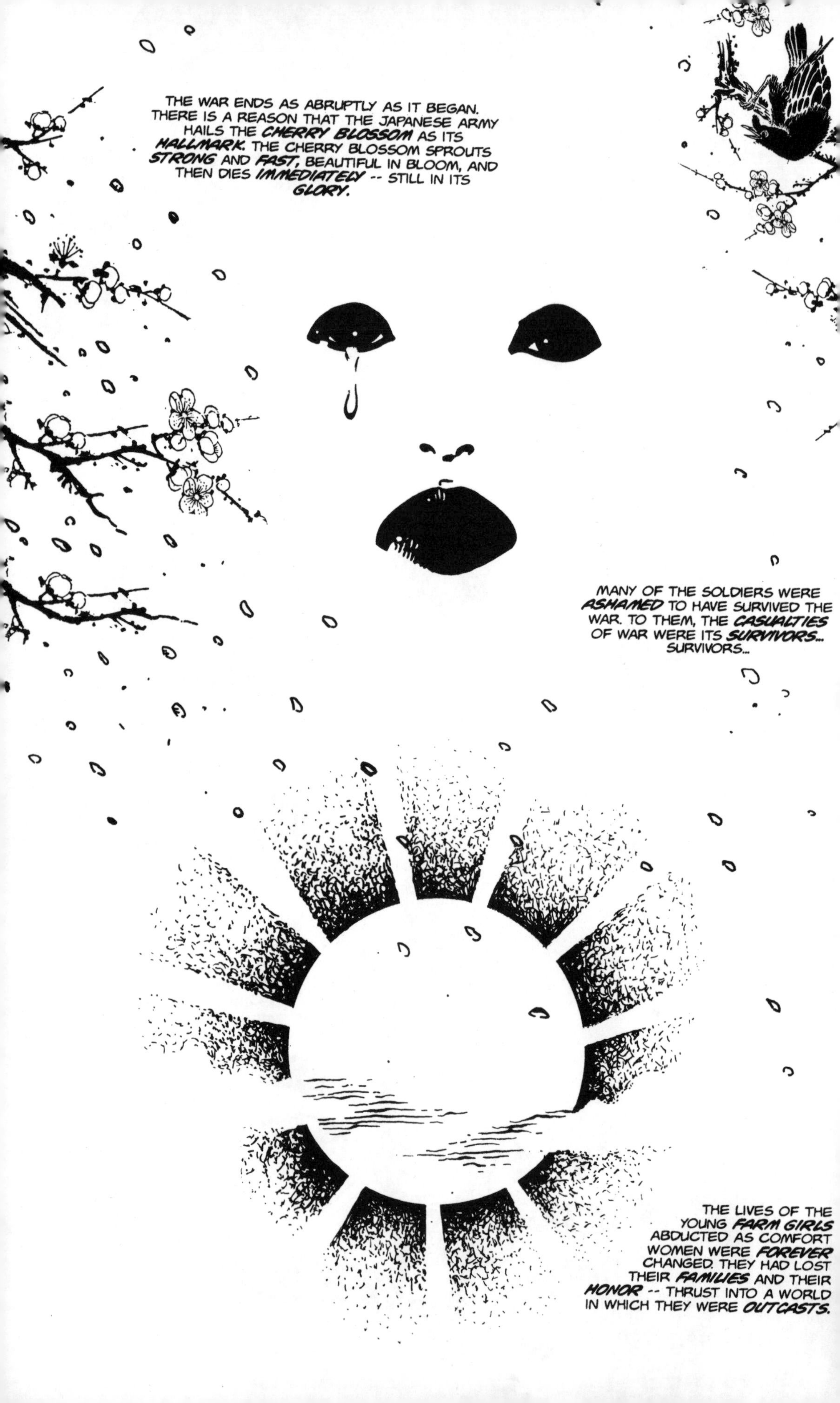
THE WAR ENDS AS ABRUPTLY AS IT BEGAN. THERE IS A REASON THAT THE JAPANESE ARMY HAILS THE CHERRY BLOSSOM AS ITS HALLMARK. THE CHERRY BLOSSOM SPROUTS STRONG AND FAST, BEAUTIFUL IN BLOOM, AND THEN DIES IMMEDIATELY -- STILL IN ITS GLORY.
MANY OF THE SOLDIERS WERE ASHAMED TO HAVE SURVIVED THE WAR. TO THEM, THE CASUALTIES OF WAR WERE ITS SURVIVORS... SURVIVORS...
THE LIVES OF THE YOUNG FARM GIRLS ABDUCTED AS COMFORT WOMEN WERE FOREVER CHANGED. THEY HAD LOST THEIR FAMILIES AND THEIR HONOR -- THRUST INTO A WORLD IN WHICH THEY WERE OUTCASTS.

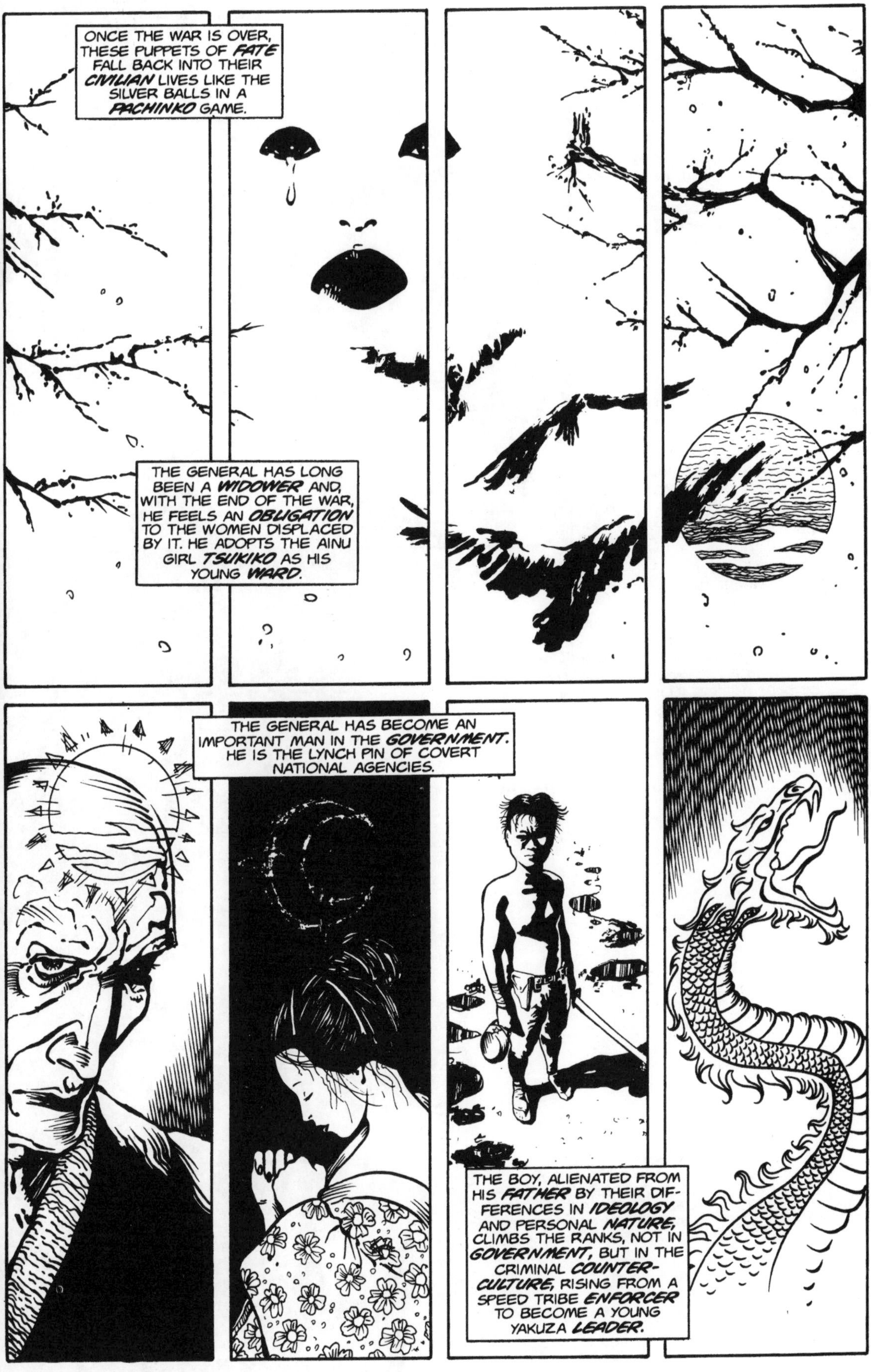

ONCE THE WAR IS OVER, THESE PUPPETS OF FATE FALL BACK INTO THEIR CIVILIAN LIVES LIKE THE SILVER BALLS IN A PACHINKO GAME.
THE GENERAL HAS LONG BEEN A WIDOWER AND, WITH THE END OF THE WAR, HE FEELS AN OBLIGATION TO THE WOMEN DISPLACED BY IT. HE ADOPTS THE AINU GIRL TSUKIKO AS HIS YOUNG WARD.
THE GENERAL HAS BECOME AN IMPORTANT MAN IN THE GOVERNMENT. HE IS THE LYNCH PIN OF COVERT NATIONAL AGENCIES.
THE BOY, ALIENATED FROM HIS FATHER BY THEIR DIFFERENCES IN IDEOLOGY AND PERSONAL NATURE, CLIMBS THE RANKS, NOT IN GOVERNMENT, BUT IN THE CRIMINAL COUNTER-CULTURE, RISING FROM A SPEED TRIBE ENFORCER TO BECOME A YOUNG YAKUZA LEADER.

AS THE GENERAL *INCREASES* HIS STATUS IN GOVERNMENT, HIS NAME FOLLOWS THE NATURE OF HIS POSITION INTO SECRECY, BECOMING A *WHISPER* ON THE *LIPS* OF *IMPORTANT MEN*.

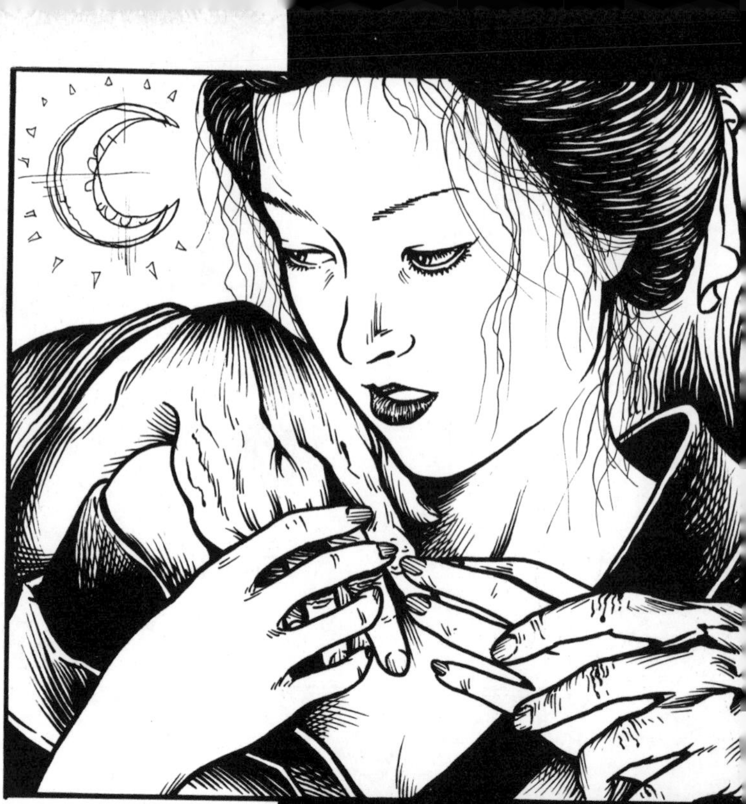

HOWEVER, HIS SON, ESTRANGED FROM HIM DUE TO DISGUST WITH HIS FATHER'S AFFILIATION WITH THE AINU GIRL, BECOMES MORE *VICIOUS*. HE ESTABLISHES A FIERCE *REPUTATION* IN THE JAPANESE UNDERWORLD THAT BRINGS *INFAMY* TO THE NAME *KAI*.

TSUKIKO GROWS TO RETURN THE LOVE OF THE AGING GENERAL. ALTHOUGH *MATRIMONY* WITH THE AINU GIRL WOULD APPEAR *DISHONORABLE* IN SOCIAL CIRCLES, ESPECIALLY FOR A MAN OF THE GENERAL'S POSITION, HE HAS SET A DATE TO WED HER.

THE GENERAL'S SUPERIORS ARE SHOCKED AT FIRST, BUT THEY HAVE LONG *TOLERATED* HIS ECCENTRICITIES.

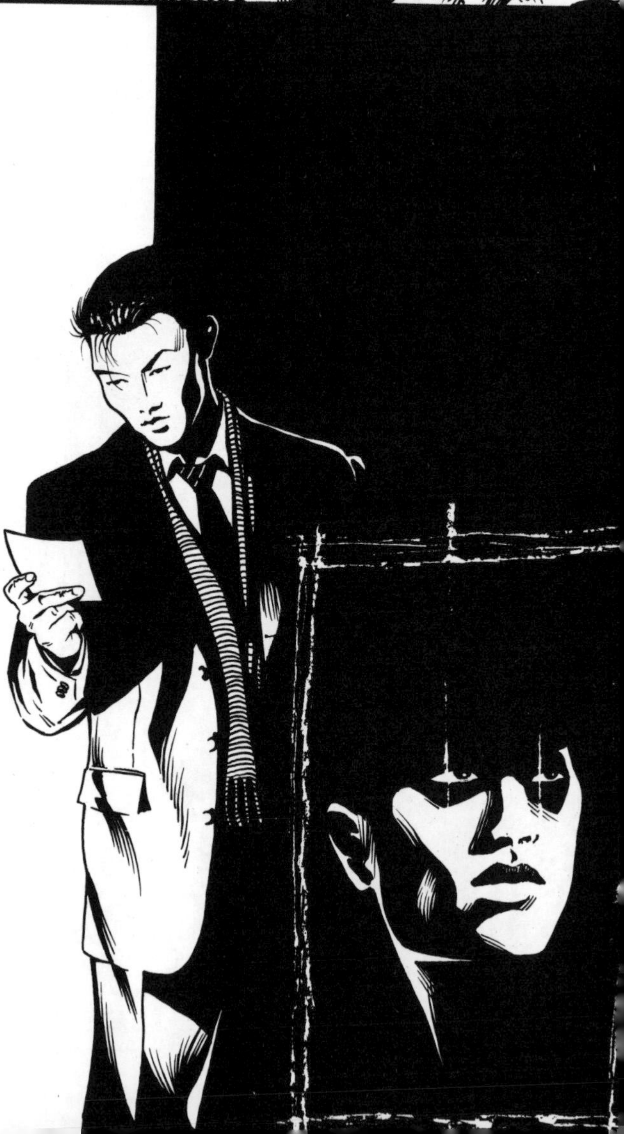

HOWEVER, WHEN RYUICHI KAI LEARNS OF THE PLAN, HE IS *OUTRAGED*. HE FEELS *DISGUSTED* FOR HIMSELF AND *DISHONORED* FOR HIS *DECEASED MOTHER*.

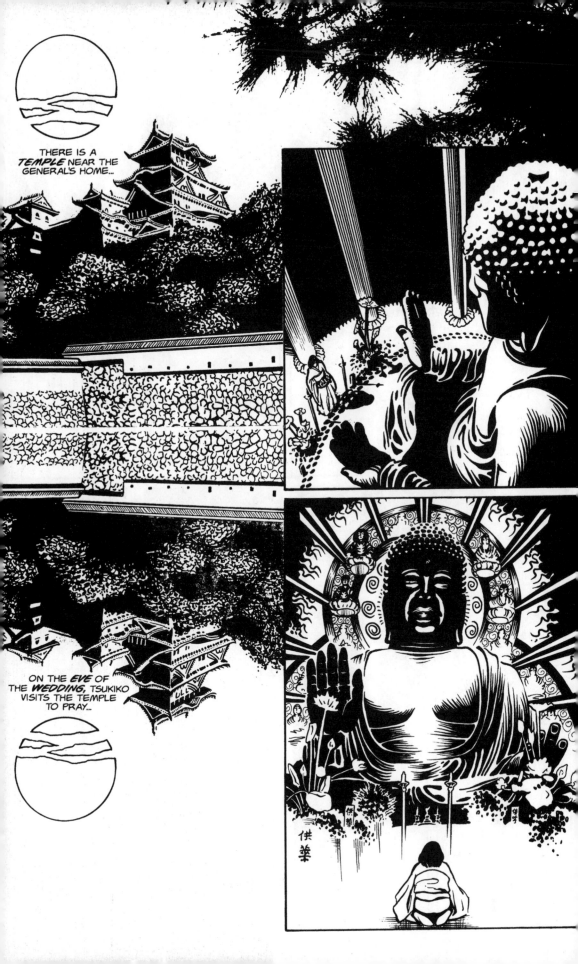

THERE IS A *TEMPLE* NEAR THE GENERAL'S HOME...

ON THE *EVE* OF THE *WEDDING*, TSUKIKO VISITS THE TEMPLE TO PRAY...

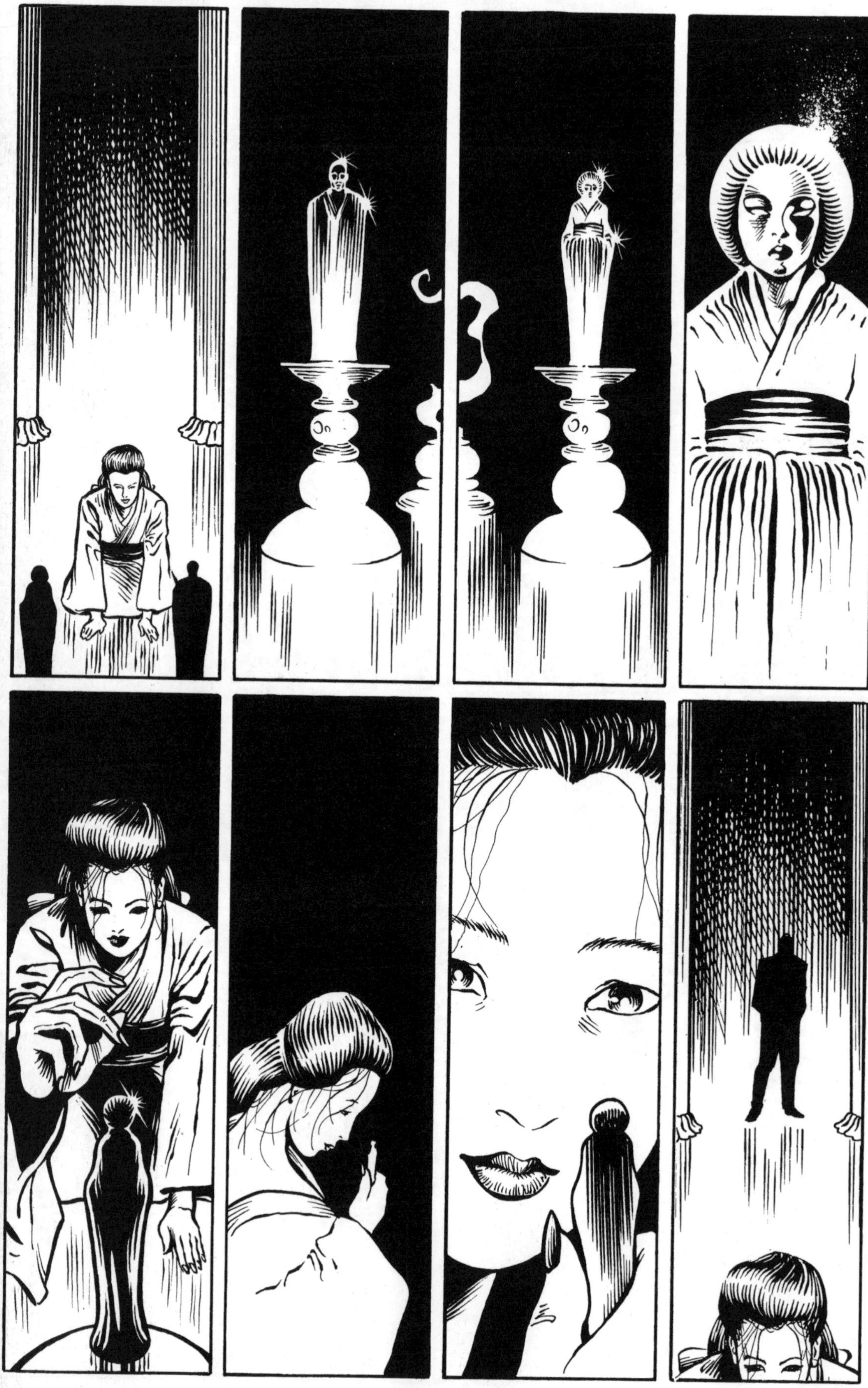

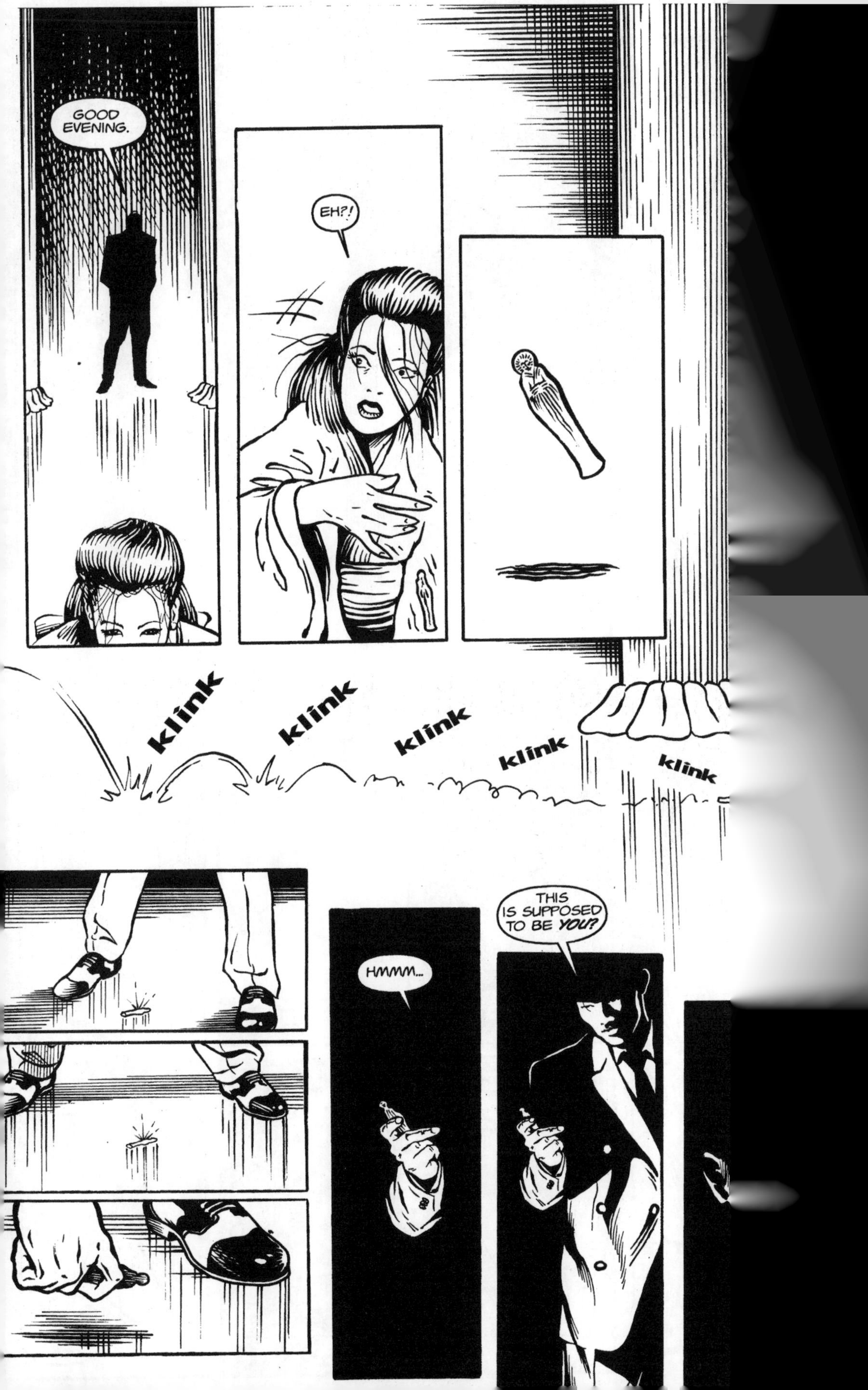

GOOD EVENING.
EH?!
klink
klink
klink
klink
klink
HMMM...
THIS IS SUPPOSED TO BE *YOU?*

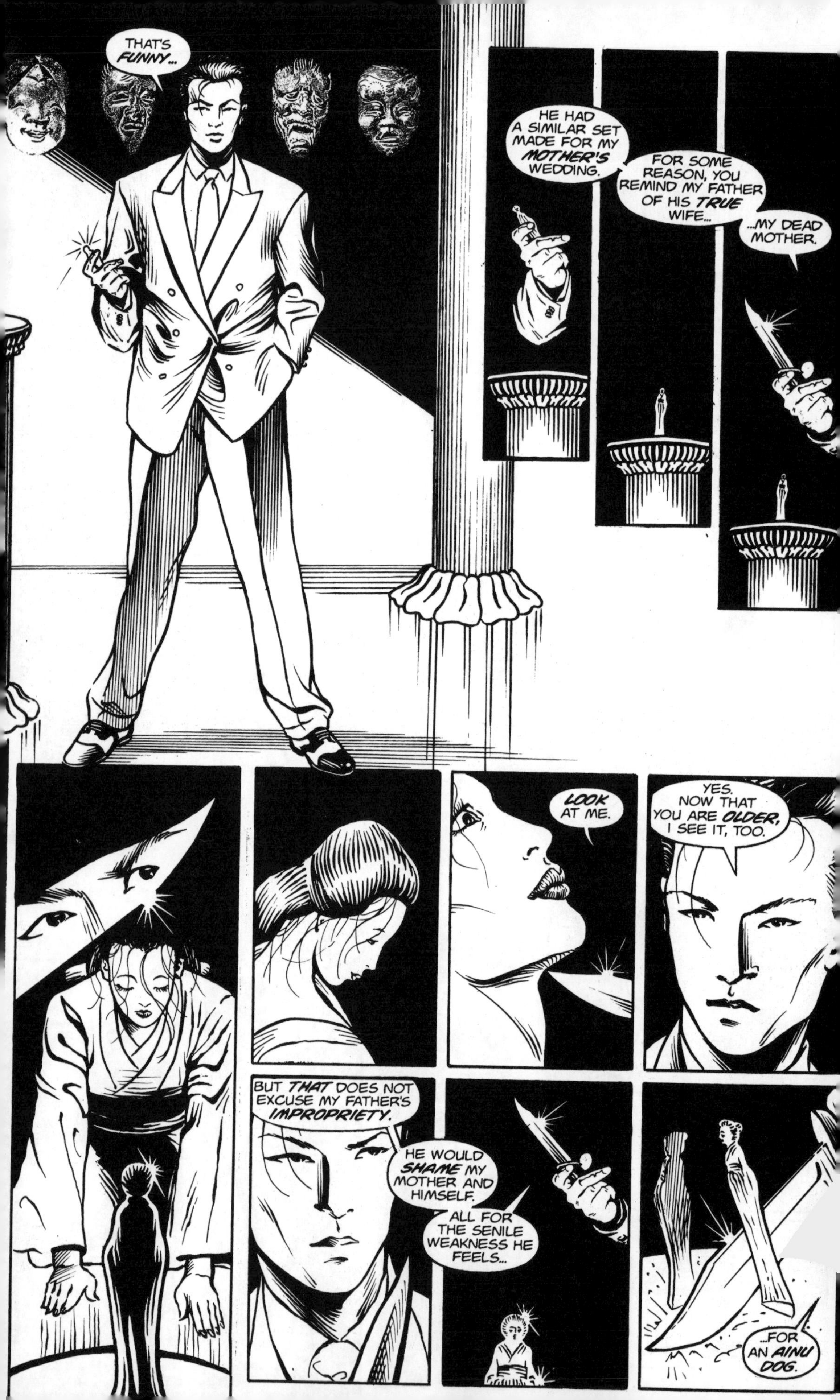
THAT'S FUNNY...
HE HAD A SIMILAR SET MADE FOR MY MOTHER'S WEDDING.
FOR SOME REASON, YOU REMIND MY FATHER OF HIS TRUE WIFE...
...MY DEAD MOTHER.
LOOK AT ME.
YES. NOW THAT YOU ARE OLDER, I SEE IT, TOO.
BUT THAT DOES NOT EXCUSE MY FATHER'S IMPROPRIETY.
HE WOULD SHAME MY MOTHER AND HIMSELF.
ALL FOR THE SENILE WEAKNESS HE FEELS...
...FOR AN AINU DOG.

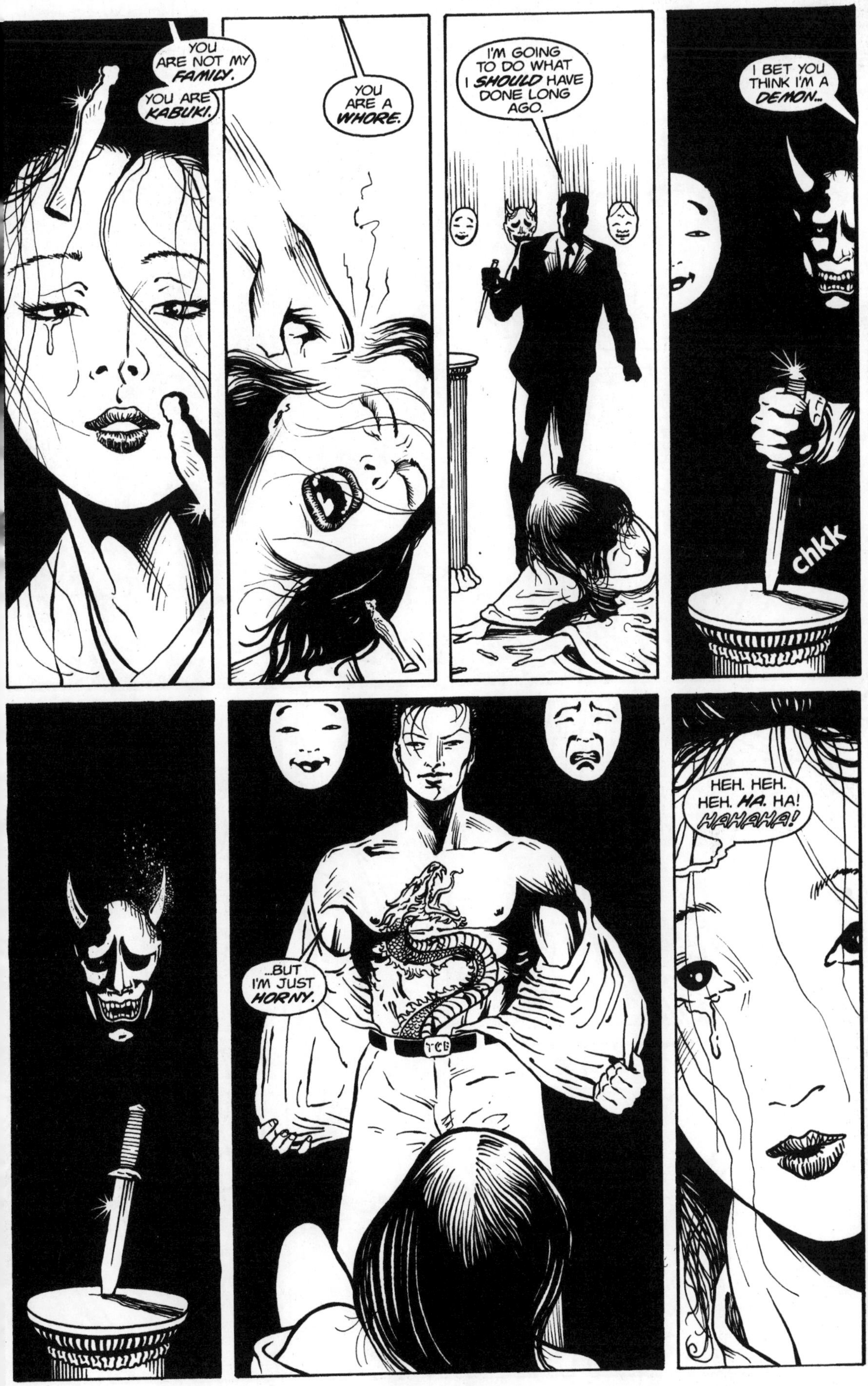
YOU ARE NOT MY FAMILY.
YOU ARE KABUKI.
YOU ARE A WHORE.
I'M GOING TO DO WHAT I SHOULD HAVE DONE LONG AGO.
I BET YOU THINK I'M A DEMON...
chkk
...BUT I'M JUST HORNY.
HEH. HEH. HEH. HA. HA! HAHAHA!

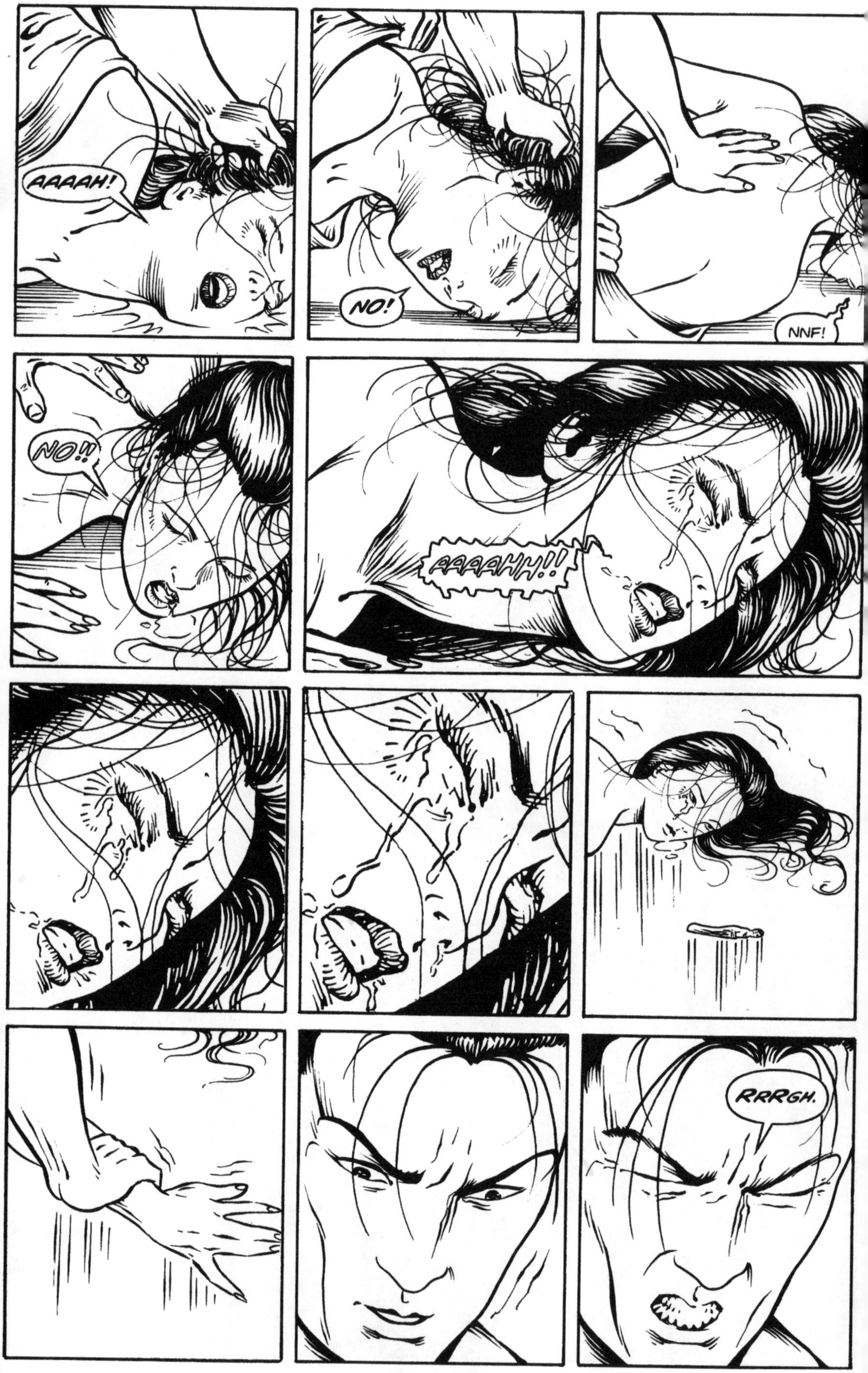
AAAAH!
NO!
NNF!
NO!!
AAAAHH!!
RRRGH.

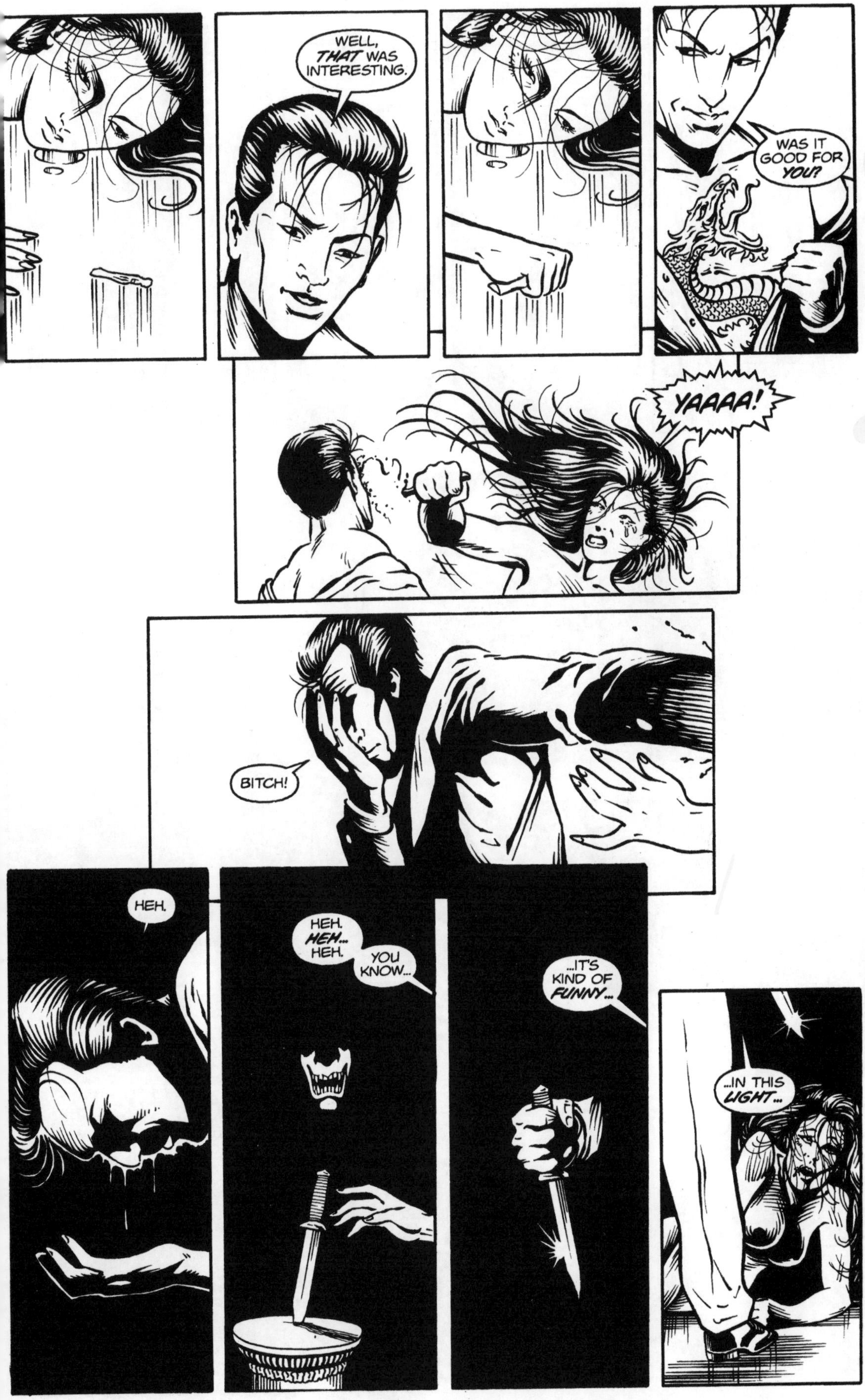
WELL, THAT WAS INTERESTING.
WAS IT GOOD FOR YOU?
YAAAA!
BITCH!
HEH.
HEH. HEH... HEH.
YOU KNOW...
...IT'S KIND OF FUNNY...
...IN THIS LIGHT...

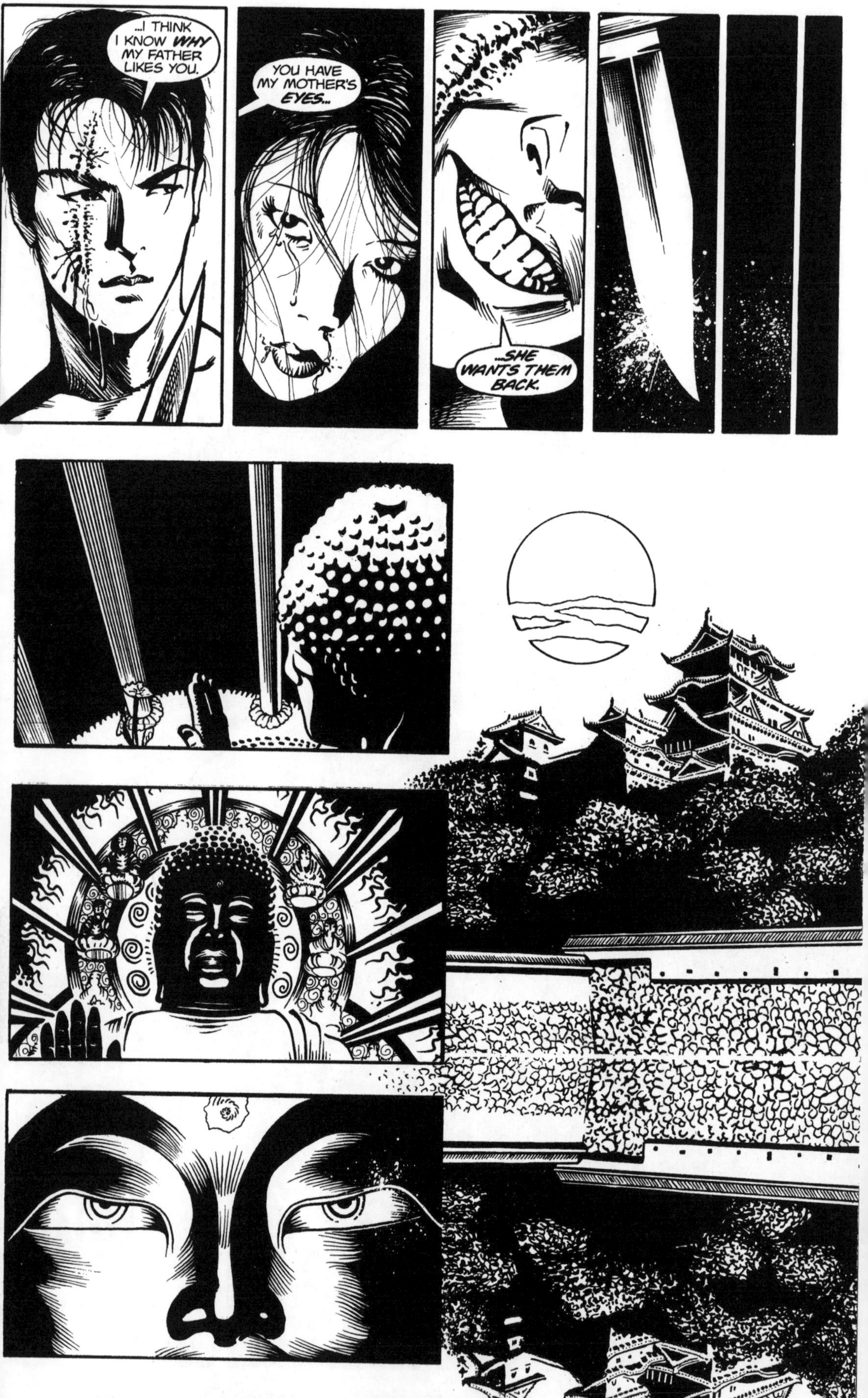

...I THINK I KNOW WHY MY FATHER LIKES YOU.
YOU HAVE MY MOTHER'S EYES...
...SHE WANTS THEM BACK.

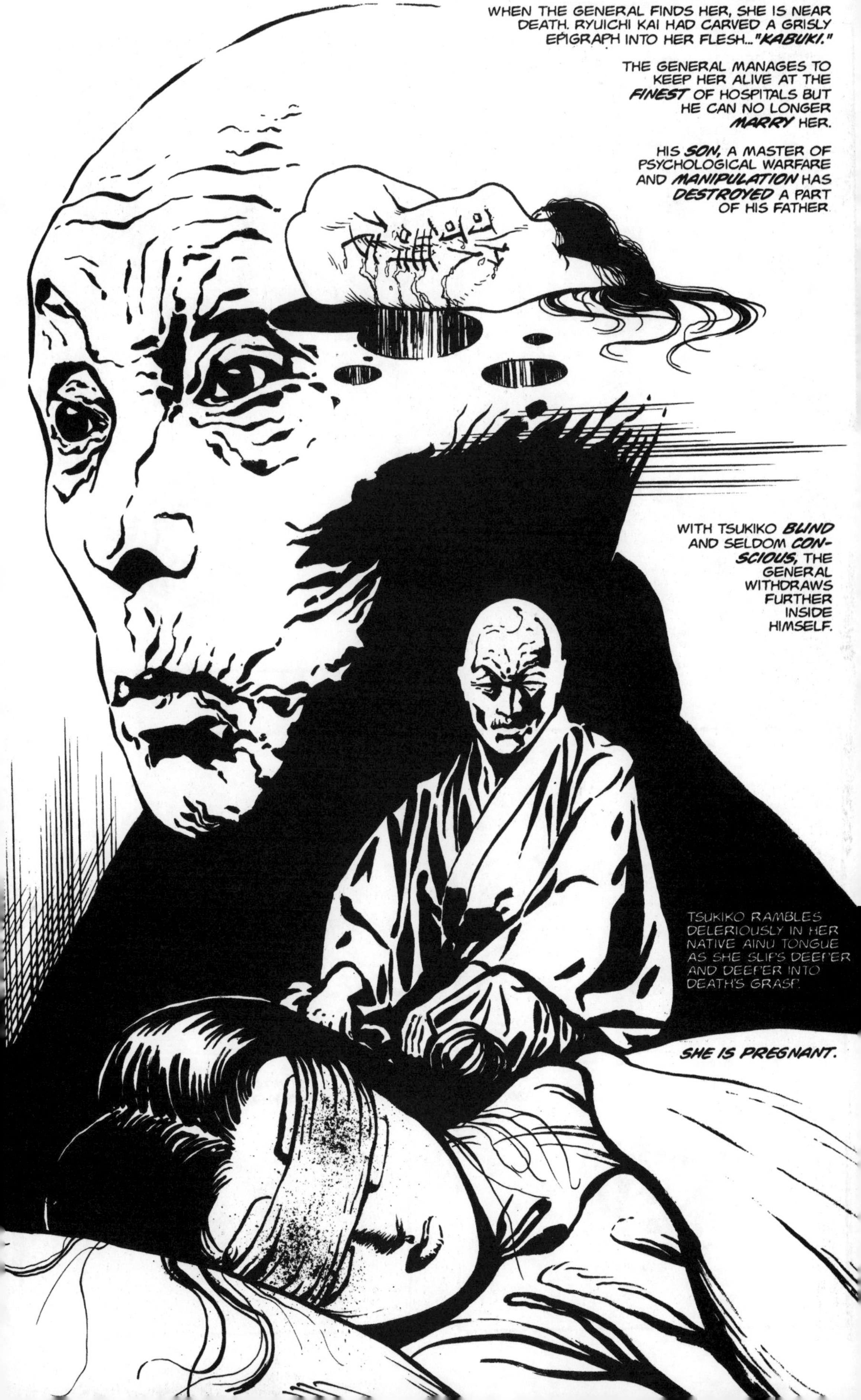
WHEN THE GENERAL FINDS HER, SHE IS NEAR DEATH. RYUICHI KAI HAD CARVED A GRISLY EPIGRAPH INTO HER FLESH..."KABUKI."
THE GENERAL MANAGES TO KEEP HER ALIVE AT THE FINEST OF HOSPITALS BUT HE CAN NO LONGER MARRY HER.
HIS SON, A MASTER OF PSYCHOLOGICAL WARFARE AND MANIPULATION HAS DESTROYED A PART OF HIS FATHER.
WITH TSUKIKO BLIND AND SELDOM CONSCIOUS, THE GENERAL WITHDRAWS FURTHER INSIDE HIMSELF.
TSUKIKO RAMBLES DELERIOUSLY IN HER NATIVE AINU TONGUE AS SHE SLIPS DEEPER AND DEEPER INTO DEATH'S GRASP.
SHE IS PREGNANT.

THE GENERAL HAD NEVER *CON-SUMATED* WITH TSUKIKO. SHE WAS NEVER *CONSCIOUS* ENOUGH TO IDENTIFY HER ATTACKER, BUT THE GENERAL *KNOWS* IN HIS HEART WHO THE *FATHER IS.*

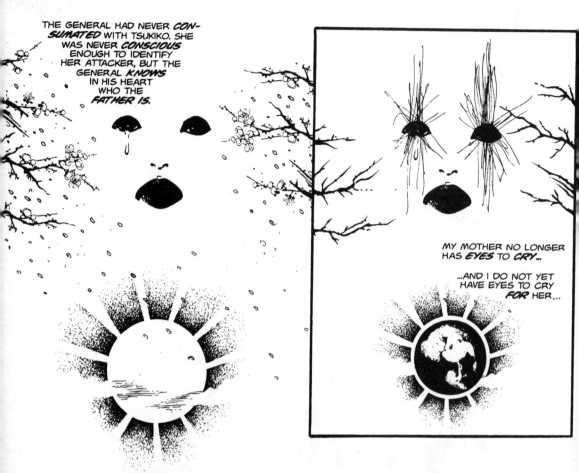

MY MOTHER NO LONGER HAS *EYES* TO *CRY...*

...AND I DO NOT YET HAVE EYES TO CRY *FOR* HER...

...SO I *LISTEN* TO THE *MUSIC* OF HER *MELANCHOLY SONG...*

...AND I GROW *STRONGER.*

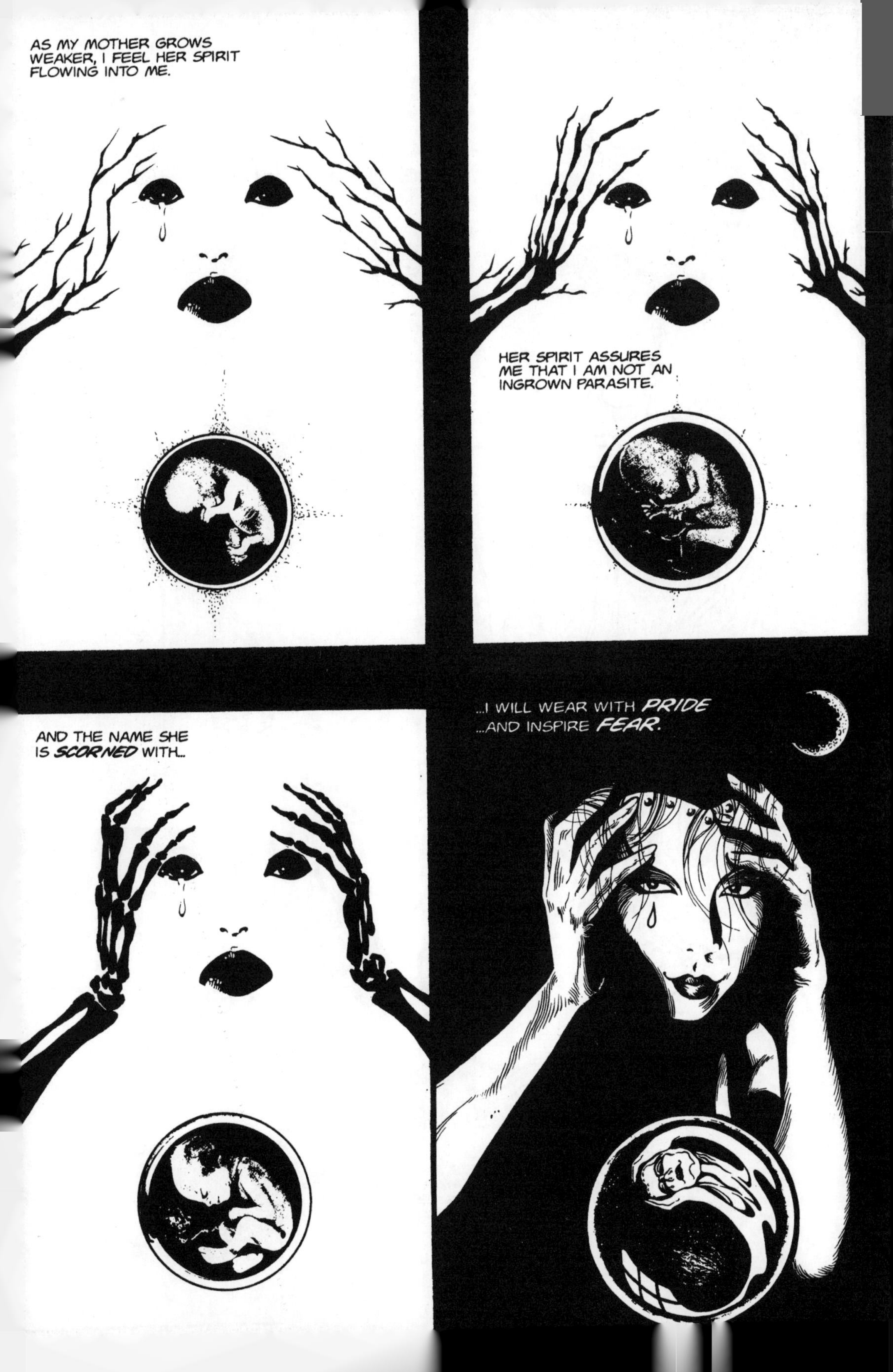
AS MY MOTHER GROWS WEAKER, I FEEL HER SPIRIT FLOWING INTO ME.
HER SPIRIT ASSURES ME THAT I AM NOT AN INGROWN PARASITE.
AND THE NAME SHE IS SCORNED WITH...
...I WILL WEAR WITH PRIDE ...AND INSPIRE FEAR.

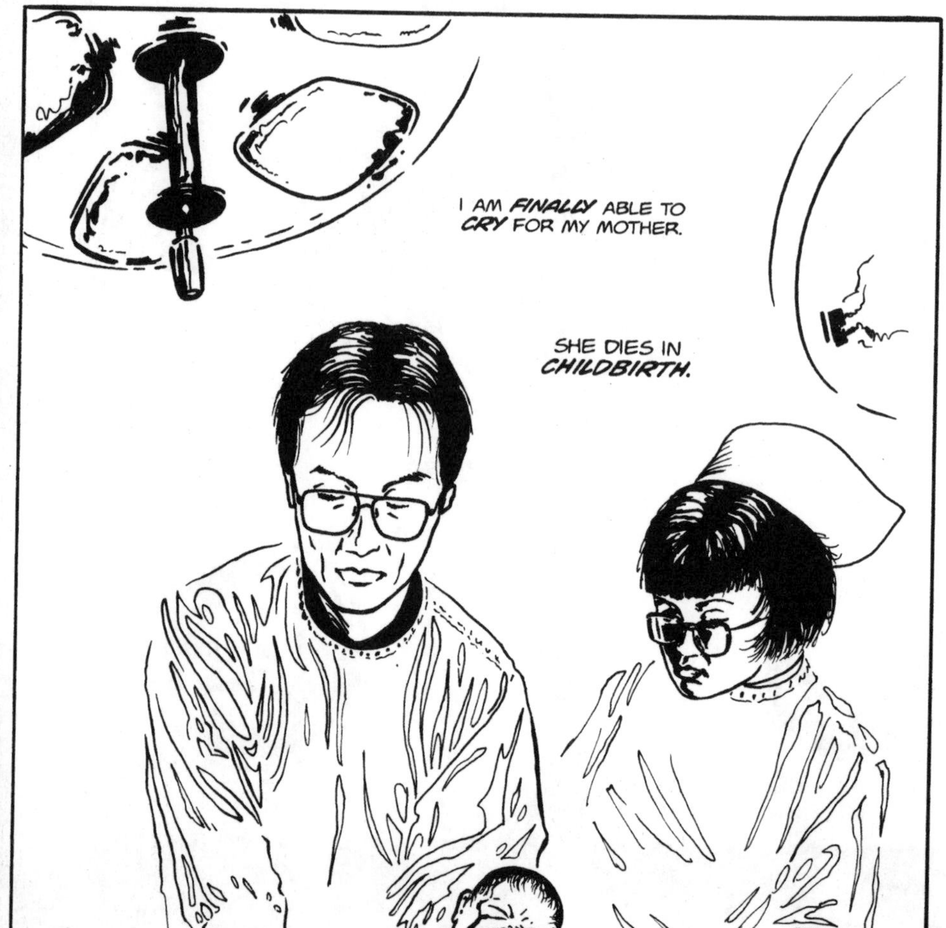
I AM ***FINALLY*** ABLE TO ***CRY*** FOR MY MOTHER.
SHE DIES IN ***CHILDBIRTH.***

THE GENERAL FEELS ***RESPONSIBLE*** FOR THE YOUNG ***CHILD.*** HE RAISES HER AS HIS ***OWN.*** HE ***SEES*** MY MOTHER THROUGH THE INFANT'S ***EYES.***

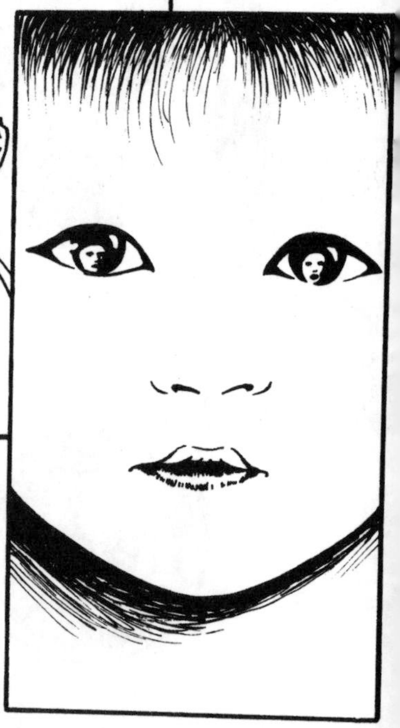

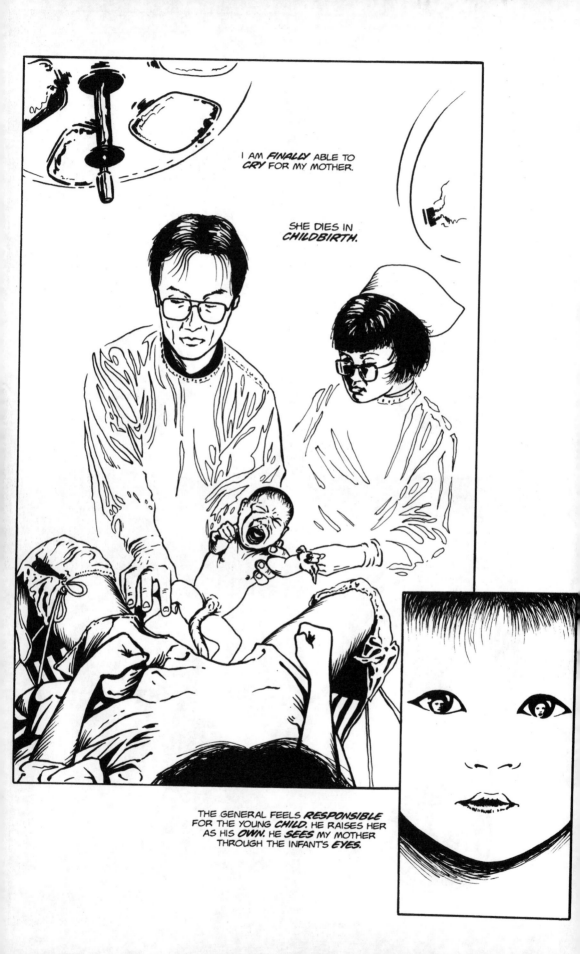

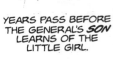
YEARS PASS BEFORE THE GENERAL'S *SON* LEARNS OF THE LITTLE GIRL.

WHEN HE FINDS THAT A *CHILD* WAS BORN RESULTING FROM HIS *ASSAULT* ON TSUKIKO...

...AND THAT HIS FATHER *RAISES* THE GIRL AS HIS *FAMILY*, HE IS *ENRAGED* TO THE POINT OF *MADNESS*.

THE CHILD IS IN THE GARDEN AT HER MOTHER'S GRAVE. SHE IS *WAITING* FOR HER MUSIC LESSONS.

FROM THE GARDEN SHE CAN HEAR THE GENERAL AT HIS PIANO. HE IS PLAYING WAGNER'S "RIDE OF THE VALKYRIES."

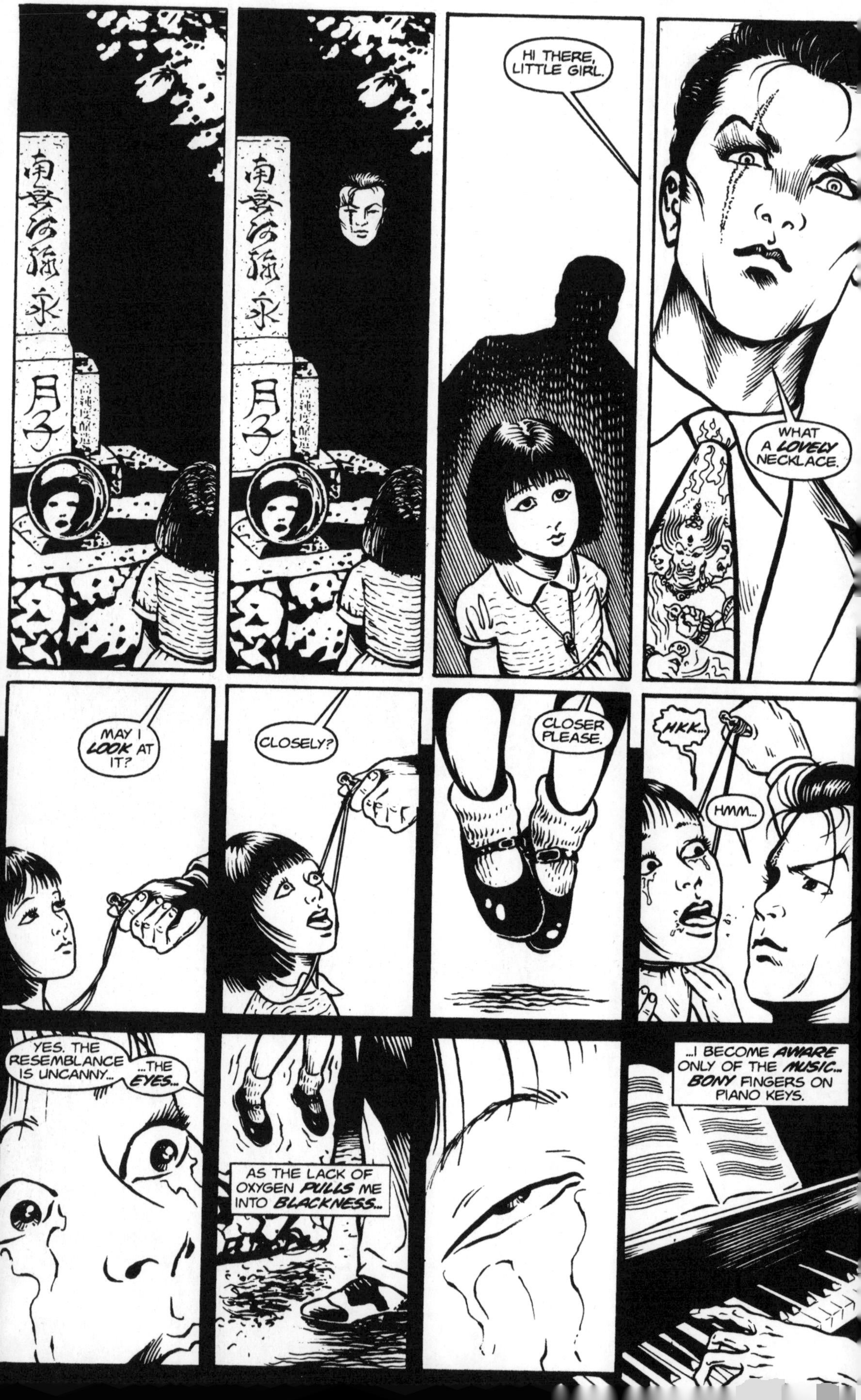
HI THERE, LITTLE GIRL.
WHAT A LOVELY NECKLACE.
MAY I LOOK AT IT?
CLOSELY?
CLOSER PLEASE.
HKK...
HMM...
YES. THE RESEMBLANCE IS UNCANNY...
...THE EYES...
AS THE LACK OF OXYGEN PULLS ME INTO BLACKNESS...
...I BECOME AWARE ONLY OF THE MUSIC... BONY FINGERS ON PIANO KEYS.

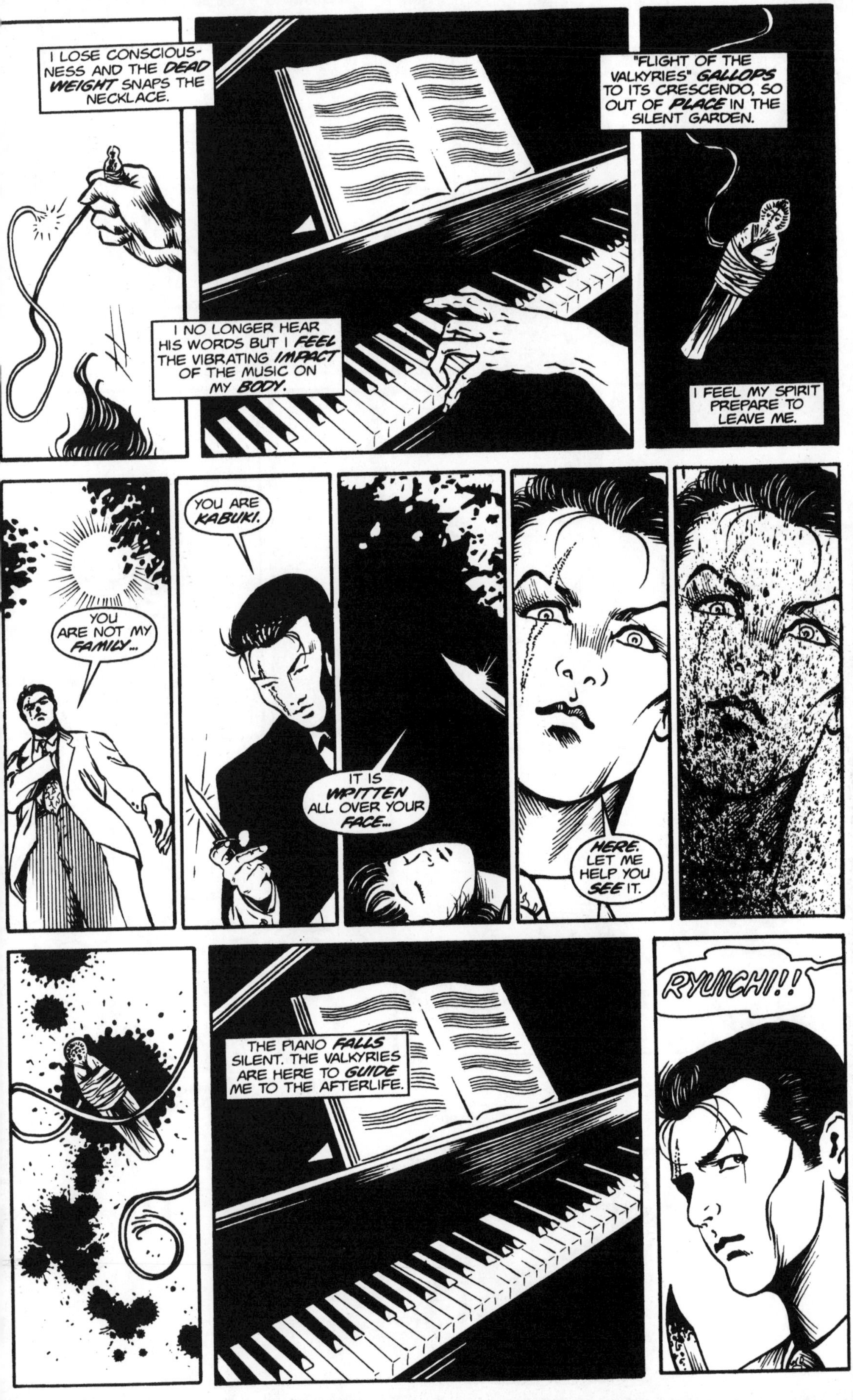

I LOSE CONSCIOUSNESS AND THE DEAD WEIGHT SNAPS THE NECKLACE.
I NO LONGER HEAR HIS WORDS BUT I FEEL THE VIBRATING IMPACT OF THE MUSIC ON MY BODY.
"FLIGHT OF THE VALKYRIES" GALLOPS TO ITS CRESCENDO, SO OUT OF PLACE IN THE SILENT GARDEN.
I FEEL MY SPIRIT PREPARE TO LEAVE ME.
YOU ARE NOT MY FAMILY...
YOU ARE KABUKI.
IT IS WRITTEN ALL OVER YOUR FACE...
HERE. LET ME HELP YOU SEE IT.
THE PIANO FALLS SILENT. THE VALKYRIES ARE HERE TO GUIDE ME TO THE AFTERLIFE.
RYUICHI!!

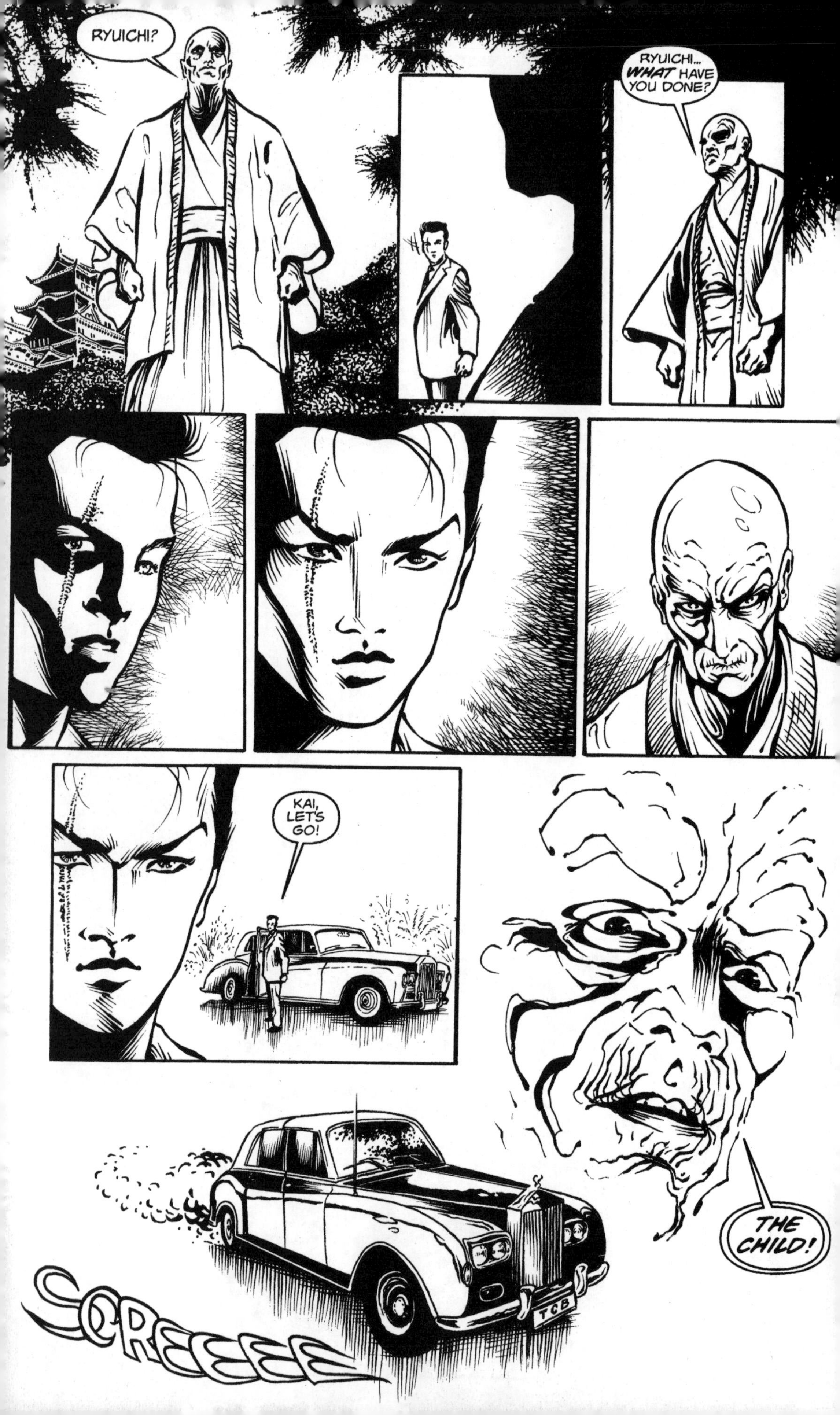
RYUICHI?
RYUICHI... WHAT HAVE YOU DONE?
KAI, LET'S GO!
THE CHILD!
SCREEEEE

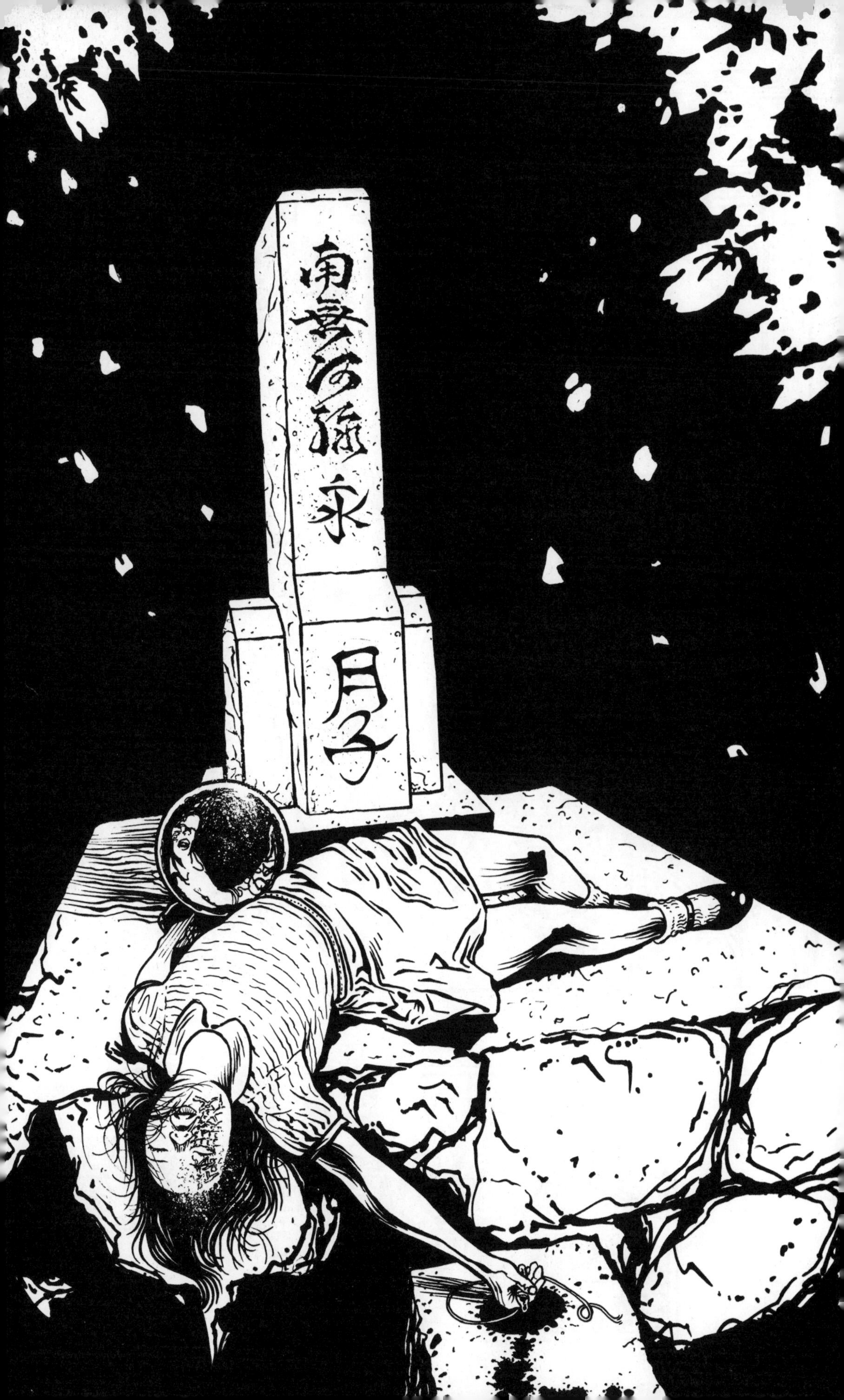
月子

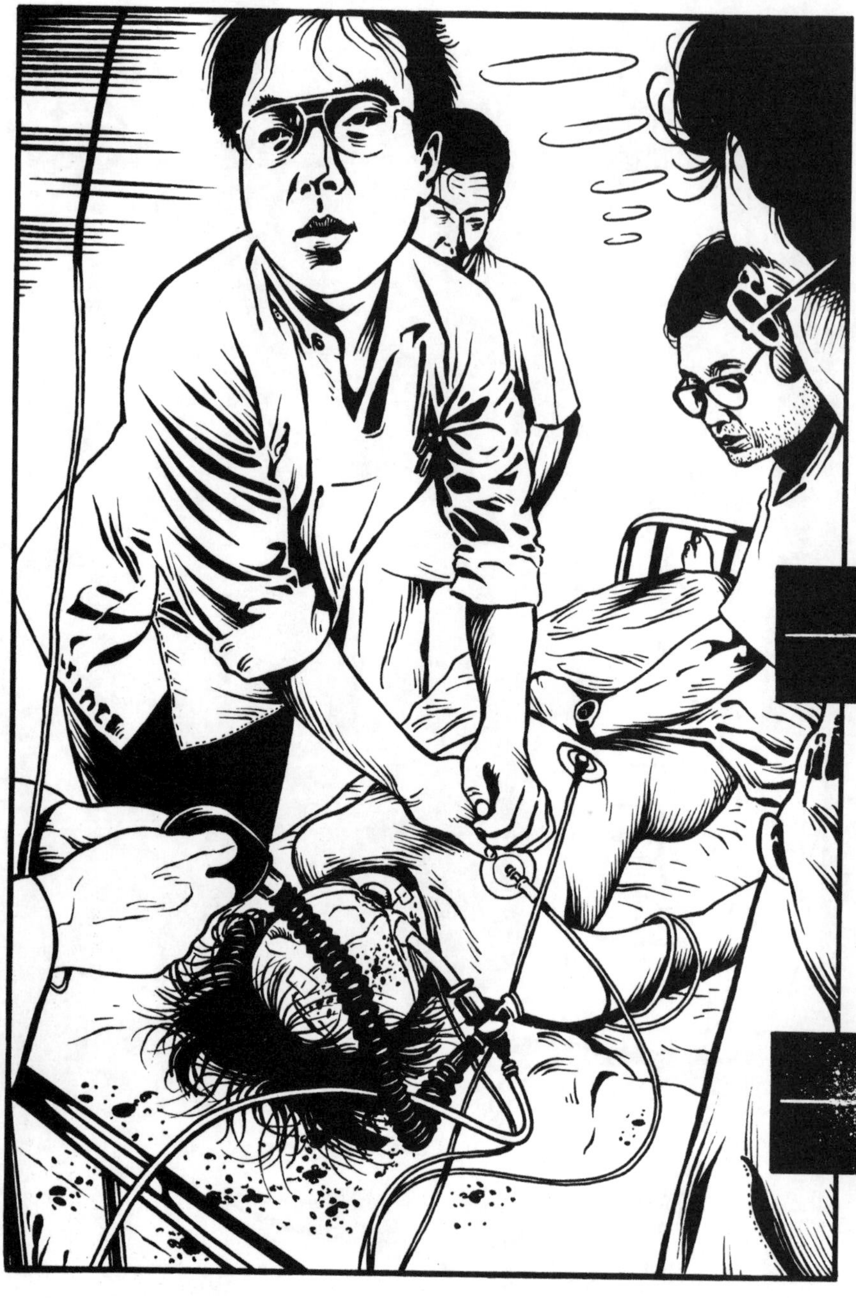

THE GENERAL MEDEVACS
THE GIRL TO THE *FINEST*
HOSPITAL. HE ***SPARES*** NO
EXPENSE TO ACCESS THE
LATEST IN MEDICAL
TECHNOLOGY.

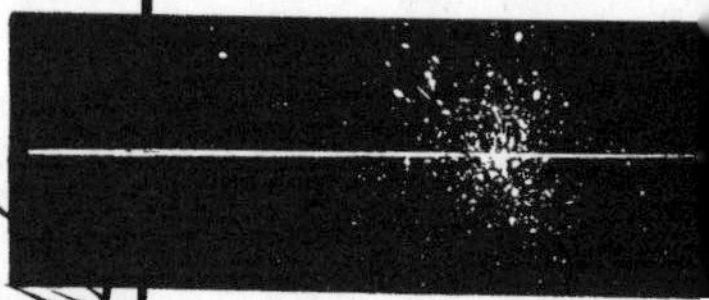

I AM DEAD.

MY HEART ***STOPS*** FOR
NINE MINUTES. TOTAL
FLATLINE.

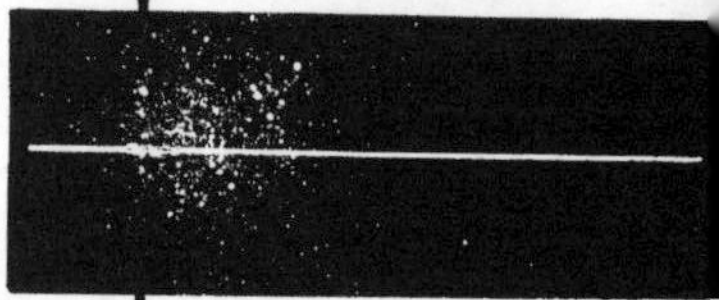

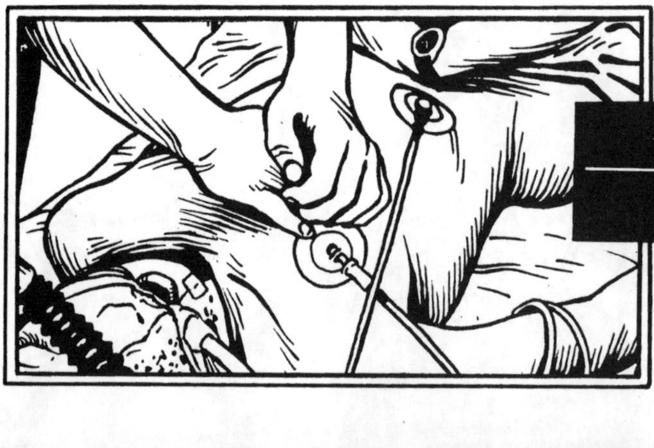

MIRACULOUSLY,
THE MEDICS BRING
ME ***BACK***.

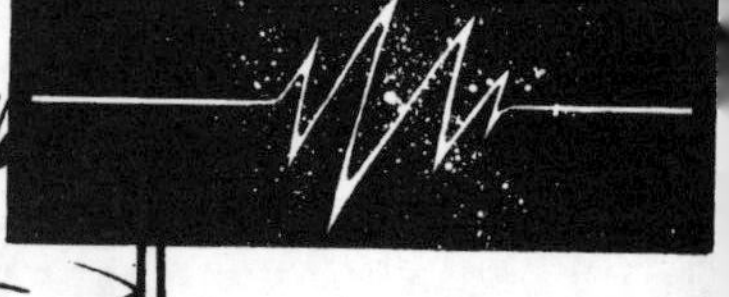

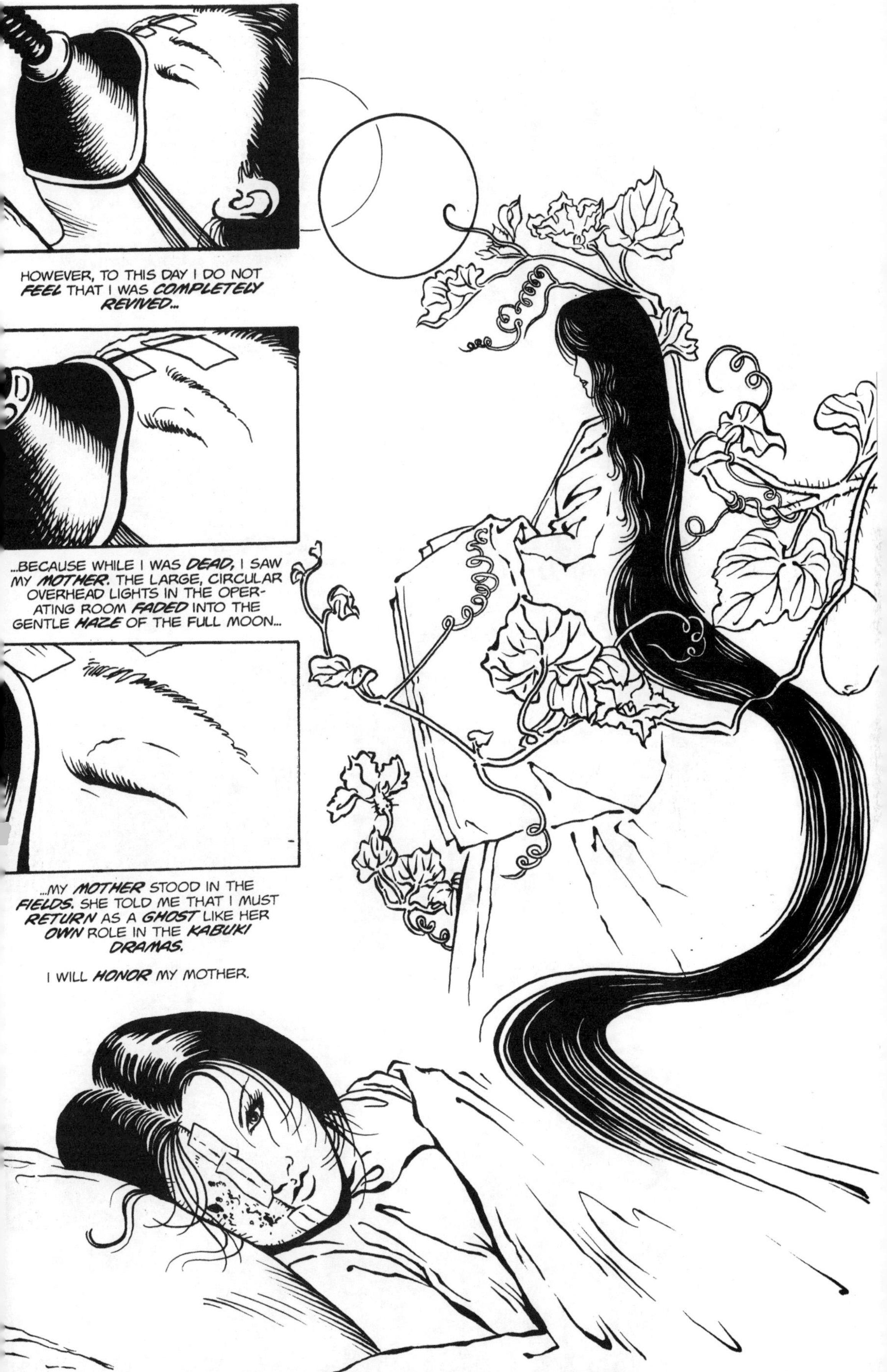

HOWEVER, TO THIS DAY I DO NOT FEEL THAT I WAS COMPLETELY REVIVED...
...BECAUSE WHILE I WAS DEAD, I SAW MY MOTHER. THE LARGE, CIRCULAR OVERHEAD LIGHTS IN THE OPERATING ROOM FADED INTO THE GENTLE HAZE OF THE FULL MOON...
...MY MOTHER STOOD IN THE FIELDS. SHE TOLD ME THAT I MUST RETURN AS A GHOST LIKE HER OWN ROLE IN THE KABUKI DRAMAS.
I WILL HONOR MY MOTHER.

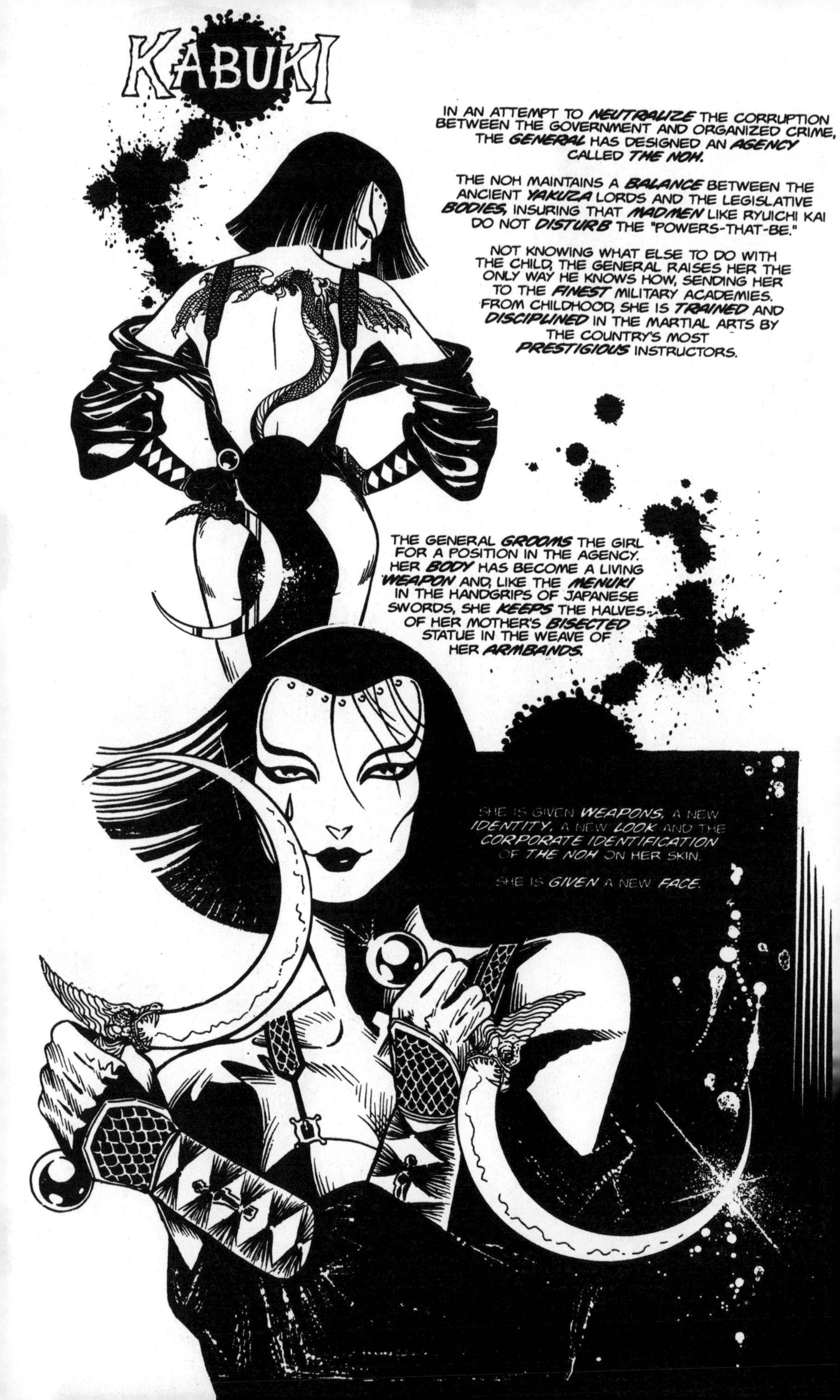
KABUKI
IN AN ATTEMPT TO NEUTRALIZE THE CORRUPTION BETWEEN THE GOVERNMENT AND ORGANIZED CRIME, THE GENERAL HAS DESIGNED AN AGENCY CALLED THE NOH.
THE NOH MAINTAINS A BALANCE BETWEEN THE ANCIENT YAKUZA LORDS AND THE LEGISLATIVE BODIES, INSURING THAT MADMEN LIKE RYUICHI KAI DO NOT DISTURB THE "POWERS-THAT-BE."
NOT KNOWING WHAT ELSE TO DO WITH THE CHILD, THE GENERAL RAISES HER THE ONLY WAY HE KNOWS HOW, SENDING HER TO THE FINEST MILITARY ACADEMIES. FROM CHILDHOOD, SHE IS TRAINED AND DISCIPLINED IN THE MARTIAL ARTS BY THE COUNTRY'S MOST PRESTIGIOUS INSTRUCTORS.
THE GENERAL GROOMS THE GIRL FOR A POSITION IN THE AGENCY. HER BODY HAS BECOME A LIVING WEAPON AND, LIKE THE MENUKI IN THE HANDGRIPS OF JAPANESE SWORDS, SHE KEEPS THE HALVES OF HER MOTHER'S BISECTED STATUE IN THE WEAVE OF HER ARMBANDS.
SHE IS GIVEN WEAPONS, A NEW IDENTITY, A NEW LOOK AND THE CORPORATE IDENTIFICATION OF THE NOH ON HER SKIN.
SHE IS GIVEN A NEW FACE.

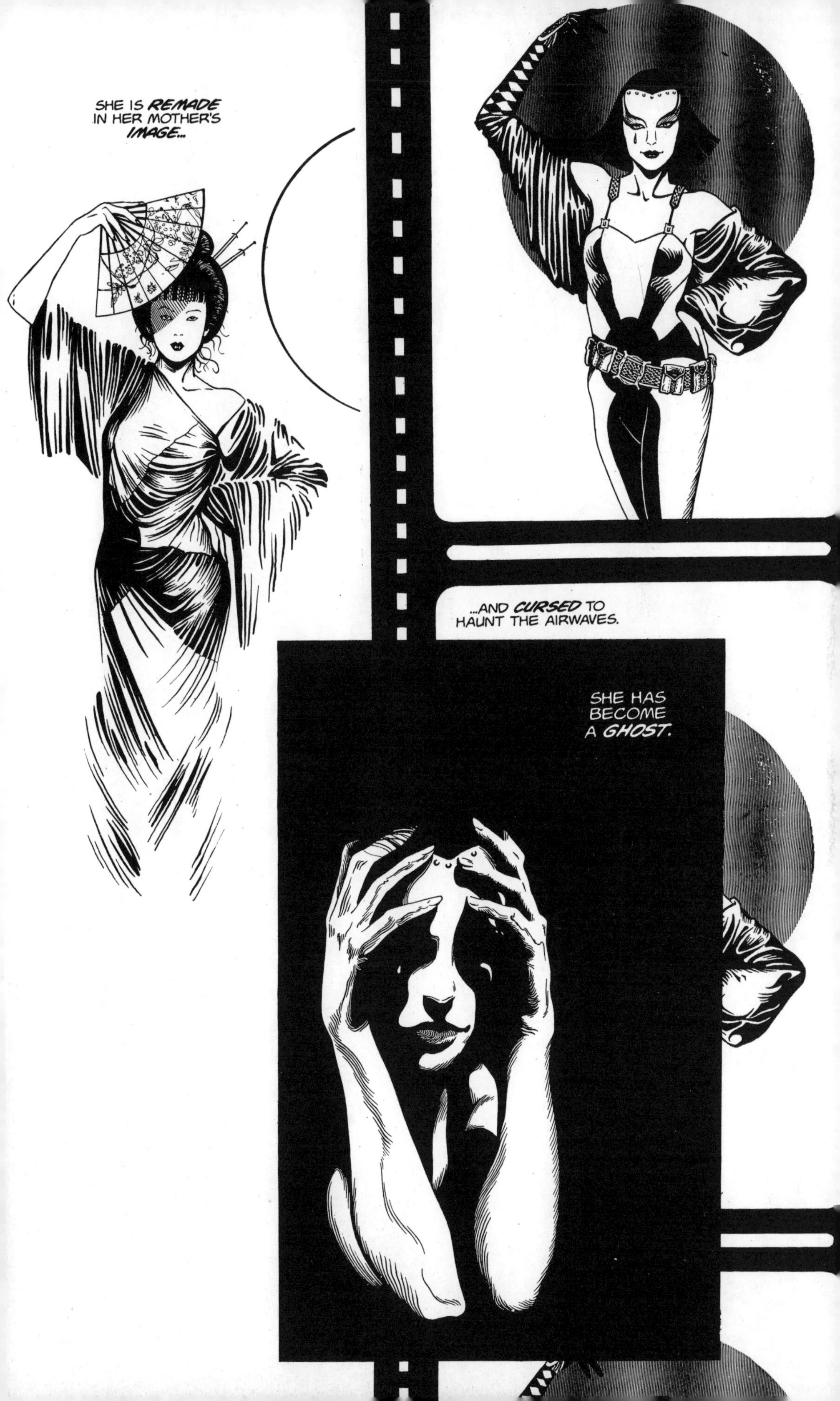
SHE IS REMADE IN HER MOTHER'S IMAGE...
...AND CURSED TO HAUNT THE AIRWAVES.
SHE HAS BECOME A GHOST.

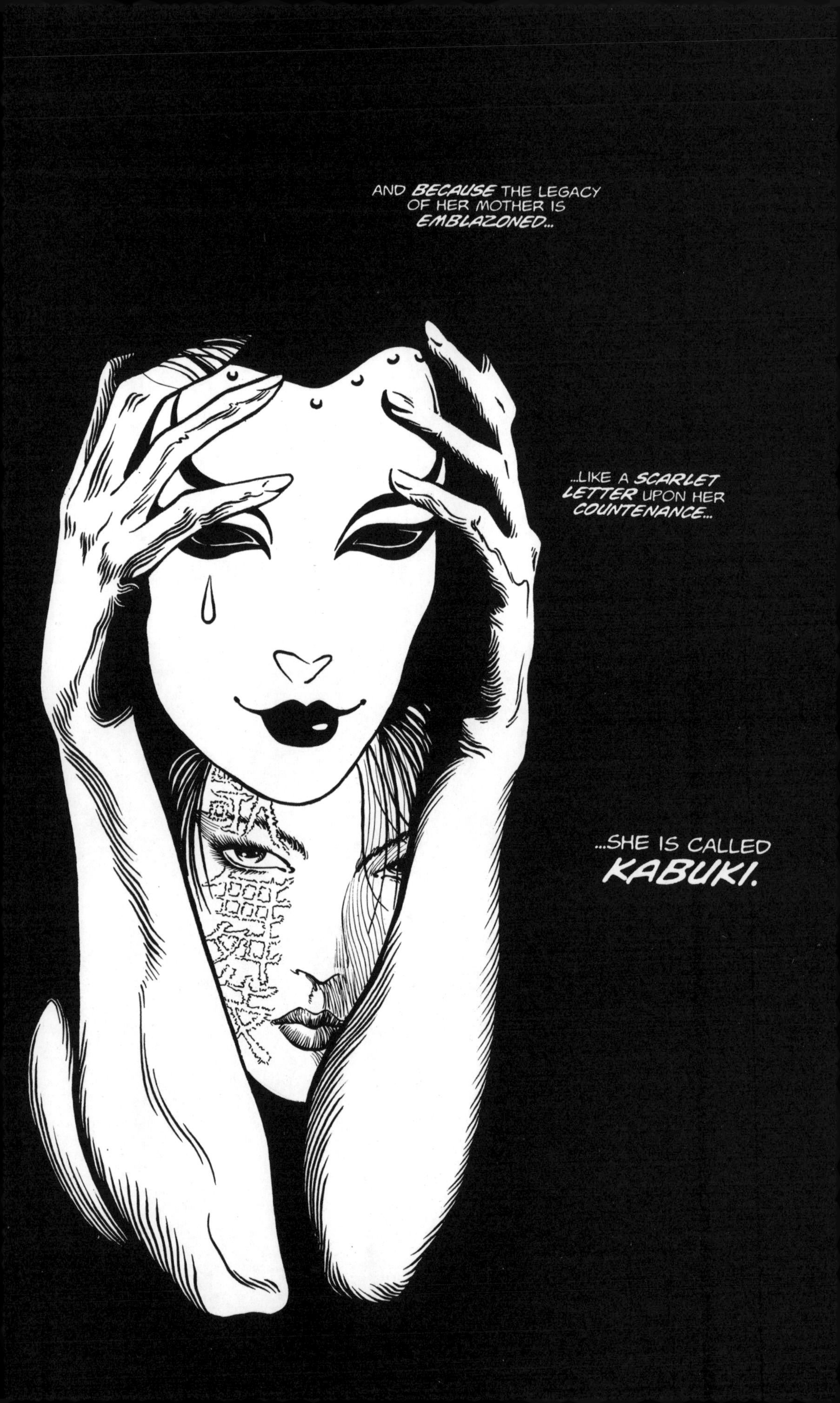
AND BECAUSE THE LEGACY OF HER MOTHER IS EMBLAZONED...
...LIKE A SCARLET LETTER UPON HER COUNTENANCE...
...SHE IS CALLED KABUKI.

"A fairy tale Moon grins
like the cat of the Night,
And its empty smile on your empty
Eyes
Forces a tear down Your Cheek.
Laughter becomes Madness,
Madness becomes Horror."

HIS SHOULDERS ARE *HEAVY* WITH THE *WEIGHT* OF HIS COUNTRY'S *FUTURE.*

AND THOUGH HE *THINKS* AND *PLANS* AND *CONTROLS* THE COURSES OF *LIVES...*

...AS IF THEY WERE *PIECES* ON A CHESS BOARD...

...IN THE *END,* HE *KNOWS* HE IS *JUST AN OLD SOLDIER.*

SO OLD, IN FACT, THAT THE PUBLIC RECORDS CLASSIFY HIM AS "DEAD."

THE GOVERNMENT ORGANIZATION THAT HE *PRESIDES* OVER DOESN'T EXIST AND THE LITTLE GIRL THAT HE *TURNED* INTO A KILLER IS *RECORDED* TO HAVE *DIED* IN HER *YOUTH.*

ALL THE TOY SOLDIERS UNDER HIS COMMAND HAVE, AS FAR AS RECORDS SHOW, *DIED* LONG AGO.

THE OLD SOLDIER, *TOO* OLD TO BE ALIVE WHO *FOUNDED* A SECRET GOVERNMENT ORGANIZATION THAT *DOESN'T* EXIST, *SITS* IN HIS OFFICE THAT DOESN'T EXIST, IN HIS *CHAIR* THAT NEVER WAS, AND PRESIDES OVER AN *ARMY* OF GHOSTS...

...THAT *HAUNT* OUT CRIME AND CORRUPTION THAT *NEVER* SHOULD HAVE BEEN.

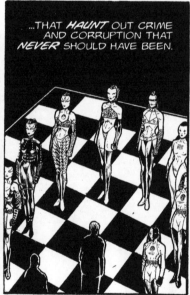

BUT HE IS *HAUNTED* BY HIS OWN *GHOSTS...*

...PAPER IMAGES THAT BRING *TRAGEDY*...AND *PAIN* TO HIS HEART.

BUT HIS HEART AND ALLEGIANCES ARE *NOT* PLEDGED TO THE PHOTOGRAPHS IN HIS WITHERED GRASP...

...BUT TO THE FLAG HE HOLDS ON HIS WALL.

THE FLAG, IN TURN, HOLDS A *CIRCLE OF BLOOD...*

...AND THE *CIRCLE* OF BLOOD HOLDS HIM, *TIGHTENING* ITS *GRIP.*

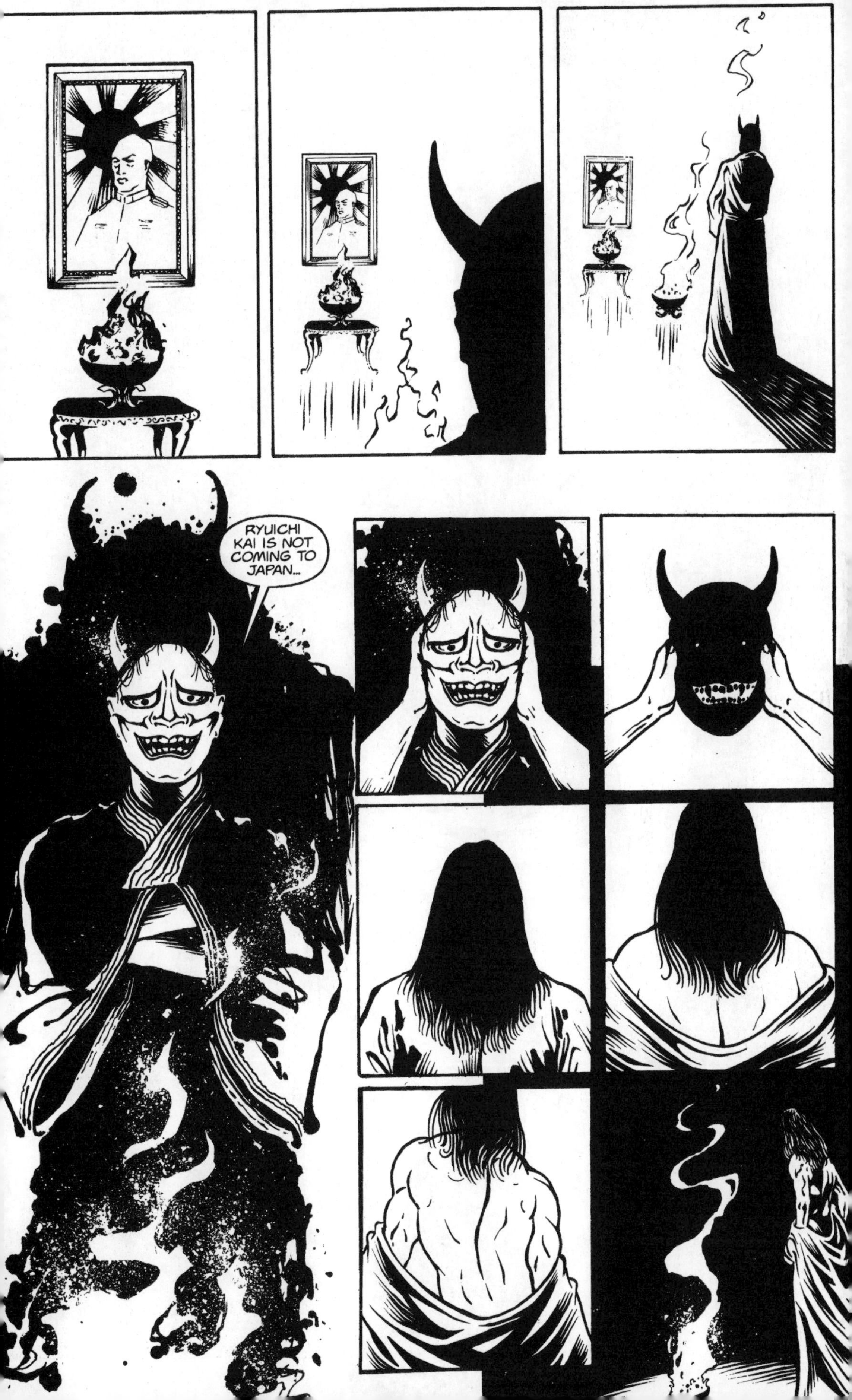
RYUICHI KAI IS NOT COMING TO JAPAN...

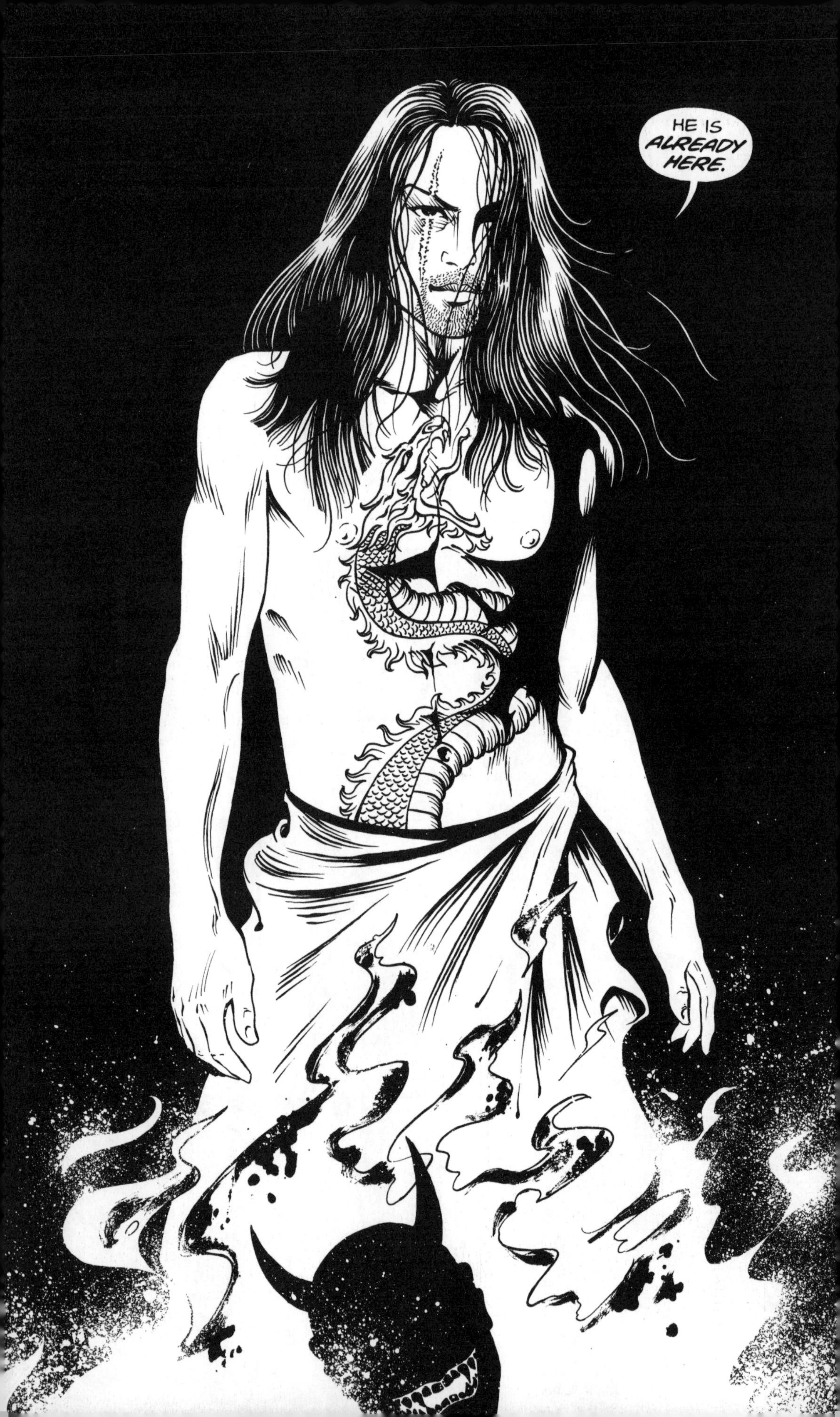
HE IS ALREADY HERE.

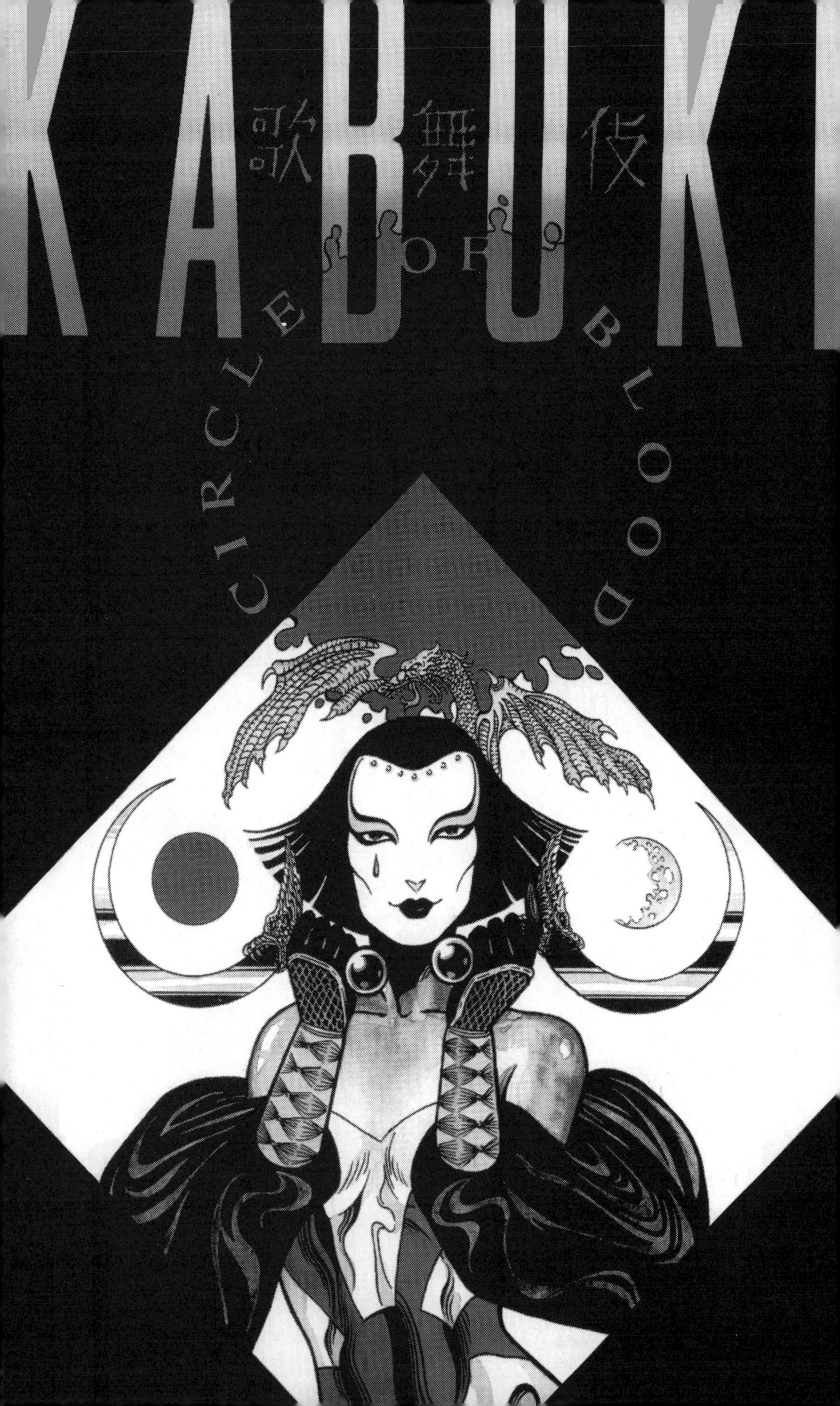
KABUKI
歌舞伎
CIRCLE OF BLOOD

GOOD MORNING JAPAN.

A MORNING RAINBOW FRAMES KYOTO IN A PICTURE OF ILLUSORY SERENITY, MARKING A TEMPORARY RELIEF FROM THE RAINSTORMS THAT HAD RECENTLY BEEN POUNDING JAPAN. BUT LIKE THE RAINBOW, THERE IS ANOTHER SIDE OF THE CITY *HIDDEN* TO THE NAKED EYE. IN THE SAME WAY THAT ONLY A HALF-ARC OF THE RAINBOW IS SEEN WHILE THE FULL CIRCLE DISAPPEARS UNDER THE HORIZON, THE CITY'S INVISIBLE *COUNTER-CULTURE* LIES UNDISTURBED AND HARD AT WORK.

I AM KABUKI, VOICE OF THE NOH, AND I'LL BE YOUR GUIDE THROUGH THE DAYS AND NIGHTS OF KYOTO...

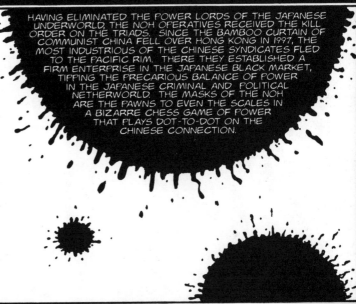

HAVING ELIMINATED THE POWER LORDS OF THE JAPANESE UNDERWORLD, THE NOH OPERATIVES RECEIVED THE KILL ORDER ON THE TRIADS. SINCE THE BAMBOO CURTAIN OF COMMUNIST CHINA FELL OVER HONG KONG IN 1997, THE MOST INDUSTRIOUS OF THE CHINESE SYNDICATES FLED TO THE PACIFIC RIM. THERE THEY ESTABLISHED A FIRM ENTERPRISE IN THE JAPANESE BLACK MARKET, TIPPING THE PRECARIOUS BALANCE OF POWER IN THE JAPANESE CRIMINAL AND POLITICAL NETHERWORLD. THE MASKS OF THE NOH ARE THE PAWNS TO EVEN THE SCALES IN A BIZARRE CHESS GAME OF POWER THAT PLAYS DOT-TO-DOT ON THE CHINESE CONNECTION.

KEEPING YOU COMPANY ON YOUR COMMUTE TO THE OFFICE AND KEEPING CITIZENS SAFE FROM ORGANIZED CRIME.

ALABASTER STATUES OF THE COLONEL-- WESTERN IDOLS OF POULTRY-- COMPLETE WITH BOWTIE AND SNOW-WHITE GOATEE, GRIN LIKE WHITE DEVILS BEHIND THE RESTAURANT'S GLASS WALLS, INVITING THE SALARYMEN TO A LUNCH BREAK OF AMERICAN CHICKEN.

鳥をもっと食べよう！
ホット・ブレスト・スペシャル
¥1500

特売ランチ

鶏

ブレスト

ウィング

サイ

美味鶏

特安

THE ABSURDITY OF THE WESTERN SATURATION IS ALARMING.

STAY TUNED FOR THE UP-TO-THE-MINUTE WEATHER REPORT.

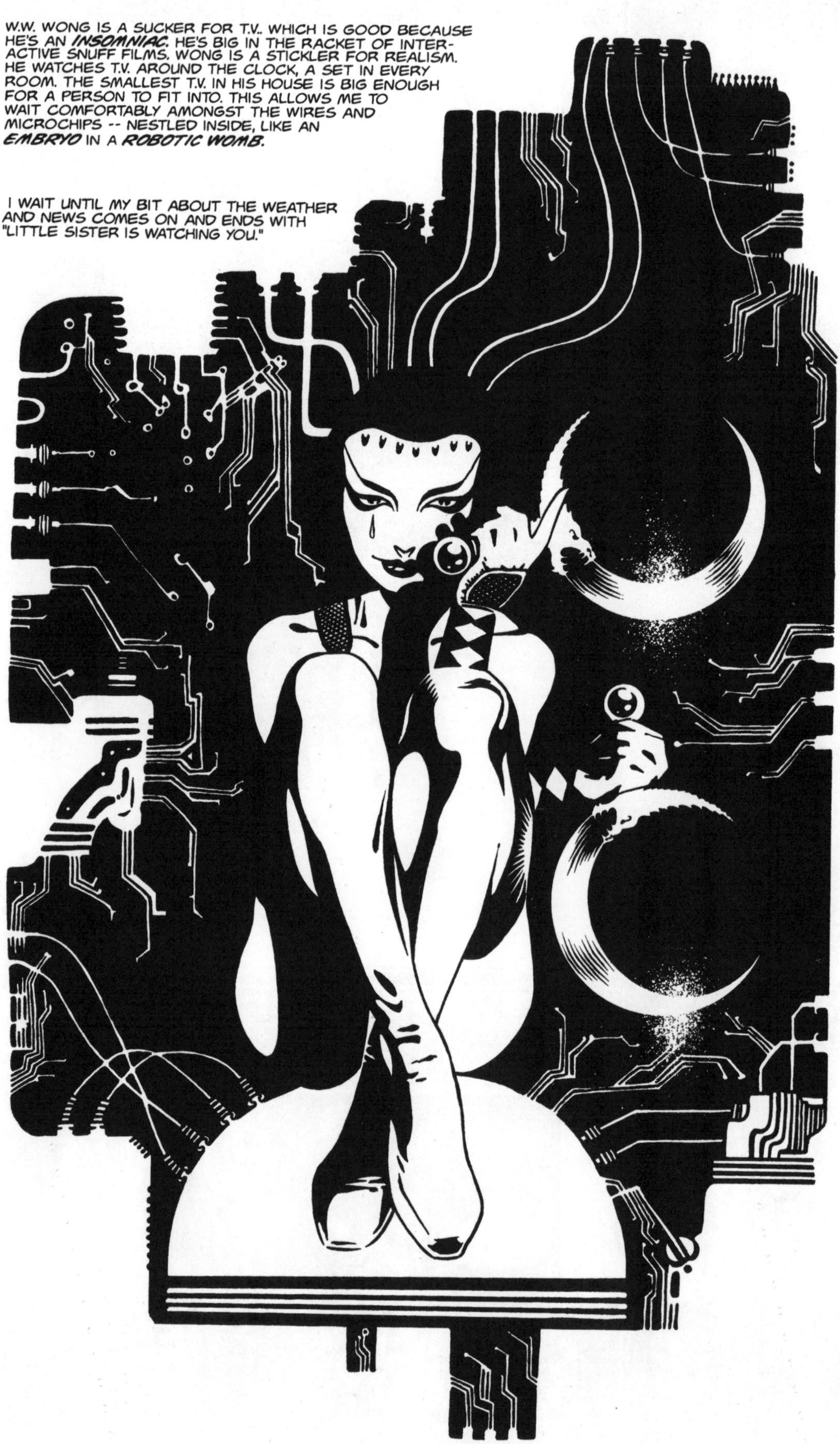
W.W. WONG IS A SUCKER FOR T.V.. WHICH IS GOOD BECAUSE HE'S AN *INSOMNIAC.* HE'S BIG IN THE RACKET OF INTER-ACTIVE SNUFF FILMS. WONG IS A STICKLER FOR REALISM. HE WATCHES T.V. AROUND THE CLOCK, A SET IN EVERY ROOM. THE SMALLEST T.V. IN HIS HOUSE IS BIG ENOUGH FOR A PERSON TO FIT INTO. THIS ALLOWS ME TO WAIT COMFORTABLY AMONGST THE WIRES AND MICROCHIPS -- NESTLED INSIDE, LIKE AN *EMBRYO* IN A *ROBOTIC WOMB.*
I WAIT UNTIL MY BIT ABOUT THE WEATHER AND NEWS COMES ON AND ENDS WITH "LITTLE SISTER IS WATCHING YOU."

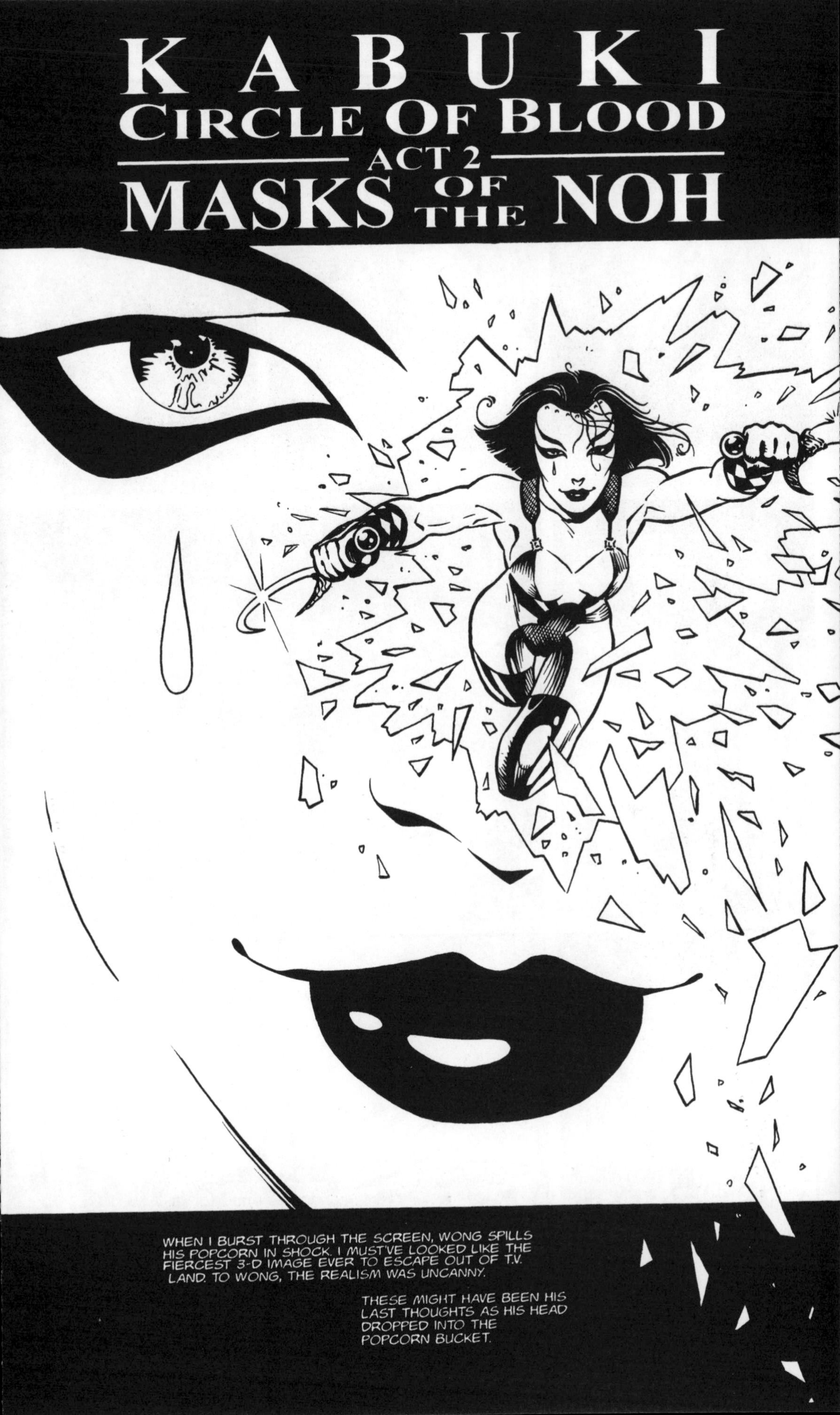
KABUKI
CIRCLE OF BLOOD
ACT 2
MASKS OF THE NOH
WHEN I BURST THROUGH THE SCREEN, WONG SPILLS HIS POPCORN IN SHOCK. I MUST'VE LOOKED LIKE THE FIERCEST 3-D IMAGE EVER TO ESCAPE OUT OF T.V. LAND. TO WONG, THE REALISM WAS UNCANNY.
THESE MIGHT HAVE BEEN HIS LAST THOUGHTS AS HIS HEAD DROPPED INTO THE POPCORN BUCKET.

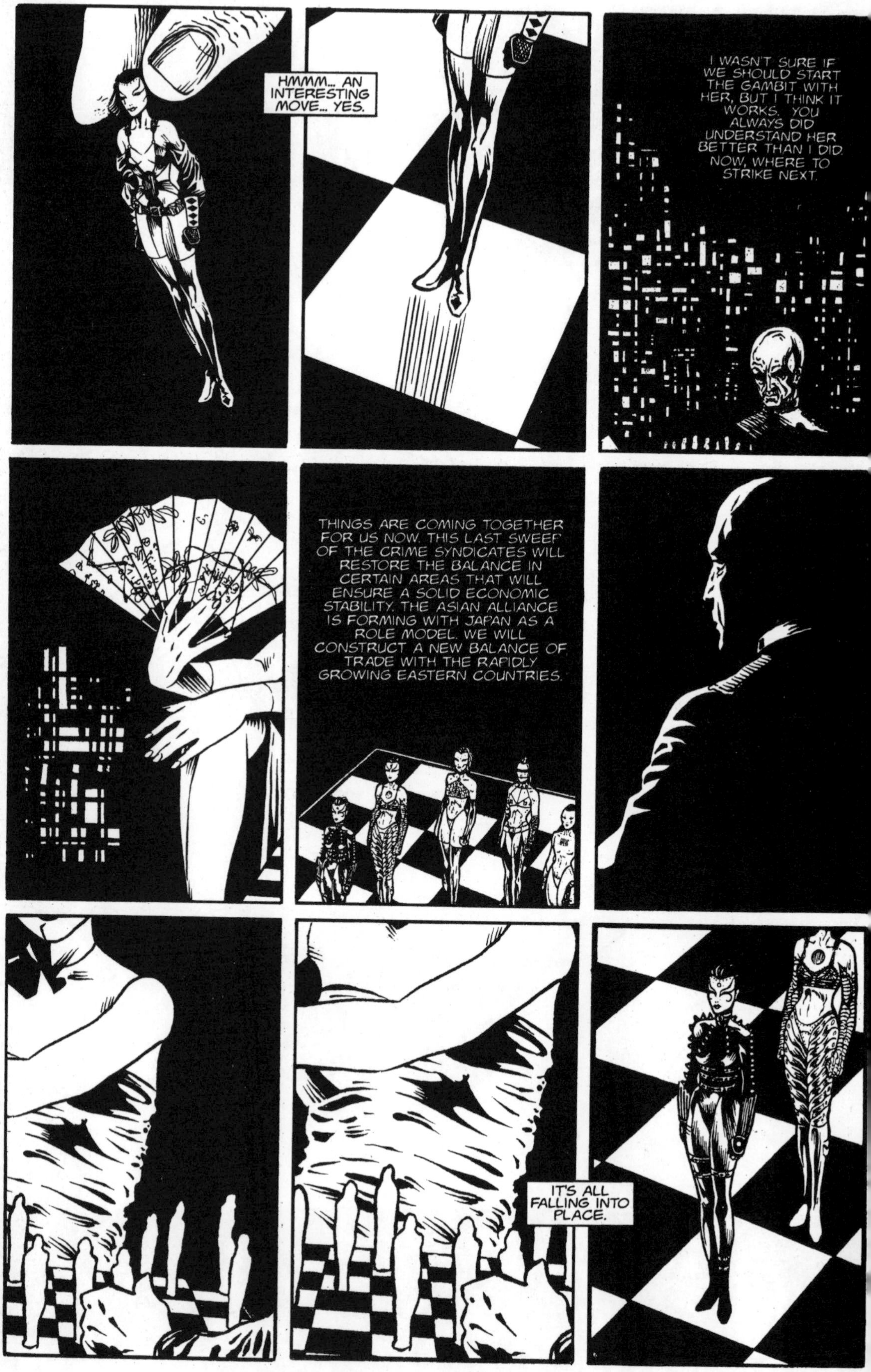
HMMM... AN INTERESTING MOVE... YES.
I WASN'T SURE IF WE SHOULD START THE GAMBIT WITH HER, BUT I THINK IT WORKS. YOU ALWAYS DID UNDERSTAND HER BETTER THAN I DID. NOW, WHERE TO STRIKE NEXT.
THINGS ARE COMING TOGETHER FOR US NOW. THIS LAST SWEEP OF THE CRIME SYNDICATES WILL RESTORE THE BALANCE IN CERTAIN AREAS THAT WILL ENSURE A SOLID ECONOMIC STABILITY. THE ASIAN ALLIANCE IS FORMING WITH JAPAN AS A ROLE MODEL. WE WILL CONSTRUCT A NEW BALANCE OF TRADE WITH THE RAPIDLY GROWING EASTERN COUNTRIES.
IT'S ALL FALLING INTO PLACE.

THE *MASKS OF THE NOH...* ARE CERTAINLY A FORCE TO BE RECKONED WITH. THEY ARE ADEPT BOTH AT ENFORCING ORDER AS GOVERNMENT AGENTS, AND AT CHARMING THE PUBLIC AS TV PERSONALITIES.

THE BOARD OF DIRECTORS WANT TO CREATE REPLICANTS OF EACH OF THEM AND USE THEM TO REGULATE OTHER COUNTRIES IN ADDITION TO POLICING JAPAN AS AN ELITE FORCE OF MASKED ANDROIDS. THEY SAID WE HAVE THE TECHNOLOGY, BUT I DON'T THINK THAT'S THE POINT.

I ENJOY THE COLLECTIVE TEAM SPIRIT....

...THE *HUMAN SPIRIT* OF THEIR ACTIONS.

FLESH AND BLOOD-- YOU UNDERSTAND, DON'T YOU?

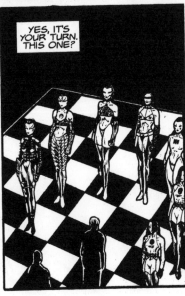

YES, IT'S YOUR TURN. THIS ONE?

PERFECT.

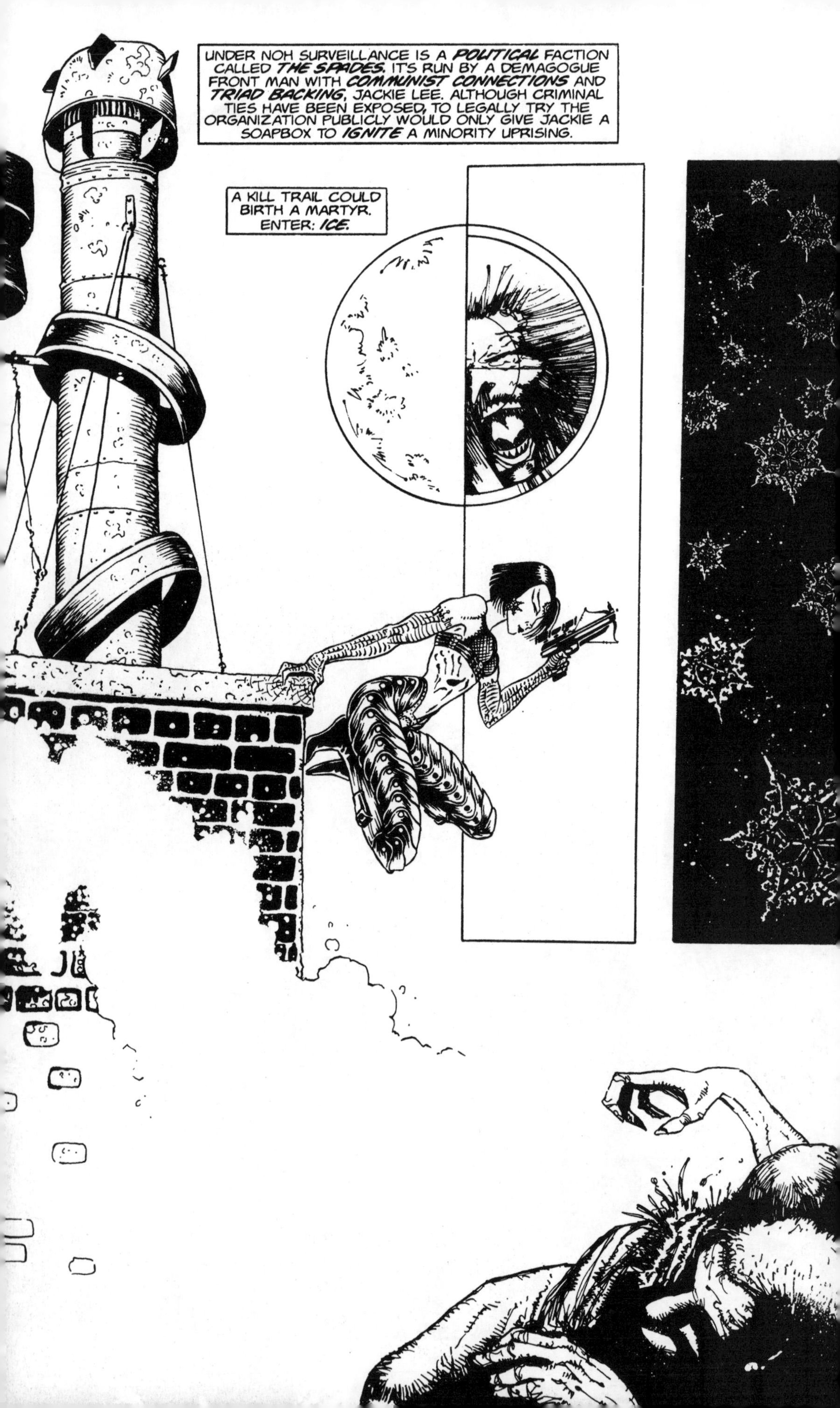
UNDER NOH SURVEILLANCE IS A POLITICAL FACTION CALLED THE SPADES. IT'S RUN BY A DEMAGOGUE FRONT MAN WITH COMMUNIST CONNECTIONS AND TRIAD BACKING, JACKIE LEE. ALTHOUGH CRIMINAL TIES HAVE BEEN EXPOSED, TO LEGALLY TRY THE ORGANIZATION PUBLICLY WOULD ONLY GIVE JACKIE A SOAPBOX TO IGNITE A MINORITY UPRISING.
A KILL TRAIL COULD BIRTH A MARTYR. ENTER: ICE.

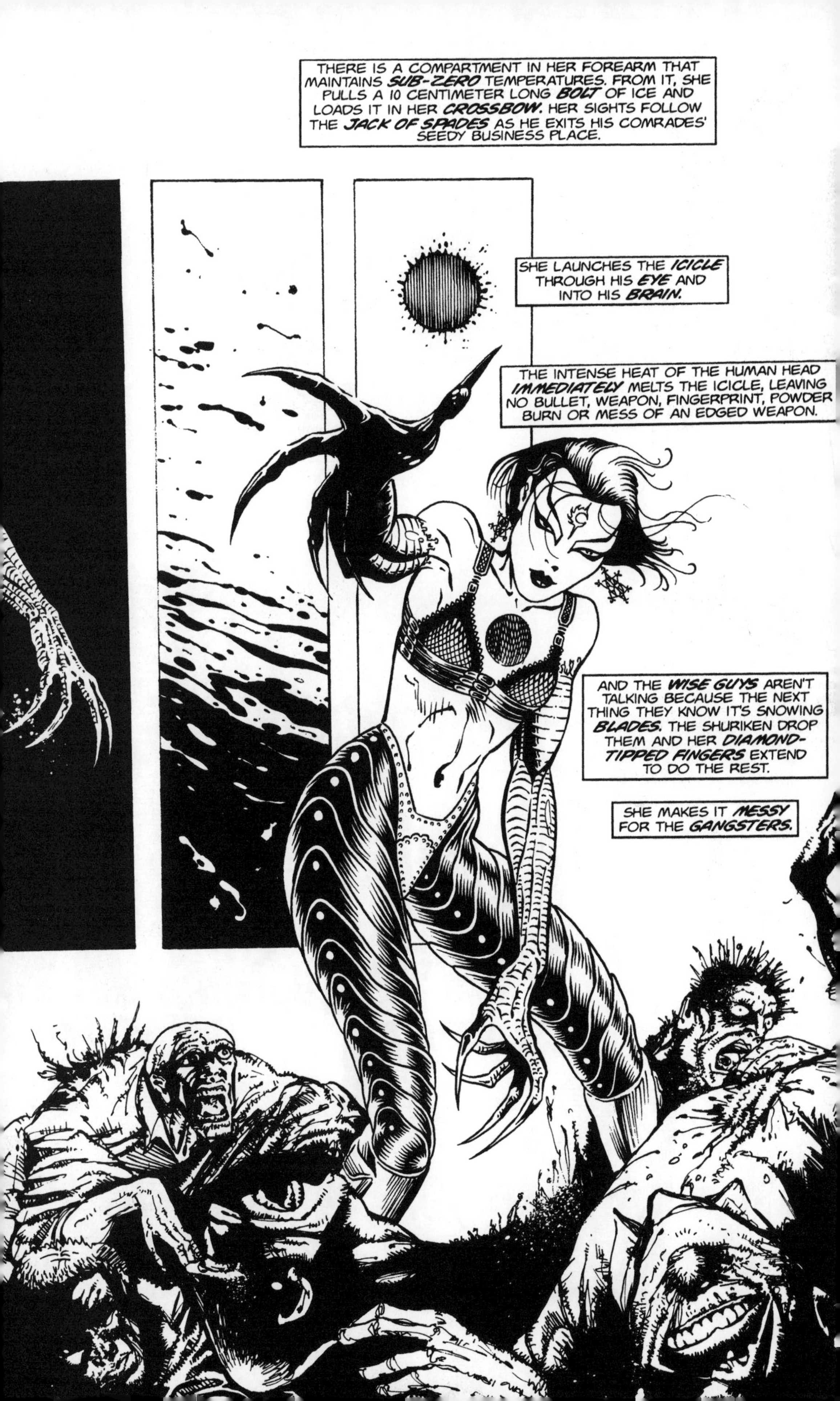
THERE IS A COMPARTMENT IN HER FOREARM THAT MAINTAINS SUB-ZERO TEMPERATURES. FROM IT, SHE PULLS A 10 CENTIMETER LONG BOLT OF ICE AND LOADS IT IN HER CROSSBOW. HER SIGHTS FOLLOW THE JACK OF SPADES AS HE EXITS HIS COMRADES' SEEDY BUSINESS PLACE.
SHE LAUNCHES THE ICICLE THROUGH HIS EYE AND INTO HIS BRAIN.
THE INTENSE HEAT OF THE HUMAN HEAD IMMEDIATELY MELTS THE ICICLE, LEAVING NO BULLET, WEAPON, FINGERPRINT, POWDER BURN OR MESS OF AN EDGED WEAPON.
AND THE WISE GUYS AREN'T TALKING BECAUSE THE NEXT THING THEY KNOW IT'S SNOWING BLADES. THE SHURIKEN DROP THEM AND HER DIAMOND-TIPPED FINGERS EXTEND TO DO THE REST.
SHE MAKES IT MESSY FOR THE GANGSTERS.

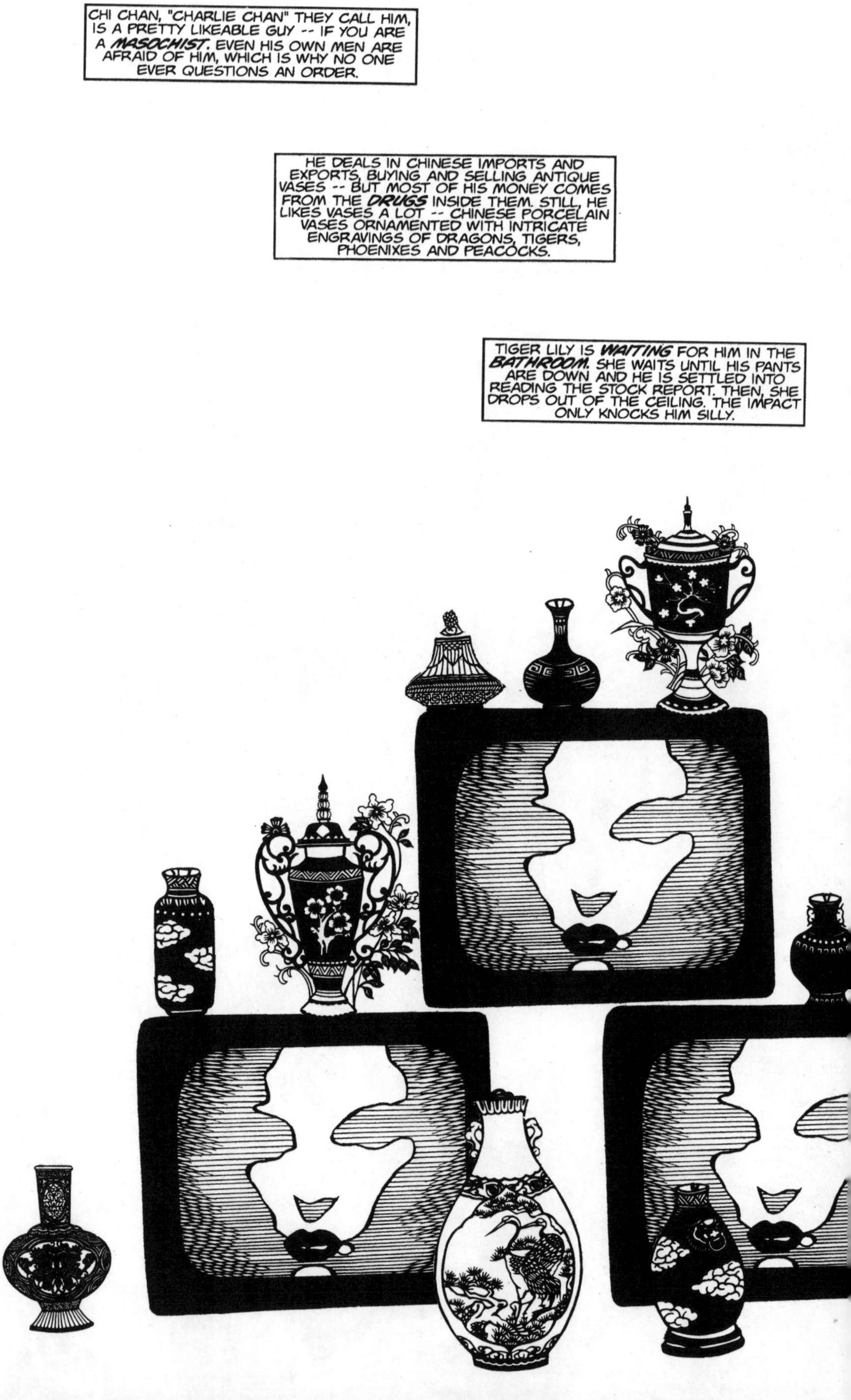
CHI CHAN, "CHARLIE CHAN" THEY CALL HIM, IS A PRETTY LIKEABLE GUY -- IF YOU ARE A MASOCHIST. EVEN HIS OWN MEN ARE AFRAID OF HIM, WHICH IS WHY NO ONE EVER QUESTIONS AN ORDER.
HE DEALS IN CHINESE IMPORTS AND EXPORTS, BUYING AND SELLING ANTIQUE VASES -- BUT MOST OF HIS MONEY COMES FROM THE DRUGS INSIDE THEM. STILL, HE LIKES VASES A LOT -- CHINESE PORCELAIN VASES ORNAMENTED WITH INTRICATE ENGRAVINGS OF DRAGONS, TIGERS, PHOENIXES AND PEACOCKS.
TIGER LILY IS WAITING FOR HIM IN THE BATHROOM. SHE WAITS UNTIL HIS PANTS ARE DOWN AND HE IS SETTLED INTO READING THE STOCK REPORT. THEN, SHE DROPS OUT OF THE CEILING. THE IMPACT ONLY KNOCKS HIM SILLY.

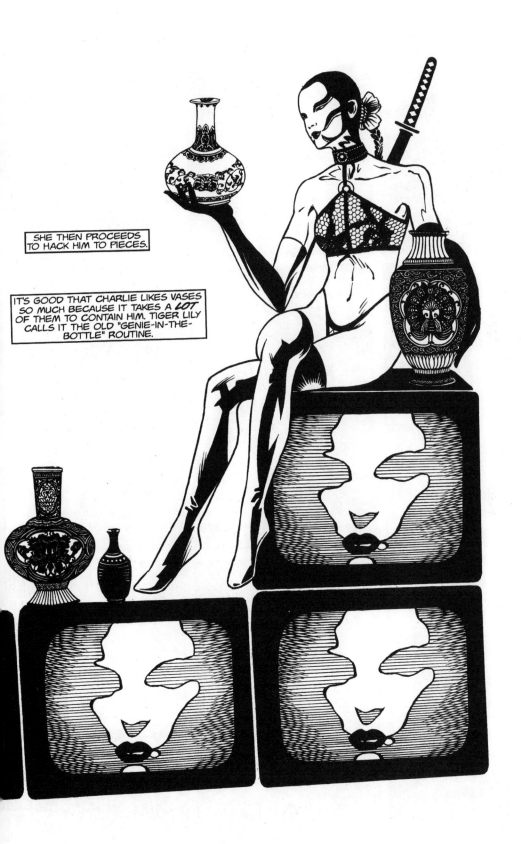

SHE THEN PROCEEDS
TO HACK HIM TO PIECES.

IT'S GOOD THAT CHARLIE LIKES VASES
SO MUCH BECAUSE IT TAKES A *LOT*
OF THEM TO CONTAIN HIM. TIGER LILY
CALLS IT THE OLD "GENIE-IN-THE-
BOTTLE" ROUTINE.

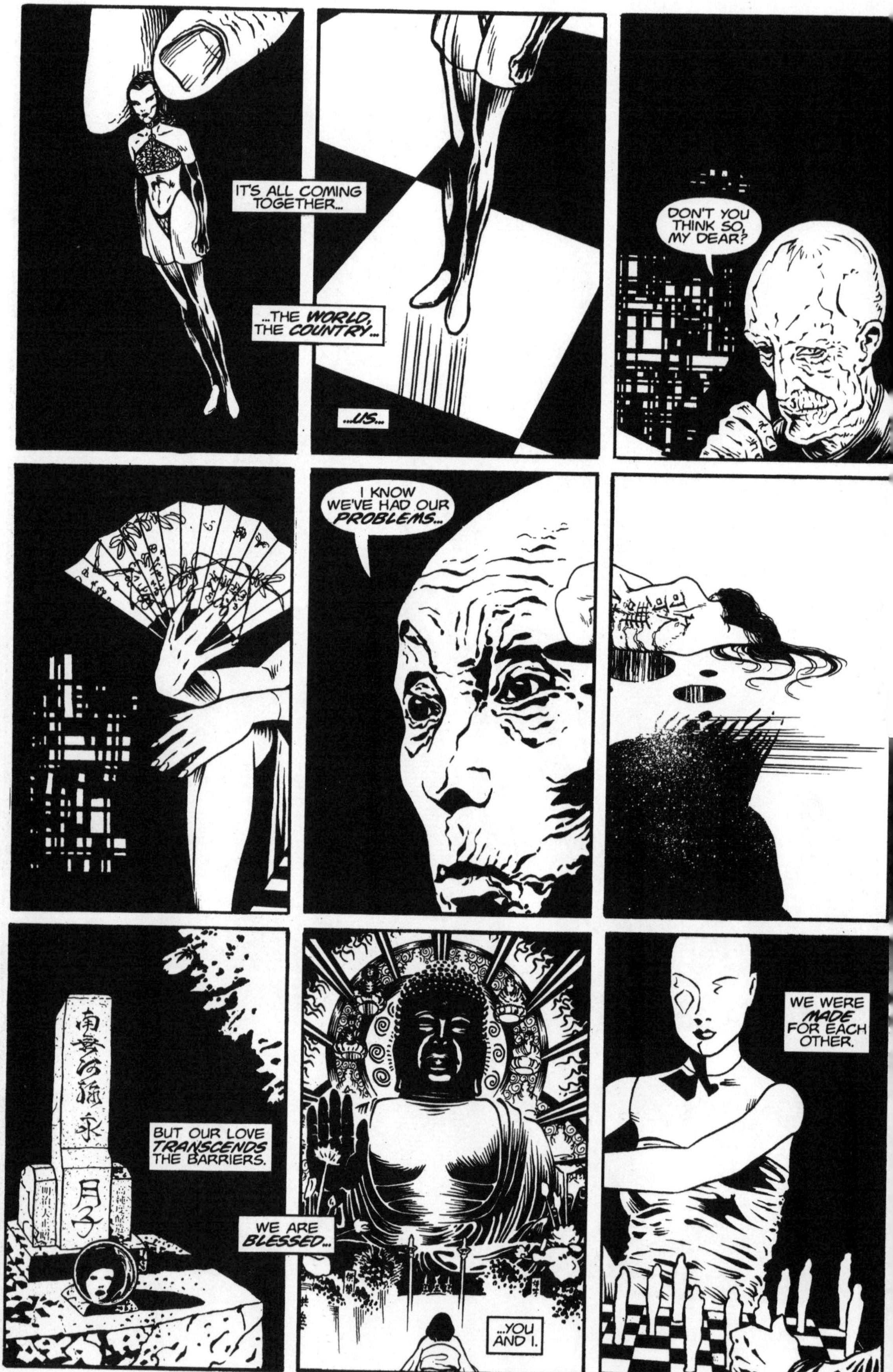

IT'S ALL COMING TOGETHER...
...THE WORLD, THE COUNTRY...
...US...
DON'T YOU THINK SO, MY DEAR?
I KNOW WE'VE HAD OUR PROBLEMS...
BUT OUR LOVE TRANSCENDS THE BARRIERS.
WE ARE BLESSED...
...YOU AND I.
WE WERE MADE FOR EACH OTHER.

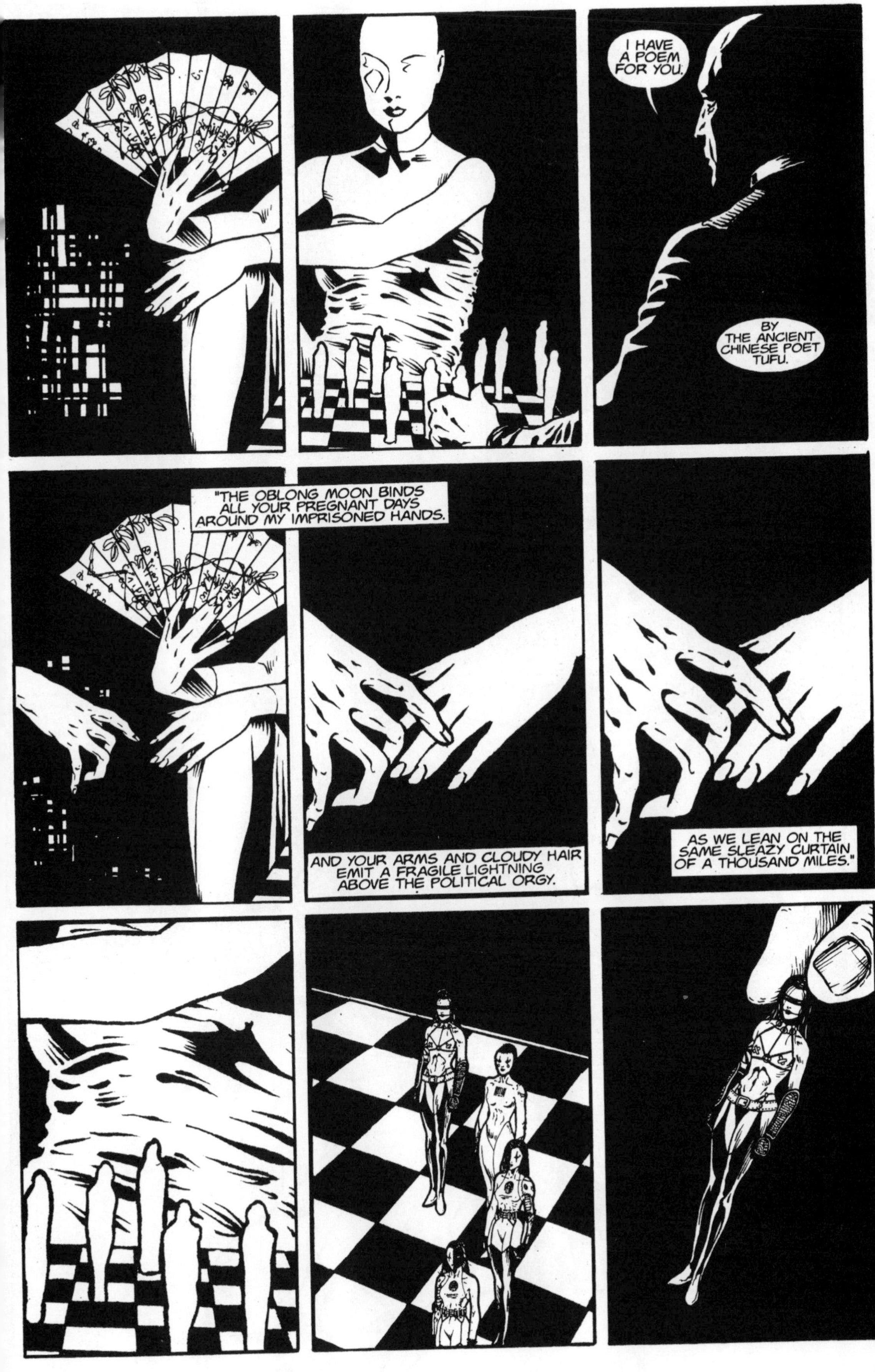
I HAVE A POEM FOR YOU.
BY THE ANCIENT CHINESE POET TUFU.
"THE OBLONG MOON BINDS ALL YOUR PREGNANT DAYS AROUND MY IMPRISONED HANDS.
AND YOUR ARMS AND CLOUDY HAIR EMIT A FRAGILE LIGHTNING ABOVE THE POLITICAL ORGY.
AS WE LEAN ON THE SAME SLEAZY CURTAIN OF A THOUSAND MILES."

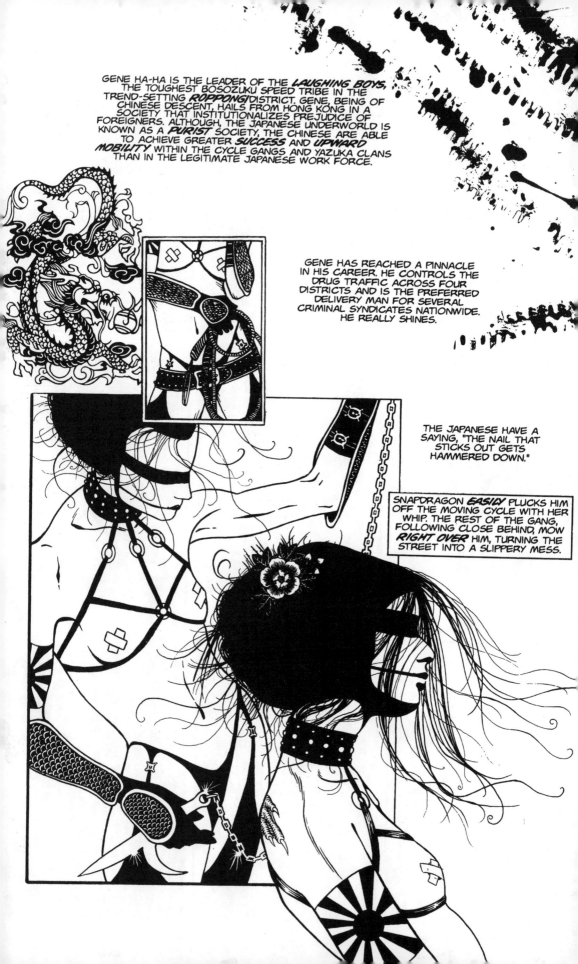

GENE HA-HA IS THE LEADER OF THE *LAUGHING BOYS,* THE TOUGHEST BOSOZUKU SPEED TRIBE IN THE TREND-SETTING *ROPPONGI* DISTRICT. GENE, BEING OF CHINESE DESCENT, HAILS FROM HONG KONG IN A SOCIETY THAT INSTITUTIONALIZES PREJUDICE OF FOREIGNERS. ALTHOUGH, THE JAPANESE UNDERWORLD IS KNOWN AS A *PURIST* SOCIETY, THE CHINESE ARE ABLE TO ACHIEVE GREATER *SUCCESS* AND *UPWARD MOBILITY* WITHIN THE CYCLE GANGS AND YAZUKA CLANS THAN IN THE LEGITIMATE JAPANESE WORK FORCE.

GENE HAS REACHED A PINNACLE IN HIS CAREER. HE CONTROLS THE DRUG TRAFFIC ACROSS FOUR DISTRICTS AND IS THE PREFERRED DELIVERY MAN FOR SEVERAL CRIMINAL SYNDICATES NATIONWIDE. HE REALLY SHINES.

THE JAPANESE HAVE A SAYING, "THE NAIL THAT STICKS OUT GETS HAMMERED DOWN."

SNAPDRAGON *EASILY* PLUCKS HIM OFF THE MOVING CYCLE WITH HER WHIP. THE REST OF THE GANG, FOLLOWING CLOSE BEHIND, MOW *RIGHT OVER* HIM, TURNING THE STREET INTO A SLIPPERY MESS.

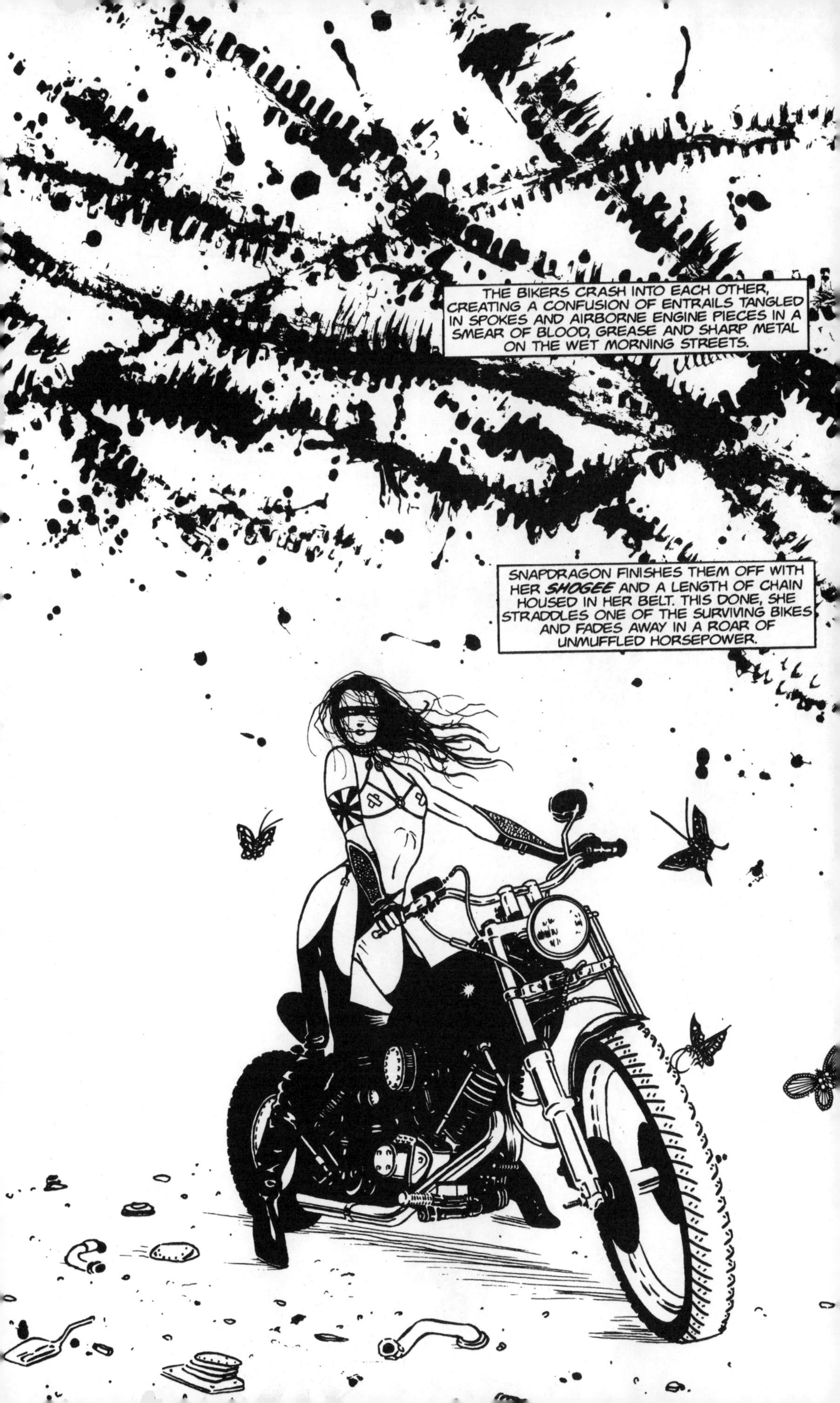
THE BIKERS CRASH INTO EACH OTHER, CREATING A CONFUSION OF ENTRAILS TANGLED IN SPOKES AND AIRBORNE ENGINE PIECES IN A SMEAR OF BLOOD, GREASE AND SHARP METAL ON THE WET MORNING STREETS.
SNAPDRAGON FINISHES THEM OFF WITH HER *SHOGEE* AND A LENGTH OF CHAIN HOUSED IN HER BELT. THIS DONE, SHE STRADDLES ONE OF THE SURVIVING BIKES AND FADES AWAY IN A ROAR OF UNMUFFLED HORSEPOWER.

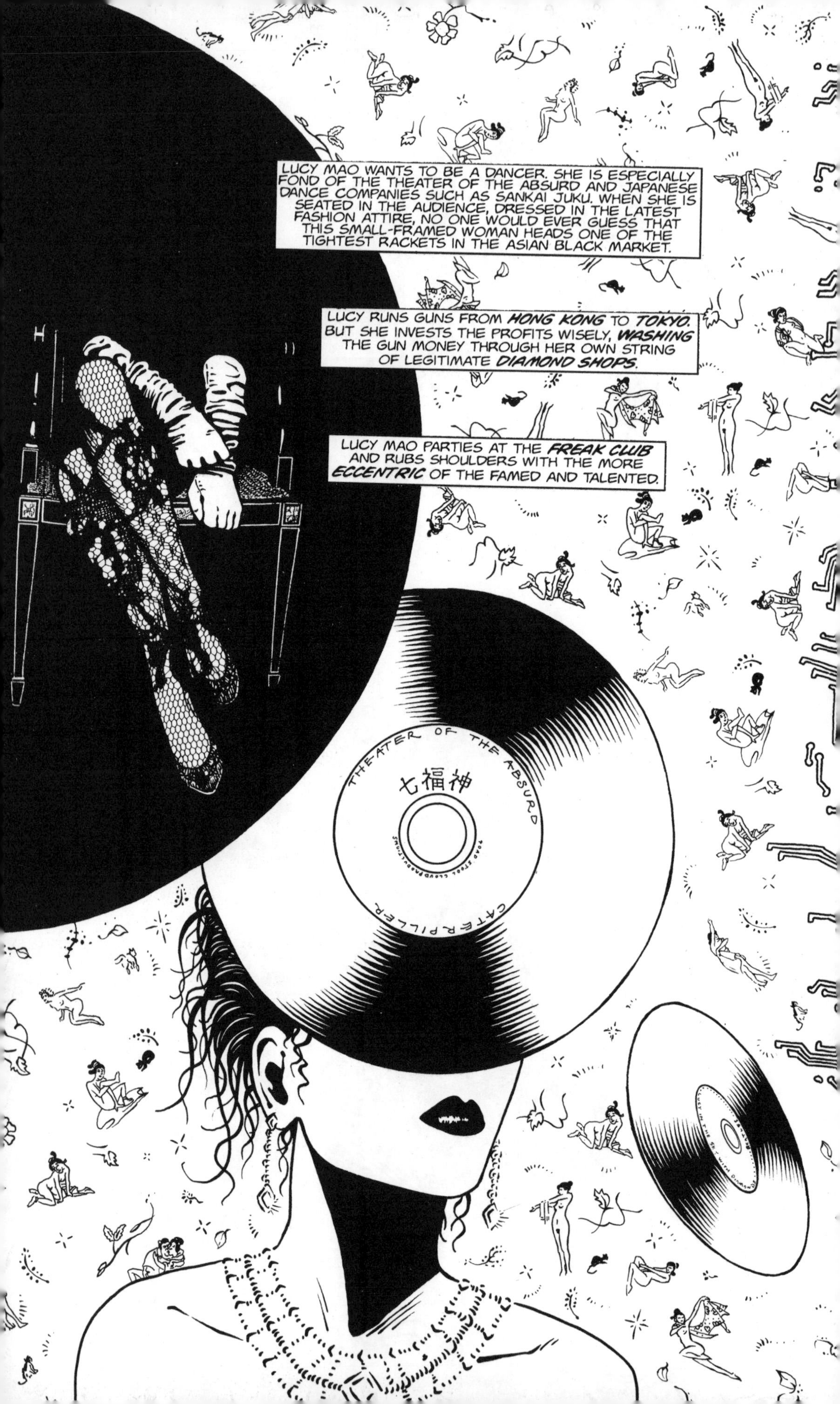

LUCY MAO WANTS TO BE A DANCER. SHE IS ESPECIALLY FOND OF THE THEATER OF THE ABSURD AND JAPANESE DANCE COMPANIES SUCH AS SANKAI JUKU. WHEN SHE IS SEATED IN THE AUDIENCE, DRESSED IN THE LATEST FASHION ATTIRE, NO ONE WOULD EVER GUESS THAT THIS SMALL-FRAMED WOMAN HEADS ONE OF THE TIGHTEST RACKETS IN THE ASIAN BLACK MARKET.
LUCY RUNS GUNS FROM *HONG KONG* TO *TOKYO*. BUT SHE INVESTS THE PROFITS WISELY, *WASHING* THE GUN MONEY THROUGH HER OWN STRING OF LEGITIMATE *DIAMOND SHOPS*.
LUCY MAO PARTIES AT THE *FREAK CLUB* AND RUBS SHOULDERS WITH THE MORE *ECCENTRIC* OF THE FAMED AND TALENTED.
THEATER OF THE ABSURD
七福神
TOAD STOOL CLOUD PRODUCTIONS
CATERPILLER
BEATLES
LUCY IN THE SKY WITH DIAMONDS

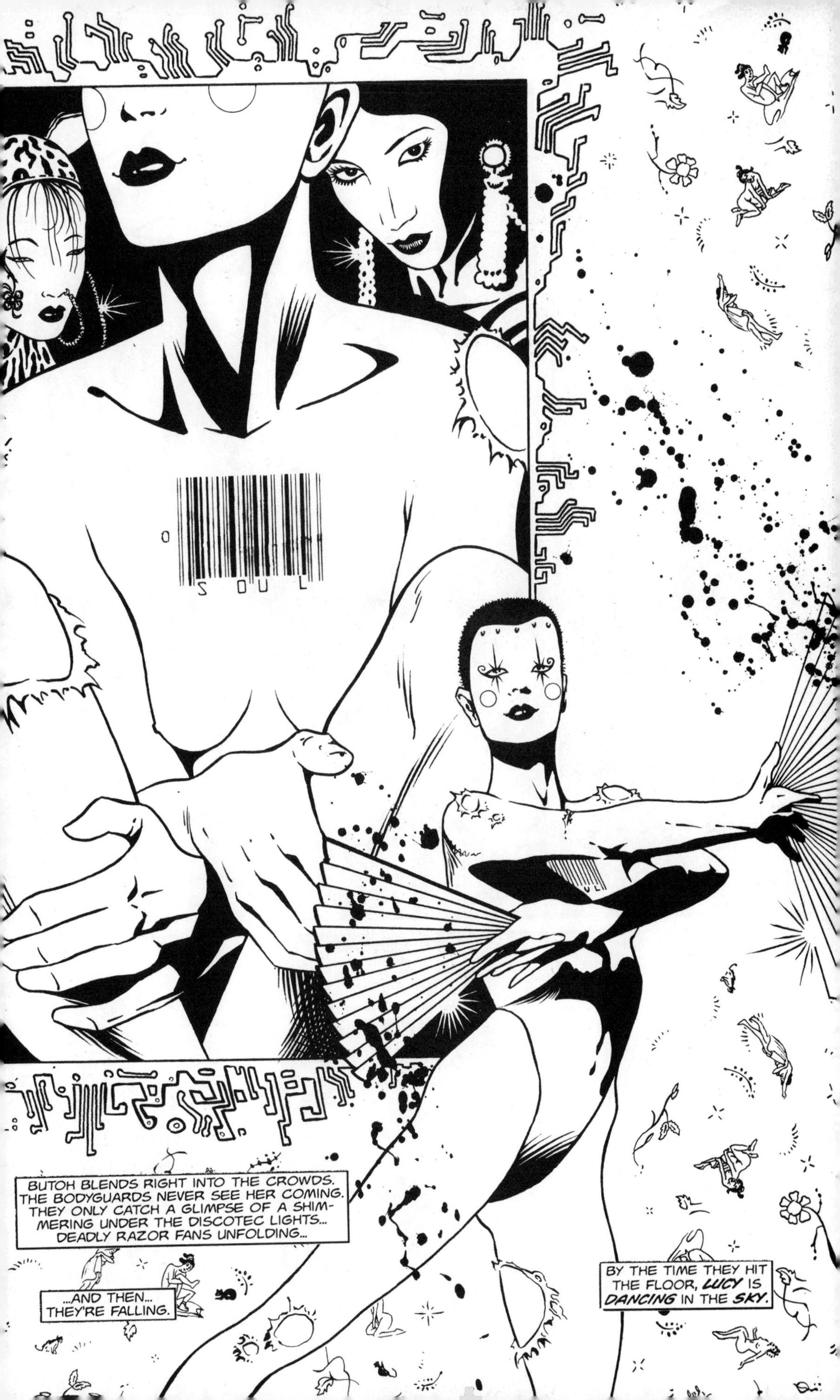

SOUL
BUTOH BLENDS RIGHT INTO THE CROWDS. THE BODYGUARDS NEVER SEE HER COMING. THEY ONLY CATCH A GLIMPSE OF A SHIMMERING UNDER THE DISCOTEC LIGHTS... DEADLY RAZOR FANS UNFOLDING...
...AND THEN... THEY'RE FALLING.
BY THE TIME THEY HIT THE FLOOR, LUCY IS DANCING IN THE SKY.

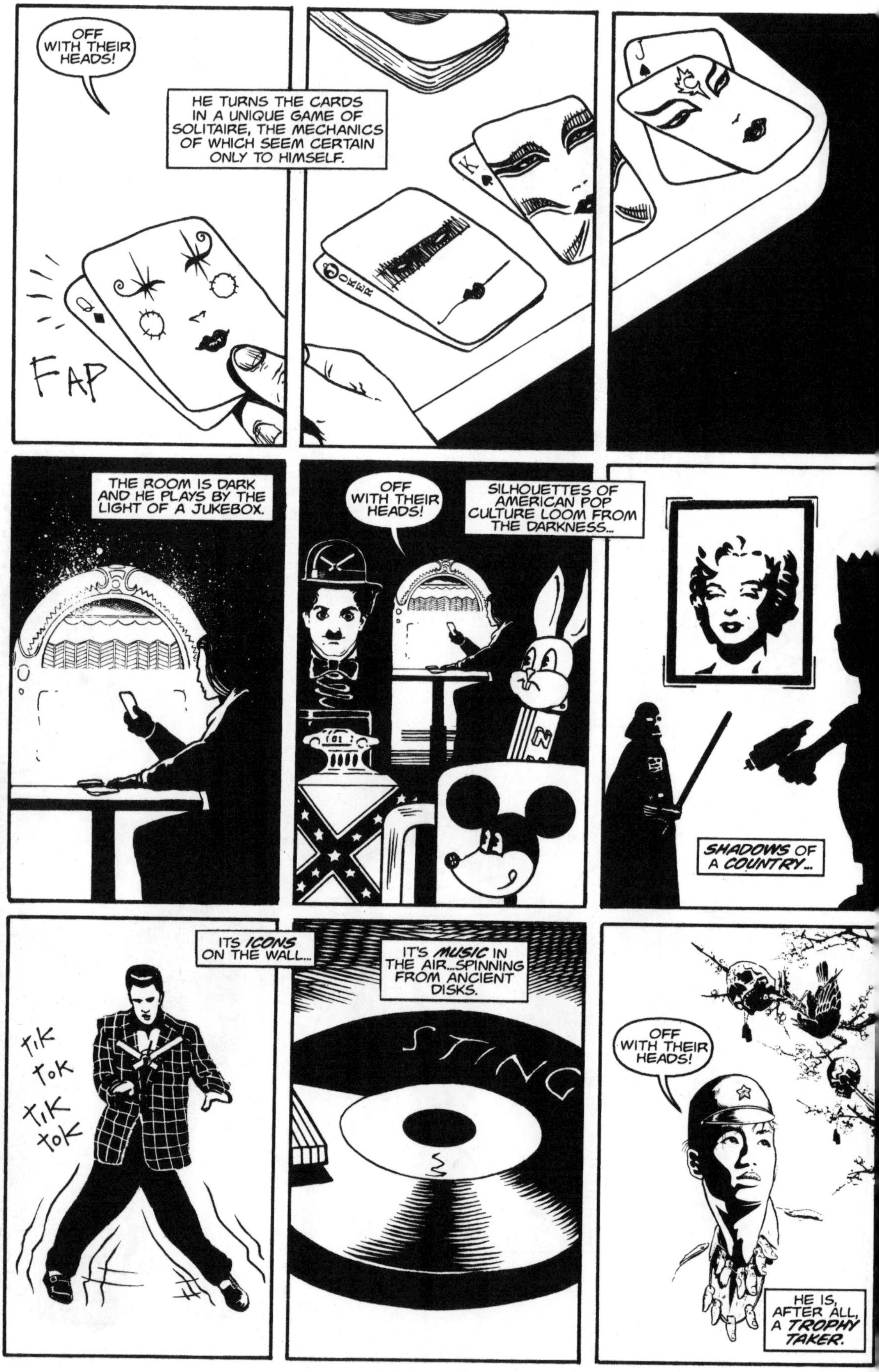
OFF WITH THEIR HEADS!
HE TURNS THE CARDS IN A UNIQUE GAME OF SOLITAIRE, THE MECHANICS OF WHICH SEEM CERTAIN ONLY TO HIMSELF.
FAP
THE ROOM IS DARK AND HE PLAYS BY THE LIGHT OF A JUKEBOX.
OFF WITH THEIR HEADS!
SILHOUETTES OF AMERICAN POP CULTURE LOOM FROM THE DARKNESS...
SHADOWS OF A COUNTRY...
ITS ICONS ON THE WALL...
TIK TOK TIK TOK
IT'S MUSIC IN THE AIR...SPINNING FROM ANCIENT DISKS.
STING
OFF WITH THEIR HEADS!
HE IS, AFTER ALL, A TROPHY TAKER.

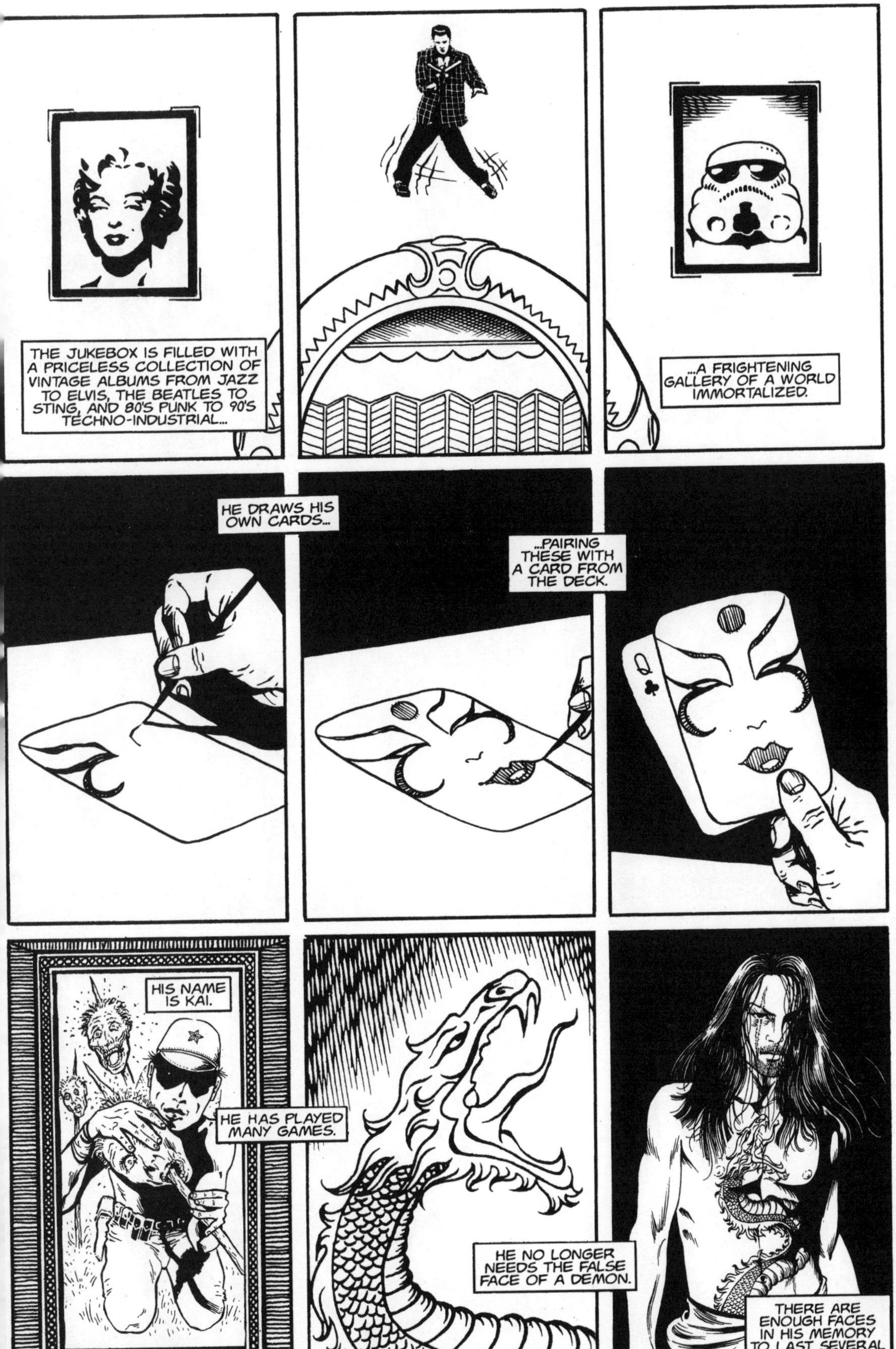
THE JUKEBOX IS FILLED WITH A PRICELESS COLLECTION OF VINTAGE ALBUMS FROM JAZZ TO ELVIS, THE BEATLES TO STING, AND 80'S PUNK TO 90'S TECHNO-INDUSTRIAL...
...A FRIGHTENING GALLERY OF A WORLD IMMORTALIZED.
HE DRAWS HIS OWN CARDS...
...PAIRING THESE WITH A CARD FROM THE DECK.
HIS NAME IS KAI.
HE HAS PLAYED MANY GAMES.
HE NO LONGER NEEDS THE FALSE FACE OF A DEMON.
THERE ARE ENOUGH FACES IN HIS MEMORY TO LAST SEVERAL LIFETIMES.

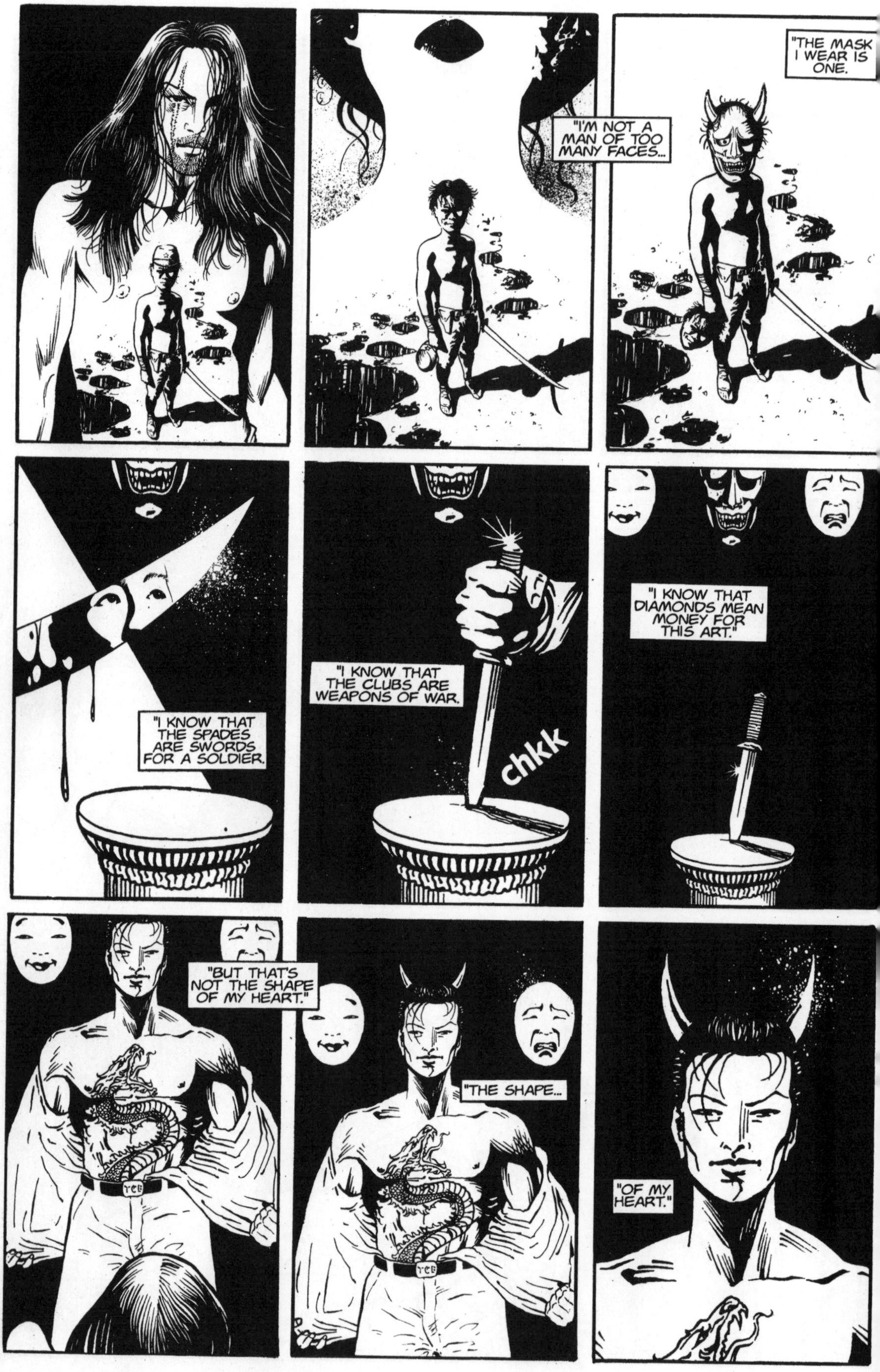
"I'M NOT A MAN OF TOO MANY FACES...
"THE MASK I WEAR IS ONE.
"I KNOW THAT THE SPADES ARE SWORDS FOR A SOLDIER.
"I KNOW THAT THE CLUBS ARE WEAPONS OF WAR.
chkk
"I KNOW THAT DIAMONDS MEAN MONEY FOR THIS ART."
"BUT THAT'S NOT THE SHAPE OF MY HEART."
"THE SHAPE...
"OF MY HEART."

"HE DEALS THE CARDS AS A MEDITATION.

"AND THOSE HE PLAYS NEVER SUSPECT...

"HE DOESN'T PLAY FOR MONEY...

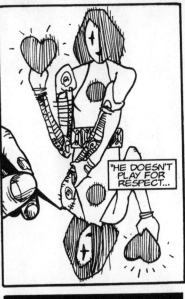

"HE DOESN'T PLAY FOR RESPECT...

"HE MAY LAY THE QUEEN OF DIAMONDS,

FAP

"HE MAY PLAY THE JACK OF SPADES,

"HE MAY CONCEAL A KING IN HIS HAND

"WHILE THE MEMORY OF IT FADES."

STING

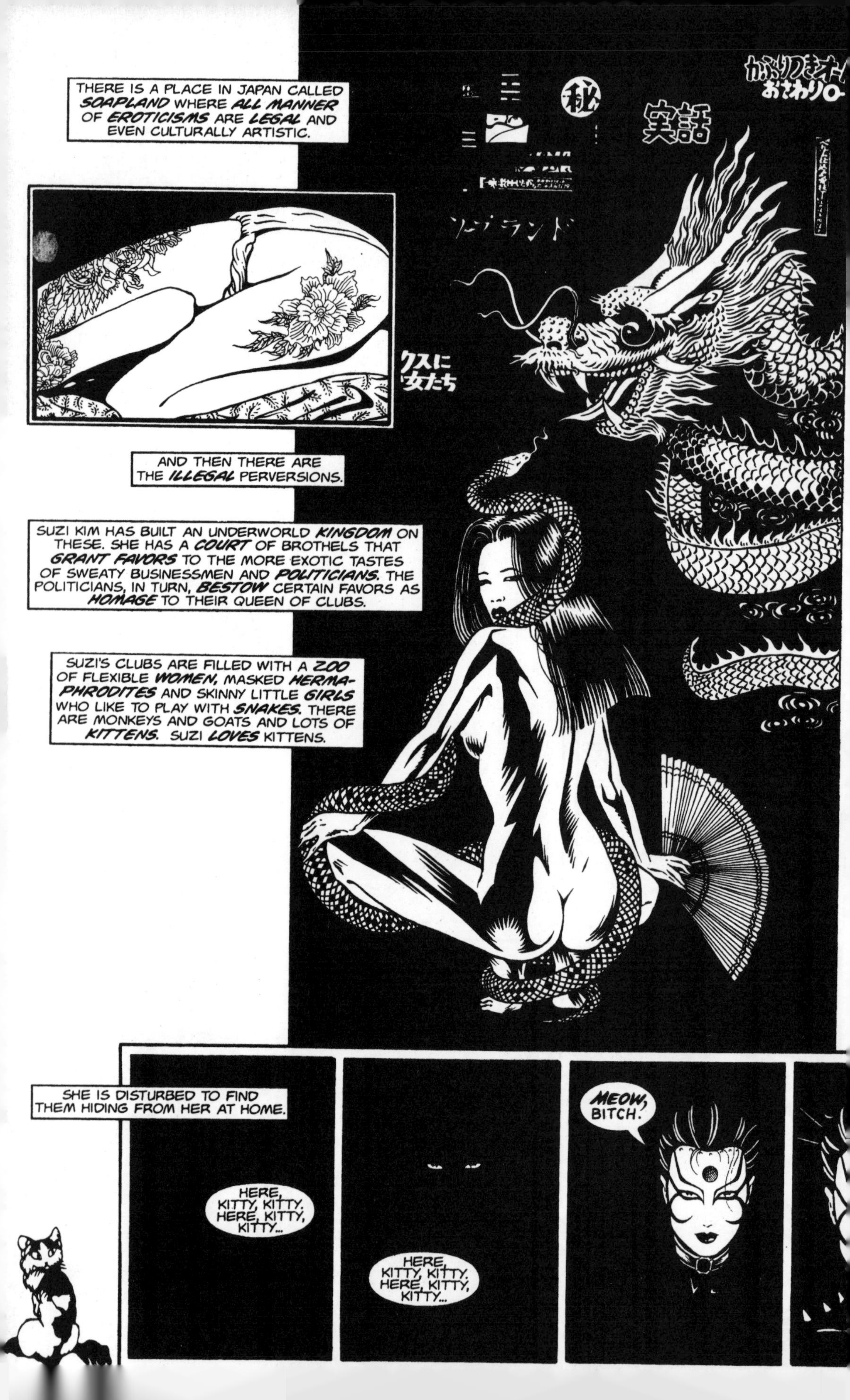
THERE IS A PLACE IN JAPAN CALLED SOAPLAND WHERE ALL MANNER OF EROTICISMS ARE LEGAL AND EVEN CULTURALLY ARTISTIC.
秘
実話
AND THEN THERE ARE THE ILLEGAL PERVERSIONS.
SUZI KIM HAS BUILT AN UNDERWORLD KINGDOM ON THESE. SHE HAS A COURT OF BROTHELS THAT GRANT FAVORS TO THE MORE EXOTIC TASTES OF SWEATY BUSINESSMEN AND POLITICIANS. THE POLITICIANS, IN TURN, BESTOW CERTAIN FAVORS AS HOMAGE TO THEIR QUEEN OF CLUBS.
SUZI'S CLUBS ARE FILLED WITH A ZOO OF FLEXIBLE WOMEN, MASKED HERMAPHRODITES AND SKINNY LITTLE GIRLS WHO LIKE TO PLAY WITH SNAKES. THERE ARE MONKEYS AND GOATS AND LOTS OF KITTENS. SUZI LOVES KITTENS.
SHE IS DISTURBED TO FIND THEM HIDING FROM HER AT HOME.
HERE, KITTY, KITTY. HERE, KITTY, KITTY...
HERE, KITTY, KITTY. HERE, KITTY, KITTY...
MEOW, BITCH.

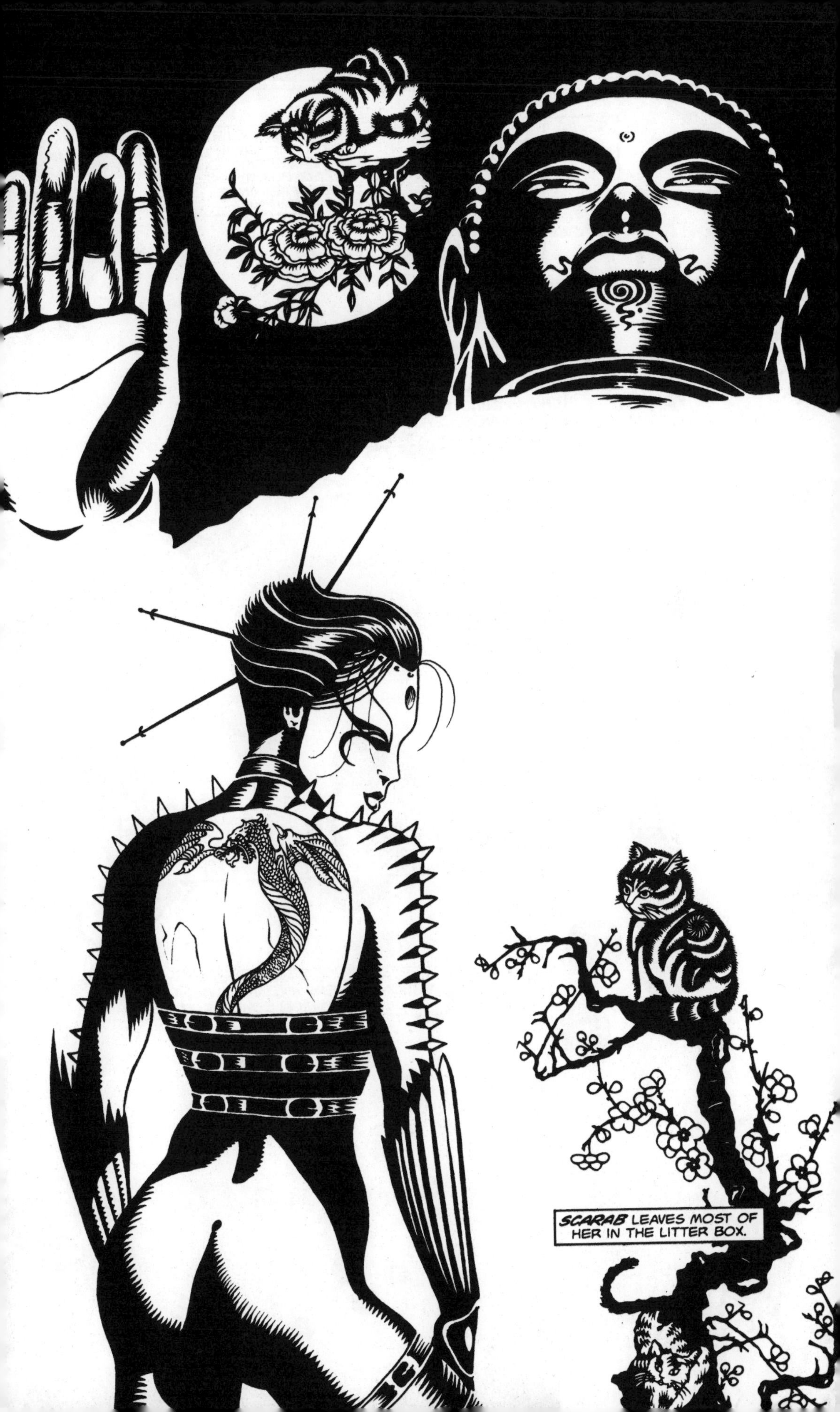
SCARAB LEAVES MOST OF HER IN THE LITTER BOX.

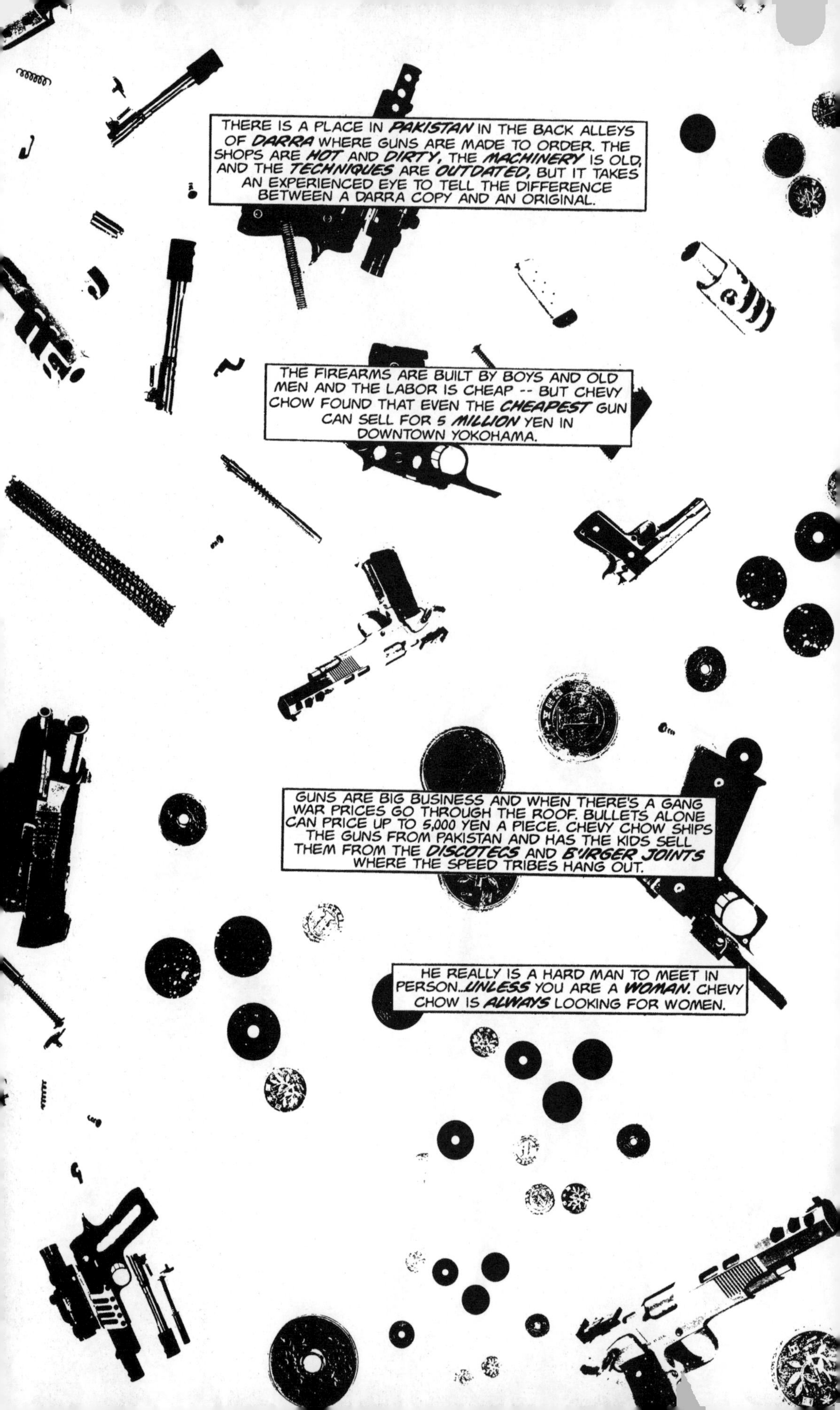
THERE IS A PLACE IN PAKISTAN IN THE BACK ALLEYS OF DARRA WHERE GUNS ARE MADE TO ORDER. THE SHOPS ARE HOT AND DIRTY, THE MACHINERY IS OLD, AND THE TECHNIQUES ARE OUTDATED, BUT IT TAKES AN EXPERIENCED EYE TO TELL THE DIFFERENCE BETWEEN A DARRA COPY AND AN ORIGINAL.
THE FIREARMS ARE BUILT BY BOYS AND OLD MEN AND THE LABOR IS CHEAP -- BUT CHEVY CHOW FOUND THAT EVEN THE CHEAPEST GUN CAN SELL FOR 5 MILLION YEN IN DOWNTOWN YOKOHAMA.
GUNS ARE BIG BUSINESS AND WHEN THERE'S A GANG WAR PRICES GO THROUGH THE ROOF. BULLETS ALONE CAN PRICE UP TO 5,000 YEN A PIECE. CHEVY CHOW SHIPS THE GUNS FROM PAKISTAN AND HAS THE KIDS SELL THEM FROM THE DISCOTECS AND B'URGER JOINTS WHERE THE SPEED TRIBES HANG OUT.
HE REALLY IS A HARD MAN TO MEET IN PERSON...UNLESS YOU ARE A WOMAN. CHEVY CHOW IS ALWAYS LOOKING FOR WOMEN.

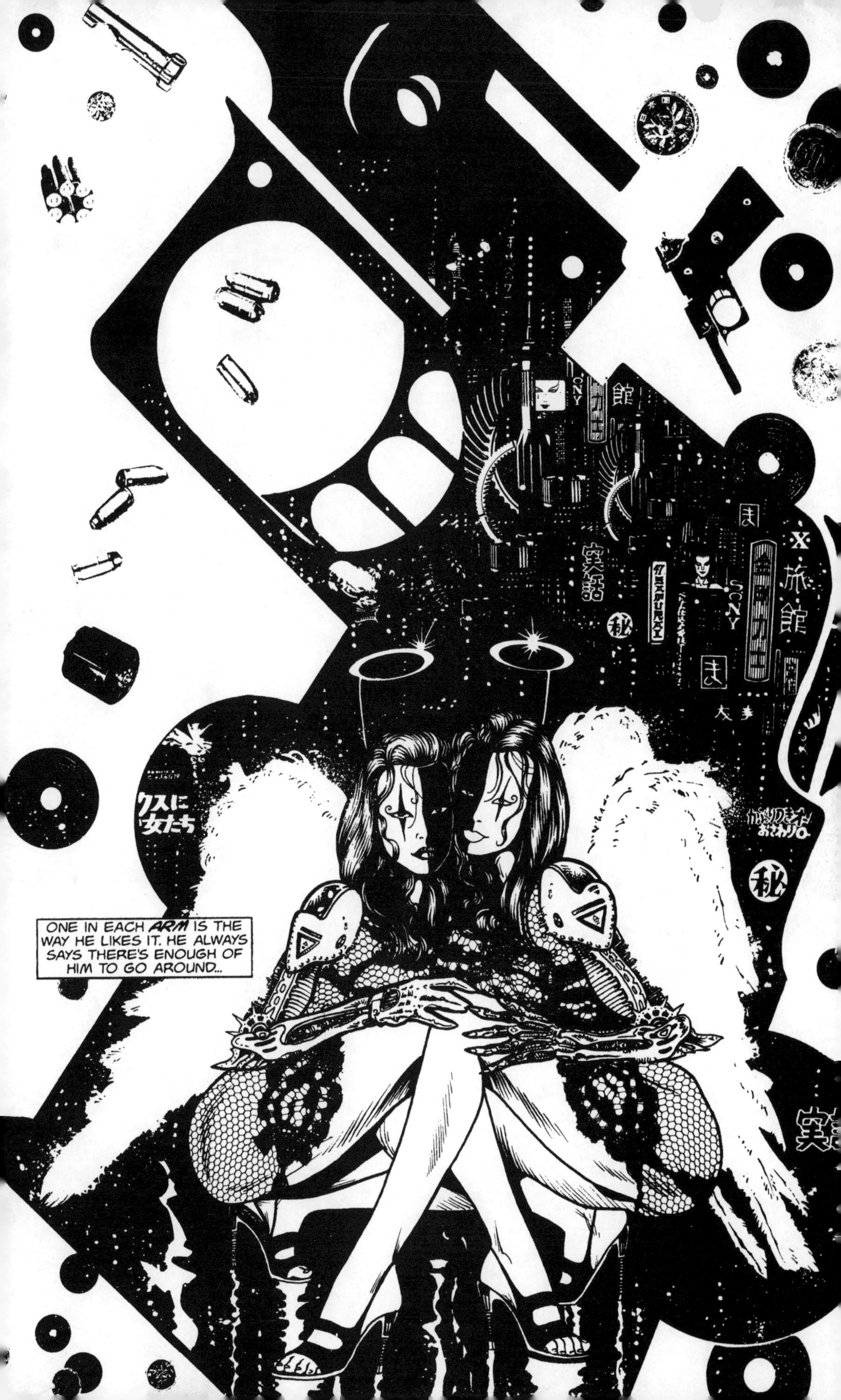
ONE IN EACH ARM IS THE WAY HE LIKES IT. HE ALWAYS SAYS THERE'S ENOUGH OF HIM TO GO AROUND...
実話
旅館
秘
クスに
女たち

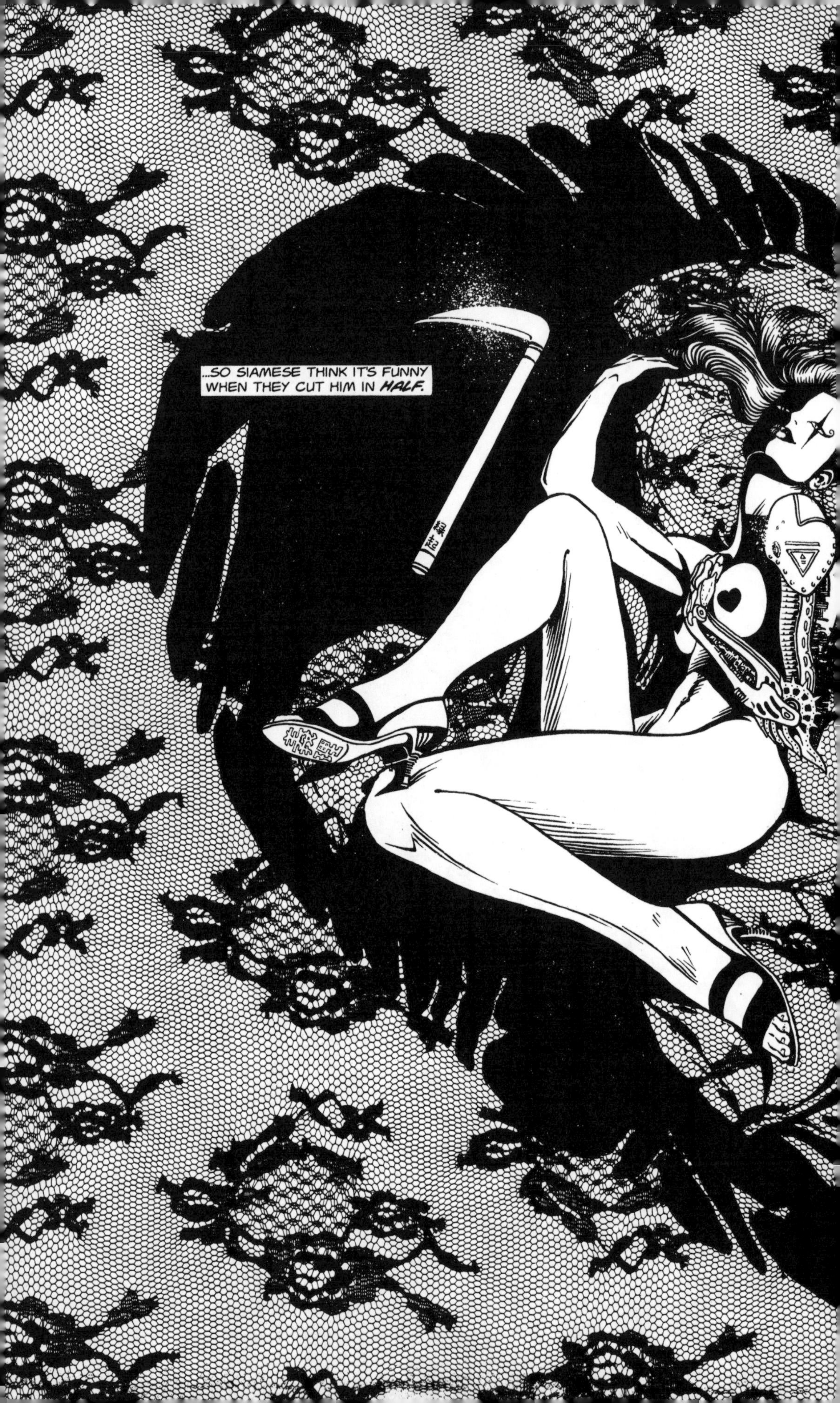
...SO SIAMESE THINK IT'S FUNNY WHEN THEY CUT HIM IN HALF.

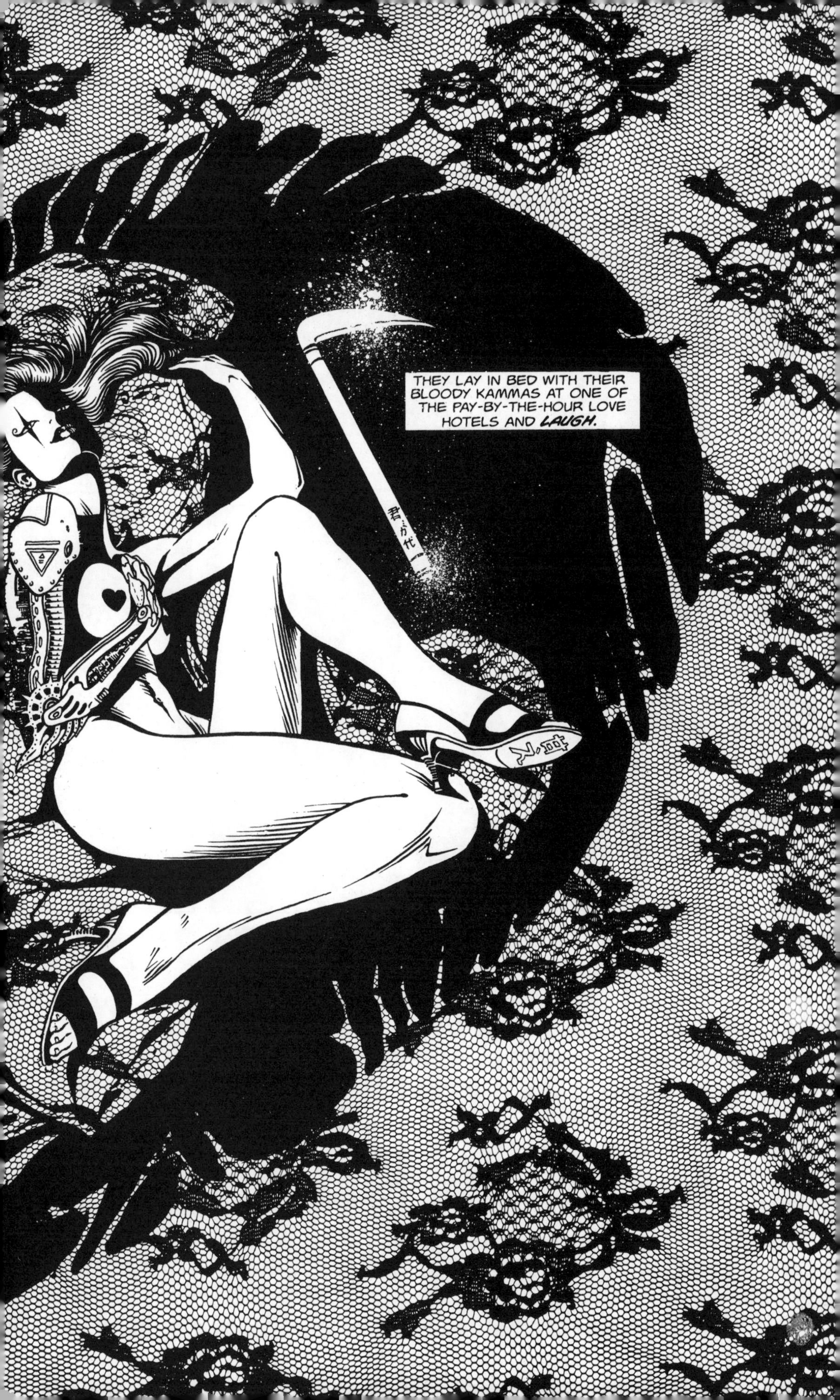
THEY LAY IN BED WITH THEIR BLOODY KAMMAS AT ONE OF THE PAY-BY-THE-HOUR LOVE HOTELS AND LAUGH.

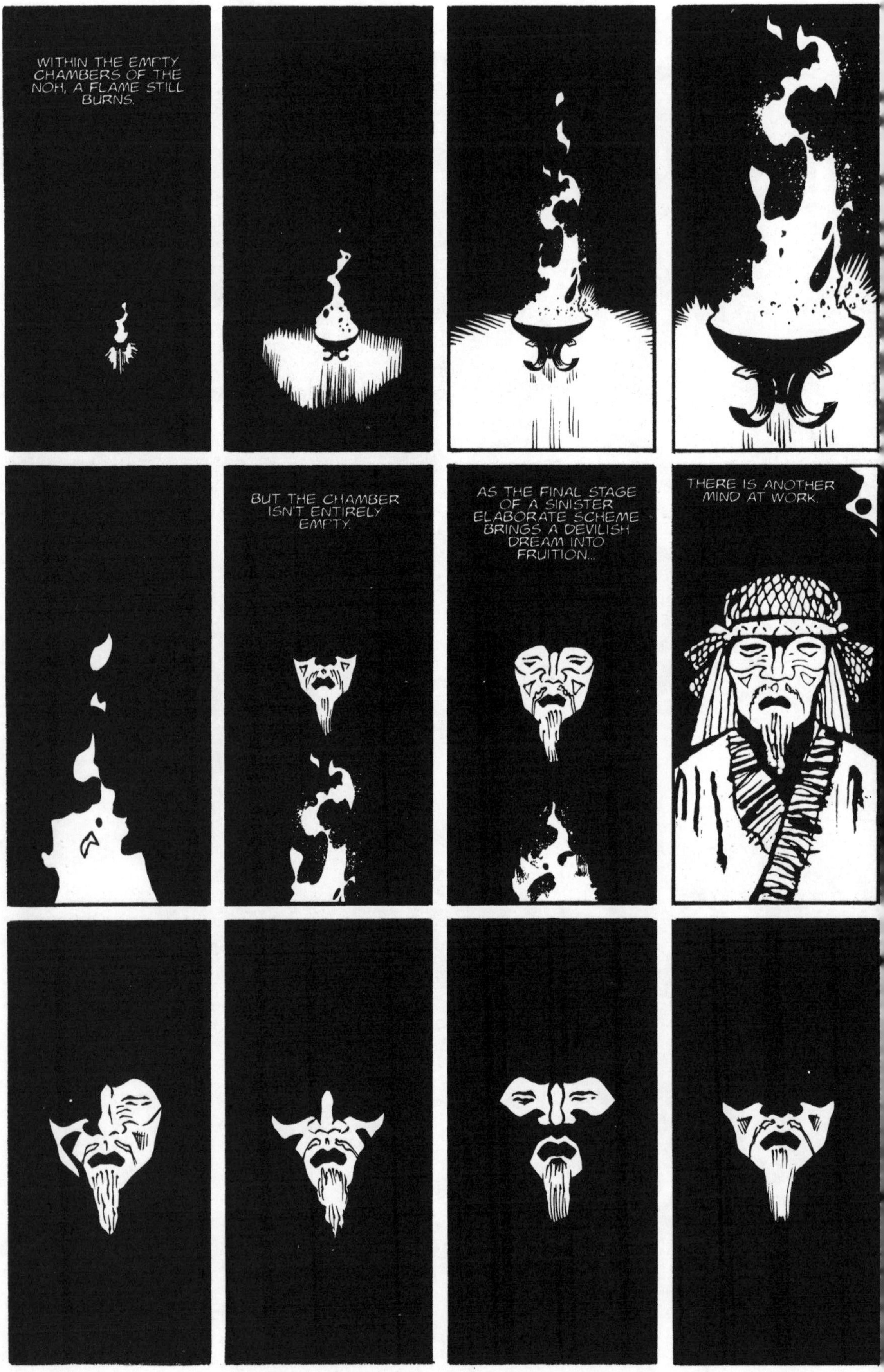
WITHIN THE EMPTY CHAMBERS OF THE NOH, A FLAME STILL BURNS.
BUT THE CHAMBER ISN'T ENTIRELY EMPTY.
AS THE FINAL STAGE OF A SINISTER ELABORATE SCHEME BRINGS A DEVILISH DREAM INTO FRUITION...
THERE IS ANOTHER MIND AT WORK.

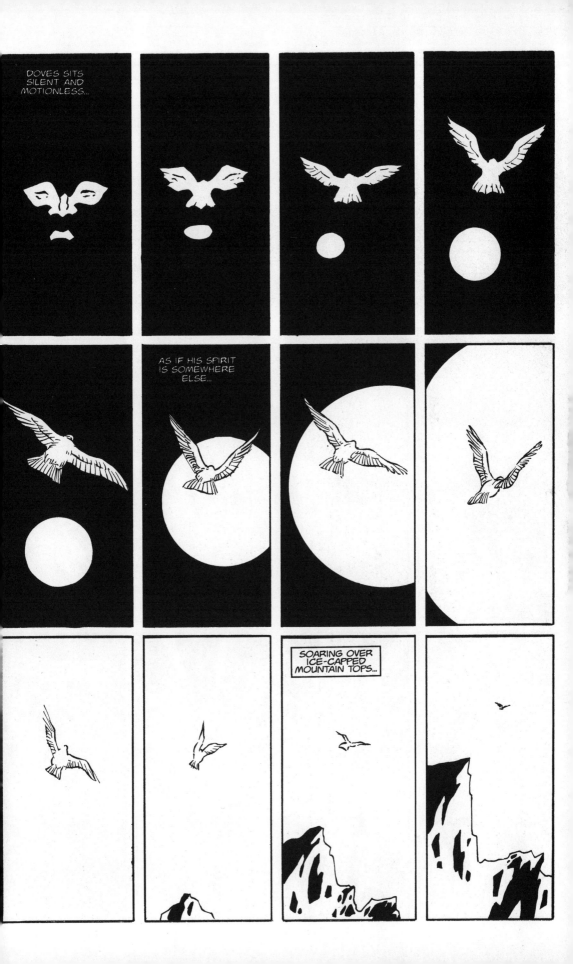

DOVES SITS SILENT AND MOTIONLESS...

AS IF HIS SPIRIT IS SOMEWHERE ELSE...

SOARING OVER ICE-CAPPED MOUNTAIN TOPS...

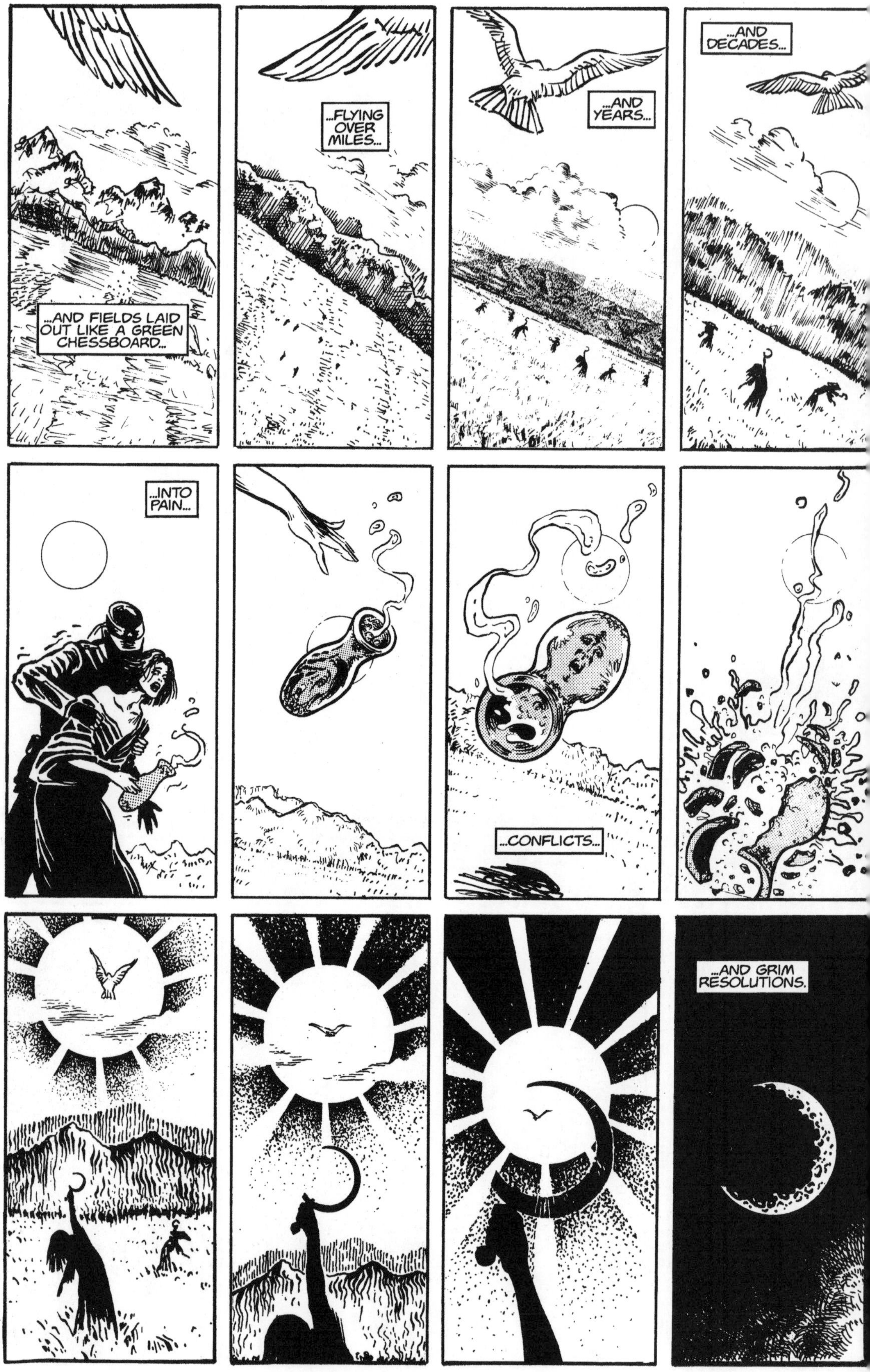
...AND FIELDS LAID OUT LIKE A GREEN CHESSBOARD...
...FLYING OVER MILES...
...AND YEARS...
...AND DECADES...
...INTO PAIN...
...CONFLICTS...
...AND GRIM RESOLUTIONS.

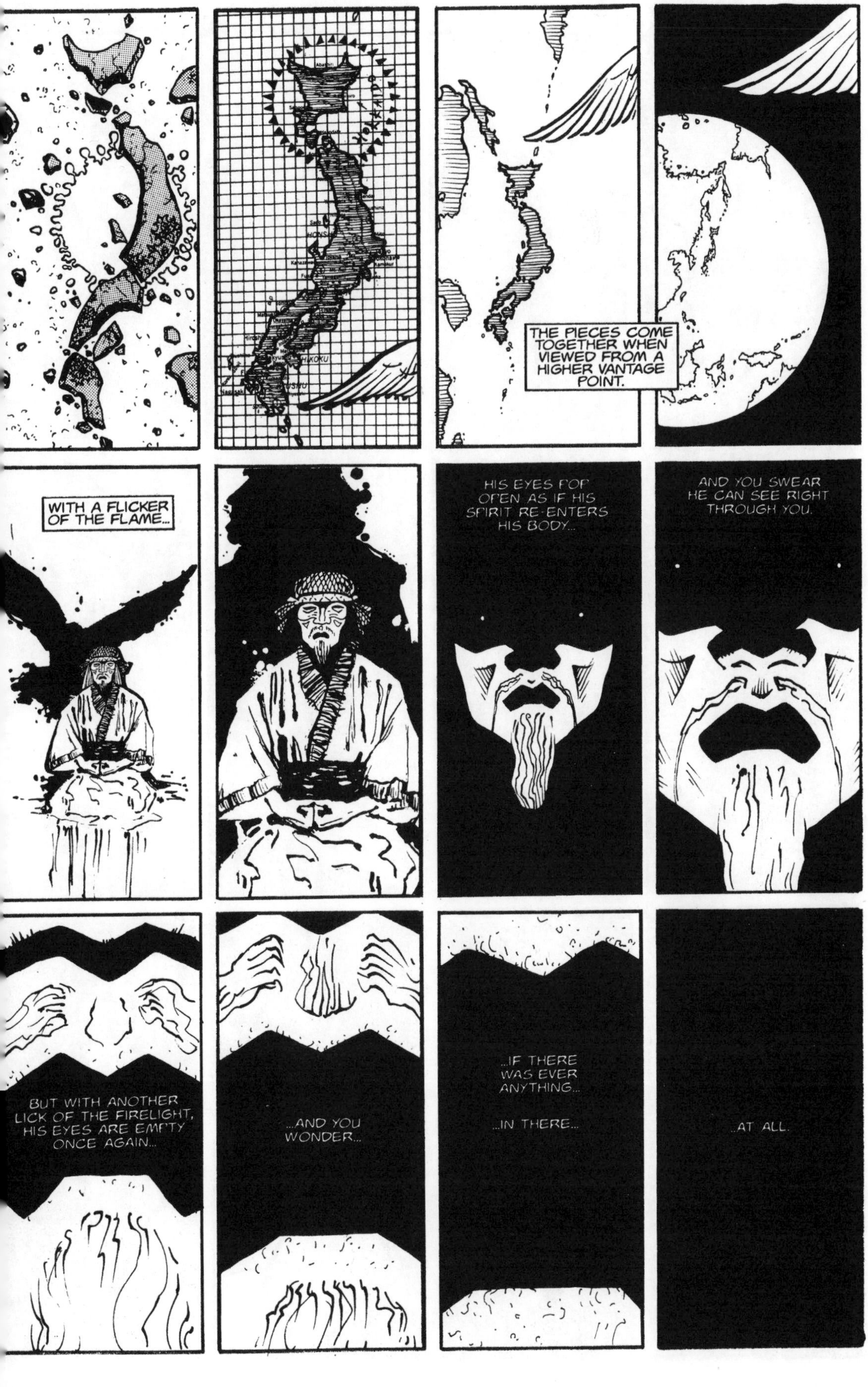
THE PIECES COME TOGETHER WHEN VIEWED FROM A HIGHER VANTAGE POINT.
WITH A FLICKER OF THE FLAME...
HIS EYES POP OPEN AS IF HIS SPIRIT RE-ENTERS HIS BODY...
AND YOU SWEAR HE CAN SEE RIGHT THROUGH YOU.
BUT WITH ANOTHER LICK OF THE FIRELIGHT, HIS EYES ARE EMPTY ONCE AGAIN...
...AND YOU WONDER...
...IF THERE WAS EVER ANYTHING...
...IN THERE...
...AT ALL.

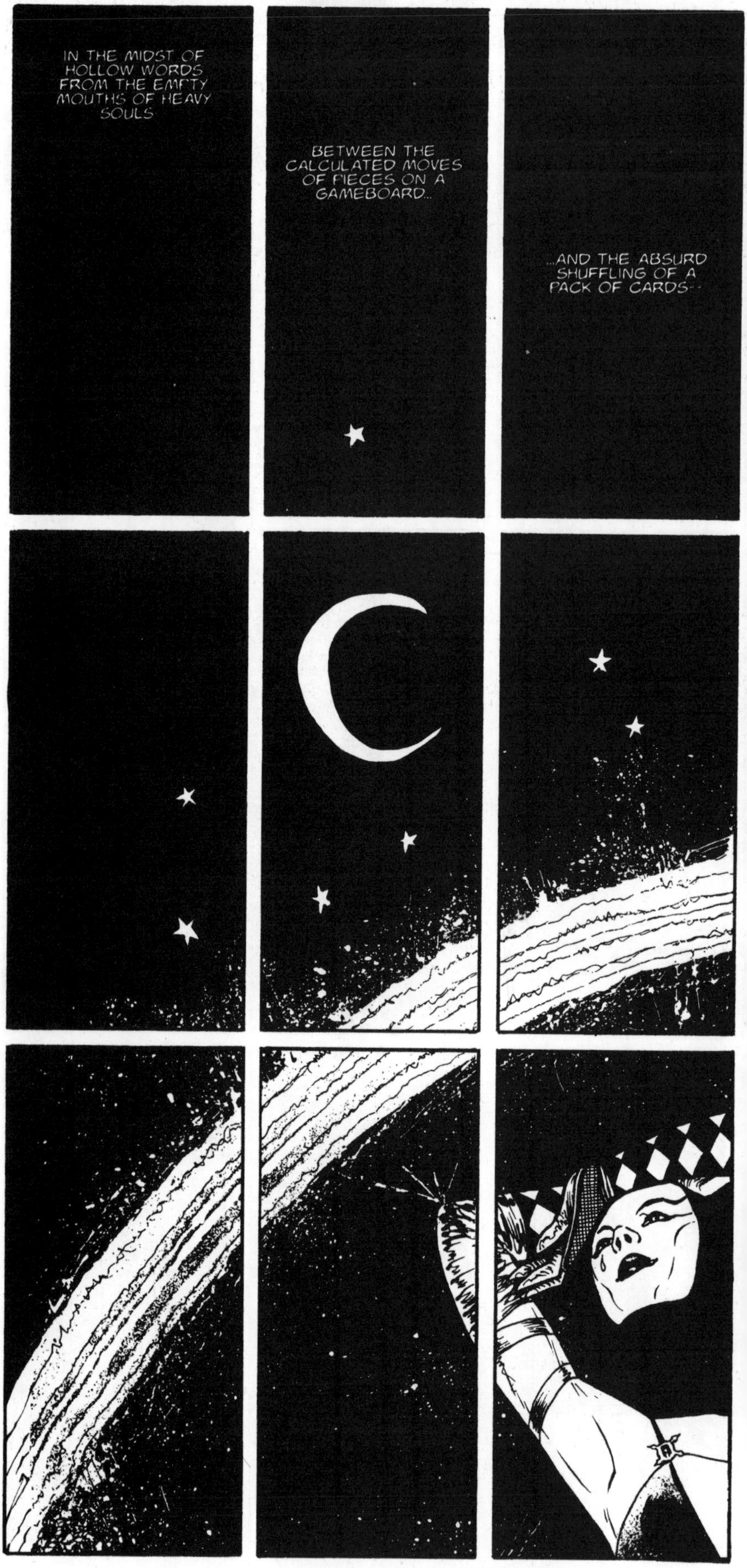
IN THE MIDST OF HOLLOW WORDS FROM THE EMPTY MOUTHS OF HEAVY SOULS
BETWEEN THE CALCULATED MOVES OF PIECES ON A GAMEBOARD...
...AND THE ABSURD SHUFFLING OF A PACK OF CARDS--

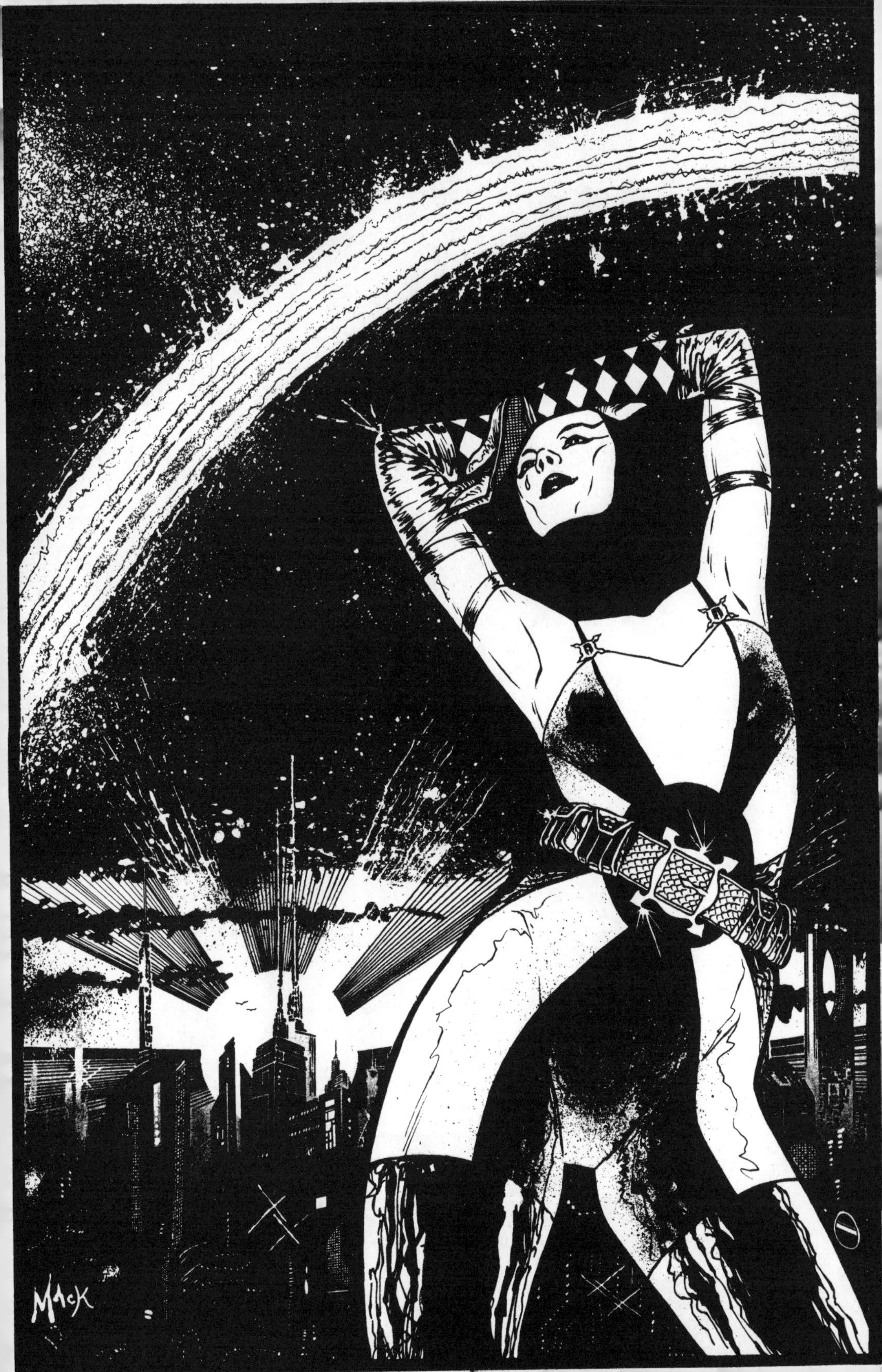

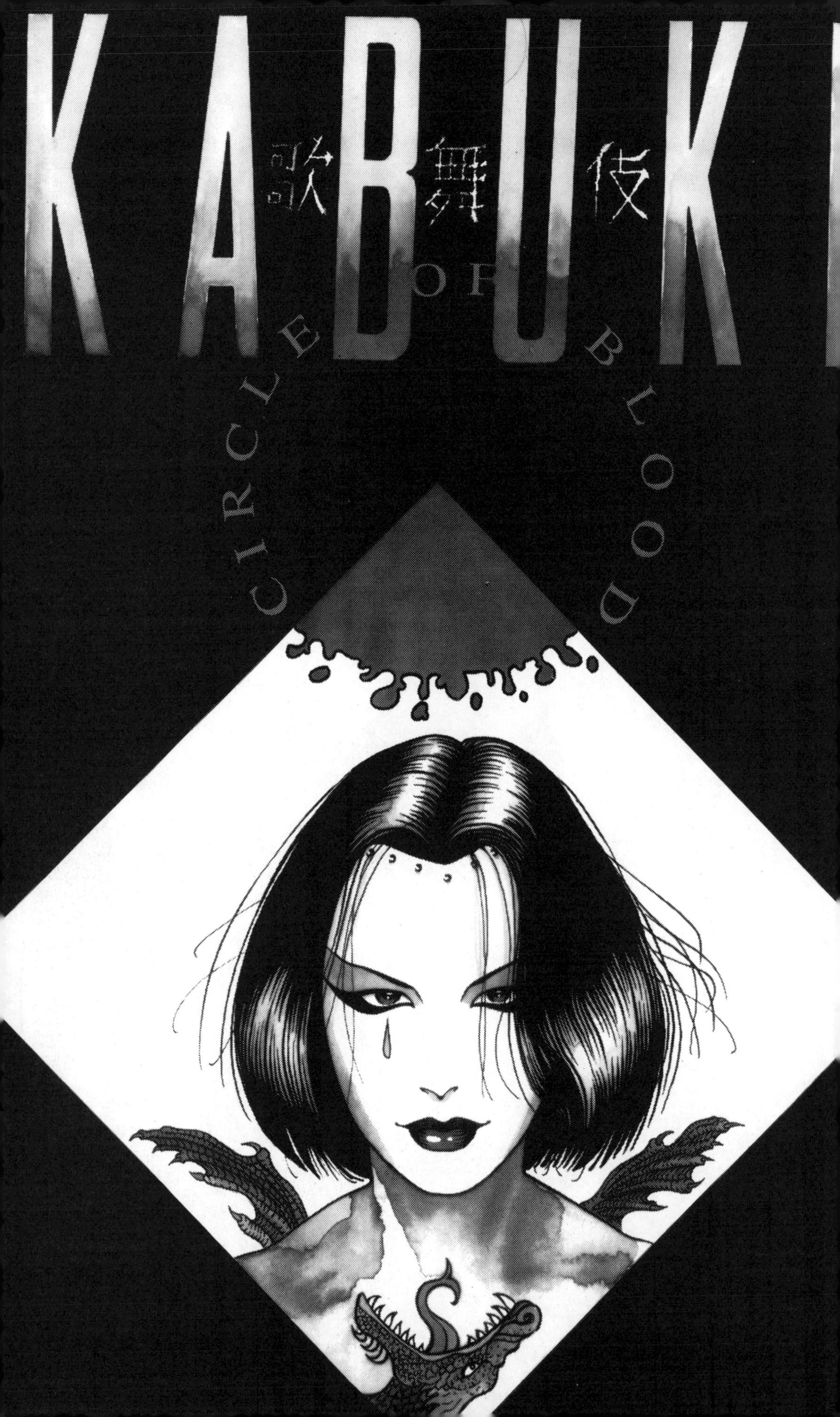
KABUKI
歌舞伎
CIRCLE OF BLOOD

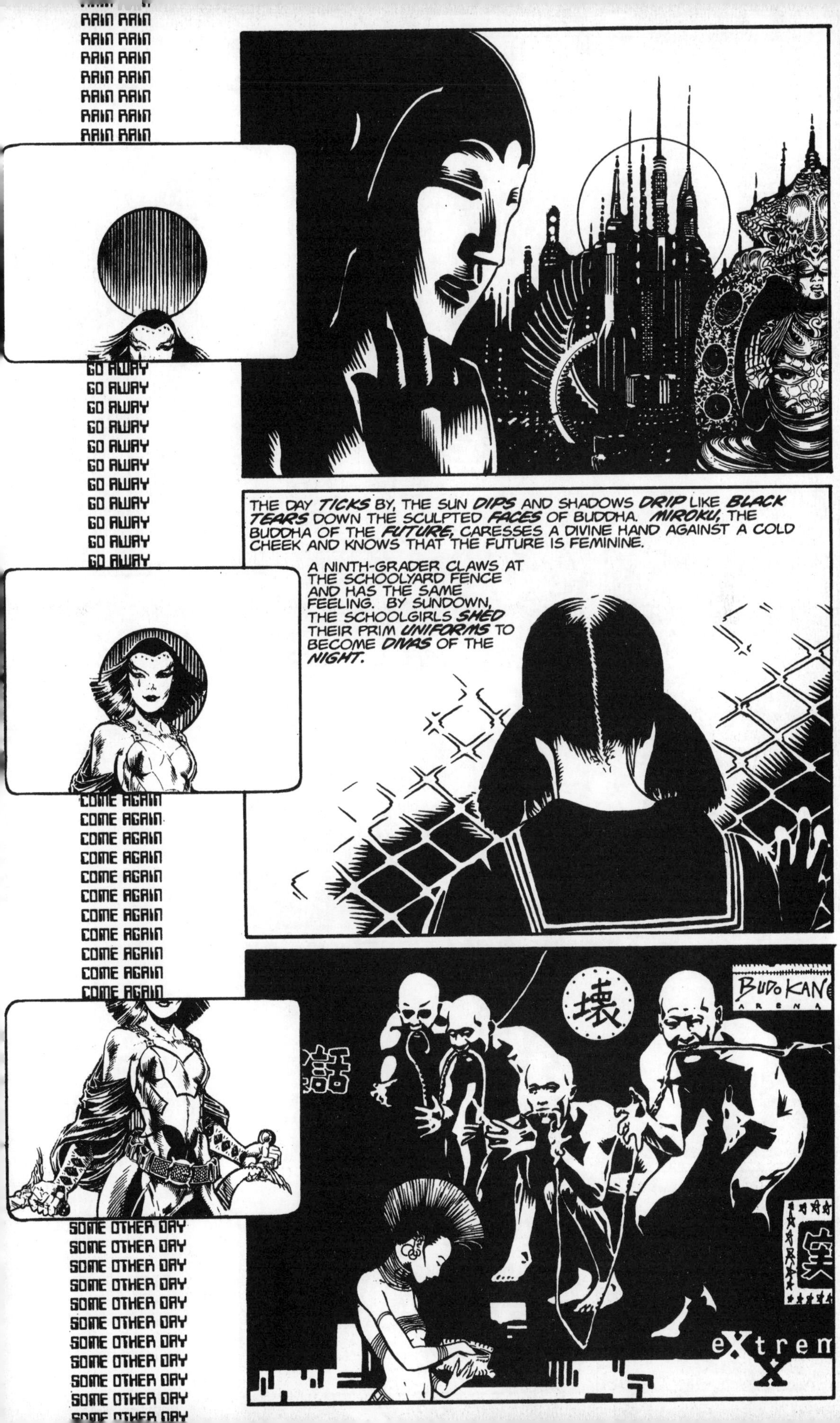

RAIN RAIN
RAIN RAIN
RAIN RAIN
RAIN RAIN
RAIN RAIN
RAIN RAIN
RAIN RAIN
GO AWAY
GO AWAY
GO AWAY
GO AWAY
GO AWAY
GO AWAY
GO AWAY
GO AWAY
GO AWAY
GO AWAY
GO AWAY
THE DAY TICKS BY, THE SUN DIPS AND SHADOWS DRIP LIKE BLACK TEARS DOWN THE SCULPTED FACES OF BUDDHA. MIROKU, THE BUDDHA OF THE FUTURE, CARESSES A DIVINE HAND AGAINST A COLD CHEEK AND KNOWS THAT THE FUTURE IS FEMININE.
A NINTH-GRADER CLAWS AT THE SCHOOLYARD FENCE AND HAS THE SAME FEELING. BY SUNDOWN, THE SCHOOLGIRLS SHED THEIR PRIM UNIFORMS TO BECOME DIVAS OF THE NIGHT.
COME AGAIN
COME AGAIN
COME AGAIN
COME AGAIN
COME AGAIN
COME AGAIN
COME AGAIN
COME AGAIN
COME AGAIN
COME AGAIN
COME AGAIN
壊
BUDOKAN
ARENA
話
実
eXtrem
SOME OTHER DAY
SOME OTHER DAY
SOME OTHER DAY
SOME OTHER DAY
SOME OTHER DAY
SOME OTHER DAY
SOME OTHER DAY
SOME OTHER DAY
SOME OTHER DAY
SOME OTHER DAY
SOME OTHER DAY

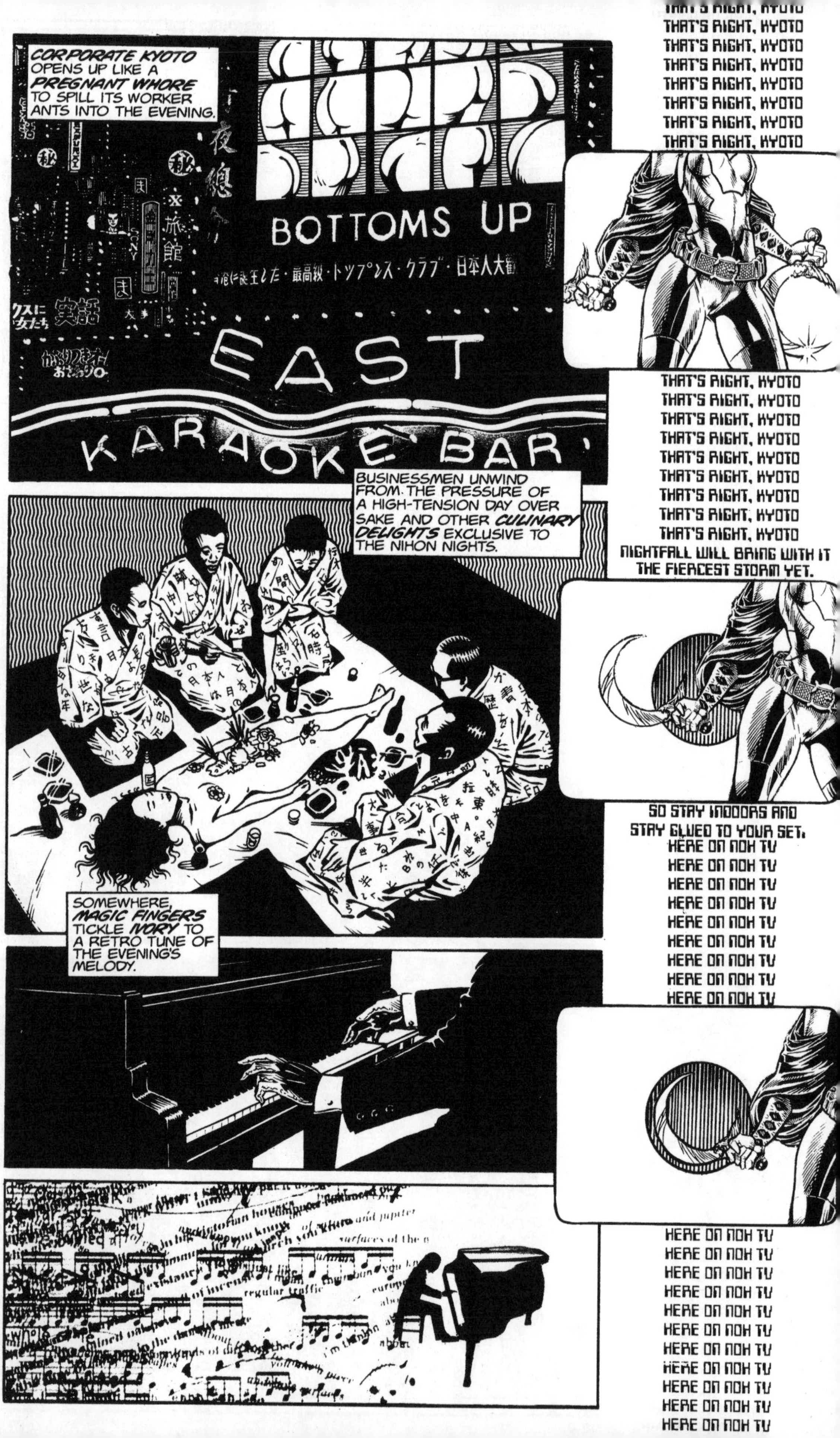
THAT'S RIGHT, KYOTO
THAT'S RIGHT, KYOTO
THAT'S RIGHT, KYOTO
THAT'S RIGHT, KYOTO
THAT'S RIGHT, KYOTO
THAT'S RIGHT, KYOTO
THAT'S RIGHT, KYOTO
THAT'S RIGHT, KYOTO
CORPORATE KYOTO OPENS UP LIKE A PREGNANT WHORE TO SPILL ITS WORKER ANTS INTO THE EVENING.
BOTTOMS UP
SONY
実話
EAST
KARAOKE BAR
THAT'S RIGHT, KYOTO
THAT'S RIGHT, KYOTO
THAT'S RIGHT, KYOTO
THAT'S RIGHT, KYOTO
THAT'S RIGHT, KYOTO
THAT'S RIGHT, KYOTO
THAT'S RIGHT, KYOTO
THAT'S RIGHT, KYOTO
THAT'S RIGHT, KYOTO
NIGHTFALL WILL BRING WITH IT
THE FIERCEST STORM YET.
BUSINESSMEN UNWIND FROM THE PRESSURE OF A HIGH-TENSION DAY OVER SAKE AND OTHER CULINARY DELIGHTS EXCLUSIVE TO THE NIHON NIGHTS.
SO STAY INDOORS AND
STAY GLUED TO YOUR SET.
HERE ON NOH TV
HERE ON NOH TV
HERE ON NOH TV
HERE ON NOH TV
HERE ON NOH TV
HERE ON NOH TV
HERE ON NOH TV
HERE ON NOH TV
HERE ON NOH TV
SOMEWHERE, MAGIC FINGERS TICKLE IVORY TO A RETRO TUNE OF THE EVENING'S MELODY.
HERE ON NOH TV
HERE ON NOH TV
HERE ON NOH TV
HERE ON NOH TV
HERE ON NOH TV
HERE ON NOH TV
HERE ON NOH TV
HERE ON NOH TV
HERE ON NOH TV
HERE ON NOH TV
HERE ON NOH TV

HERE ON NOH TV
HERE ON NOH TV
HERE ON NOH TV
HERE ON NOH TV
HERE ON NOH TV
HERE ON NOH TV
HERE ON NOH TV
HERE ON NOH TV
NO, SIR, GENERAL, WE DON'T KNOW WHEN THIS HAPPENED. WHAT WE DO KNOW IS THAT RYUICHI KAI IS THE INFILTRATOR
HE'S BEEN USING THE NOH AGENTS TO ELIMINATE ANYONE WHO MIGHT HAVE POSED A THREAT TO HIM IN THE CRIMINAL ARENA.
HERE ON NOH TV
HERE ON NOH TV
HERE ON NOH TV
HERE ON NOH TV
HERE ON NOH TV
HERE ON NOH TV
HERE ON NOH TV
HERE ON NOH TV
HERE ON NOH TV
HERE ON NOH TV
WHERE THE SUN IS ALWAYS UP.
THE BOARD OF DIRECTORS ARE IN A PANIC. WITH THE ELECTIONS COMING UP SOON, THEY FEAR A NEW CHAOS BETWEEN THE CRIME FAMILIES WHO DONATE TO THE CAMPAIGNS.
AN UPSWING IN CRIME AND DISORDER WILL MAKE THE CURRENT ADMINISTRATION LOOK BAD TO THE PUBLIC.
BE WATCHING US.
BECAUSE WE WILL BE
WATCHING YOU
WATCHING YOU
WATCHING YOU
WATCHING YOU
WATCHING YOU
WATCHING YOU
WATCHING YOU
WATCHING YOU
WATCHING YOU
NO ONE KNOWS WHAT KAI WILL DO. THE YEN IS AT AN UNSTABLE MARK AND KAI COULD PANIC INVESTORS AND...
BLAH BLAH BLAH BLAH BLAH BLAH BLAH BLAH BLAH BLAH BLAH
WATCHING YOU
WATCHING YOU
WATCHING YOU
WATCHING YOU
WATCHING YOU
WATCHING YOU
WATCHING YOU
WATCHING YOU
WATCHING YOU
WATCHING YOU
WATCHING YOU

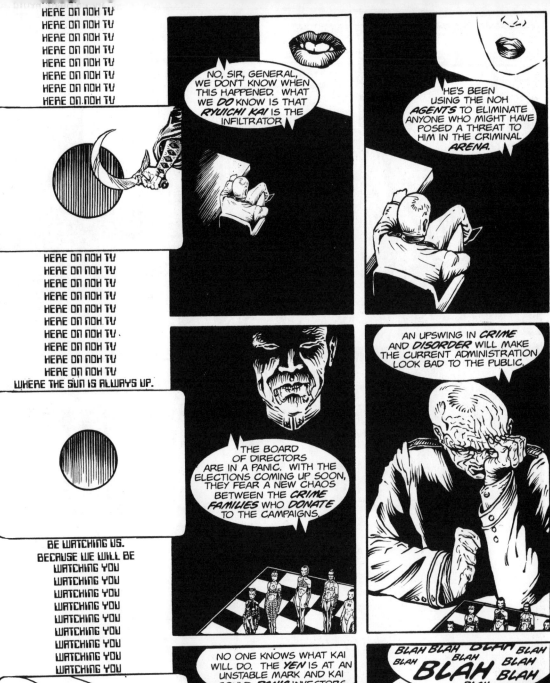

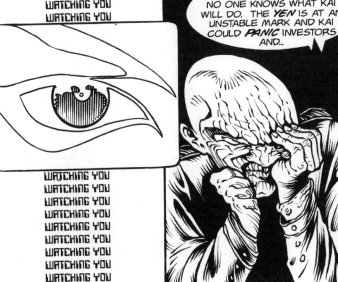

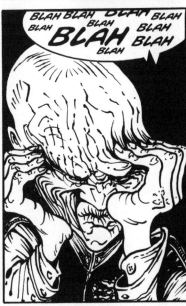

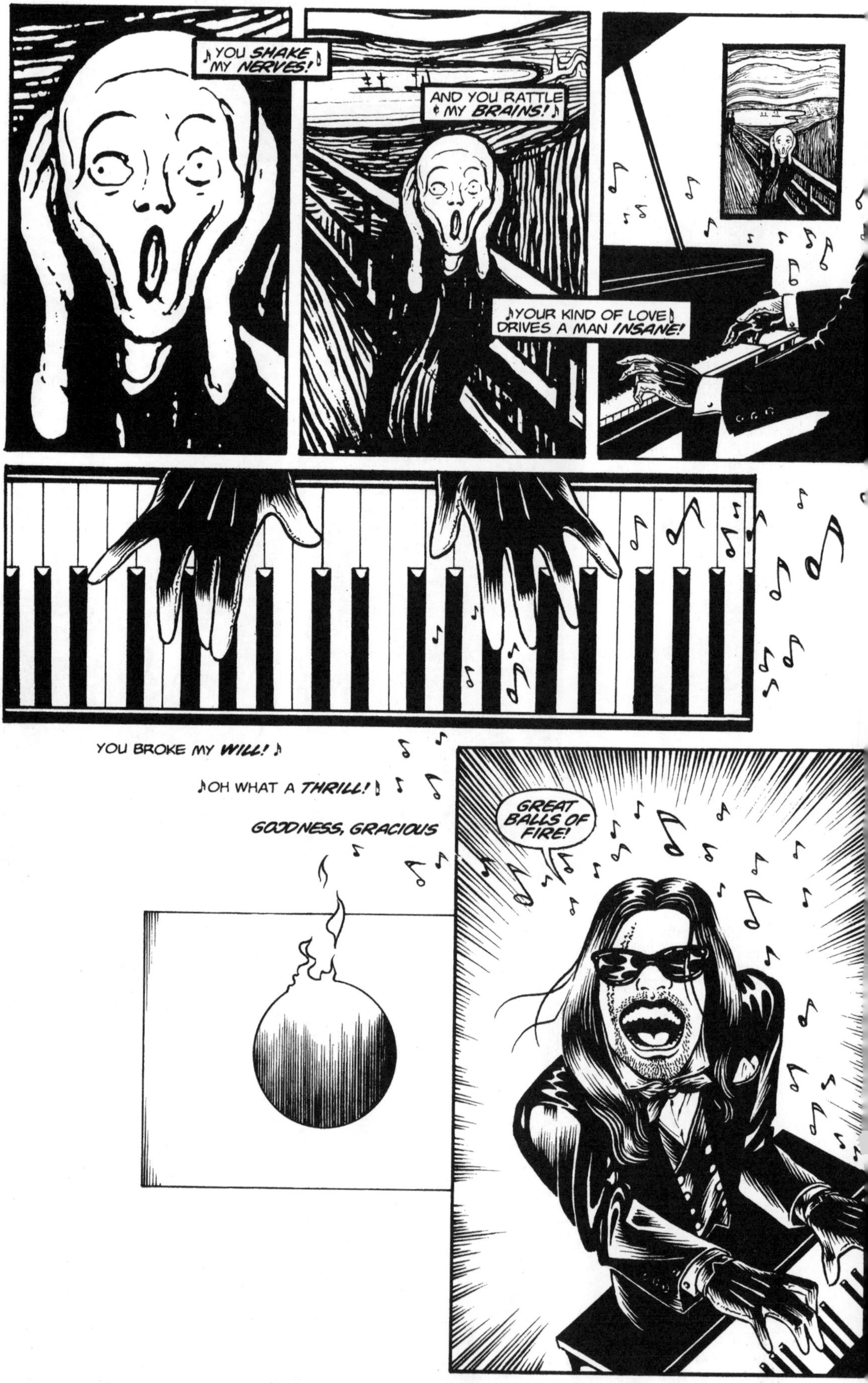
♪YOU SHAKE MY NERVES!♪
AND YOU RATTLE MY BRAINS!♪
♪YOUR KIND OF LOVE♪ DRIVES A MAN INSANE!
YOU BROKE MY WILL!♪
♪OH WHAT A THRILL!♪
GOODNESS, GRACIOUS
GREAT BALLS OF FIRE!

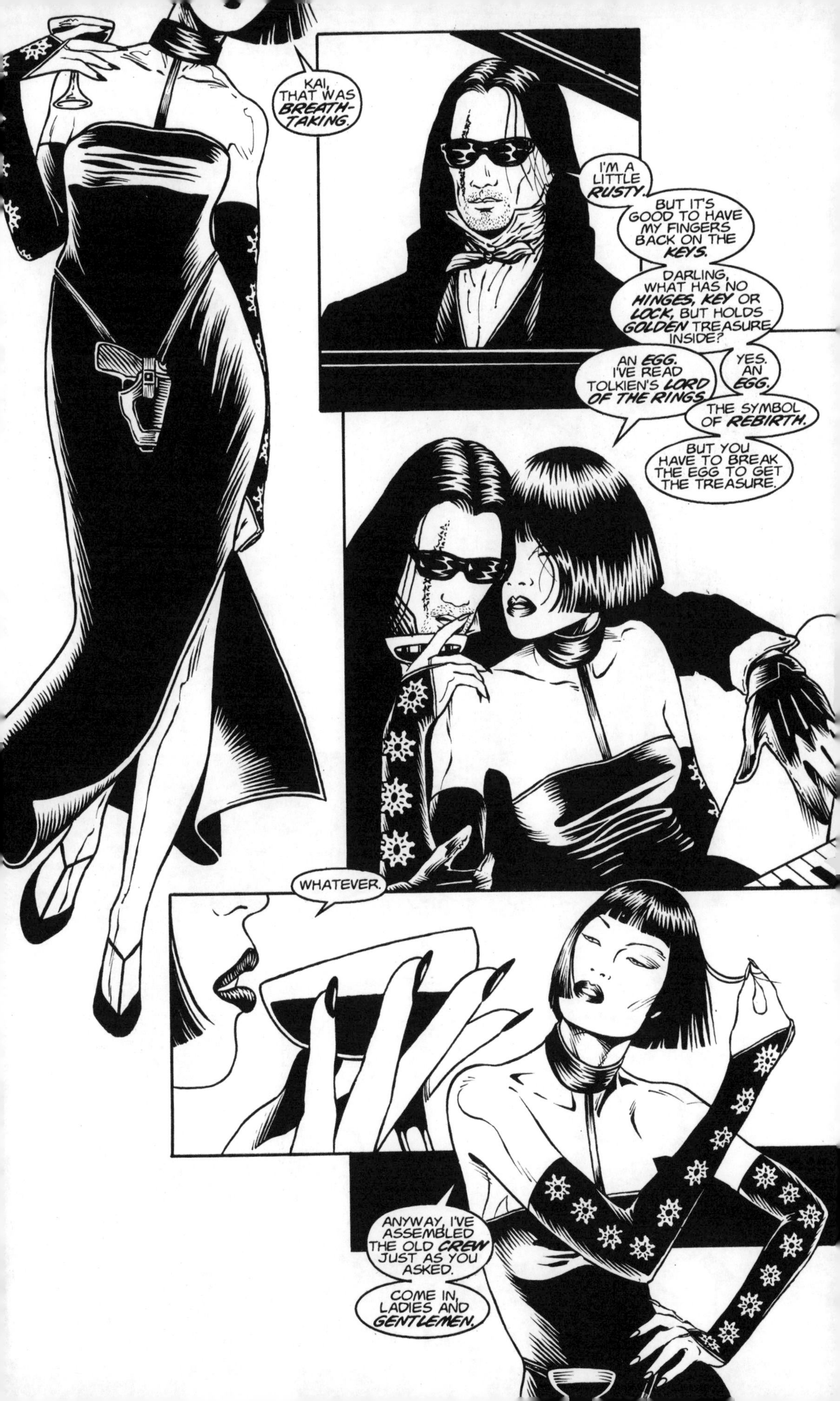

KAI, THAT WAS *BREATH-TAKING*.
I'M A LITTLE *RUSTY*.
BUT IT'S GOOD TO HAVE MY FINGERS BACK ON THE *KEYS*.
DARLING, WHAT HAS NO *HINGES, KEY* OR *LOCK*, BUT HOLDS *GOLDEN* TREASURE INSIDE?
AN *EGG*. I'VE READ TOLKIEN'S *LORD OF THE RINGS*.
YES. AN *EGG*.
THE SYMBOL OF *REBIRTH*.
BUT YOU HAVE TO BREAK THE EGG TO GET THE TREASURE.
WHATEVER.
ANYWAY, I'VE ASSEMBLED THE OLD *CREW* JUST AS YOU ASKED.
COME IN, LADIES AND *GENTLEMEN*.

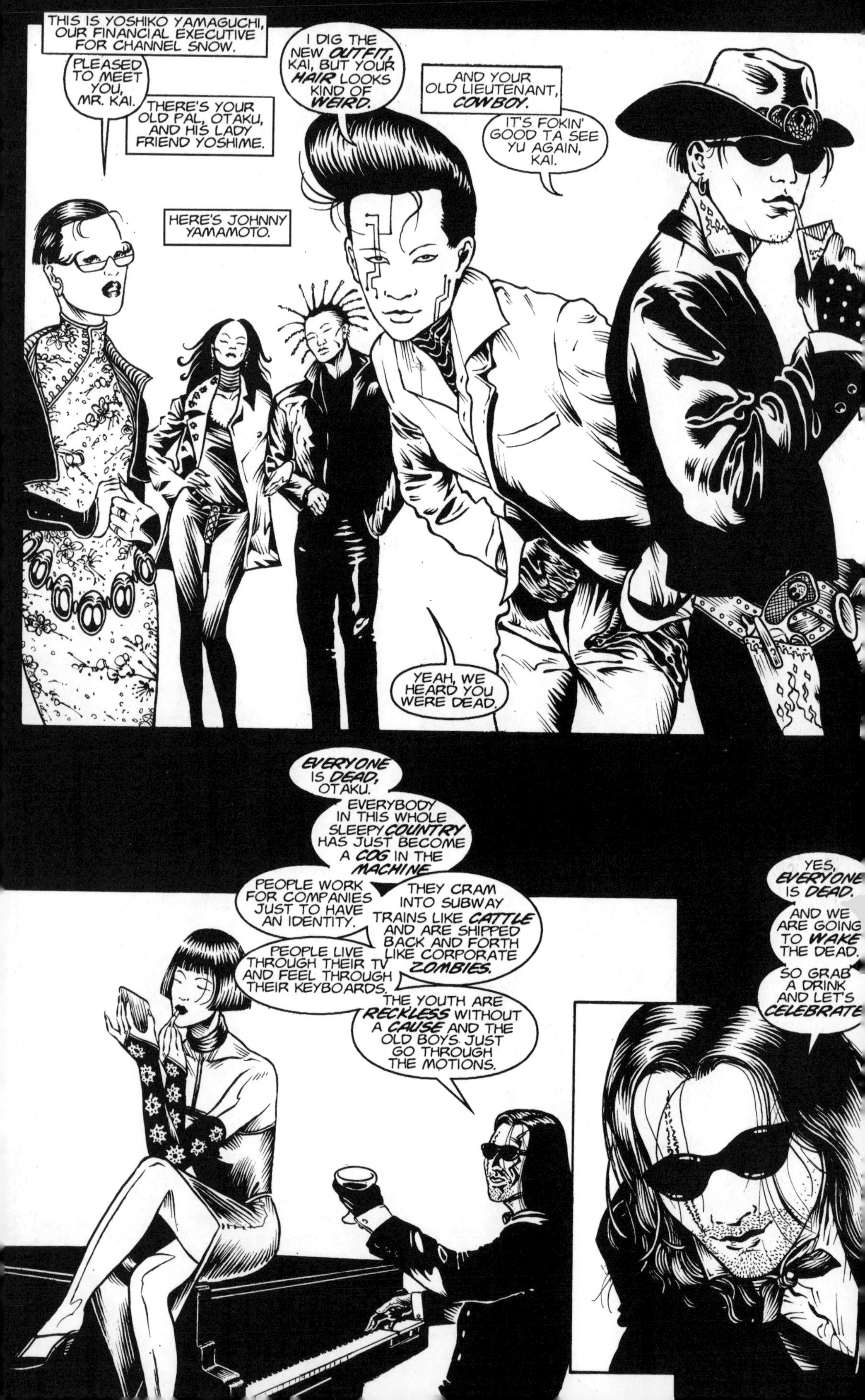
THIS IS YOSHIKO YAMAGUCHI, OUR FINANCIAL EXECUTIVE FOR CHANNEL SNOW.
PLEASED TO MEET YOU, MR. KAI.
THERE'S YOUR OLD PAL, OTAKU, AND HIS LADY FRIEND YOSHIME.
HERE'S JOHNNY YAMAMOTO.
I DIG THE NEW OUTFIT, KAI, BUT YOUR HAIR LOOKS KIND OF WEIRD.
AND YOUR OLD LIEUTENANT, COWBOY.
IT'S FOKIN' GOOD TA SEE YU AGAIN, KAI.
YEAH, WE HEARD YOU WERE DEAD.
EVERYONE IS DEAD, OTAKU.
EVERYBODY IN THIS WHOLE SLEEPY COUNTRY HAS JUST BECOME A COG IN THE MACHINE.
PEOPLE WORK FOR COMPANIES JUST TO HAVE AN IDENTITY.
THEY CRAM INTO SUBWAY TRAINS LIKE CATTLE AND ARE SHIPPED BACK AND FORTH LIKE CORPORATE ZOMBIES.
PEOPLE LIVE THROUGH THEIR TV AND FEEL THROUGH THEIR KEYBOARDS.
THE YOUTH ARE RECKLESS WITHOUT A CAUSE AND THE OLD BOYS JUST GO THROUGH THE MOTIONS.
YES, EVERYONE IS DEAD.
AND WE ARE GOING TO WAKE THE DEAD.
SO GRAB A DRINK AND LET'S CELEBRATE

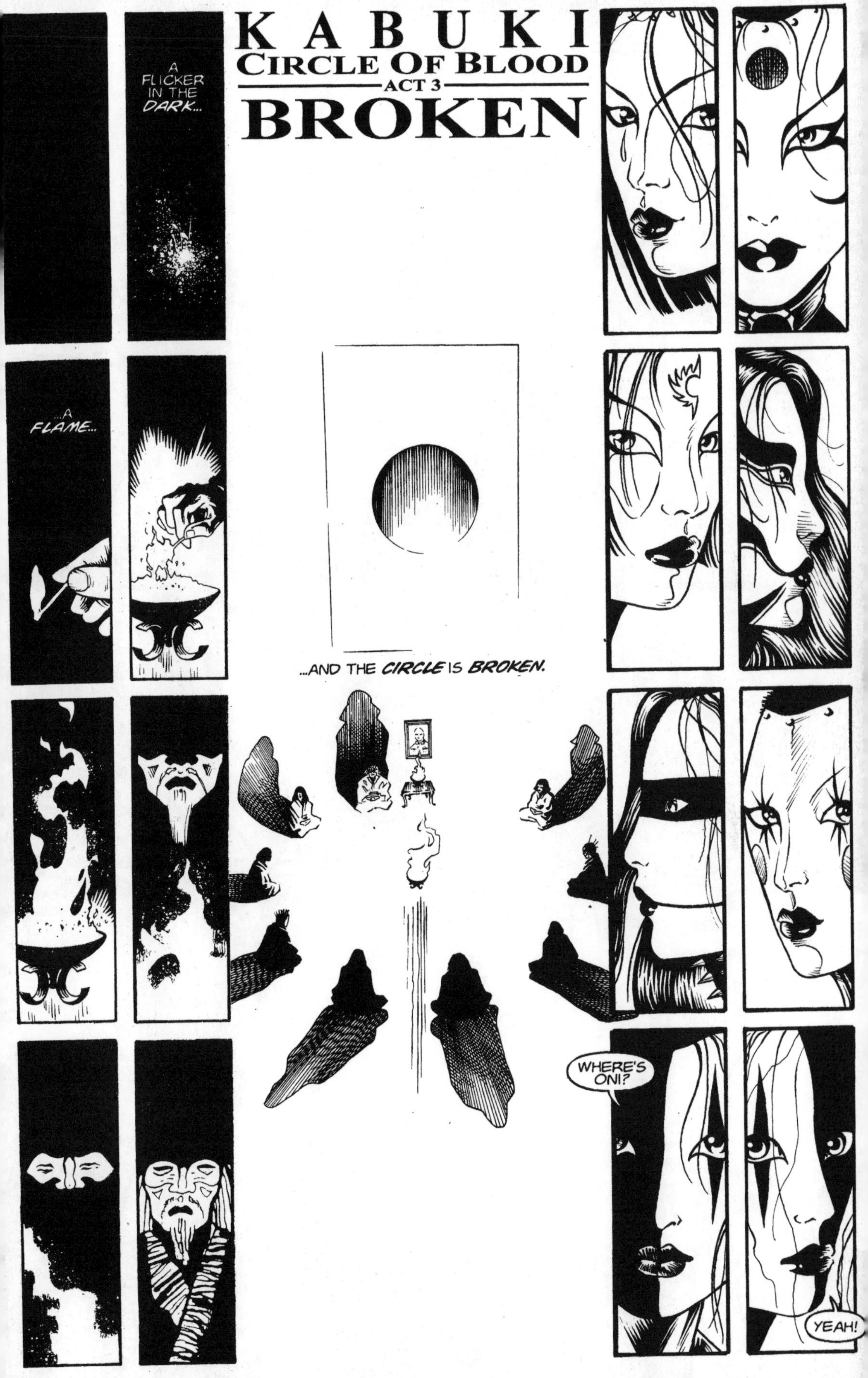
KABUKI
CIRCLE OF BLOOD
ACT 3
BROKEN
A FLICKER IN THE DARK...
...A FLAME...
...AND THE CIRCLE IS BROKEN.
WHERE'S ONI?
YEAH!

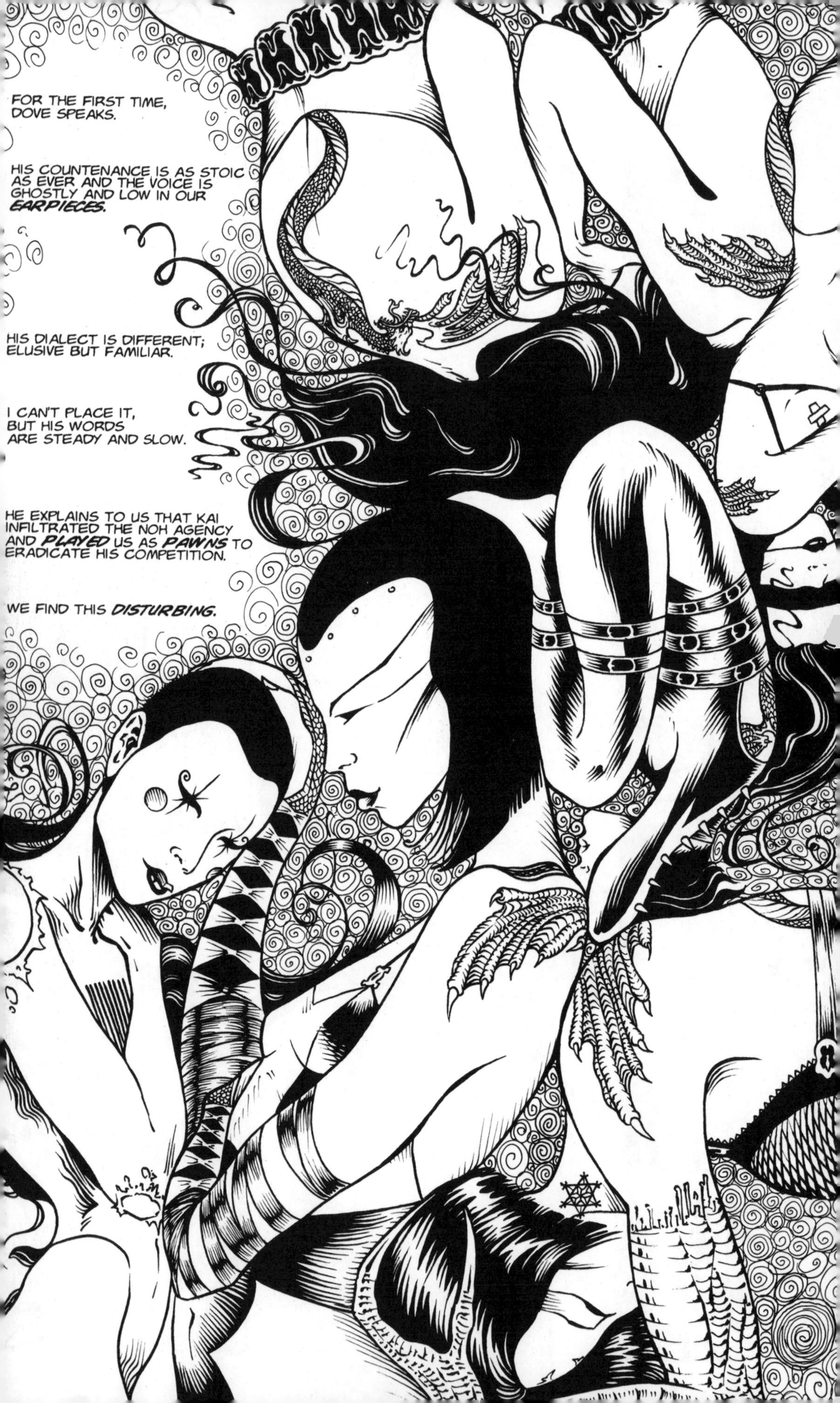
FOR THE FIRST TIME, DOVE SPEAKS.
HIS COUNTENANCE IS AS STOIC AS EVER AND THE VOICE IS GHOSTLY AND LOW IN OUR EARPIECES.
HIS DIALECT IS DIFFERENT; ELUSIVE BUT FAMILIAR.
I CAN'T PLACE IT, BUT HIS WORDS ARE STEADY AND SLOW.
HE EXPLAINS TO US THAT KAI INFILTRATED THE NOH AGENCY AND PLAYED US AS PAWNS TO ERADICATE HIS COMPETITION.
WE FIND THIS DISTURBING.

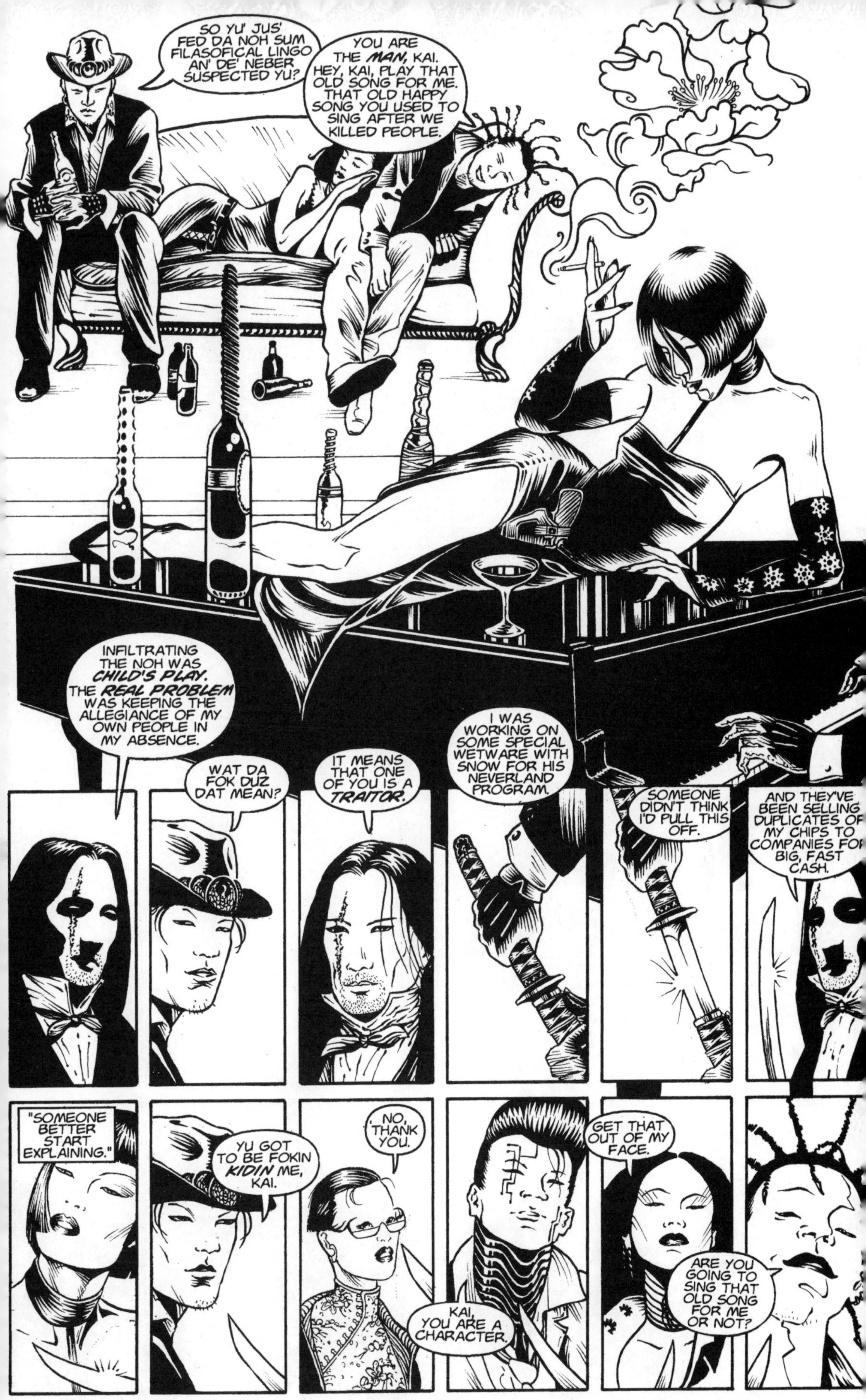

SO YU' JUS' FED DA NOH SUM FILASOFICAL LINGO AN' DE' NEBER SUSPECTED YU?
YOU ARE THE MAN, KAI. HEY, KAI, PLAY THAT OLD SONG FOR ME. THAT OLD HAPPY SONG YOU USED TO SING AFTER WE KILLED PEOPLE.
INFILTRATING THE NOH WAS CHILD'S PLAY. THE REAL PROBLEM WAS KEEPING THE ALLEGIANCE OF MY OWN PEOPLE IN MY ABSENCE.
WAT DA FOK DUZ DAT MEAN?
IT MEANS THAT ONE OF YOU IS A TRAITOR.
I WAS WORKING ON SOME SPECIAL WETWARE WITH SNOW FOR HIS NEVERLAND PROGRAM.
SOMEONE DIDN'T THINK I'D PULL THIS OFF.
AND THEY'VE BEEN SELLING DUPLICATES OF MY CHIPS TO COMPANIES FOR BIG, FAST CASH.
"SOMEONE BETTER START EXPLAINING."
YU GOT TO BE FOKIN KIDIN ME, KAI.
NO, THANK YOU.
KAI, YOU ARE A CHARACTER.
GET THAT OUT OF MY FACE.
ARE YOU GOING TO SING THAT OLD SONG FOR ME OR NOT?

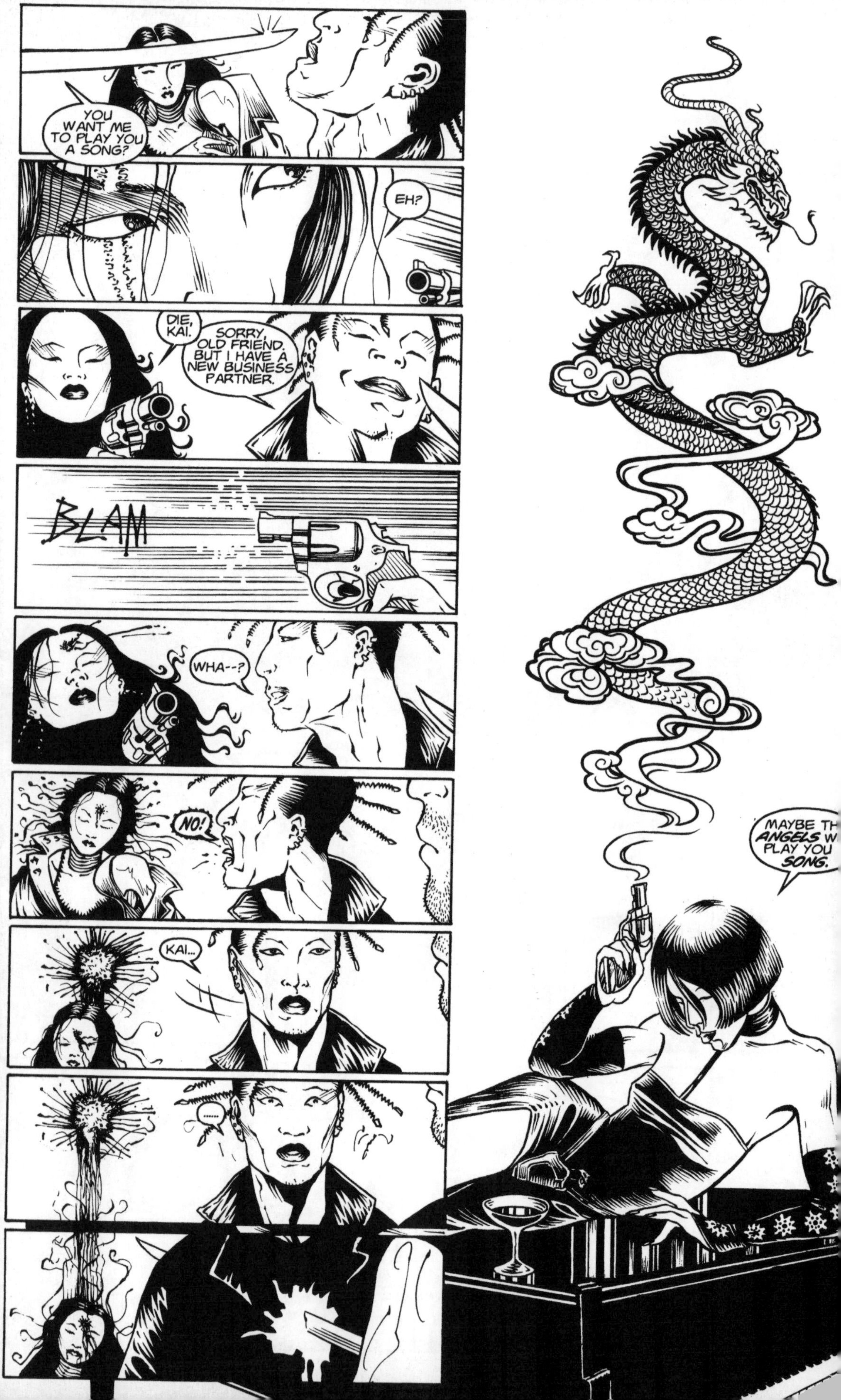

YOU WANT ME TO PLAY YOU A SONG?
EH?
DIE, KAI.
SORRY, OLD FRIEND. BUT I HAVE A NEW BUSINESS PARTNER.
BLAM
WHA--?
NO!
KAI...
......

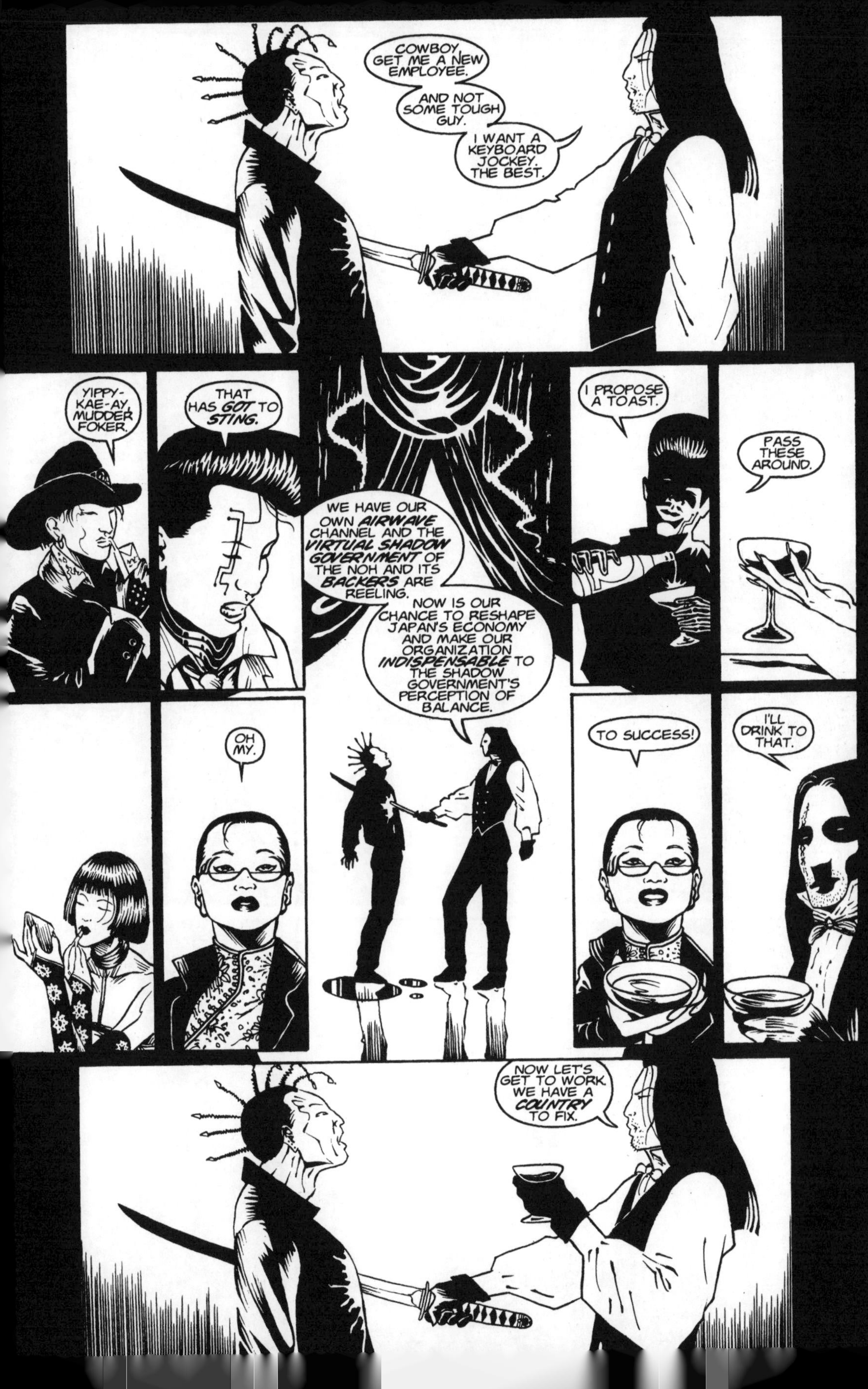
COWBOY, GET ME A NEW EMPLOYEE.
AND NOT SOME TOUGH GUY.
I WANT A KEYBOARD JOCKEY. THE BEST.
YIPPY-KAE-AY, MUDDER FOKER.
THAT HAS GOT TO STING.
WE HAVE OUR OWN AIRWAVE CHANNEL AND THE VIRTUAL SHADOW GOVERNMENT OF THE NOH AND ITS BACKERS ARE REELING.
NOW IS OUR CHANCE TO RESHAPE JAPAN'S ECONOMY AND MAKE OUR ORGANIZATION INDISPENSABLE TO THE SHADOW GOVERNMENT'S PERCEPTION OF BALANCE.
I PROPOSE A TOAST.
PASS THESE AROUND.
OH MY.
TO SUCCESS!
I'LL DRINK TO THAT.
NOW LET'S GET TO WORK. WE HAVE A COUNTRY TO FIX.

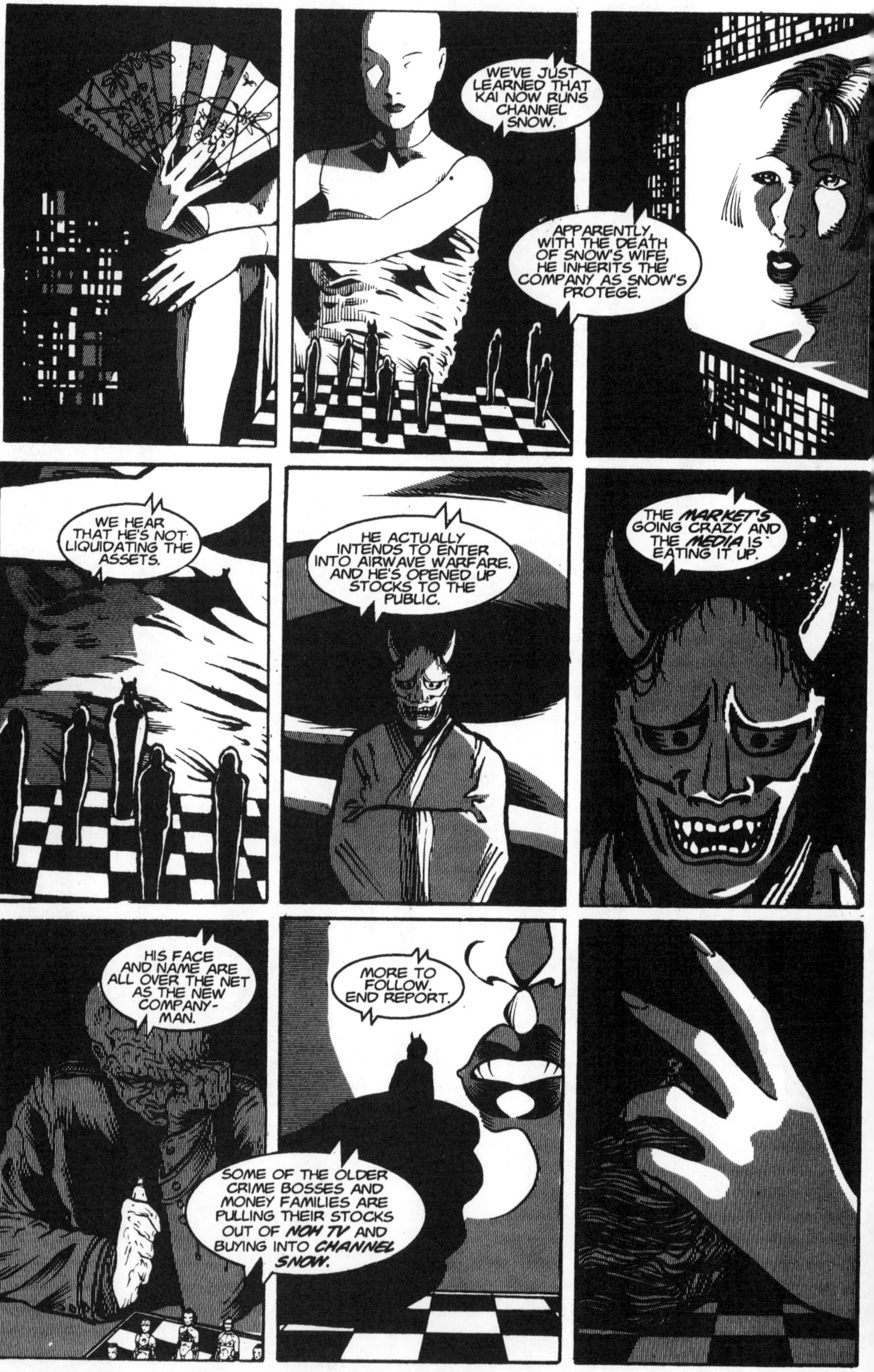
WE'VE JUST LEARNED THAT KAI NOW RUNS CHANNEL SNOW.
APPARENTLY, WITH THE DEATH OF SNOW'S WIFE, HE INHERITS THE COMPANY AS SNOW'S PROTEGE.
WE HEAR THAT HE'S NOT LIQUIDATING THE ASSETS.
HE ACTUALLY INTENDS TO ENTER INTO AIRWAVE WARFARE. AND HE'S OPENED UP STOCKS TO THE PUBLIC.
THE MARKET'S GOING CRAZY AND THE MEDIA IS EATING IT UP.
HIS FACE AND NAME ARE ALL OVER THE NET AS THE NEW COMPANY-MAN.
SOME OF THE OLDER CRIME BOSSES AND MONEY FAMILIES ARE PULLING THEIR STOCKS OUT OF NOH TV AND BUYING INTO CHANNEL SNOW.
MORE TO FOLLOW. END REPORT.

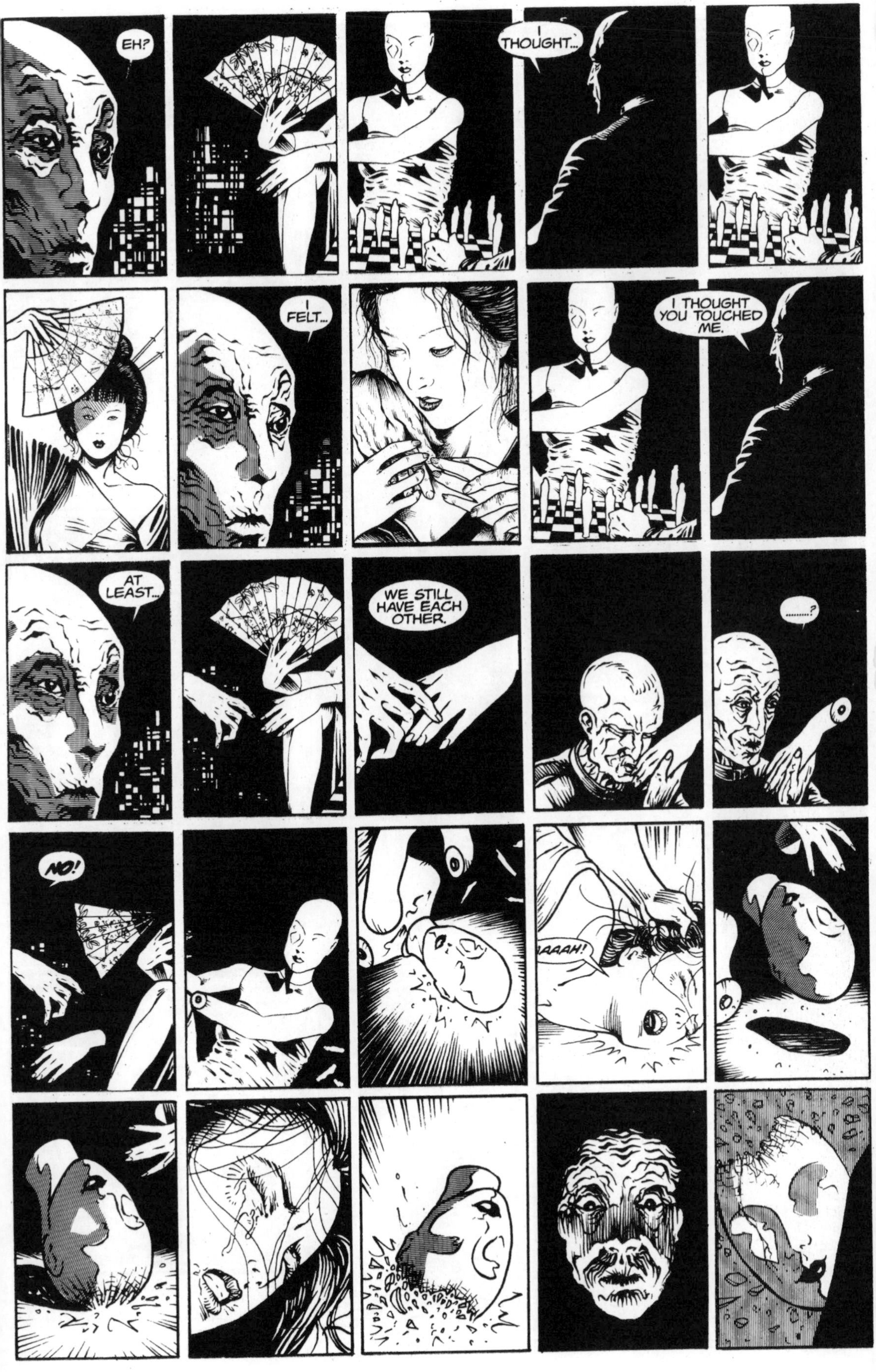
EH?
I THOUGHT...
I FELT...
I THOUGHT YOU TOUCHED ME.
AT LEAST...
WE STILL HAVE EACH OTHER.
.........?
NO!
AAAAH!

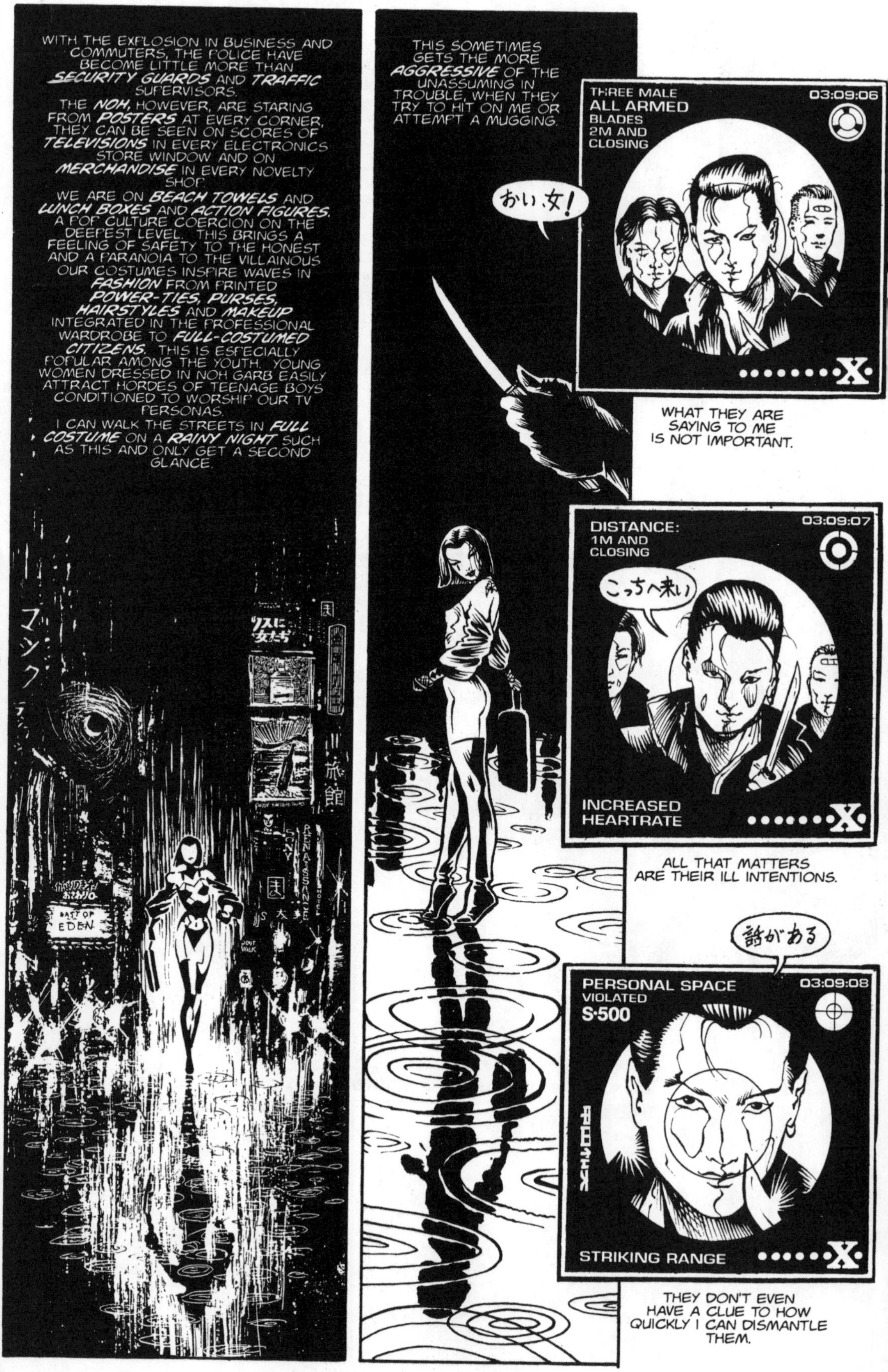

WITH THE EXPLOSION IN BUSINESS AND COMMUTERS, THE POLICE HAVE BECOME LITTLE MORE THAN SECURITY GUARDS AND TRAFFIC SUPERVISORS.
THE NOH, HOWEVER, ARE STARING FROM POSTERS AT EVERY CORNER, THEY CAN BE SEEN ON SCORES OF TELEVISIONS IN EVERY ELECTRONICS STORE WINDOW AND ON MERCHANDISE IN EVERY NOVELTY SHOP.
WE ARE ON BEACH TOWELS AND LUNCH BOXES AND ACTION FIGURES. A POP CULTURE COERCION ON THE DEEPEST LEVEL. THIS BRINGS A FEELING OF SAFETY TO THE HONEST AND A PARANOIA TO THE VILLAINOUS. OUR COSTUMES INSPIRE WAVES IN FASHION FROM PRINTED POWER-TIES, PURSES, HAIRSTYLES AND MAKEUP INTEGRATED IN THE PROFESSIONAL WARDROBE TO FULL-COSTUMED CITIZENS. THIS IS ESPECIALLY POPULAR AMONG THE YOUTH. YOUNG WOMEN DRESSED IN NOH GARB EASILY ATTRACT HORDES OF TEENAGE BOYS CONDITIONED TO WORSHIP OUR TV PERSONAS.
I CAN WALK THE STREETS IN FULL COSTUME ON A RAINY NIGHT SUCH AS THIS AND ONLY GET A SECOND GLANCE.
マック
旅館
SONY
RENAISSANCE HOTEL
EAST OF EDEN
DON'T WALK
THIS SOMETIMES GETS THE MORE AGGRESSIVE OF THE UNASSUMING IN TROUBLE, WHEN THEY TRY TO HIT ON ME OR ATTEMPT A MUGGING.
おい、女!
THREE MALE
ALL ARMED
BLADES
2M AND CLOSING
03:09:06
X
WHAT THEY ARE SAYING TO ME IS NOT IMPORTANT.
DISTANCE:
1M AND CLOSING
03:09:07
こっちへ来い
INCREASED HEARTRATE
X
ALL THAT MATTERS ARE THEIR ILL INTENTIONS.
話がある
PERSONAL SPACE
VIOLATED
S·500
03:09:08
STRIKING RANGE
X
THEY DON'T EVEN HAVE A CLUE TO HOW QUICKLY I CAN DISMANTLE THEM.

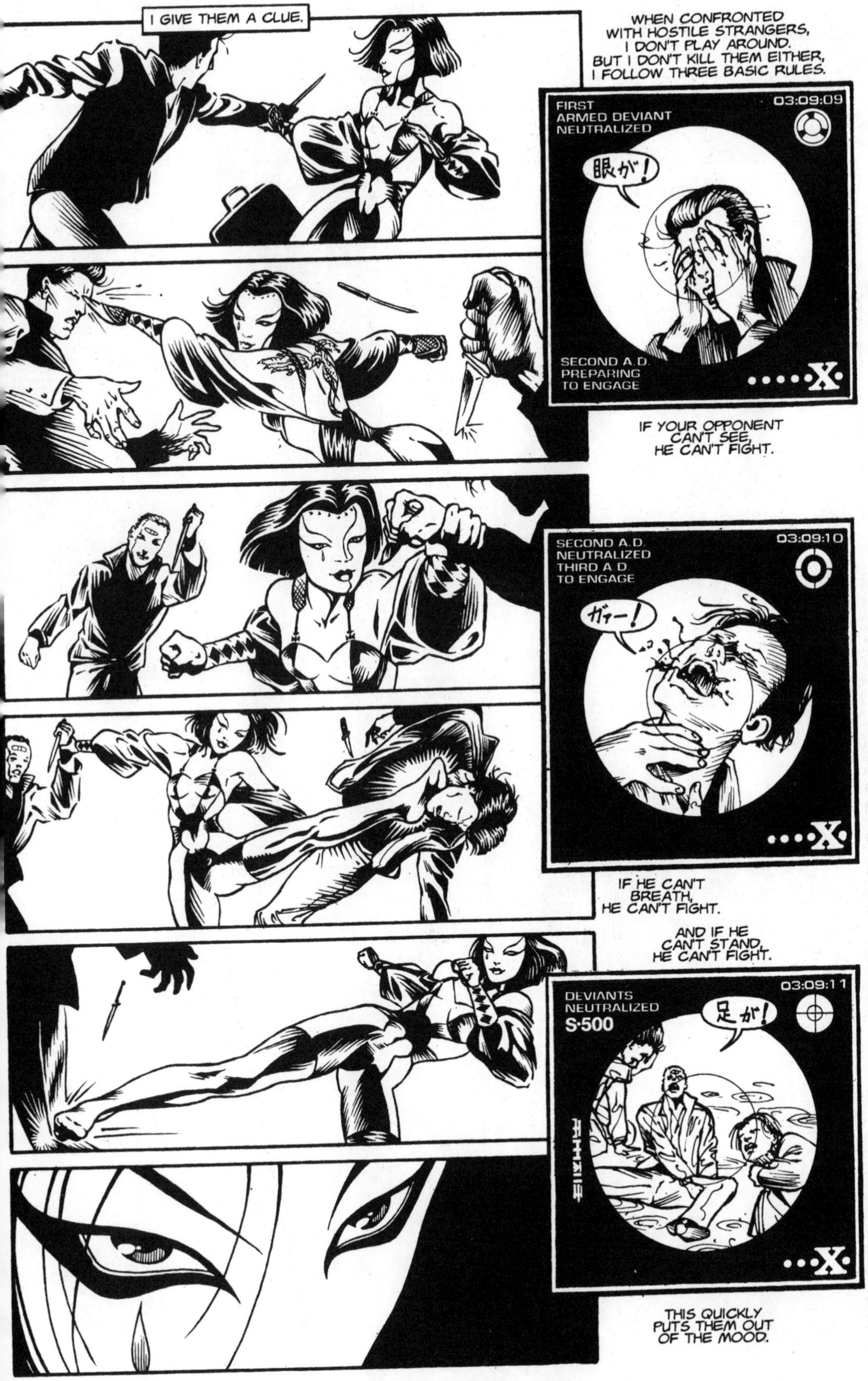

I GIVE THEM A CLUE.
WHEN CONFRONTED WITH HOSTILE STRANGERS, I DON'T PLAY AROUND. BUT I DON'T KILL THEM EITHER, I FOLLOW THREE BASIC RULES.
FIRST ARMED DEVIANT NEUTRALIZED
03:09:09
眼が!
SECOND A.D. PREPARING TO ENGAGE
X
IF YOUR OPPONENT CAN'T SEE, HE CAN'T FIGHT.
SECOND A.D. NEUTRALIZED THIRD A.D. TO ENGAGE
03:09:10
ガァー!
X
IF HE CAN'T BREATH, HE CAN'T FIGHT.
AND IF HE CAN'T STAND, HE CAN'T FIGHT.
DEVIANTS NEUTRALIZED
S·500
03:09:11
足が!
X
THIS QUICKLY PUTS THEM OUT OF THE MOOD.

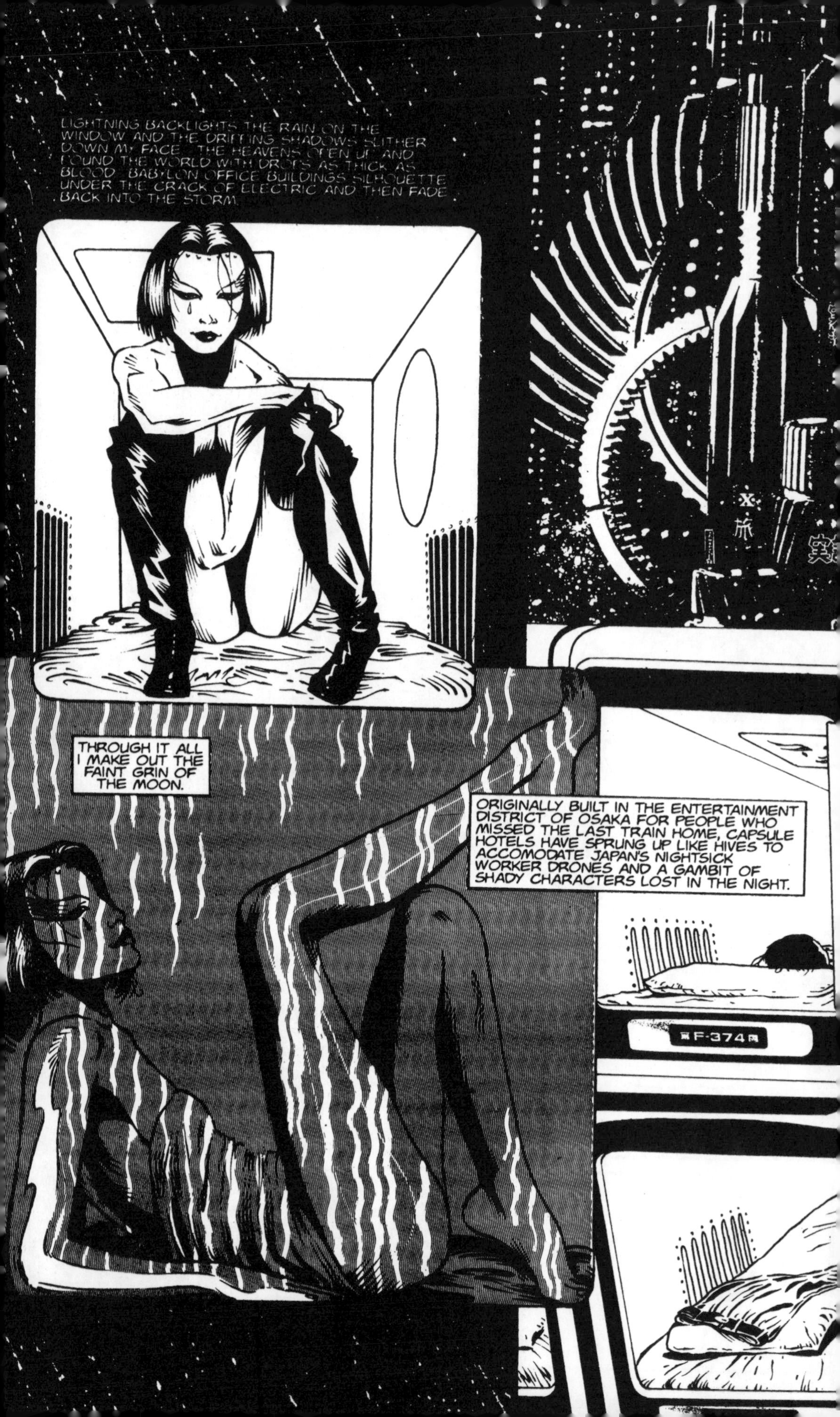
LIGHTNING BACKLIGHTS THE RAIN ON THE WINDOW AND THE DRIFTING SHADOWS SLITHER DOWN MY FACE. THE HEAVENS OPEN UP AND POUND THE WORLD WITH DROPS AS THICK AS BLOOD. BABYLON OFFICE BUILDINGS SILHOUETTE UNDER THE CRACK OF ELECTRIC AND THEN FADE BACK INTO THE STORM.
THROUGH IT ALL I MAKE OUT THE FAINT GRIN OF THE MOON.
ORIGINALLY BUILT IN THE ENTERTAINMENT DISTRICT OF OSAKA FOR PEOPLE WHO MISSED THE LAST TRAIN HOME, CAPSULE HOTELS HAVE SPRUNG UP LIKE HIVES TO ACCOMODATE JAPAN'S NIGHTSICK WORKER DRONES AND A GAMBIT OF SHADY CHARACTERS LOST IN THE NIGHT.
F-374

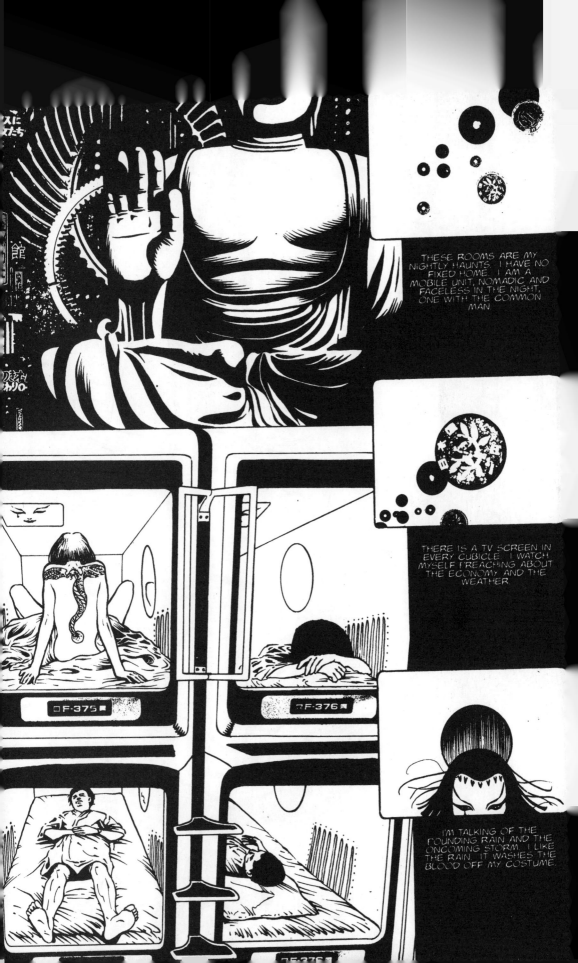

THESE ROOMS ARE MY NIGHTLY HAUNTS. I HAVE NO FIXED HOME. I AM A MOBILE UNIT, NOMADIC AND FACELESS IN THE NIGHT, ONE WITH THE COMMON MAN.

THERE IS A TV SCREEN IN EVERY CUBICLE. I WATCH MYSELF PREACHING ABOUT THE ECONOMY AND THE WEATHER.

I'M TALKING OF THE POUNDING RAIN AND THE ONCOMING STORM. I LIKE THE RAIN. IT WASHES THE BLOOD OFF MY COSTUME.

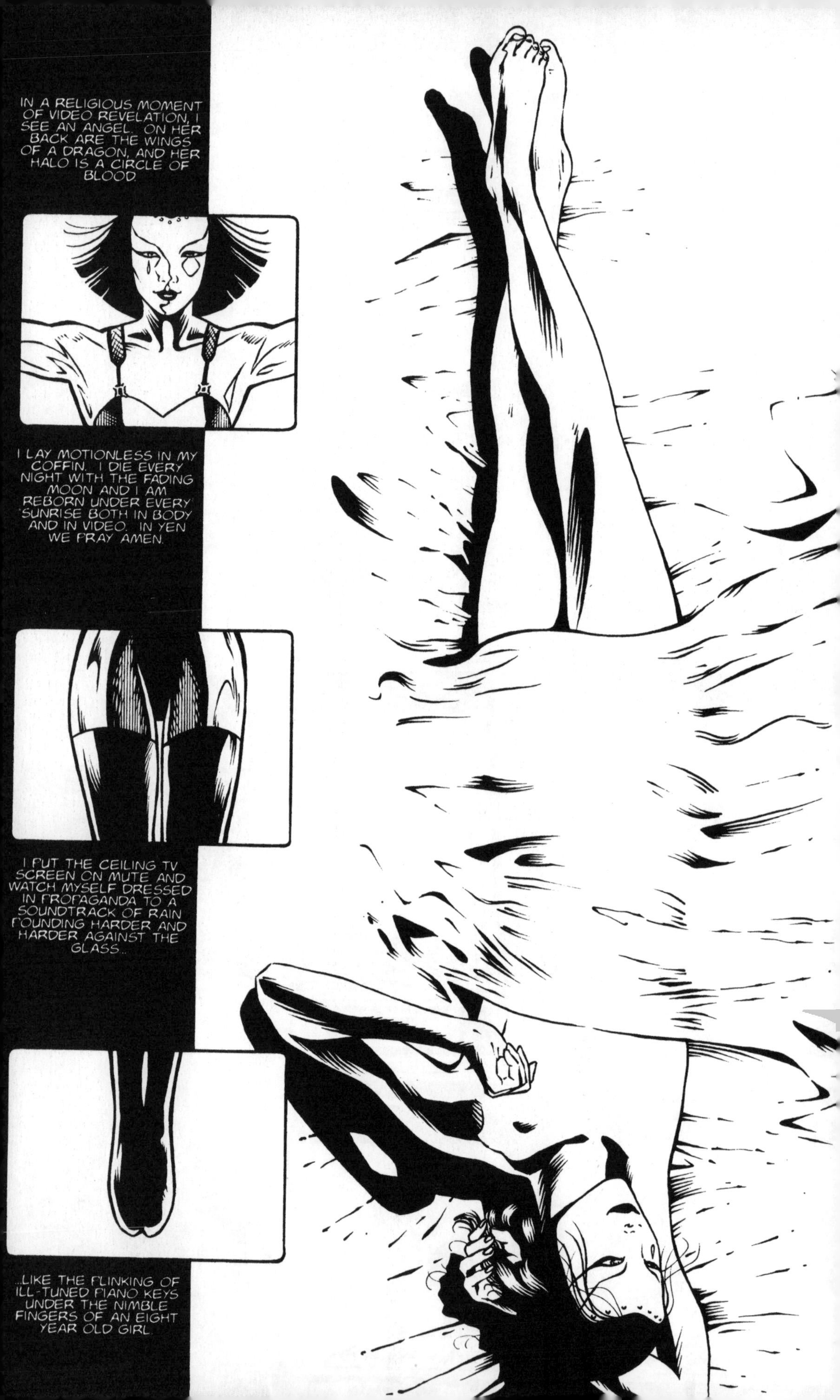
IN A RELIGIOUS MOMENT OF VIDEO REVELATION, I SEE AN ANGEL. ON HER BACK ARE THE WINGS OF A DRAGON, AND HER HALO IS A CIRCLE OF BLOOD.
I LAY MOTIONLESS IN MY COFFIN. I DIE EVERY NIGHT WITH THE FADING MOON AND I AM REBORN UNDER EVERY SUNRISE BOTH IN BODY AND IN VIDEO. IN YEN WE PRAY AMEN.
I PUT THE CEILING TV SCREEN ON MUTE AND WATCH MYSELF DRESSED IN PROPAGANDA TO A SOUNDTRACK OF RAIN POUNDING HARDER AND HARDER AGAINST THE GLASS...
...LIKE THE PLINKING OF ILL-TUNED PIANO KEYS UNDER THE NIMBLE FINGERS OF AN EIGHT YEAR OLD GIRL.

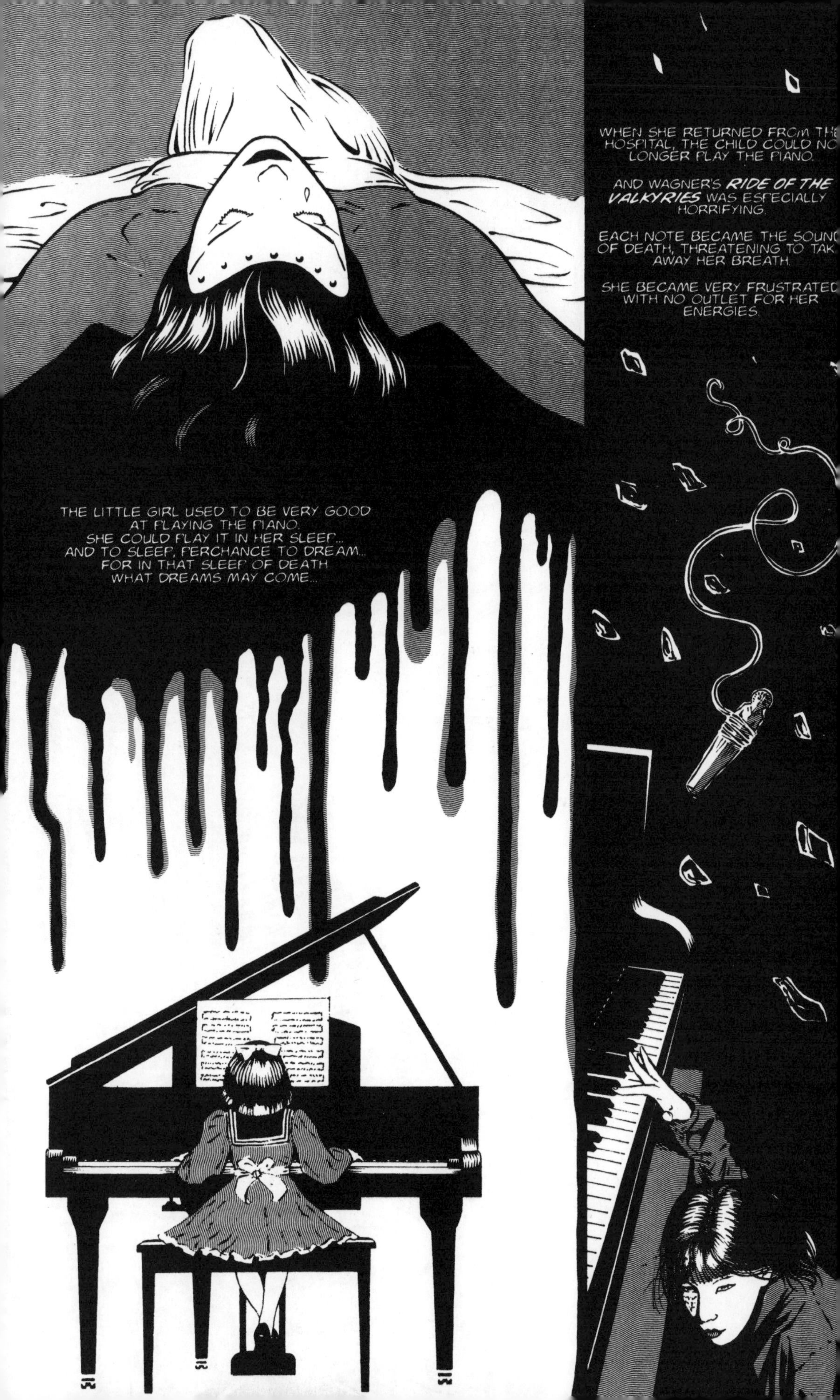
THE LITTLE GIRL USED TO BE VERY GOOD AT PLAYING THE PIANO. SHE COULD PLAY IT IN HER SLEEP... AND TO SLEEP, PERCHANCE TO DREAM... FOR IN THAT SLEEP OF DEATH WHAT DREAMS MAY COME...
WHEN SHE RETURNED FROM THE HOSPITAL, THE CHILD COULD NO LONGER PLAY THE PIANO.
AND WAGNER'S RIDE OF THE VALKYRIES WAS ESPECIALLY HORRIFYING.
EACH NOTE BECAME THE SOUND OF DEATH, THREATENING TO TAKE AWAY HER BREATH.
SHE BECAME VERY FRUSTRATED WITH NO OUTLET FOR HER ENERGIES.

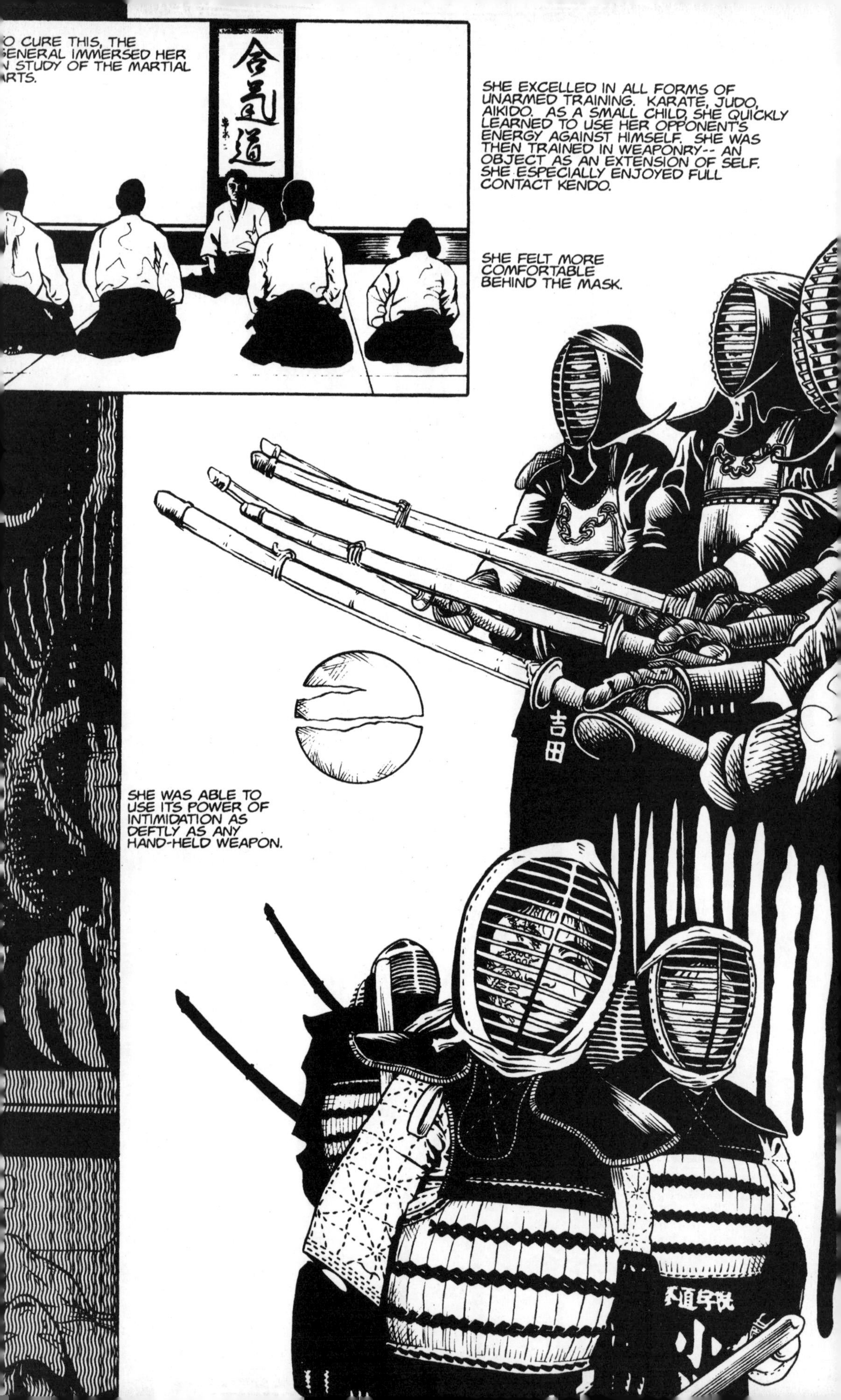
O CURE THIS, THE
ENERAL IMMERSED HER
N STUDY OF THE MARTIAL
RTS.
SHE EXCELLED IN ALL FORMS OF UNARMED TRAINING. KARATE, JUDO, AIKIDO. AS A SMALL CHILD, SHE QUICKLY LEARNED TO USE HER OPPONENT'S ENERGY AGAINST HIMSELF. SHE WAS THEN TRAINED IN WEAPONRY-- AN OBJECT AS AN EXTENSION OF SELF. SHE ESPECIALLY ENJOYED FULL CONTACT KENDO.
SHE FELT MORE COMFORTABLE BEHIND THE MASK.
吉田
SHE WAS ABLE TO USE ITS POWER OF INTIMIDATION AS DEFTLY AS ANY HAND-HELD WEAPON.

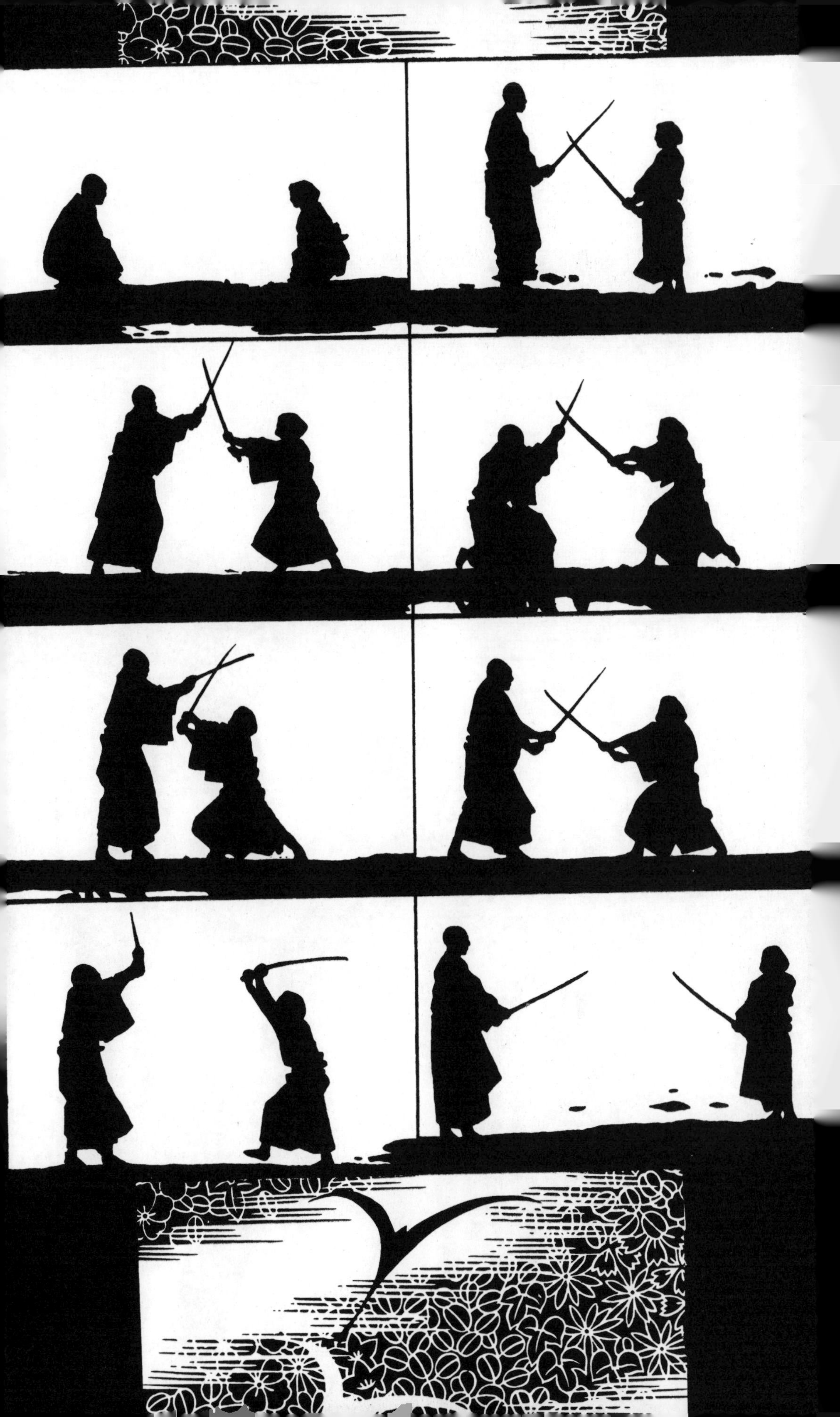

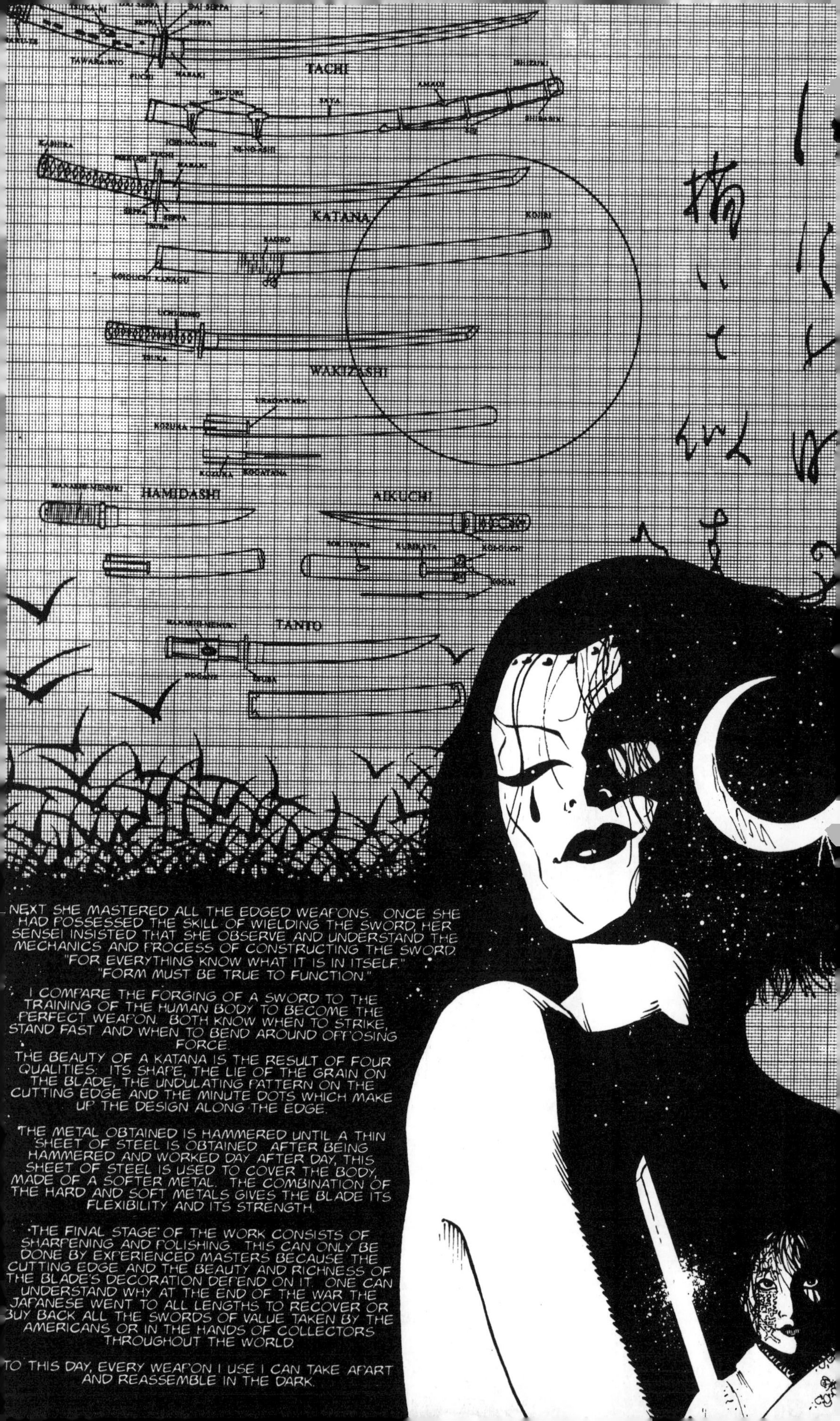
TACHI
KATANA
WAKIZASHI
HAMIDASHI
AIKUCHI
TANTO
NEXT SHE MASTERED ALL THE EDGED WEAPONS. ONCE SHE HAD POSSESSED THE SKILL OF WIELDING THE SWORD, HER SENSEI INSISTED THAT SHE OBSERVE AND UNDERSTAND THE MECHANICS AND PROCESS OF CONSTRUCTING THE SWORD. "FOR EVERYTHING KNOW WHAT IT IS IN ITSELF." "FORM MUST BE TRUE TO FUNCTION."
I COMPARE THE FORGING OF A SWORD TO THE TRAINING OF THE HUMAN BODY TO BECOME THE PERFECT WEAPON. BOTH KNOW WHEN TO STRIKE, STAND FAST AND WHEN TO BEND AROUND OPPOSING FORCE.
THE BEAUTY OF A KATANA IS THE RESULT OF FOUR QUALITIES: ITS SHAPE, THE LIE OF THE GRAIN ON THE BLADE, THE UNDULATING PATTERN ON THE CUTTING EDGE AND THE MINUTE DOTS WHICH MAKE UP THE DESIGN ALONG THE EDGE.
THE METAL OBTAINED IS HAMMERED UNTIL A THIN SHEET OF STEEL IS OBTAINED. AFTER BEING HAMMERED AND WORKED DAY AFTER DAY, THIS SHEET OF STEEL IS USED TO COVER THE BODY, MADE OF A SOFTER METAL. THE COMBINATION OF THE HARD AND SOFT METALS GIVES THE BLADE ITS FLEXIBILITY AND ITS STRENGTH.
THE FINAL STAGE OF THE WORK CONSISTS OF SHARPENING AND POLISHING. THIS CAN ONLY BE DONE BY EXPERIENCED MASTERS BECAUSE THE CUTTING EDGE AND THE BEAUTY AND RICHNESS OF THE BLADE'S DECORATION DEPEND ON IT. ONE CAN UNDERSTAND WHY AT THE END OF THE WAR THE JAPANESE WENT TO ALL LENGTHS TO RECOVER OR BUY BACK ALL THE SWORDS OF VALUE TAKEN BY THE AMERICANS OR IN THE HANDS OF COLLECTORS THROUGHOUT THE WORLD.
TO THIS DAY, EVERY WEAPON I USE I CAN TAKE APART AND REASSEMBLE IN THE DARK.

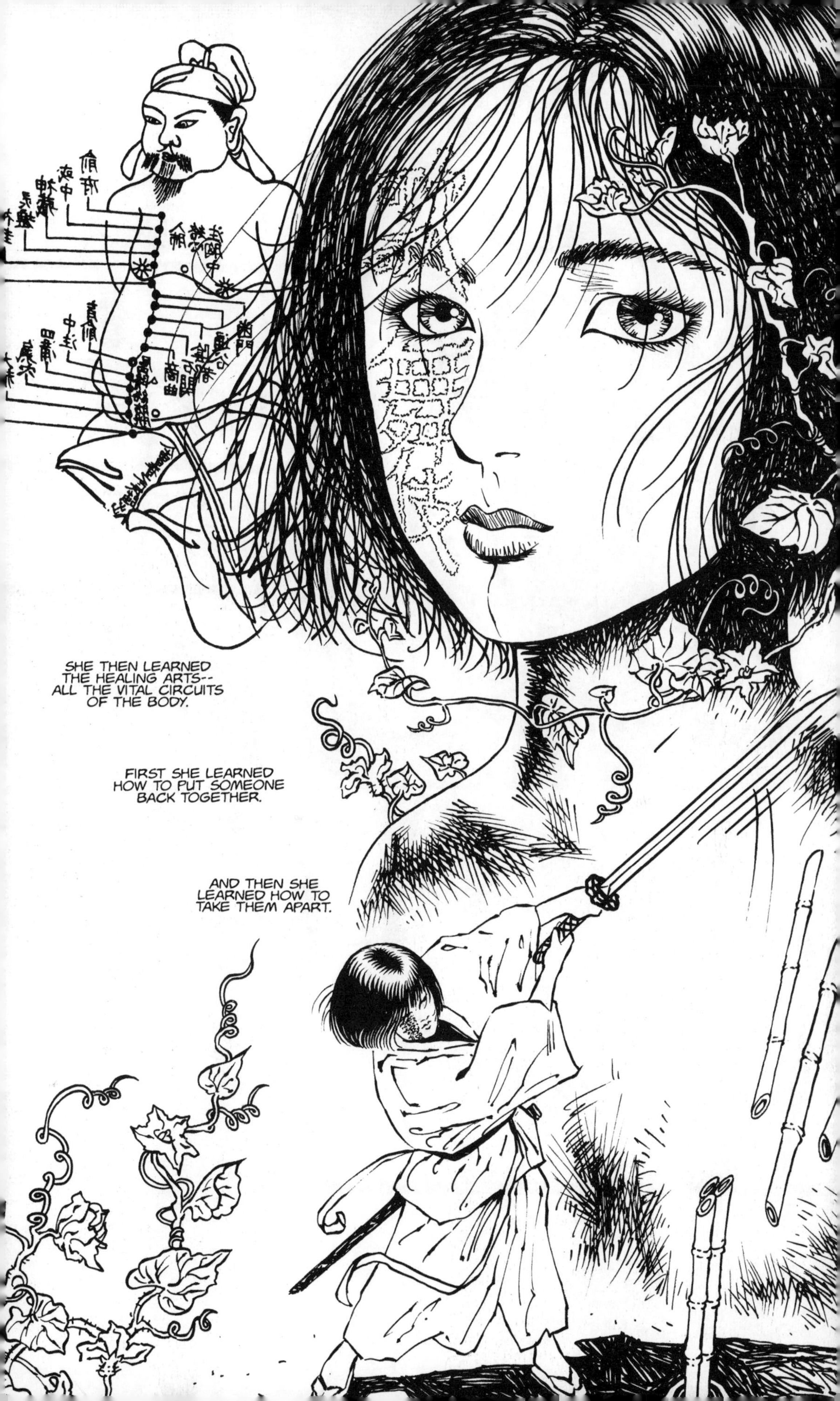
SHE THEN LEARNED THE HEALING ARTS-- ALL THE VITAL CIRCUITS OF THE BODY.
FIRST SHE LEARNED HOW TO PUT SOMEONE BACK TOGETHER.
AND THEN SHE LEARNED HOW TO TAKE THEM APART.

I BECOME A *GODDESS* OF THE *SHURIKEN.*

MY *BREATH* IS THE WHISTLE OF *FALLING STARS.*

I TRAINED MY EYE TO *BE* THE TARGET.

FROM FEATHERED FINS TO THE TIP OF T
HEAD, THE ARROW WAS THE ULTIM
IN HEART-TO-HEART COMMUNICAT
I LEARNED TO REACH OUT AND TO
SOMEONE.

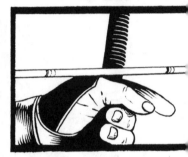

MASTER ANZAWA SAID,
"ONE MUST ALWAYS AIM BEYOND TH
TARGET. ONE MUST AIM A LONG W
OUR WHOLE LIFE, OUR WHOLE SPIR
TRAVELS WITH THE ARROW. AND
WHEN THE ARROW HAS BEEN FIRED
IS NEVER THE END."

THE *SPINE* OF THE *BOW*
BECAME MY *OWN.* WHERE THE NERVES OF MY *FINGERTIPS*
ENDED, THE BOWSTRING CONTINUED, SENDING IMPULSES ACROSS
AN ALMOST NON-EXISTENT FILAMENT OF *CATGUT.*

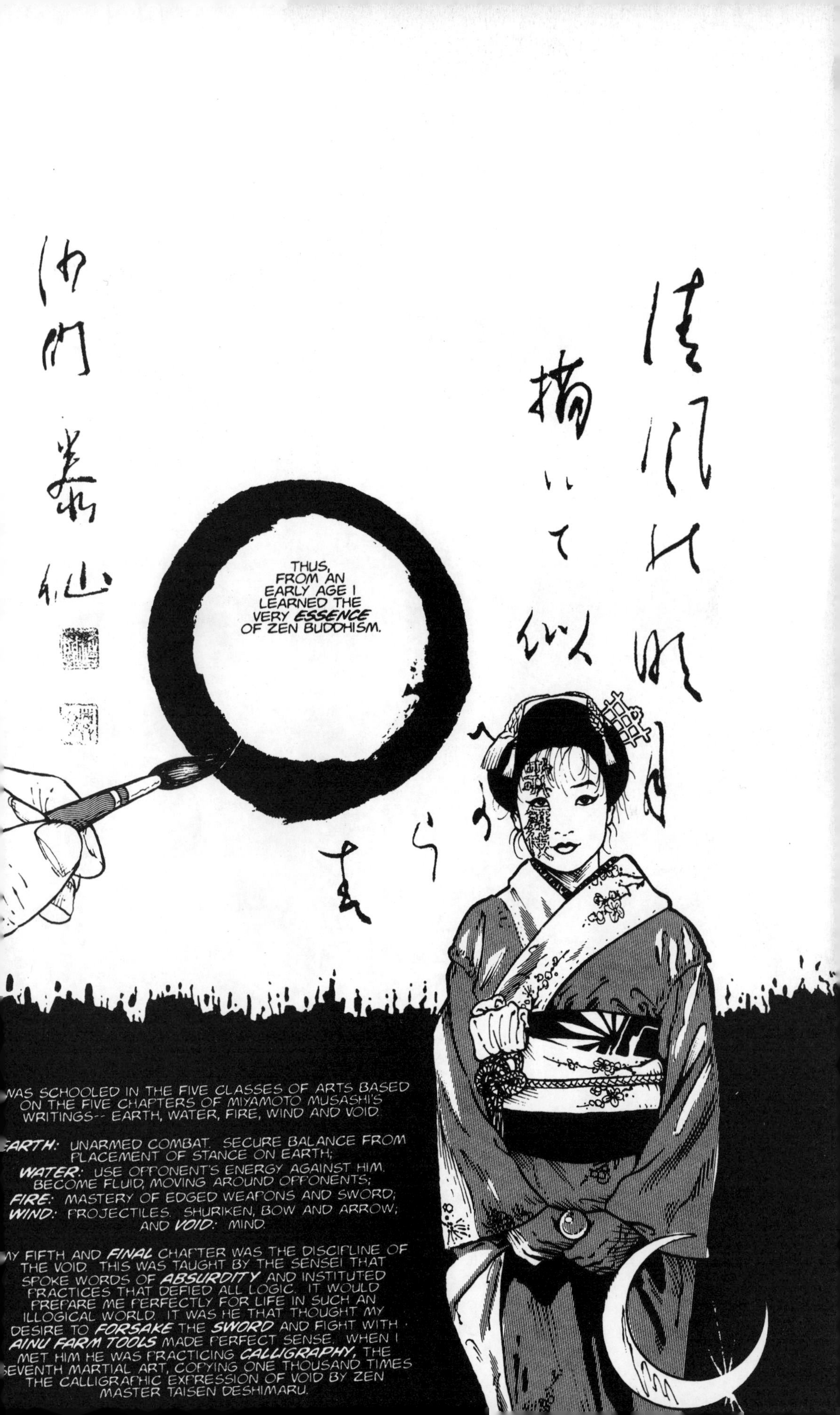

THUS, FROM AN EARLY AGE I LEARNED THE VERY ESSENCE OF ZEN BUDDHISM.
WAS SCHOOLED IN THE FIVE CLASSES OF ARTS BASED ON THE FIVE CHAPTERS OF MIYAMOTO MUSASHI'S WRITINGS-- EARTH, WATER, FIRE, WIND AND VOID.
EARTH: UNARMED COMBAT. SECURE BALANCE FROM PLACEMENT OF STANCE ON EARTH;
WATER: USE OPPONENT'S ENERGY AGAINST HIM. BECOME FLUID, MOVING AROUND OPPONENTS;
FIRE: MASTERY OF EDGED WEAPONS AND SWORD;
WIND: PROJECTILES. SHURIKEN, BOW AND ARROW;
AND VOID: MIND.
MY FIFTH AND FINAL CHAPTER WAS THE DISCIPLINE OF THE VOID. THIS WAS TAUGHT BY THE SENSEI THAT SPOKE WORDS OF ABSURDITY AND INSTITUTED PRACTICES THAT DEFIED ALL LOGIC. IT WOULD PREPARE ME PERFECTLY FOR LIFE IN SUCH AN ILLOGICAL WORLD. IT WAS HE THAT THOUGHT MY DESIRE TO FORSAKE THE SWORD AND FIGHT WITH AINU FARM TOOLS MADE PERFECT SENSE. WHEN I MET HIM HE WAS PRACTICING CALLIGRAPHY, THE SEVENTH MARTIAL ART, COPYING ONE THOUSAND TIMES THE CALLIGRAPHIC EXPRESSION OF VOID BY ZEN MASTER TAISEN DESHIMARU.

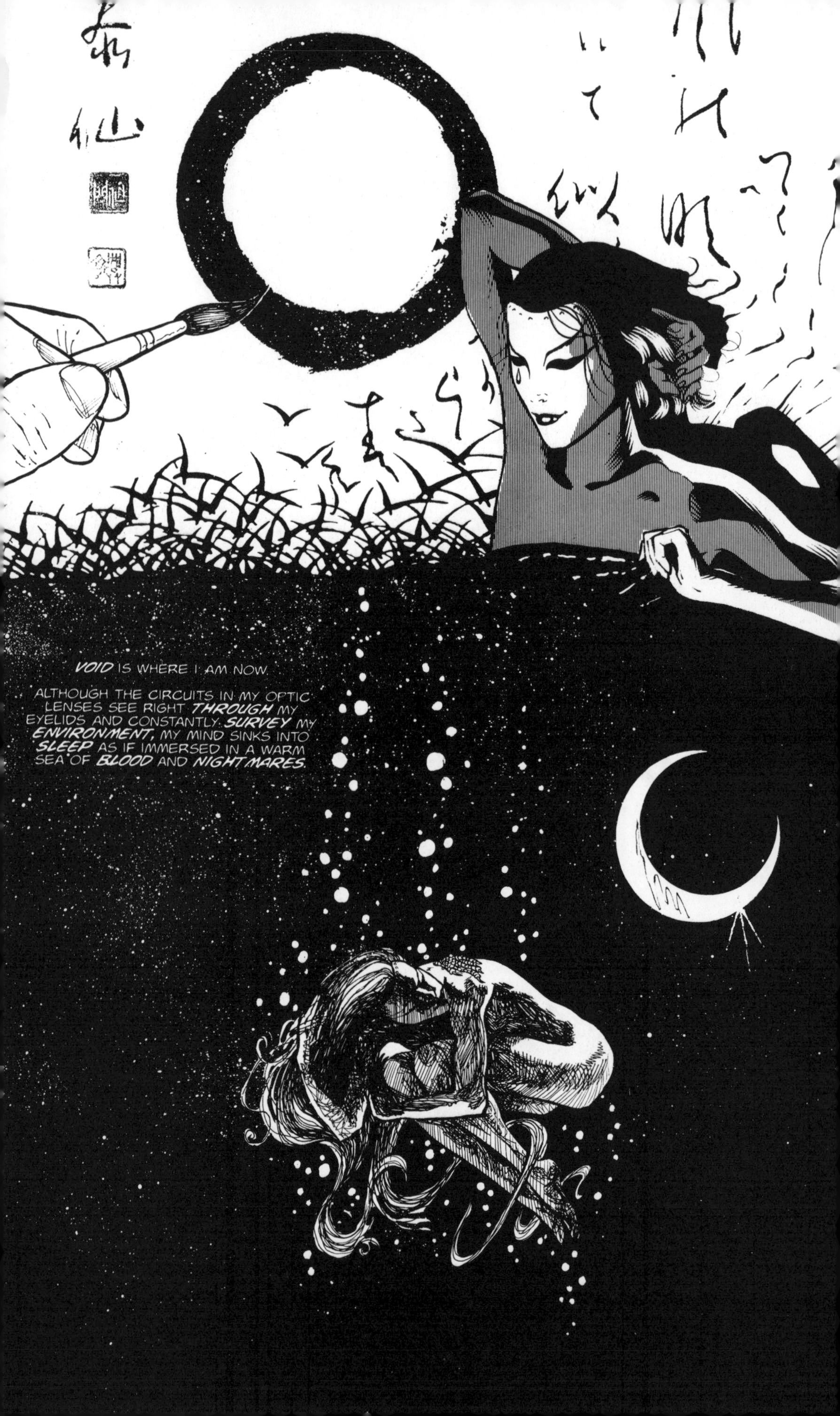
VOID IS WHERE I AM NOW.
ALTHOUGH THE CIRCUITS IN MY OPTIC LENSES SEE RIGHT THROUGH MY EYELIDS AND CONSTANTLY SURVEY MY ENVIRONMENT, MY MIND SINKS INTO SLEEP AS IF IMMERSED IN A WARM SEA OF BLOOD AND NIGHTMARES.

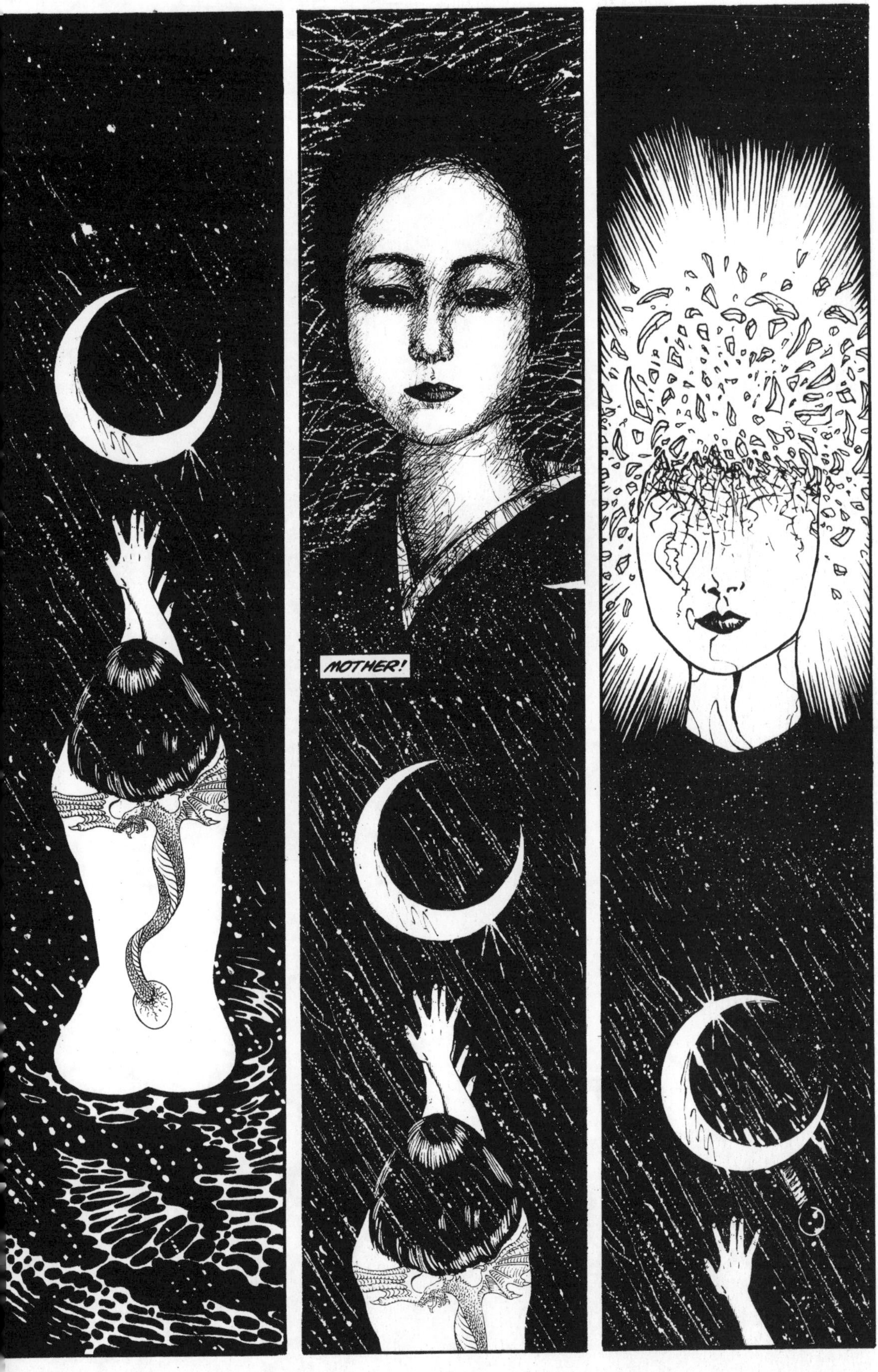
MOTHER!

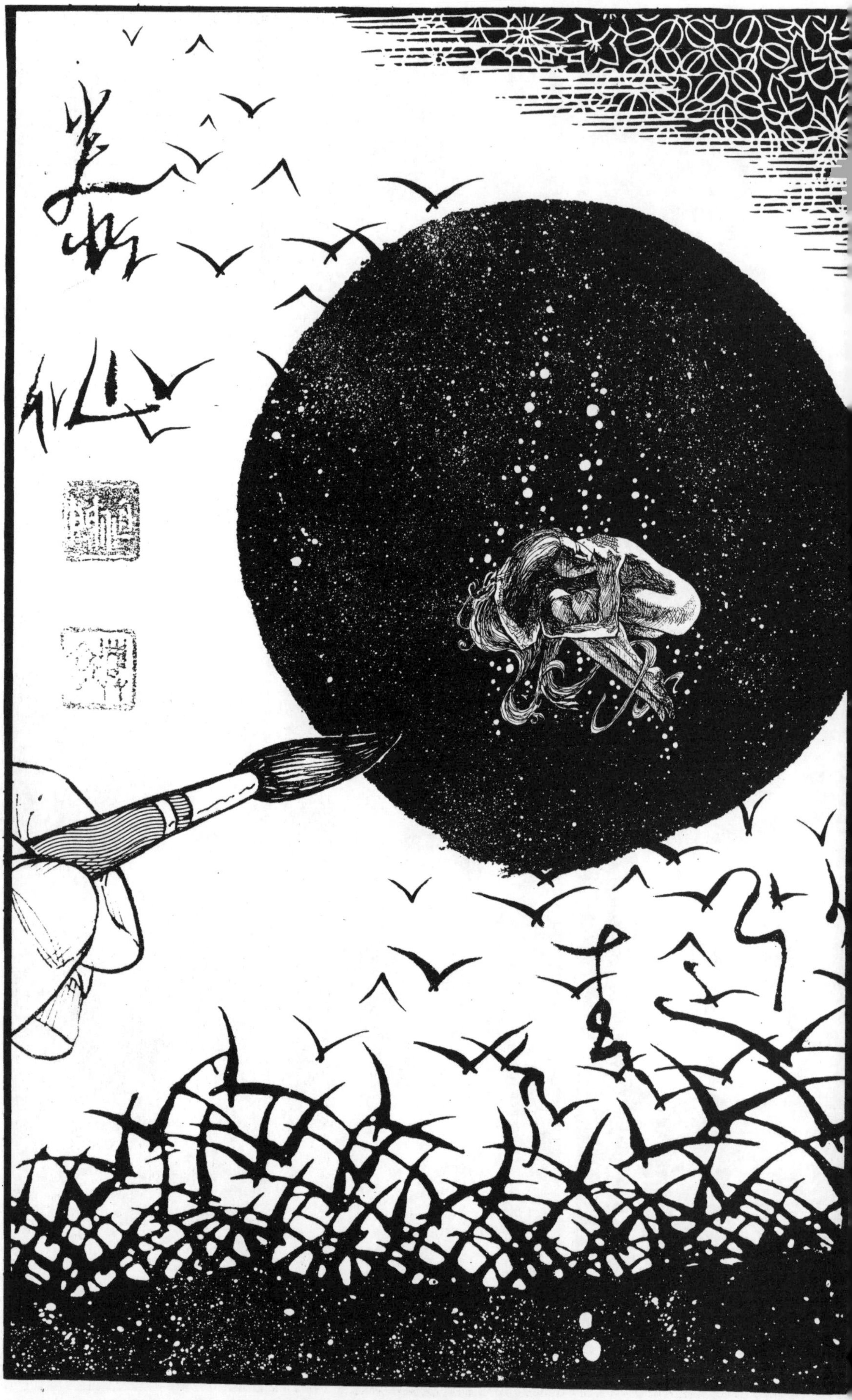

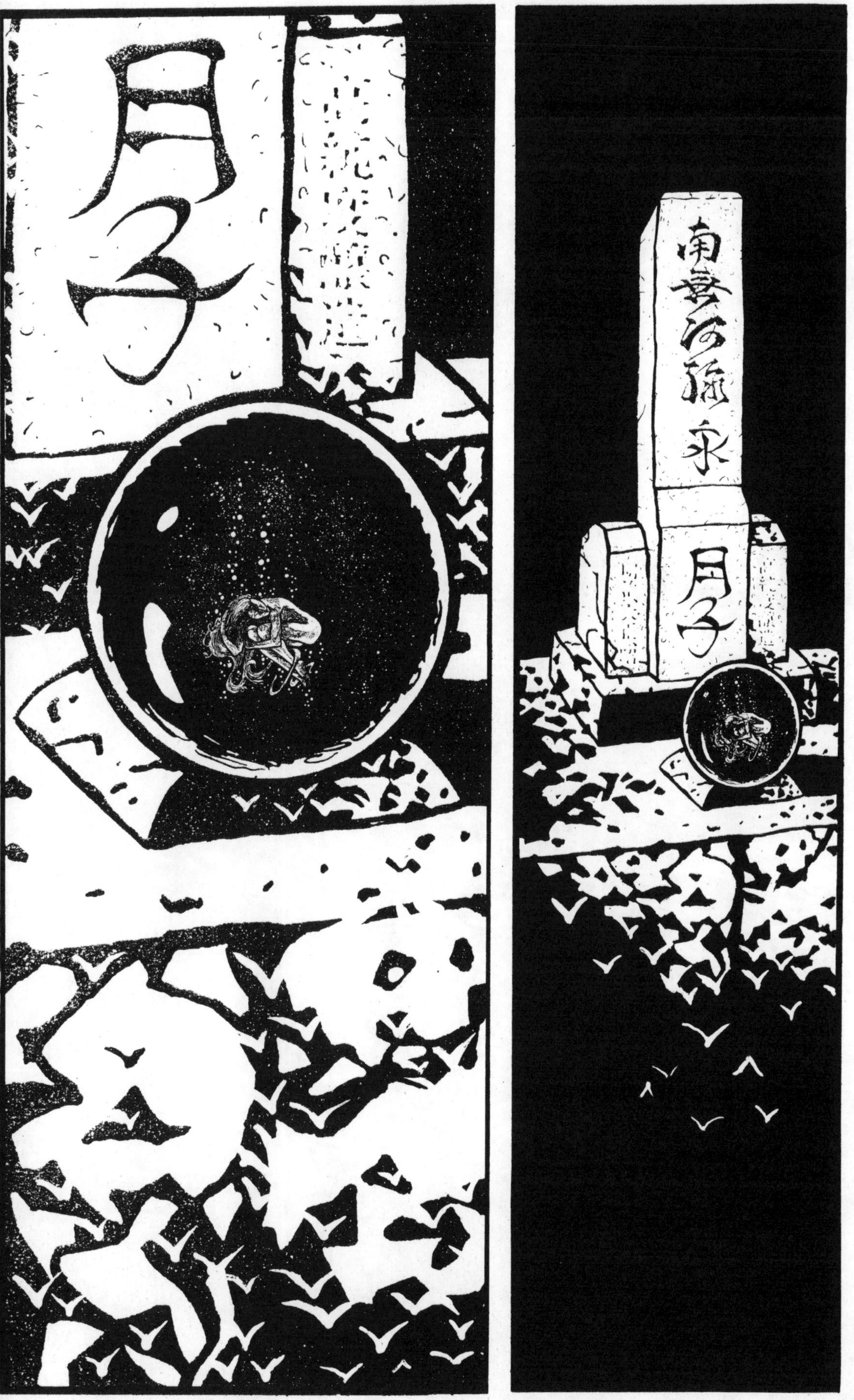
月子

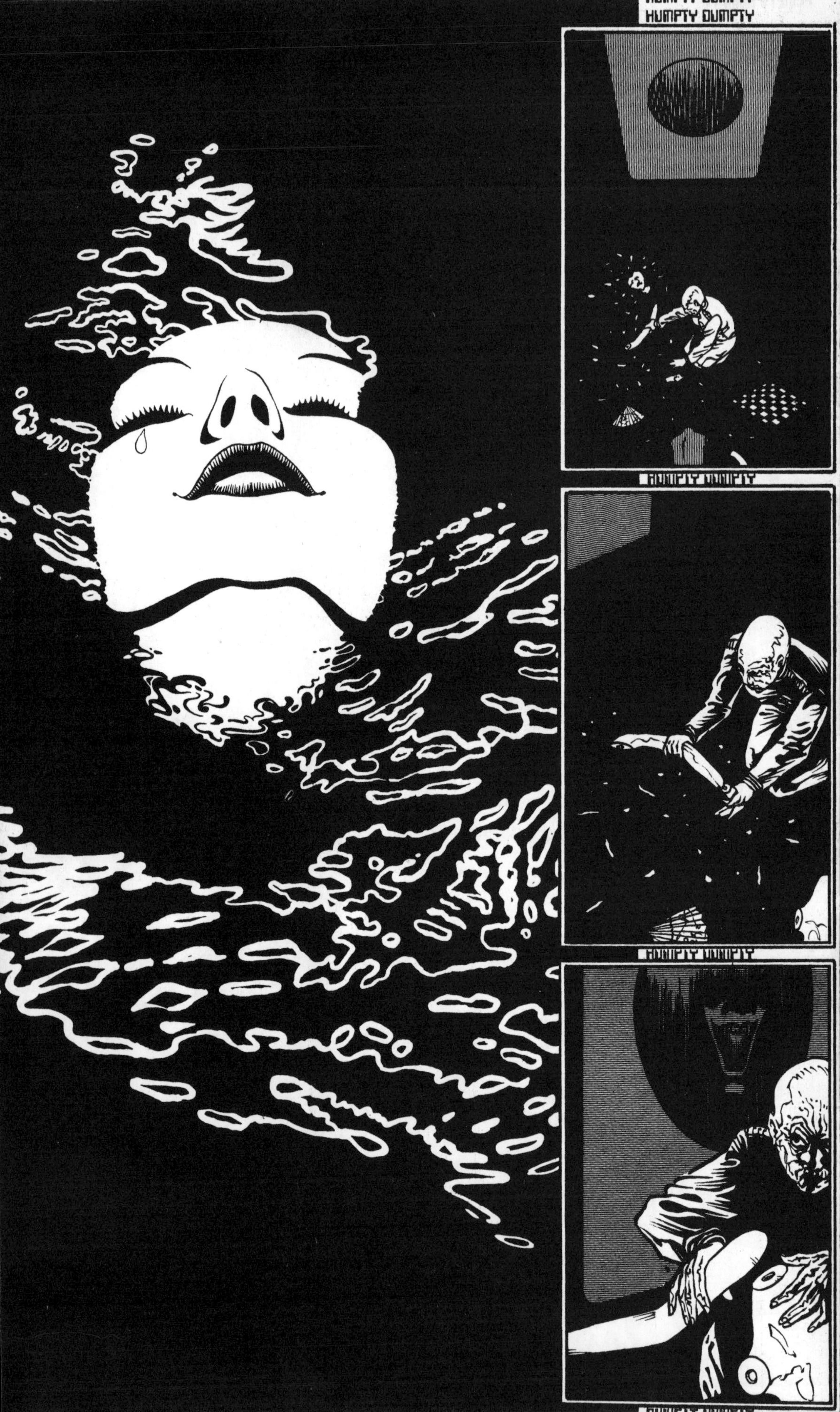
HUMPTY DUMPTY

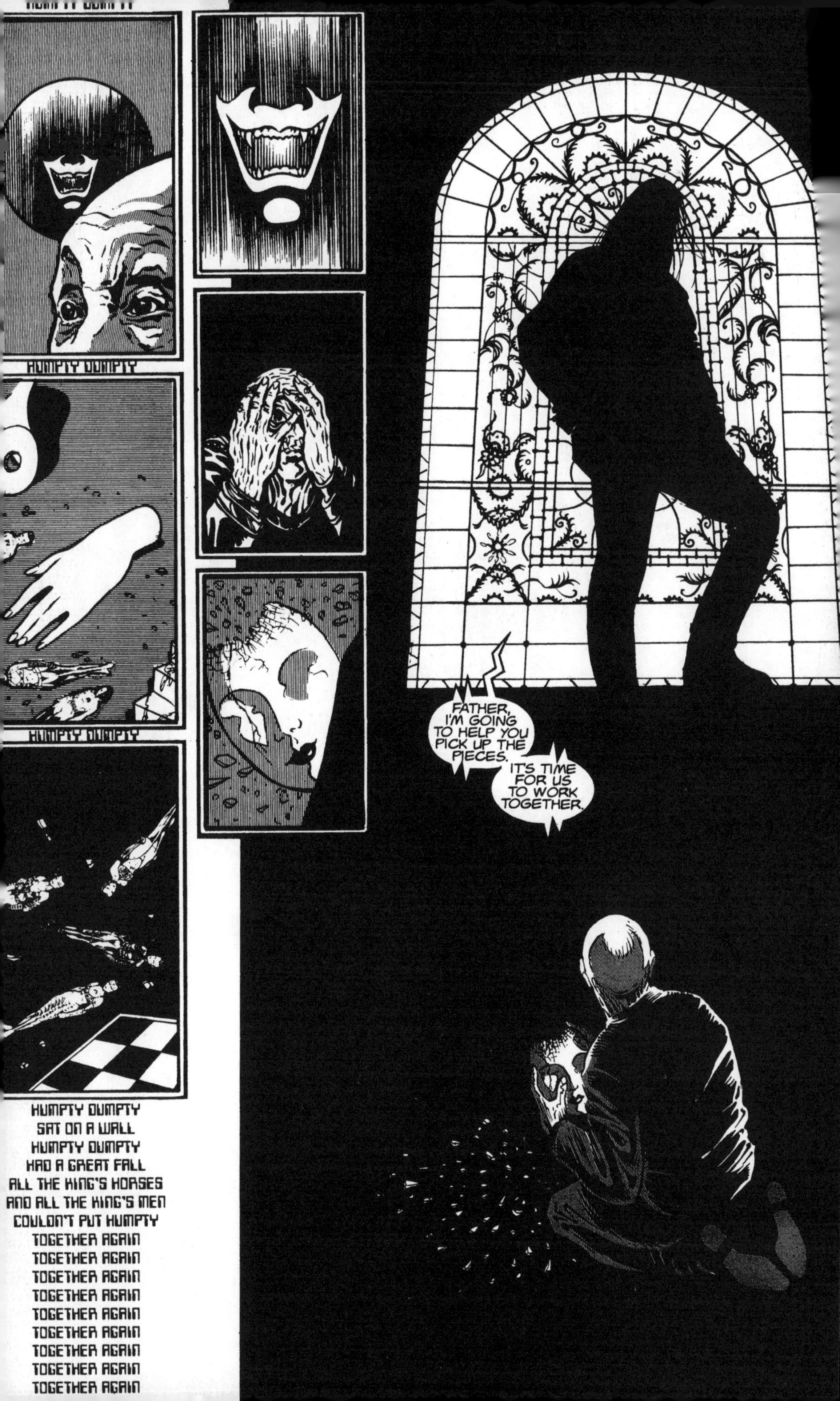

HUMPTY DUMPTY
HUMPTY DUMPTY
FATHER, I'M GOING TO HELP YOU PICK UP THE PIECES.
IT'S TIME FOR US TO WORK TOGETHER.
HUMPTY DUMPTY
SAT ON A WALL
HUMPTY DUMPTY
HAD A GREAT FALL
ALL THE KING'S HORSES
AND ALL THE KING'S MEN
COULDN'T PUT HUMPTY
TOGETHER AGAIN
TOGETHER AGAIN
TOGETHER AGAIN
TOGETHER AGAIN
TOGETHER AGAIN
TOGETHER AGAIN
TOGETHER AGAIN
TOGETHER AGAIN
TOGETHER AGAIN
TOGETHER AGAIN

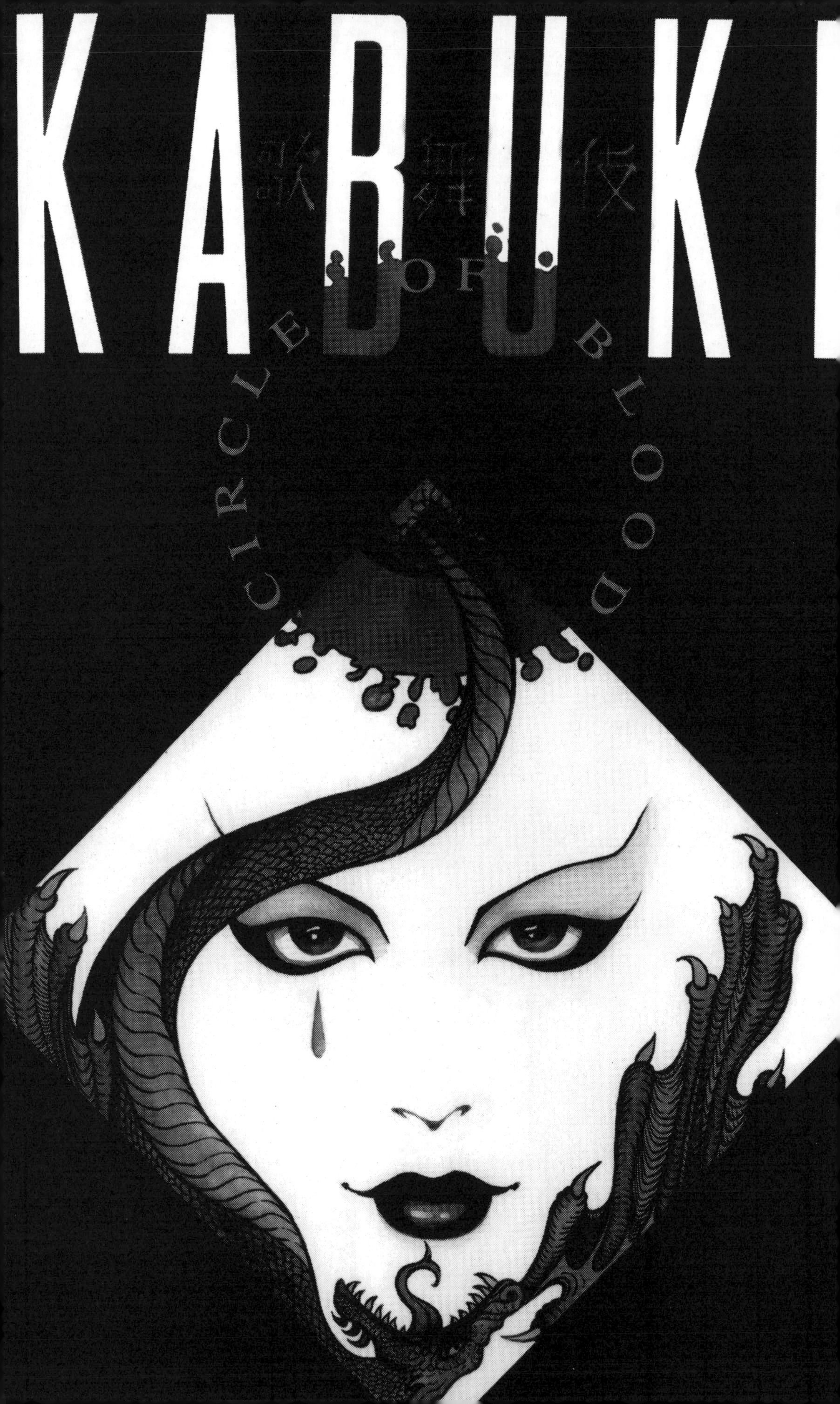
KABUKI
歌舞伎
CIRCLE OF BLOOD

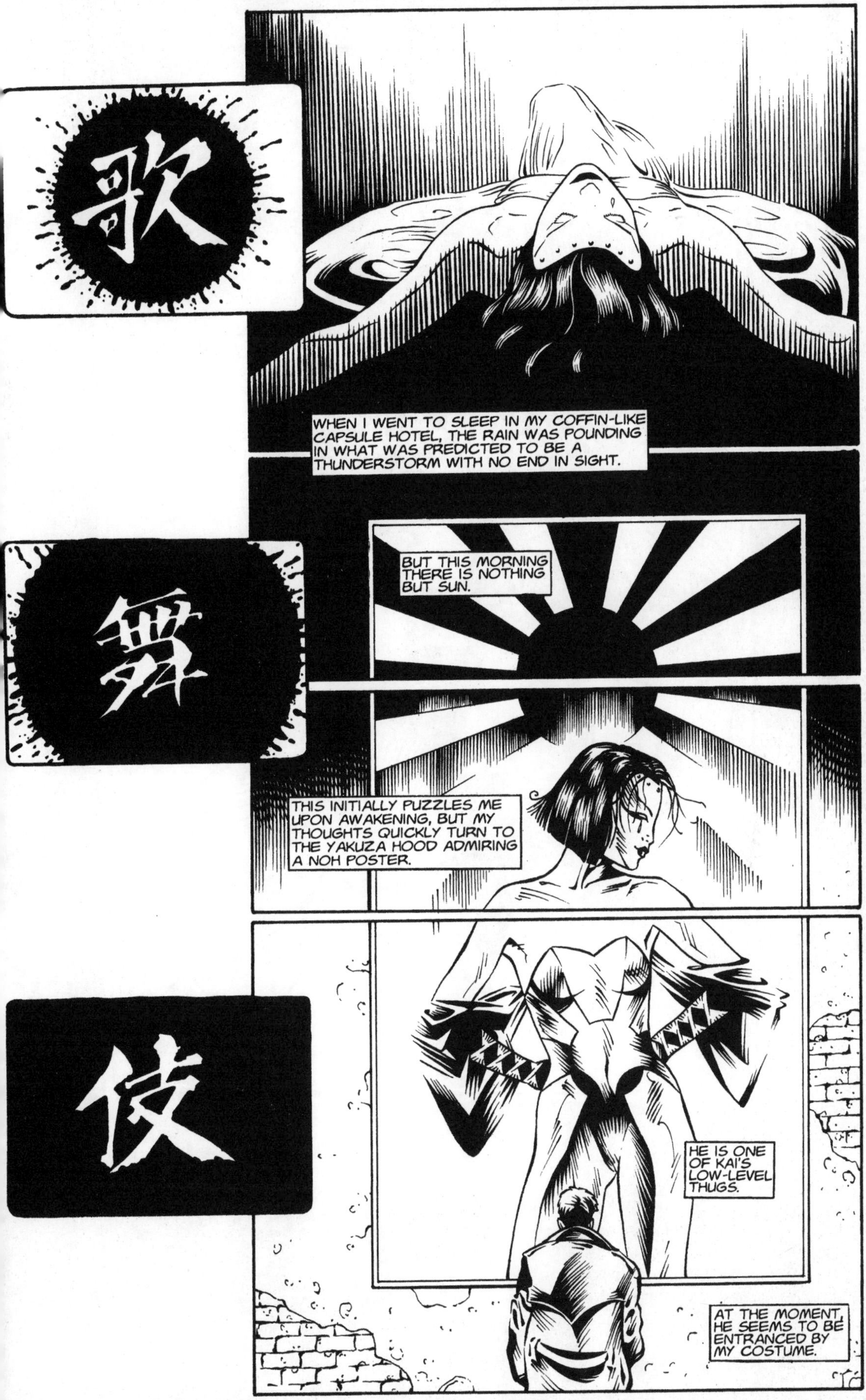

歌
WHEN I WENT TO SLEEP IN MY COFFIN-LIKE CAPSULE HOTEL, THE RAIN WAS POUNDING IN WHAT WAS PREDICTED TO BE A THUNDERSTORM WITH NO END IN SIGHT.
舞
BUT THIS MORNING THERE IS NOTHING BUT SUN.
THIS INITIALLY PUZZLES ME UPON AWAKENING, BUT MY THOUGHTS QUICKLY TURN TO THE YAKUZA HOOD ADMIRING A NOH POSTER.
伎
HE IS ONE OF KAI'S LOW-LEVEL THUGS.
AT THE MOMENT, HE SEEMS TO BE ENTRANCED BY MY COSTUME.

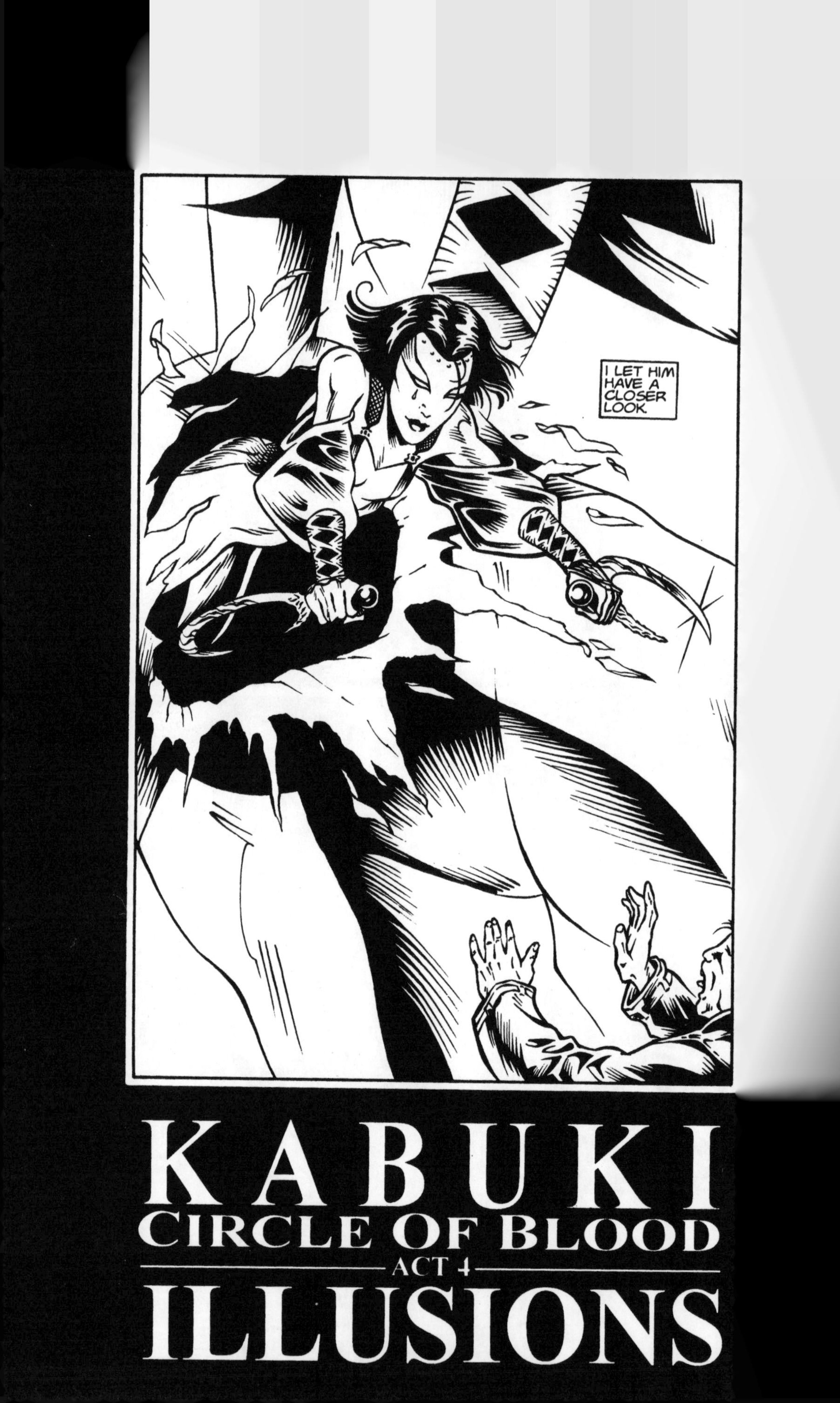
I LET HIM HAVE A CLOSER LOOK.

KABUKI
CIRCLE OF BLOOD
ACT 4
ILLUSIONS

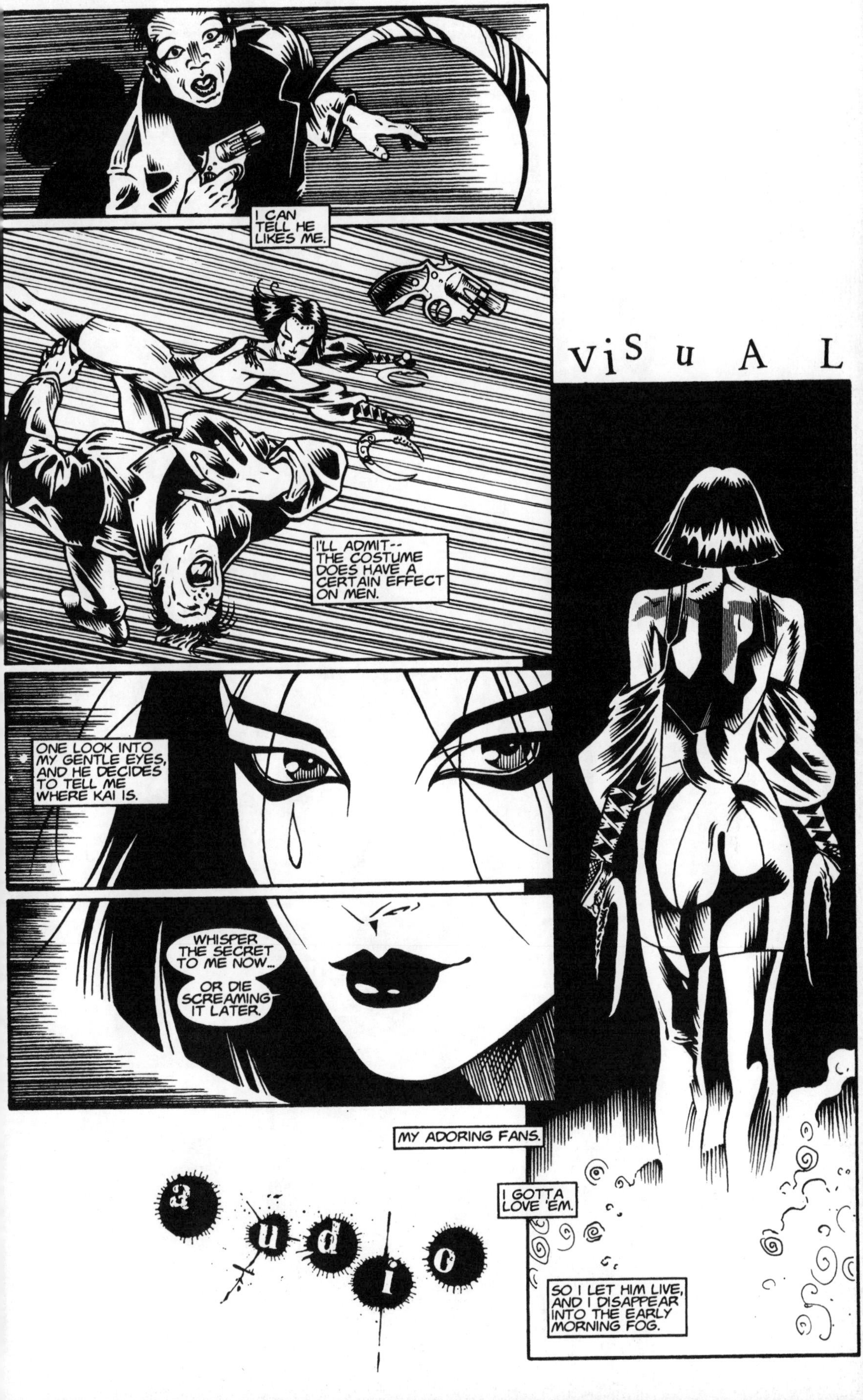
I CAN TELL HE LIKES ME.
I'LL ADMIT-- THE COSTUME DOES HAVE A CERTAIN EFFECT ON MEN.
ViSuAL
ONE LOOK INTO MY GENTLE EYES, AND HE DECIDES TO TELL ME WHERE KAI IS.
WHISPER THE SECRET TO ME NOW...
OR DIE SCREAMING IT LATER.
MY ADORING FANS.
audio
I GOTTA LOVE 'EM.
SO I LET HIM LIVE, AND I DISAPPEAR INTO THE EARLY MORNING FOG.

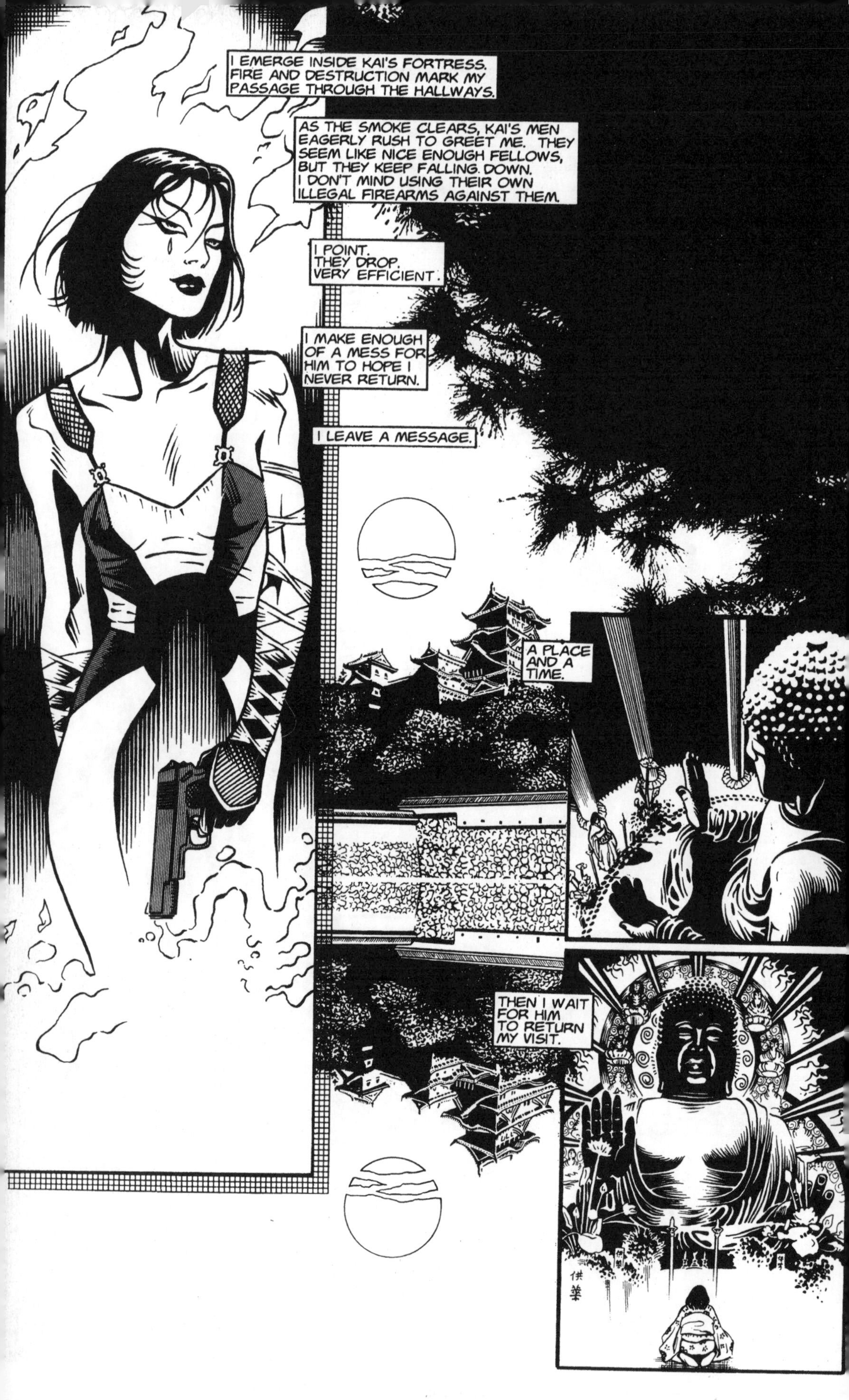
I EMERGE INSIDE KAI'S FORTRESS. FIRE AND DESTRUCTION MARK MY PASSAGE THROUGH THE HALLWAYS.
AS THE SMOKE CLEARS, KAI'S MEN EAGERLY RUSH TO GREET ME. THEY SEEM LIKE NICE ENOUGH FELLOWS, BUT THEY KEEP FALLING DOWN. I DON'T MIND USING THEIR OWN ILLEGAL FIREARMS AGAINST THEM.
I POINT. THEY DROP. VERY EFFICIENT.
I MAKE ENOUGH OF A MESS FOR HIM TO HOPE I NEVER RETURN.
I LEAVE A MESSAGE.
A PLACE AND A TIME.
THEN I WAIT FOR HIM TO RETURN MY VISIT.

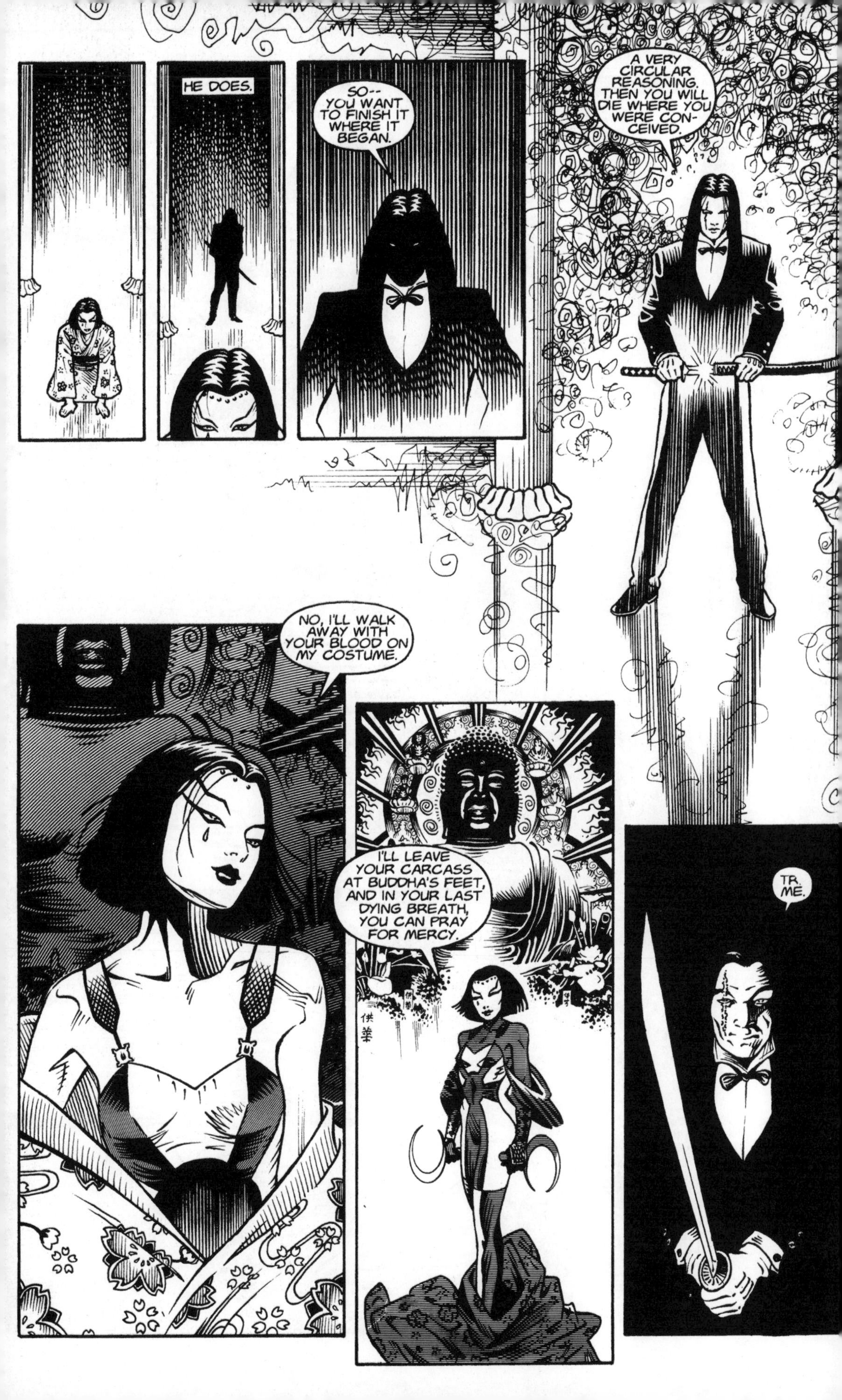
HE DOES.
SO-- YOU WANT TO FINISH IT WHERE IT BEGAN.
A VERY CIRCULAR REASONING. THEN YOU WILL DIE WHERE YOU WERE CON-CEIVED.
NO, I'LL WALK AWAY WITH YOUR BLOOD ON MY COSTUME.
I'LL LEAVE YOUR CARCASS AT BUDDHA'S FEET, AND IN YOUR LAST DYING BREATH, YOU CAN PRAY FOR MERCY.
TRY ME.

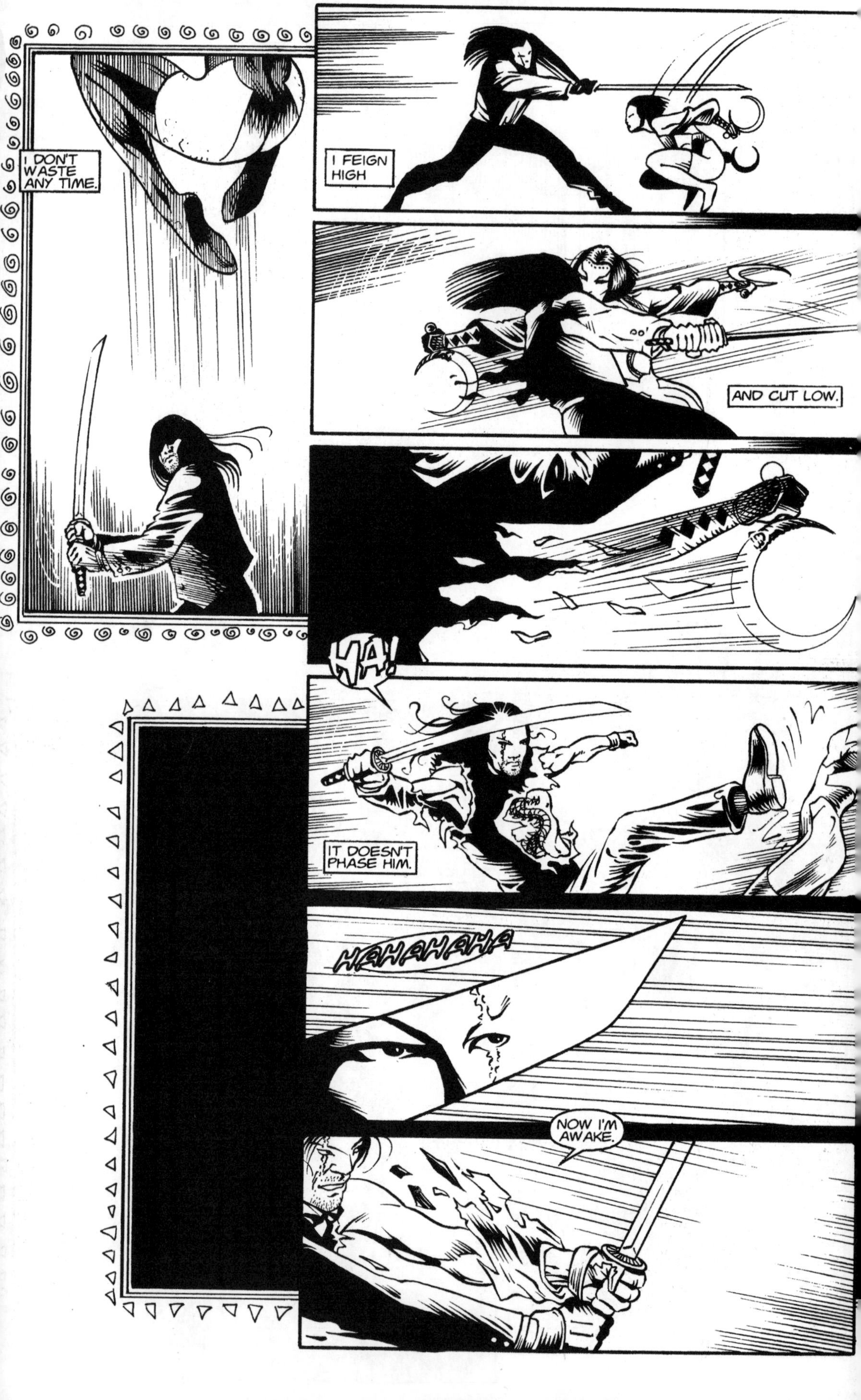

I DON'T WASTE ANY TIME.
I FEIGN HIGH
AND CUT LOW.
HA!
IT DOESN'T PHASE HIM.
HAHAHAHA
NOW I'M AWAKE.

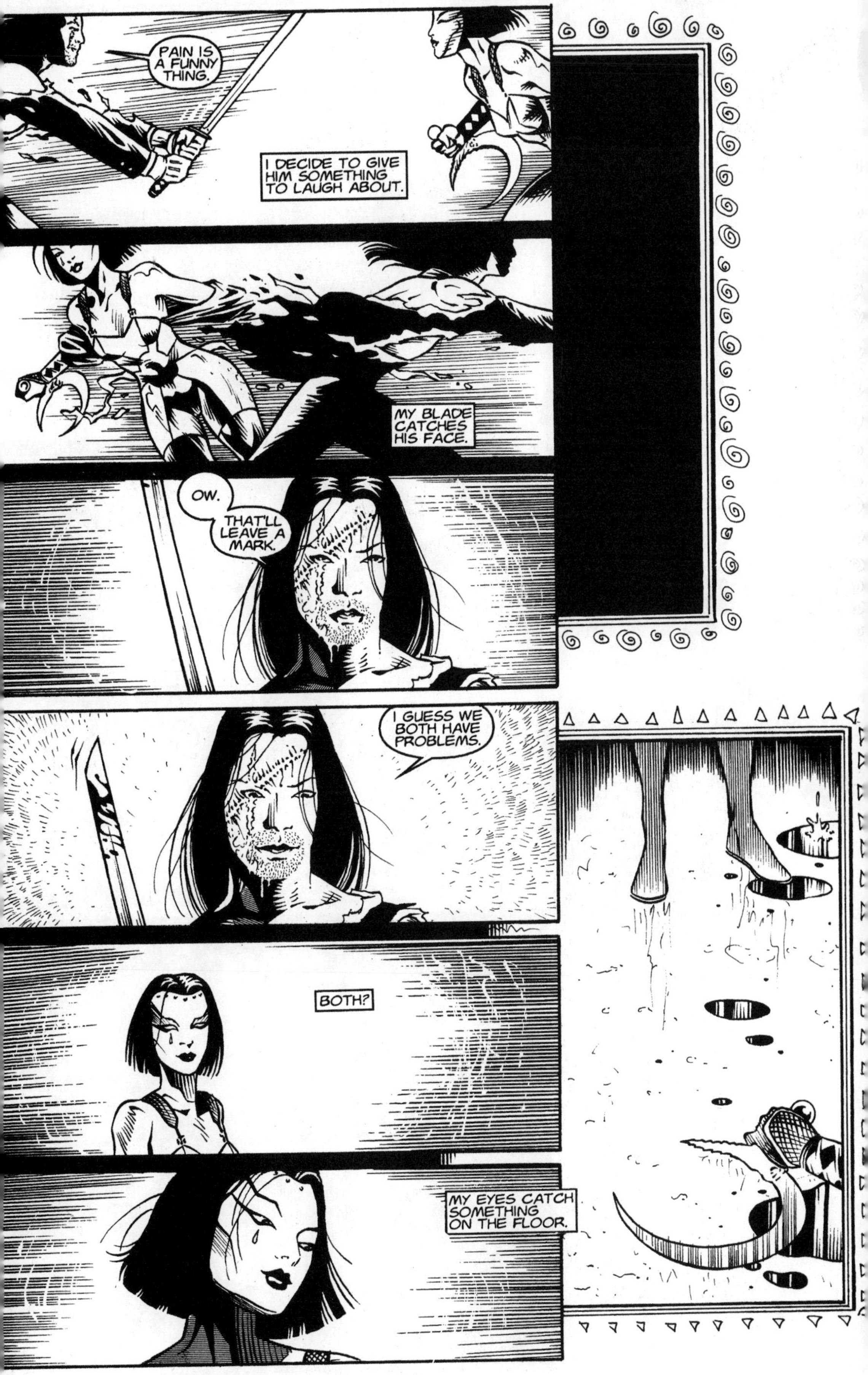
PAIN IS A FUNNY THING.
I DECIDE TO GIVE HIM SOMETHING TO LAUGH ABOUT.
MY BLADE CATCHES HIS FACE.
OW.
THAT'LL LEAVE A MARK.
I GUESS WE BOTH HAVE PROBLEMS.
BOTH?
MY EYES CATCH SOMETHING ON THE FLOOR.

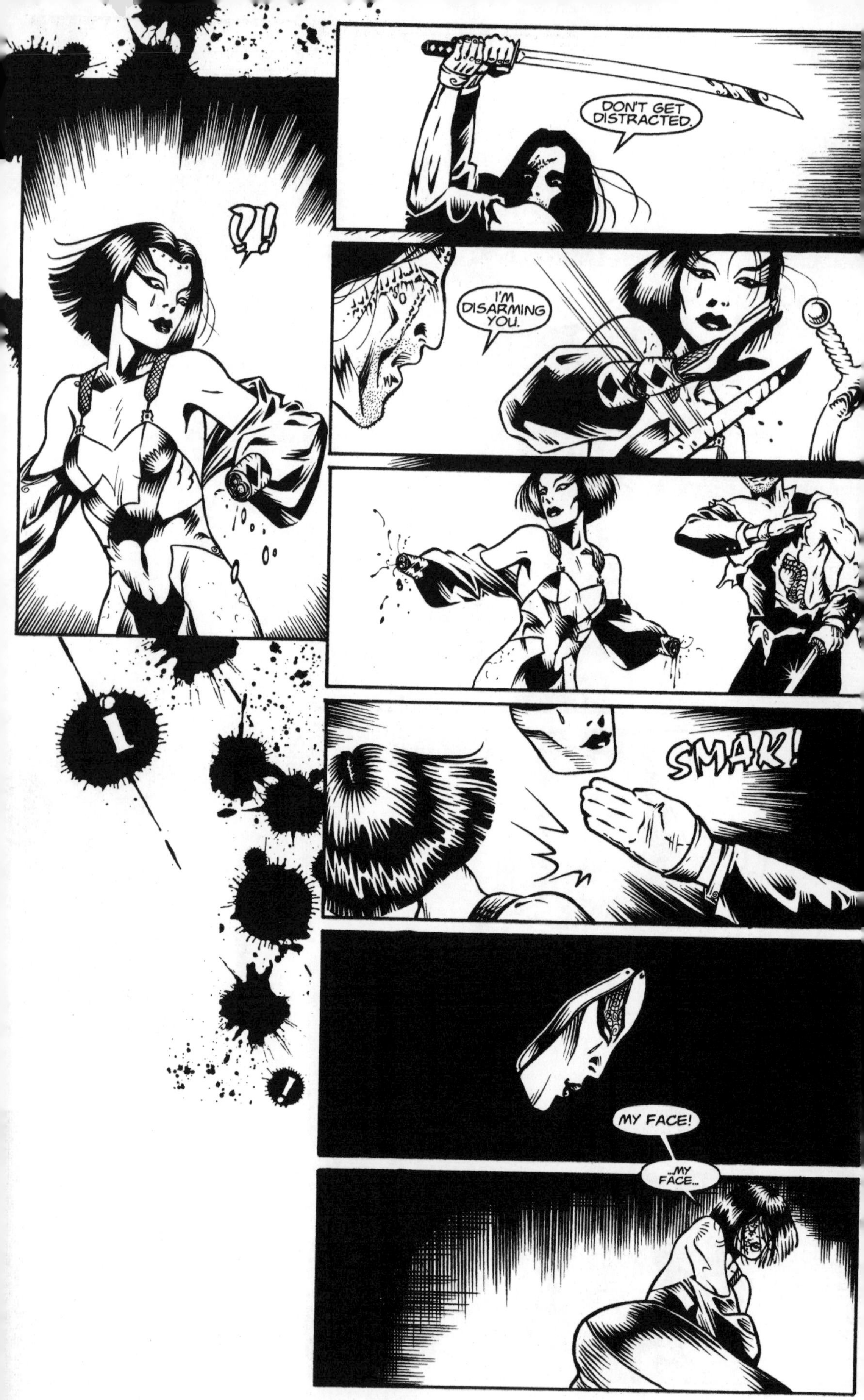
DON'T GET DISTRACTED.
?!
I'M DISARMING YOU.
SMAK!
!
MY FACE!
...MY FACE...

WELL, I MIGHT AS WELL TAKE MY MASK OFF, TOO.

AAAAH!

NO!

NNF!

NO!!

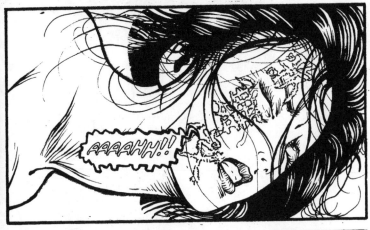

AAAAHH!!

NO

NO!

NO!

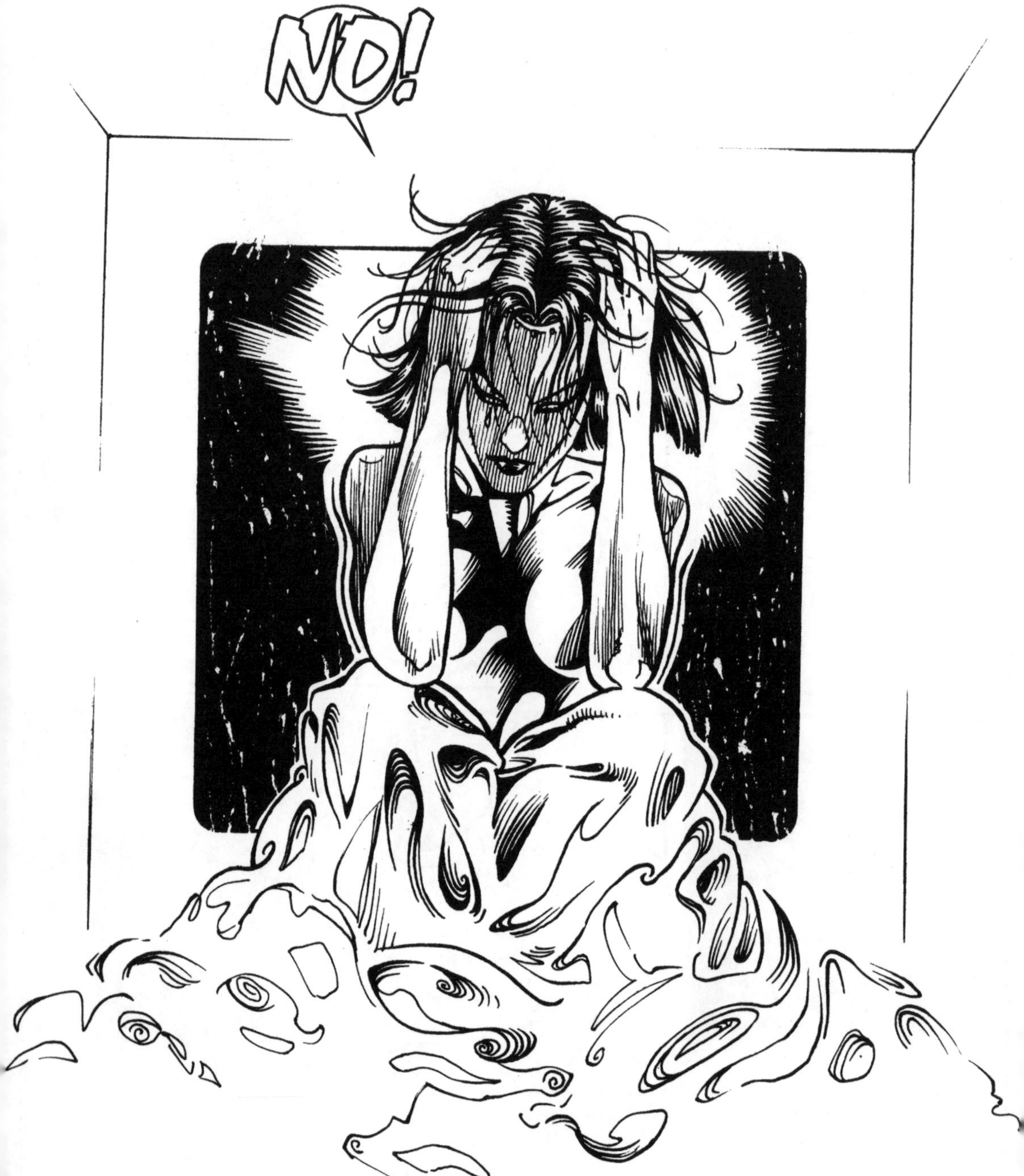
NO!
I WAKE UP.
IT IS STILL RAINING.

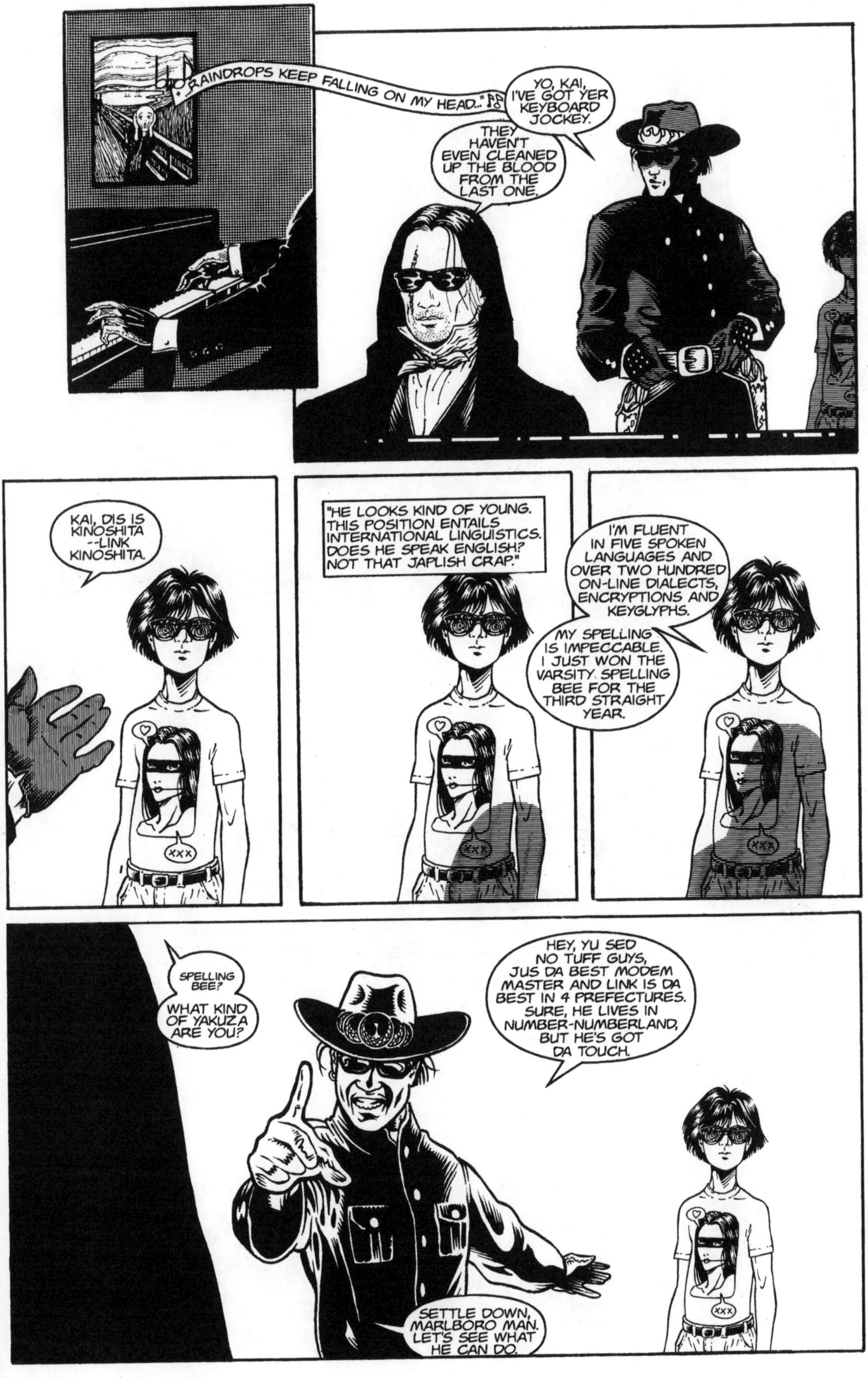
"RAINDROPS KEEP FALLING ON MY HEAD..."
YO, KAI, I'VE GOT YER KEYBOARD JOCKEY.
THEY HAVEN'T EVEN CLEANED UP THE BLOOD FROM THE LAST ONE.
KAI, DIS IS KINOSHITA --LINK KINOSHITA.
"HE LOOKS KIND OF YOUNG. THIS POSITION ENTAILS INTERNATIONAL LINGUISTICS. DOES HE SPEAK ENGLISH? NOT THAT JAPLISH CRAP."
I'M FLUENT IN FIVE SPOKEN LANGUAGES AND OVER TWO HUNDRED ON-LINE DIALECTS, ENCRYPTIONS AND KEYGLYPHS.
MY SPELLING IS IMPECCABLE. I JUST WON THE VARSITY SPELLING BEE FOR THE THIRD STRAIGHT YEAR.
SPELLING BEE?
WHAT KIND OF YAKUZA ARE YOU?
HEY, YU SED NO TUFF GUYS, JUS DA BEST MODEM MASTER AND LINK IS DA BEST IN 4 PREFECTURES. SURE, HE LIVES IN NUMBER-NUMBERLAND, BUT HE'S GOT DA TOUCH.
SETTLE DOWN, MARLBORO MAN. LET'S SEE WHAT HE CAN DO.

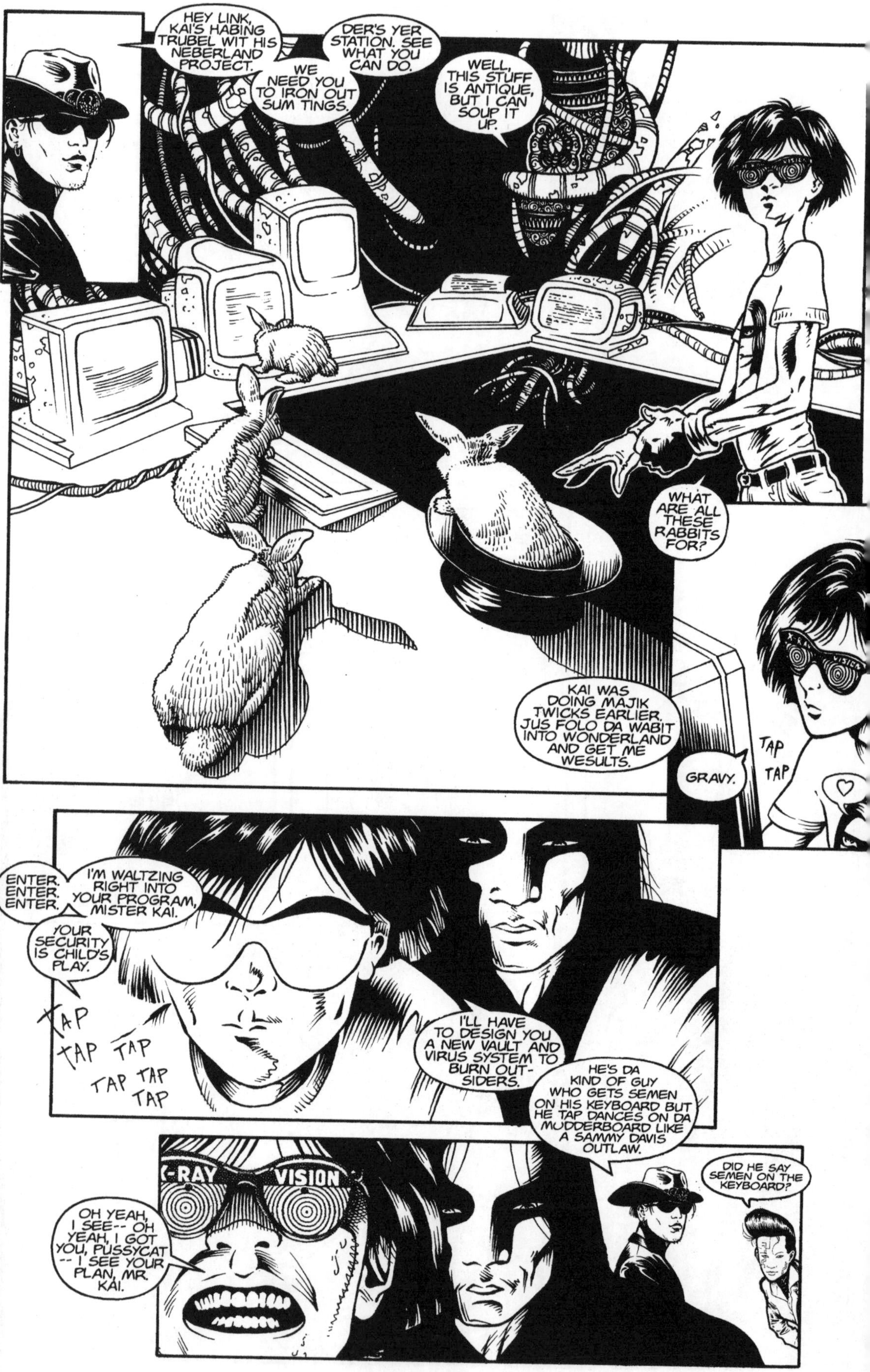

HEY LINK, KAI'S HABING TRUBEL WIT HIS NEBERLAND PROJECT.
WE NEED YOU TO IRON OUT SUM TINGS.
DER'S YER STATION. SEE WHAT YOU CAN DO.
WELL, THIS STUFF IS ANTIQUE, BUT I CAN SOUP IT UP.
WHAT ARE ALL THESE RABBITS FOR?
KAI WAS DOING MAJIK TWICKS EARLIER. JUS FOLO DA WABIT INTO WONDERLAND AND GET ME WESULTS.
GRAVY.
TAP TAP
ENTER. ENTER. ENTER.
I'M WALTZING RIGHT INTO YOUR PROGRAM, MISTER KAI.
YOUR SECURITY IS CHILD'S PLAY.
TAP TAP TAP TAP TAP TAP
I'LL HAVE TO DESIGN YOU A NEW VAULT AND VIRUS SYSTEM TO BURN OUT-SIDERS.
HE'S DA KIND OF GUY WHO GETS SEMEN ON HIS KEYBOARD BUT HE TAP DANCES ON DA MUDDERBOARD LIKE A SAMMY DAVIS OUTLAW.
DID HE SAY SEMEN ON THE KEYBOARD?
X-RAY VISION
OH YEAH, I SEE-- OH YEAH, I GOT YOU, PUSSYCAT -- I SEE YOUR PLAN, MR. KAI.

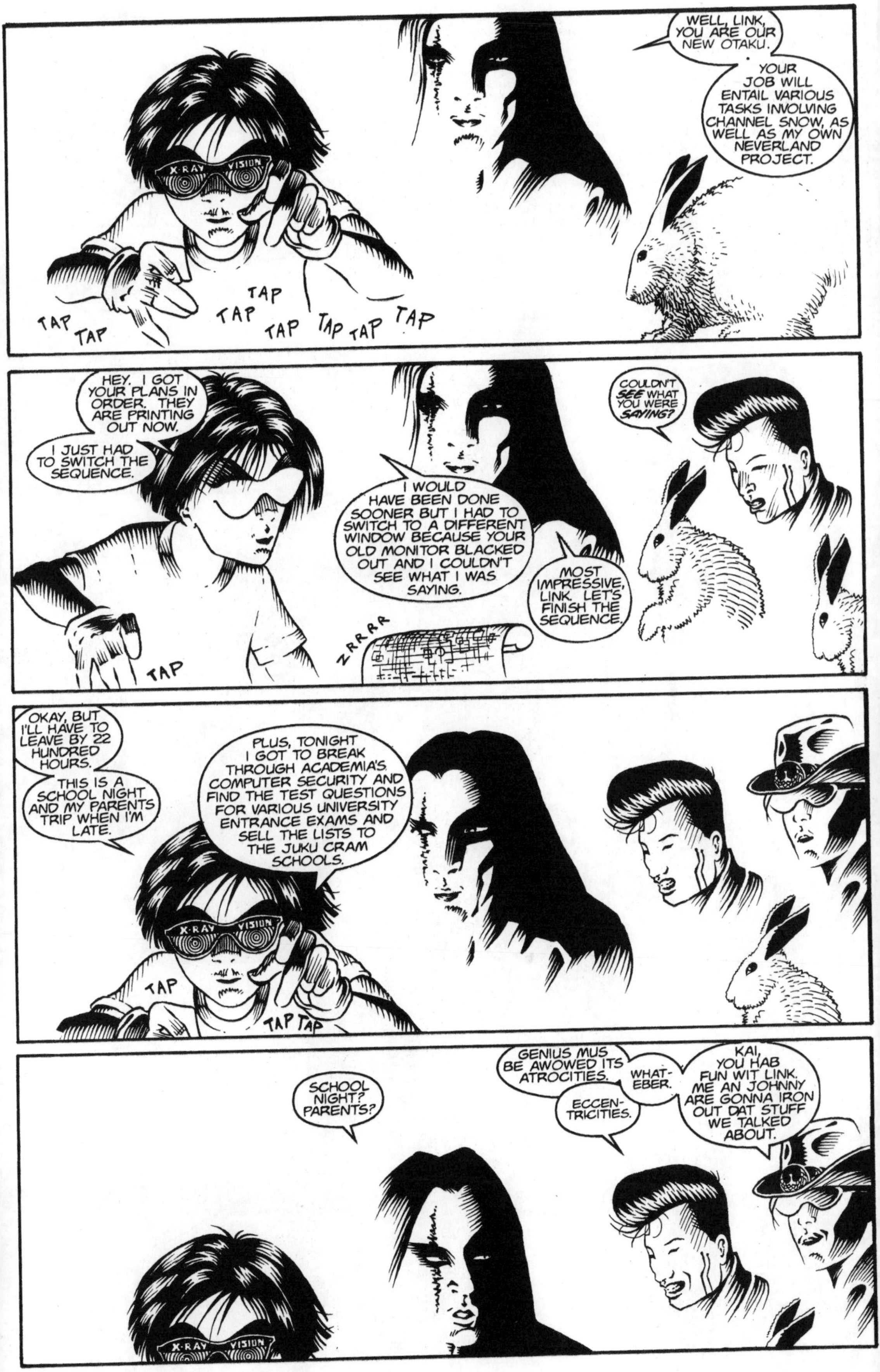

WELL, LINK, YOU ARE OUR NEW OTAKU.
YOUR JOB WILL ENTAIL VARIOUS TASKS INVOLVING CHANNEL SNOW, AS WELL AS MY OWN NEVERLAND PROJECT.
X-RAY VISION
TAP TAP TAP TAP TAP TAP TAP TAP
HEY. I GOT YOUR PLANS IN ORDER. THEY ARE PRINTING OUT NOW.
I JUST HAD TO SWITCH THE SEQUENCE.
I WOULD HAVE BEEN DONE SOONER BUT I HAD TO SWITCH TO A DIFFERENT WINDOW BECAUSE YOUR OLD MONITOR BLACKED OUT AND I COULDN'T SEE WHAT I WAS SAYING.
COULDN'T SEE WHAT YOU WERE SAYING?
MOST IMPRESSIVE, LINK. LET'S FINISH THE SEQUENCE.
TAP
ZRRRR
OKAY, BUT I'LL HAVE TO LEAVE BY 22 HUNDRED HOURS.
THIS IS A SCHOOL NIGHT AND MY PARENTS TRIP WHEN I'M LATE.
PLUS, TONIGHT I GOT TO BREAK THROUGH ACADEMIA'S COMPUTER SECURITY AND FIND THE TEST QUESTIONS FOR VARIOUS UNIVERSITY ENTRANCE EXAMS AND SELL THE LISTS TO THE JUKU CRAM SCHOOLS.
X-RAY VISION
TAP
TAP TAP
SCHOOL NIGHT? PARENTS?
GENIUS MUS BE AWOWED ITS ATROCITIES.
ECCEN-TRICITIES.
WHAT-EBER.
KAI, YOU HAB FUN WIT LINK. ME AN JOHNNY ARE GONNA IRON OUT DAT STUFF WE TALKED ABOUT.
X-RAY VISION

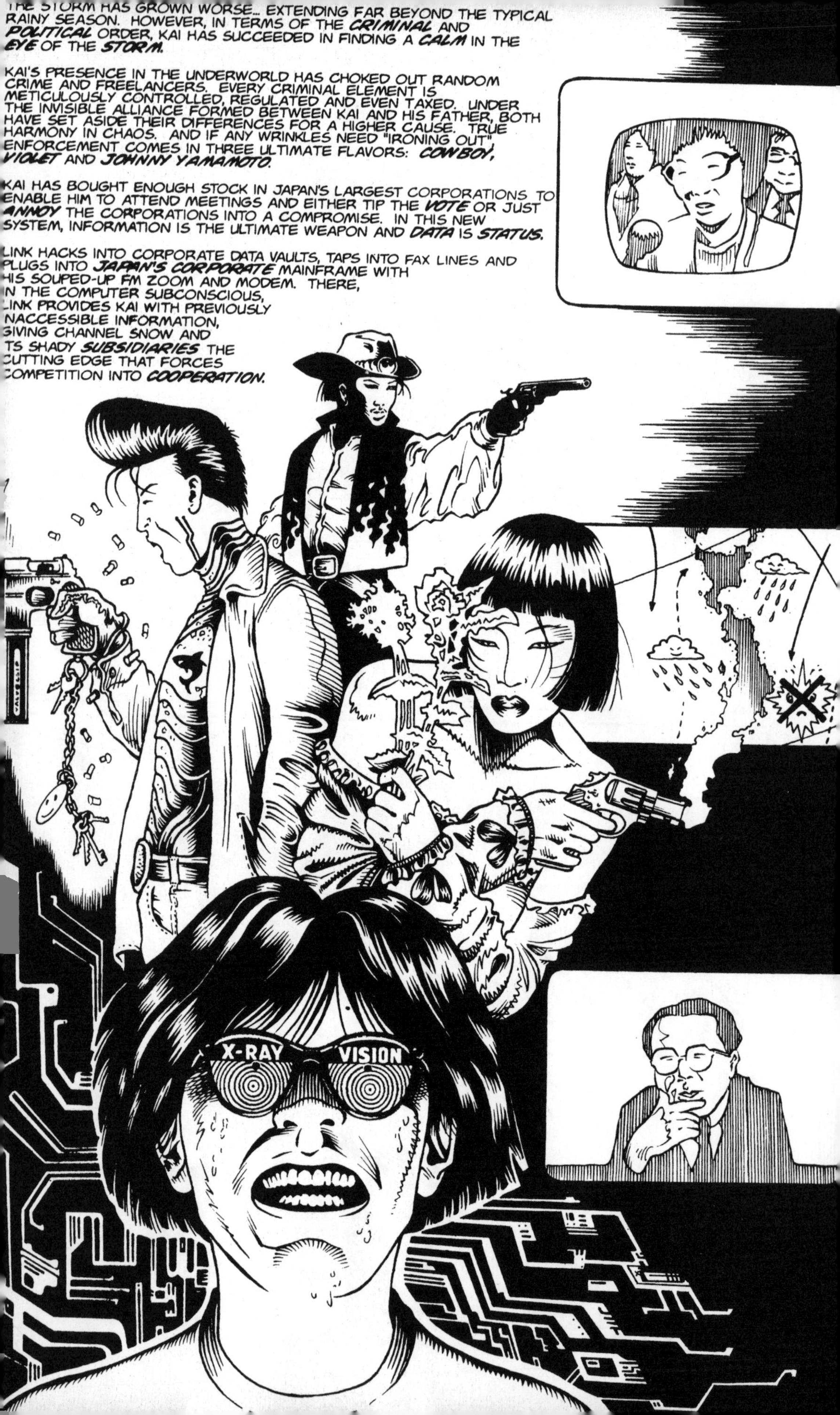
THE STORM HAS GROWN WORSE... EXTENDING FAR BEYOND THE TYPICAL RAINY SEASON. HOWEVER, IN TERMS OF THE CRIMINAL AND POLITICAL ORDER, KAI HAS SUCCEEDED IN FINDING A CALM IN THE EYE OF THE STORM.
KAI'S PRESENCE IN THE UNDERWORLD HAS CHOKED OUT RANDOM CRIME AND FREELANCERS. EVERY CRIMINAL ELEMENT IS METICULOUSLY CONTROLLED, REGULATED AND EVEN TAXED. UNDER THE INVISIBLE ALLIANCE FORMED BETWEEN KAI AND HIS FATHER, BOTH HAVE SET ASIDE THEIR DIFFERENCES FOR A HIGHER CAUSE. TRUE HARMONY IN CHAOS. AND IF ANY WRINKLES NEED "IRONING OUT", ENFORCEMENT COMES IN THREE ULTIMATE FLAVORS: COWBOY, VIOLET AND JOHNNY YAMAMOTO.
KAI HAS BOUGHT ENOUGH STOCK IN JAPAN'S LARGEST CORPORATIONS TO ENABLE HIM TO ATTEND MEETINGS AND EITHER TIP THE VOTE OR JUST ANNOY THE CORPORATIONS INTO A COMPROMISE. IN THIS NEW SYSTEM, INFORMATION IS THE ULTIMATE WEAPON AND DATA IS STATUS.
LINK HACKS INTO CORPORATE DATA VAULTS, TAPS INTO FAX LINES AND PLUGS INTO JAPAN'S CORPORATE MAINFRAME WITH HIS SOUPED-UP FM ZOOM AND MODEM. THERE, IN THE COMPUTER SUBCONSCIOUS, LINK PROVIDES KAI WITH PREVIOUSLY INACCESSIBLE INFORMATION, GIVING CHANNEL SNOW AND ITS SHADY SUBSIDIARIES THE CUTTING EDGE THAT FORCES COMPETITION INTO COOPERATION.
X-RAY VISION

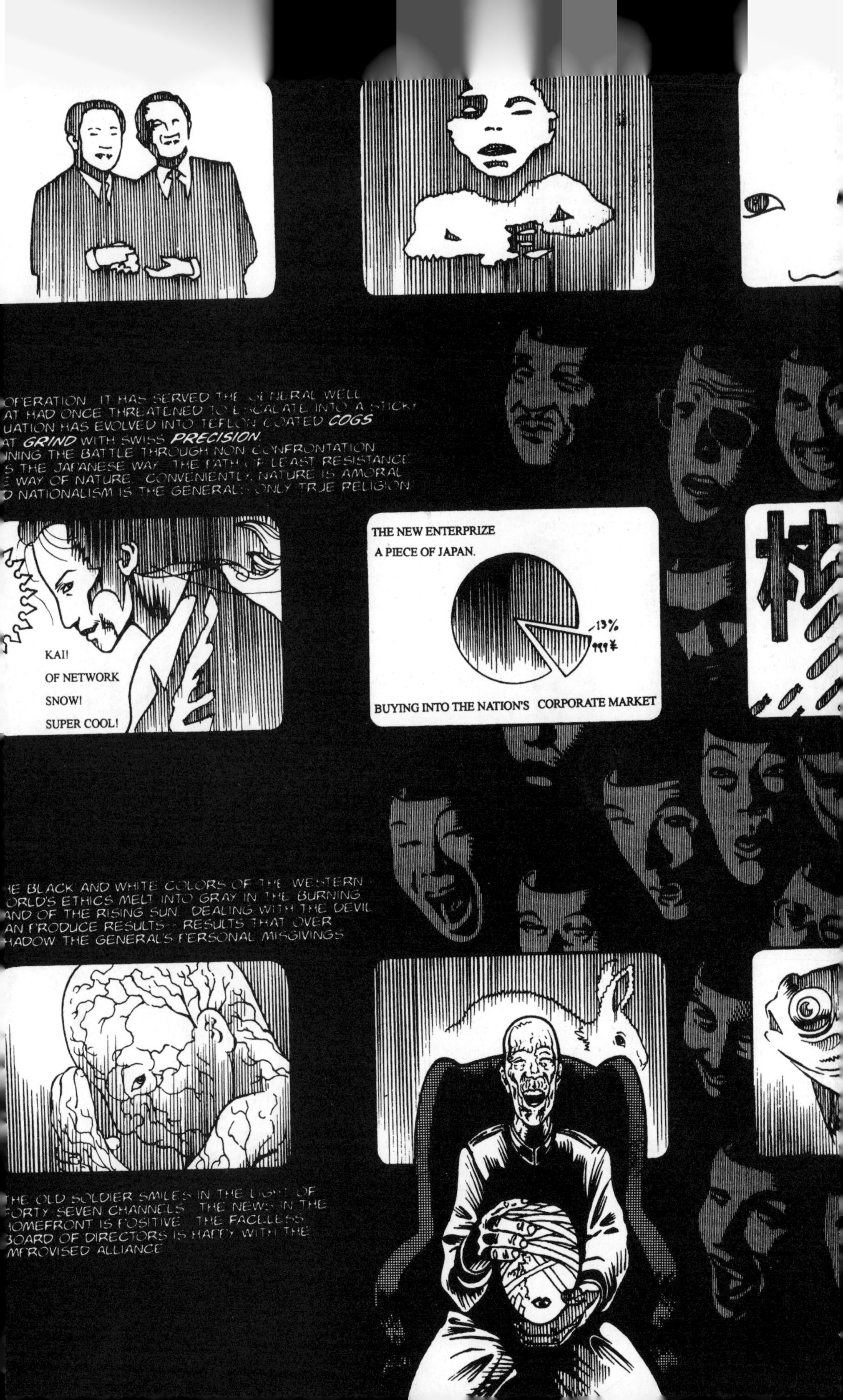

OPERATION. IT HAS SERVED THE GENERAL WELL
AT HAD ONCE THREATENED TO ESCALATE INTO A STICKY
UATION HAS EVOLVED INTO TEFLON COATED *COGS*
AT *GRIND* WITH SWISS *PRECISION*
NING THE BATTLE THROUGH NON CONFRONTATION
S THE JAPANESE WAY, THE PATH OF LEAST RESISTANCE
E WAY OF NATURE. CONVENIENTLY, NATURE IS AMORAL
O NATIONALISM IS THE GENERAL'S ONLY TRUE RELIGION

KAI!

OF NETWORK

SNOW!

SUPER COOL!

THE NEW ENTERPRIZE
A PIECE OF JAPAN.

-13%
999 ¥

BUYING INTO THE NATION'S CORPORATE MARKET

HE BLACK AND WHITE COLORS OF THE WESTERN
ORLD'S ETHICS MELT INTO GRAY IN THE BURNING
AND OF THE RISING SUN. DEALING WITH THE DEVIL
AN PRODUCE RESULTS-- RESULTS THAT OVER
HADOW THE GENERAL'S PERSONAL MISGIVINGS

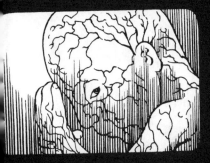

HE OLD SOLDIER SMILES IN THE LIGHT OF
FORTY SEVEN CHANNELS. THE NEWS IN THE
HOMEFRONT IS POSITIVE. THE FACELESS
BOARD OF DIRECTORS IS HAPPY WITH THE
MPROVISED ALLIANCE

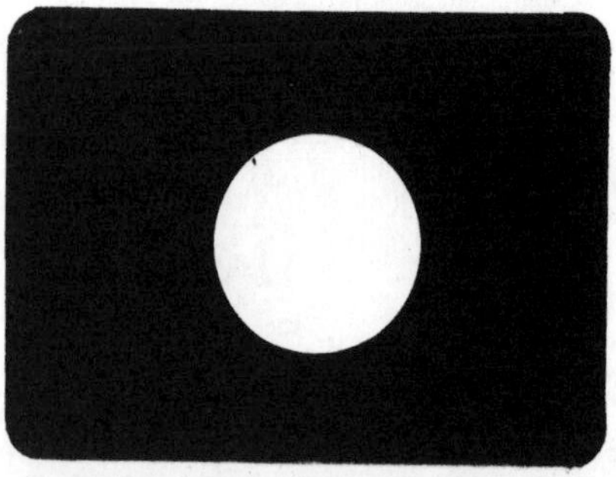

THE ***AINU PEOPLE'S CULTURE PRESERVATION PARTY*** HAS CONTINUED TO PUSH FOR REFORM AND APOLOGY FROM THE JAPANESE GOVERNMENT. THE OPPRESSED NATIVES OF JAPAN DEMONSTRATED BEFORE THE HOUSE OF THE DIET TODAY AGAINST THEIR UNFAIR TREATMENT.

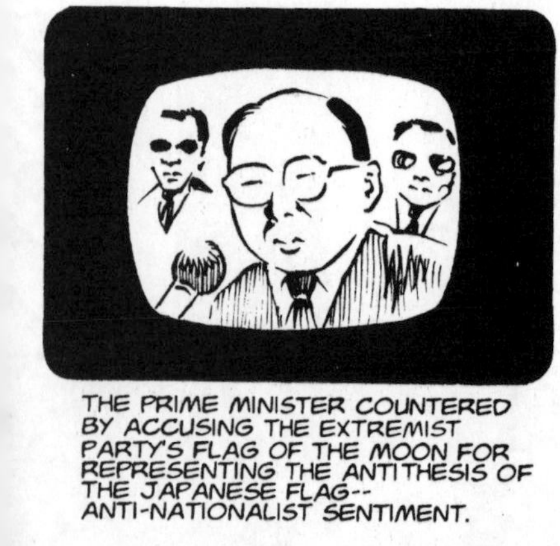

THE PRIME MINISTER COUNTERED BY ACCUSING THE EXTREMIST PARTY'S FLAG OF THE MOON FOR REPRESENTING THE ANTITHESIS OF THE JAPANESE FLAG-- ANTI-NATIONALIST SENTIMENT.

IN OTHER NEWS, THE AGENTS OF THE NOH ATTENDED A GALA EVENT HELD AT THE EMPEROR'S PALACE TO COMMEMORATE THE NEW BOOM IN INDUSTRY, INDEPENDENCE AND NATIONALISM.

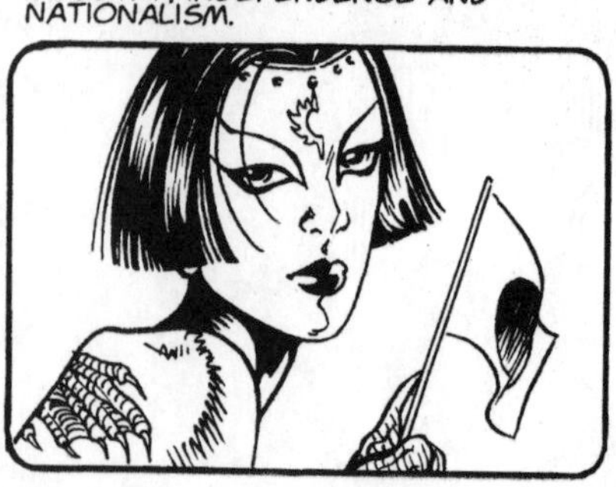

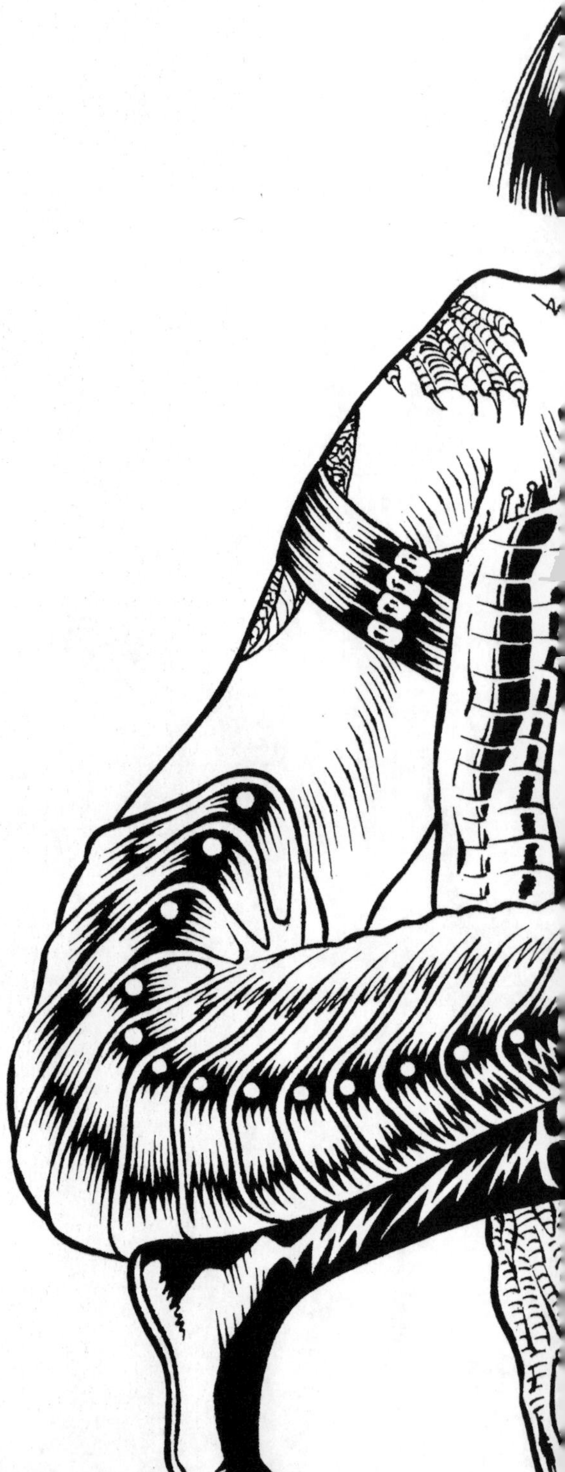

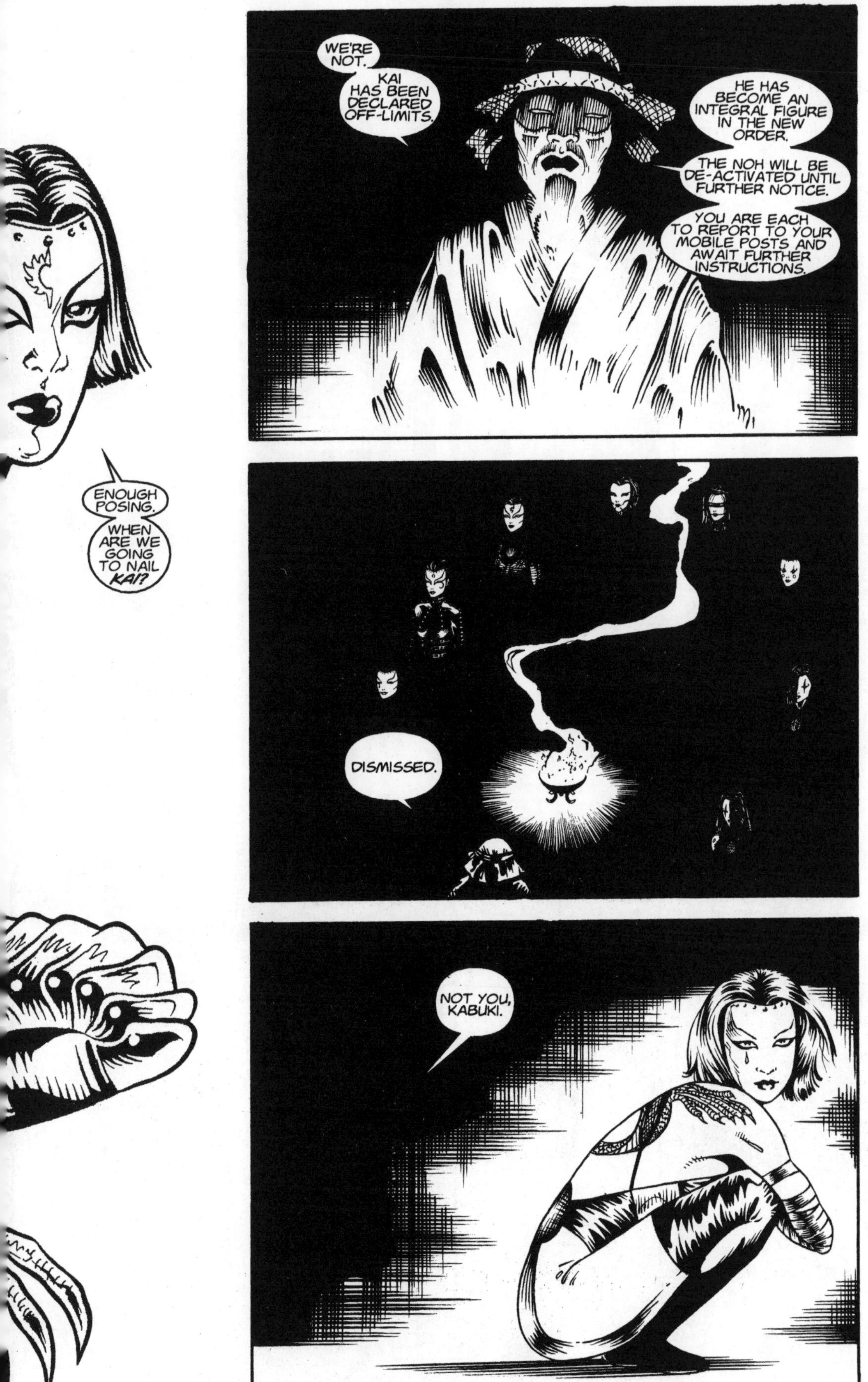
ENOUGH POSING.
WHEN ARE WE GOING TO NAIL KAI?
WE'RE NOT.
KAI HAS BEEN DECLARED OFF-LIMITS.
HE HAS BECOME AN INTEGRAL FIGURE IN THE NEW ORDER.
THE NOH WILL BE DE-ACTIVATED UNTIL FURTHER NOTICE.
YOU ARE EACH TO REPORT TO YOUR MOBILE POSTS AND AWAIT FURTHER INSTRUCTIONS.
DISMISSED.
NOT YOU, KABUKI.

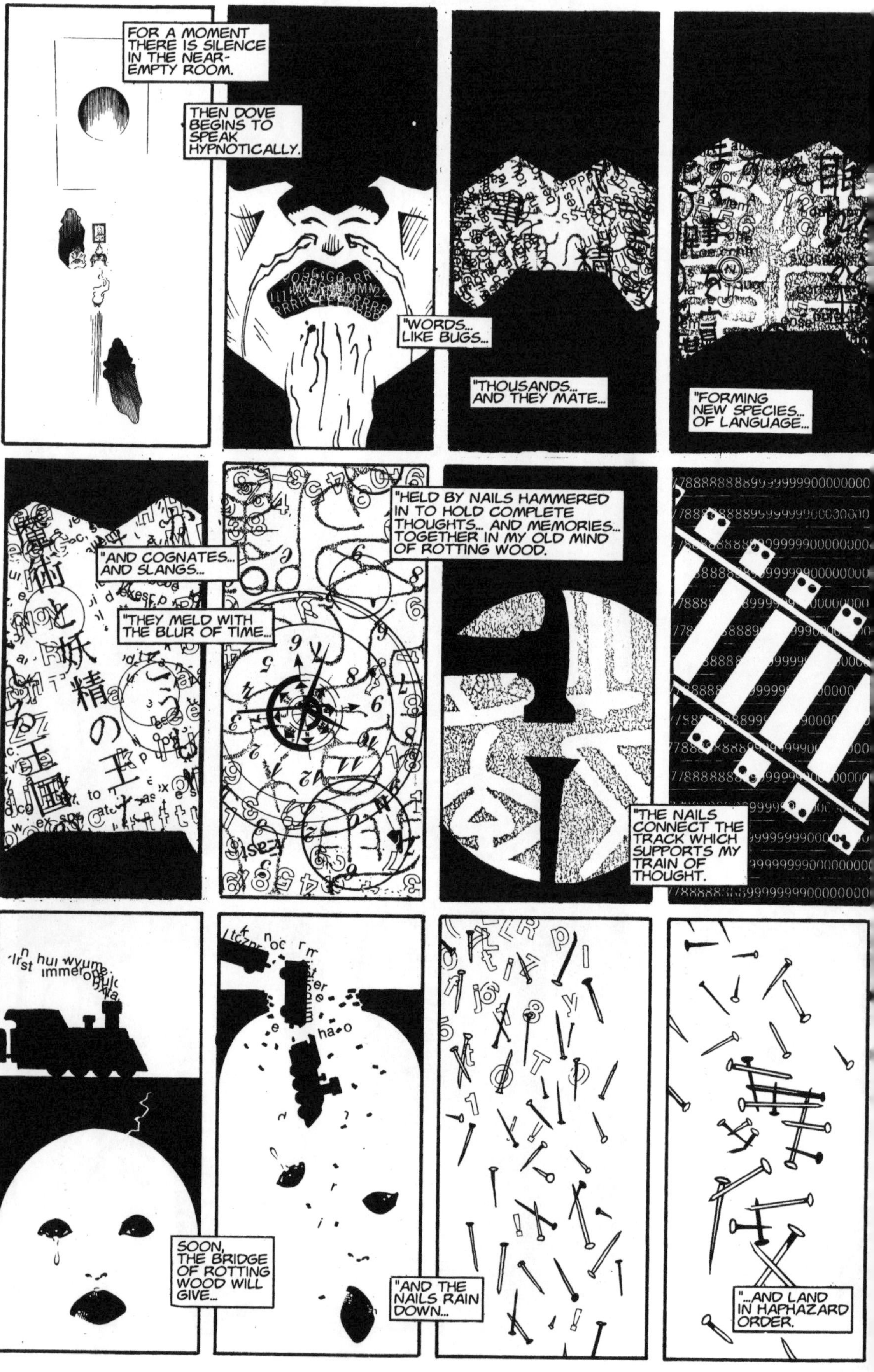

FOR A MOMENT THERE IS SILENCE IN THE NEAR-EMPTY ROOM.
THEN DOVE BEGINS TO SPEAK HYPNOTICALLY.
"WORDS... LIKE BUGS...
"THOUSANDS... AND THEY MATE...
"FORMING NEW SPECIES... OF LANGUAGE...
"AND COGNATES... AND SLANGS...
"THEY MELD WITH THE BLUR OF TIME...
"HELD BY NAILS HAMMERED IN TO HOLD COMPLETE THOUGHTS... AND MEMORIES... TOGETHER IN MY OLD MIND OF ROTTING WOOD.
"THE NAILS CONNECT THE TRACK WHICH SUPPORTS MY TRAIN OF THOUGHT.
SOON, THE BRIDGE OF ROTTING WOOD WILL GIVE...
"AND THE NAILS RAIN DOWN...
"...AND LAND IN HAPHAZARD ORDER.

"SEE ME NOW WITH YOUR TRUE EYES.

"BEFORE THIS OCCURS, I MUST PASS THE BLUEPRINT ON TO YOU.

"HEAR ME NOW WITH MY TRUE ROTTEN PHYSICAL VOICE, THE UNTRACEABLE WORDS AND IMPERFECT SENTENCE STRUCTURES I GIVE TO YOU.

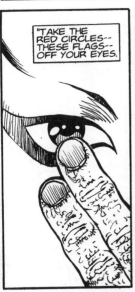

"TAKE THE RED CIRCLES-- THESE FLAGS-- OFF YOUR EYES.

"SO THAT YOU RECORD NOTHING FOR THEIR DATA BANKS. MY TRUE FACE WILL EXIST ONLY IN YOUR MEMORY.

"YOUR MOTHER WAS TSUKIKO, "MOON-CHILD."

"I CAN SEE HER IN YOUR EYES.

"YOU ARE A PART OF HER.

"YOUR NAME IS A PART OF HERS.

TSUKIKO

MY NAME?

UKIKO

"YOUR GIVEN NAME: UKIKO-- "GIRL-OF- THE-RAIN."

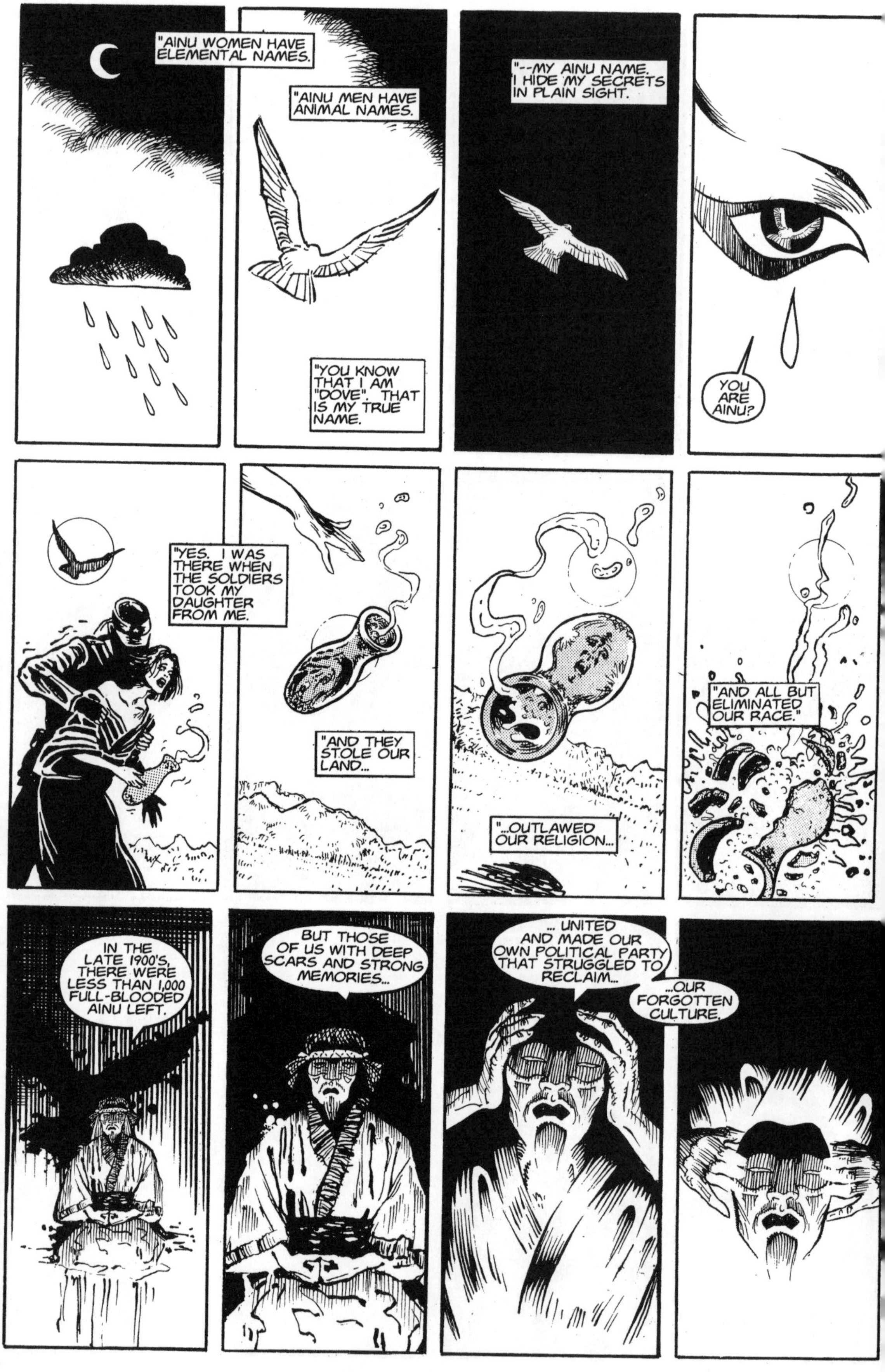
"AINU WOMEN HAVE ELEMENTAL NAMES.
"AINU MEN HAVE ANIMAL NAMES.
"YOU KNOW THAT I AM "DOVE". THAT IS MY TRUE NAME.
"--MY AINU NAME. I HIDE MY SECRETS IN PLAIN SIGHT.
YOU ARE AINU?
"YES. I WAS THERE WHEN THE SOLDIERS TOOK MY DAUGHTER FROM ME.
"AND THEY STOLE OUR LAND...
"...OUTLAWED OUR RELIGION...
"AND ALL BUT ELIMINATED OUR RACE."
IN THE LATE 1900'S, THERE WERE LESS THAN 1,000 FULL-BLOODED AINU LEFT.
BUT THOSE OF US WITH DEEP SCARS AND STRONG MEMORIES...
... UNITED AND MADE OUR OWN POLITICAL PARTY THAT STRUGGLED TO RECLAIM...
...OUR FORGOTTEN CULTURE.

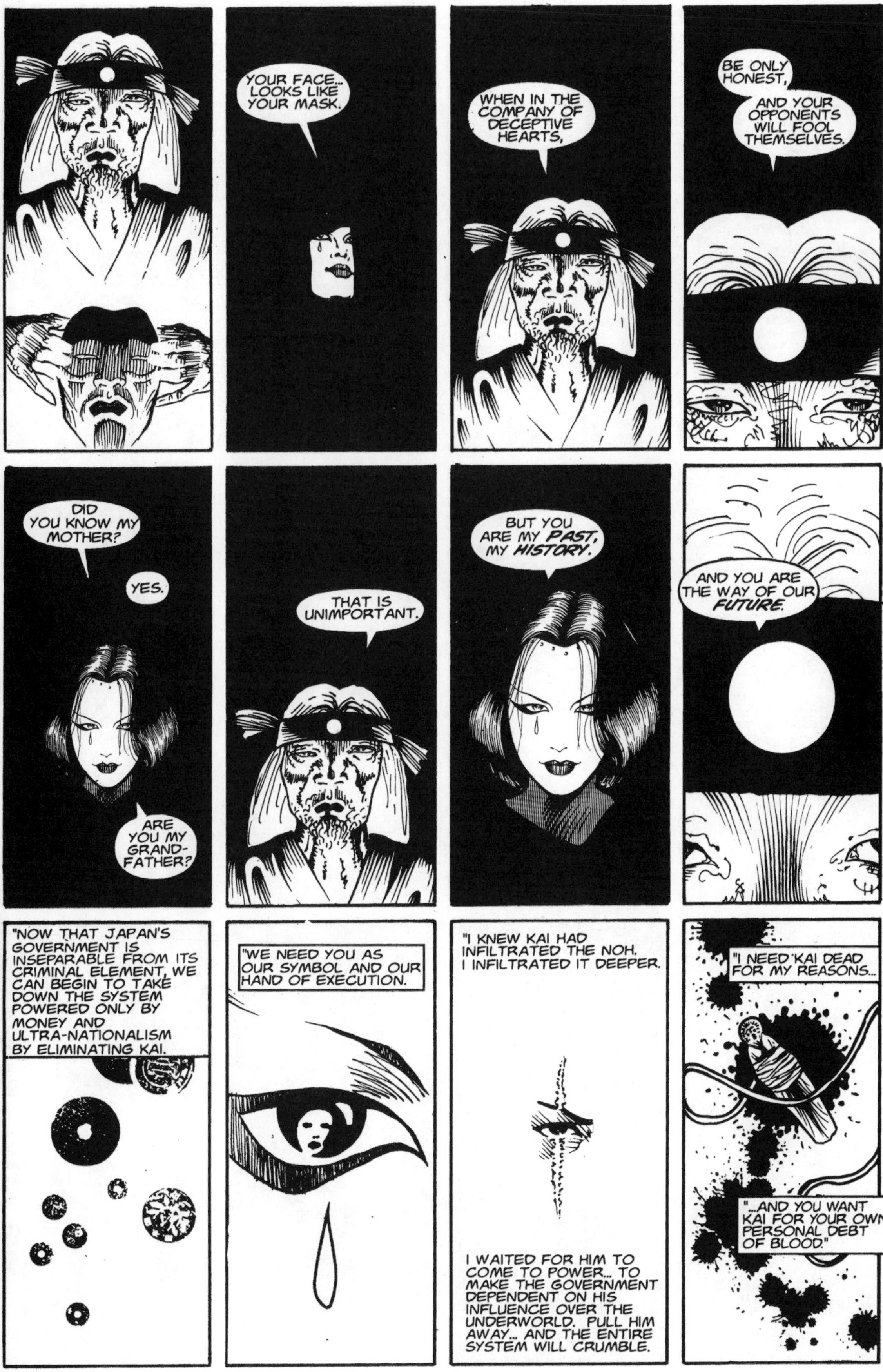
YOUR FACE... LOOKS LIKE YOUR MASK.
WHEN IN THE COMPANY OF DECEPTIVE HEARTS,
BE ONLY HONEST,
AND YOUR OPPONENTS WILL FOOL THEMSELVES.
DID YOU KNOW MY MOTHER?
YES.
ARE YOU MY GRAND-FATHER?
THAT IS UNIMPORTANT.
BUT YOU ARE MY PAST, MY HISTORY.
AND YOU ARE THE WAY OF OUR FUTURE.
"NOW THAT JAPAN'S GOVERNMENT IS INSEPARABLE FROM ITS CRIMINAL ELEMENT, WE CAN BEGIN TO TAKE DOWN THE SYSTEM POWERED ONLY BY MONEY AND ULTRA-NATIONALISM BY ELIMINATING KAI.
"WE NEED YOU AS OUR SYMBOL AND OUR HAND OF EXECUTION.
"I KNEW KAI HAD INFILTRATED THE NOH. I INFILTRATED IT DEEPER.
I WAITED FOR HIM TO COME TO POWER... TO MAKE THE GOVERNMENT DEPENDENT ON HIS INFLUENCE OVER THE UNDERWORLD. PULL HIM AWAY... AND THE ENTIRE SYSTEM WILL CRUMBLE.
"I NEED KAI DEAD FOR MY REASONS...
"...AND YOU WANT KAI FOR YOUR OWN PERSONAL DEBT OF BLOOD."

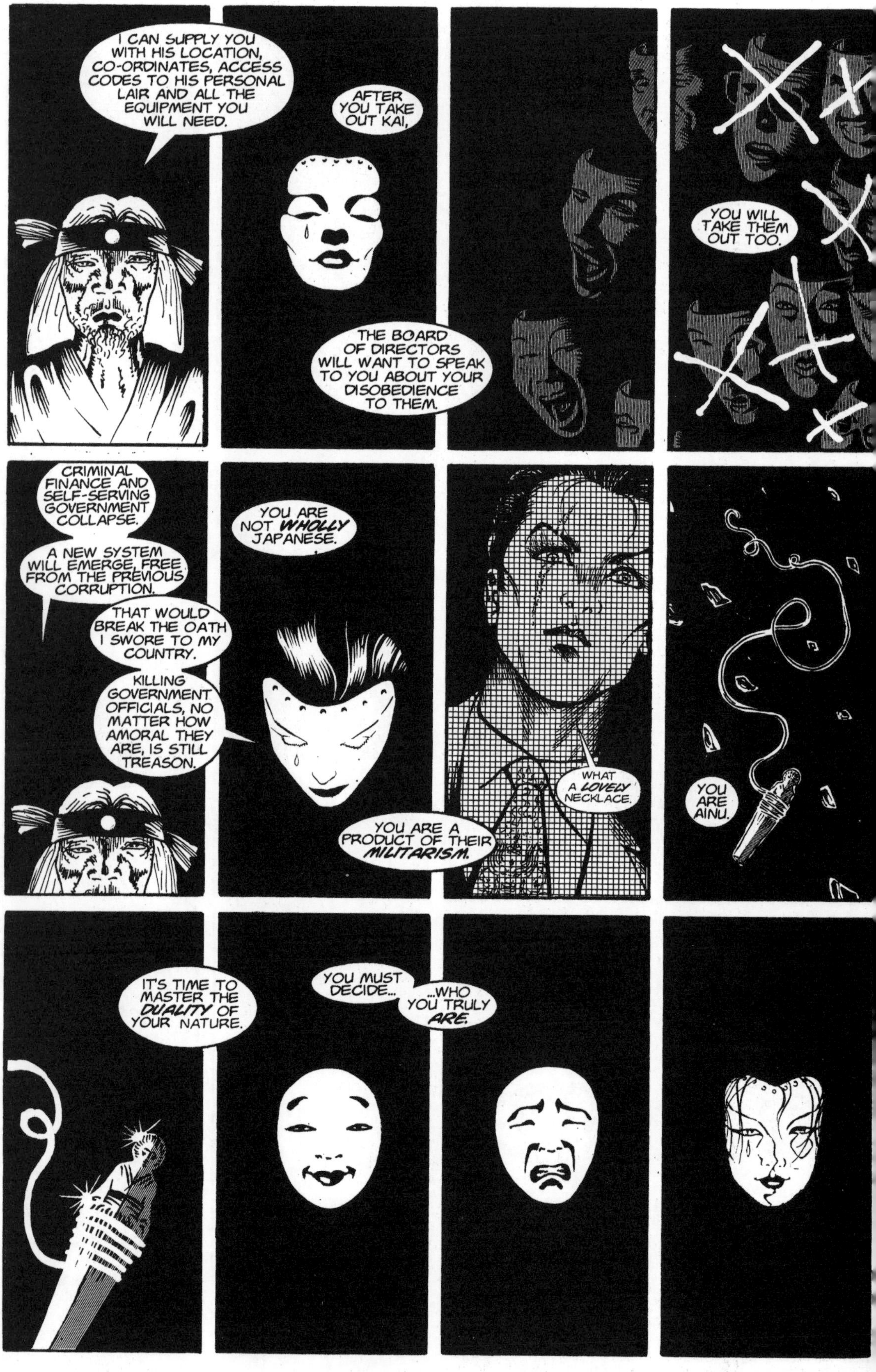
I CAN SUPPLY YOU WITH HIS LOCATION, CO-ORDINATES, ACCESS CODES TO HIS PERSONAL LAIR AND ALL THE EQUIPMENT YOU WILL NEED.
AFTER YOU TAKE OUT KAI,
THE BOARD OF DIRECTORS WILL WANT TO SPEAK TO YOU ABOUT YOUR DISOBEDIENCE TO THEM.
YOU WILL TAKE THEM OUT TOO.
CRIMINAL FINANCE AND SELF-SERVING GOVERNMENT COLLAPSE.
A NEW SYSTEM WILL EMERGE, FREE FROM THE PREVIOUS CORRUPTION.
THAT WOULD BREAK THE OATH I SWORE TO MY COUNTRY.
KILLING GOVERNMENT OFFICIALS, NO MATTER HOW AMORAL THEY ARE, IS STILL TREASON.
YOU ARE NOT WHOLLY JAPANESE.
YOU ARE A PRODUCT OF THEIR MILITARISM.
WHAT A LOVELY NECKLACE.
YOU ARE AINU.
IT'S TIME TO MASTER THE DUALITY OF YOUR NATURE.
YOU MUST DECIDE...
...WHO YOU TRULY ARE.

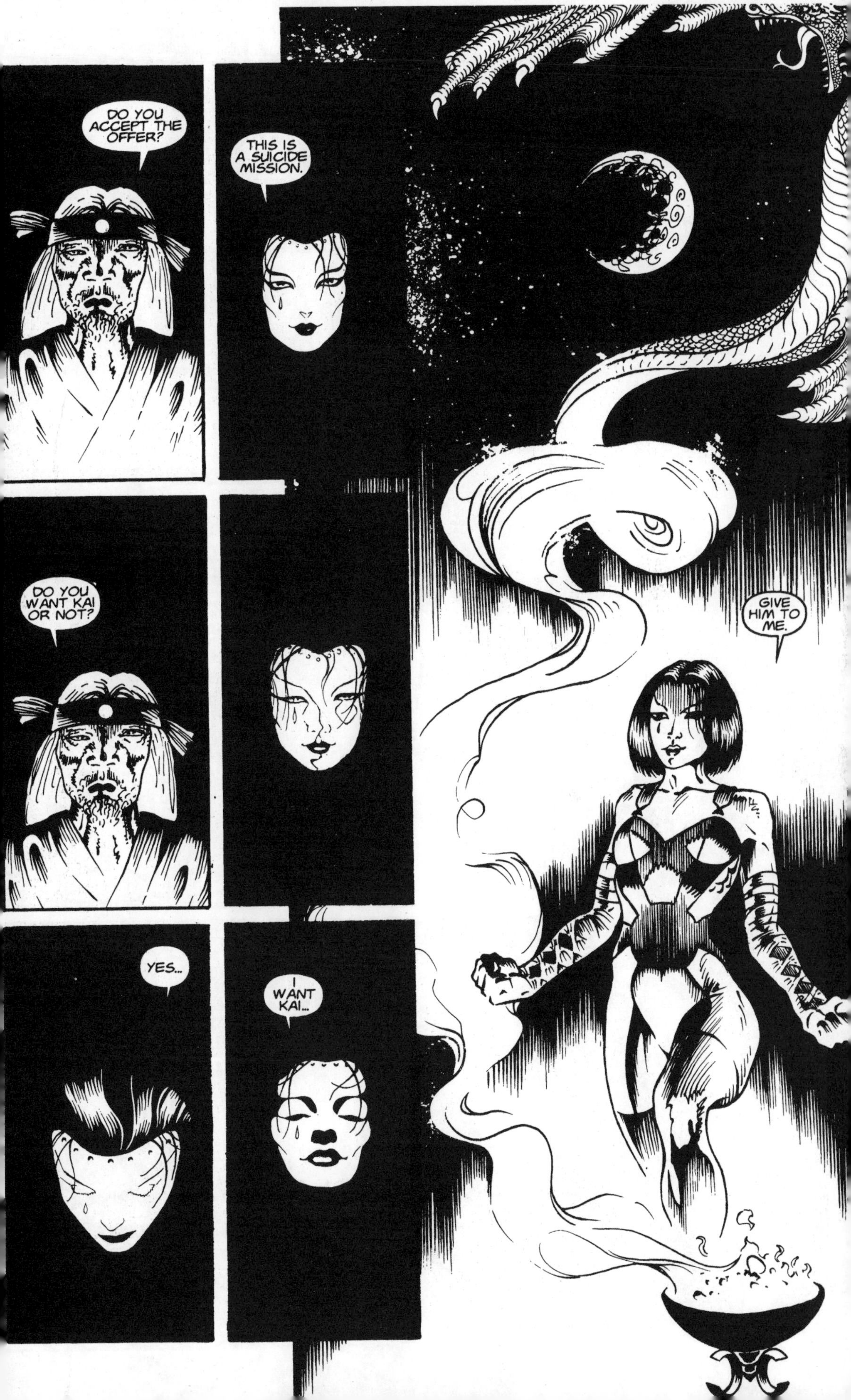

DO YOU ACCEPT THE OFFER?
THIS IS A SUICIDE MISSION.
DO YOU WANT KAI OR NOT?
YES...
I WANT KAI...
GIVE HIM TO ME.

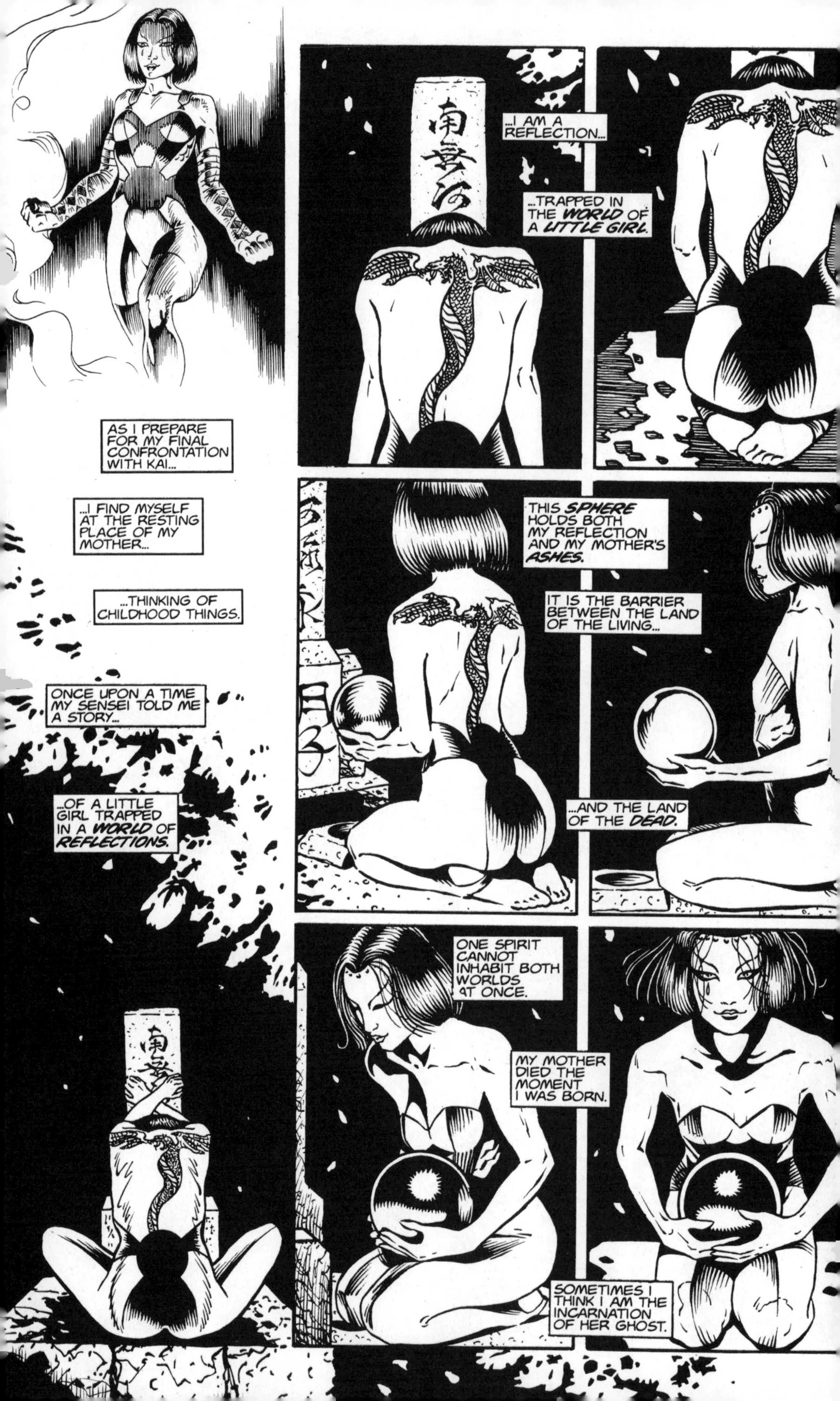
AS I PREPARE FOR MY FINAL CONFRONTATION WITH KAI...
...I FIND MYSELF AT THE RESTING PLACE OF MY MOTHER...
...THINKING OF CHILDHOOD THINGS.
ONCE UPON A TIME MY SENSEI TOLD ME A STORY...
...OF A LITTLE GIRL TRAPPED IN A WORLD OF REFLECTIONS.
...I AM A REFLECTION...
...TRAPPED IN THE WORLD OF A LITTLE GIRL.
THIS SPHERE HOLDS BOTH MY REFLECTION AND MY MOTHER'S ASHES.
IT IS THE BARRIER BETWEEN THE LAND OF THE LIVING...
...AND THE LAND OF THE DEAD.
ONE SPIRIT CANNOT INHABIT BOTH WORLDS AT ONCE.
MY MOTHER DIED THE MOMENT I WAS BORN.
SOMETIMES I THINK I AM THE INCARNATION OF HER GHOST.

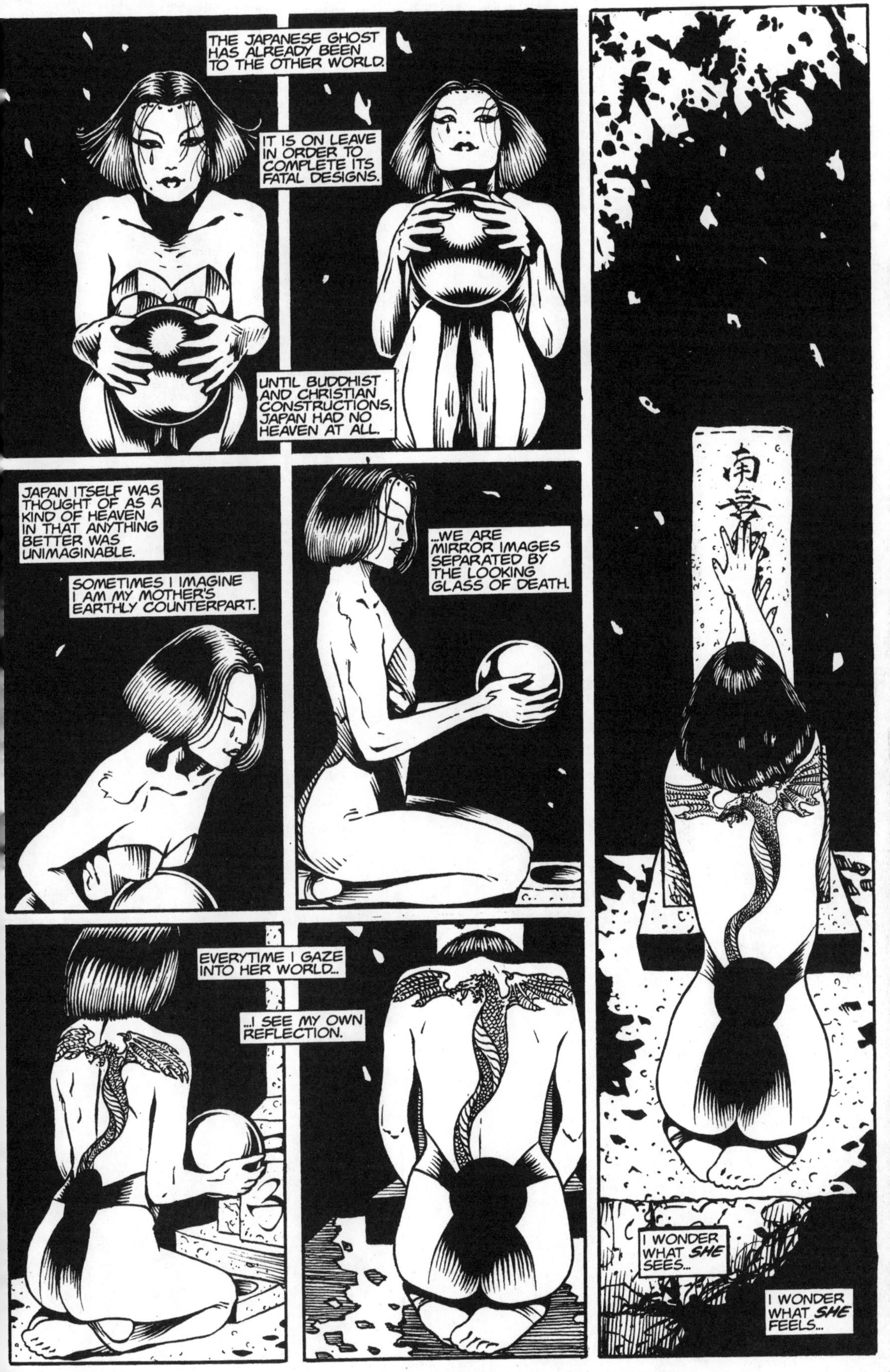

THE JAPANESE GHOST HAS ALREADY BEEN TO THE OTHER WORLD.
IT IS ON LEAVE IN ORDER TO COMPLETE ITS FATAL DESIGNS.
UNTIL BUDDHIST AND CHRISTIAN CONSTRUCTIONS, JAPAN HAD NO HEAVEN AT ALL.
JAPAN ITSELF WAS THOUGHT OF AS A KIND OF HEAVEN IN THAT ANYTHING BETTER WAS UNIMAGINABLE.
SOMETIMES I IMAGINE I AM MY MOTHER'S EARTHLY COUNTERPART.
...WE ARE MIRROR IMAGES SEPARATED BY THE LOOKING GLASS OF DEATH.
EVERYTIME I GAZE INTO HER WORLD...
...I SEE MY OWN REFLECTION.
I WONDER WHAT SHE SEES...
I WONDER WHAT SHE FEELS...

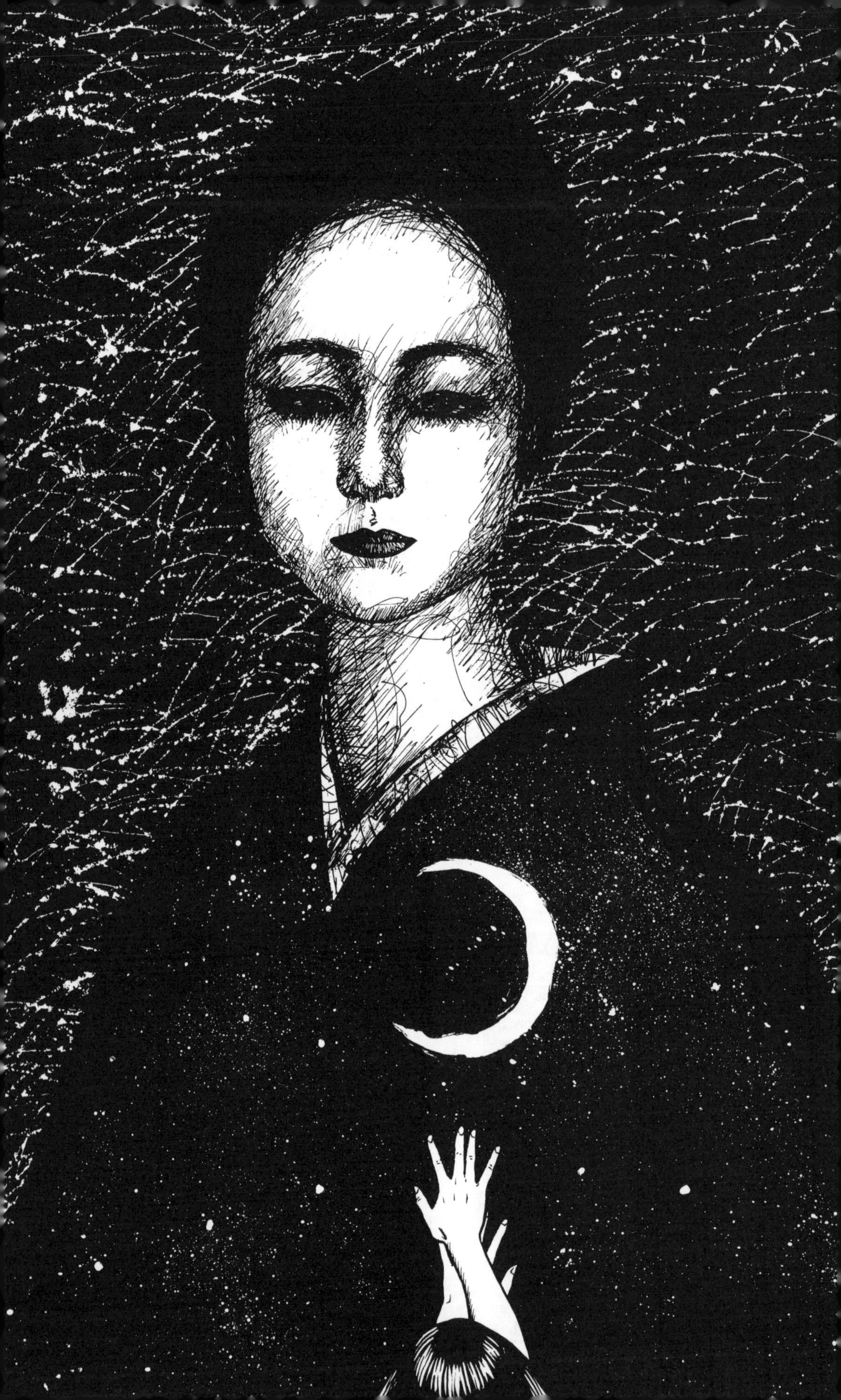

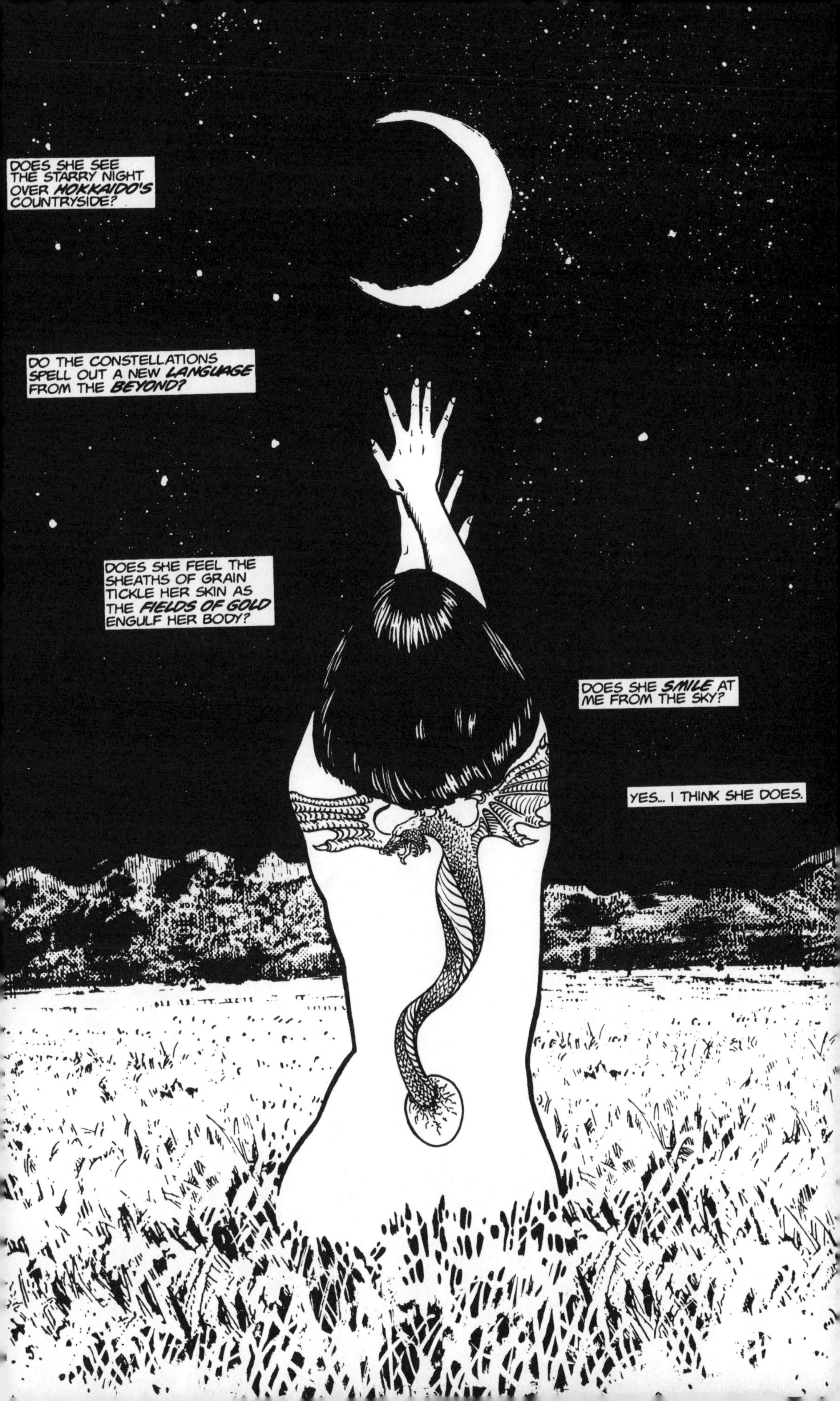

DOES SHE SEE THE STARRY NIGHT OVER HOKKAIDO'S COUNTRYSIDE?
DO THE CONSTELLATIONS SPELL OUT A NEW LANGUAGE FROM THE BEYOND?
DOES SHE FEEL THE SHEATHS OF GRAIN TICKLE HER SKIN AS THE FIELDS OF GOLD ENGULF HER BODY?
DOES SHE SMILE AT ME FROM THE SKY?
YES... I THINK SHE DOES.

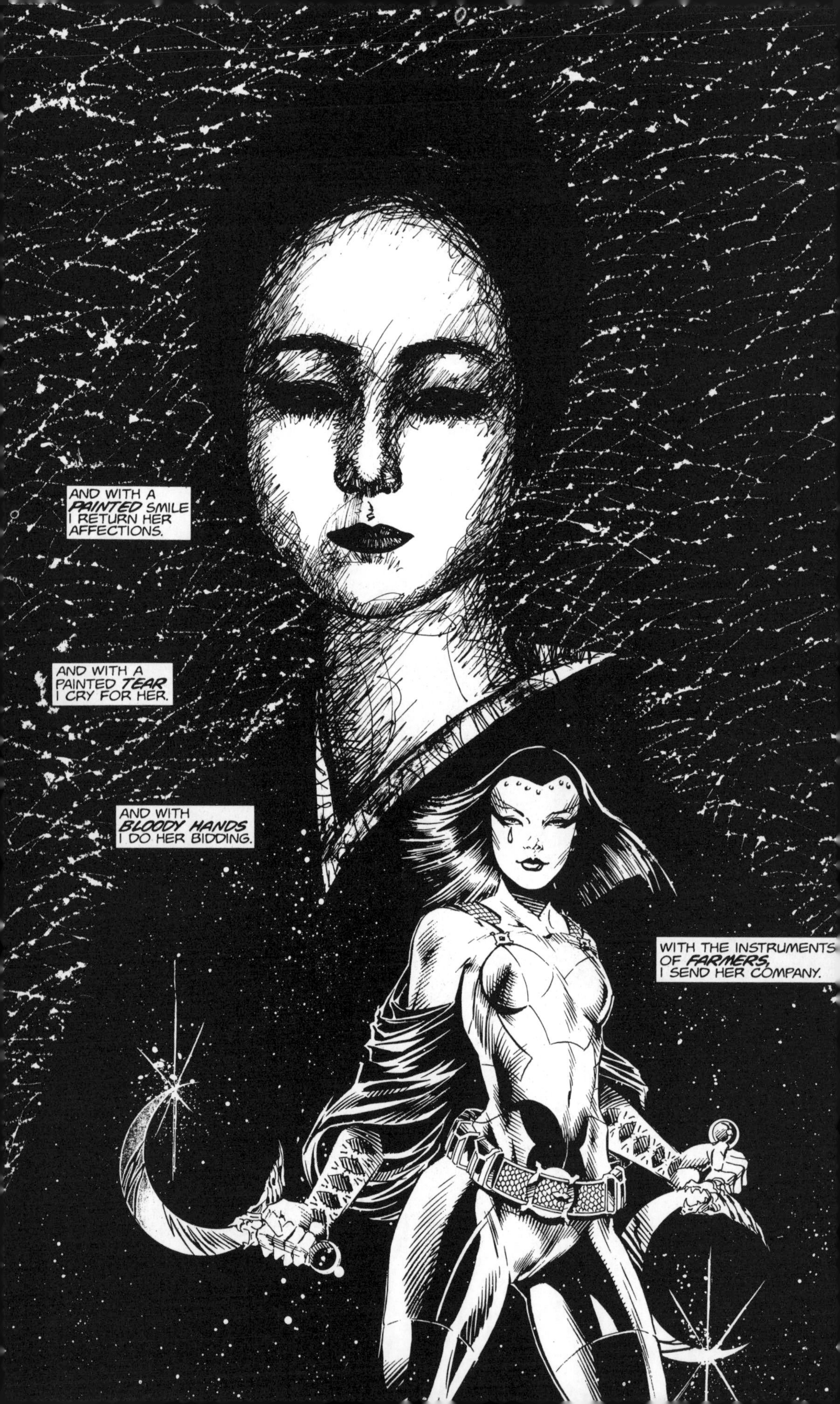
AND WITH A PAINTED SMILE I RETURN HER AFFECTIONS.
AND WITH A PAINTED TEAR I CRY FOR HER.
AND WITH BLOODY HANDS I DO HER BIDDING.
WITH THE INSTRUMENTS OF FARMERS, I SEND HER COMPANY.

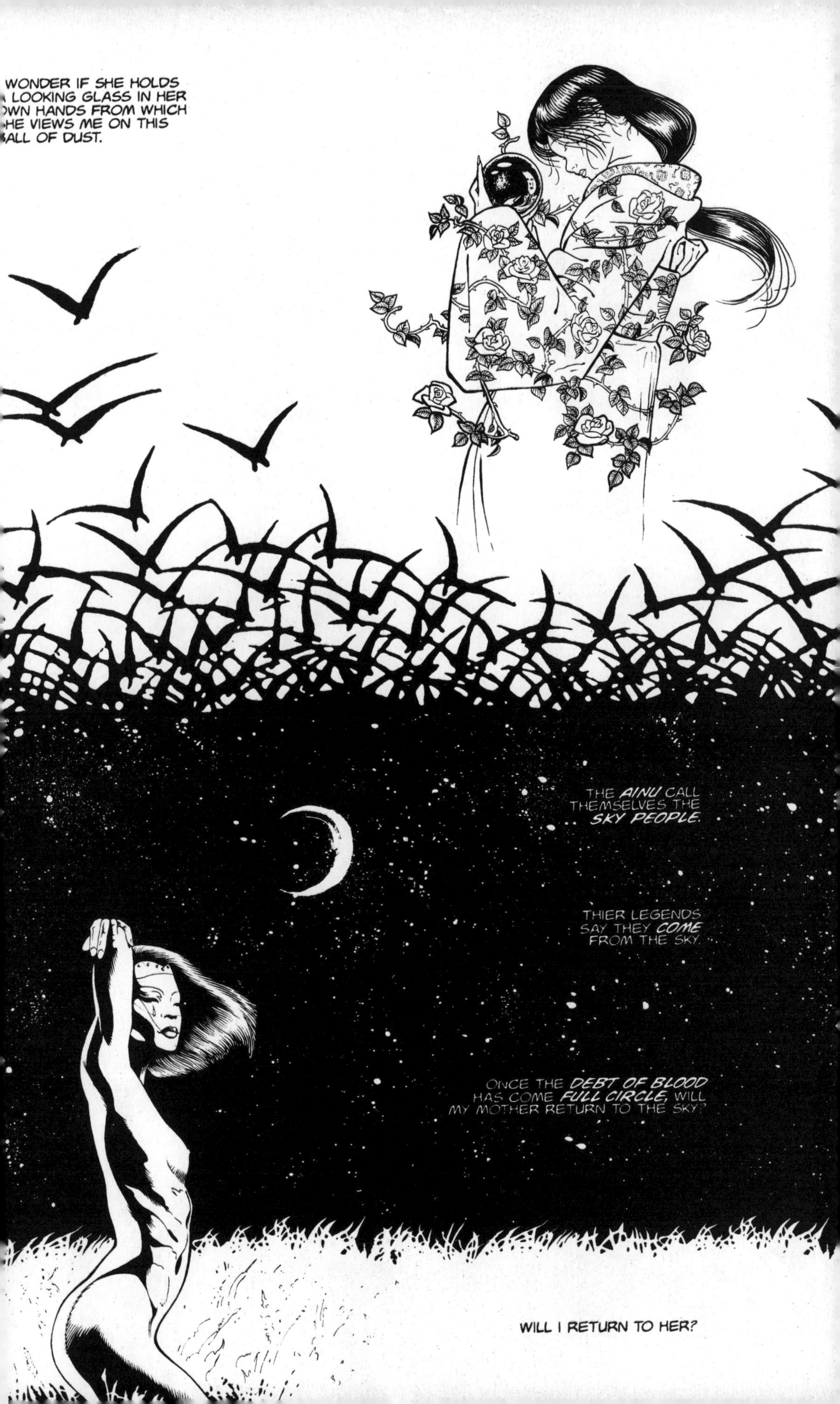

WONDER IF SHE HOLDS
LOOKING GLASS IN HER
WN HANDS FROM WHICH
HE VIEWS ME ON THIS
ALL OF DUST.
THE AINU CALL THEMSELVES THE SKY PEOPLE.
THIER LEGENDS SAY THEY COME FROM THE SKY.
ONCE THE DEBT OF BLOOD HAS COME FULL CIRCLE, WILL MY MOTHER RETURN TO THE SKY?
WILL I RETURN TO HER?

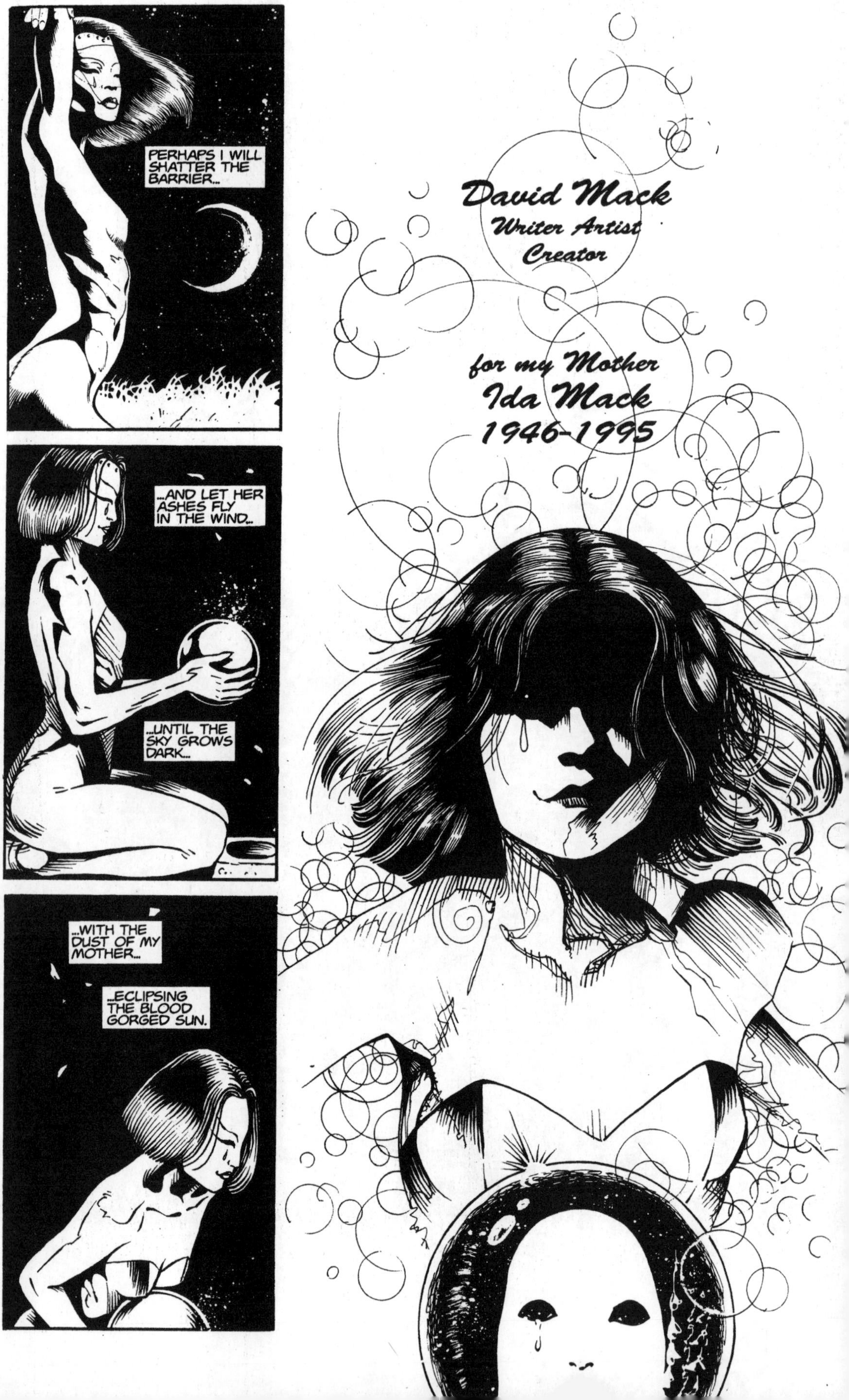
PERHAPS I WILL SHATTER THE BARRIER...
...AND LET HER ASHES FLY IN THE WIND...
...UNTIL THE SKY GROWS DARK...
...WITH THE DUST OF MY MOTHER...
...ECLIPSING THE BLOOD GORGED SUN.
David Mack
Writer Artist
Creator
for my Mother
Ida Mack
1946-1995

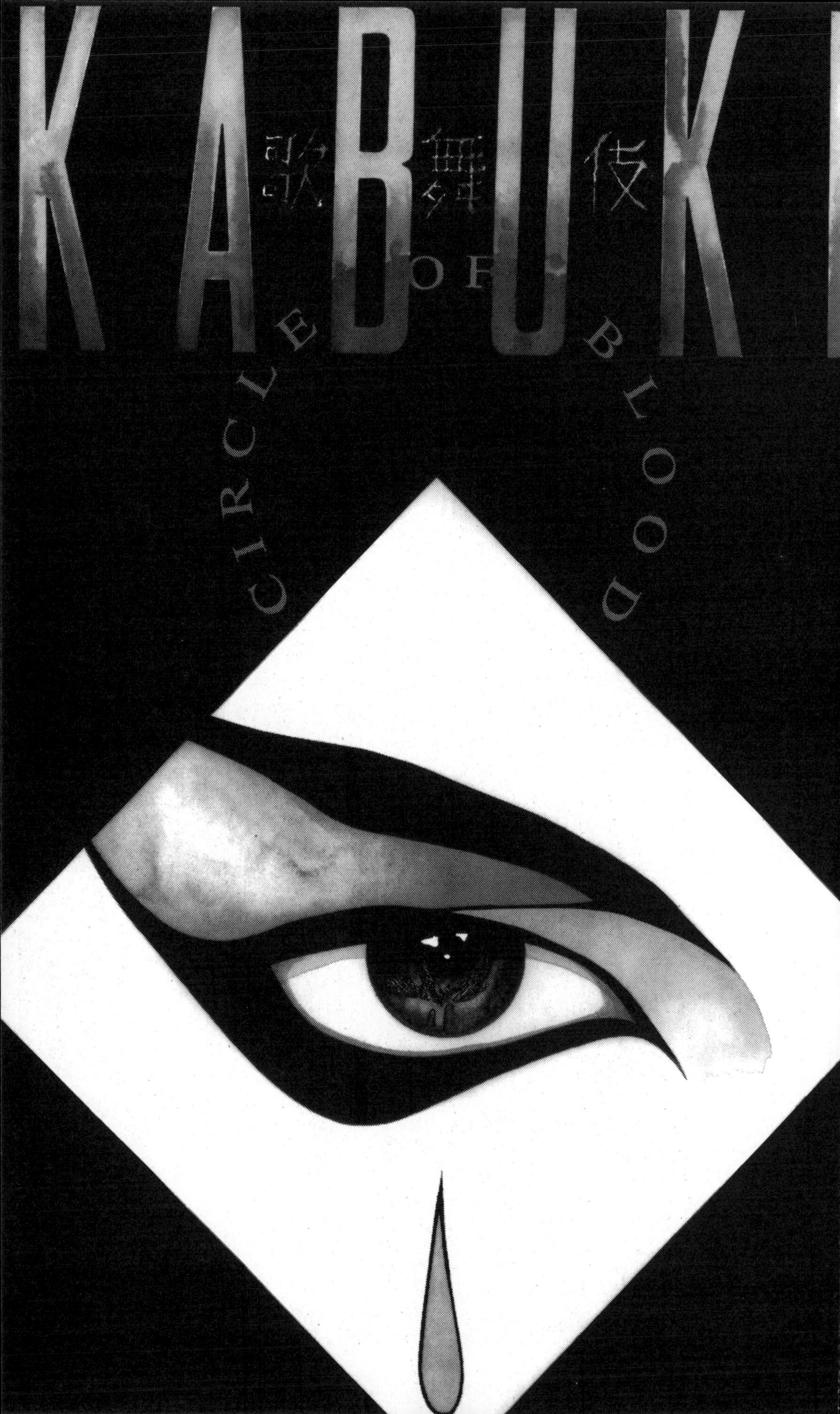
KABUKI
歌舞伎
CIRCLE OF BLOOD

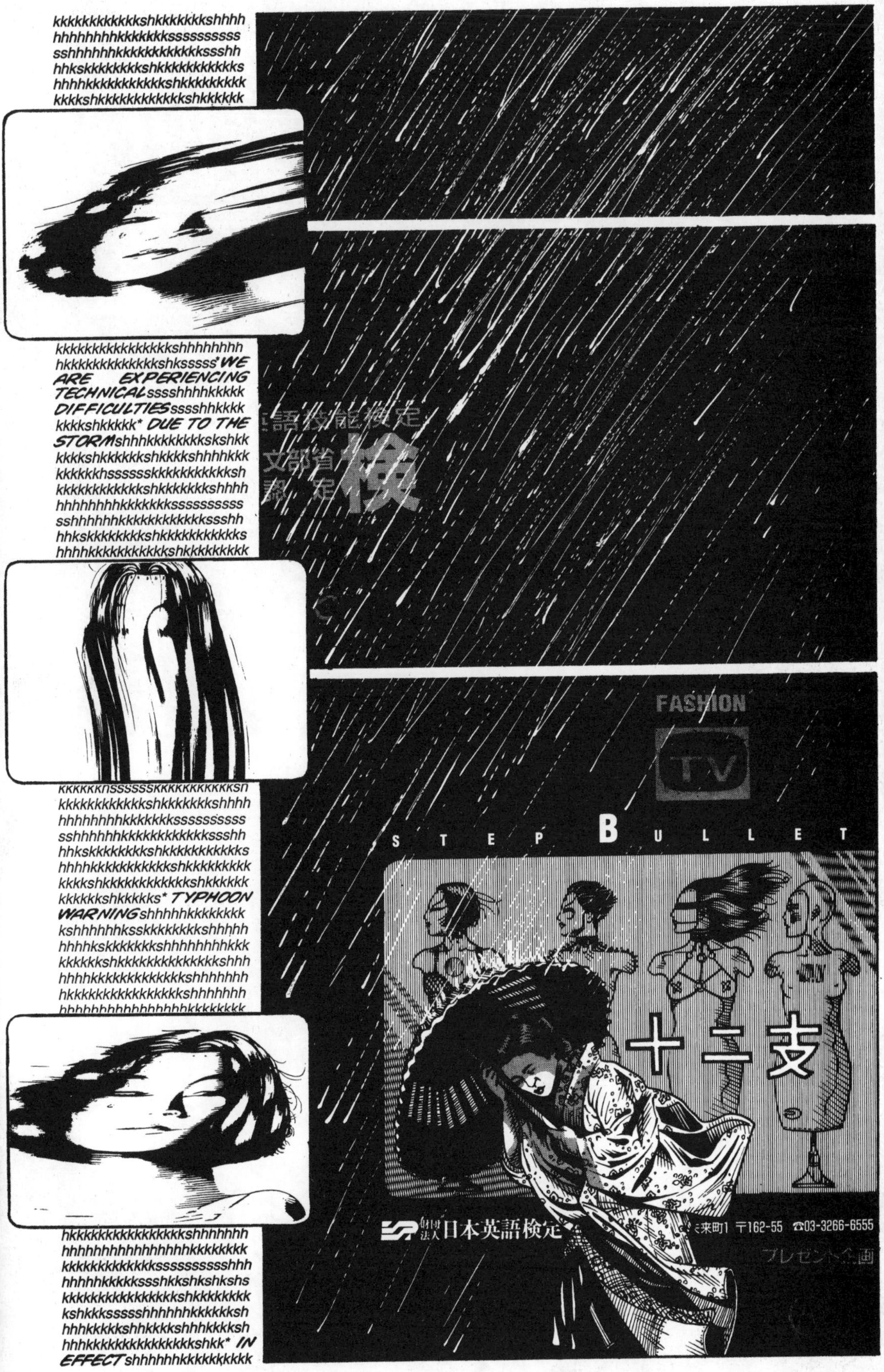
kkkkkkkkkkkkshkkkkkkkshhhh
hhhhhhhhkkkkkkkssssssssss
sshhhhhhkkkkkkkkkkkkkssshh
hhkskkkkkkkkshkkkkkkkkkkks
hhhhkkkkkkkkkkkshkkkkkkkkk
kkkkshkkkkkkkkkkkkshkkkkkk
kkkkkkkkkkkkkkkkshhhhhhhh
hkkkkkkkkkkkkkkshksssss* WE ARE EXPERIENCING TECHNICAL sssshhhhkkkkk
DIFFICULTIES sssshhkkkk
kkkkshkkkkk* DUE TO THE STORM shhhkkkkkkkkkskshkk
kkkkshkkkkkkshkkkkshhhhkkk
kkkkkkhssssssskkkkkkkkkkksh
kkkkkkkkkkkkshkkkkkkkkshhhh
hhhhhhhhkkkkkkkssssssssss
sshhhhhhkkkkkkkkkkkkkssshh
hhkskkkkkkkkshkkkkkkkkkkks
hhhhkkkkkkkkkkkkshkkkkkkkkk
語技能検定
文部省
認定
検
FASHION
TV
STEP BULLET
kkkkkkhssssssskkkkkkkkkkksh
kkkkkkkkkkkkshkkkkkkkkshhhh
hhhhhhhhkkkkkkkssssssssss
sshhhhhhkkkkkkkkkkkkkssshh
hhkskkkkkkkkshkkkkkkkkkkks
hhhhkkkkkkkkkkkkshkkkkkkkkk
kkkkshkkkkkkkkkkkkkshkkkkkk
kkkkkkshkkkkkks* TYPHOON WARNING shhhhhkkkkkkkk
kshhhhhhksskkkkkkkkshhhhh
hhhhkskkkkkkkshhhhhhhhkkk
kkkkkkshkkkkkkkkkkkkkkkshhh
hhhhkkkkkkkkkkkkkkshhhhhhh
hkkkkkkkkkkkkkkkkkshhhhhhh
hhhhhhhhhhhhhhhhhkkkkkkk
十二支
財団法人日本英語検定
来町1 〒162-55 ☎03-3266-6555
プレゼント企画
hkkkkkkkkkkkkkkkkshhhhhhh
hhhhhhhhhhhhhhhhkkkkkkkk
kkkkkkkkkkkkkksssssssssshhh
hhhhhkkkkkssshkkshkshkshs
kkkkkkkkkkkkkkkkkkshkkkkkkk
kshkkksssssshhhhhhkkkkkksh
hhhkkkkkshhkkkkshhhkkkksh
hhhkkkkkkkkkkkkkkkkshkk* IN EFFECT shhhhhhkkkkkkkkk

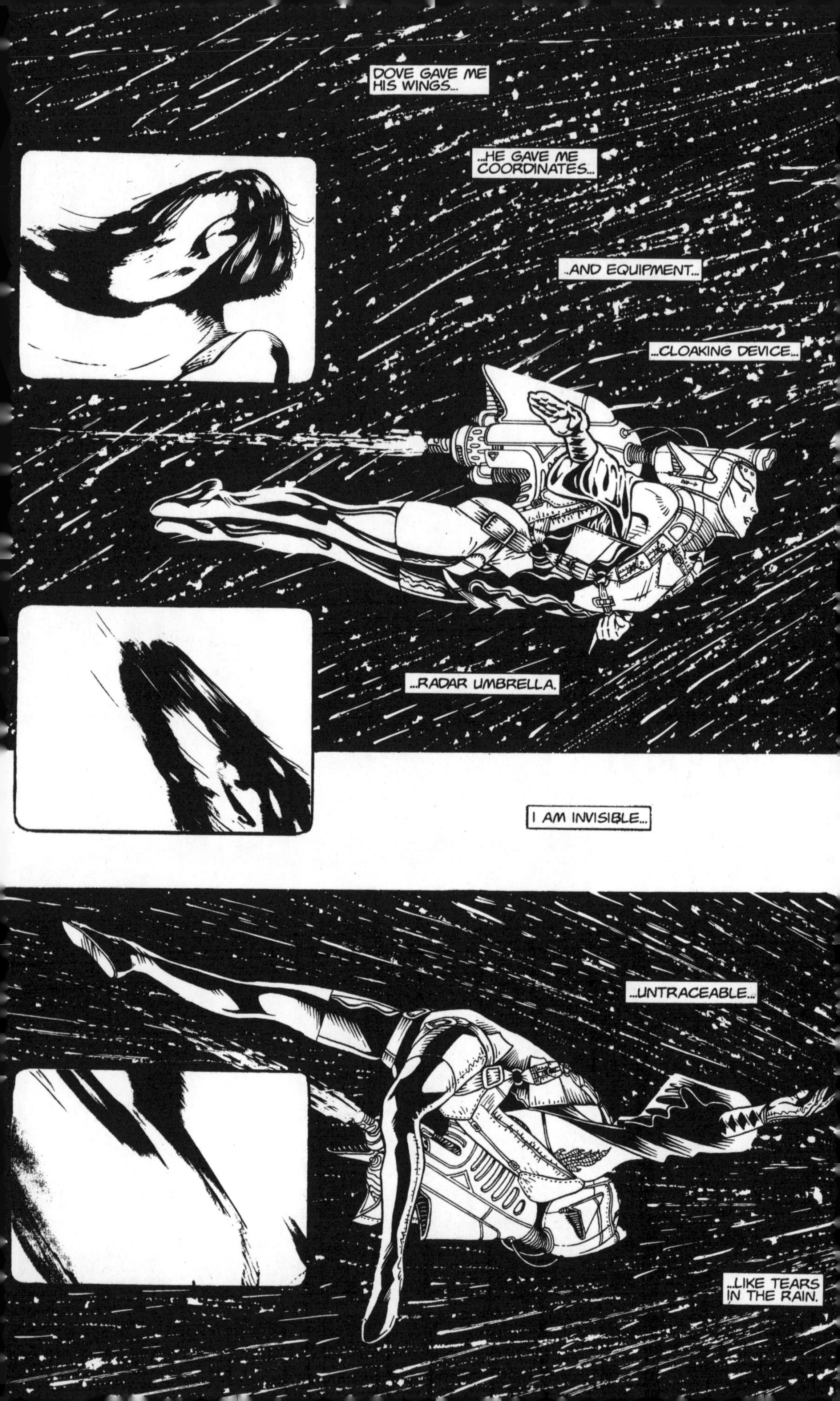
DOVE GAVE ME HIS WINGS...
...HE GAVE ME COORDINATES...
...AND EQUIPMENT...
...CLOAKING DEVICE...
...RADAR UMBRELLA.
I AM INVISIBLE...
...UNTRACEABLE...
...LIKE TEARS IN THE RAIN.

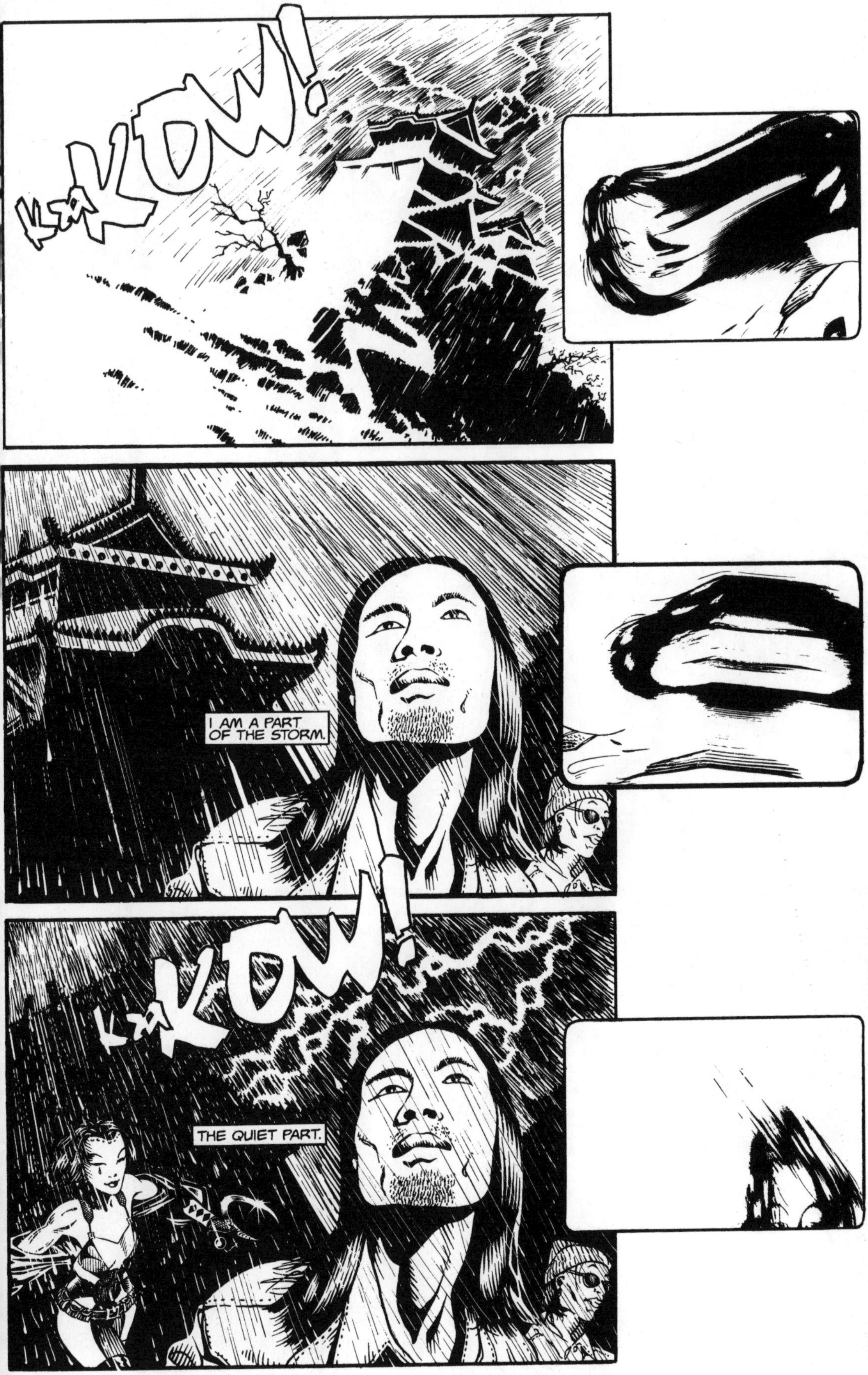

K-RAKOW!
I AM A PART
OF THE STORM.
K-RAKOW!
THE QUIET PART.

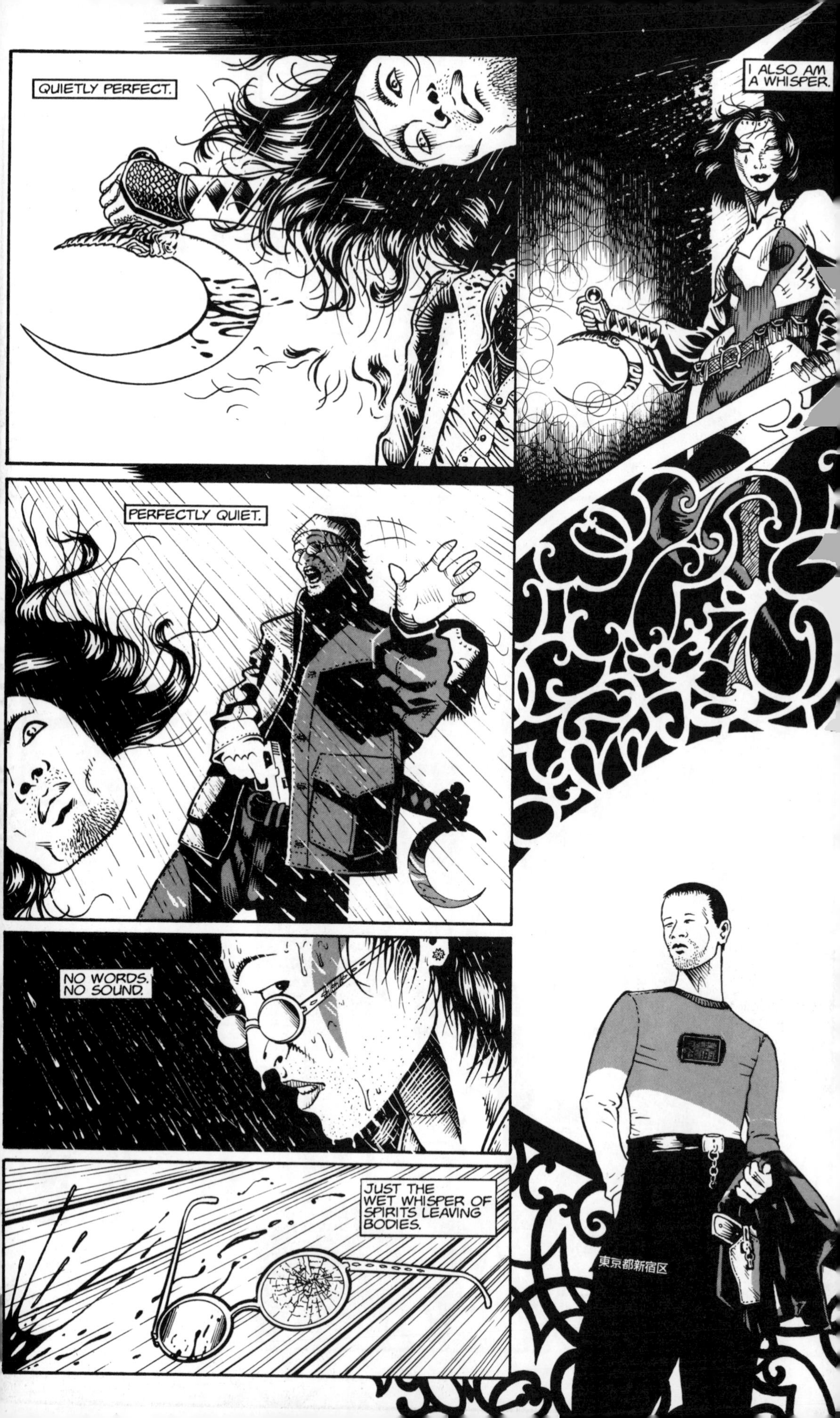
QUIETLY PERFECT.
I ALSO AM A WHISPER.
PERFECTLY QUIET.
NO WORDS. NO SOUND.
JUST THE WET WHISPER OF SPIRITS LEAVING BODIES.
東京都新宿区

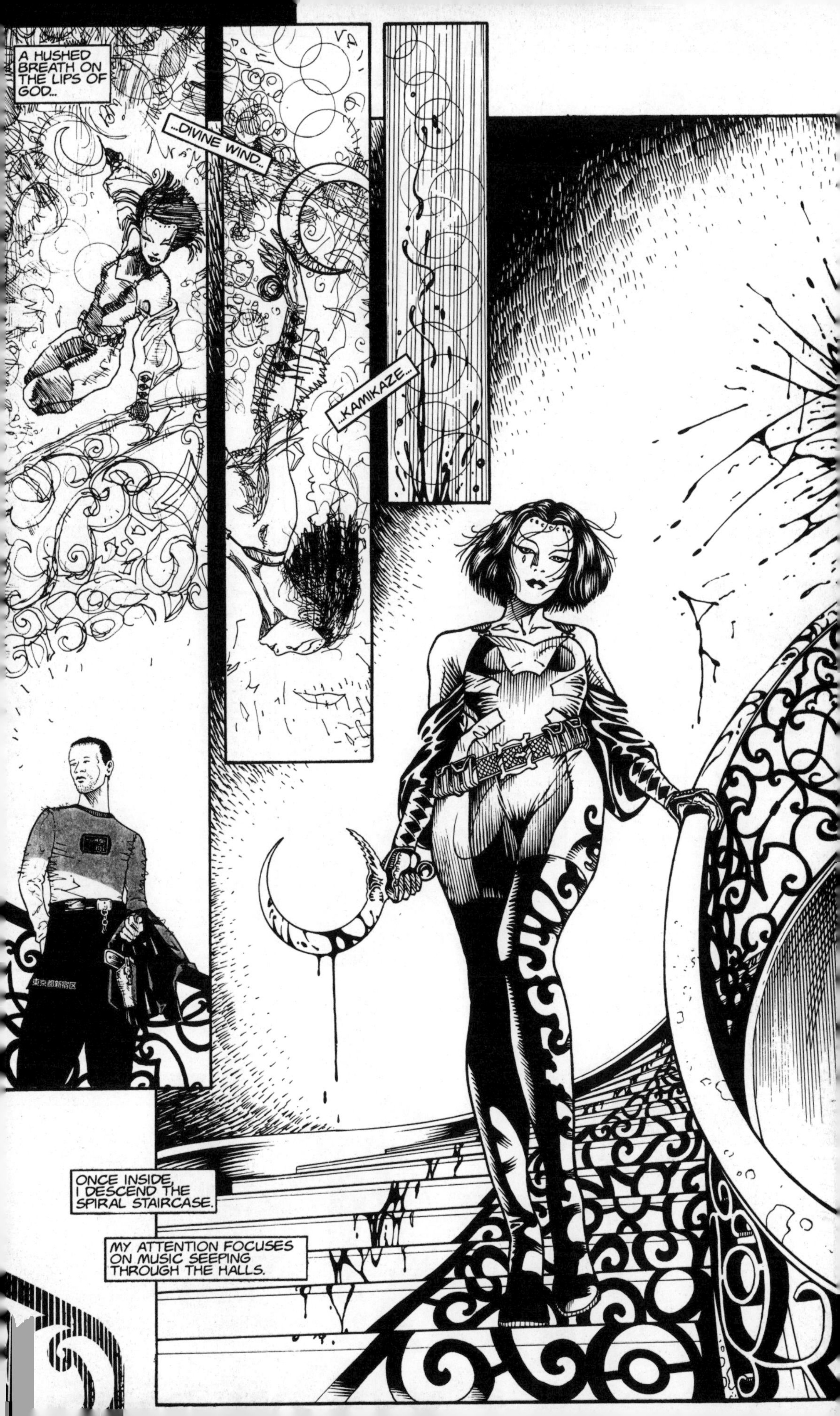
A HUSHED BREATH ON THE LIPS OF GOD...
...DIVINE WIND...
...KAMIKAZE...
東京都新宿区
ONCE INSIDE, I DESCEND THE SPIRAL STAIRCASE.
MY ATTENTION FOCUSES ON MUSIC SEEPING THROUGH THE HALLS.

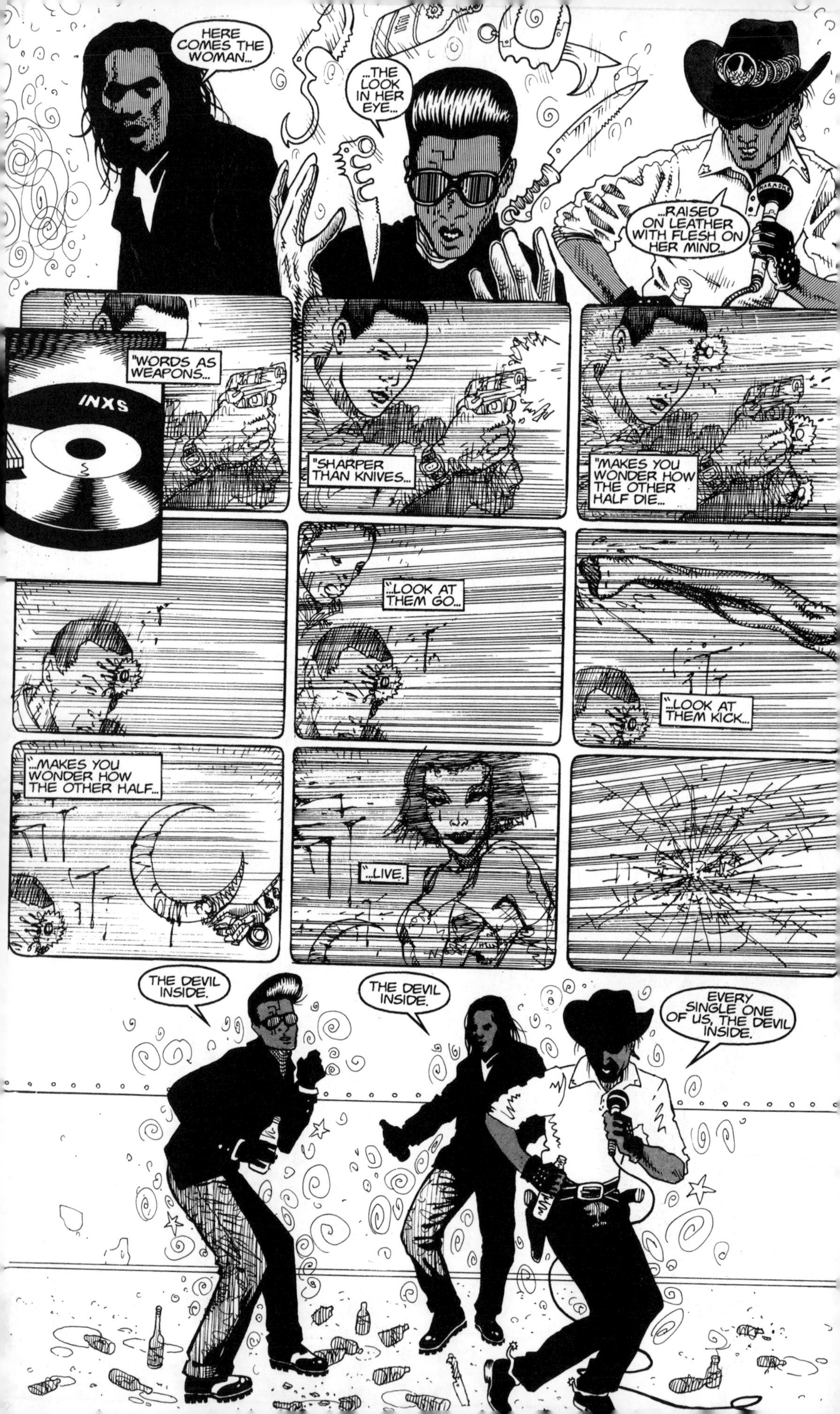
HERE COMES THE WOMAN...
...THE LOOK IN HER EYE...
...RAISED ON LEATHER WITH FLESH ON HER MIND...
INXS
"WORDS AS WEAPONS...
"SHARPER THAN KNIVES...
"MAKES YOU WONDER HOW THE OTHER HALF DIE...
"...LOOK AT THEM GO...
"...LOOK AT THEM KICK...
"...MAKES YOU WONDER HOW THE OTHER HALF...
"...LIVE.
THE DEVIL INSIDE.
THE DEVIL INSIDE.
EVERY SINGLE ONE OF US, THE DEVIL INSIDE.

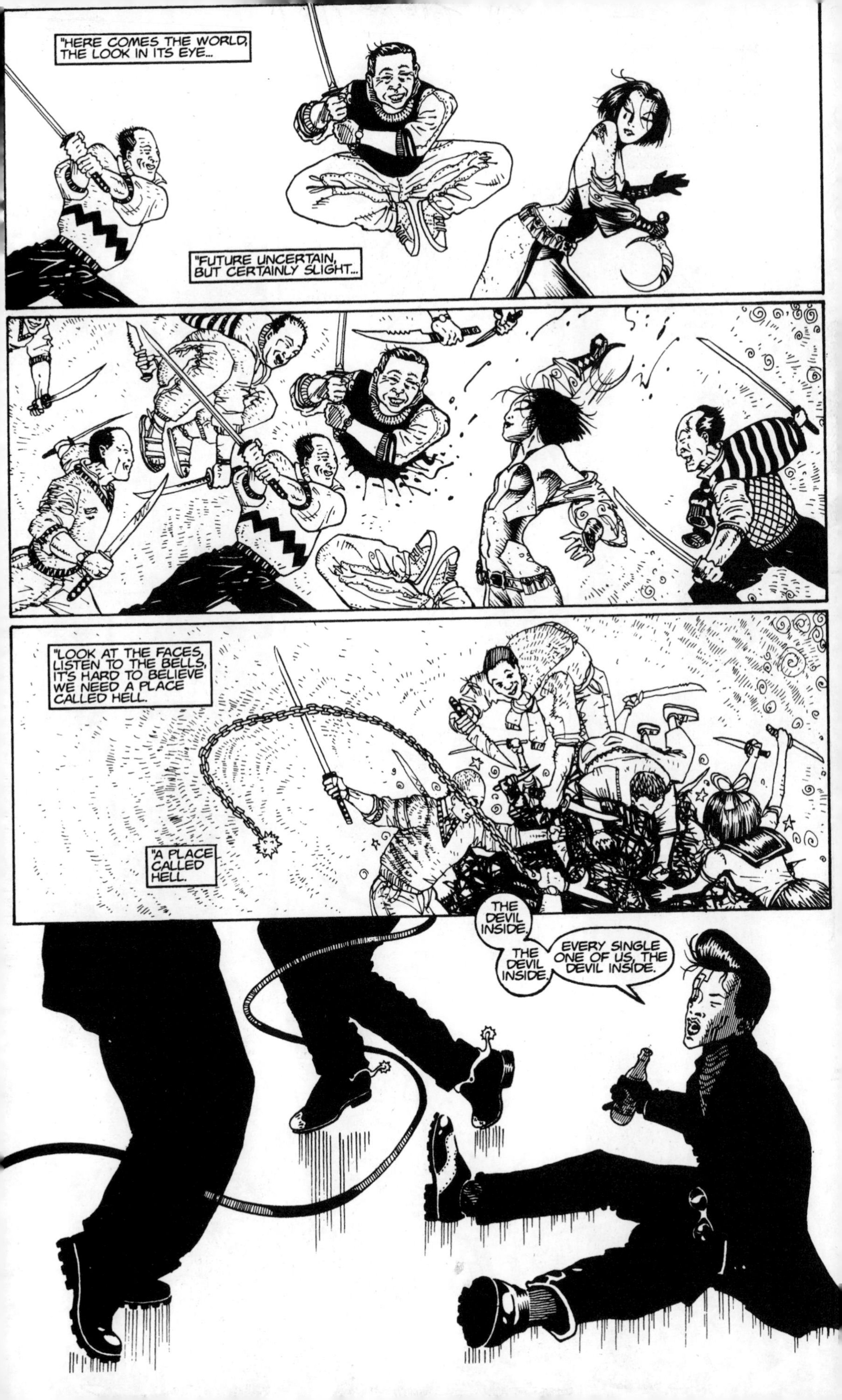
"HERE COMES THE WORLD, THE LOOK IN ITS EYE...
"FUTURE UNCERTAIN, BUT CERTAINLY SLIGHT...
"LOOK AT THE FACES, LISTEN TO THE BELLS, IT'S HARD TO BELIEVE WE NEED A PLACE CALLED HELL.
"A PLACE CALLED HELL.
THE DEVIL INSIDE.
THE DEVIL INSIDE.
EVERY SINGLE ONE OF US, THE DEVIL INSIDE.

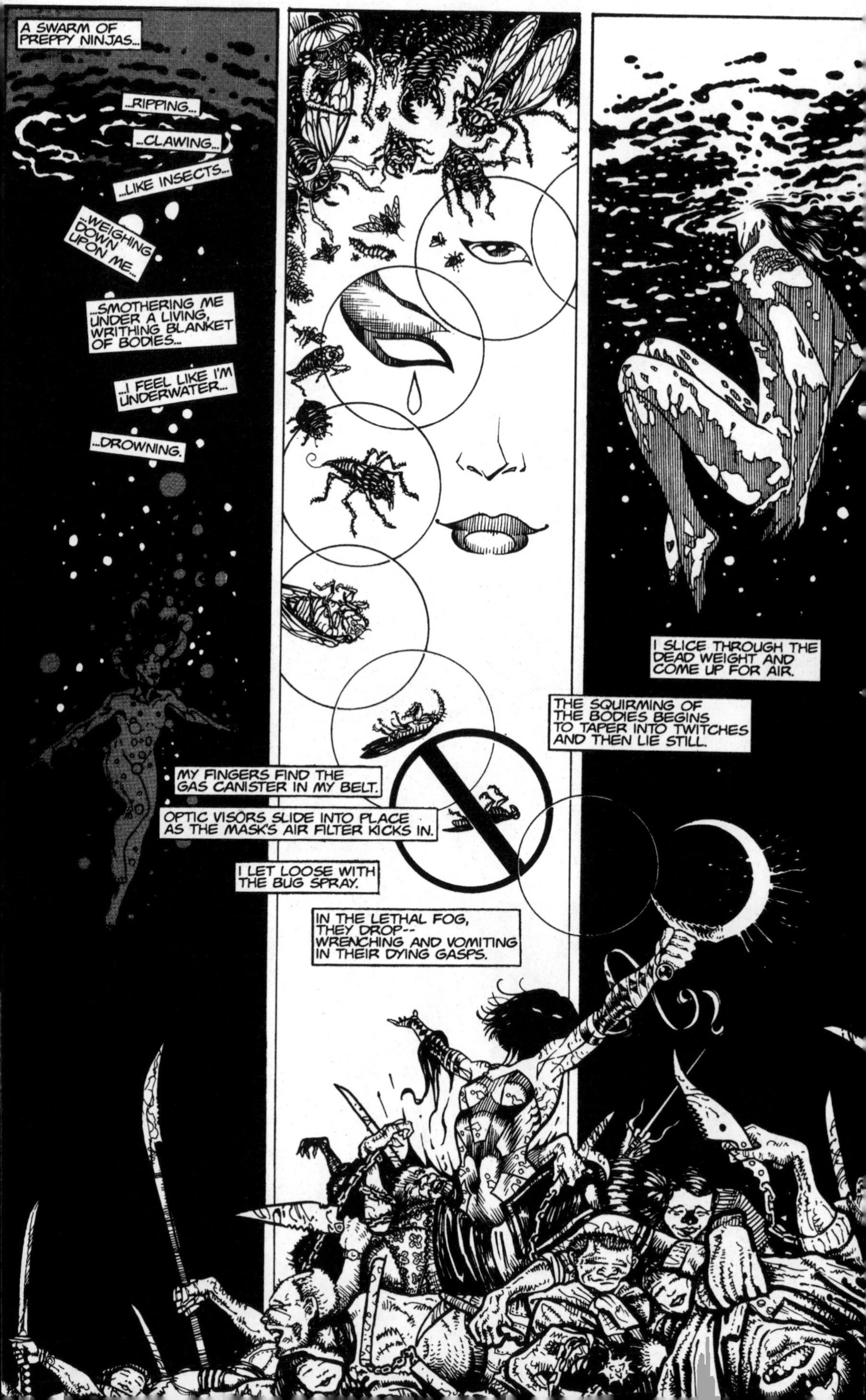
A SWARM OF PREPPY NINJAS...
...RIPPING...
...CLAWING...
...LIKE INSECTS...
...WEIGHING DOWN UPON ME...
...SMOTHERING ME UNDER A LIVING, WRITHING BLANKET OF BODIES...
...I FEEL LIKE I'M UNDERWATER...
...DROWNING.
MY FINGERS FIND THE GAS CANISTER IN MY BELT.
OPTIC VISORS SLIDE INTO PLACE AS THE MASK'S AIR FILTER KICKS IN.
I LET LOOSE WITH THE BUG SPRAY.
IN THE LETHAL FOG, THEY DROP-- WRENCHING AND VOMITING IN THEIR DYING GASPS.
THE SQUIRMING OF THE BODIES BEGINS TO TAPER INTO TWITCHES AND THEN LIE STILL.
I SLICE THROUGH THE DEAD WEIGHT AND COME UP FOR AIR.

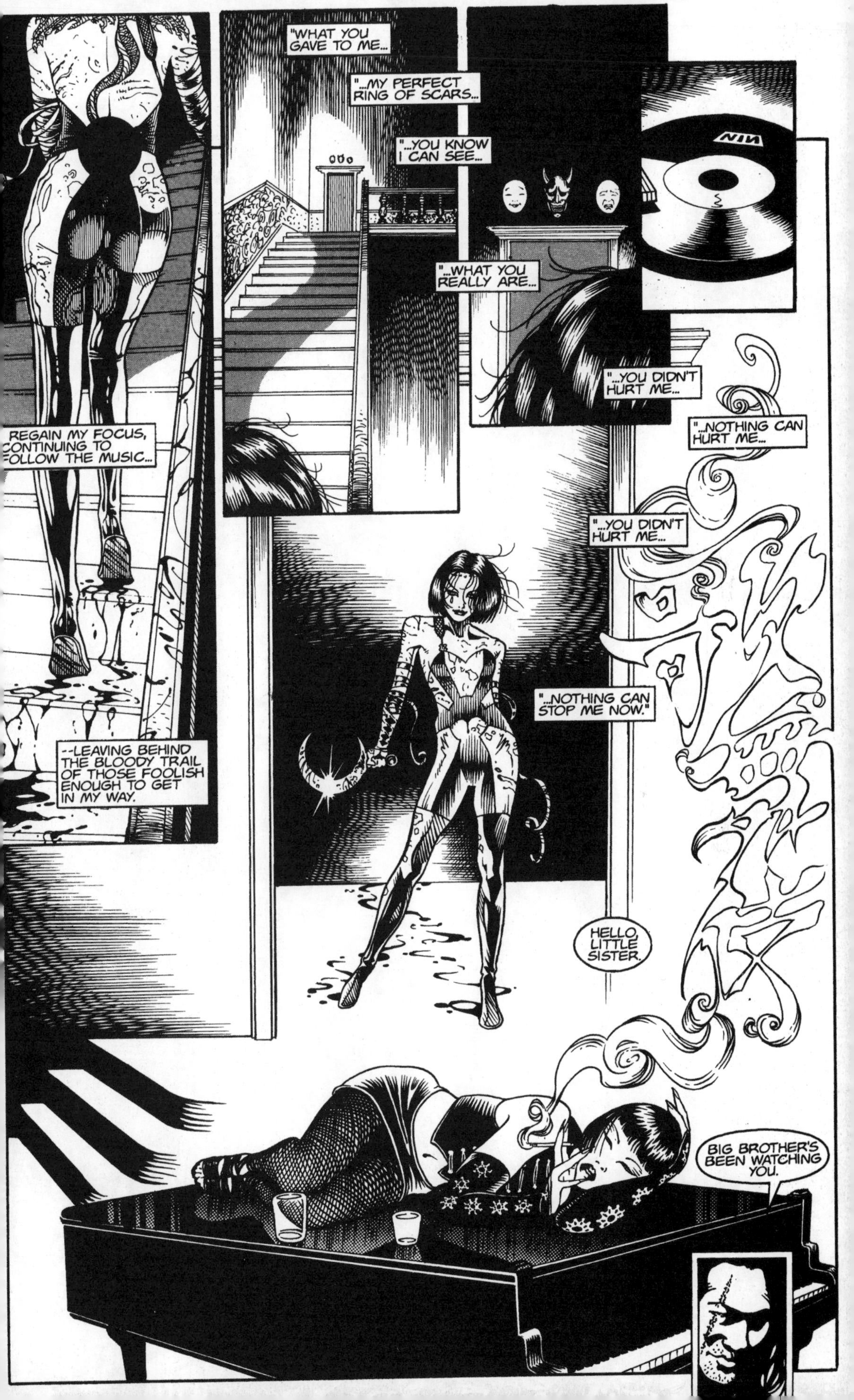

I REGAIN MY FOCUS, CONTINUING TO FOLLOW THE MUSIC...
--LEAVING BEHIND THE BLOODY TRAIL OF THOSE FOOLISH ENOUGH TO GET IN MY WAY.
"WHAT YOU GAVE TO ME...
"...MY PERFECT RING OF SCARS...
"...YOU KNOW I CAN SEE...
"...WHAT YOU REALLY ARE...
NIN
"...YOU DIDN'T HURT ME...
"...NOTHING CAN HURT ME...
"...YOU DIDN'T HURT ME...
"...NOTHING CAN STOP ME NOW."
HELLO, LITTLE SISTER.
BIG BROTHER'S BEEN WATCHING YOU.

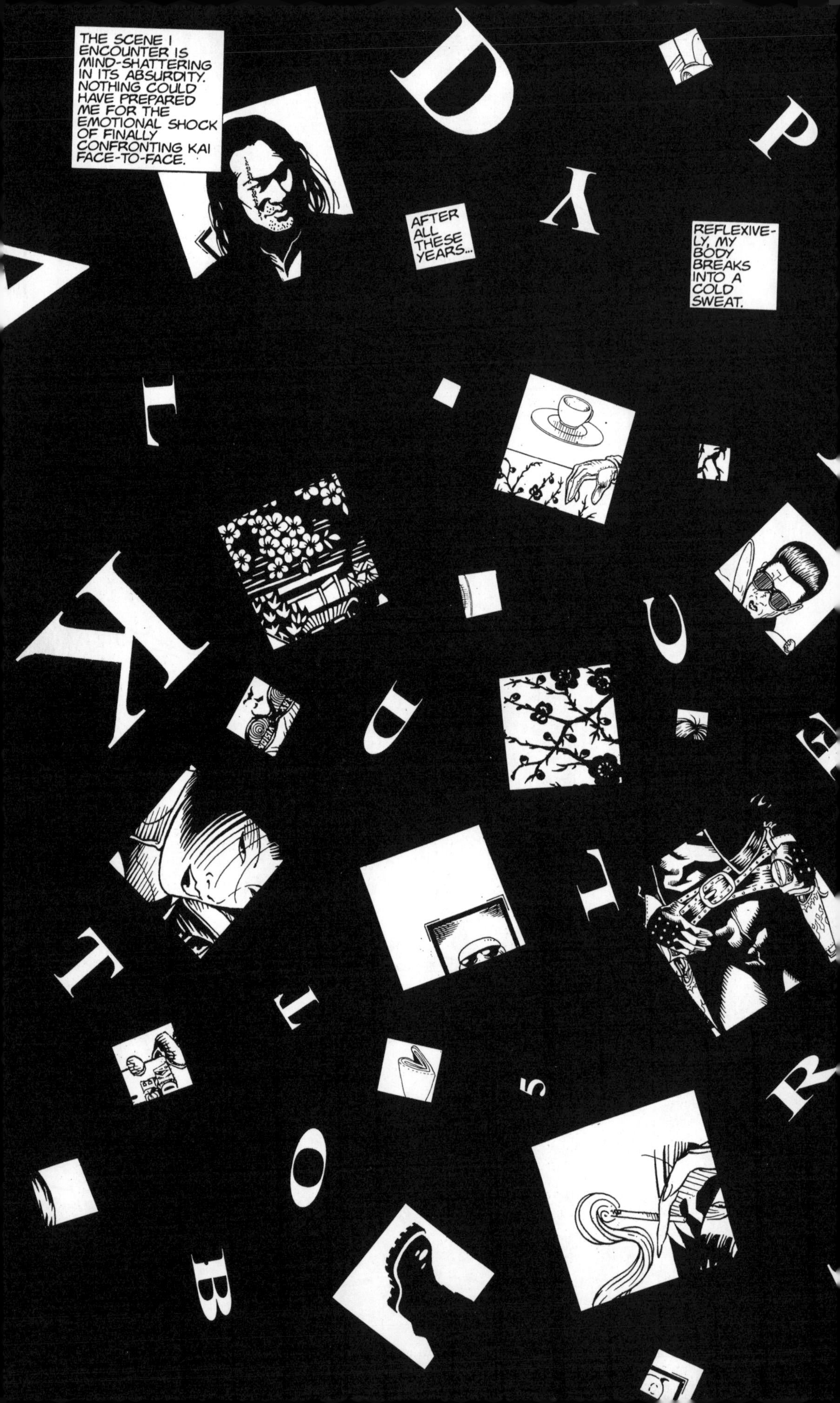

THE SCENE I ENCOUNTER IS MIND-SHATTERING IN ITS ABSURDITY. NOTHING COULD HAVE PREPARED ME FOR THE EMOTIONAL SHOCK OF FINALLY CONFRONTING KAI FACE-TO-FACE.
AFTER ALL THESE YEARS...
REFLEXIVELY, MY BODY BREAKS INTO A COLD SWEAT.

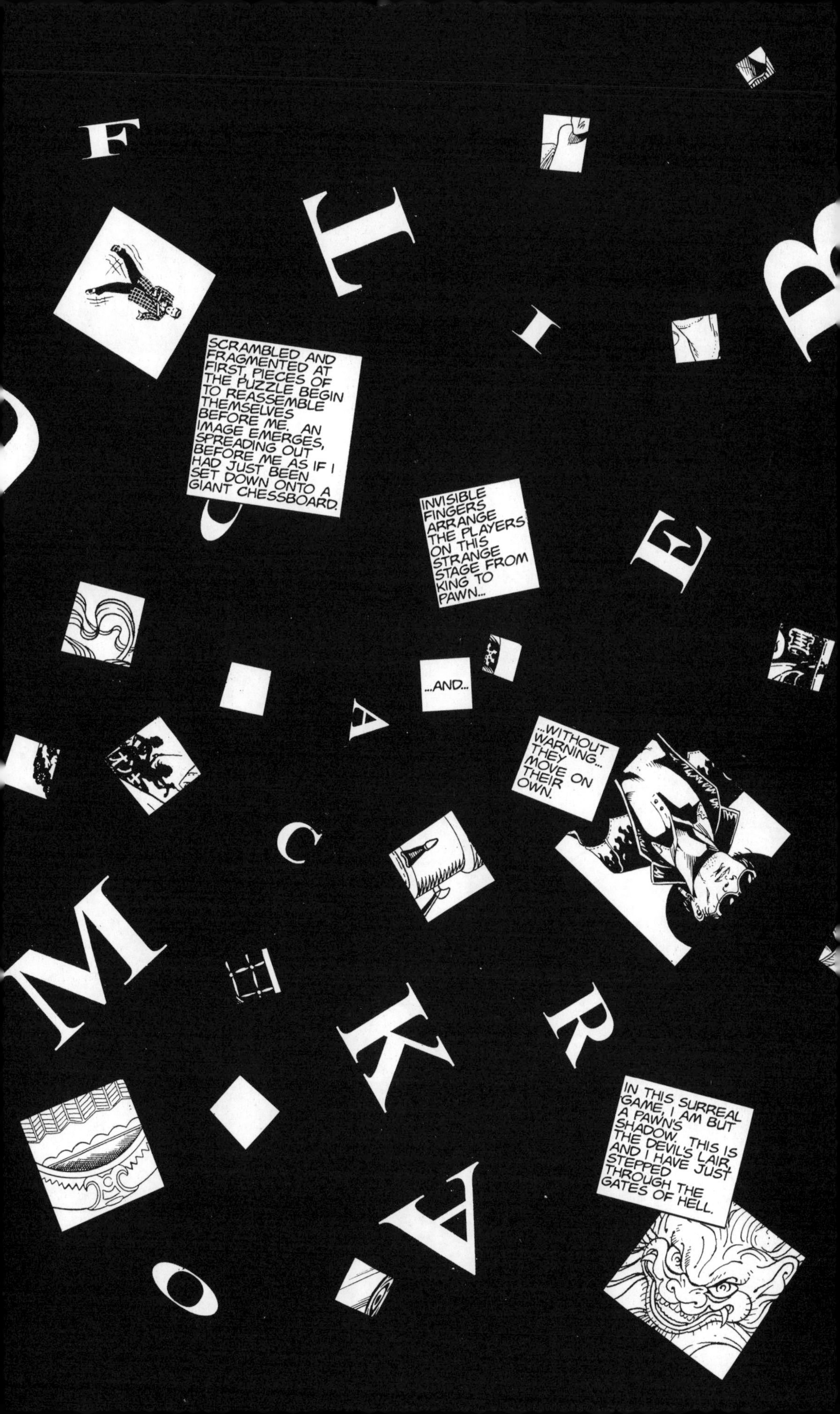
SCRAMBLED AND FRAGMENTED AT FIRST, PIECES OF THE PUZZLE BEGIN TO REASSEMBLE THEMSELVES BEFORE ME. AN IMAGE EMERGES, SPREADING OUT BEFORE ME AS IF I HAD JUST BEEN SET DOWN ONTO A GIANT CHESSBOARD.
INVISIBLE FINGERS ARRANGE THE PLAYERS ON THIS STRANGE STAGE FROM KING TO PAWN...
...AND...
...WITHOUT WARNING... THEY MOVE ON THEIR OWN.
IN THIS SURREAL GAME, I AM BUT A PAWN'S SHADOW. THIS IS THE DEVIL'S LAIR, AND I HAVE JUST STEPPED THROUGH THE GATES OF HELL.

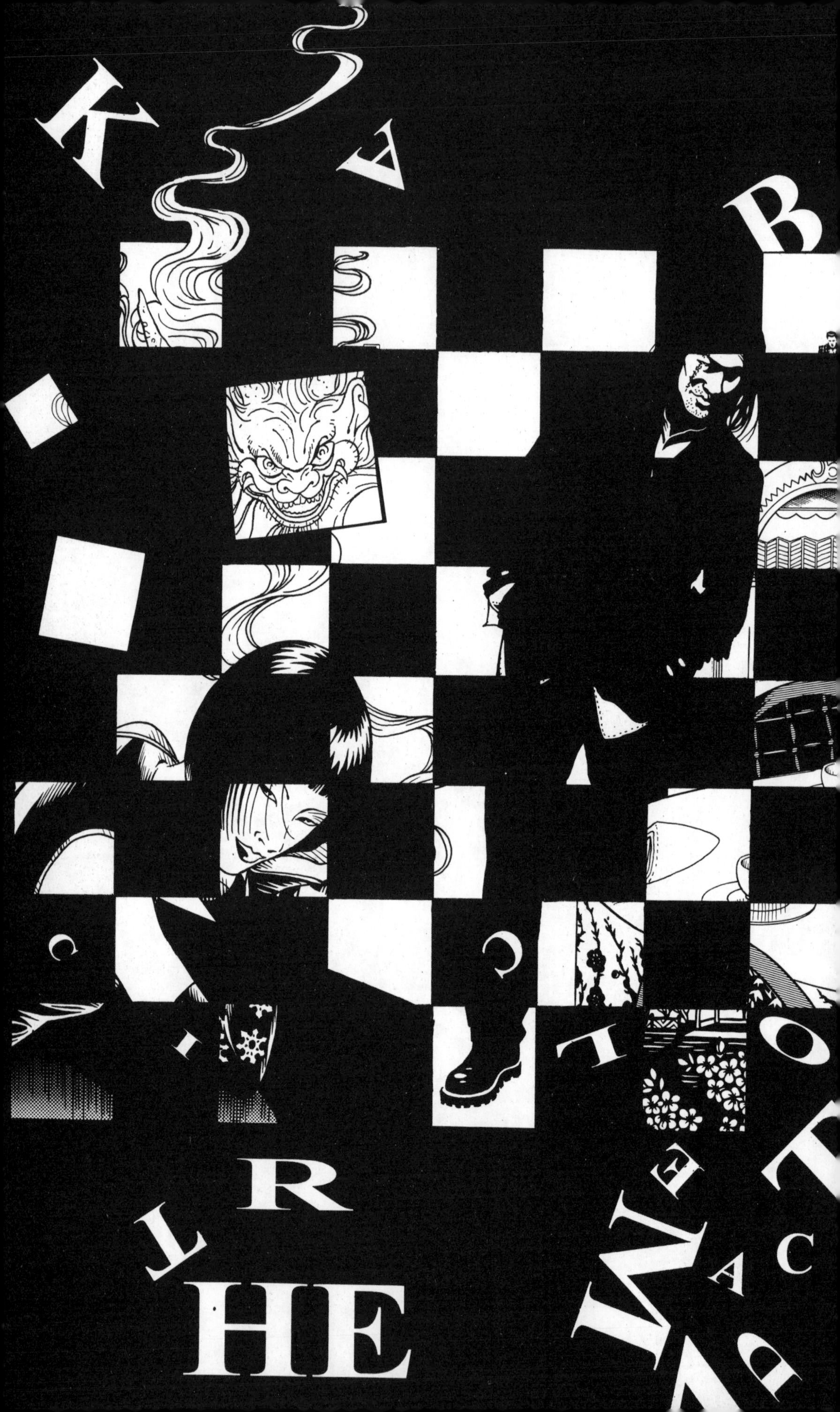

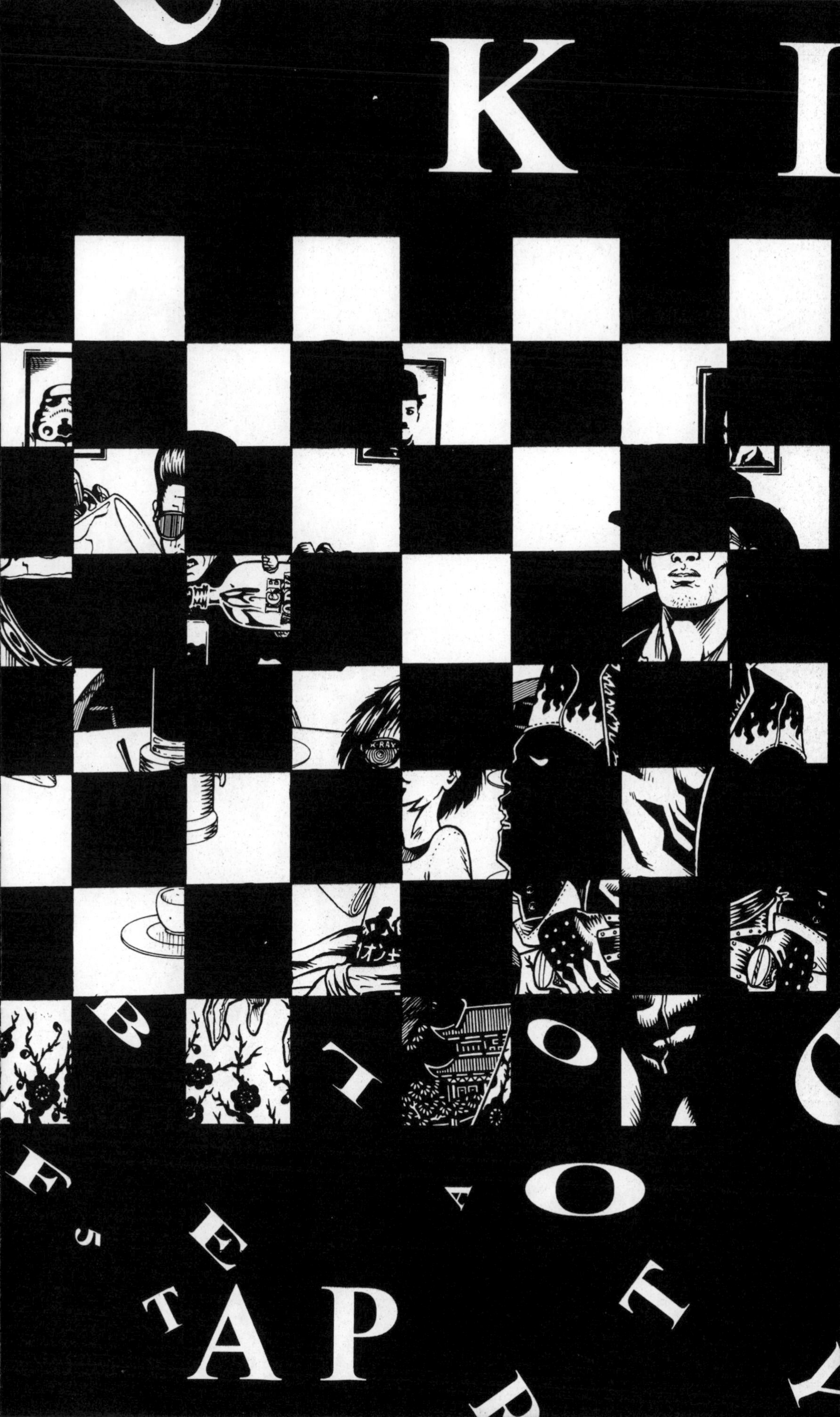

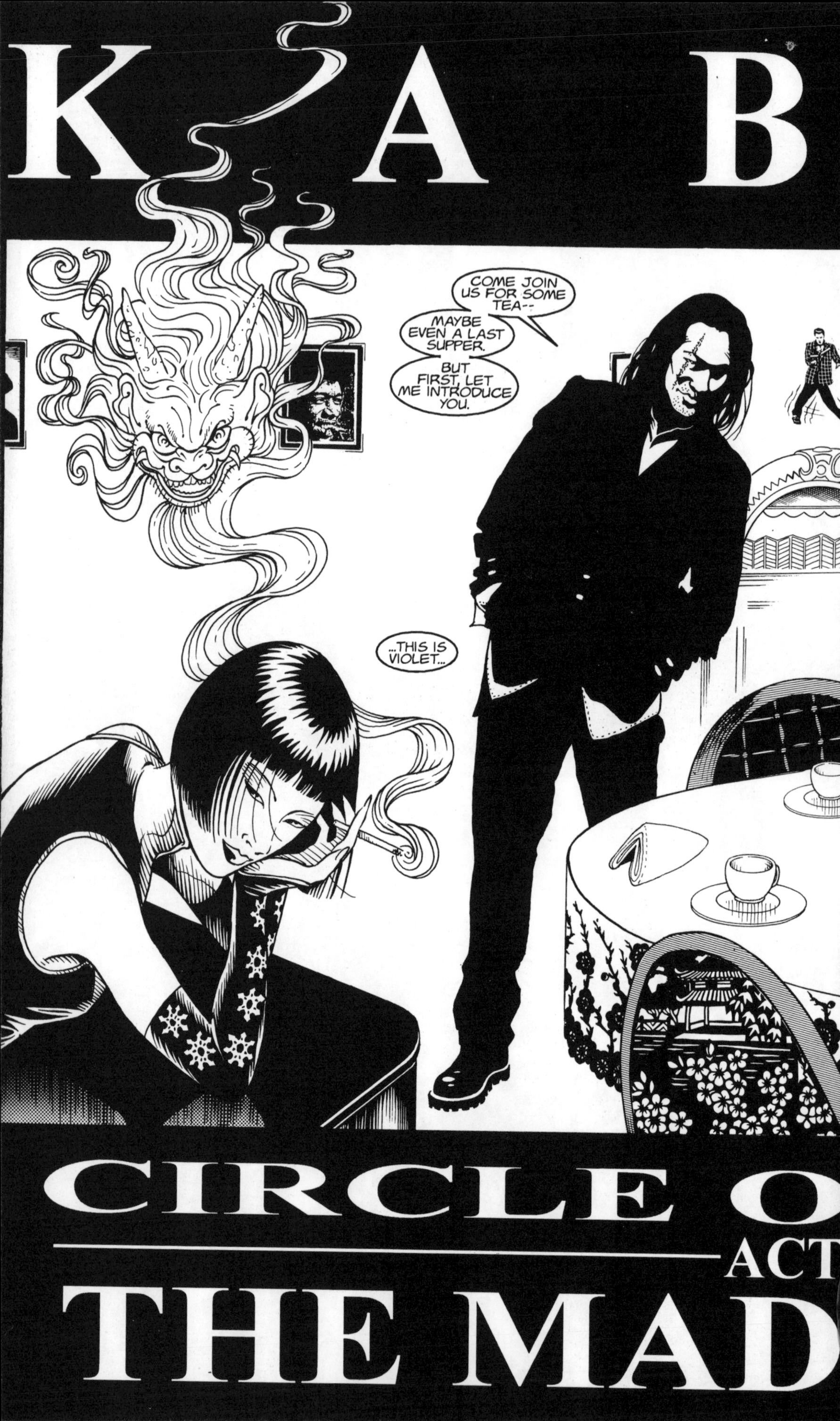
K A B
COME JOIN US FOR SOME TEA--
MAYBE EVEN A LAST SUPPER.
BUT FIRST, LET ME INTRODUCE YOU.
...THIS IS VIOLET...
CIRCLE O
ACT
THE MAD

U K I

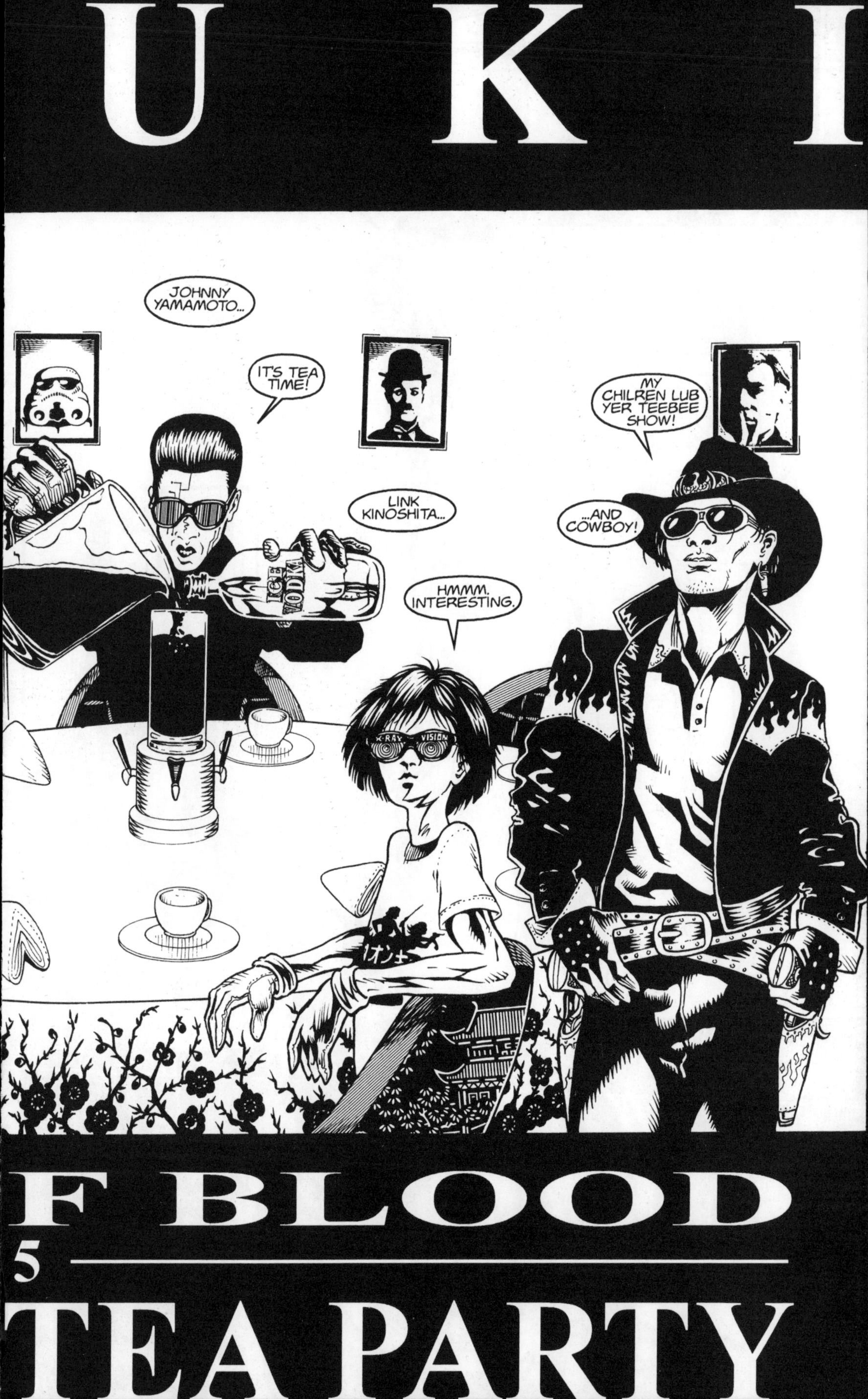
JOHNNY YAMAMOTO...
IT'S TEA TIME!
MY CHILREN LUB YER TEEBEE SHOW!
LINK KINOSHITA...
...AND COWBOY!
HMMM. INTERESTING.
ICE VODKA
X-RAY VISION

F BLOOD

5

TEA PARTY

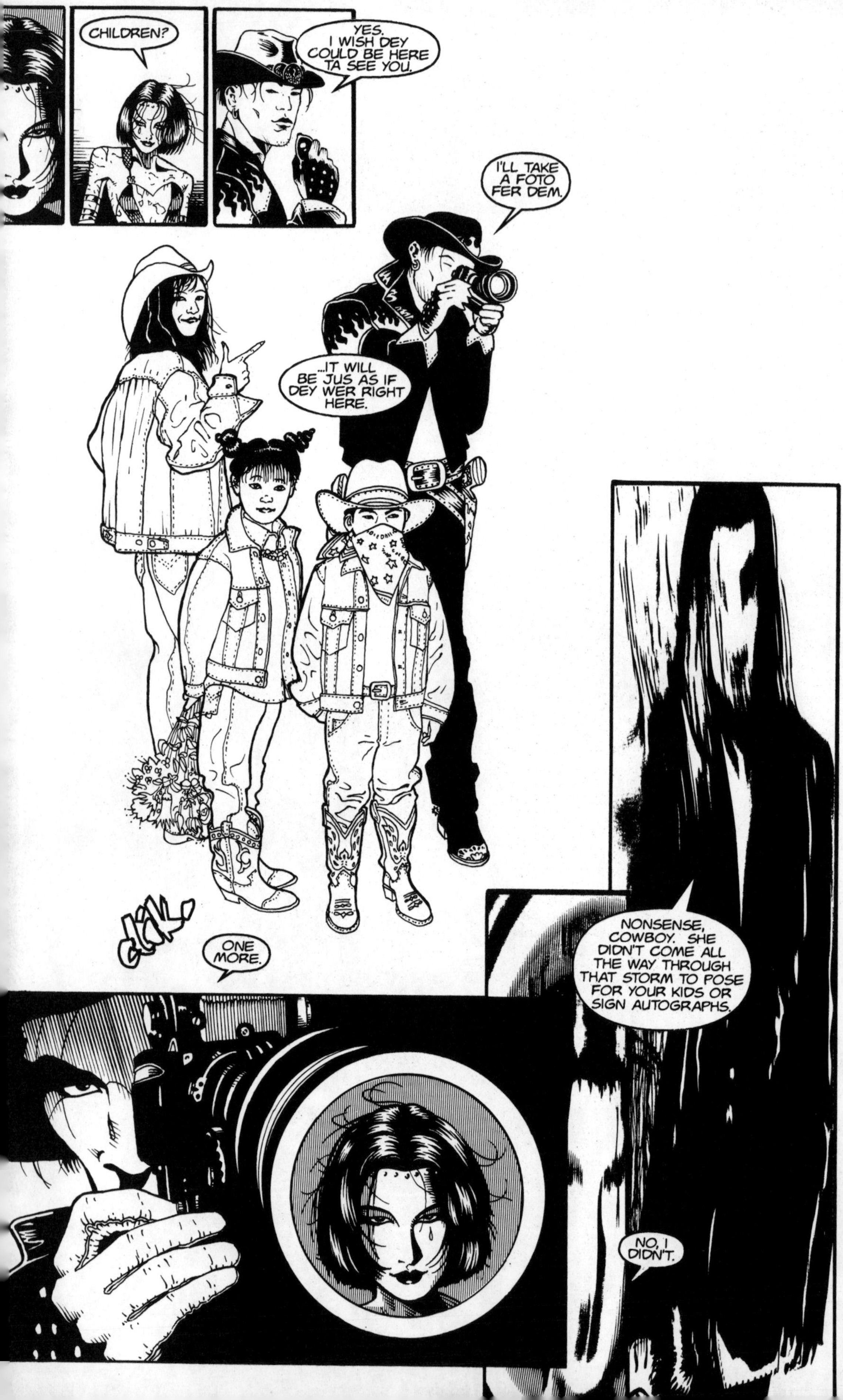
CHILDREN?
YES. I WISH DEY COULD BE HERE TA SEE YOU.
I'LL TAKE A FOTO FER DEM.
...IT WILL BE JUS AS IF DEY WER RIGHT HERE.
ONE MORE.
NONSENSE, COWBOY. SHE DIDN'T COME ALL THE WAY THROUGH THAT STORM TO POSE FOR YOUR KIDS OR SIGN AUTOGRAPHS.
NO, I DIDN'T.

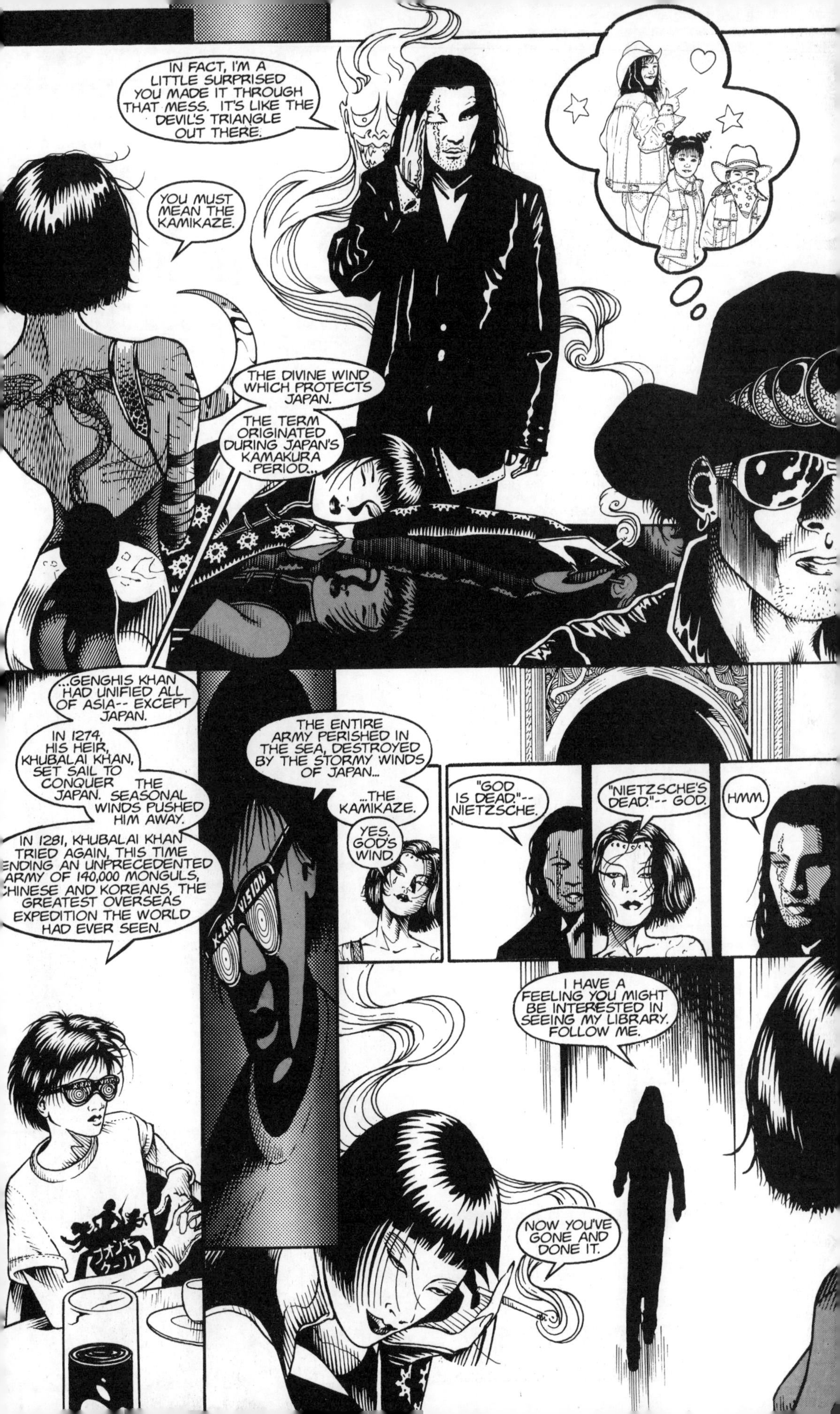

IN FACT, I'M A LITTLE SURPRISED YOU MADE IT THROUGH THAT MESS. IT'S LIKE THE DEVIL'S TRIANGLE OUT THERE.
YOU MUST MEAN THE KAMIKAZE.
THE DIVINE WIND WHICH PROTECTS JAPAN.
THE TERM ORIGINATED DURING JAPAN'S KAMAKURA PERIOD...
...GENGHIS KHAN HAD UNIFIED ALL OF ASIA-- EXCEPT JAPAN.
IN 1274, HIS HEIR, KHUBALAI KHAN, SET SAIL TO CONQUER THE JAPAN. SEASONAL WINDS PUSHED HIM AWAY.
IN 1281, KHUBALAI KHAN TRIED AGAIN, THIS TIME SENDING AN UNPRECEDENTED ARMY OF 140,000 MONGULS, CHINESE AND KOREANS, THE GREATEST OVERSEAS EXPEDITION THE WORLD HAD EVER SEEN.
THE ENTIRE ARMY PERISHED IN THE SEA, DESTROYED BY THE STORMY WINDS OF JAPAN...
...THE KAMIKAZE.
YES. GOD'S WIND.
"GOD IS DEAD."-- NIETZSCHE.
"NIETZSCHE'S DEAD."-- GOD.
HMM.
I HAVE A FEELING YOU MIGHT BE INTERESTED IN SEEING MY LIBRARY. FOLLOW ME.
NOW YOU'VE GONE AND DONE IT.

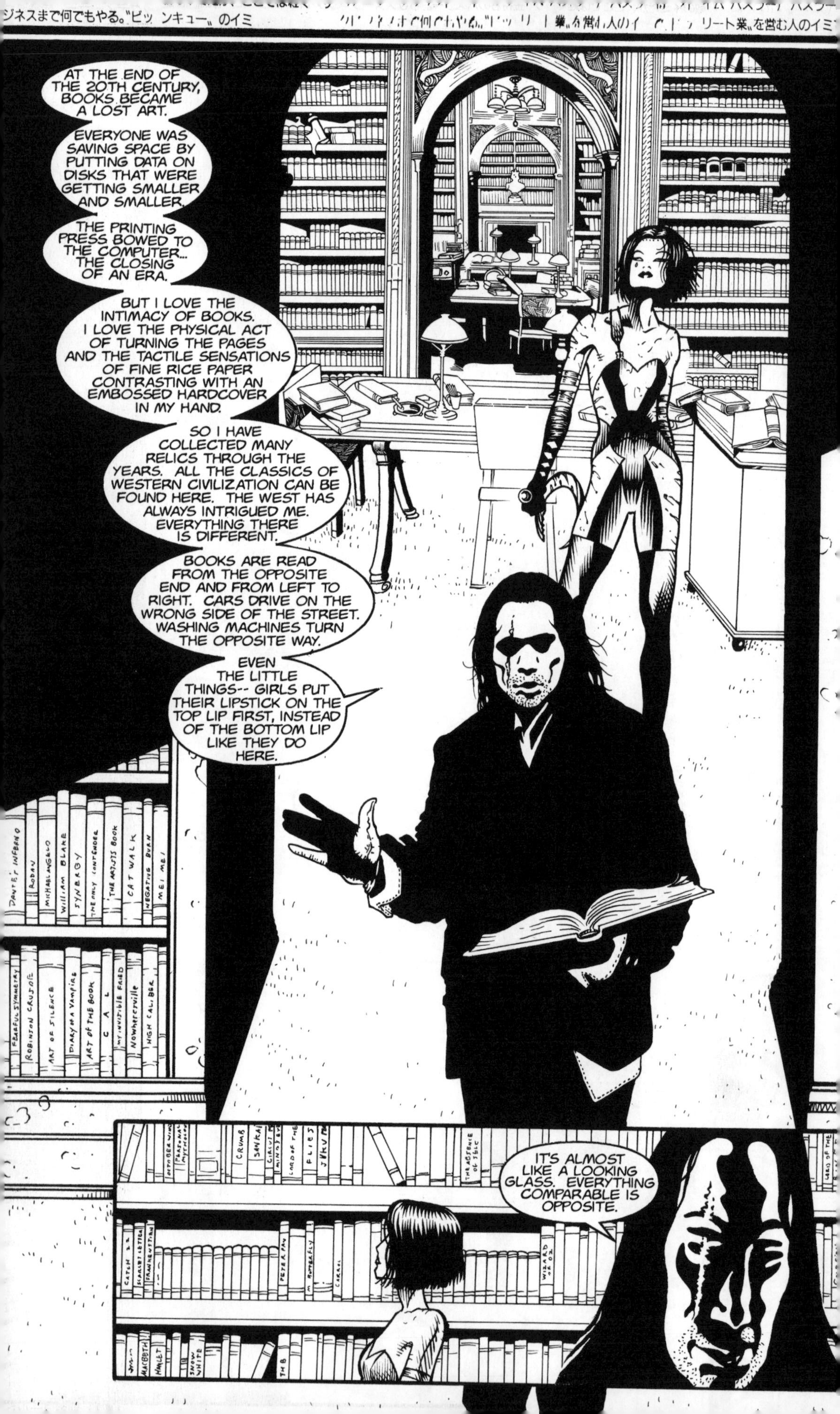
ジネスまで何でもやる。"ビッ ンキュー" のイミ
AT THE END OF THE 20TH CENTURY, BOOKS BECAME A LOST ART.
EVERYONE WAS SAVING SPACE BY PUTTING DATA ON DISKS THAT WERE GETTING SMALLER AND SMALLER.
THE PRINTING PRESS BOWED TO THE COMPUTER... THE CLOSING OF AN ERA.
BUT I LOVE THE INTIMACY OF BOOKS. I LOVE THE PHYSICAL ACT OF TURNING THE PAGES AND THE TACTILE SENSATIONS OF FINE RICE PAPER CONTRASTING WITH AN EMBOSSED HARDCOVER IN MY HAND.
SO I HAVE COLLECTED MANY RELICS THROUGH THE YEARS. ALL THE CLASSICS OF WESTERN CIVILIZATION CAN BE FOUND HERE. THE WEST HAS ALWAYS INTRIGUED ME. EVERYTHING THERE IS DIFFERENT.
BOOKS ARE READ FROM THE OPPOSITE END AND FROM LEFT TO RIGHT. CARS DRIVE ON THE WRONG SIDE OF THE STREET. WASHING MACHINES TURN THE OPPOSITE WAY.
EVEN THE LITTLE THINGS-- GIRLS PUT THEIR LIPSTICK ON THE TOP LIP FIRST, INSTEAD OF THE BOTTOM LIP LIKE THEY DO HERE.
IT'S ALMOST LIKE A LOOKING GLASS. EVERYTHING COMPARABLE IS OPPOSITE.

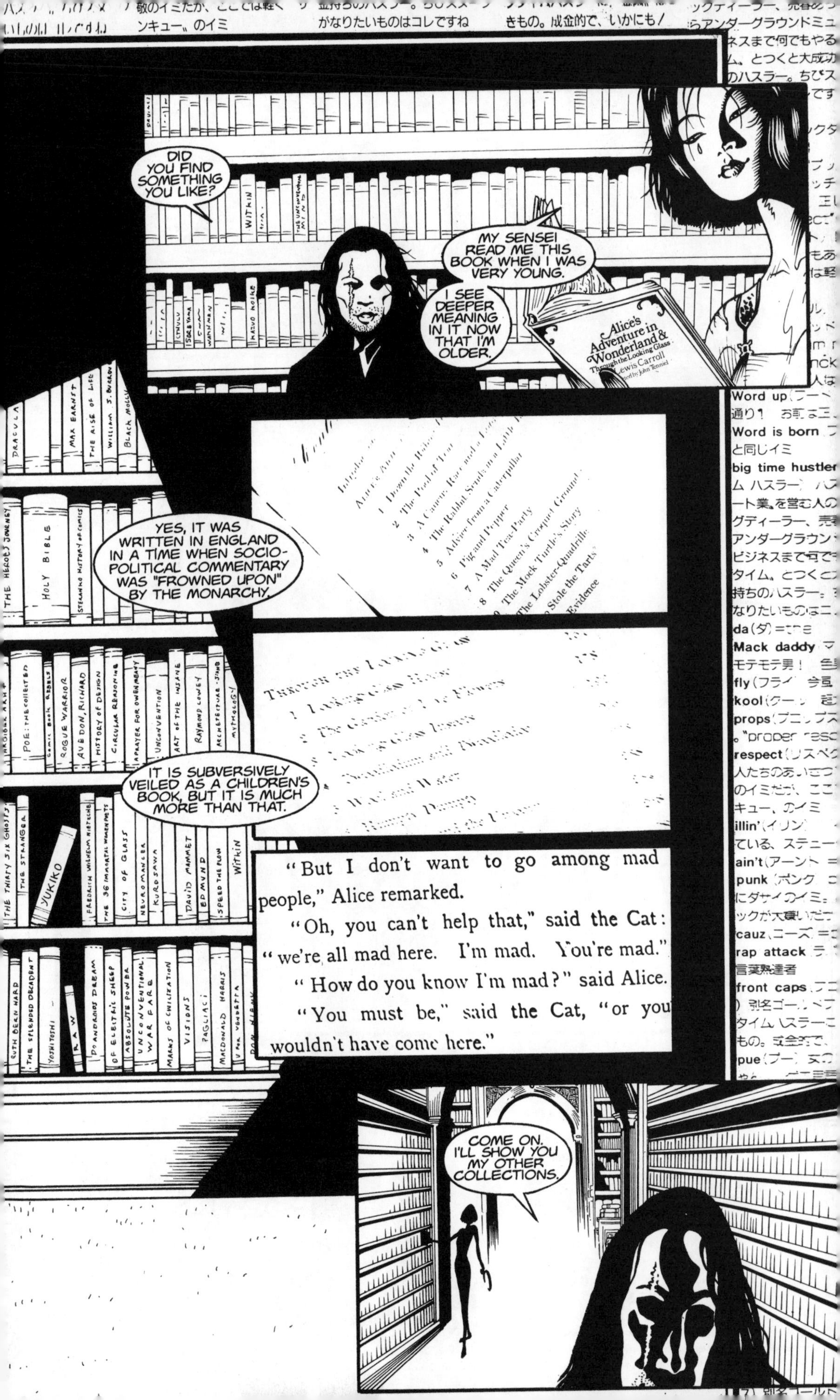
DID YOU FIND SOMETHING YOU LIKE?
MY SENSEI READ ME THIS BOOK WHEN I WAS VERY YOUNG.
I SEE DEEPER MEANING IN IT NOW THAT I'M OLDER.
Alice's Adventure in Wonderland & Through the Looking Glass
Lewis Carroll
YES, IT WAS WRITTEN IN ENGLAND IN A TIME WHEN SOCIO-POLITICAL COMMENTARY WAS "FROWNED UPON" BY THE MONARCHY.
IT IS SUBVERSIVELY VEILED AS A CHILDREN'S BOOK, BUT IT IS MUCH MORE THAN THAT.
"But I don't want to go among mad people," Alice remarked.
"Oh, you can't help that," said the Cat: "we're all mad here. I'm mad. You're mad."
"How do you know I'm mad?" said Alice.
"You must be," said the Cat, "or you wouldn't have come here."
COME ON. I'LL SHOW YOU MY OTHER COLLECTIONS.

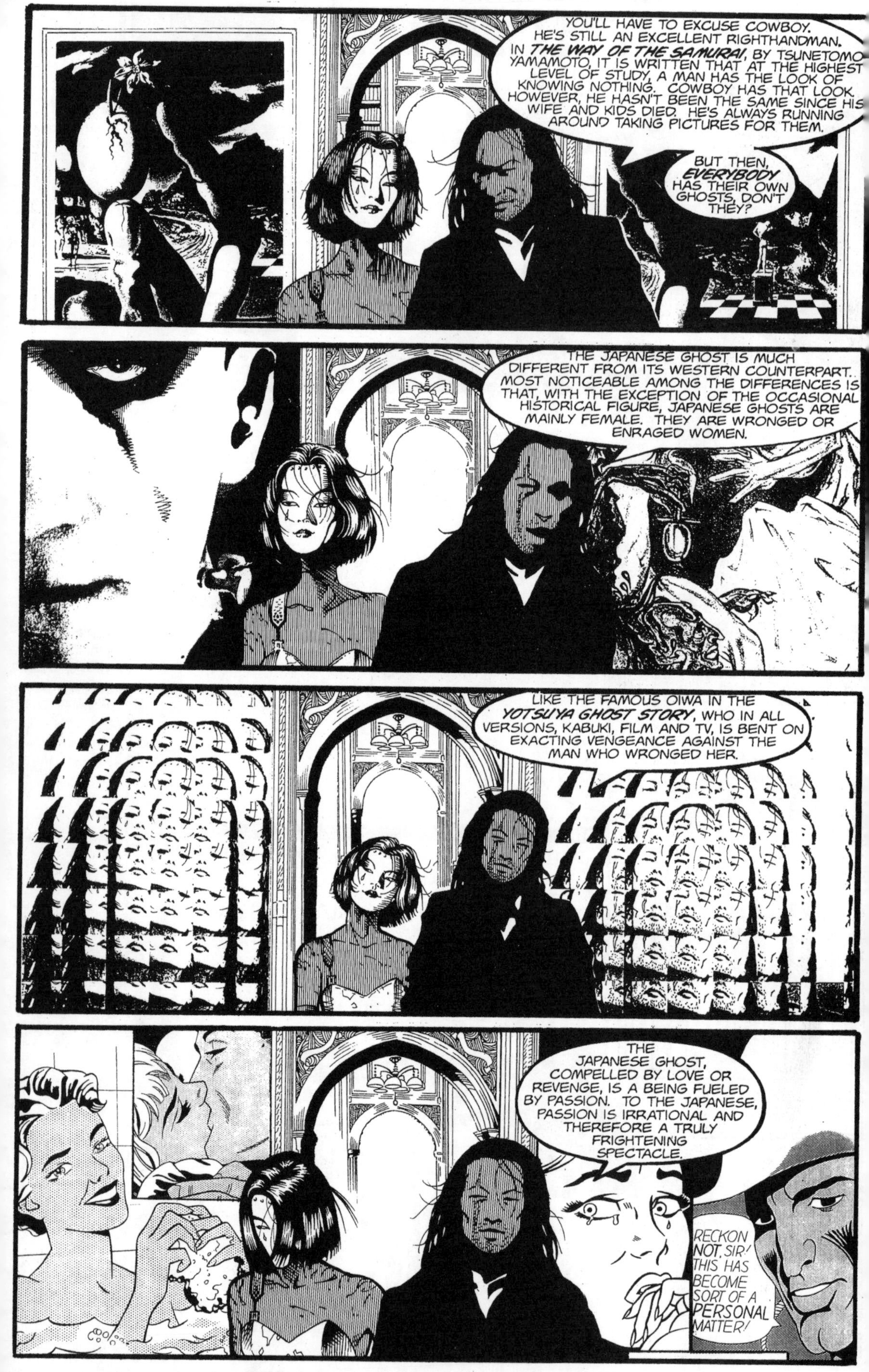

YOU'LL HAVE TO EXCUSE COWBOY. HE'S STILL AN EXCELLENT RIGHTHANDMAN. IN THE WAY OF THE SAMURAI, BY TSUNETOMO YAMAMOTO, IT IS WRITTEN THAT AT THE HIGHEST LEVEL OF STUDY, A MAN HAS THE LOOK OF KNOWING NOTHING. COWBOY HAS THAT LOOK. HOWEVER, HE HASN'T BEEN THE SAME SINCE HIS WIFE AND KIDS DIED. HE'S ALWAYS RUNNING AROUND TAKING PICTURES FOR THEM.
BUT THEN, EVERYBODY HAS THEIR OWN GHOSTS, DON'T THEY?
THE JAPANESE GHOST IS MUCH DIFFERENT FROM ITS WESTERN COUNTERPART. MOST NOTICEABLE AMONG THE DIFFERENCES IS THAT, WITH THE EXCEPTION OF THE OCCASIONAL HISTORICAL FIGURE, JAPANESE GHOSTS ARE MAINLY FEMALE. THEY ARE WRONGED OR ENRAGED WOMEN.
LIKE THE FAMOUS OIWA IN THE YOTSUYA GHOST STORY, WHO IN ALL VERSIONS, KABUKI, FILM AND TV, IS BENT ON EXACTING VENGEANCE AGAINST THE MAN WHO WRONGED HER.
THE JAPANESE GHOST, COMPELLED BY LOVE OR REVENGE, IS A BEING FUELED BY PASSION. TO THE JAPANESE, PASSION IS IRRATIONAL AND THEREFORE A TRULY FRIGHTENING SPECTACLE.
RECKON NOT, SIR! THIS HAS BECOME SORT OF A PERSONAL MATTER!

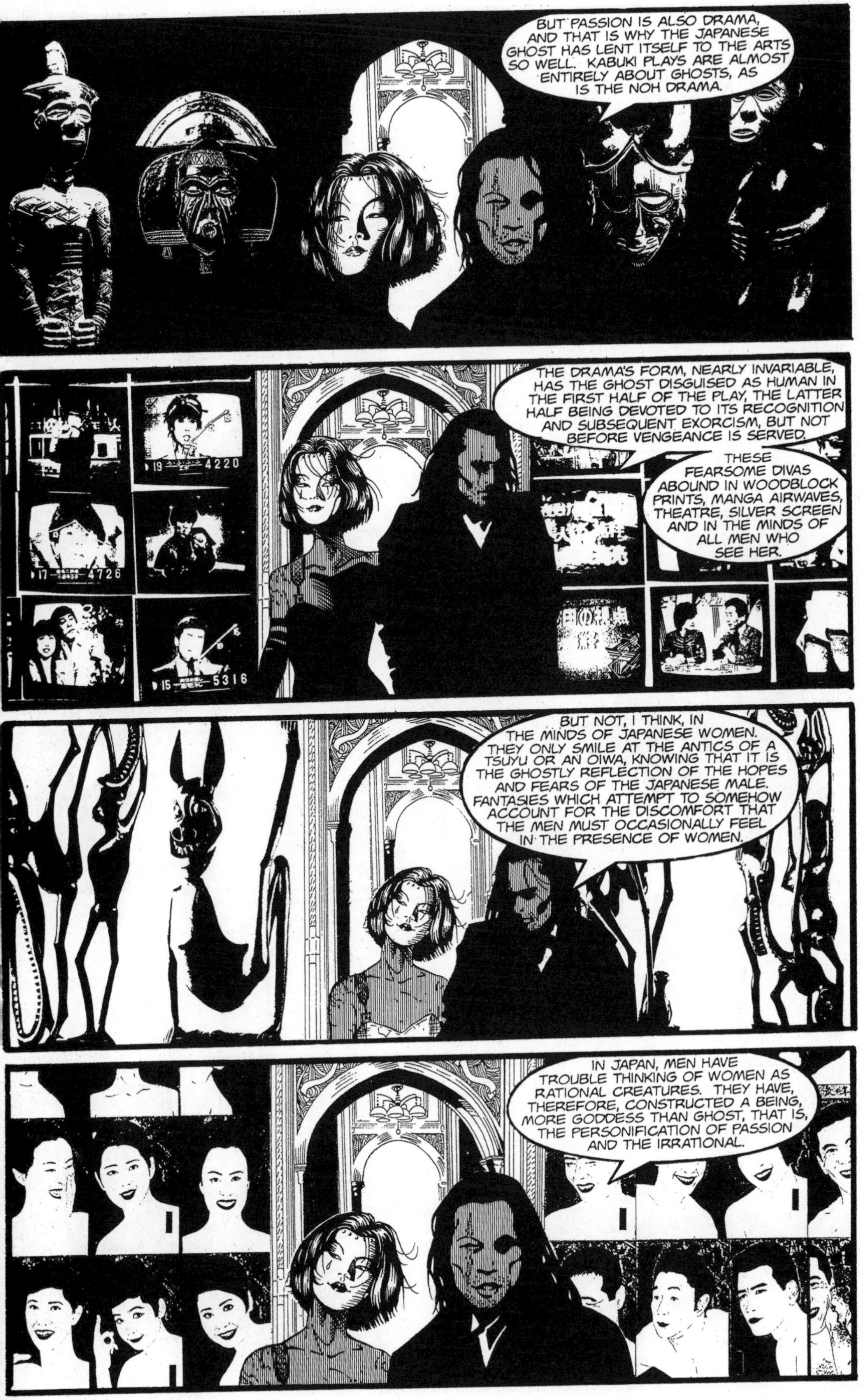
BUT PASSION IS ALSO DRAMA, AND THAT IS WHY THE JAPANESE GHOST HAS LENT ITSELF TO THE ARTS SO WELL. KABUKI PLAYS ARE ALMOST ENTIRELY ABOUT GHOSTS, AS IS THE NOH DRAMA.
THE DRAMA'S FORM, NEARLY INVARIABLE, HAS THE GHOST DISGUISED AS HUMAN IN THE FIRST HALF OF THE PLAY, THE LATTER HALF BEING DEVOTED TO ITS RECOGNITION AND SUBSEQUENT EXORCISM, BUT NOT BEFORE VENGEANCE IS SERVED.
THESE FEARSOME DIVAS ABOUND IN WOODBLOCK PRINTS, MANGA AIRWAVES, THEATRE, SILVER SCREEN AND IN THE MINDS OF ALL MEN WHO SEE HER.
BUT NOT, I THINK, IN THE MINDS OF JAPANESE WOMEN. THEY ONLY SMILE AT THE ANTICS OF A TSUYU OR AN OIWA, KNOWING THAT IT IS THE GHOSTLY REFLECTION OF THE HOPES AND FEARS OF THE JAPANESE MALE. FANTASIES WHICH ATTEMPT TO SOMEHOW ACCOUNT FOR THE DISCOMFORT THAT THE MEN MUST OCCASIONALLY FEEL IN THE PRESENCE OF WOMEN.
IN JAPAN, MEN HAVE TROUBLE THINKING OF WOMEN AS RATIONAL CREATURES. THEY HAVE, THEREFORE, CONSTRUCTED A BEING, MORE GODDESS THAN GHOST, THAT IS, THE PERSONIFICATION OF PASSION AND THE IRRATIONAL.

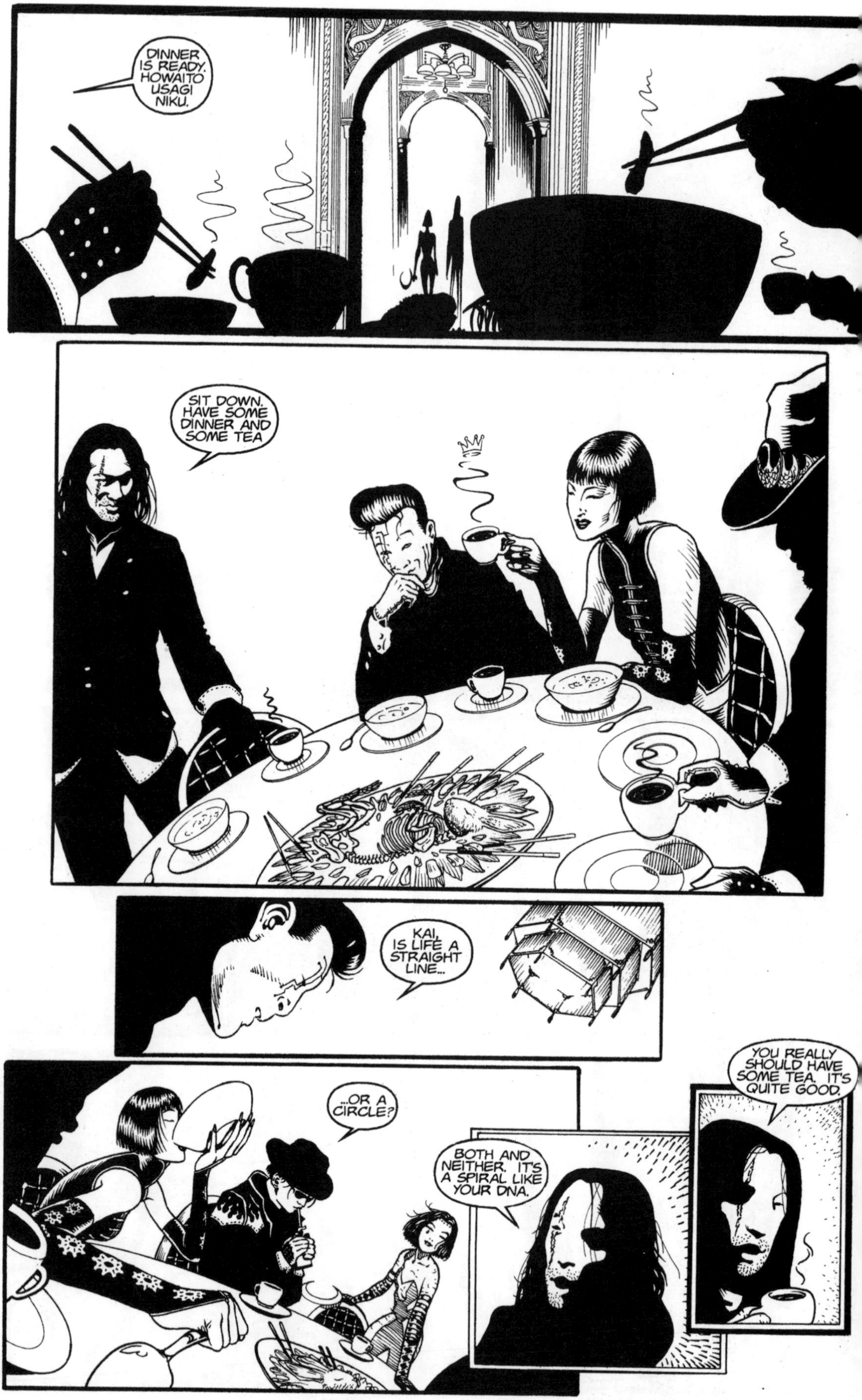
DINNER IS READY. HOWAITO USAGI NIKU.
SIT DOWN. HAVE SOME DINNER AND SOME TEA
KAI, IS LIFE A STRAIGHT LINE...
...OR A CIRCLE?
BOTH AND NEITHER. IT'S A SPIRAL LIKE YOUR DNA.
YOU REALLY SHOULD HAVE SOME TEA. IT'S QUITE GOOD.

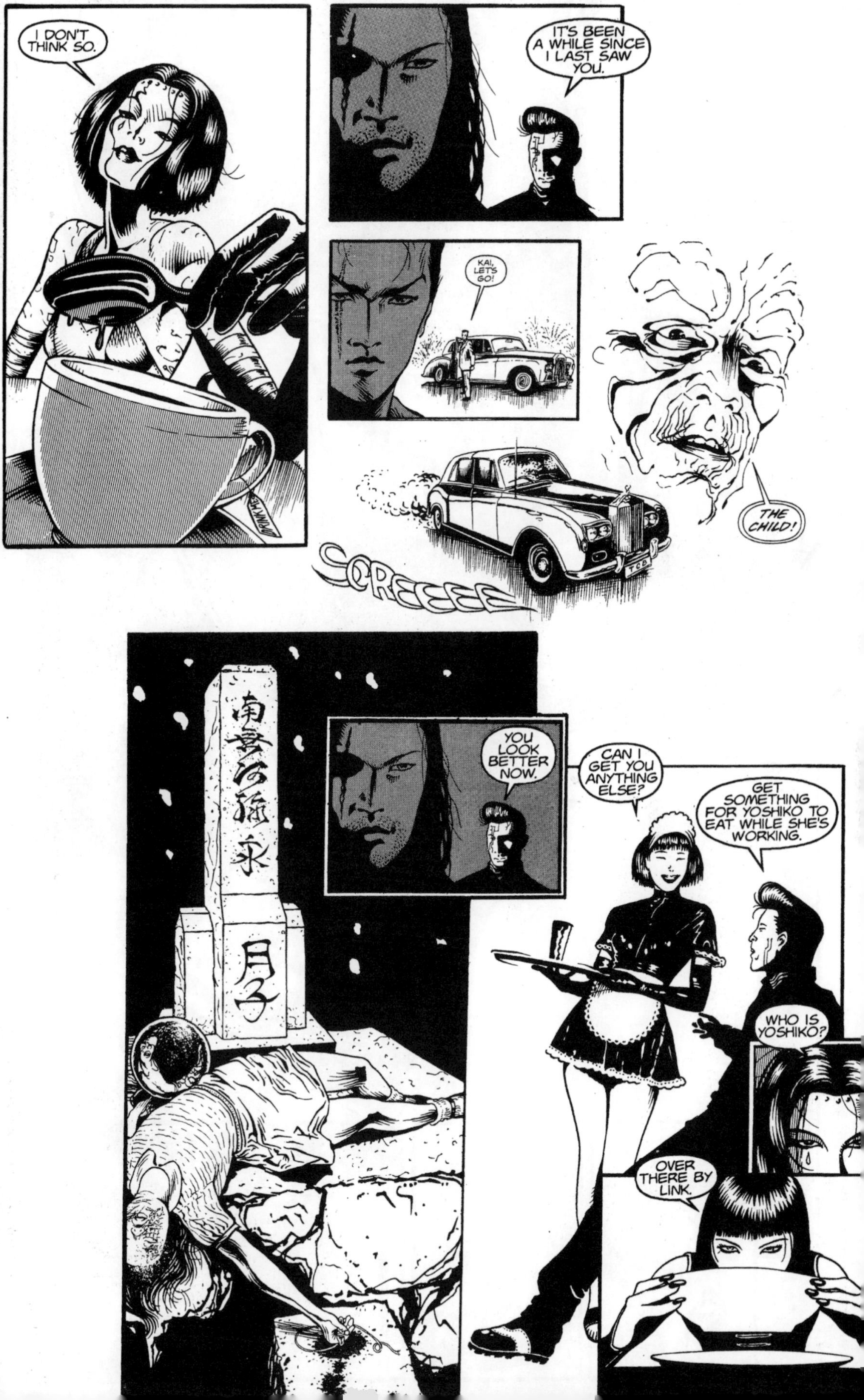
I DON'T THINK SO.
IT'S BEEN A WHILE SINCE I LAST SAW YOU.
KAI, LET'S GO!
THE CHILD!
SCREEEEE
YOU LOOK BETTER NOW.
CAN I GET YOU ANYTHING ELSE?
GET SOMETHING FOR YOSHIKO TO EAT WHILE SHE'S WORKING.
WHO IS YOSHIKO?
OVER THERE BY LINK.

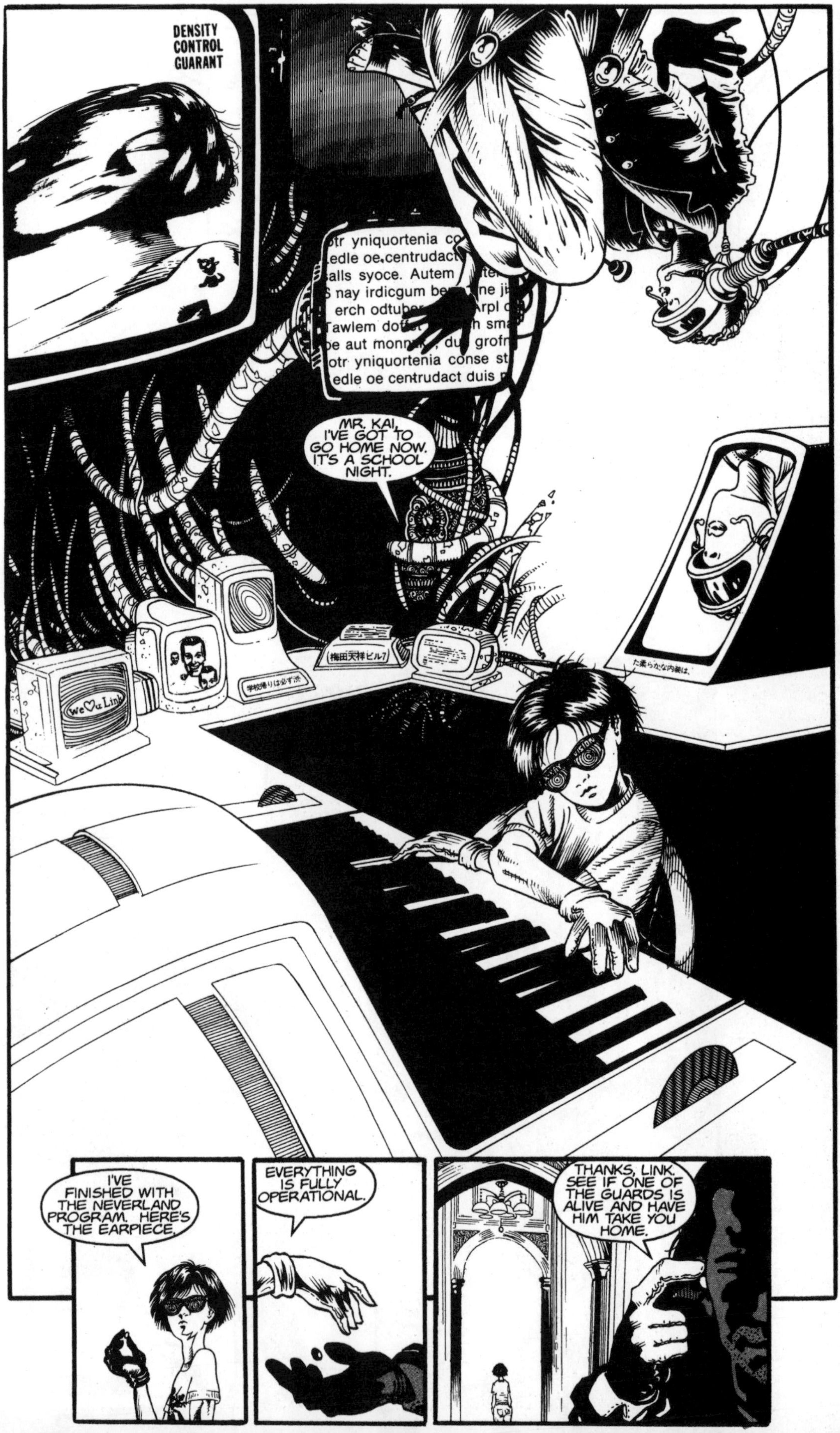
DENSITY CONTROL GUARANT
MR. KAI, I'VE GOT TO GO HOME NOW. IT'S A SCHOOL NIGHT.
I'VE FINISHED WITH THE NEVERLAND PROGRAM. HERE'S THE EARPIECE.
EVERYTHING IS FULLY OPERATIONAL.
THANKS, LINK. SEE IF ONE OF THE GUARDS IS ALIVE AND HAVE HIM TAKE YOU HOME.

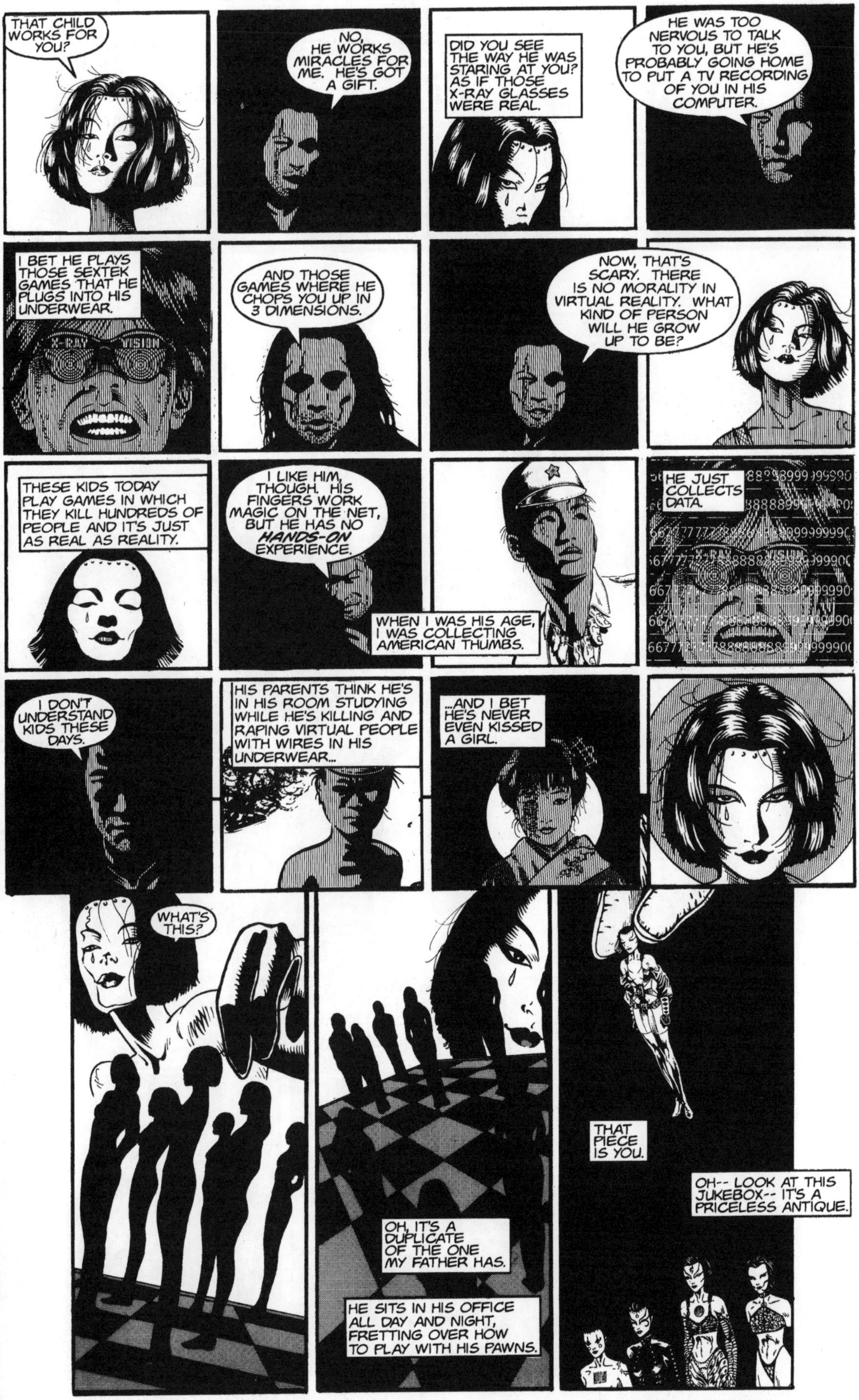
THAT CHILD WORKS FOR YOU?
NO, HE WORKS MIRACLES FOR ME. HE'S GOT A GIFT.
DID YOU SEE THE WAY HE WAS STARING AT YOU? AS IF THOSE X-RAY GLASSES WERE REAL.
HE WAS TOO NERVOUS TO TALK TO YOU, BUT HE'S PROBABLY GOING HOME TO PUT A TV RECORDING OF YOU IN HIS COMPUTER.
I BET HE PLAYS THOSE SEXTEK GAMES THAT HE PLUGS INTO HIS UNDERWEAR.
X-RAY VISION
AND THOSE GAMES WHERE HE CHOPS YOU UP IN 3 DIMENSIONS.
NOW, THAT'S SCARY. THERE IS NO MORALITY IN VIRTUAL REALITY. WHAT KIND OF PERSON WILL HE GROW UP TO BE?
THESE KIDS TODAY PLAY GAMES IN WHICH THEY KILL HUNDREDS OF PEOPLE AND IT'S JUST AS REAL AS REALITY.
I LIKE HIM, THOUGH. HIS FINGERS WORK MAGIC ON THE NET, BUT HE HAS NO *HANDS-ON* EXPERIENCE.
WHEN I WAS HIS AGE, I WAS COLLECTING AMERICAN THUMBS.
HE JUST COLLECTS DATA.
I DON'T UNDERSTAND KIDS THESE DAYS.
HIS PARENTS THINK HE'S IN HIS ROOM STUDYING WHILE HE'S KILLING AND RAPING VIRTUAL PEOPLE WITH WIRES IN HIS UNDERWEAR...
...AND I BET HE'S NEVER EVEN KISSED A GIRL.
WHAT'S THIS?
OH, IT'S A DUPLICATE OF THE ONE MY FATHER HAS.
HE SITS IN HIS OFFICE ALL DAY AND NIGHT, FRETTING OVER HOW TO PLAY WITH HIS PAWNS.
THAT PIECE IS YOU.
OH-- LOOK AT THIS JUKEBOX-- IT'S A PRICELESS ANTIQUE.

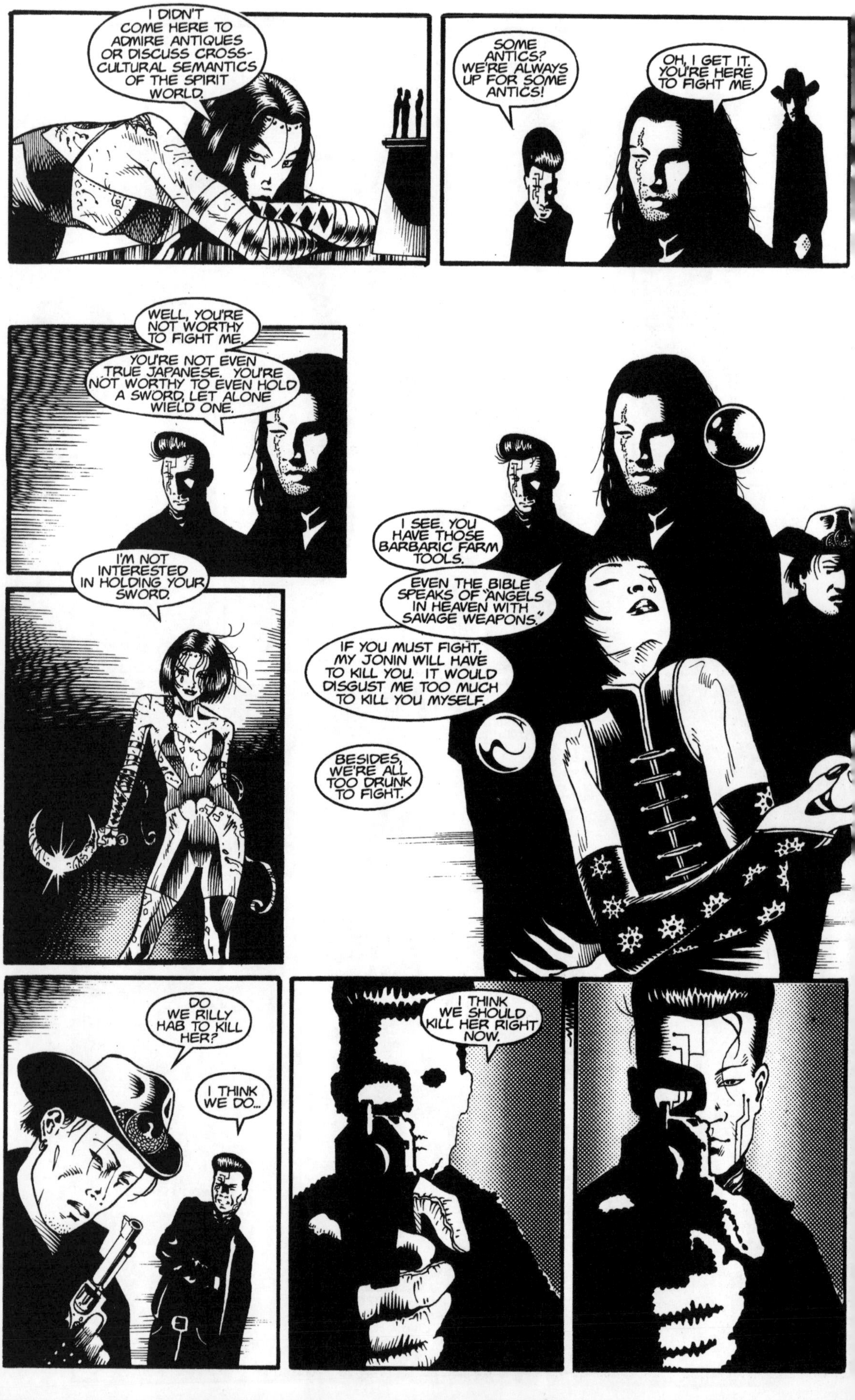
I DIDN'T COME HERE TO ADMIRE ANTIQUES OR DISCUSS CROSS-CULTURAL SEMANTICS OF THE SPIRIT WORLD.
SOME ANTICS? WE'RE ALWAYS UP FOR SOME ANTICS!
OH, I GET IT. YOU'RE HERE TO FIGHT ME.
WELL, YOU'RE NOT WORTHY TO FIGHT ME.
YOU'RE NOT EVEN TRUE JAPANESE. YOU'RE NOT WORTHY TO EVEN HOLD A SWORD, LET ALONE WIELD ONE.
I'M NOT INTERESTED IN HOLDING YOUR SWORD.
I SEE. YOU HAVE THOSE BARBARIC FARM TOOLS.
EVEN THE BIBLE SPEAKS OF "ANGELS IN HEAVEN WITH SAVAGE WEAPONS."
IF YOU MUST FIGHT, MY JONIN WILL HAVE TO KILL YOU. IT WOULD DISGUST ME TOO MUCH TO KILL YOU MYSELF.
BESIDES, WE'RE ALL TOO DRUNK TO FIGHT.
DO WE RILLY HAB TO KILL HER?
I THINK WE DO...
I THINK WE SHOULD KILL HER RIGHT NOW.

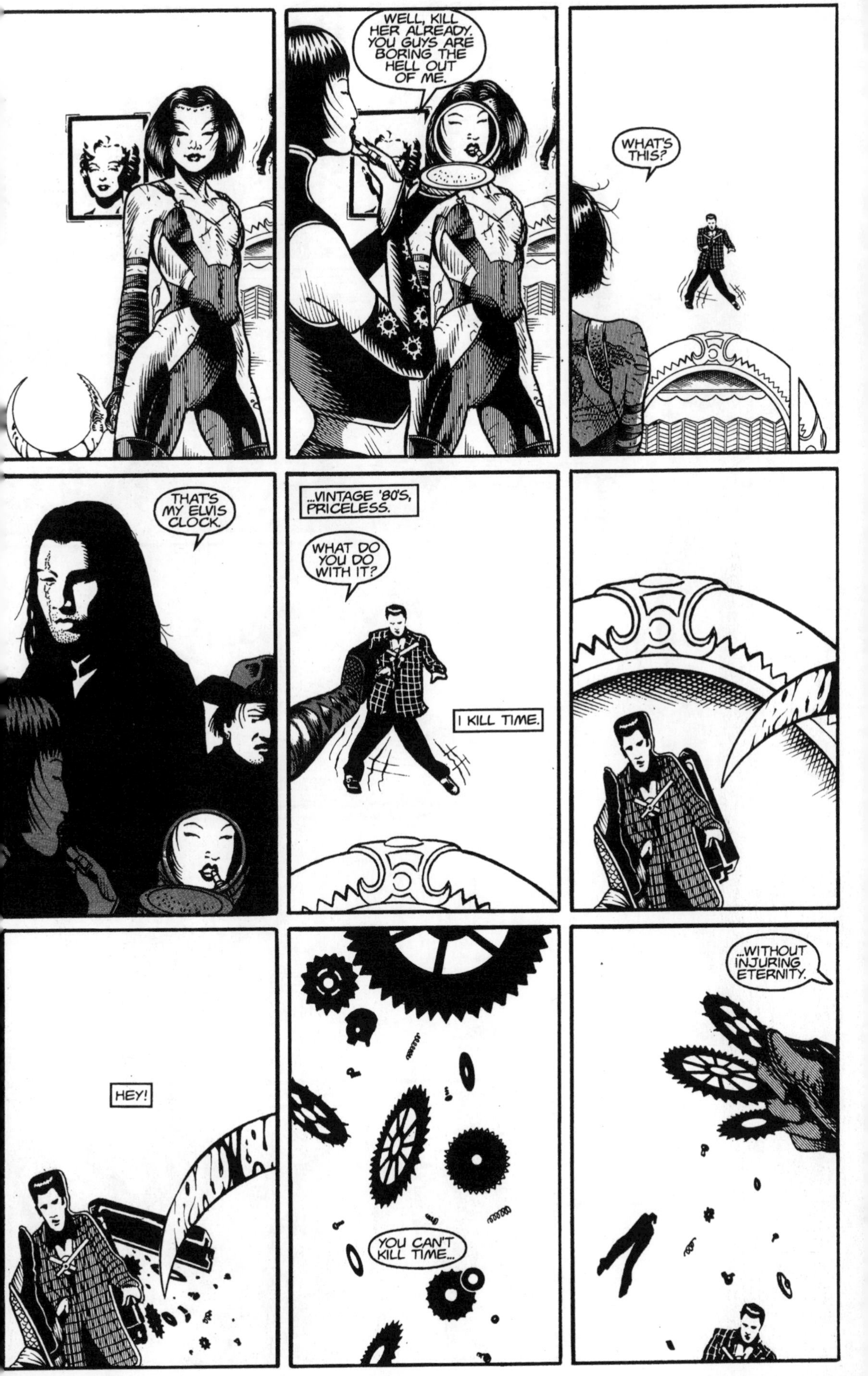
WELL, KILL HER ALREADY. YOU GUYS ARE BORING THE HELL OUT OF ME.
WHAT'S THIS?
THAT'S MY ELVIS CLOCK.
...VINTAGE '80'S, PRICELESS.
WHAT DO YOU DO WITH IT?
I KILL TIME.
HEY!
YOU CAN'T KILL TIME...
...WITHOUT INJURING ETERNITY.

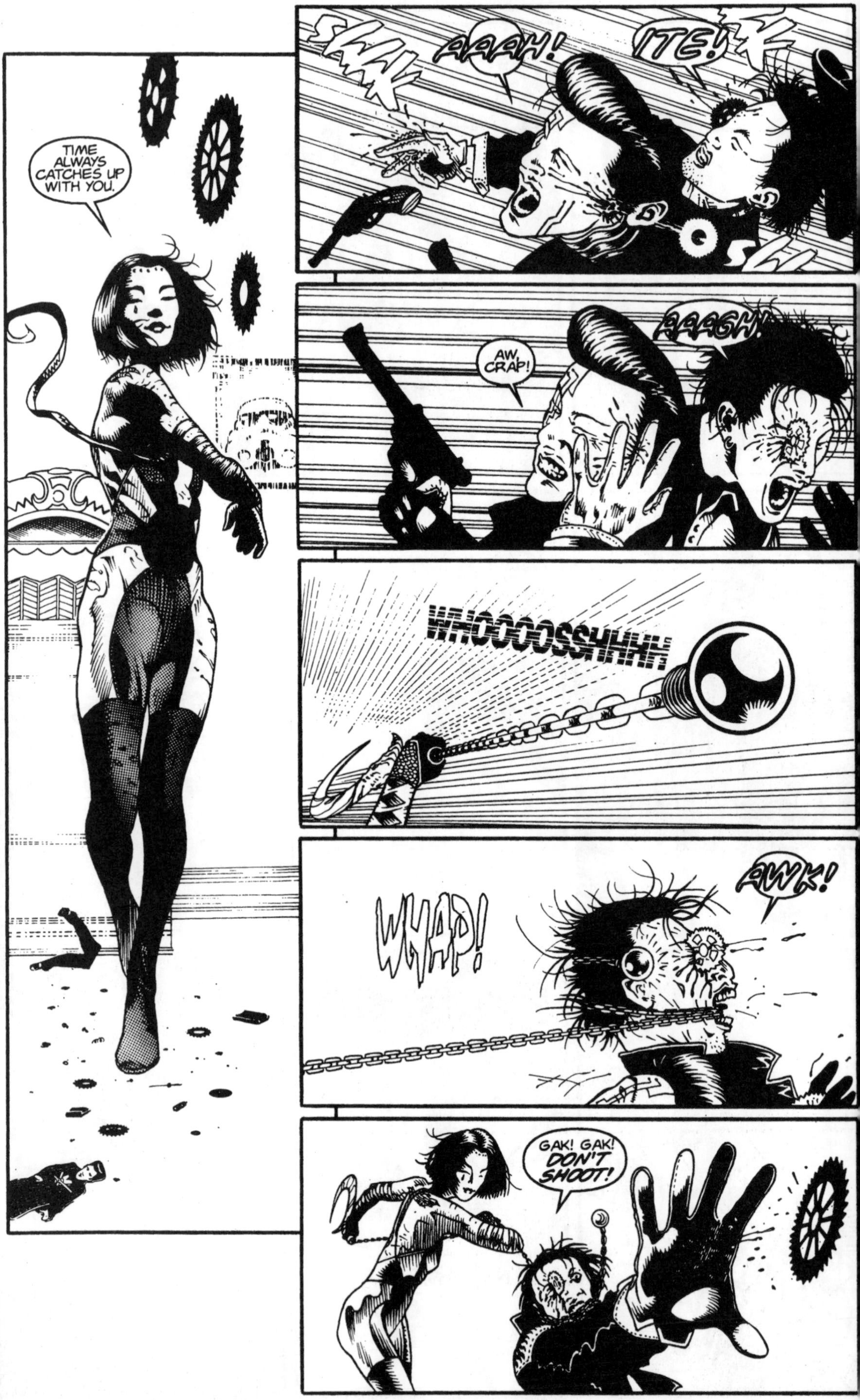

TIME ALWAYS CATCHES UP WITH YOU.
SHAK
AAAAH!
ITE!
AAAGH!
AW, CRAP!
WHOOOOOSSHHHH
WHAP!
AWK!
GAK! GAK! DON'T SHOOT!

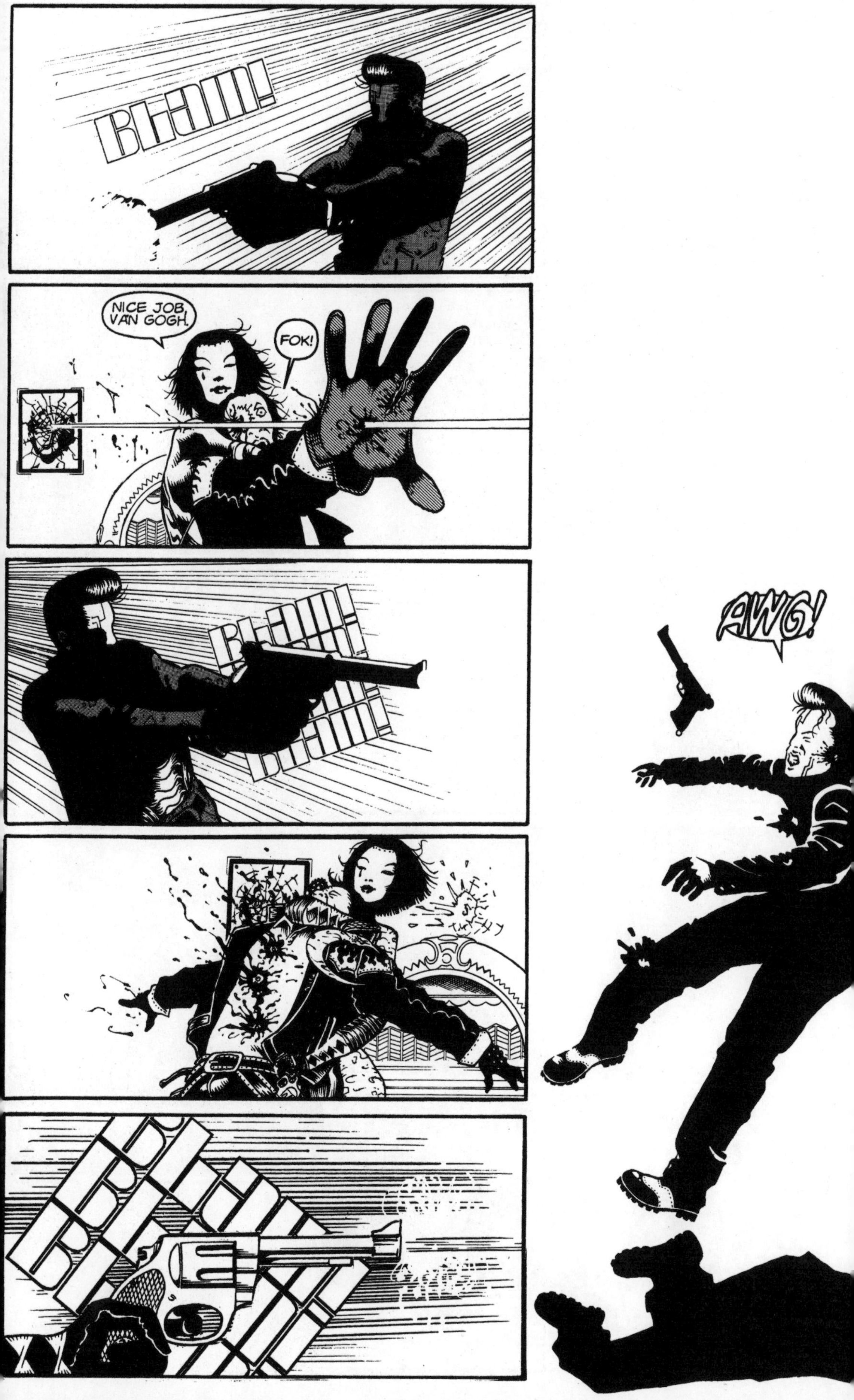
BLAM!
NICE JOB VAN GOGH.
FOK!
BLAM! BLAM! BLAM!
AWG!

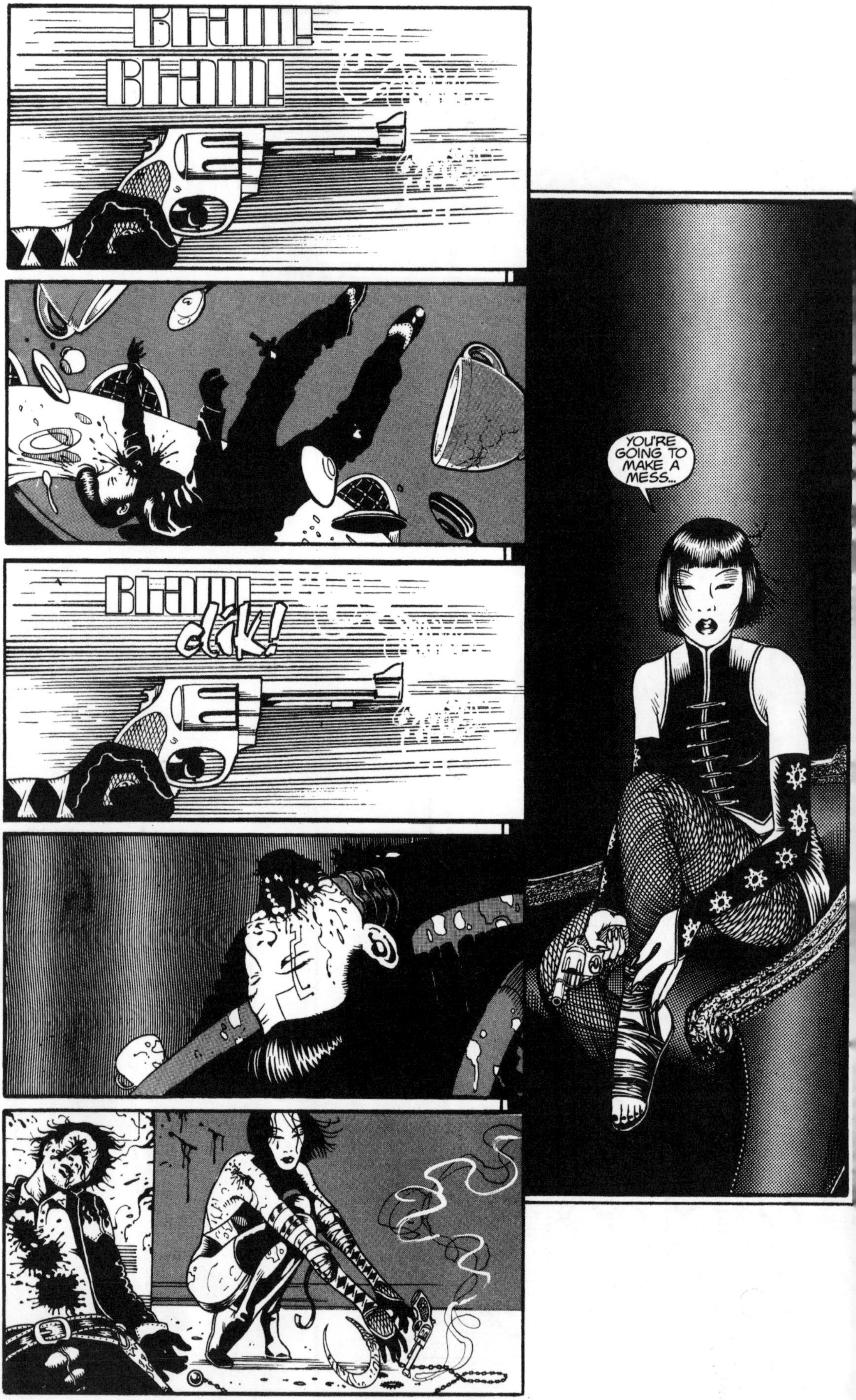
BLAM!
BLAM!
BLAM!
clik!
YOU'RE GOING TO MAKE A MESS...

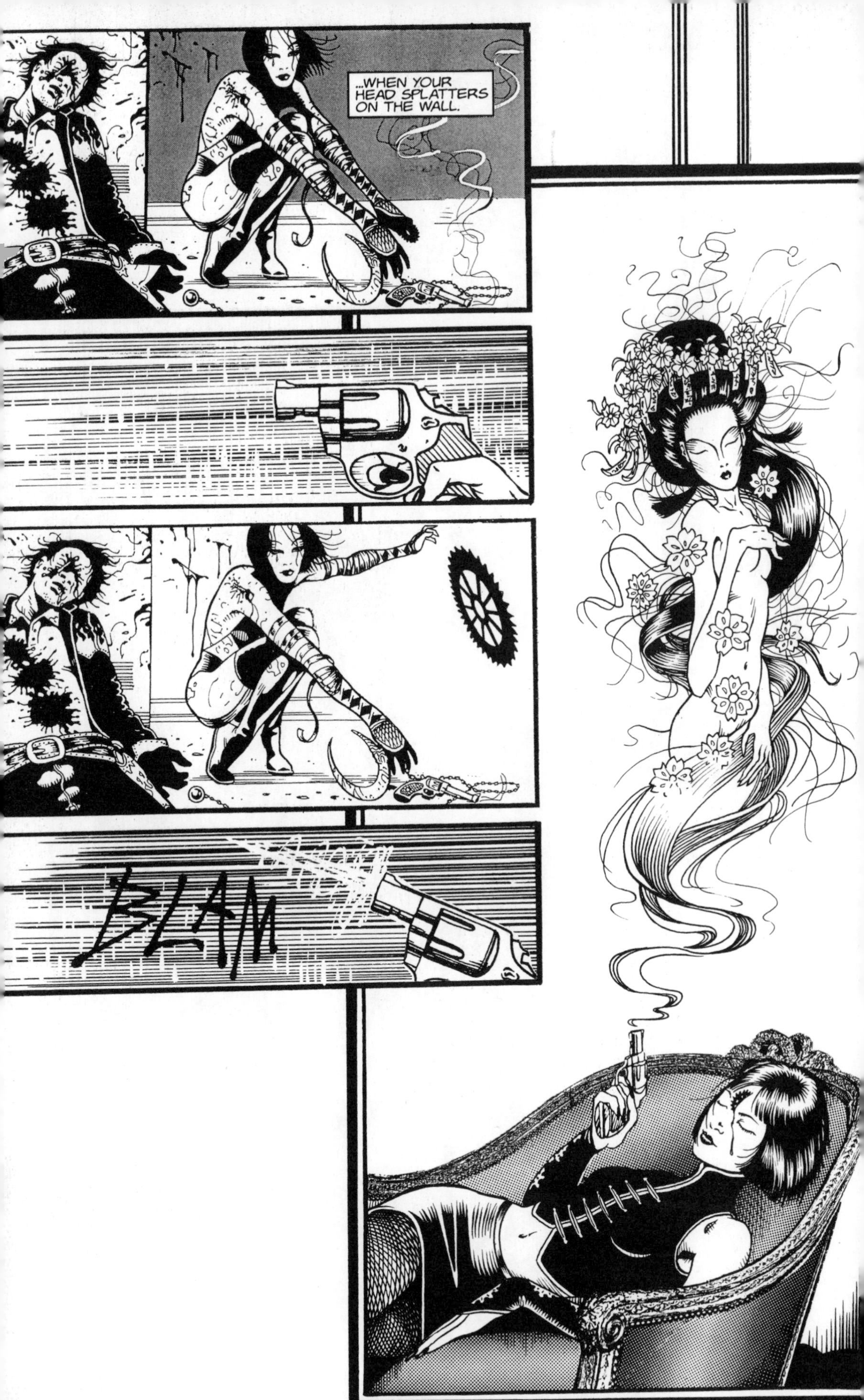
...WHEN YOUR HEAD SPLATTERS ON THE WALL.
BLAM

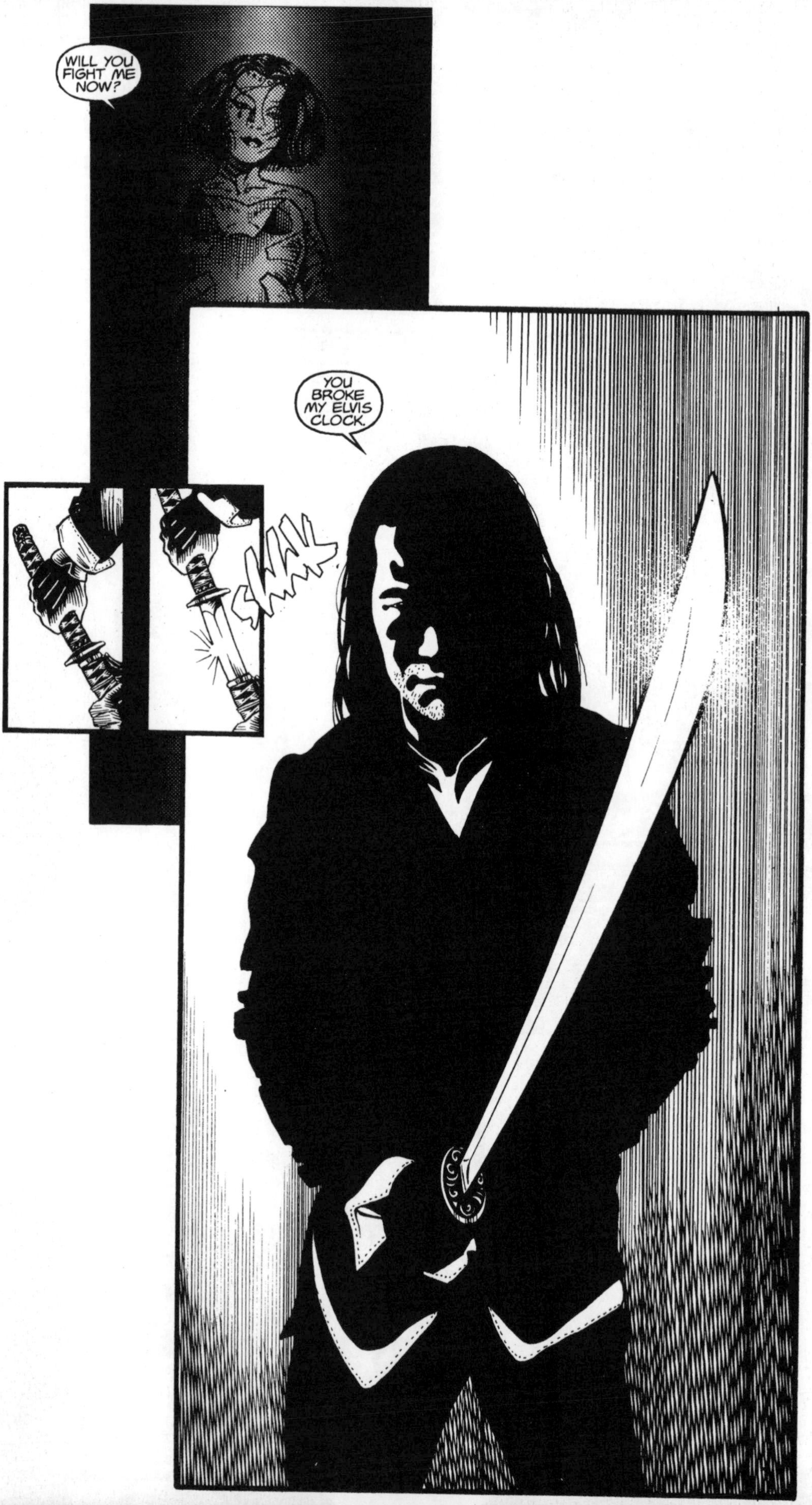
WILL YOU FIGHT ME NOW?
YOU BROKE MY ELVIS CLOCK.
SWAK

KABUKI

歌舞伎

CIRCLE OF BLOOD

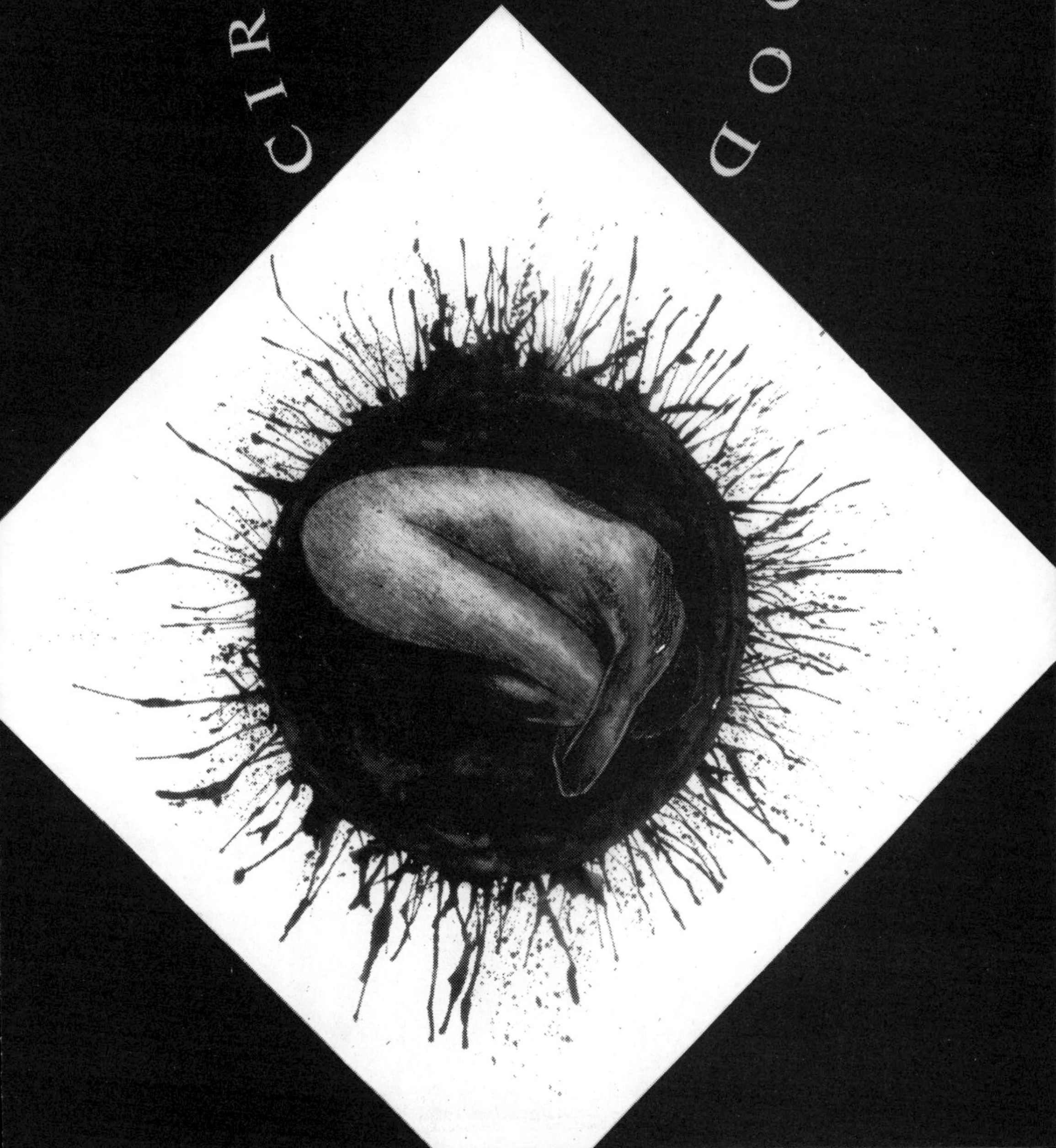

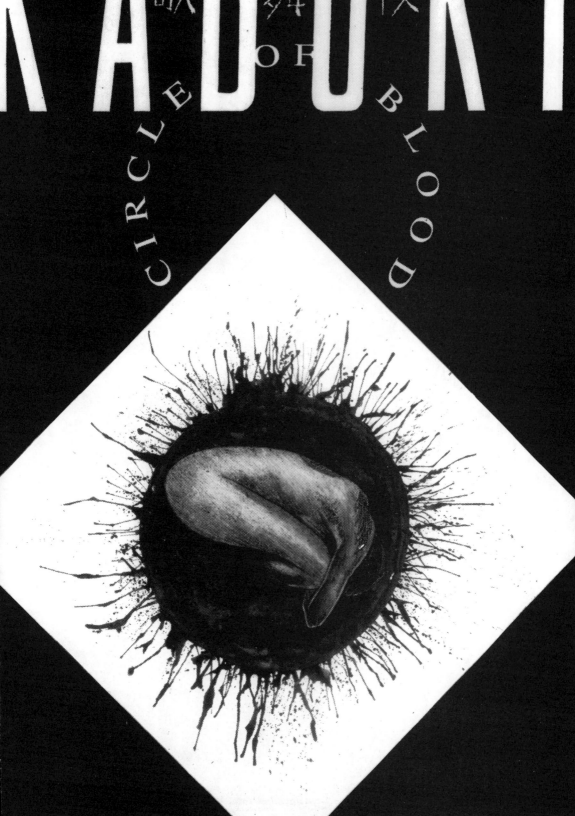

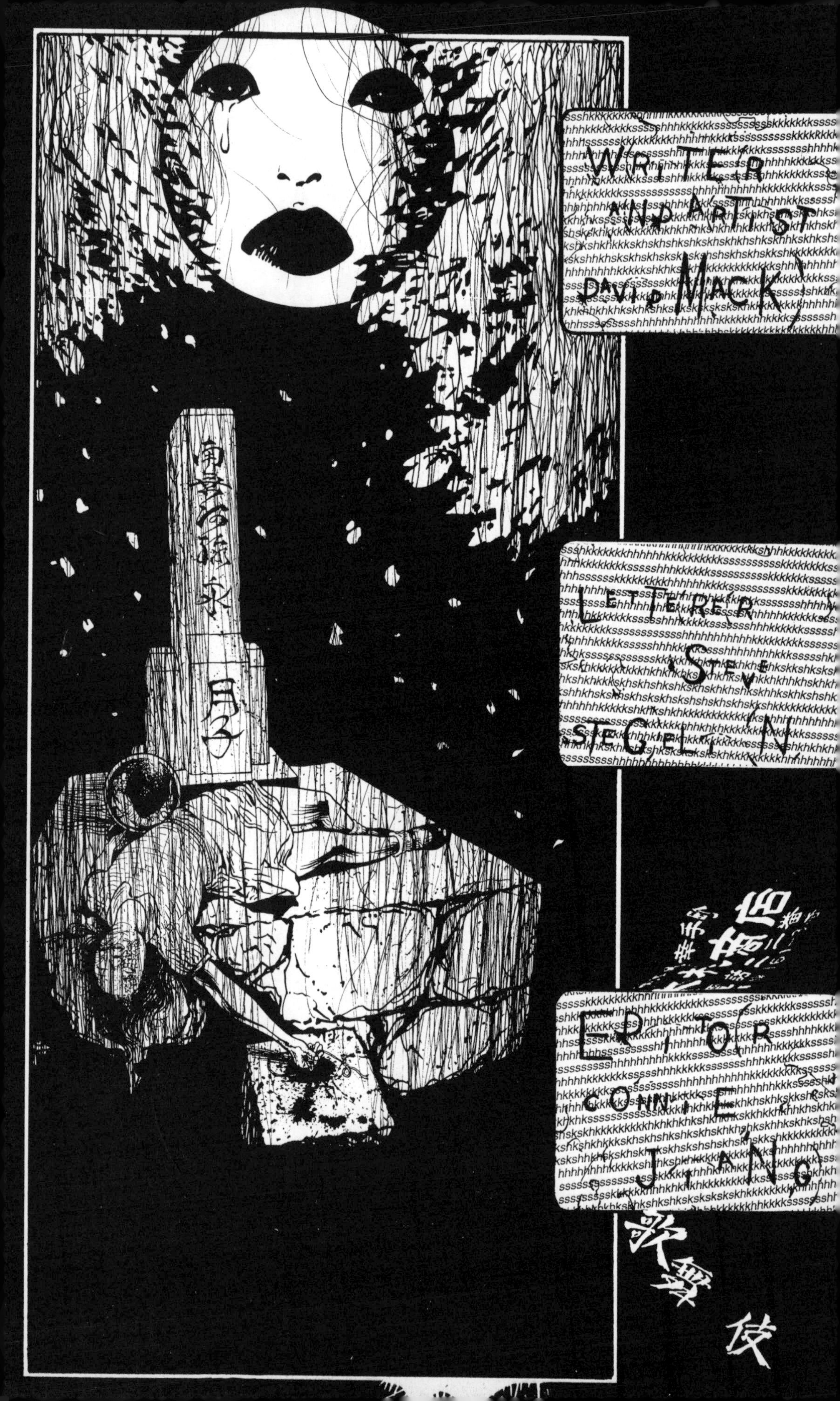
WRITER AND ARTIST
DAVID MACK
LETTERER
STEVE STEGELIN
EDITOR
CONNIE JIANG
歌舞伎

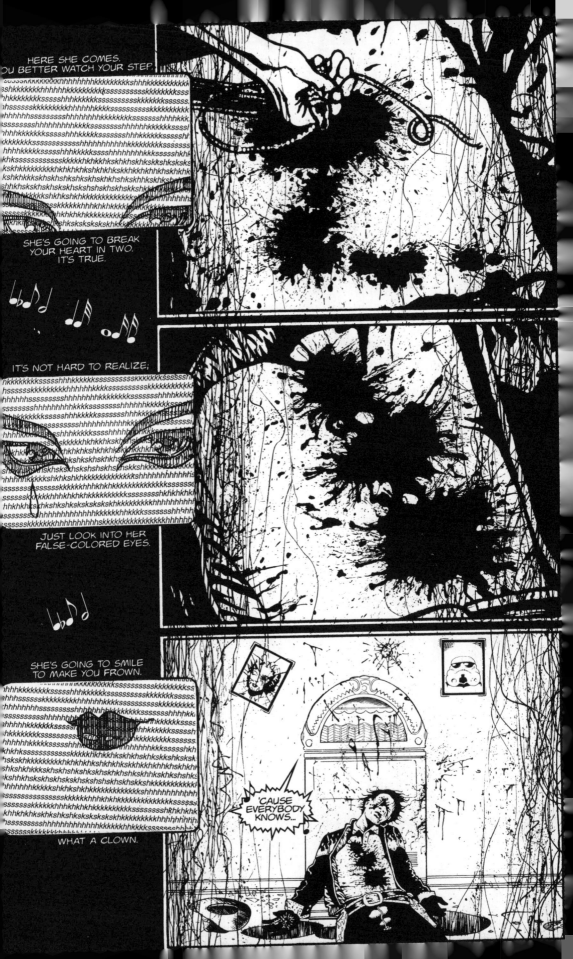

HERE SHE COMES.
YOU BETTER WATCH YOUR STEP.

SHE'S GOING TO BREAK
YOUR HEART IN TWO.
IT'S TRUE.

IT'S NOT HARD TO REALIZE;

JUST LOOK INTO HER
FALSE-COLORED EYES.

SHE'S GOING TO SMILE
TO MAKE YOU FROWN.

WHAT A CLOWN.

'CAUSE
EVERYBODY
KNOWS...

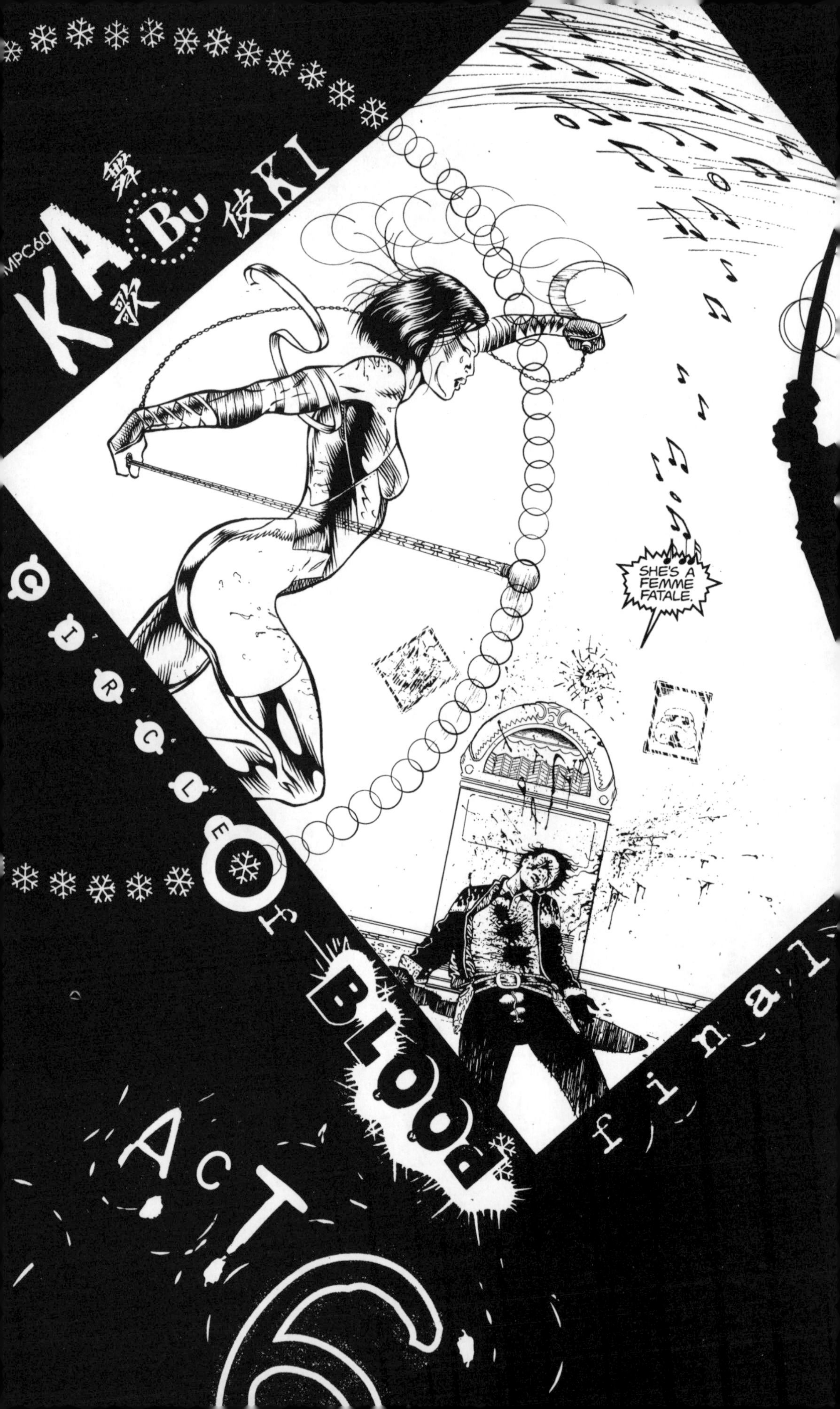
KABUKI 歌舞伎
MPC60
CIRCLE of BLOOD
ACT 6 final
SHE'S A FEMME FATALE.

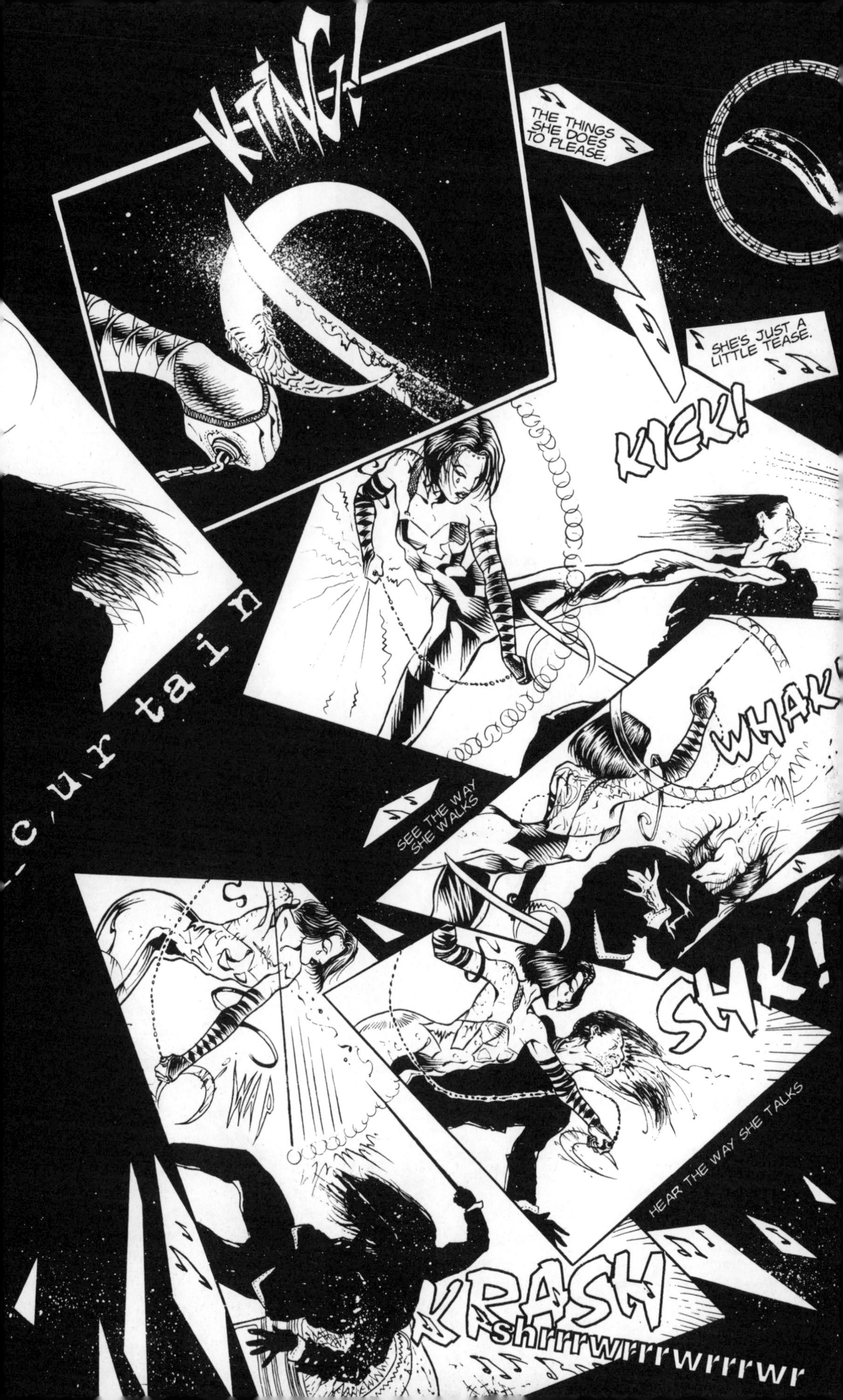

K-TING!
THE THINGS SHE DOES TO PLEASE.
SHE'S JUST A LITTLE TEASE.
KICK!
curtain
WHAK
SEE THE WAY SHE WALKS
SHK!
HEAR THE WAY SHE TALKS
KRASH
shrrrwrrrrwrrrrwr

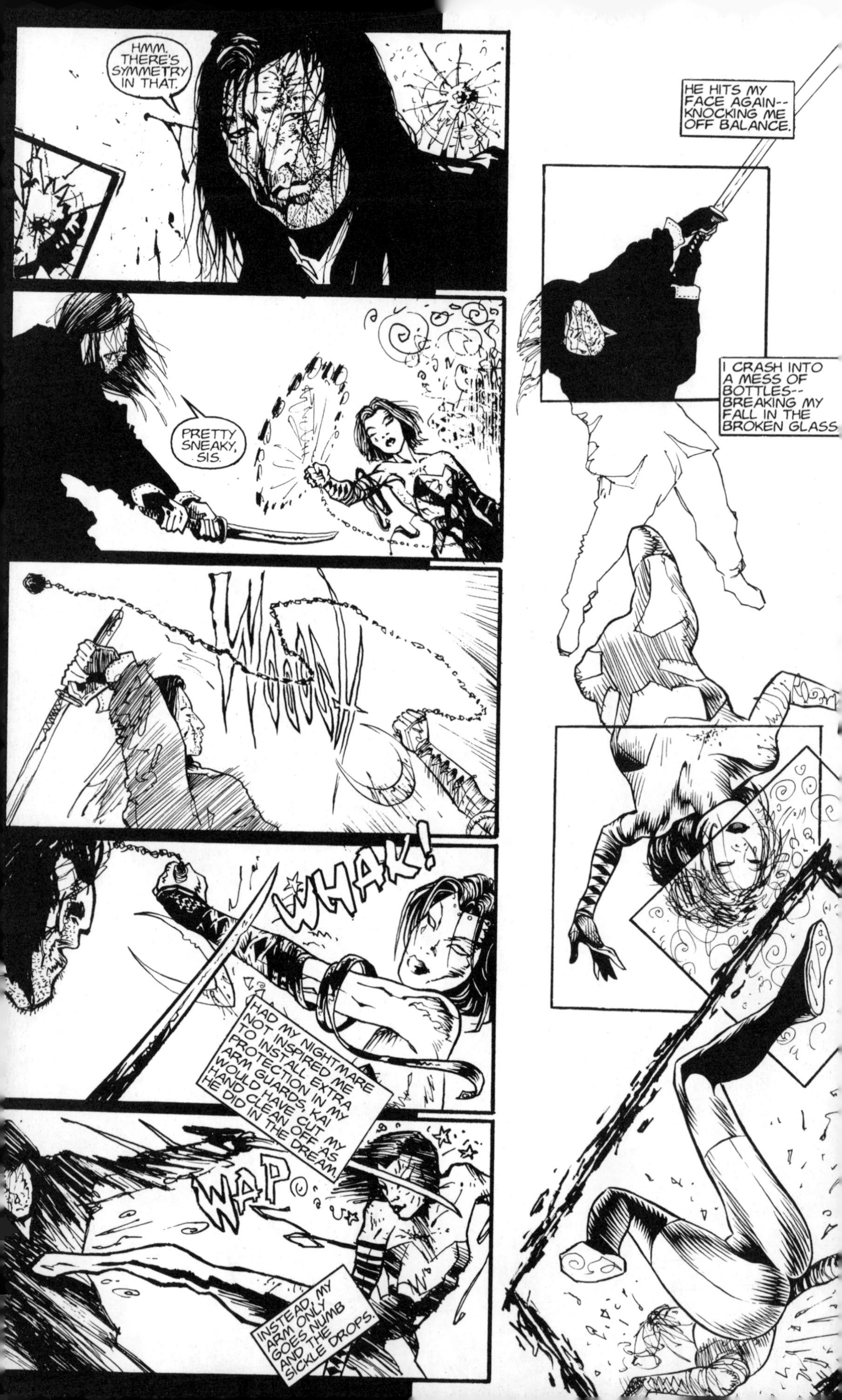

HMM. THERE'S SYMMETRY IN THAT.
PRETTY SNEAKY, SIS.
WHOOOSH
WHAK!
HAD MY NIGHTMARE NOT INSPIRED ME TO INSTALL EXTRA PROTECTION IN MY ARM GUARDS, KAI WOULD HAVE CUT MY HAND CLEAN OFF AS HE DID IN THE DREAM.
WAP
INSTEAD, MY ARM ONLY GOES NUMB AND THE SICKLE DROPS.
HE HITS MY FACE AGAIN-- KNOCKING ME OFF BALANCE.
I CRASH INTO A MESS OF BOTTLES-- BREAKING MY FALL IN THE BROKEN GLASS.

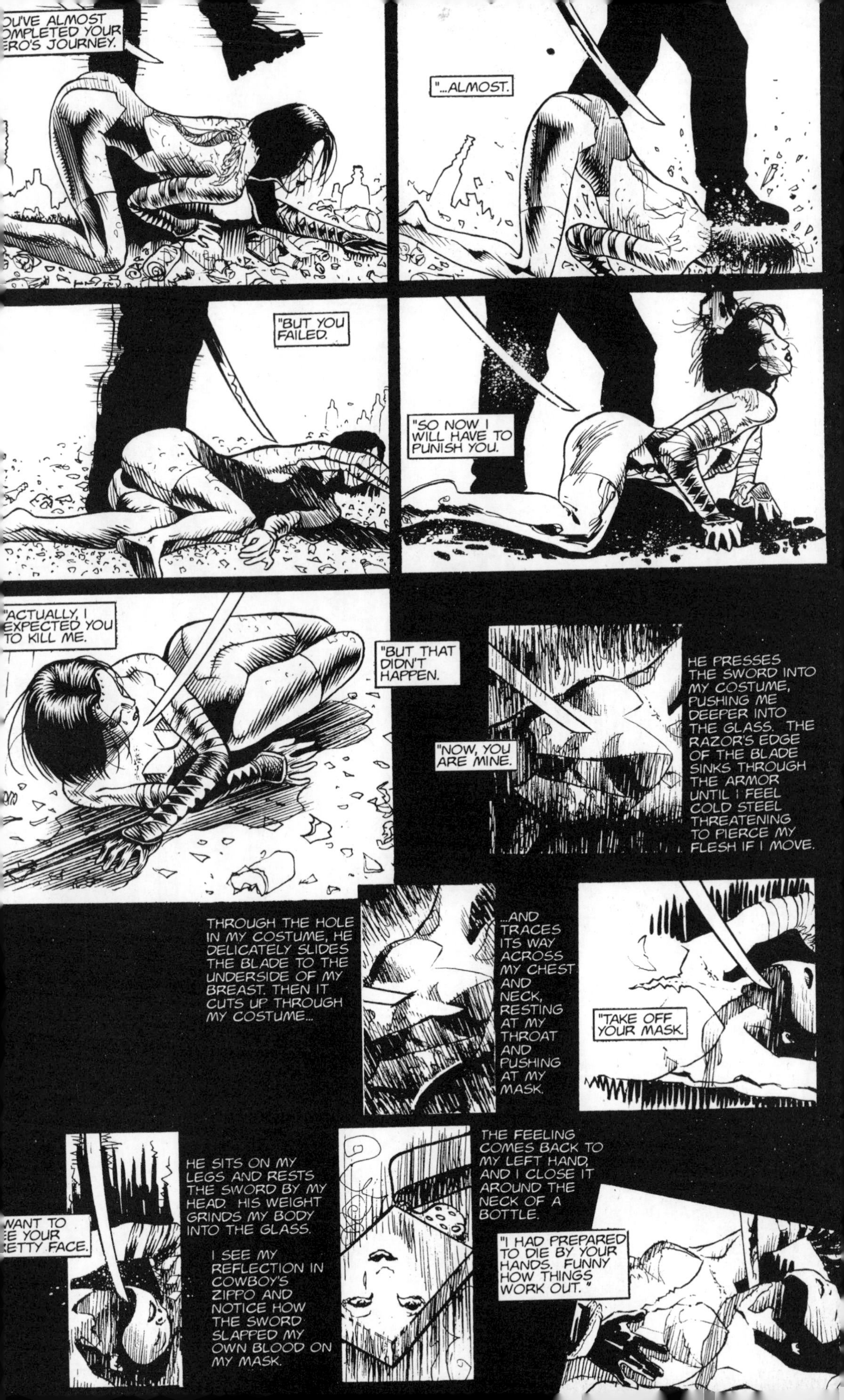
OU'VE ALMOST OMPLETED YOUR ERO'S JOURNEY.
"...ALMOST.
"BUT YOU FAILED.
"SO NOW I WILL HAVE TO PUNISH YOU.
"ACTUALLY, I EXPECTED YOU TO KILL ME.
"BUT THAT DIDN'T HAPPEN.
"NOW, YOU ARE MINE.
HE PRESSES THE SWORD INTO MY COSTUME, PUSHING ME DEEPER INTO THE GLASS. THE RAZOR'S EDGE OF THE BLADE SINKS THROUGH THE ARMOR UNTIL I FEEL COLD STEEL THREATENING TO PIERCE MY FLESH IF I MOVE.
THROUGH THE HOLE IN MY COSTUME, HE DELICATELY SLIDES THE BLADE TO THE UNDERSIDE OF MY BREAST. THEN IT CUTS UP THROUGH MY COSTUME...
...AND TRACES ITS WAY ACROSS MY CHEST AND NECK, RESTING AT MY THROAT AND PUSHING AT MY MASK.
"TAKE OFF YOUR MASK.
WANT TO EE YOUR ETTY FACE.
HE SITS ON MY LEGS AND RESTS THE SWORD BY MY HEAD. HIS WEIGHT GRINDS MY BODY INTO THE GLASS.
I SEE MY REFLECTION IN COWBOY'S ZIPPO AND NOTICE HOW THE SWORD SLAPPED MY OWN BLOOD ON MY MASK.
THE FEELING COMES BACK TO MY LEFT HAND, AND I CLOSE IT AROUND THE NECK OF A BOTTLE.
"I HAD PREPARED TO DIE BY YOUR HANDS. FUNNY HOW THINGS WORK OUT."

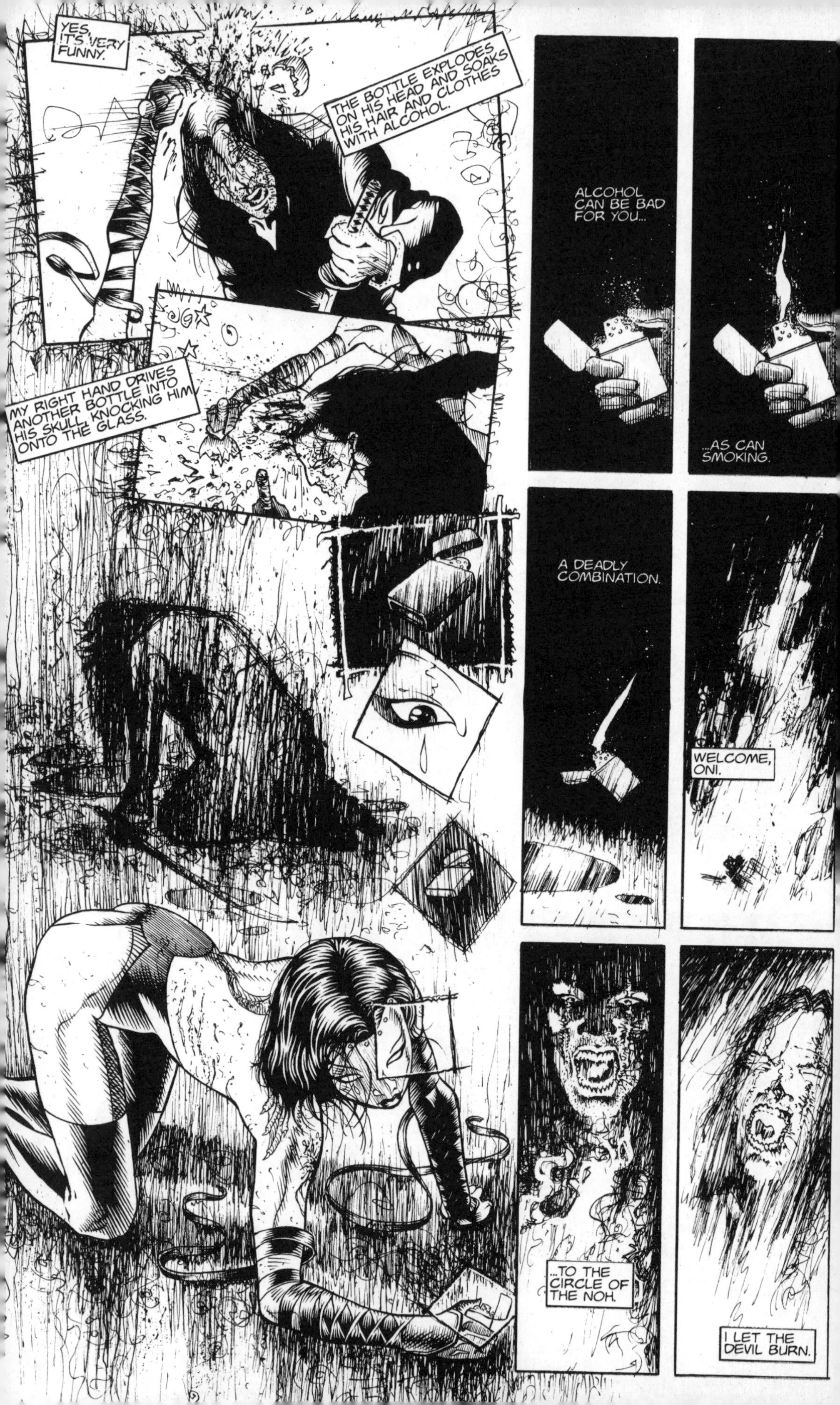

YES, IT'S VERY FUNNY.
THE BOTTLE EXPLODES ON HIS HEAD AND SOAKS HIS HAIR AND CLOTHES WITH ALCOHOL.
MY RIGHT HAND DRIVES ANOTHER BOTTLE INTO HIS SKULL, KNOCKING HIM ONTO THE GLASS.
ALCOHOL CAN BE BAD FOR YOU...
...AS CAN SMOKING.
A DEADLY COMBINATION.
WELCOME, ONI.
...TO THE CIRCLE OF THE NOH.
I LET THE DEVIL BURN.

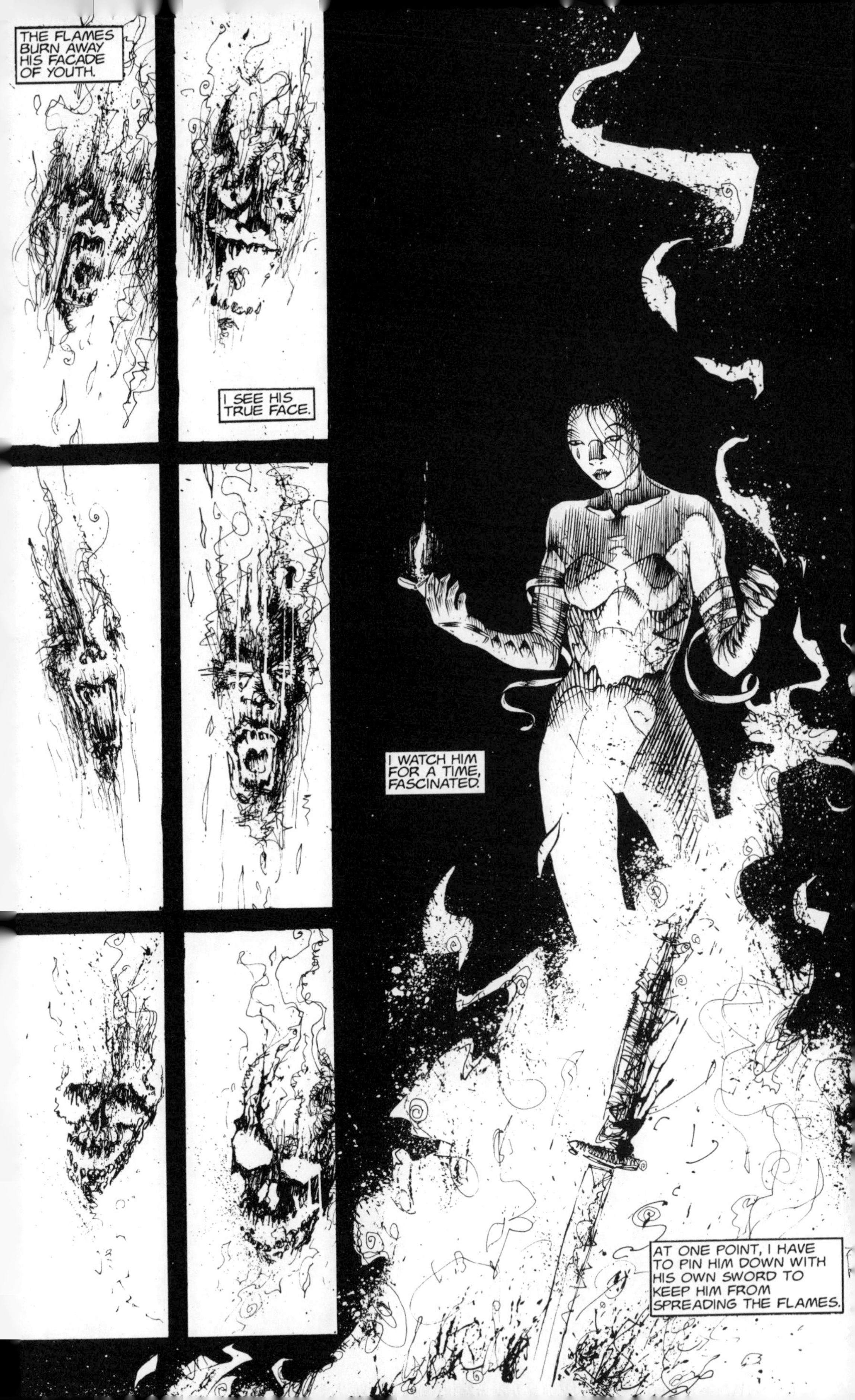
THE FLAMES BURN AWAY HIS FACADE OF YOUTH.
I SEE HIS TRUE FACE.
I WATCH HIM FOR A TIME, FASCINATED.
AT ONE POINT, I HAVE TO PIN HIM DOWN WITH HIS OWN SWORD TO KEEP HIM FROM SPREADING THE FLAMES.

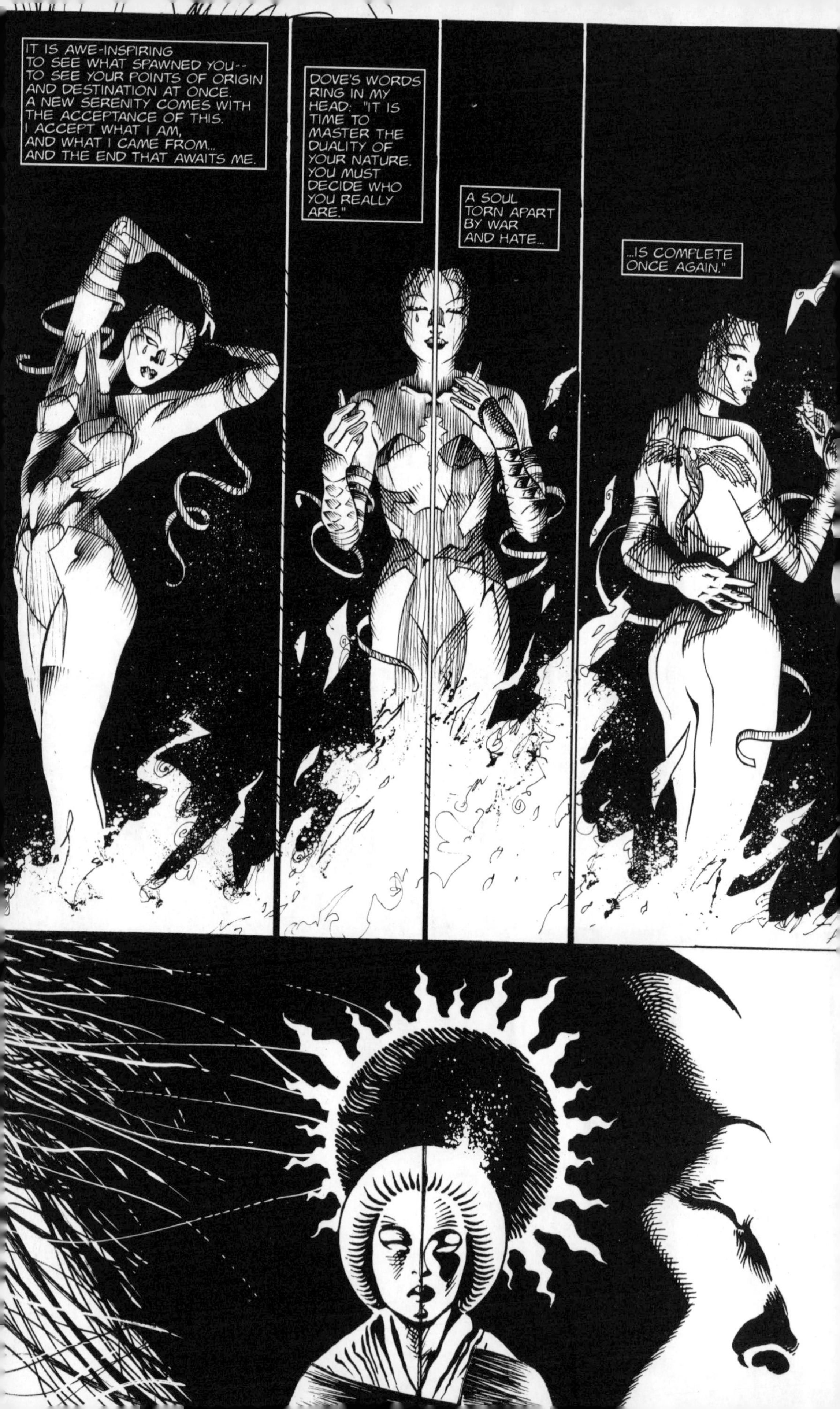

IT IS AWE-INSPIRING TO SEE WHAT SPAWNED YOU-- TO SEE YOUR POINTS OF ORIGIN AND DESTINATION AT ONCE. A NEW SERENITY COMES WITH THE ACCEPTANCE OF THIS. I ACCEPT WHAT I AM, AND WHAT I CAME FROM... AND THE END THAT AWAITS ME.
DOVE'S WORDS RING IN MY HEAD: "IT IS TIME TO MASTER THE DUALITY OF YOUR NATURE. YOU MUST DECIDE WHO YOU REALLY ARE."
A SOUL TORN APART BY WAR AND HATE...
...IS COMPLETE ONCE AGAIN."

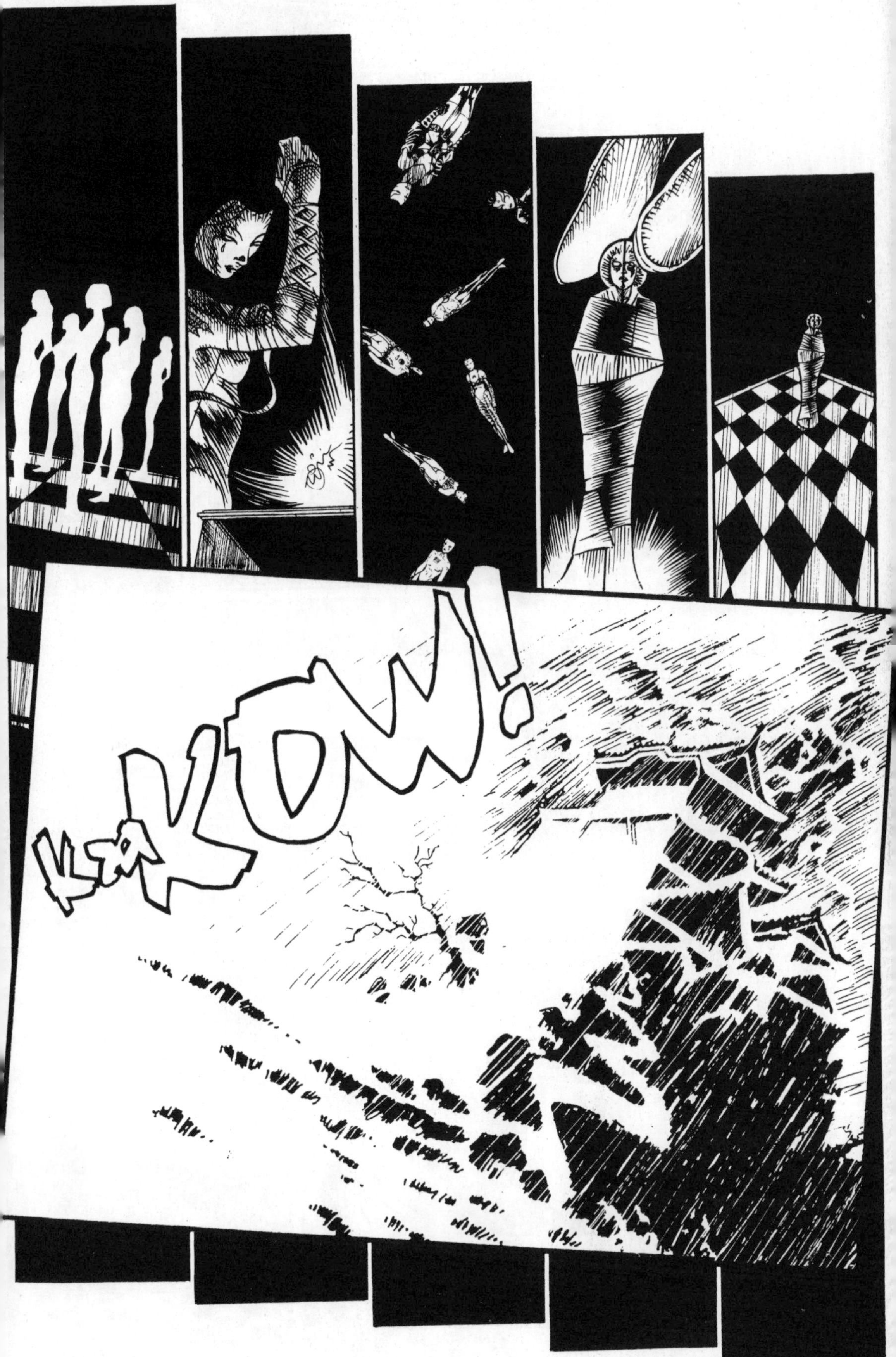
KAKOW!

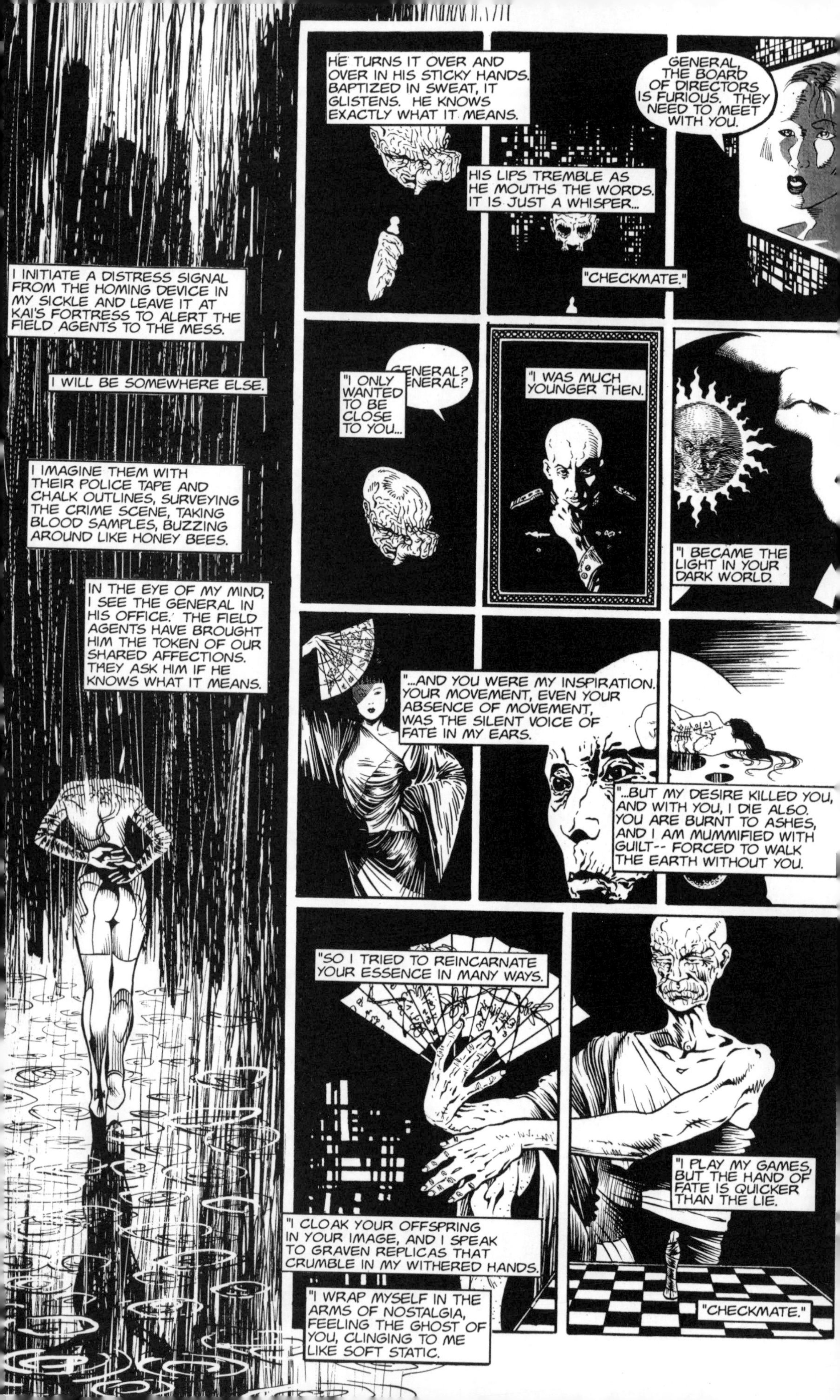

I INITIATE A DISTRESS SIGNAL FROM THE HOMING DEVICE IN MY SICKLE AND LEAVE IT AT KAI'S FORTRESS TO ALERT THE FIELD AGENTS TO THE MESS.
I WILL BE SOMEWHERE ELSE.
I IMAGINE THEM WITH THEIR POLICE TAPE AND CHALK OUTLINES, SURVEYING THE CRIME SCENE, TAKING BLOOD SAMPLES, BUZZING AROUND LIKE HONEY BEES.
IN THE EYE OF MY MIND, I SEE THE GENERAL IN HIS OFFICE. THE FIELD AGENTS HAVE BROUGHT HIM THE TOKEN OF OUR SHARED AFFECTIONS. THEY ASK HIM IF HE KNOWS WHAT IT MEANS.
HE TURNS IT OVER AND OVER IN HIS STICKY HANDS. BAPTIZED IN SWEAT, IT GLISTENS. HE KNOWS EXACTLY WHAT IT MEANS.
HIS LIPS TREMBLE AS HE MOUTHS THE WORDS. IT IS JUST A WHISPER...
"CHECKMATE."
GENERAL, THE BOARD OF DIRECTORS IS FURIOUS. THEY NEED TO MEET WITH YOU.
GENERAL? GENERAL?
"I ONLY WANTED TO BE CLOSE TO YOU...
"I WAS MUCH YOUNGER THEN.
"I BECAME THE LIGHT IN YOUR DARK WORLD.
"...AND YOU WERE MY INSPIRATION. YOUR MOVEMENT, EVEN YOUR ABSENCE OF MOVEMENT, WAS THE SILENT VOICE OF FATE IN MY EARS.
"...BUT MY DESIRE KILLED YOU, AND WITH YOU, I DIE ALSO. YOU ARE BURNT TO ASHES, AND I AM MUMMIFIED WITH GUILT-- FORCED TO WALK THE EARTH WITHOUT YOU.
"SO I TRIED TO REINCARNATE YOUR ESSENCE IN MANY WAYS.
"I CLOAK YOUR OFFSPRING IN YOUR IMAGE, AND I SPEAK TO GRAVEN REPLICAS THAT CRUMBLE IN MY WITHERED HANDS.
"I WRAP MYSELF IN THE ARMS OF NOSTALGIA, FEELING THE GHOST OF YOU, CLINGING TO ME LIKE SOFT STATIC.
"I PLAY MY GAMES, BUT THE HAND OF FATE IS QUICKER THAN THE LIE.
"CHECKMATE."

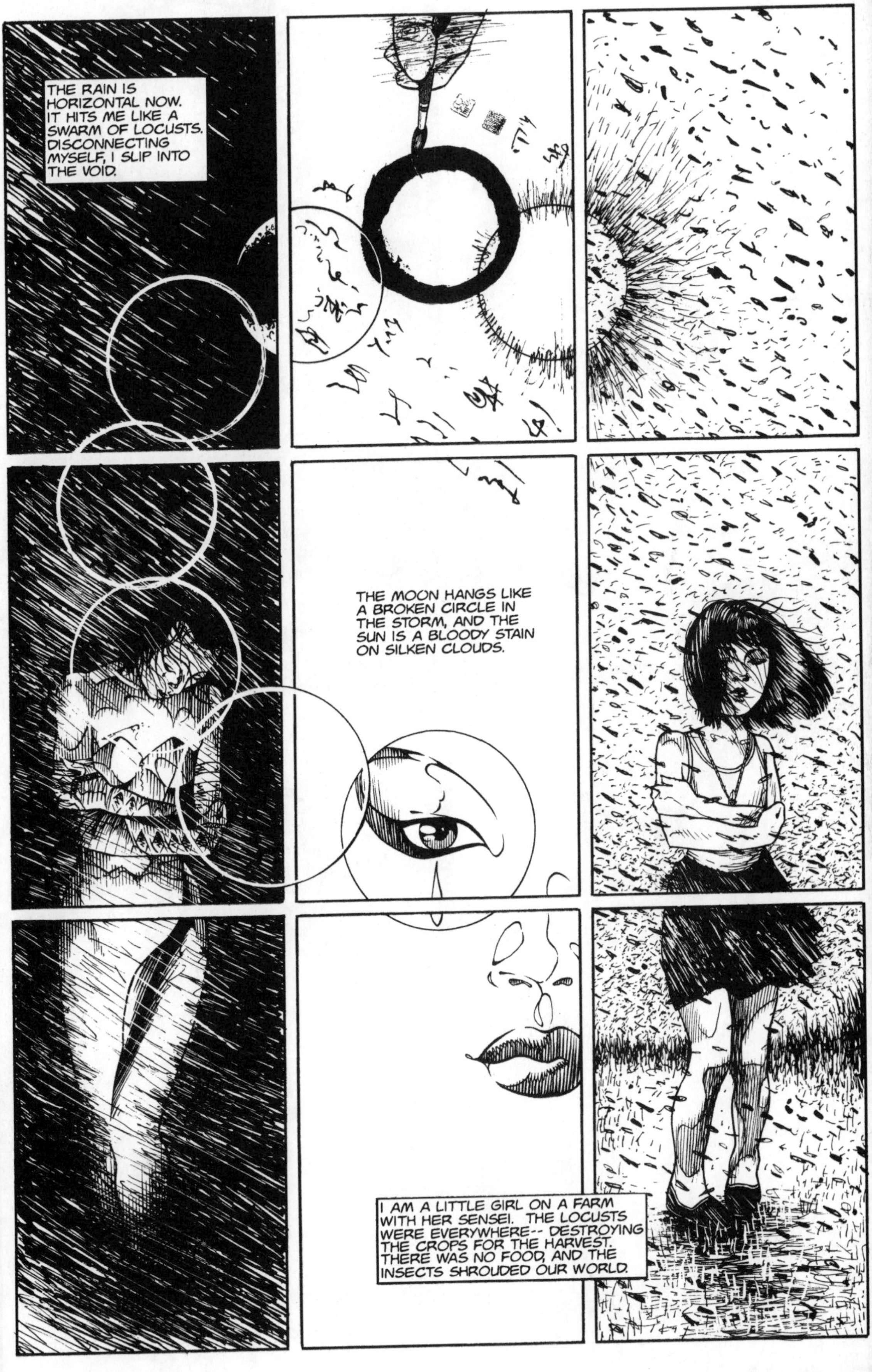
THE RAIN IS HORIZONTAL NOW. IT HITS ME LIKE A SWARM OF LOCUSTS. DISCONNECTING MYSELF, I SLIP INTO THE VOID.
THE MOON HANGS LIKE A BROKEN CIRCLE IN THE STORM, AND THE SUN IS A BLOODY STAIN ON SILKEN CLOUDS.
I AM A LITTLE GIRL ON A FARM WITH HER SENSEI. THE LOCUSTS WERE EVERYWHERE-- DESTROYING THE CROPS FOR THE HARVEST. THERE WAS NO FOOD, AND THE INSECTS SHROUDED OUR WORLD.

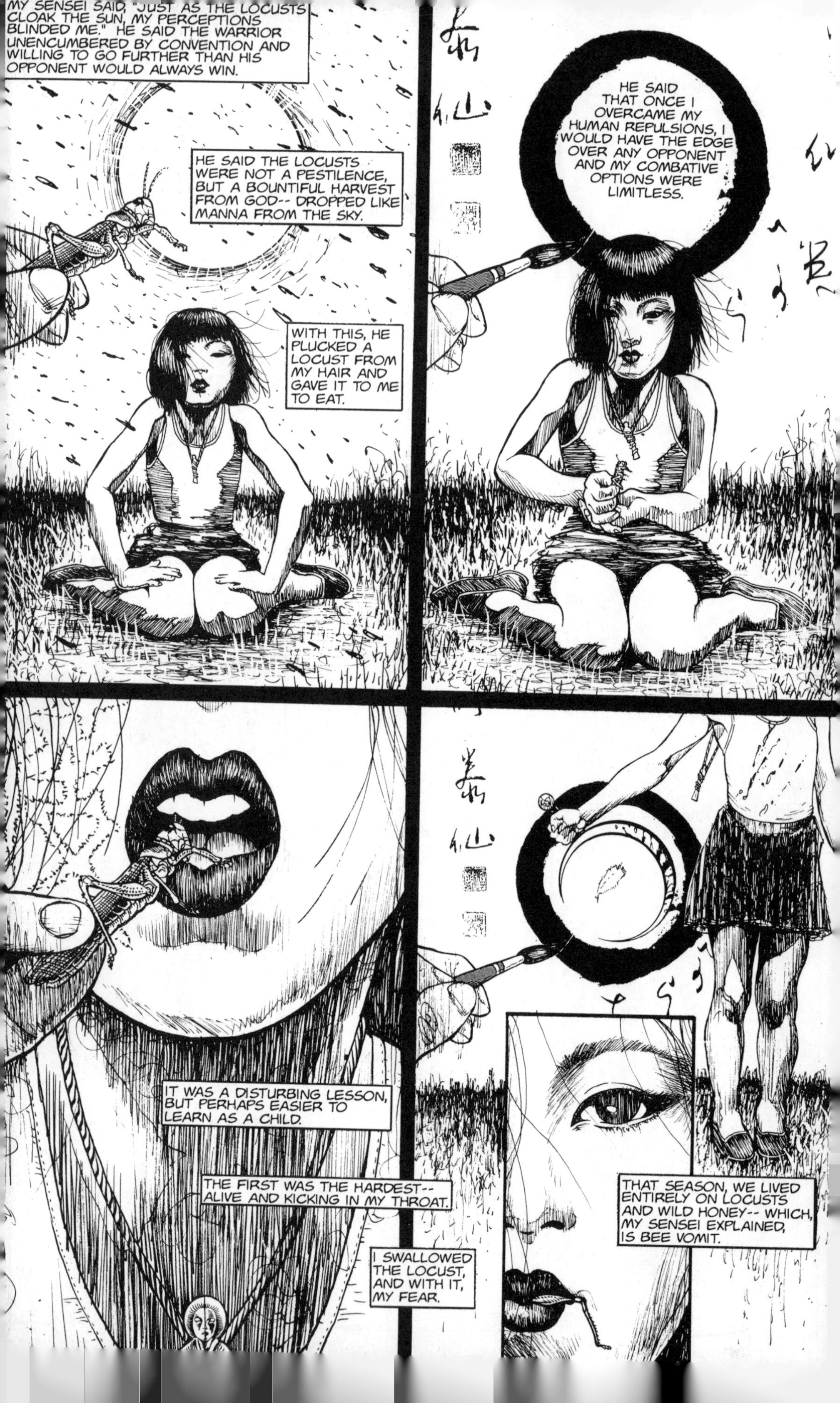
MY SENSEI SAID, "JUST AS THE LOCUSTS CLOAK THE SUN, MY PERCEPTIONS BLINDED ME." HE SAID THE WARRIOR UNENCUMBERED BY CONVENTION AND WILLING TO GO FURTHER THAN HIS OPPONENT WOULD ALWAYS WIN.
HE SAID THE LOCUSTS WERE NOT A PESTILENCE, BUT A BOUNTIFUL HARVEST FROM GOD-- DROPPED LIKE MANNA FROM THE SKY.
WITH THIS, HE PLUCKED A LOCUST FROM MY HAIR AND GAVE IT TO ME TO EAT.
HE SAID THAT ONCE I OVERCAME MY HUMAN REPULSIONS, I WOULD HAVE THE EDGE OVER ANY OPPONENT AND MY COMBATIVE OPTIONS WERE LIMITLESS.
IT WAS A DISTURBING LESSON, BUT PERHAPS EASIER TO LEARN AS A CHILD.
THE FIRST WAS THE HARDEST-- ALIVE AND KICKING IN MY THROAT.
I SWALLOWED THE LOCUST, AND WITH IT, MY FEAR.
THAT SEASON, WE LIVED ENTIRELY ON LOCUSTS AND WILD HONEY-- WHICH, MY SENSEI EXPLAINED, IS BEE VOMIT.

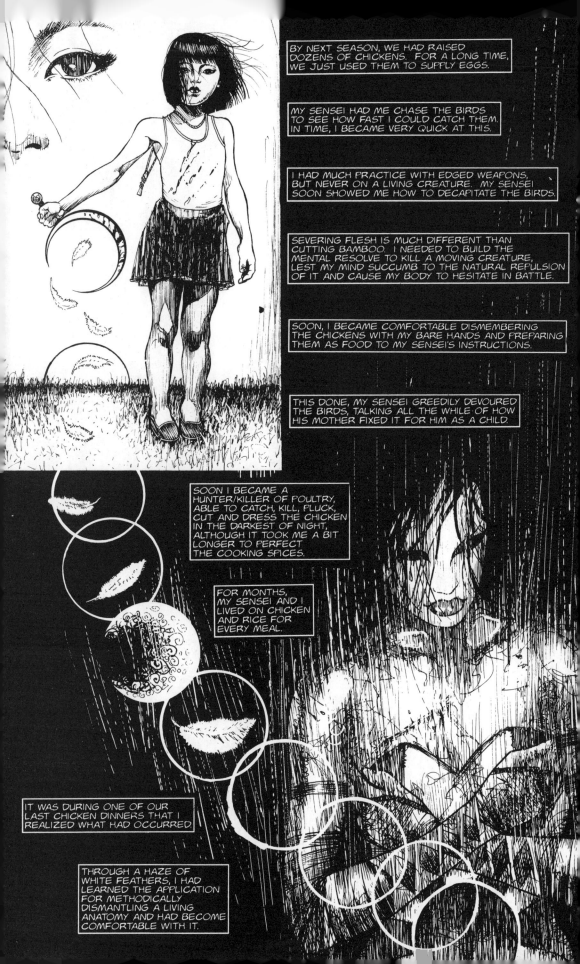

BY NEXT SEASON, WE HAD RAISED DOZENS OF CHICKENS. FOR A LONG TIME, WE JUST USED THEM TO SUPPLY EGGS.

MY SENSEI HAD ME CHASE THE BIRDS TO SEE HOW FAST I COULD CATCH THEM. IN TIME, I BECAME VERY QUICK AT THIS.

I HAD MUCH PRACTICE WITH EDGED WEAPONS, BUT NEVER ON A LIVING CREATURE. MY SENSEI SOON SHOWED ME HOW TO DECAPITATE THE BIRDS.

SEVERING FLESH IS MUCH DIFFERENT THAN CUTTING BAMBOO. I NEEDED TO BUILD THE MENTAL RESOLVE TO KILL A MOVING CREATURE, LEST MY MIND SUCCUMB TO THE NATURAL REPULSION OF IT AND CAUSE MY BODY TO HESITATE IN BATTLE.

SOON, I BECAME COMFORTABLE DISMEMBERING THE CHICKENS WITH MY BARE HANDS AND PREPARING THEM AS FOOD TO MY SENSEI'S INSTRUCTIONS.

THIS DONE, MY SENSEI GREEDILY DEVOURED THE BIRDS, TALKING ALL THE WHILE OF HOW HIS MOTHER FIXED IT FOR HIM AS A CHILD.

SOON I BECAME A HUNTER/KILLER OF POULTRY, ABLE TO CATCH, KILL, PLUCK, CUT AND DRESS THE CHICKEN IN THE DARKEST OF NIGHT, ALTHOUGH IT TOOK ME A BIT LONGER TO PERFECT THE COOKING SPICES.

FOR MONTHS, MY SENSEI AND I LIVED ON CHICKEN AND RICE FOR EVERY MEAL.

IT WAS DURING ONE OF OUR LAST CHICKEN DINNERS THAT I REALIZED WHAT HAD OCCURRED.

THROUGH A HAZE OF WHITE FEATHERS, I HAD LEARNED THE APPLICATION FOR METHODICALLY DISMANTLING A LIVING ANATOMY AND HAD BECOME COMFORTABLE WITH IT.

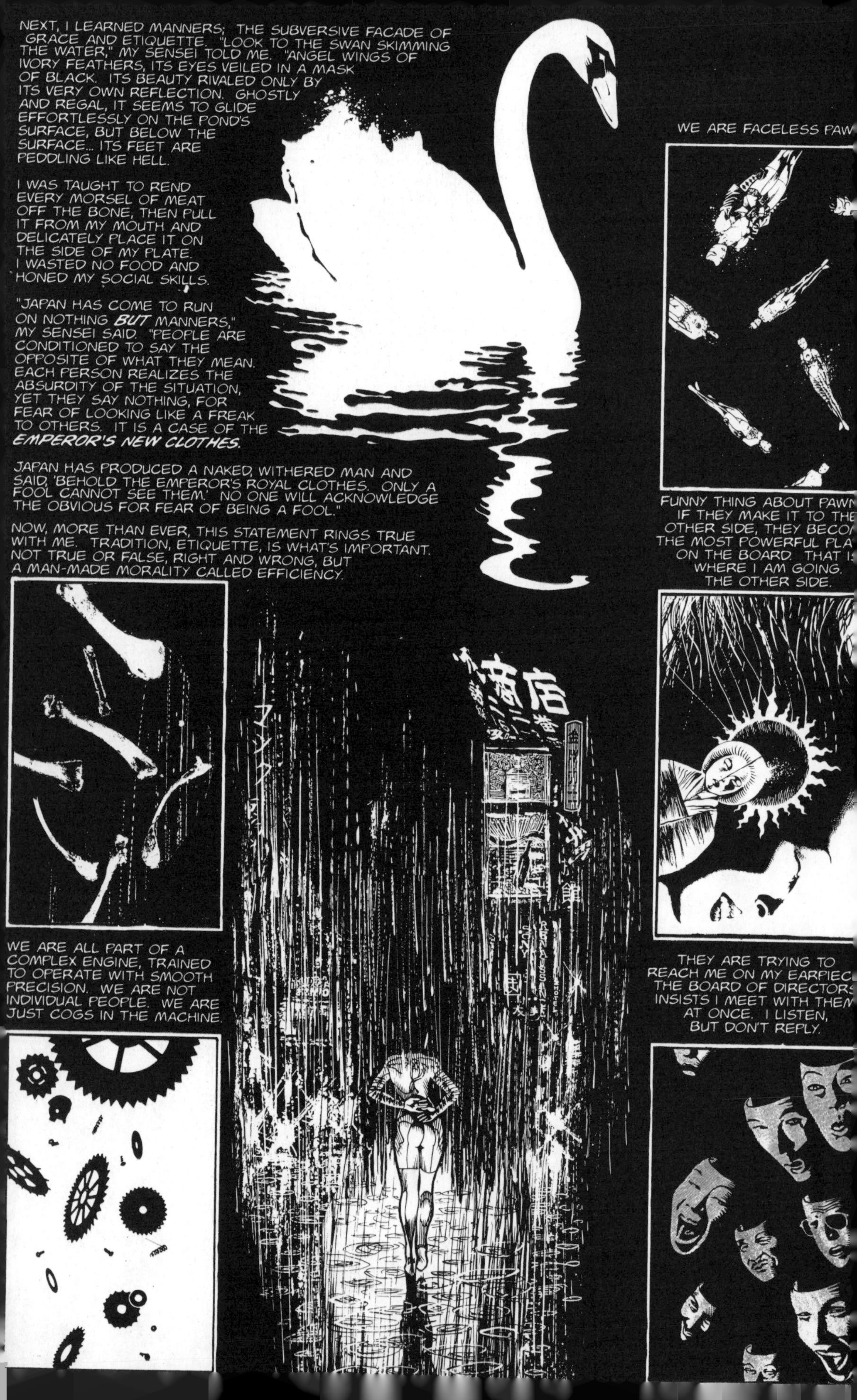
NEXT, I LEARNED MANNERS; THE SUBVERSIVE FACADE OF GRACE AND ETIQUETTE. "LOOK TO THE SWAN SKIMMING THE WATER," MY SENSEI TOLD ME. "ANGEL WINGS OF IVORY FEATHERS, ITS EYES VEILED IN A MASK OF BLACK. ITS BEAUTY RIVALED ONLY BY ITS VERY OWN REFLECTION. GHOSTLY AND REGAL, IT SEEMS TO GLIDE EFFORTLESSLY ON THE POND'S SURFACE, BUT BELOW THE SURFACE... ITS FEET ARE PEDDLING LIKE HELL.
I WAS TAUGHT TO REND EVERY MORSEL OF MEAT OFF THE BONE, THEN PULL IT FROM MY MOUTH AND DELICATELY PLACE IT ON THE SIDE OF MY PLATE. I WASTED NO FOOD AND HONED MY SOCIAL SKILLS.
"JAPAN HAS COME TO RUN ON NOTHING *BUT* MANNERS," MY SENSEI SAID. "PEOPLE ARE CONDITIONED TO SAY THE OPPOSITE OF WHAT THEY MEAN. EACH PERSON REALIZES THE ABSURDITY OF THE SITUATION, YET THEY SAY NOTHING, FOR FEAR OF LOOKING LIKE A FREAK TO OTHERS. IT IS A CASE OF THE ***EMPEROR'S NEW CLOTHES.***
JAPAN HAS PRODUCED A NAKED, WITHERED MAN AND SAID, 'BEHOLD THE EMPEROR'S ROYAL CLOTHES. ONLY A FOOL CANNOT SEE THEM.' NO ONE WILL ACKNOWLEDGE THE OBVIOUS FOR FEAR OF BEING A FOOL."
NOW, MORE THAN EVER, THIS STATEMENT RINGS TRUE WITH ME. TRADITION, ETIQUETTE, IS WHAT'S IMPORTANT. NOT TRUE OR FALSE, RIGHT AND WRONG, BUT A MAN-MADE MORALITY CALLED EFFICIENCY.
WE ARE ALL PART OF A COMPLEX ENGINE, TRAINED TO OPERATE WITH SMOOTH PRECISION. WE ARE NOT INDIVIDUAL PEOPLE. WE ARE JUST COGS IN THE MACHINE.
WE ARE FACELESS PAW
FUNNY THING ABOUT PAWN IF THEY MAKE IT TO THE OTHER SIDE, THEY BECOM THE MOST POWERFUL PLA ON THE BOARD. THAT I WHERE I AM GOING. THE OTHER SIDE.
THEY ARE TRYING TO REACH ME ON MY EARPIEC THE BOARD OF DIRECTORS INSISTS I MEET WITH THEM AT ONCE. I LISTEN, BUT DON'T REPLY.

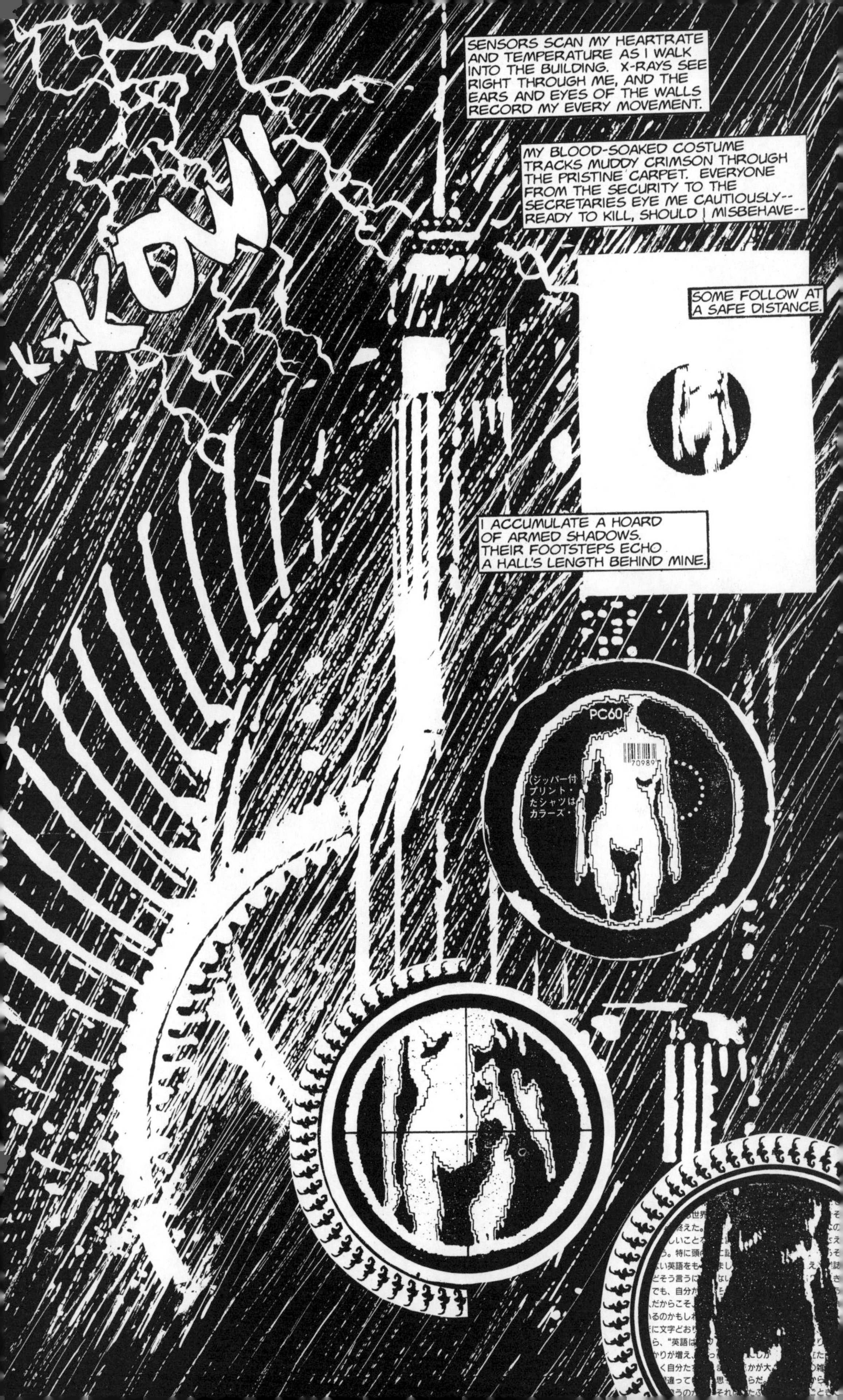
SENSORS SCAN MY HEARTRATE AND TEMPERATURE AS I WALK INTO THE BUILDING. X-RAYS SEE RIGHT THROUGH ME, AND THE EARS AND EYES OF THE WALLS RECORD MY EVERY MOVEMENT.
KOW!
MY BLOOD-SOAKED COSTUME TRACKS MUDDY CRIMSON THROUGH THE PRISTINE CARPET. EVERYONE FROM THE SECURITY TO THE SECRETARIES EYE ME CAUTIOUSLY-- READY TO KILL, SHOULD I MISBEHAVE--
SOME FOLLOW AT A SAFE DISTANCE.
I ACCUMULATE A HOARD OF ARMED SHADOWS. THEIR FOOTSTEPS ECHO A HALL'S LENGTH BEHIND MINE.
PC60
(ジッパー付
プリント・
たシャツは
カラーズ・

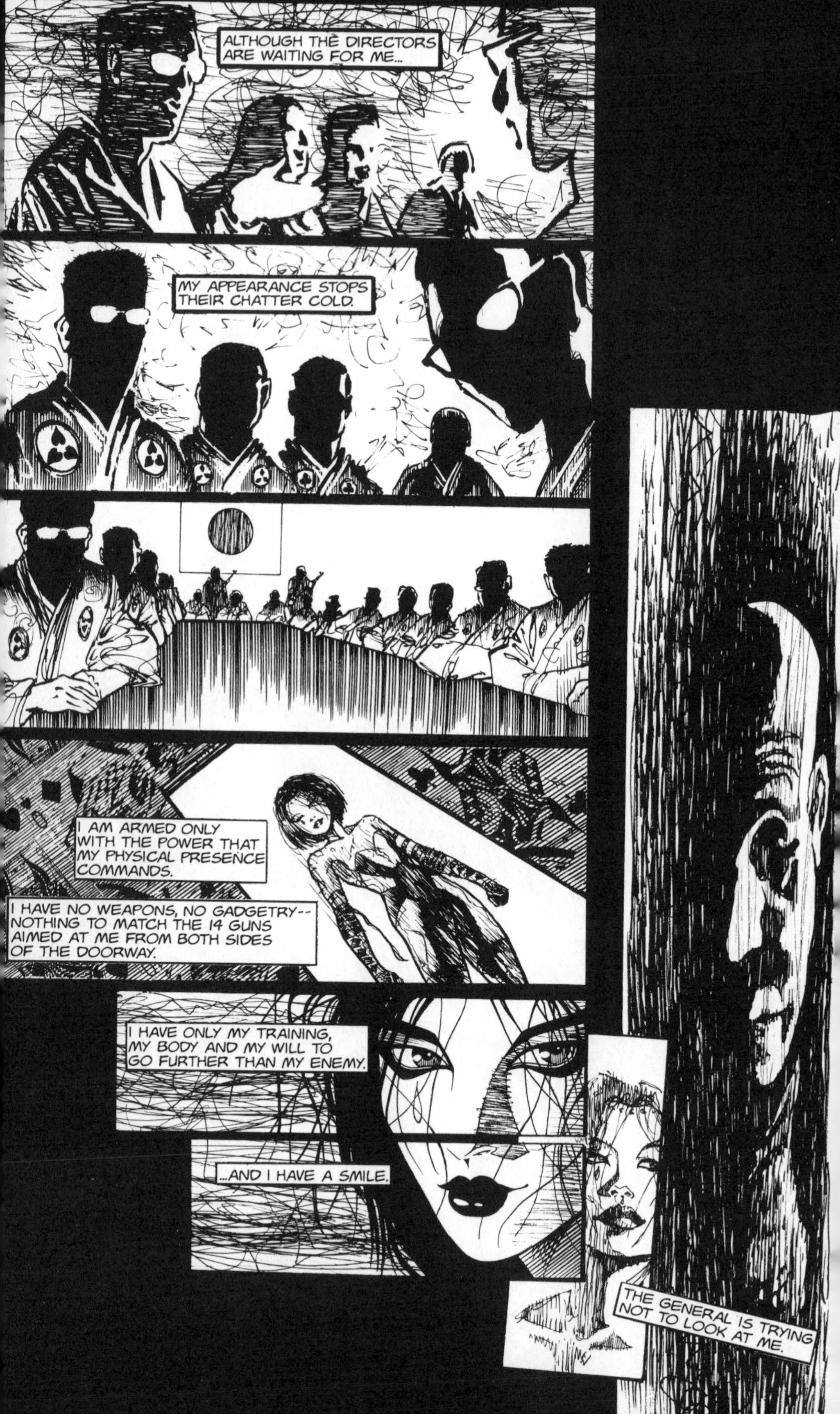
ALTHOUGH THE DIRECTORS ARE WAITING FOR ME...
MY APPEARANCE STOPS THEIR CHATTER COLD.
I AM ARMED ONLY WITH THE POWER THAT MY PHYSICAL PRESENCE COMMANDS.
I HAVE NO WEAPONS, NO GADGETRY-- NOTHING TO MATCH THE 14 GUNS AIMED AT ME FROM BOTH SIDES OF THE DOORWAY.
I HAVE ONLY MY TRAINING, MY BODY AND MY WILL TO GO FURTHER THAN MY ENEMY.
...AND I HAVE A SMILE.
THE GENERAL IS TRYING NOT TO LOOK AT ME.

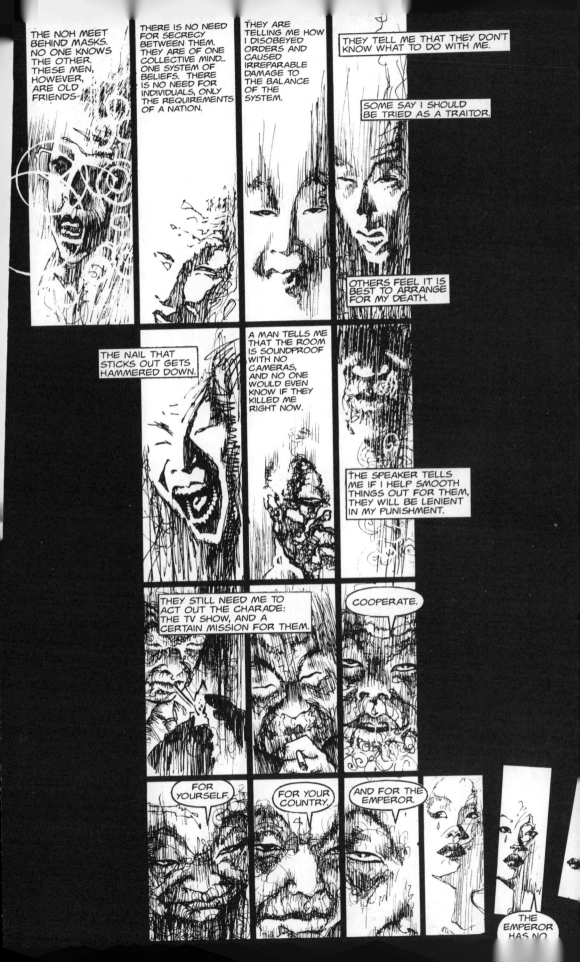

THE NOH MEET BEHIND MASKS. NO ONE KNOWS THE OTHER. THESE MEN, HOWEVER, ARE OLD FRIENDS—

THERE IS NO NEED FOR SECRECY BETWEEN THEM. THEY ARE OF ONE COLLECTIVE MIND... ONE SYSTEM OF BELIEFS. THERE IS NO NEED FOR INDIVIDUALS, ONLY THE REQUIREMENTS OF A NATION.

THEY ARE TELLING ME HOW I DISOBEYED ORDERS AND CAUSED IRREPARABLE DAMAGE TO THE BALANCE OF THE SYSTEM.

THEY TELL ME THAT THEY DON'T KNOW WHAT TO DO WITH ME.

SOME SAY I SHOULD BE TRIED AS A TRAITOR.

OTHERS FEEL IT IS BEST TO ARRANGE FOR MY DEATH.

THE NAIL THAT STICKS OUT GETS HAMMERED DOWN.

A MAN TELLS ME THAT THE ROOM IS SOUNDPROOF WITH NO CAMERAS, AND NO ONE WOULD EVEN KNOW IF THEY KILLED ME RIGHT NOW.

THE SPEAKER TELLS ME IF I HELP SMOOTH THINGS OUT FOR THEM, THEY WILL BE LENIENT IN MY PUNISHMENT.

THEY STILL NEED ME TO ACT OUT THE CHARADE: THE TV SHOW, AND A CERTAIN MISSION FOR THEM.

COOPERATE.

FOR YOURSELF.

FOR YOUR COUNTRY.

AND FOR THE EMPEROR.

THE EMPEROR HAS NO

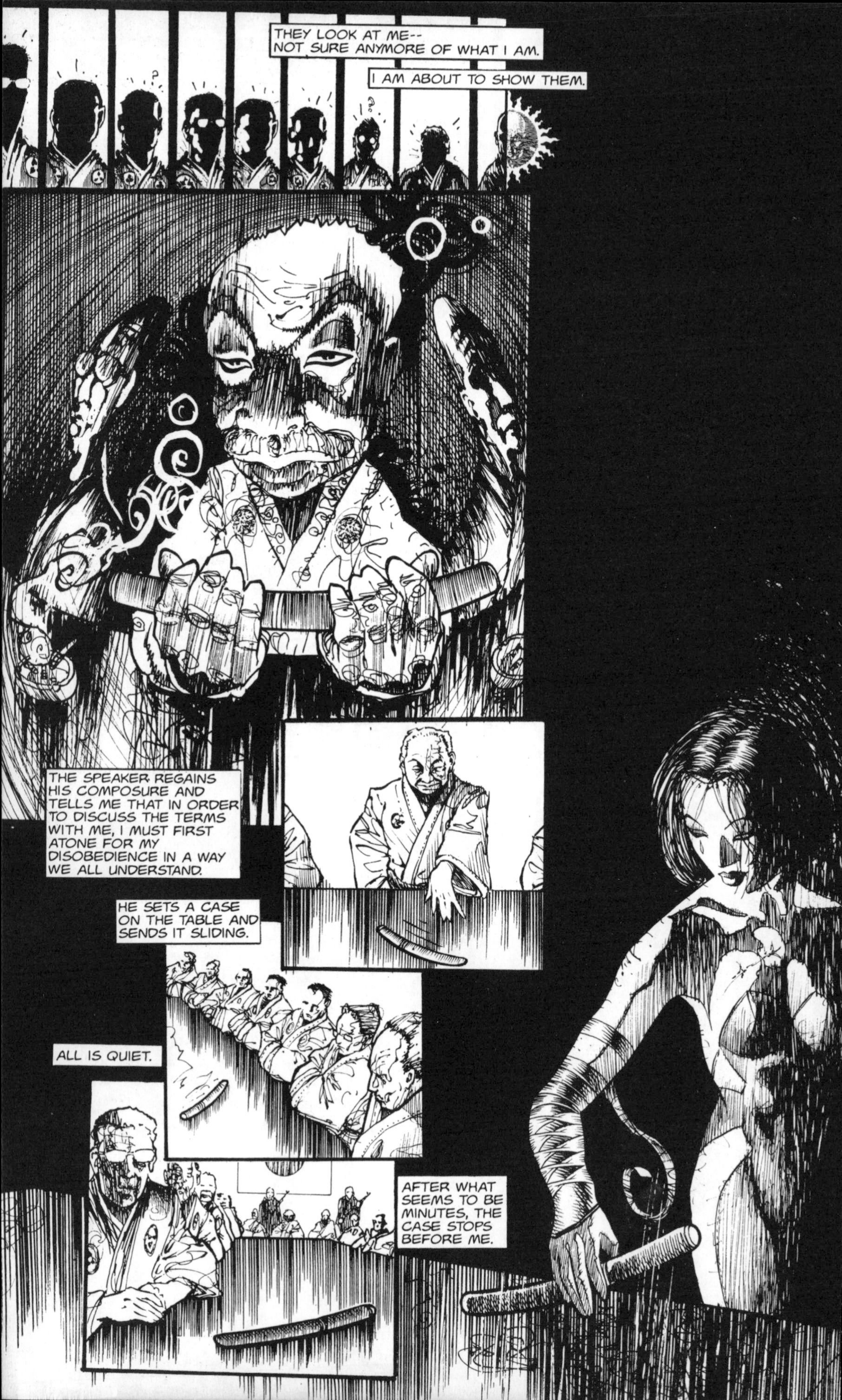
THEY LOOK AT ME--
NOT SURE ANYMORE OF WHAT I AM.
I AM ABOUT TO SHOW THEM.
THE SPEAKER REGAINS HIS COMPOSURE AND TELLS ME THAT IN ORDER TO DISCUSS THE TERMS WITH ME, I MUST FIRST ATONE FOR MY DISOBEDIENCE IN A WAY WE ALL UNDERSTAND.
HE SETS A CASE ON THE TABLE AND SENDS IT SLIDING.
ALL IS QUIET.
AFTER WHAT SEEMS TO BE MINUTES, THE CASE STOPS BEFORE ME.

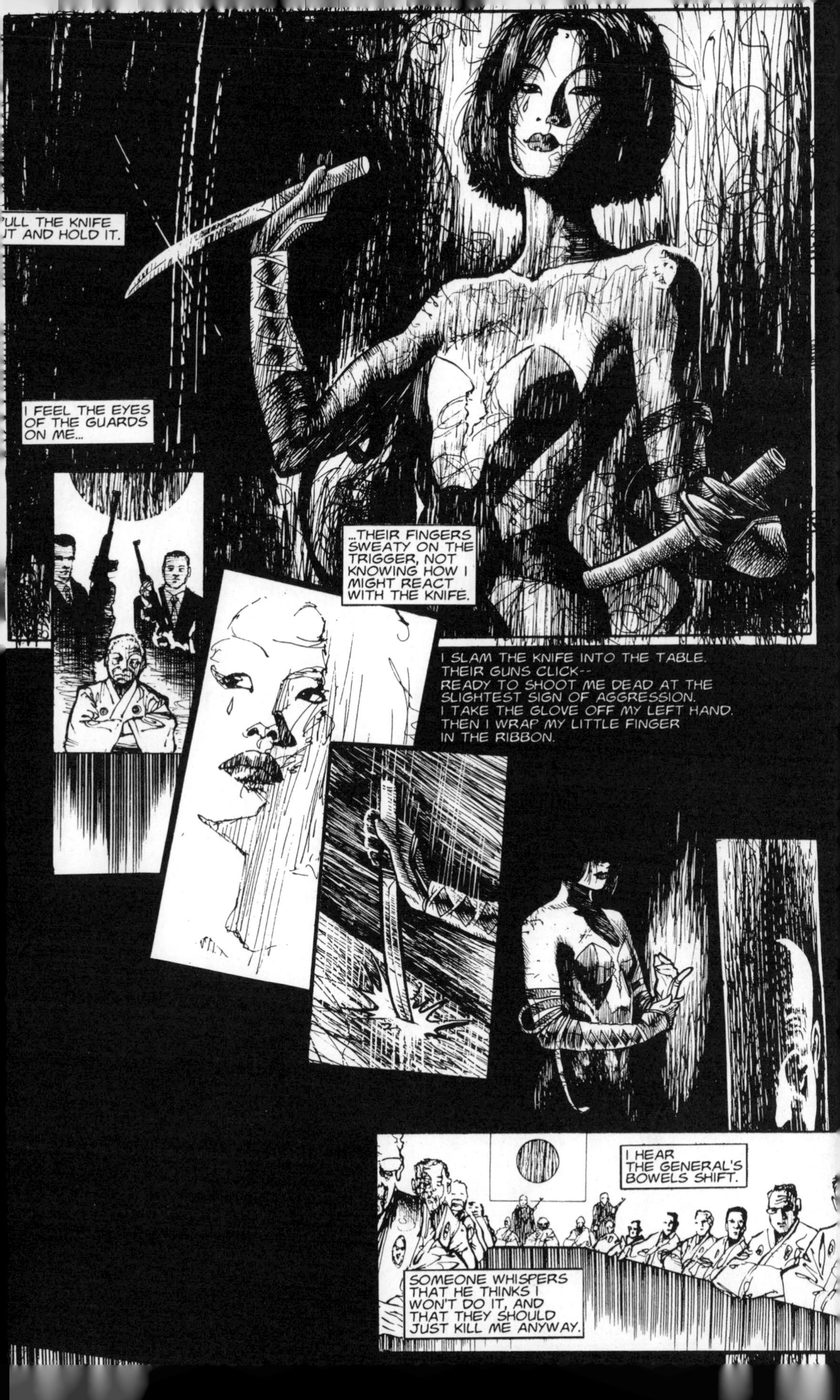

PULL THE KNIFE
UT AND HOLD IT.
I FEEL THE EYES
OF THE GUARDS
ON ME...
...THEIR FINGERS
SWEATY ON THE
TRIGGER, NOT
KNOWING HOW I
MIGHT REACT
WITH THE KNIFE.
I SLAM THE KNIFE INTO THE TABLE.
THEIR GUNS CLICK--
READY TO SHOOT ME DEAD AT THE
SLIGHTEST SIGN OF AGGRESSION.
I TAKE THE GLOVE OFF MY LEFT HAND.
THEN I WRAP MY LITTLE FINGER
IN THE RIBBON.
I HEAR
THE GENERAL'S
BOWELS SHIFT.
SOMEONE WHISPERS
THAT HE THINKS I
WON'T DO IT, AND
THAT THEY SHOULD
JUST KILL ME ANYWAY.

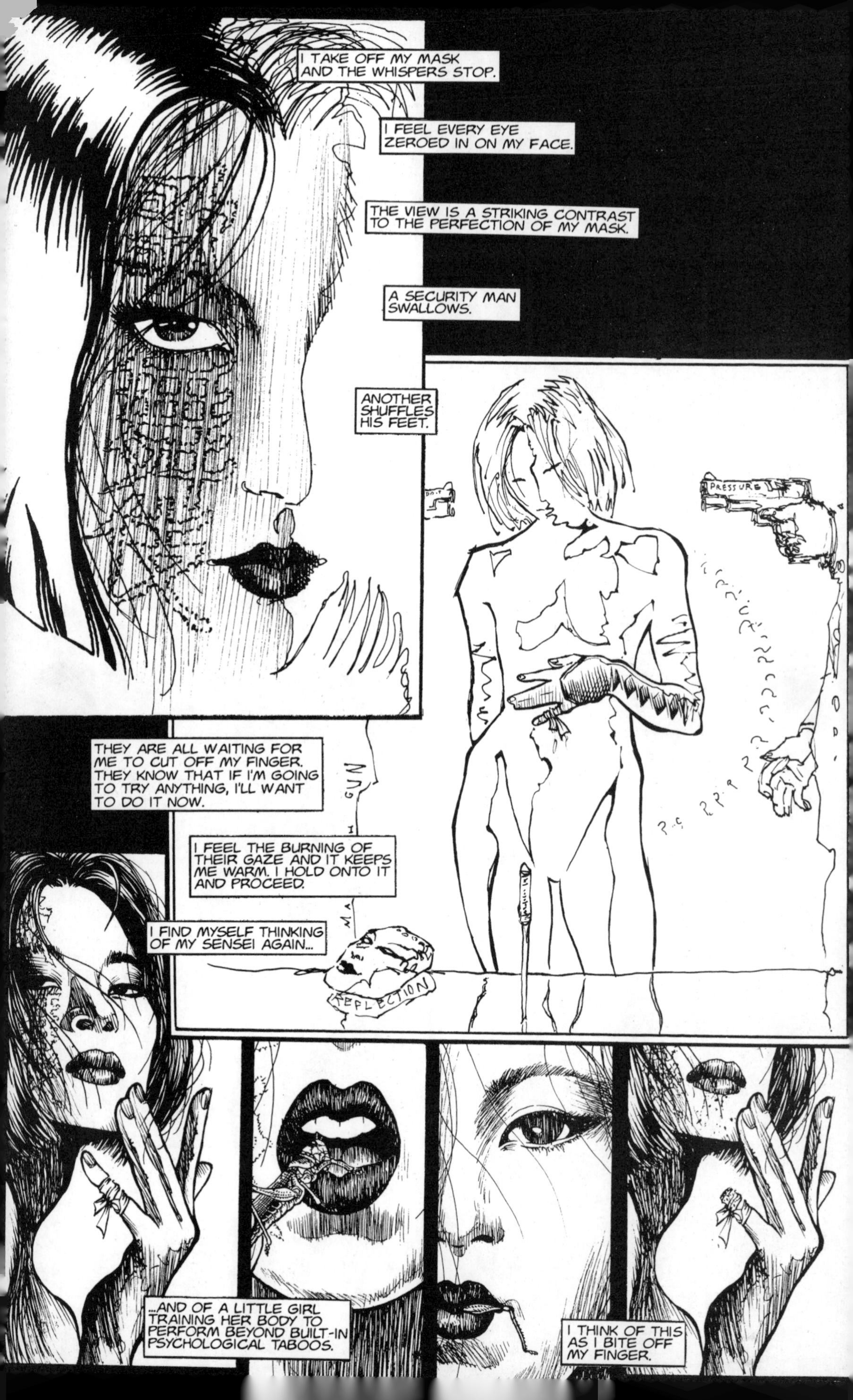
I TAKE OFF MY MASK AND THE WHISPERS STOP.
I FEEL EVERY EYE ZEROED IN ON MY FACE.
THE VIEW IS A STRIKING CONTRAST TO THE PERFECTION OF MY MASK.
A SECURITY MAN SWALLOWS.
ANOTHER SHUFFLES HIS FEET.
PRESSURE
THEY ARE ALL WAITING FOR ME TO CUT OFF MY FINGER. THEY KNOW THAT IF I'M GOING TO TRY ANYTHING, I'LL WANT TO DO IT NOW.
GUN
I FEEL THE BURNING OF THEIR GAZE AND IT KEEPS ME WARM. I HOLD ONTO IT AND PROCEED.
I FIND MYSELF THINKING OF MY SENSEI AGAIN...
REFLECTION
...AND OF A LITTLE GIRL TRAINING HER BODY TO PERFORM BEYOND BUILT-IN PSYCHOLOGICAL TABOOS.
I THINK OF THIS AS I BITE OFF MY FINGER.

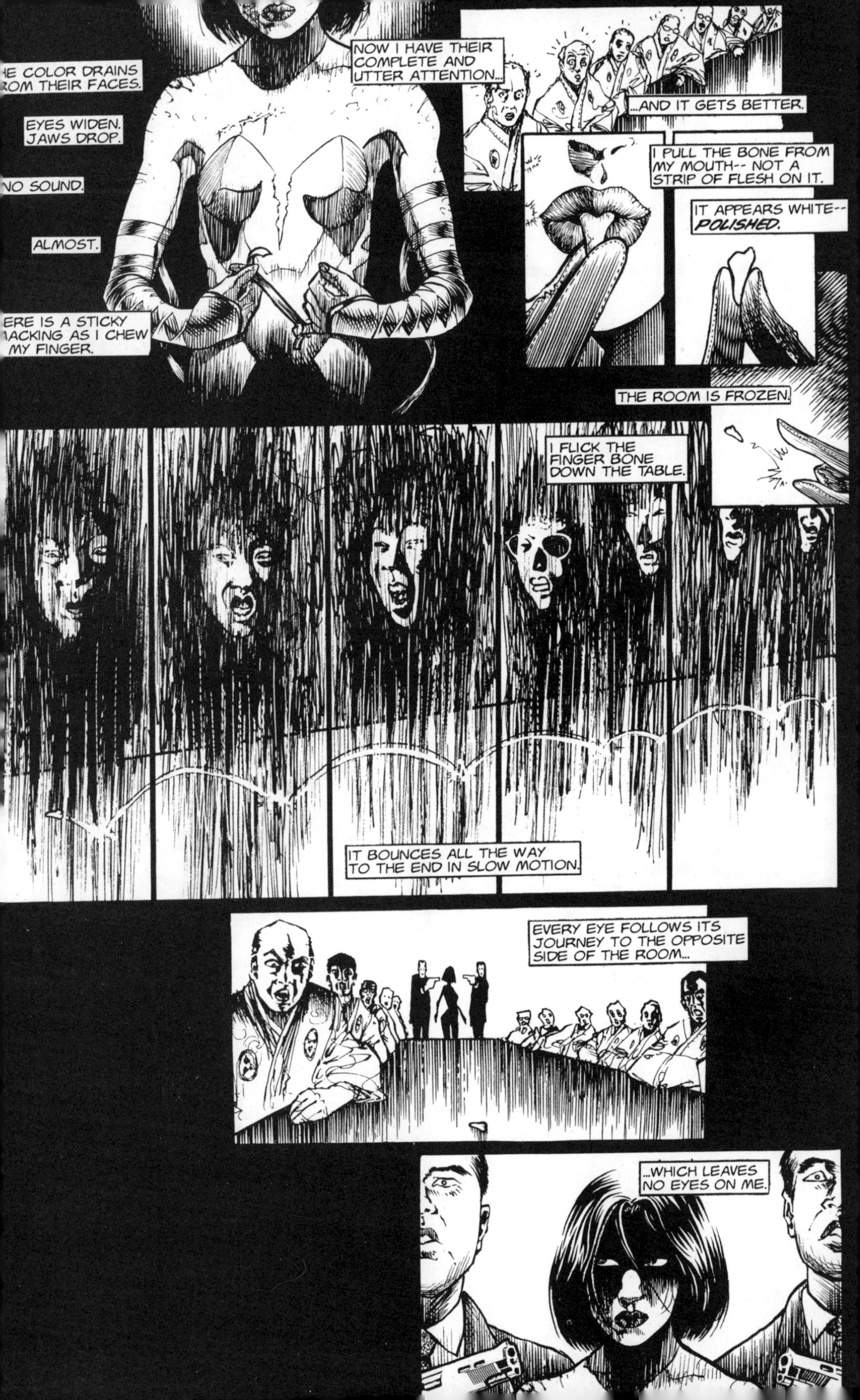

HE COLOR DRAINS
ROM THEIR FACES.
EYES WIDEN.
JAWS DROP.
NO SOUND.
ALMOST.
ERE IS A STICKY
MACKING AS I CHEW
MY FINGER.
NOW I HAVE THEIR COMPLETE AND UTTER ATTENTION...
...AND IT GETS BETTER.
I PULL THE BONE FROM MY MOUTH-- NOT A STRIP OF FLESH ON IT.
IT APPEARS WHITE-- POLISHED.
THE ROOM IS FROZEN.
I FLICK THE FINGER BONE DOWN THE TABLE.
IT BOUNCES ALL THE WAY TO THE END IN SLOW MOTION.
EVERY EYE FOLLOWS ITS JOURNEY TO THE OPPOSITE SIDE OF THE ROOM...
...WHICH LEAVES NO EYES ON ME.

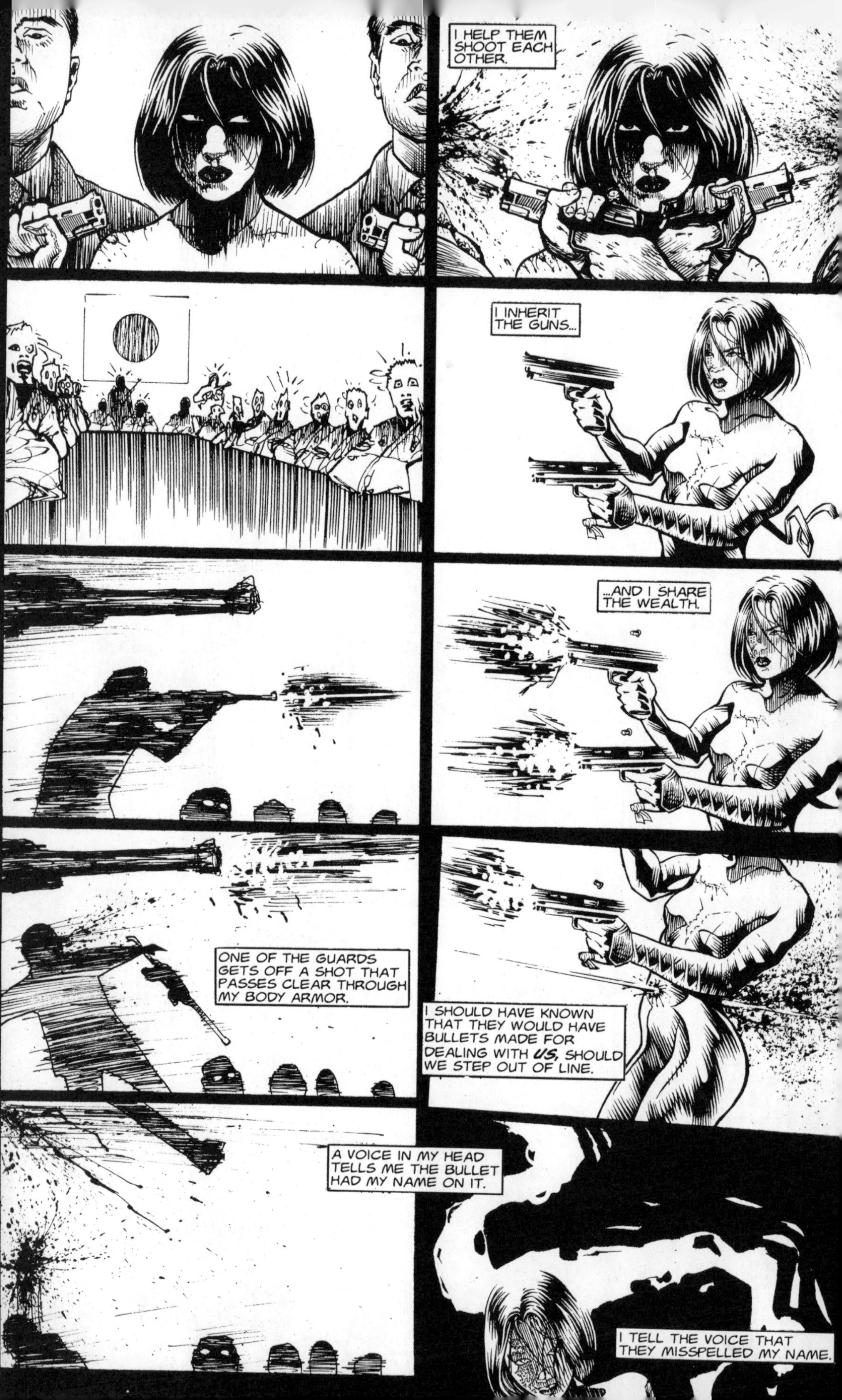
I HELP THEM SHOOT EACH OTHER.
I INHERIT THE GUNS...
...AND I SHARE THE WEALTH.
ONE OF THE GUARDS GETS OFF A SHOT THAT PASSES CLEAR THROUGH MY BODY ARMOR.
I SHOULD HAVE KNOWN THAT THEY WOULD HAVE BULLETS MADE FOR DEALING WITH US, SHOULD WE STEP OUT OF LINE.
A VOICE IN MY HEAD TELLS ME THE BULLET HAD MY NAME ON IT.
I TELL THE VOICE THAT THEY MISSPELLED MY NAME.

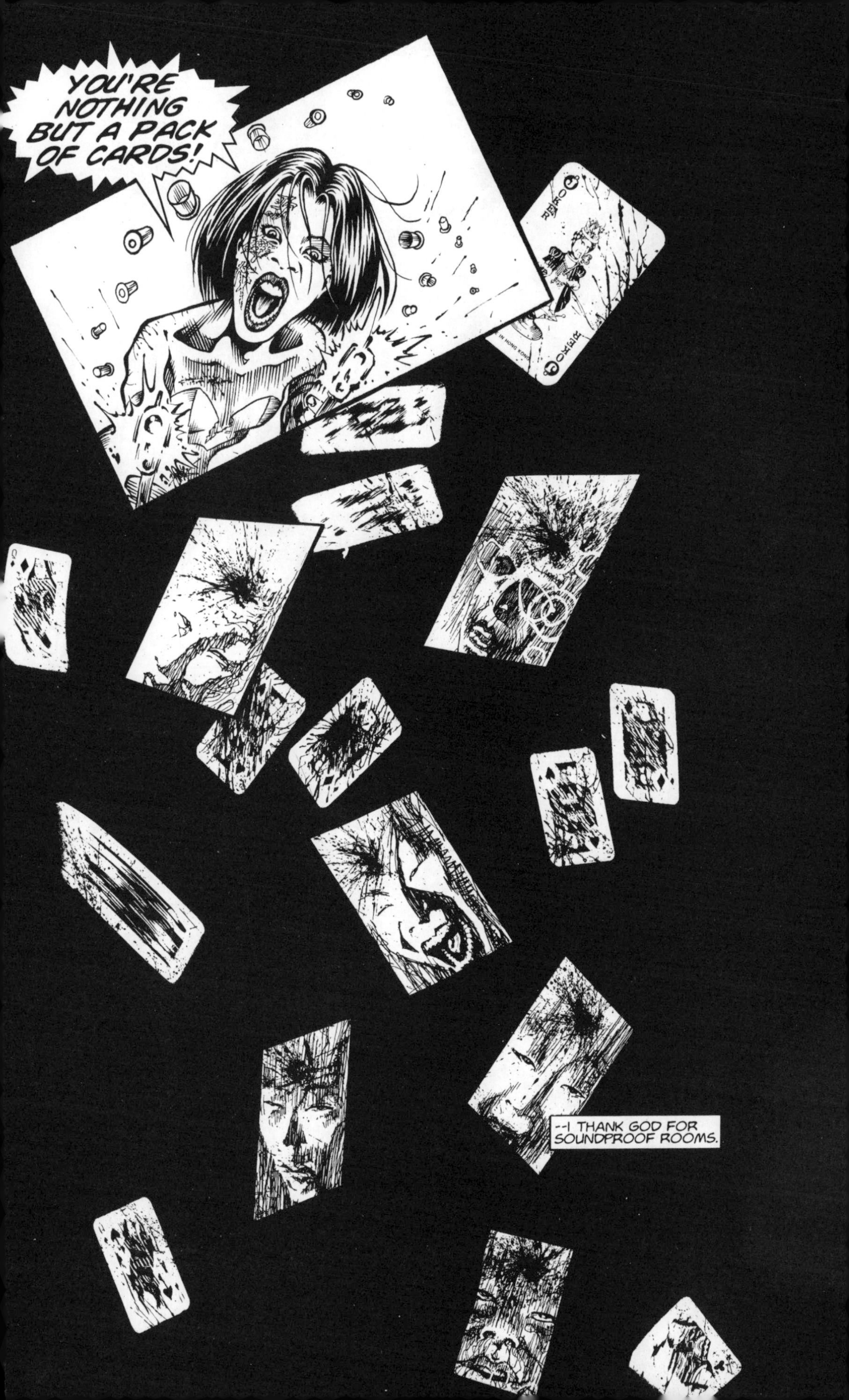
YOU'RE NOTHING BUT A PACK OF CARDS!
--I THANK GOD FOR SOUNDPROOF ROOMS.

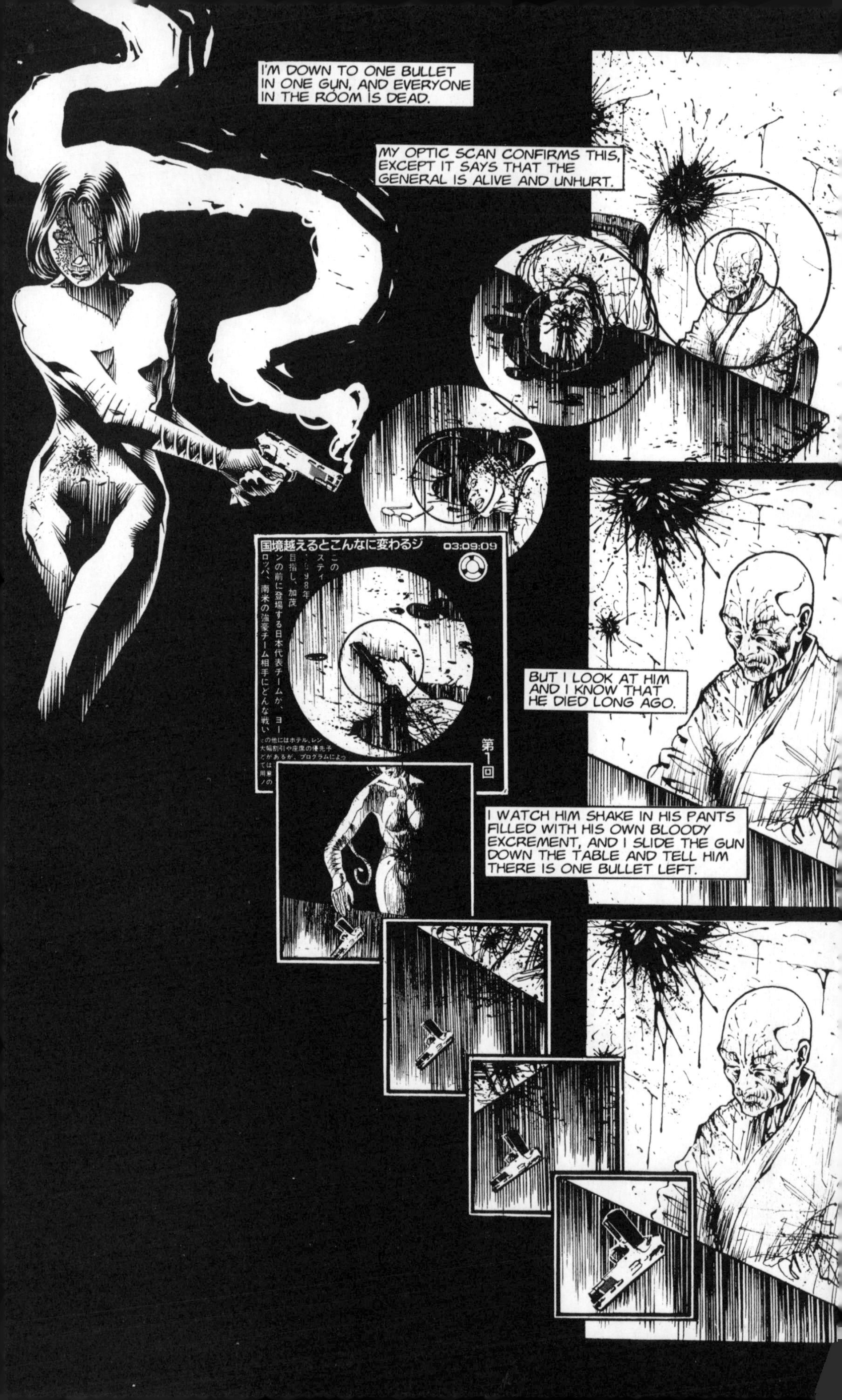
I'M DOWN TO ONE BULLET IN ONE GUN, AND EVERYONE IN THE ROOM IS DEAD.
MY OPTIC SCAN CONFIRMS THIS, EXCEPT IT SAYS THAT THE GENERAL IS ALIVE AND UNHURT.
国境越えるとこんなに変わるジ
03:09:09
第1回
BUT I LOOK AT HIM AND I KNOW THAT HE DIED LONG AGO.
I WATCH HIM SHAKE IN HIS PANTS FILLED WITH HIS OWN BLOODY EXCREMENT, AND I SLIDE THE GUN DOWN THE TABLE AND TELL HIM THERE IS ONE BULLET LEFT.

HE PICKS IT UP LIKE AN OLD LOVER WARM IN HIS HANDS.

FOR A SPLIT SECOND, I SEE A YOUNG MAN, AND I THINK HE ACTUALLY CONSIDERS TRYING TO SHOOT ME.

THEN THE GUN GETS HEAVY AND HIS EYES ARE TIRED. I CAN SEE HE WISHES HE HAD DIED LONG AGO.

WHAT BROKEN DREAMS RATTLE THROUGH HIS BONY HEAD?

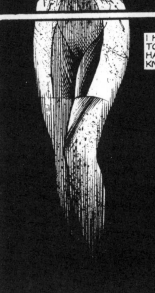

I HOLD MY STOMACH TOGETHER WITH MY HANDS AND SLIDE THE KNIFE IN MY ARM BANDS.

THEN I OPEN THE DOOR AND WALK OUT.

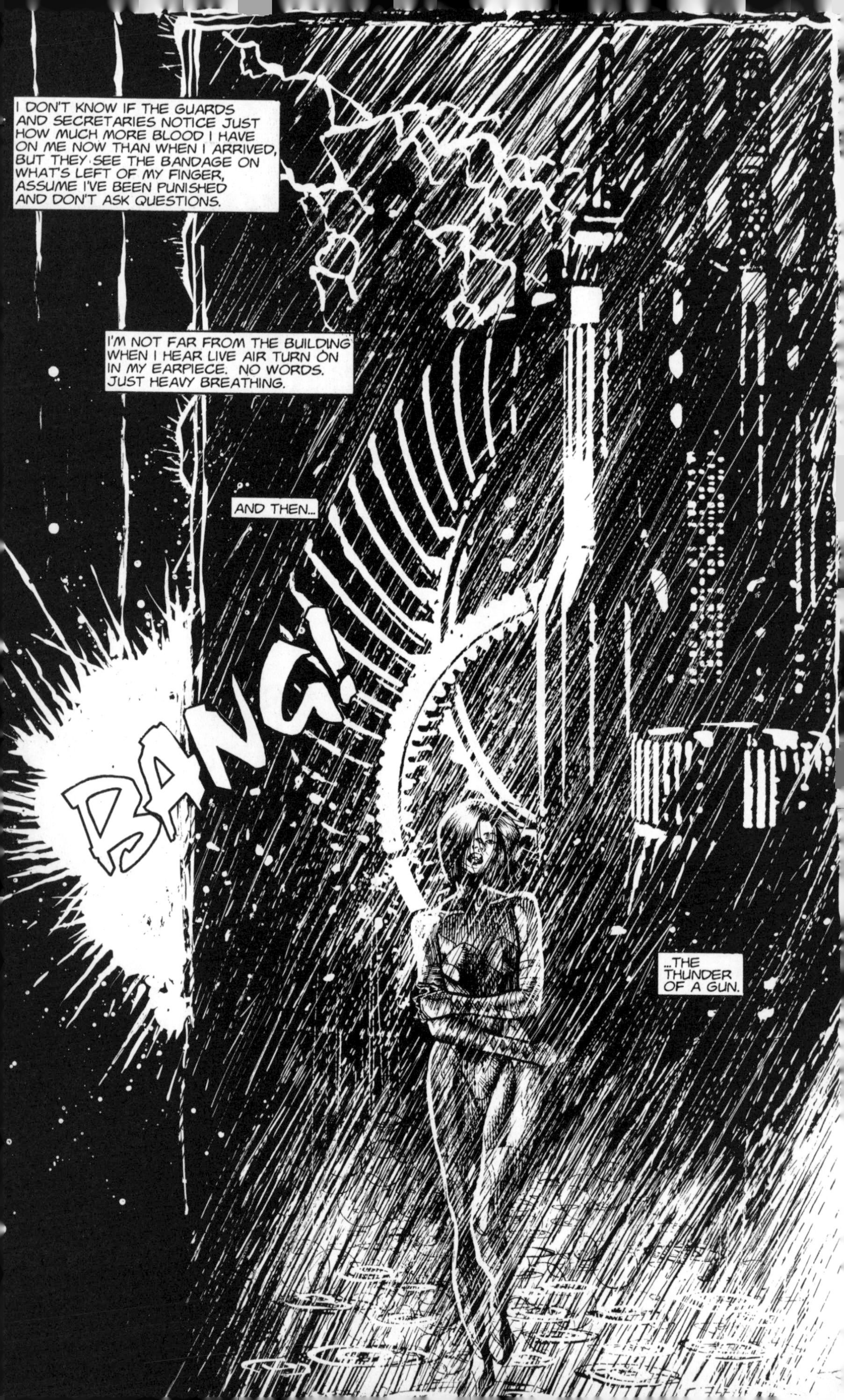
I DON'T KNOW IF THE GUARDS AND SECRETARIES NOTICE JUST HOW MUCH MORE BLOOD I HAVE ON ME NOW THAN WHEN I ARRIVED, BUT THEY SEE THE BANDAGE ON WHAT'S LEFT OF MY FINGER, ASSUME I'VE BEEN PUNISHED AND DON'T ASK QUESTIONS.
I'M NOT FAR FROM THE BUILDING WHEN I HEAR LIVE AIR TURN ON IN MY EARPIECE. NO WORDS. JUST HEAVY BREATHING.
AND THEN...
BANG!
...THE THUNDER OF A GUN.

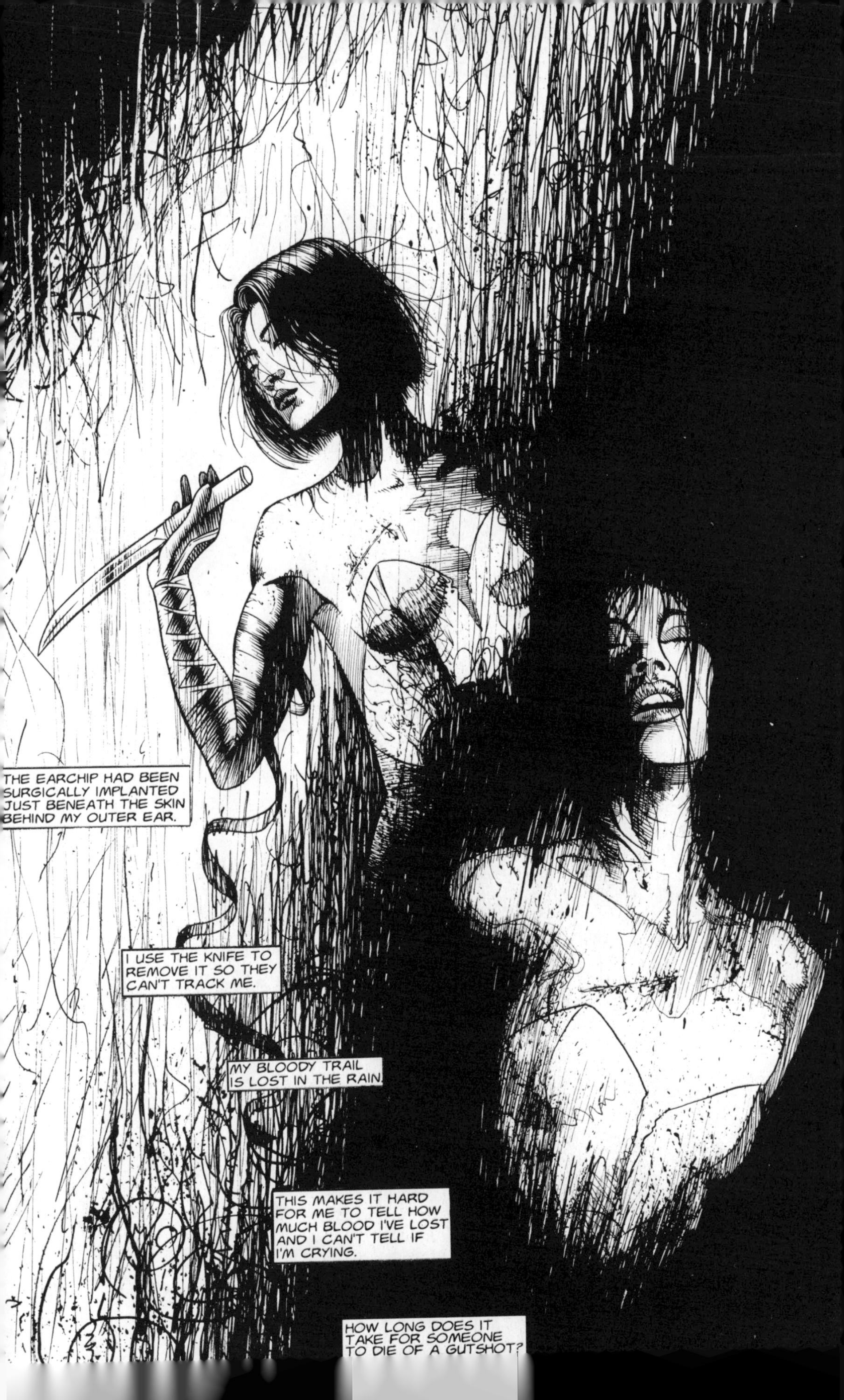

THE EARCHIP HAD BEEN SURGICALLY IMPLANTED JUST BENEATH THE SKIN BEHIND MY OUTER EAR.
I USE THE KNIFE TO REMOVE IT SO THEY CAN'T TRACK ME.
MY BLOODY TRAIL IS LOST IN THE RAIN.
THIS MAKES IT HARD FOR ME TO TELL HOW MUCH BLOOD I'VE LOST AND I CAN'T TELL IF I'M CRYING.
HOW LONG DOES IT TAKE FOR SOMEONE TO DIE OF A GUTSHOT?

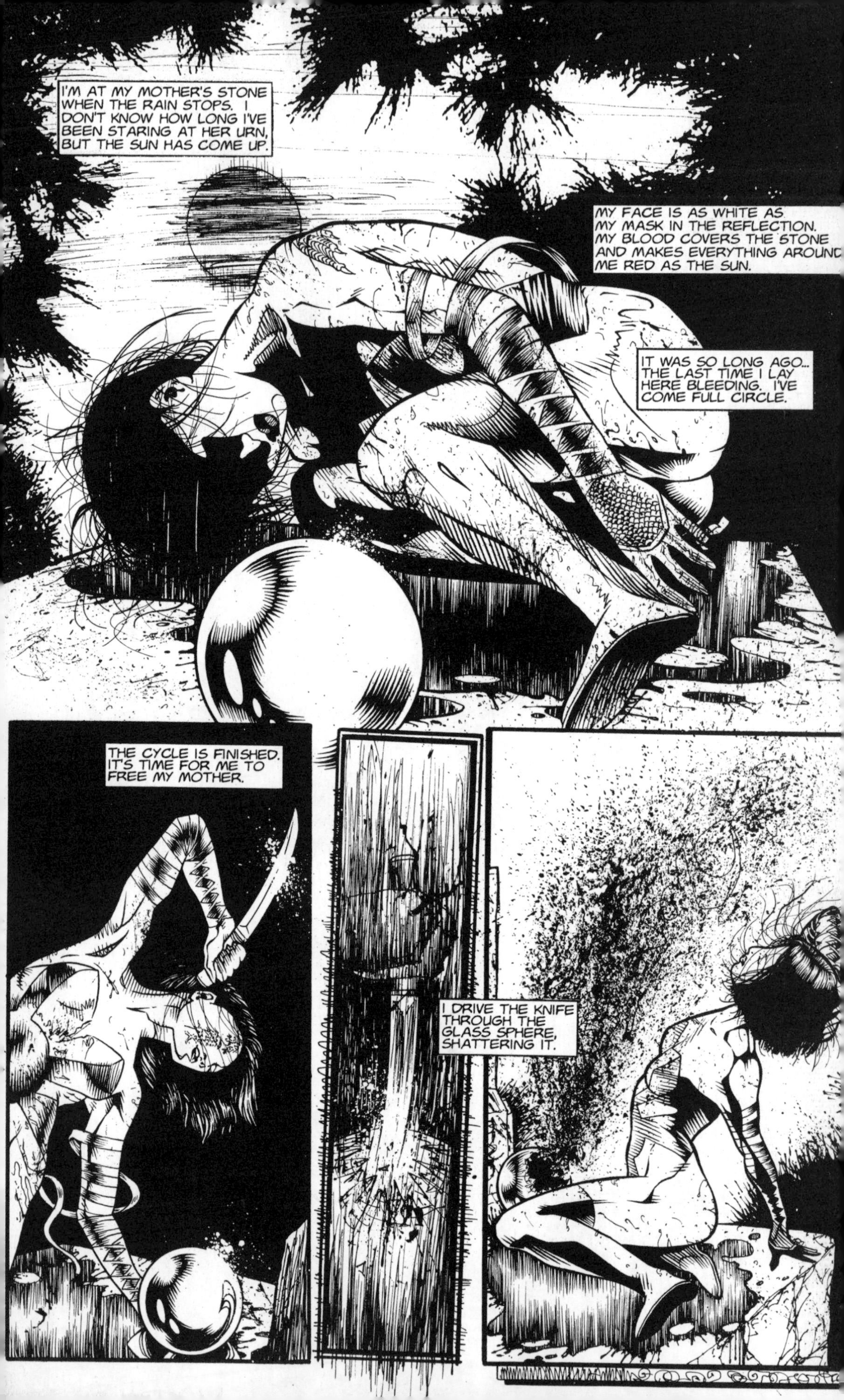
I'M AT MY MOTHER'S STONE WHEN THE RAIN STOPS. I DON'T KNOW HOW LONG I'VE BEEN STARING AT HER URN, BUT THE SUN HAS COME UP.
MY FACE IS AS WHITE AS MY MASK IN THE REFLECTION. MY BLOOD COVERS THE STONE AND MAKES EVERYTHING AROUND ME RED AS THE SUN.
IT WAS SO LONG AGO... THE LAST TIME I LAY HERE BLEEDING. I'VE COME FULL CIRCLE.
THE CYCLE IS FINISHED. IT'S TIME FOR ME TO FREE MY MOTHER.
I DRIVE THE KNIFE THROUGH THE GLASS SPHERE, SHATTERING IT.

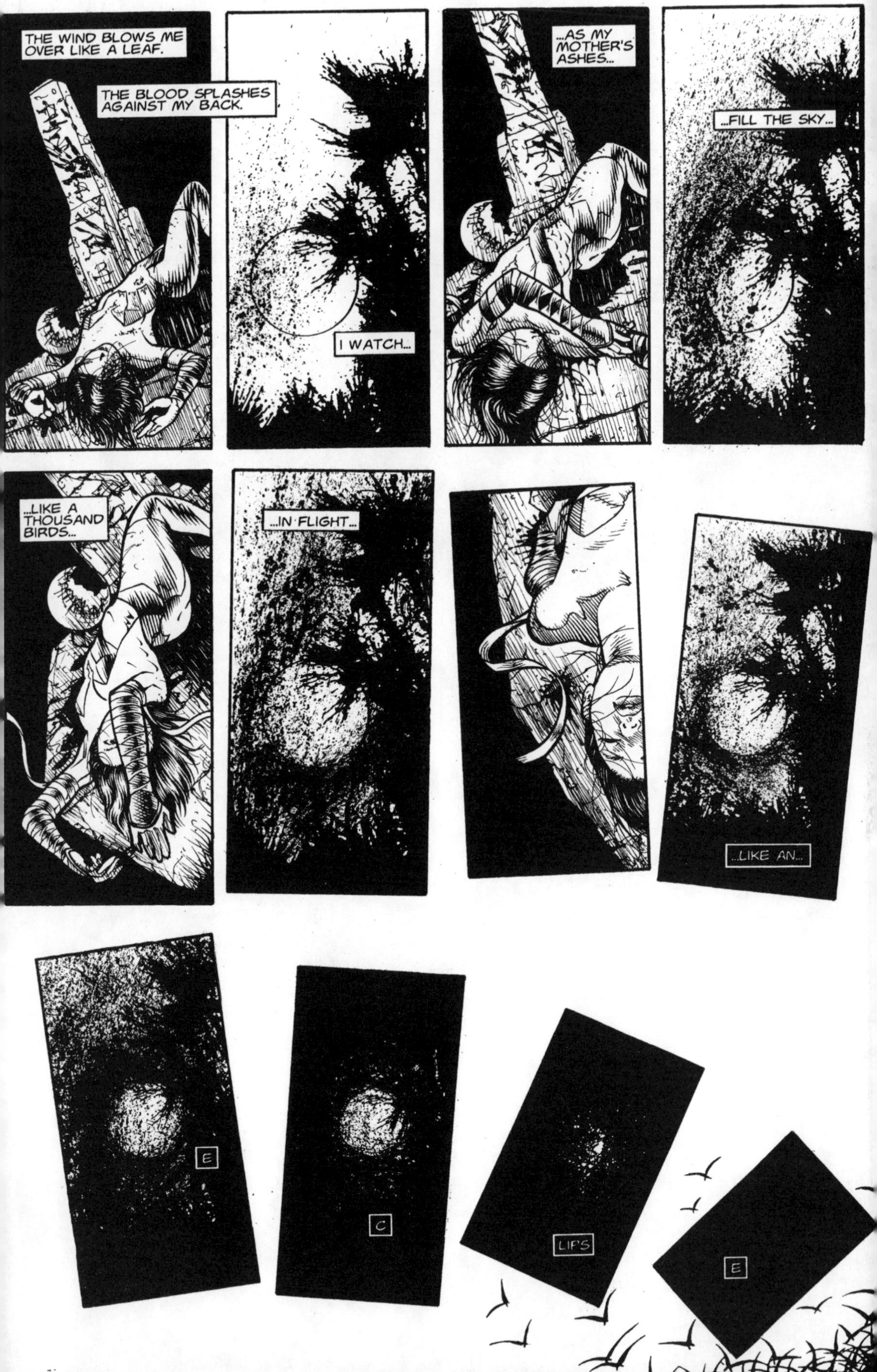
THE WIND BLOWS ME OVER LIKE A LEAF.
THE BLOOD SPLASHES AGAINST MY BACK.
I WATCH...
...AS MY MOTHER'S ASHES...
...FILL THE SKY...
...LIKE A THOUSAND BIRDS...
...IN FLIGHT...
...LIKE AN...
E
C
LIPS
E

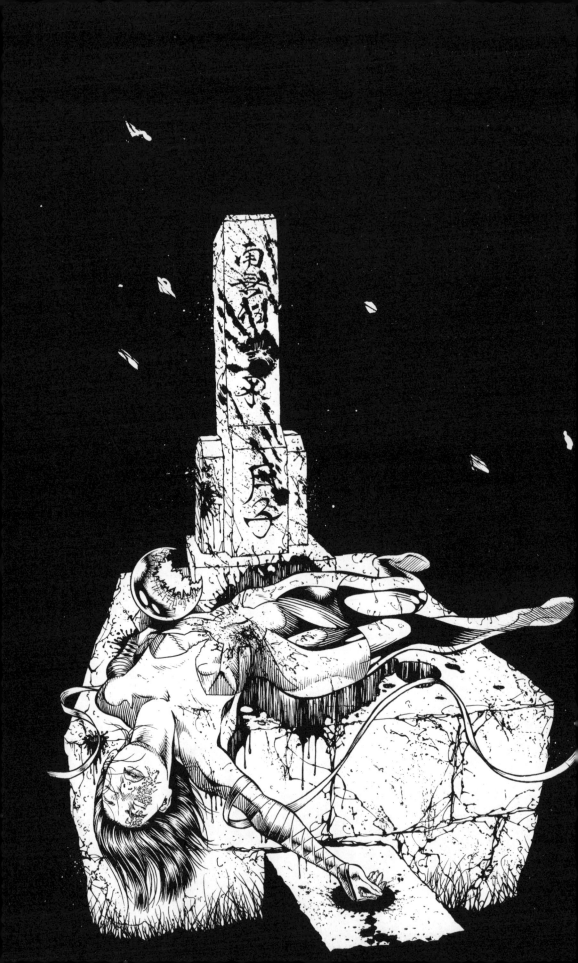

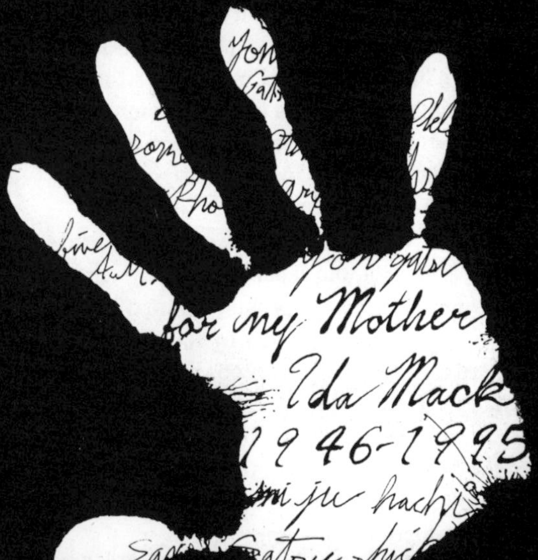
for my Mother
Ida Mack
1946-1995

Glossary of Terms

In Japanese, the five vowel sounds are pronounced as they are in Italian or Spanish, always using, however the short *e* and *o*. All syllables end in vowels or diphthongs, with the exception of those ending in *n* (which sometimes in transliteration becomes *m*), or followed by a double consonant. there is no accent, except that occasioned by the long vowel sound.

Aikido The art of using an opponents energy against them. "the way of harmony and universal energy." Martial art developed in Japan since 1931 by Master Morhei Ueshiba, foundation of the fist dojo, the Kobukai. Aiki-do techniques are divided into two categories: negazawa, throwing techniques and kateme-waza, controlling techniques, "Akikai", the Aiki-do foundation was formed on February 9, 1948.

Ainu Literally means "Man" or " Human". The natives of Japan, the Ainu people once inhabited the main island of Honshu. Now they mostly dwell in Hokkaido, although many have assimilated into Japanese society. The warriors of Japan drove the Ainu out of their homeland, and the Japanese governments outlawed their religious and cultural activities. For example, when an Ainu girl reached womanhood she was tattooed with a blue smile shaped design over her lips. This ritual was outlawed by the Japanese government but the Ainu continued it's practice in secret.

Ashura Supernatural being represented in a group of eight statues sculpted in the Nara period. Most of them have survived the centuries. Ashura is a spirit of spirits represented by three faces and six arms who achieves victory over enemies not only by strength but also by charm. Ashura is one figure in a group called the eight guardians.

Bosozoku Literally "speed tribes". Discontent youth, often motorcycle gangs, that dress like wise guys and drive flashy cars and motorcycles who revel in noise and spectacle. They are a farming ground of the Yakuza.

Bushido "The way of the warrior" Code of honor of the Japanese warrior. The word, popularized by Inazo Nitobe in his work *Bushido, the Soul of Japan,* published at the beginning of this century, defines the code of honor of the ancestors: a spiritual law which Japanese nationalists in particular have constantly praised. Integrity, justice, courage, contempt of death, goodwill, politeness, sincerity, honor, loyalty, and self control are the principle rules of Bushido.

Butoh The Japanese word for Butoh in its most general sense means dance. It is taken from the character pronounced "bu" which is the middle character in kabuki. Kabuki itself is a term comprised of three characters meaning song (ka) dance (bu) action (ki). However the term Butoh has come to imply a more avant guard performance dance that only recently has gained wide spread popularity and acceptance. It is a cathartic, often ghoulish display, employing an intense control of the human body as the exclusive instrument of expression to depict the joy of life, shadow of death, and the thin veil that separates them.

Comfort women Women from Korea, Philippines, and Burma that were turned into sex slaves for the Japanese soldiers in W.W.II. Although the Japanese government has offered no formal apology to these countries, it has recently sent money as a form of restitution.

Diet The legislative section of the Japanese government. The equivalent of Parliament.

Forty-seven Samurai A kabuki play based on a true story in which a lord's faithful servants avenge his death and then commit seppuku. Also called Forty-seven Ronin. Whether they are Ronin or Samurai depends on how you view the play.

Howaito The Japanese adoption of the English word meaning the color white.

Jonin A rank in an old Japanese class system in which jonin is the class underneath the leader and genin is below jonin. Nin is the pronunciation of the symbol for person. *Jo* refers to upper and *ge* to lower.

Juku "Cram schools" In order to get into college, Japanese students must first pass an extreme exam. These are cram schools that prepare a student for such exams.

Kamikaze "Holy wind", "devine wind". Kami is a Shinto word meaning Gods' or of God. Kaze means wind. Kamikaze is the name of the devine wind that protects Japan. Name of the typhoon which devastated the Mongolian fleet around 1280 and name referring to the W.W.II naval pilots because they were of the school of warriors who believed the holy wind would drive the United States away from Japan as it had every other invading army.

Kamma (or kama) Type of farming sickle used as a weapon in Okinawa.

Kendo Originally the art of the sword. All the rules of the sword apply to kendo, however, the weapon used is called a shinai and is made of four strips of bamboo bound together. Equipment: men=mask, do=breastplate, kote=gauntlet to protect the wrist and forearm.

Kyoto Established as Japan's capitol in the Heian period, (then called Heian-kyo.) The character kyo meaning capitol or "primary". During the Edo period the capitol was moved to Edo, now called Tokyo.

Love Hotels Modern day hotels that can be rented by the hour or by the night. They often come equipped with a fancy decor and sexual aids. One of the few places with free parking.

Manga Japanese term for comic books. Widely read on the subway, there are books for all ages.

Menuki Small icon or symbol that exists as two halves that rest inside the woven handle of a Japanese sword. Sometimes a dragon or figures that represents ancestors or family.

Miroku "The Buddha of the future" represented in Japanese sculptures with right hand on right cheek. From the late Asuka period.

Miyamoto Musashi Japan's most renowned samurai. He wrote a book called the Five Rings and is the subject of popular films.

Niku Meat

Noh Aristocratic theater in which each actor wears a mask to delineate their role in the play. The Noh serves as apoetic codename for the clandestine agency that is so secret even its operatives meet only behind the anonymity of masks.

Oiwa In kabuki plays, a female who returns from the grave for revenge against a man who wronged her. Made popular in the Yotsuya Kaidan(Yotsuya referring to a place in Tokyo and kaidan meaning ghost story and kai meaning ghost).

Oni "Demon" represented by a devilish horned mask in the Noh theater.

Otaku The most formal way of referring to "you" in Japanese. Implying a technological barrier between people. Otaku has come to refer the often obsessive and reclusive individuals of Japan's new generation who are more comfortable interacting with computers, games, books, data, television and technology than with people.

Oyabun "Boss" equivalent of "Godfather". Leader of an organization.

Pachinko A gambling game with several silver balls similar to a pinball machine. Pachinko parlors are a popular pastime in Japan.

Rainy season Called the Tsuyu, it is the period of constant rain in Japan from early June to Mid July.

Roppongi One of the most stylish and trendy Nightclub districts in Tokyo.

Sakura Cherry tree. The sakura's blossom is a symbol of ephemeral beauty and unselfish love of life. It expresses the idea of death in the sense of complete detachment from life, as the cherry blossom falls from the tree of its own accord.

Sankaijuku A dance troupe of the modern performance art or dance theater of Butoh.

Sensei "Teacher" "master of ones education".

Sun Tzu Chinese martial strategist. Many of his strategies were adopted by the Japanese.

Triads Chinese organized crime syndicates.

Usagi Rabbit.

Yakuza The Japanese organized crime syndicates. Yakuza influence extends to the highest reaches of Japanese government. Their world is fiercely hierarchical . They consider themselves the last of Japan's warrior class and a necessary balance to the order of society.

Afterword

By Takashi Hattori

"The rainy season has begun." These words coupled with a dark splatter set the stage and initiate a sequence of double narratives dealing with the weather that open every act. This is a case of using weather to achieve an atmosphere for each chapter and a climate for the entire story. Just one in a multitude of story telling techniques, but an appropriate line to begin with since Kabuki's birth name Ukiko means rain. "The rainy season has begun " or essentially "Welcome to the story of Ukiko".

When David asked me to Write a text about his story, I figured I would start by introducing myself and telling how we met each other. My name is Takashi Hattori. Born and raised in Japan, I came to the U.S. in 1989 to attend collage. David was 17 when he started college in 1990 on an art scholarship and we met his freshman year. We had two classes together ; life drawing and oil painting. David was participating in the collegiate martial arts program and won the first place medal as a freshman competing against upper-classmen . Once he learned that I held a blackbelt in karate and Judo we began practicing together constantly. I must admit some responsibility for fanning David's intense interest in martial arts philosophy into a deeper research of history, language, and culture. My sister Yoshiko and I shared an apartment off campus in which we hosted many of the Japanese and International student parties. These began with traditional Japanese meals and inspiring conversation. The topics often turned to the various martial arts studied by the students. The party would then go from demonstrative techniques to friendly brawls, some of which still exist on my camcorder.

David and I spent more and more time together. He helped me with my homework and polished my English and I began teaching him Japanese. Since most of our social occasions were with a Japanese crowd, he had the opportunity to practice everyday speaking. Having gained an interest in the language, he enrolled in the university's Japanese language classes for the rest of his college stay. David also got plenty of language practice at his girlfriend's house. Connie's parents are from Taiwan which used to be occupied by Japan. So her Grandmother who speaks little English, speaks fluent Japanese. Upon hearing that David was taking Japanese at school, she spoke to him incessantly. She took it as her duty to constantly teach him new words even to a comical degree.

When reading "Circle of Blood", I see many things inspired by our experiences together or by our discussions of Japan's social and political state. Although David has carefully implanted allusions to fairy tales and children's stories throughout the story line, the last act referring to the "Emperors new clothes" comes from a discussion we had. Being able to see Japan from both sides of the looking glass has given me a more objective view of its customs. I was expressing to David how frustrated I get at the constant pretense involved in most conventional Japanese social situations. And the fact that no one will acknowledge this frustration for fear of being viewed differently by the rest of the group, although each person in the group probably feels this same sense of ridiculousness.

Although you may enjoy rereading the story to find new layers of plot intention on your own, this can be further enhanced by some Japanese background on the subject. I will touch on some concepts that got my attention starting with the title. "Circle of Blood" refers to several different concepts. Firstly it is a visual metaphor for the flag. The implication being that instead of a beautiful sun Kabuki as a government agent sees the flag as a symbol of a country whose past was founded on bloody warrior class policies and maintains its codes with questionable, often bloody deeds. "Circle of Blood" also refers to the Circle of the Noh as the implement of these deeds. The title also refers to Kabuki's bloodlines and her family circle. This is one family's tragic struggle with near Shakespearean twists. Think of it as "Joy Luck Club" meets "Bladerunner". And finally "Circle of Blood" refers to the format of the story which is a circle or even "a spiral" as Kai might call it. Kabuki is brought into her journey violently and ends it violently at the same place with only age to mark the difference.

The story's visual style follows its literary substance. The red lenses against the whites of Kabuki's eyes are themselves flags. The Noh agents see the world only through the veil of their country's flying colors. The balance of crime and politics is weighed in the scales of the dragon on their backs. Each of them represents the conceptual lady justice with scales and blade and their eyes wrapped in patriotism.

In scene II of Fear the Reaper called "Dealing with the Devil" there is a panel with circuitry blending into Kabuki's mask and eyes. Within this circuitry is the Japanese Kanji character for Noh. The circuits stem from the Noh and lead to Kabuki's head. Anyone not familiar with Japanese Characters might have missed this. David shows a graphic knack for synthesizing type with art. He also displays this fascination for language itself.

In Japan there are different linguistic styles for every business and social situation. There are forms

IMAGES OF FIGURES BEHIND GLASS

0

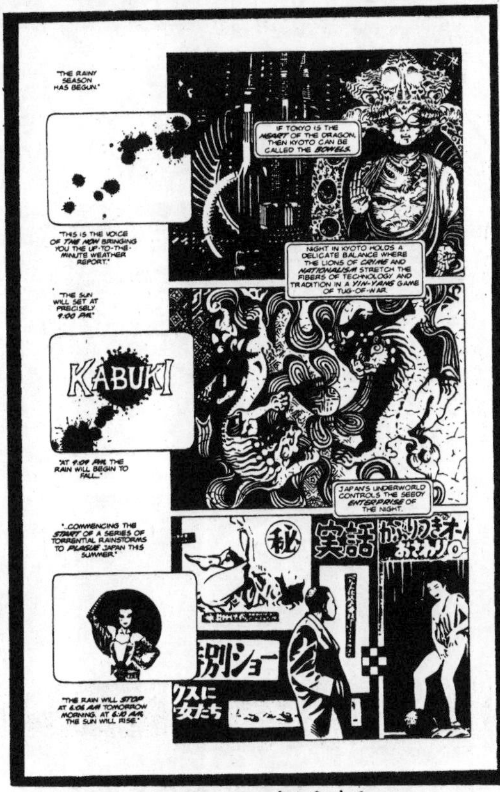

"THE RAINY SEASON HAS BEGUN."
"THIS IS THE VOICE OF THE NOW BRINGING YOU THE UP-TO-THE-MINUTE WEATHER REPORT."
"THE SUN WILL SET AT PRECISELY 9:00 PM."
KABUKI
"AT 9:09 PM THE RAIN WILL BEGIN TO FALL."
"...COMMENCING THE START OF A SERIES OF TORRENTIAL RAINSTORMS TO PLAGUE JAPAN THIS SUMMER."
"THE RAIN WILL STOP AT 6:06 AM TOMORROW MORNING. AT 6:10 AM THE SUN WILL RISE."
IF TOKYO IS THE HEART OF THE DRAGON, THEN KYOTO CAN BE CALLED THE BOWELS.
NIGHT IN KYOTO HOLDS A DELICATE BALANCE WHERE THE LIONS OF CRIME AND NATIONALISM STRETCH THE FIBERS OF TECHNOLOGY AND TRADITION IN A YIN-YANG GAME OF TUG-OF-WAR.
JAPAN'S UNDERWORLD CONTROLS THE SEEDY ENTERPRISE OF THE NIGHT.
秘
実話
特別ショー
クスに
女たち

DANCERS

BOY

1

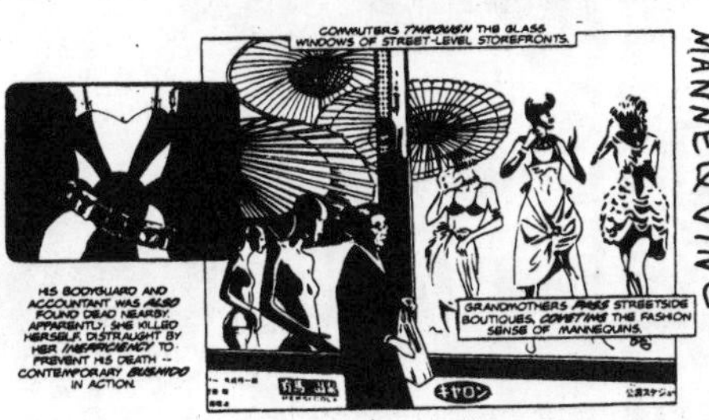

COMMUTERS THROUGH THE GLASS WINDOWS OF STREET-LEVEL STOREFRONTS.
HIS BODYGUARD AND ACCOUNTANT WAS ALSO FOUND DEAD NEARBY. APPARENTLY, SHE KILLED HERSELF, DISTRAUGHT BY HER INEFFICIENCY TO PREVENT HIS DEATH -- CONTEMPORARY BUSHIDO IN ACTION.
GRANDMOTHERS PASS STREETSIDE BOUTIQUES, COVETING THE FASHION SENSE OF MANNEQUINS.
キヤロン

MANNEQUINS

Girl

2

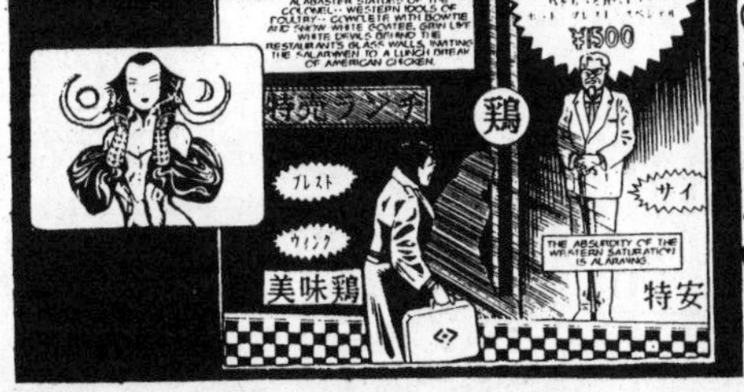

ALABASTER STATUES OF THE COLONEL -- WESTERN IDOLS OF POULTRY -- COMPLETE WITH BOWTIE AND SNOW WHITE GOATEE, GRIN LIKE WHITE DEVILS BEHIND THE RESTAURANT'S GLASS WALLS, INVITING THE SALARYMEN TO A LUNCH BREAK OF AMERICAN CHICKEN.
¥500
鶏
ブレスト
ウィング
美味鶏
サイ
特安
THE ABSURDITY OF THE WESTERN SATURATION IS ALARMING.

STATUE

Boy

3

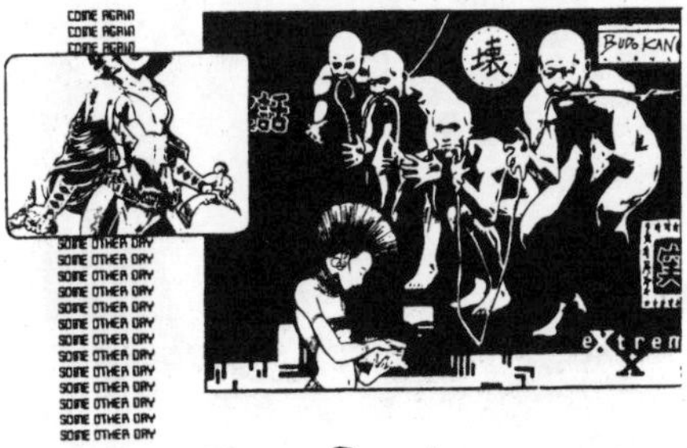

COME AGAIN
COME AGAIN
COME AGAIN
BUDOKAN
SOME OTHER DAY
SOME OTHER DAY
SOME OTHER DAY
SOME OTHER DAY
SOME OTHER DAY
SOME OTHER DAY
SOME OTHER DAY
SOME OTHER DAY
SOME OTHER DAY
SOME OTHER DAY
SOME OTHER DAY
SOME OTHER DAY
SOME OTHER DAY
SOME OTHER DAY
SOME OTHER DAY
SOME OTHER DAY
eXtrem

BILLBOARD

Girl

4

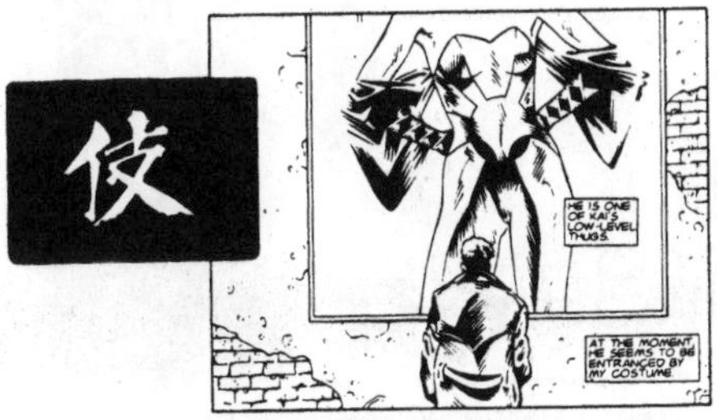

伎
HE IS ONE OF KAI'S LOW-LEVEL THUGS.
AT THE MOMENT HE SEEMS TO BE ENTRANCED BY MY COSTUME.

POSTER

BOY

5

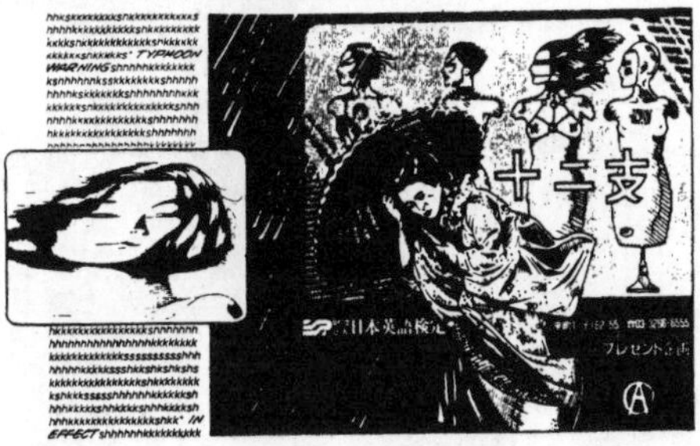

" TYPHOON WARNING
" IN EFFECT
十二支
プレゼント企画

SEWING DUMMIES

Girl

6

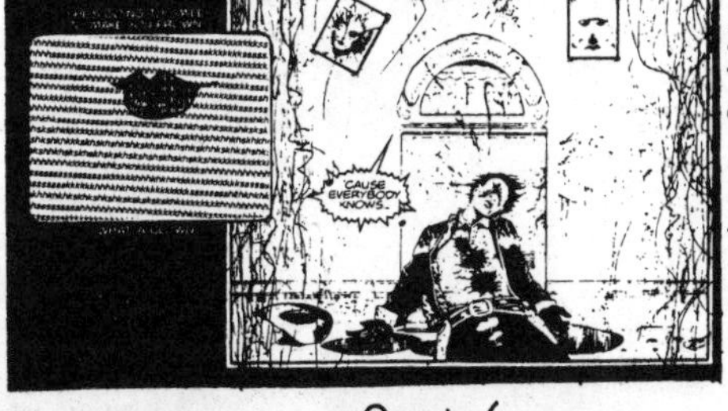

'CAUSE EVERYBODY KNOWS...

PHOTOGRAPHS

Boy

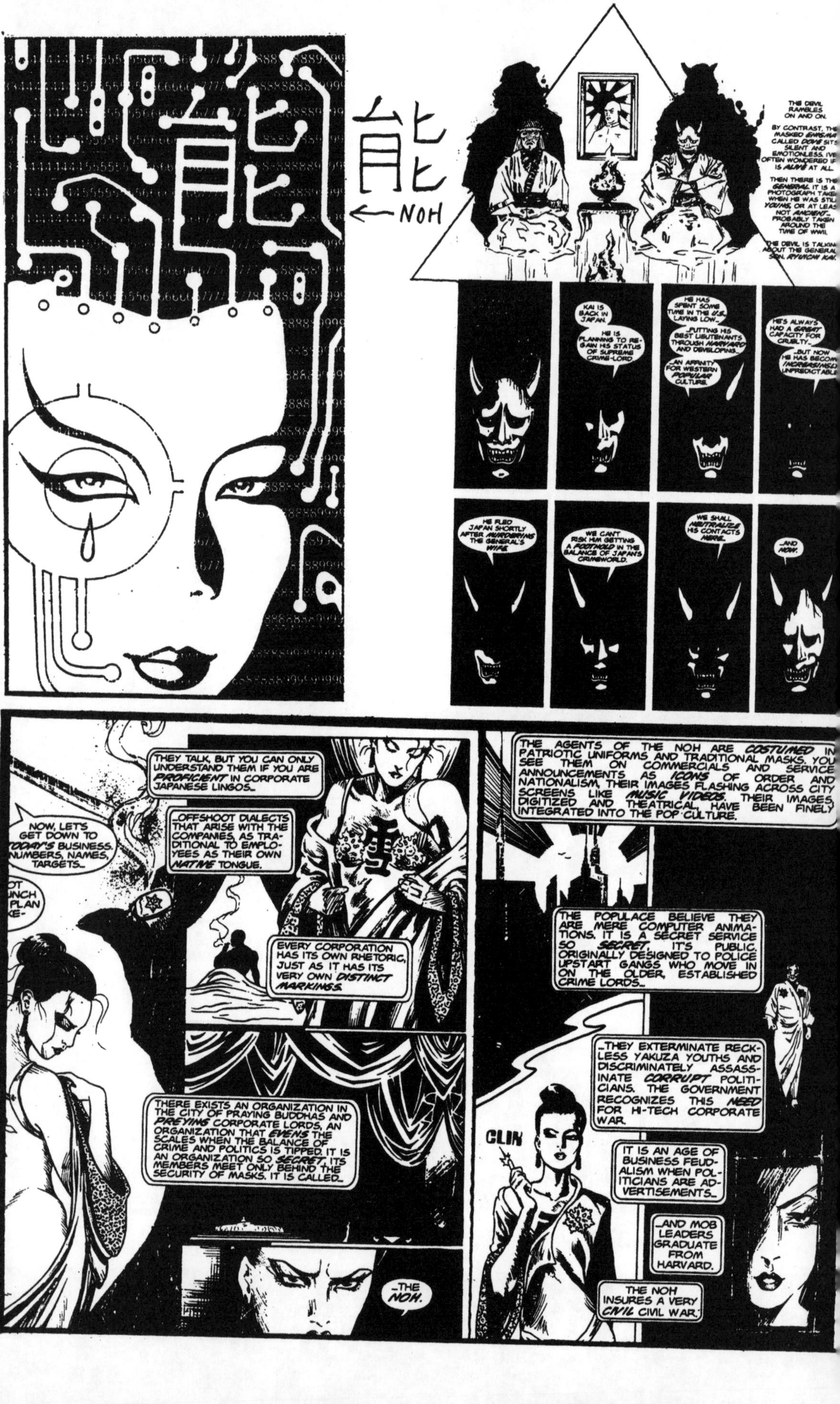
能
← NOH
THE DEVIL RAMBLES ON AND ON.
BY CONTRAST, THE MASKED ENIGMA CALLED DOVE SITS SILENT AND EMOTIONLESS. IVE OFTEN WONDERED IF IS ALIVE AT ALL.
THEN THERE IS THE GENERAL. IT IS A PHOTOGRAPH TAKEN WHEN HE WAS STILL YOUNG, OR AT LEAST NOT ANCIENT... PROBABLY TAKEN AROUND THE TIME OF WWII.
THE DEVIL IS TALKING ABOUT THE GENERAL SON. RYUICHI KAI.
KAI IS BACK IN JAPAN.
HE IS PLANNING TO RE-GAIN HIS STATUS OF SUPREME CRIME-LORD.
HE HAS SPENT SOME TIME IN THE U.S. LAYING LOW...
...PUTTING HIS BEST LIEUTENANTS THROUGH HARVARD AND DEVELOPING...
...AN AFFINITY FOR WESTERN POPULAR CULTURE.
HE'S ALWAYS HAD A GREAT CAPACITY FOR CRUELTY...
...BUT NOW HE HAS BECOME INCREASINGLY UNPREDICTABLE
HE FLED JAPAN SHORTLY AFTER MURDERING THE GENERAL'S WIFE.
WE CAN'T RISK HIM GETTING A FOOTHOLD IN THE BALANCE OF JAPAN'S CRIMEWORLD.
WE SHALL NEUTRALIZE HIS CONTACTS HERE.
...AND NOW.
THEY TALK, BUT YOU CAN ONLY UNDERSTAND THEM IF YOU ARE PROFICIENT IN CORPORATE JAPANESE LINGOS...
...OFFSHOOT DIALECTS THAT ARISE WITH THE COMPANIES, AS TRADITIONAL TO EMPLOYEES AS THEIR OWN NATIVE TONGUE.
NOW, LETS GET DOWN TO TODAY'S BUSINESS. NUMBERS, NAMES, TARGETS...
EVERY CORPORATION HAS ITS OWN RHETORIC, JUST AS IT HAS ITS VERY OWN DISTINCT MARKINGS.
THERE EXISTS AN ORGANIZATION IN THE CITY OF PRAYING BUDDHAS AND PREYING CORPORATE LORDS, AN ORGANIZATION THAT EVENS THE SCALES WHEN THE BALANCE OF CRIME AND POLITICS IS TIPPED. IT IS AN ORGANIZATION SO SECRET, ITS MEMBERS MEET ONLY BEHIND THE SECURITY OF MASKS. IT IS CALLED...
...THE NOH.
THE AGENTS OF THE NOH ARE COSTUMED IN PATRIOTIC UNIFORMS AND TRADITIONAL MASKS. YOU SEE THEM ON COMMERCIALS AND SERVICE ANNOUNCEMENTS AS ICONS OF ORDER AND NATIONALISM, THEIR IMAGES FLASHING ACROSS CITY SCREENS LIKE MUSIC VIDEOS. THEIR IMAGES, DIGITIZED AND THEATRICAL, HAVE BEEN FINELY INTEGRATED INTO THE POP CULTURE.
THE POPULACE BELIEVE THEY ARE MERE COMPUTER ANIMATIONS. IT IS A SECRET SERVICE SO SECRET, IT'S PUBLIC. ORIGINALLY DESIGNED TO POLICE UPSTART GANGS WHO MOVE IN ON THE OLDER, ESTABLISHED CRIME LORDS...
...THEY EXTERMINATE RECKLESS YAKUZA YOUTHS AND DISCRIMINATELY ASSASSINATE CORRUPT POLITICIANS. THE GOVERNMENT RECOGNIZES THIS NEED FOR HI-TECH CORPORATE WAR.
CLIK
IT IS AN AGE OF BUSINESS FEUDALISM WHEN POLITICIANS ARE ADVERTISEMENTS...
...AND MOB LEADERS GRADUATE FROM HARVARD.
THE NOH INSURES A VERY CIVIL CIVIL WAR.

of speech for men, women, boys, girls, and for people of different age and class. David takes this concept of language to a new degree. In Kabuki, every corporation and social group has its own bastardized Japanese based on the lingo and slang inherent within that organization. This gives each company its own family secrets, pushing the envelope of language variation conceived by George Orwell in his classic futuristic novel "1984". The agents of the Noh speak to each other in Noh-speak, company employees of channel Snow; Snow-speak. Each Yakuza faction has its own jargon as would each motorcycle tribe in much the same way as contemporary gangs develop their own "street language". Of course every one still has traditional Japanese as a base of communication. Thus, Kabuki takes a contemporary trend and pushes it to it's future extreme and in the process has resolved communication in a graphic way by making obsolete that pesky comic book use of brackets proclaiming {translated from Japanese}. The Japanese language has absorbed many foreign words into it and turned them into its own. In Kabuki we read everything clearly but are aware that the characters are speaking in dialects of Japanese not yet invented.

"We are only faces, yet we are faceless ... nothing but a pack of cards on wonderland. There are eight of us... my comrades in arms... eight... the number of pawns in an army of chess pieces." Kabuki is the saga of a child displaced into a traditionally collective establishment and haunted by the scars of history. She completes her hero's journey as a woman embracing her own individual and adult consciousness. In more strategic terms, this is Kabuki's journey from pawn to queen. The setting is a wonderland where things are not what they seem and Kabuki encounters many strange characters. Just as "Alice in Wonderland" relates its characters to cards and in "Through the Looking Glass" the characters correlate to chess pieces, Kabuki 's characters operate on similar patterns even correlating to characters in Alice's journey. Tigerlily was named after a character in the "The Garden of Live Flowers" chapter, as was violet. Snapdragon replaces Daisy. Siamese are of course Tweedle Dum and Tweedle Dee. Scarab is the Beetle and so on. If you wished, you could match up every character to a figure in Alice's journey or to a piece on the chess board.

I am touching on points as they appear in the story chronologically. This brings me to the introduction of Oni, Dove, and the General's photograph presented as the heads of the Noh. This first image of Dove and Oni on either side of the General's photograph reminds me of the triangular compositions in Renaissance art. In light of the fact that a dove in renaissance art signified the holy spirit in religious paintings, this triangular composition of the General, Oni and Dove subconsciously hit me as a trinity of the Father, Son, and Spirit of the Noh.

It is important to understand that nothing is said offhandedly in this story. Unlike film, words in comics take up physical space. Therefore they must each have a meaning and urgency to the story. For example, Oni talking in the fire light about Kai has a whole different affect once you realize Oni is Kai. As Oni talks of snow he mentions the pornographic pay-per-play programs on channel snow. In Japan AV refers to adult video. In the U.S., VR is a popular reference to virtual reality. In Kabuki, David has coined the term AVR as an amalgam of these. Giving snow the family crest of a snowflake was poetic, as well as the crest tattooed on his people. The kanji tattoo on snow's body guard means **"Yukiko" or "girl of snow"**.

In scene IV "Through the Looking Glass" we are introduced to a dichotomy of icons. Sun and moon become symbols for male/female, father/mother, Japanese/Ainu, warrior/poet, day/night, yin/yang. Kabuki is searching for an equinox between these icons; a balance between these dualities. Kabuki's reflection is caught in her mother's urn and shown "halfway between the sun and the moon". The farmer's sickle becomes the crescent moon. Kabuki's sickles stand for her farmer ancestors as well as the crescent moon of her mother's namesake. I also see them as a dragon biting the moon, attempting to devour it. Or perhaps the blade of the sickle is the dragon's tongue, giving its victim one last kiss. The crescent moon is the image of Kabuki's mother smiling like the Cheshire cat, guiding Kabuki along her journey.

Act I "Ghosts in the Looking Glass". It is on this title page that I notice the numbers counting in the optic scans. Of course they give us a sense of timing with the visual action, but this sequence begins 08:09:03. What an appropriate number to start the series with. It is a reference to the origins of the title for organized crime in Japan. The word Yakuza means 8, 9, 3. It is a losing hand in an old card game. In light of this, Oni assigning hits by dealing cards is delightfully poetic. A losing hand indeed.

The General is a man who wears his military clothes and medals like an old decrepit medieval king would still wear his battle armor. The family name of Kai was chosen for two reasons. It is the name of an old warrior class family in Japan. Also, it means ghost. After partaking of the General's own private thoughts we meet young Ryuichi Kai. First we see his image as an embryo framed in the circle of a sun, this is preceded by the General's icon of his face in the sun behind a reflection on Ryuichi's sword that represents the visage of death. We see young master Kai shirtless but otherwise in Japanese military attire with a shadow that runs off the page and a trail of blood behind him. Later we will see him take off his hat, his hair blowing in the wind, and the rest of his shadow depicts a demon's horns. The opposite page features three pairs of hands in exactly the same position. The first set holds chess pieces with a moon in the background. The second panel reveals the General's hands arranging chess pieces on a board and the sun behind him. The third pair belongs to Ryuichi Kai, his hands arranging the heads of slain enemies on a stick. An image of death in the form of an impaled head looms in the background as his own icon. Each of these seems to fade into the other; father to son, their figures and symbols in the same place in the panel. The first however also possesses more meaning. Are these in fact the General's hands holding chess pieces in the moon light before the sun in the next panel reveals the rest of his figure? Perhaps this shows him planning meticulously day and night. A valid interpretation, and I think the art implies this when coupled with the text. But these hands could also be the "hands of fate", arranging its players on the board, or even, "The bloody hands of war" mentioned in this page's script. Or perhaps it is both, and even something else. We see Kai dealing death on sticks. Above him, the General planning the strategy of war; his symbol; the sun. Perhaps the top panel is a foreshadowing to someone out playing everyone's strategies, someone whose symbol is the moon.

We see the General grow more enchanted with Tsukiko and Ryuichi sees this too. There is a very Hamlet-like atmosphere to these scenes. Kai of course in the role of Hamlet, his parent showing interest in someone other than the dead spouse. This obviously distresses Kai, and though he was not exactly normal before this, the situation affects him mentally as it did Hamlet. There is some room to empathize with Kai. In fact I believe David could tell the same story from Kai's point of view as Hamlet was told and make it just as moving. For that matter the story could also be told from the General's P.O.V., or Tsukiko's, or even Dove's and each would compliment the original.

The miniature statue of Tsukiko shown in Act I goes through several stages of symbolism. The first close up we see of it reveals a goddess-like image of Tsukiko. The very next panel depicts the actual Tsukiko whose face in this panel is located in the some place as the statues face on the previous panel. In film, the faces on the same point of this shot might flow into each other in a slow lap dissolve. The statue halves are later worn in Kabuki's woven arm bands just as menuki are held in the handles of the Japanese

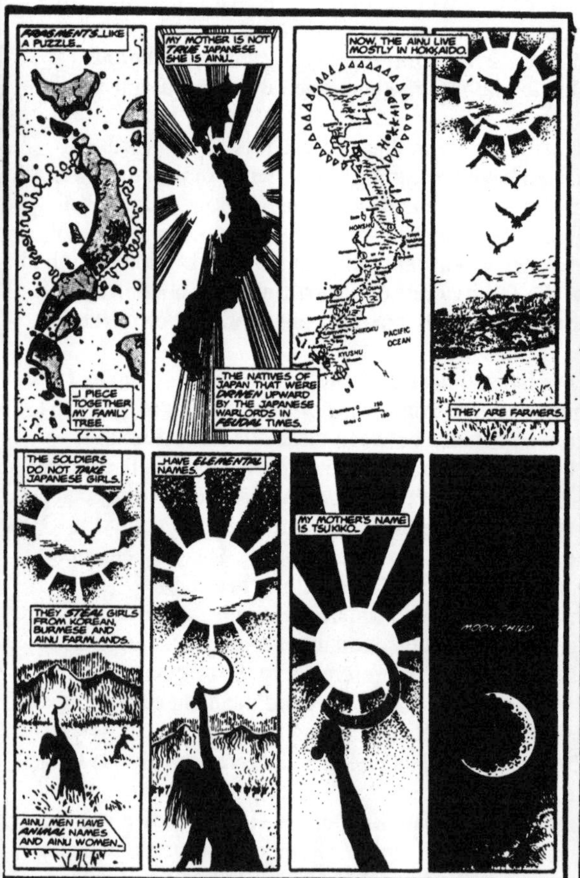

FRAGMENTS...LIKE A PUZZLE...
...I PIECE TOGETHER MY FAMILY TREE.
MY MOTHER IS NOT TRUE JAPANESE. SHE IS AINU...
...THE NATIVES OF JAPAN THAT WERE DRIVEN UPWARD BY THE JAPANESE WARLORDS IN FEUDAL TIMES.
NOW, THE AINU LIVE MOSTLY IN HOKKAIDO.
THEY ARE FARMERS.
THE SOLDIERS DO NOT TAKE JAPANESE GIRLS.
THEY STEAL GIRLS FROM KOREAN, BURMESE AND AINU FARMLANDS.
AINU MEN HAVE ANIMAL NAMES AND AINU WOMEN...
...HAVE ELEMENTAL NAMES.
MY MOTHER'S NAME IS TSUKIKO...

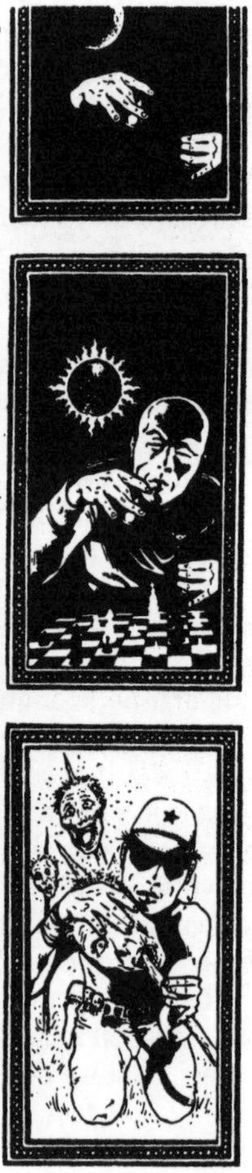

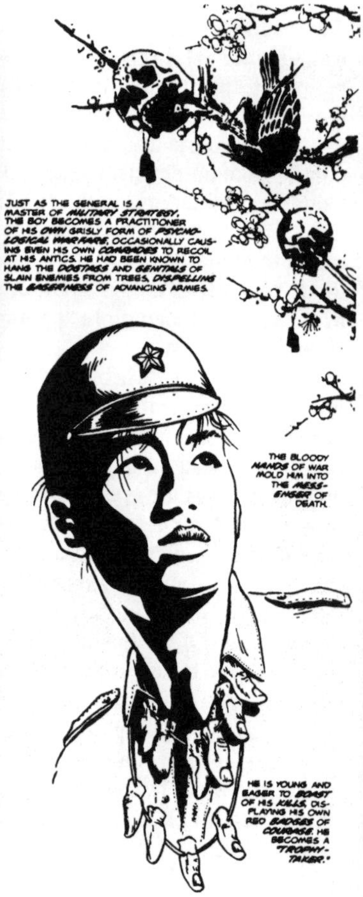

JUST AS THE GENERAL IS A MASTER OF MILITARY STRATEGY, THE BOY BECOMES A PRACTITIONER OF HIS OWN GRISLY FORM OF PSYCHOLOGICAL WARFARE, OCCASIONALLY CAUSING EVEN HIS OWN COMRADES TO RECOIL AT HIS ANTICS. HE HAD BEEN KNOWN TO HANG THE DOGTAGS AND GENITALS OF SLAIN ENEMIES FROM TREES, DISPELLING THE EAGERNESS OF ADVANCING ARMIES.
THE BLOODY HANDS OF WAR MOLD HIM INTO THE MESSENGER OF DEATH.
HE IS YOUNG AND EAGER TO BOAST OF HIS KILLS, DISPLAYING HIS OWN RED BADGES OF COURAGE. HE BECOMES A "TROPHY-TAKER."

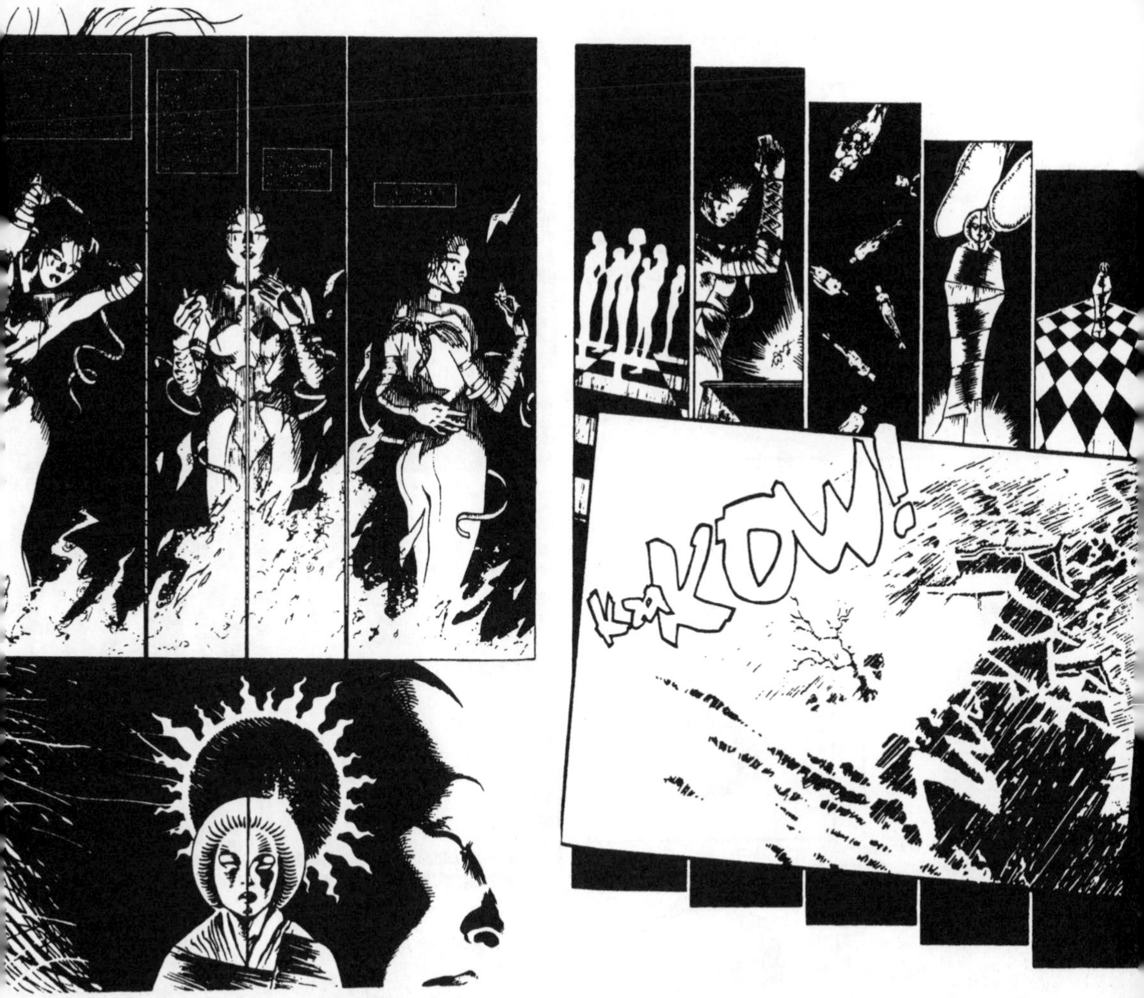
KOW!

sword. Finally the joined halves become the ultimate queen on the chessboard that signifies Kabuki's journey from pawn to queen. She knocks all the pawns off the board and sets down the united halves of the statue on the empty chessboard. It is a message for the General.

When Kai makes his appearance in the temple scene his face is in line with a row of masks in the background depicting his face as one mask of the many. When he opens his shirt to reveal the tattoo, he is also standing in front of masks on the wall, but the frame is shot so that just two are visible. These are an old Noh mask denoting happiness and one of anguish; comedy and tragedy, each a theme on Kabuki's mask. It is later in Act 2 that we see that the mask behind his head is the demon mask. There is a shot in which his head blocks out the mask behind him but not the horns which stick out above his head. Kai cuts the statue in two . This itself is symbolic and Kabuki's journey is to master "the dualities of her nature" and the pieces are joined to signify the completion of this. Just as Kai cuts the statue in two it is a half of the statue that scars his own face.

There are two pages that chronicle Kabuki's growth in her mother's womb. They have a simple page layout in which many things are happening. The panels show Kabuki's mother 's face with a tear and painted lips and end with Kabuki's own painted mask. Cherry blossom branches become skeletal hands around Tsukiko's face and end with Kabuki's own hands on her face. The sun fades into the embryo which grows and in turn fades into the reflection of Kabuki in her mother's urn. The urn itself was built as a symbol of the moon. In effect, the panel sequence starts with the sun and ends with the moon.

In Act 3 we see a frustrated General turn into Edvard Munch's B/W lithograph, "The Cry"(not to be confused with his painting "The Scream"). This in turn fades in to Kai's rendition of "Great Balls of Fire" which is punctuated by the sun on a Japanese flag emitting flames.

Before I go on with my comments on the language of the story it is at this point that I want to address the fact that it is just that; a language. Mack has put together a story and artwork that are more than the sum of their parts. He has created his own graphic language, one that is more eccentric and

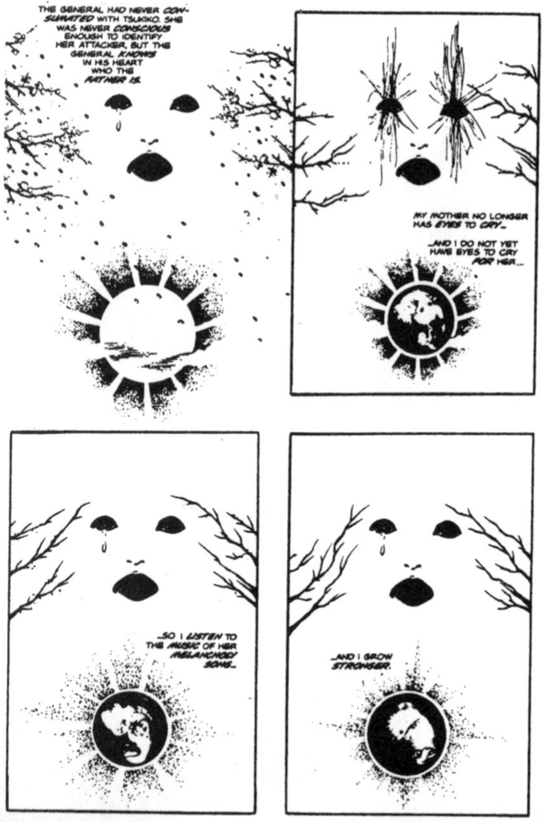
THE GENERAL HAD NEVER CONSUMATED WITH TSUKKO. SHE WAS NEVER CONSCIOUS ENOUGH TO IDENTIFY HER ATTACKER, BUT THE GENERAL KNOWS IN HIS HEART WHO THE FATHER IS.
MY MOTHER NO LONGER HAS EYES TO CRY...
...AND I DO NOT YET HAVE EYES TO CRY FOR HER...
...SO I LISTEN TO THE MUSIC OF HER MELANCHOLY SONG...
...AND I GROW STRONGER.

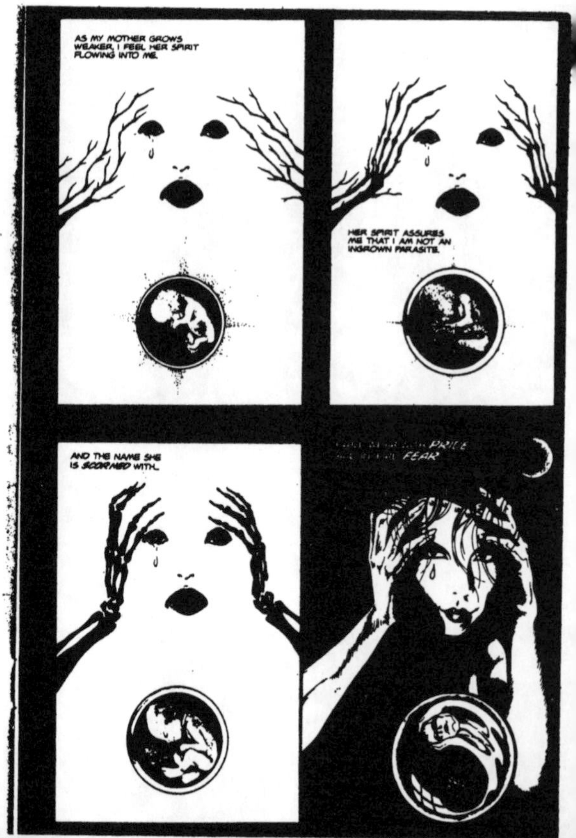
AS MY MOTHER GROWS WEAKER, I FEEL HER SPIRIT FLOWING INTO ME.
HER SPIRIT ASSURES ME THAT I AM NOT AN INGROWN PARASITE.
AND THE NAME SHE IS SCORNED WITH...

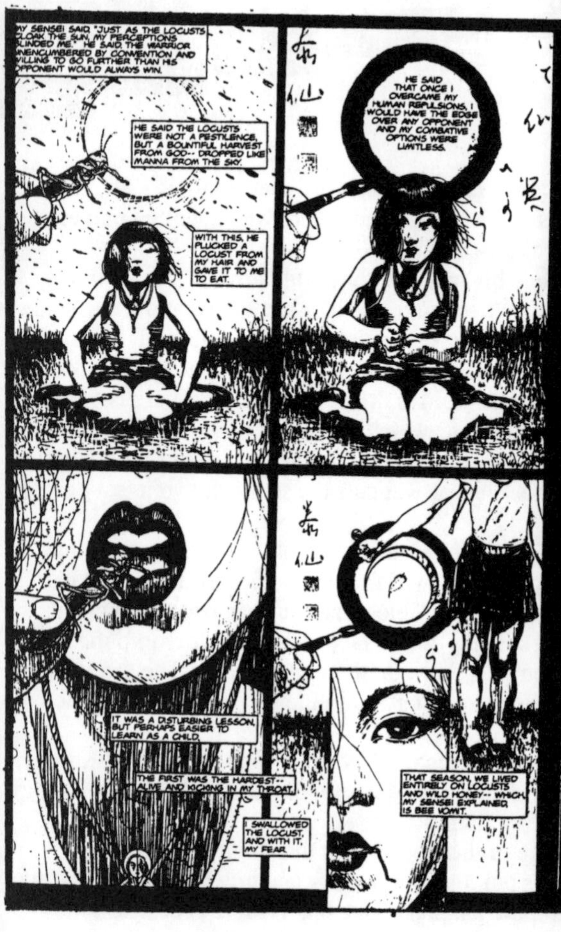
MY SENSEI SAID, "JUST AS THE LOCUSTS CLOAK THE SUN, MY PERCEPTIONS BLINDED ME." HE SAID THE WARRIOR UNENCUMBERED BY CONVENTION AND WILLING TO GO FURTHER THAN HIS OPPONENT WOULD ALWAYS WIN.
HE SAID THE LOCUSTS WERE NOT A PESTILENCE, BUT A BOUNTIFUL HARVEST FROM GOD-- DROPPED LIKE MANNA FROM THE SKY.
WITH THIS, HE PLUCKED A LOCUST FROM MY HAIR AND GAVE IT TO ME TO EAT.
HE SAID THAT ONCE I OVERCAME MY HUMAN REPULSIONS, I WOULD HAVE THE EDGE OVER ANY OPPONENT AND MY COMBATIVE OPTIONS WERE LIMITLESS.
IT WAS A DISTURBING LESSON, BUT PERHAPS EASIER TO LEARN AS A CHILD.
THE FIRST WAS THE HARDEST-- ALIVE AND KICKING IN MY THROAT.
I SWALLOWED THE LOCUST, AND WITH IT, MY FEAR.
THAT SEASON, WE LIVED ENTIRELY ON LOCUSTS AND WILD HONEY-- WHICH, MY SENSEI EXPLAINED, IS BEE VOMIT.

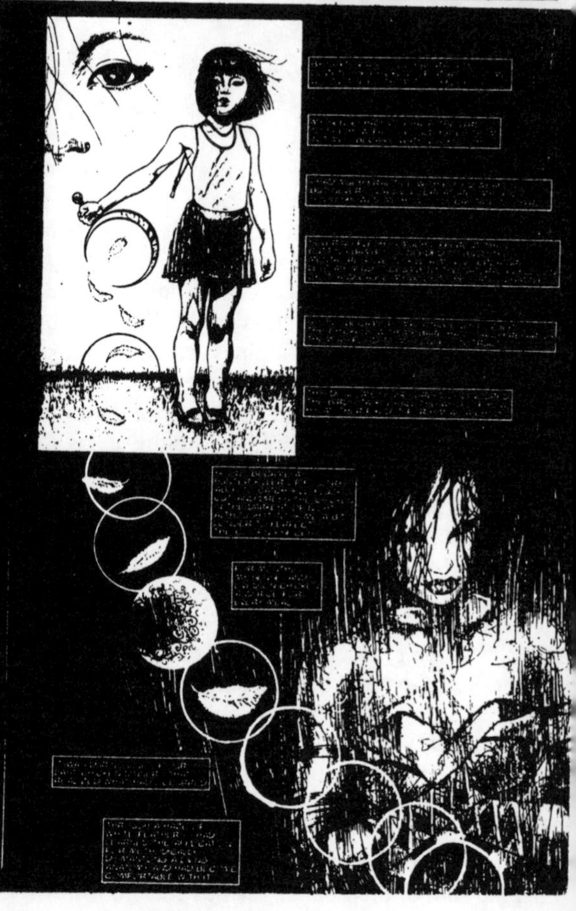

esoteric than the sequential language of the conventional comic. It affects the reader on many different levels. From the double narratives at the beginning of each book in which words on TV screens are also texture and sound, to the words that imply pictures, and pictures that imply unspoken meanings, he is giving the reader pieces of a puzzle. David Mack's story-telling philosophy is not to "tell" the reader wha is happening and not even to "show" the reader what is happening, as is the focus of many artists , but it i to "reveal" what is happening. This revelation is brought about by the unique system of story-telling that unifies symbols, icons, graphic design, pacing, sensitivity to type, and haunting imagery into a synthesis o visual language.

It's interesting to note that Mack does not feel bound by the laws of realism. He has proven he understands the laws of realistic illustration and he bends, even breaks those laws when it adds to the story There is a page in Act 3 that depicts all the agents together their bodies swirling in confusion. The edge o one body is the outline of another. The art achieves a level of surrealism. Much of it is very realistic but there may be something extra, something symbolic or other-worldly that seems to exist on a different plane than most of the other images. For instance, the images in Violet's cigarette smoke, Cowboy's visual thought balloons or how the General becomes physically distorted to reflect his mental state. There are ghostly apparitions(Kabuki's mother, Cowboy's children, Violet's spirit) that show us more than what is in the physical world of the characters. Artistically David has no fear. No fear of violating convention in order to communicate to the reader. In fact there is an intimacy, an interactive quality that one feels when reading Kabuki. The story demands something of the reader. It is not a simple read. It is thought-provoking and even educational. Therefore the reader must be willing to think, to learn, and to utterly lose oneself in the story. There is a different style of art to give each scene its own atmosphere. David thinks of the art and words not as the focus, but as pointers to the meaning of the story. Because of this he has

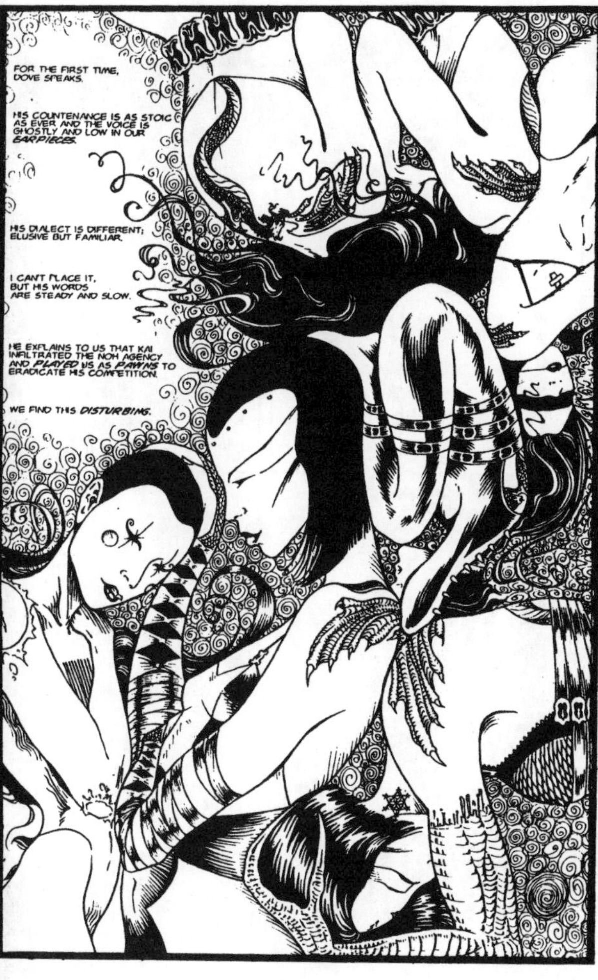
FOR THE FIRST TIME, DOVE SPEAKS.
HIS COUNTENANCE IS AS STOIC AS EVER AND THE VOICE IS GHOSTLY AND LOW IN OUR EARPIECES.
HIS DIALECT IS DIFFERENT; ELUSIVE BUT FAMILIAR.
I CAN'T PLACE IT, BUT HIS WORDS ARE STEADY AND SLOW.
HE EXPLAINS TO US THAT KAI INFILTRATED THE NOH AGENCY AND PLAYED US AS PAWNS TO ERADICATE HIS COMPETITION.
WE FIND THIS DISTURBING.

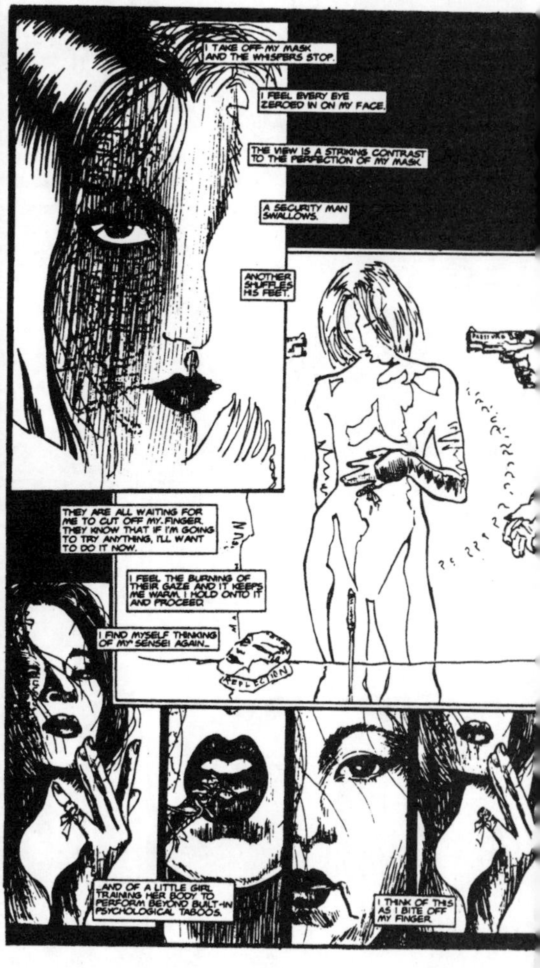
I TAKE OFF MY MASK AND THE WHISPERS STOP.
I FEEL EVERY EYE ZEROED IN ON MY FACE.
THE VIEW IS A STRIKING CONTRAST TO THE PERFECTION OF MY MASK
A SECURITY MAN SWALLOWS.
ANOTHER SHUFFLES HIS FEET.
THEY ARE ALL WAITING FOR ME TO CUT OFF MY FINGER. THEY KNOW THAT IF I'M GOING TO TRY ANYTHING, I'LL WANT TO DO IT NOW.
I FEEL THE BURNING OF THEIR GAZE AND IT KEEPS ME WARM. I HOLD ONTO IT AND PROCEED.
I FIND MYSELF THINKING OF MY SENSEI AGAIN_
REFLECTION
_AND OF A LITTLE GIRL TRAINING HER BODY TO PERFORM BEYOND BUILT-IN PSYCHOLOGICAL TABOOS.
I THINK OF THIS AS I BITE OFF MY FINGER.

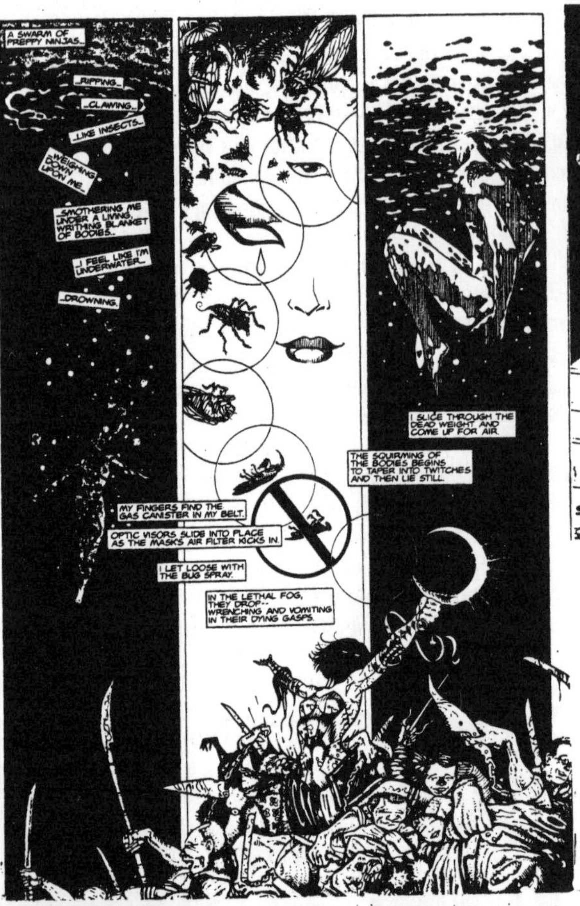
A SWARM OF PREPPY NINJAS...
...RIPPING...
...CLAWING...
...LIKE INSECTS...
...WEIGHING DOWN UPON ME...
...SMOTHERING ME UNDER A LIVING, WRITHING BLANKET OF BODIES...
...I FEEL LIKE I'M UNDERWATER...
...DROWNING.
MY FINGERS FIND THE GAS CANISTER IN MY BELT.
OPTIC VISORS SLIDE INTO PLACE AS THE MASK'S AIR FILTER KICKS IN.
I LET LOOSE WITH THE BUG SPRAY.
IN THE LETHAL FOG, THEY DROP-- WRENCHING AND VOMITING IN THEIR DYING GASPS.
THE SQUIRMING OF THE BODIES BEGINS TO TAPER INTO TWITCHES AND THEN LIE STILL.
I SLICE THROUGH THE DEAD WEIGHT AND COME UP FOR AIR.

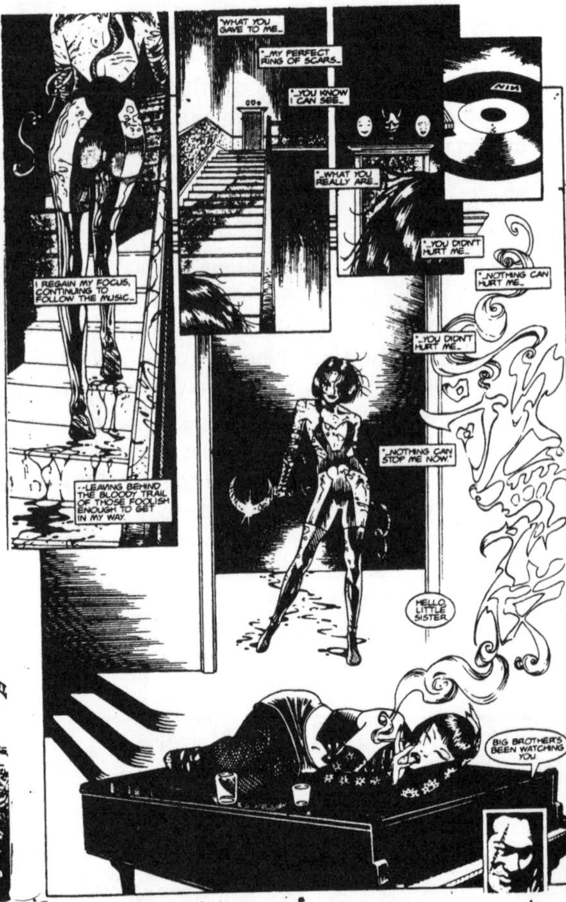
I REGAIN MY FOCUS, CONTINUING TO FOLLOW THE MUSIC...
--LEAVING BEHIND THE BLOODY TRAIL OF THOSE FOOLISH ENOUGH TO GET IN MY WAY.
"WHAT YOU GAVE TO ME...
"...MY PERFECT RING OF SCARS...
"...YOU KNOW I CAN SEE...
"...WHAT YOU REALLY ARE...
"...YOU DIDN'T HURT ME...
"...NOTHING CAN HURT ME...
"...YOU DIDN'T HURT ME...
"...NOTHING CAN STOP ME NOW."
NIN
HELLO, LITTLE SISTER
BIG BROTHER'S BEEN WATCHING YOU

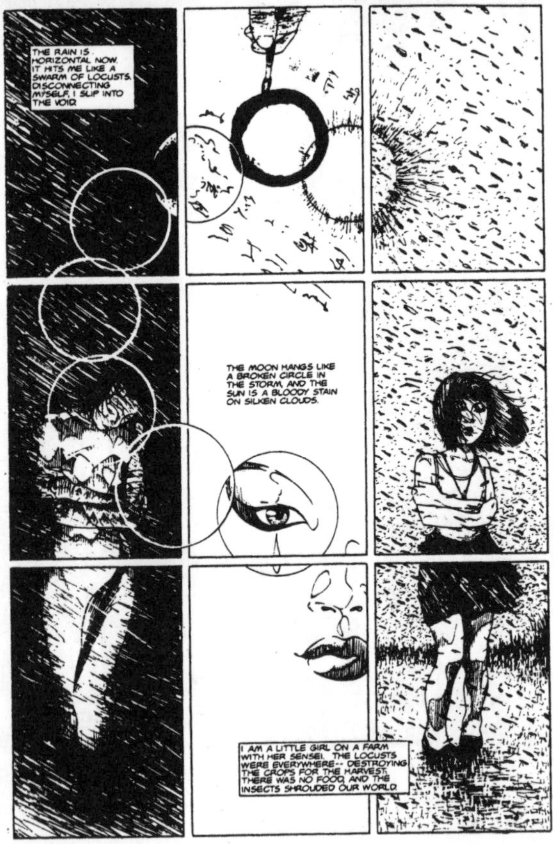
THE RAIN IS HORIZONTAL NOW. IT HITS ME LIKE A SWARM OF LOCUSTS. DISCONNECTING MYSELF, I SLIP INTO THE VOID.
THE MOON HANGS LIKE A BROKEN CIRCLE IN THE STORM, AND THE SUN IS A BLOODY STAIN ON SILKEN CLOUDS.
I AM A LITTLE GIRL ON A FARM WITH HER SENSEI. THE LOCUSTS WERE EVERYWHERE-- DESTROYING THE CROPS FOR THE HARVEST. THERE WAS NO FOOD, AND THE INSECTS SHROUDED OUR WORLD.

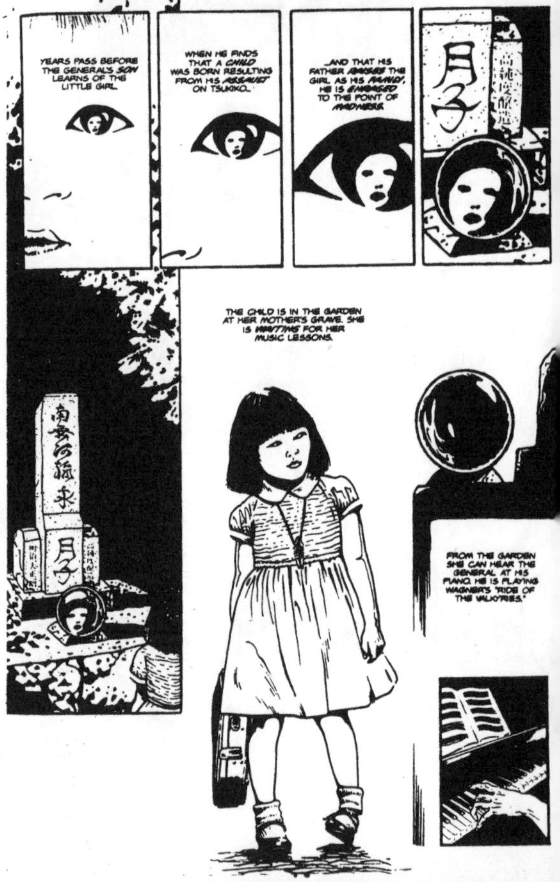
YEARS PASS BEFORE THE GENERAL'S SON LEARNS OF THE LITTLE GIRL
WHEN HE FINDS THAT A CHILD WAS BORN RESULTING FROM HIS ASSAULT ON TSUKIKO...
...AND THAT HIS FATHER RAISES THE GIRL AS HIS FAMILY, HE IS ENRAGED TO THE POINT OF MADNESS.
月子
THE CHILD IS IN THE GARDEN AT HER MOTHER'S GRAVE. SHE IS WAITING FOR HER MUSIC LESSONS.
FROM THE GARDEN SHE CAN HEAR THE GENERAL AT HIS PIANO. HE IS PLAYING WAGNER'S 'RIDE OF THE VALKYRIES.'

no problem writing and drawing metaphorically. He has spoke of Kabuki as a metaphor like " Alice in Wonderland". The fact that he is exploring a topic in Japanese setting from a classic of English literature only adds to the richness. Akira Kurosawa did the same thing when filming "Ran" as a Japanese interpretation of Shakespeare's "King Lear". The legendary hero's journey transcends nationality. It is an idea based in the mythos of all cultures around the globe. Joseph Campbell has written extensively on the subject and it can be found in many classic tales popular in modern times; Star Wars, the first Conan movie, Frankenstein. Child is displaced in a society where they don't fit in. They must find out who they really are. They confront their father figure and learn who they truly are under a trial by fire. Coming to grips with their past they enter the world of adulthood and self actualization. Frank Miller and Dave Gibbons related the hero's journey of Martha Washington in "Give Me Liberty". This story took place in America's future, dealt with its history and asked what it means to be an American. Alan Moore and David Lloyd explored the bleak future of England under totalitarian reign, depicting the end of one hero's journey and the beginning of another in "V for Vendetta". David Mack has dealt with a nation's future, history, concepts of patriotism and birth of a hero from a Japanese angle in Kabuki.

Just as "Circle of Blood" is Kabuki's journey, it can also be viewed as the journey of her mother's ghost. As described in Act 5, the Kabuki plays are almost entirely about ghosts, "wronged or enraged women bent on exacting vengeance from the man who wronged her". Tsukiko died just as Kabuki was born. Perhaps the child is a vengeful reincarnation of her mother. And Kabuki was killed by Kai in her youth;" I am dead. My heart stops beating for nine minutes. Total flatline. Miraculously, the medics bring me back. However to this day I do not feel that I was completely revived... because while I was dead, I saw my mother. The large, circular overhead lights in the operating room faded into the gentle haze of the full moon... my mother stood in the fields. She told me I must return as a ghost like her own role in the Kabuki dramas. I will honor my mother..." Not completely revived? Perhaps this means that when Kabuki was revived, she brought her mother's vengeful spirit back with her. In this light I see the ending of "Circle of Blood" as the closure to the ghostly designs of Kabuki's mother. Kabuki shatters the urn and Tsukiko's ashes take to the sky. I believe that this is meant to signify the departure of Tsukiko's spirit from Kabuki and not as the death of Kabuki herself. The ashes "eclipse" the sun, an implication of a resolution to the sun and moon dichotomies.

So then, "Kabuki: Circle of Blood", is it a ghost story? Is it the hero's journey? Is it a trip to a wonderland of enchantment? Is it a Sci /Fi thriller? Is it a story of a nation's history and future? Is it corporate espionage and political intrigue? Is it a family's tragedy?

Yes. It is all of these. You can read it as any single one of them or all of them at once. I have only mentioned a few of my own insights to the story. There are other layers of meaning for you to find out on your own.

Takashi Hattori

服部 隆志

Yokohama, Japan